D0983711

A Dangerous Liaison:
Simone de Beauvoir and Jean-Paul Sartre

A Dangerous Liaison:

Simone de Beauvoir and Jean-Paul Sartre

CAROLE SEYMOUR-JONES

C

Century · London

Published by Century 2008

2 4 6 8 10 9 7 5 3

First published in Great Britain in 2008 by
Century
Random House, 20 Vauxhall Bridge Road,
London SW1V 2SA

www.randomhouse.co.uk

Addresses for companies within The Random House Group Limited can be found at:
www.randomhouse.co.uk

The Random House Group Limited Reg. No. 954009

A CIP catalogue record for this book
is available from the British Library

ISBN 9781844138227

The Random House Group Limited supports The Forest Stewardship Council (FSC),
the leading international forest certification organisation. All our titles that are
printed on Greenpeace approved FSC certified paper carry the FSC logo. Our paper
procurement policy can be found at: www.rbooks.co.uk/environment

Mixed Sources
Product group from well-managed
forests and other controlled sources
www.fsc.org Cert no. TT-COC-2139
FSC © 1996 Forest Stewardship Council

Typeset by SX Composing DTP, Rayleigh, Essex
Printed and bound in Great Britain by
Clays Ltd, St Ives PLC

The author and publisher have made all reasonable efforts to contact copyright
holders for permission, and apologise for any omissions or errors in the form of credits
given. Corrections may be made to future printings.

For Geoffrey

List of Illustrations

Contents

Part Two: The Dark Years 1939–44

Part Three: Écrivains Engagés 1945–56

Part Four: False Gods 1952–68

Part Five: The Farewell Ceremony 1969–86

Acknowledgements

I owe a particular debt of gratitude to the following: Sylvie Le Bon de Beauvoir, for her generous permission and insightful scholarship; Oleg Gordievsky, Bianca Bienenfeld Lamblin, Laurence Nguyen, Olivier Todd, Michèle Vian, Macha Zonina, for their invaluable memories and permission; my inspirational fellow biographer, Neil McKenna, for making this book possible; Ania Corless, for unstinting support ; my partner Geoffrey Parkinson, to whom this book is dedicated, and my children, Emma, Edward and Lucy, for their patience and good humour; Kim Witherspoon, my indefatigable agent in New York; and Hannah Black, best of editors, for believing in this book from the beginning.

I am indebted to the following individuals for help, advice and encouragement of many kinds: Lisa Appignanesi, Marchesa Amalia Ginori Bornini, Gérard and Xialong Coutin, Anne-Marie Coutin, Frank Dabell and Jay Weissberg, Peter Day, Dominique Desanti, Margaret Drabble, Carl Djerassi, Ophelia Field, Sarah Glazer, Robert Gallimard, Rina Gill, Pat Grayburn, Madeleine Gobeil-Noël, Shusha Guppy, Jonathan Heawood, Sarah Hirschmann, Michael Holroyd, Bruce Hunter, Robert Jones, Deirdre Lay, Virginie Lay, Chip Martin, Jean Mattern, Ann Maughan, the late Diane Middlebrook, Mary Sebag Montefiore, Simon Sebag Montefiore, Trevor Mostyn, Dr. Jonathan Pimm, Michaela Prunus, Camille Plutarque, Diana Reich, Anne Salter, Jean-Claude Sauer, Elaine Showalter, Frances Stonor Saunders, Julia Stonor, Tricia and Julian Storey, Gillian Tindall, Moira and Michael Williams; Dr. Lyuba Vinagradova for translation from the Russian; for editorial assistance, David Smith and, at Random House, Katie Duce and Annie Lee.

To my regret, Arlette Elkaïm-Sartre and Gisèle Halimi declined my request for an interview.

I am grateful to English PEN for giving me a sabbatical from my post as Chair of the Writers in Prison Committee, and to Ania Corless for serving as Acting Chair.

I would like to thank the following librarians, archivists and institutions for their help: Mauricette Berne, Bibliothèque Nationale de France, Paris; Liliane Phan, Archives Gallimard; Nicole Fernández-Ferrer, Centre audovisuel Simone de Beauvoir; the British Library; the London Library; Ohio State University Libraries; The Society of Authors.

The author and publishers are grateful to the following for permission to reprint extracts from the works of Simone de Beauvoir: HarperCollins Publishers for *She Came to Stay*, first published in France as *L'Invitée*, ©Librairie Gallimard 1943, translated by Yvonne Moyse and Roger Senhouse (Fontana, 1984); *The Mandarins*, first published in France as *Les Mandarins*, © Librairie Gallimard 1954, translated by Leonard M.Friedman (Fontana, 1957); *When Things of the Spirit Come First*, first published in France as *Quand prime le spirituel*, © Editions Gallimard 1979, translated by Patrick O'Brian (Fontana, 1982); Random House Group and the Estate of Simone de Beauvoir for *The Second Sex*, first published as *Le Deuxième Sexe*, © Librairie Gallimard 1949, translated by H.M. Parshley (Jonathan Cape, 1953), and *Letters to Sartre*, first published in France as *Lettres à Sartre*, © Editions

Gallimard 1990, translated by Quintin Hoare (Vintage, 1991); Penguin Books for *Memoirs of A Dutiful Daughter*, first published in France as *Mémoires d'une jeune fille rangée*, © Editions Gallimard 1958, translated by James Kirkup (Penguin 1963), translation first published André Deutsch and Weidenfeld & Nicolson, 1959, translation copyright © The World Publishing Company, 1959; *The Prime of Life*, first published as *La force de l'âge*, © Editions Gallimard, 1960, translated by Peter Green, this translation first published in the USA 1962, translation copyright © The World Publishing Company, 1962, (Penguin 1965), *Force of Circumstance*, first published in France as *La force des choses*, © Editions Gallimard 1963, translated by Richard Howard, English translation © G.P. Putnam's Sons, New York, *All Said and Done*, first published in France as *Tout compte fait*, © Editions Gallimard 1972, translated by Patrick O'Brian, (André Deutsch and Weidenfeld & Nicolson, 1974); *Une mort très douce*, (Editions Gallimard 1964); *The Blood of Others*, first published as *Le Sang des Autres*, translated by Yvonne Moyse and Roger Senhouse, (Penguin 1964); *Woman Destroyed*, first published as *La Femme Rompue*, © Editions Gallimard, 1968, translated by Patrick O'Brian, (G.P Putnam's Sons, New York, 1974); *Adieux: A Farewell to Sartre*, first published in France as *La Cérémonie des Adieux*, © Editions Gallimard, 1981, translated by Patrick O'Brian, © Patrick O'Brian, (André Deutsch and Weidenfeld & Nicolson, 1984); *Correspondance croisée: Simone de Beauvoir et Jacques-Laurent Bost* © Editions Gallimard, 2004; *Journal de Guerre*, © Editions Gallimard, 1990; and *Beloved Chicago Man: Letters to Nelson Algren 1947-1964*, first published in French translation, © Editions Gallimard, 1997, (Phoenix 1999).

We are also grateful to the following for permission to reprint extracts from works by Jean-Paul Sartre: Penguin Books for *Nausea*, first published as *La Nausée*, © Editions Gallimard 1938, translated by Robert Baldick, this translation © Penguin Books 1965; *Words*, first published in France as *Les Mots*, © Editions Gallimard, 1964, translated by Irene Clephane, translation copyright © Hamish Hamilton, 1964, (Penguin 1967); *The Age of Reason*, first published as *L'Âge de Raison*, © Editions Gallimard 1945, translated by Eric Sutton, (Penguin 1961); and *Iron in the Soul*, first published as *La Mort dans l'Âme*, translated by Gerard Hopkins, (Penguin 1963); Verso for *War Diaries: Notebooks from a Phoney War 1939-1940*, first published as *Les carnets de la drôle de guerre*, © Editions Gallimard 1983, translated by Quintin Hoare, translation copyright © Verso Editions 1984; Hamish Hamilton for *Witness to My Life: The Letters of Jean-Paul Sartre to Simone de Beauvoir 1926-1939*, first published in France as *Lettres au Castor et à quelques autres*, © Editions Gallimard 1983, translation copyright © Lee Fahnstock and Norman MacAfee, 1992; *Quiet Moments in a War: The Letters of Jean-Paul Sartre to Simone de Beauvoir, 1940-1963*, translated by Lee Fahnstock and Norman MacAfree (New York: Scriben's Sons, 1993); and to Editions Gallimard for *Les Ecrits de Sartre*, © Editions Gallimard 1970, and *Témoins de Sartre*, © Editions Gallimard 2005; to New Directions Publishing Corporation for *The Wall and Other Stories*, first published as *Le Mur*, © Editions Gallimard, 1939), translated by Lloyd Alexander, © Lloyd Alexander; to Routledge for *Being and Nothingness*, first published as *L'Être et Le Néant*, (Gallimard 1943), translated by Hazel E. Barnes, English translation © 1958 Philosophical Library (Routledge 1989); also to Northeastern University Press, Boston, for quotations from Bianca Lamblin, *A Disgraceful Affair*, translated by Julie Plovnick, translation copyright © Julie Plovnick 1996, and to HarperCollins for quotations from Liliane Siegel, *In the Shadow of Sartre*, translated by Barabara Wright (Collins 1990).

Preface

AN INTRIGUING NOTE surfaced among Jean-Paul Sartre's personal papers after his death. '*Je peux me tromper*,' he had scrawled on a scrap of paper, '*mais cela n'est pas exprès*.' He'd made mistakes, but 'not on purpose.' The note was dated 29 June 1971, nine years before his death. It suggested a rare moment of contrition for the greatest error of his political life, his and Beauvoir's love affair with the Soviet Union, which lasted right up to the moment when the tanks rolled into Prague in 1968. To many commentators, then and now, Sartre's behaviour is the twentieth century's prime example of *la trahison des clercs*, the intellectuals' betrayal of freedom.

Why did he do it? What secrets lay behind his and Beauvoir's 'bad faith', their moral compromises as they became their century's most famous *compagnons de route*, fellow travellers, in contrast to their former friends, who, one by one, painfully turned their backs on the USSR as stories of the gulag emerged: Raymond Aron, Albert Camus and, even earlier, the great André Gide? Of course Sartre and Beauvoir were not alone in being seduced by Communism. Many of the Auden generation, on both sides of the Channel, had become infatuated with the socialist 'paradise', and remained blind to its atrocities. Sidney and Beatrice Webb, about whom I wrote previously, had praised Stalin's 'land of milk and honey' in 1932. And in his defence, Sartre was a writer, by definition, perhaps, unworldly. Politics was never his natural metier. Nevertheless, his naïvete appeared strangely wilful. As I began researching his and Beauvoir's lives, I began to feel that I was searching for the missing piece in a jigsaw puzzle, the one which would explain his determination to return repeatedly to Russia, until the day came when Solzhenistyn refused to shake his hand, and he became, in the words of Bernard-Henri Lévy, 'the incarnation of dishonour'.

There were more uncomfortable questions to confront. 'The biographical question,' writes Lévy in his *Le Siècle de Sartre* (2000), is: 'what was Sartre's, and to a lesser extent Beauvoir's . . . concrete attitude towards fascism' during the Occupation of France. In other words, what did he do in the war? In attempting to answer this question, Lévy went as far as he could in exonerating Sartre. But other scholars provided persuasive evidence to the contrary, notably Ingrid Galster in her *Sartre, Vichy et les intellectuels* (2001), and Gilbert Joseph in his *Sartre et Simone de Beauvoir: Une Si Douce Occupation*, a chilling indictment of the couple for not being 'intellectual resistants' as they claimed, but collaborators. Gerhard Heller, Nazi censor in Paris during the Occupation, in his memoir *Un Allemand à Paris 1940–44*, supported Joseph's contention that during *les années noires* Sartre and Beauvoir had feathered their nests at the expense of the Jews. It is difficult to avoid the conclusion that the author of *Anti-Semite and Jew* was himself, at that period, an anti-Semite. This point was forcefully made to me in interviews with Bianca Bienenfeld Lamblin, the Jewish schoolgirl Beauvoir procured for Sartre before the couple abandoned her during the war. Lamblin still lives with a profound sense of betrayal.

In recent years, therefore, *la légende noire*, the black Sartrean legend, has gradually overshadowed the 'good' legend created and rigorously controlled by Simone de Beauvoir, the couple's memoirist. A sea change has occurred since their deaths in 1980 and 1986. Then, Jean-Paul Sartre and Simone de Beauvoir were public figures whose prolific output as novelists, philosophers and memoirists seemed to leave biographers with little to say. In addition to interviews and journalistic profiles, an academic industry had grown up around the two global celebrities that was itself a deterrent to further scrutiny. Two monumental biographies, of Sartre by Annie Cohen-Solal, and of Beauvoir by Deirdre Bair, seemed to freeze the two writers in time as untouchable twentieth-century icons.

But at the Exposition Sartre of 2005 in Paris, the comprehensive exhibition celebrating his centenary, I wandered almost alone among the exhibits. 'Not many people are going to the exposition,' remarked a French friend: 'Sartre and Beauvoir did some bad things, I think. People don't believe in them any more.' Fame seemed to have morphed into infamy since Marcel Ophuls's film, *Le Chagrin et la Pitié* (*The Sorrow and the Pity*) in 1972, which opened the floodgates to a new surge of interest in Vichy France. Robert Paxton, Henri Rousso, Robert Gildea, Rod Kedward and other historians have uncovered evidence that challenges old assumptions about the nature and extent of French resistance to the Nazis, and French treatment of the Jews. In the light of this new material, reassessment of the role played by Sartre and Beauvoir during this murky period seemed overdue. And I felt a personal connection: my maternal grandmother's Huguenot family had fled to Cullompton, Devon, in the seventeenth century. Had we remained, how would we have conducted ourselves, I wondered, during the Occupation?

But in taking a fresh look at the Sartre/Beauvoir partnership, I was stepping into a historiographical minefield. I wanted to focus on the relationship between two writers: that startlingly productive complicity which lasted half a century, a 'twinship' so profound that each finished the other's sentences. Their legendary free union made them pioneers of the sexual revolution, but it was also an immutable bond which their lovers likened to a Janus stone with two faces, the altar on which the needs of the Other was always sacrificed.

The liaison between Beauvoir and Sartre, the theme of this book, had a potential for good: it was the anvil from which intellectual sparks flew. In the Café de Flore, or the Deux Magots, they flirted, smoked, drank and made books together. But it also had a dangerous potential for evil, as the 'twins' encouraged and validated each other within their private world, the basis of which was not only intellectual iconoclasm but also fierce mutual need, stemming in part from their damaged childhoods. The fascination of Beauvoir's relationship with Sartre is that it survived without sex, redefining love as a lifetime commitment based on more binding ties than physical desire, which could be found – and discarded – elsewhere. Above all, Sartre craved the intimacy he had known as a child with his mother: the tiny, squinting man who grew up crippled by his uncertain sense of self, his confidence undermined by his own sense of disfigurement, would have an obsessive need for women.

In following Sartre and Beauvoir on their life journey, my first loyalty was to the primary sources. Since Beauvoir's death important personal papers have revolutionized our view of the model couple of the counter-culture. Beauvoir, when writing her memoirs, had her reasons for concealing the facts in her lifetime: not only to protect her lovers and Sartre's, as she claimed, but to conceal the nature of her own sexuality, to whitewash the political record, and to revenge herself on his other women.

Not until after Sartre's death did the keeper of the Sartrean flame decide to allow new evidence to trickle out. It would, in time, become a flood. In 1983 Beauvoir published Sartre's letters to her (*Lettres au Castor*). Her friends were puzzled, writes Sylvie Le Bon de Beauvoir, Beauvoir's partner, adopted daughter and literary executor. '*Mais les vôtres, Castor?* What about your own, Beaver?' they asked. But Beauvoir always gave the same reply: her letters to Sartre were lost. Mislaid in the war, or destroyed when his flat was bombed. Not without reason did one of her former lovers, Jacques-Laurent Bost, consider Beauvoir a compulsive liar. In November 1986, seven months after her death, Le Bon opened a cupboard in Beauvoir's studio at rue Schoelcher and stumbled upon a 'massive packet' of letters in Beauvoir's handwriting, many still in their envelopes, addressed to 'Monsieur Sartre'.

Le Bon published the letters without cuts, believing that it was preferable 'to tell all in order to tell the truth . . . to set aside clichés, myths, images – all those lies – so that the real person, as she really was, may appear.' The letters opened a can of worms. For the first time, shocked readers saw the rose-tinted veil which protected Beauvoir's union with Sartre ripped away to reveal the truth of their sexual exploitation of their pupils. For their vulnerable partners, these liaisons were as dangerous as those of Valmont and Mme de Merteuil. Reinventing the rules had been a bolder, more anarchic and amoral enterprise than Beauvoir's readers had ever dreamed.

Censoring and sanitizing memory, Beauvoir had played an ironic, postmodern joke on her biographers, taking them into her apparent confidence, misleading them and, as Quentin Hoare, translator of Beauvor's *Lettres à Sartre* writes, 'making even the best of them into unwitting hagiographers. Outsmarted, they underestimated her toughness and savvy. How she must have chuckled into her whisky, on evenings after her earnest visits.'

Other significant unpublished papers followed: Sartre's extra-ordinary letters to his Soviet lover, Lena Zonina, generously made available to me by her daughter, Macha, unpublished material in the private archive of Sylvie Le Bon de Beauvoir, Simone de Beauvoir's youthful journals in the Bibliothèque Nationale de France, as well as the oral history of those who knew and loved – or hated – Sartre and Beauvoir. All were vital in attempting to create a dual portrait of the couple that would weave together the disparate strands of their lives, literary and philosophical, personal and political. I felt it essential to reclaim their work: the short stories, novels and essays, lying on dusty library shelves, the tattered paperbacks of *Les Chemins de la liberté* and *L'Invitée*, the volumes of autobiography and memoir, and their posthumously published war diaries, Sartre's *Notebooks from a Phoney War*, Beauvoir's own *Journal de Guerre*. In her novels Beauvoir had often told truths she felt obliged to conceal in her memoirs, the latest volumes of which became largely fictional constructs. But even when she dares not reveal the causes of her despair – often Sartre's infidelity – blaming her depression on the ageing process and her fear of the existential void, Beauvoir is painfully, movingly honest about her emotions, for example in the third volume of her memoir, *Force of Circumstance*, in which she acknowledges that her childhood dreams have melted away like water in sand.

The disillusion both Sartre and Beauvoir expressed was dwarfed by that of many of their victims. Following the biographical trail, I was astonished by the size of the gap between the public legend and the private lives of the couple. Myth and reality were shifting mirrors, in which I briefly glimpsed figures which, as rapidly as they advanced, vanished; in Beauvoir's memoirs their names did not appear, or only briefly, disguised by pseudonyms. But in grey photocopies of old letters their voices cried out, demanding pity, vindication. Occluded, lost to the record, they were the losers, spurned, the sometimes suicidal lovers, both male and female, sacrificed to the interests of the Sartre/Beauvoir partnership, whose 1929 'contract' made all other lovers expendable in the face of their own 'essential' love.

New evidence, therefore, opened a new space for a revisionist biography of Sartre and Beauvoir, and begged the question: how great had been the influence of the private upon the public life, of sex upon politics? Arthur Koestler remarked that when you scratch a politician, you find a woman. Had Sartre, as Dora Maar quipped of Picasso, changed his style every time he changed *his* women? And what had been the impact of celebrity, the new post-war monster the couple had greedily courted until it began to devour them? Sartre loved the limelight, but it burnt him up, even as he hopped aboard the global gravy train. Celebrity feuds, cranked up by the media, with Camus and Arthur Koestler in particular, had the potential to leave him isolated and open to deception, ripe for a Soviet love-trap. Sartre's intense rivalry with other writers and philosophers was, in my view, a vital factor in the 'mistakes' he made, particularly in his dangerous support for the Communist Party at a time when his global influence was immense. It was when he changed his male friends that he changed his politics.

And how had the wronged lovers omitted from Beauvoir's 'authorized' autobiography influenced her? Determined to do posthumous justice to Jacques-Laurent Bost in particular, in 2004 Le

Bon published nearly a thousand pages of letters between Beauvoir and her young lover (*Simone de Beauvoir, Jacques-Laurent Bost, Correspondance croisée* 1937–1940); this time, both sides of the correspondence were available to create a vivid picture of a passionate wartime romance. In publishing Beauvoir's letters to Nelson Algren, Le Bon also put Beauvoir's American lover back in the frame. Both collections are important in the continuing controversy over where to place Beauvoir on the sexuality spectrum, indicating how unsatisfactory is the labelling process that would seek to claim her as 'bisexual' or 'lesbian'. Her sexual fluidity enabled her to enjoy a wide range of experiences, straight and gay, at different periods in her life. I am most grateful to Sylvie Le Bon de Beauvoir for her generosity in allowing me to see unpublished material, and for sharing her recollections of Beauvoir and Sartre, and *la famille Sartre*. Without her, this book would not have been possible.

The whispering voices that I had heard among the silent manuscripts and faded photographs of the Sartre exhibitions had became more clamorous still with the publication of kiss-and-tell memoirs, such as Bianca Lamblin's *Mémoires d'une jeune fille dérangée* or Liliane Siegel's *La Clandestine*. But the most important mistress still skulked in the shadows: Lena Zonina, the Russian interpreter Sartre wanted to marry. Sartre's nine hundred pages of outpoured love to Lena provided a window into this relationship. Conversations with Oleg Gordievsky, former KGB colonel and the highest-ranking double agent to work for the British as well as the Soviets before his escape to Britain in 1985, fleshed out the Soviet side of the story. The final key to the jigsaw came with the location of Zonina's unpublished reports, buried in the state archives in Moscow and never previously translated. Was Zonina a spy, and did Sartre suspect? Was he playing *le double jeu*, a game of double-bluff? Or was it a case of knowing and not knowing? Zonina's reports, and Sartre's letters gave me the answer.

It would be wrong, however, to suppose that my admiration for both Beauvoir and Sartre, which was the genesis of this biography, has been in any way eroded. On the contrary. Paradoxically, the more I learnt about the couple, the more my sympathy grew for them and their bold attempt to 'live against' bourgeois society. Beauvoir, iconic twentieth-century feminist, a writer in her own right, had attracted me as a subject because of the contrast she presented to my last biographical subject, frail Vivienne Eliot. Sartre's own existential quest, to examine all the logical consequences which followed from a position of atheism, seemed more relevant than ever to an age debating Richard Dawkins's

The God Delusion. Undoubtedly Sartre and Beauvoir experienced anguish at the 'death of God', as together they stared into the howling, existential void. As Le Bon emphasized to me, Sartre believed that the artist's lot is to suffer, and in many ways he represents the Romantic vision of the tormented geniuses to which he compared himself, most notably Keats, Baudelaire and Flaubert. His was a lonely pilgrimage. Atheism, he wrote, is a cruel, long-term business. *L'athéisme est une enterprise cruelle et de longue haleine,* the long breath of the withdrawal of faith like the suck of the retreating tide in Matthew Arnold's *Dover Beach. Je crois l'avoir menée jusqu'au bout,* he had pursued it to the end. But not without pain: a little man, as he said, telling stories to make sense of existence.

Bound together by their lifelong mission to find meaning in a godless, random and absurd world, Sartre and Beauvoir made art out of their revolutionary ideas. Fiercely criticized as nihilistic and anti-humanist, their struggle to assume the freedom they believed to be our human birthright, and translate it into the political arena, was inspiring even when they were *égarés,* misled. It was, I believe, because he was seeking a substitute for Christianity that Sartre found Communism, the grand illusion of the twentieth century, to which he clung with all the fervour of the convert. And despite his errors, Sartre left a lasting political legacy in his contribution to the liberation struggles of the twentieth century. His ideas provided the ethical and philosophical basis for Algerian revolt, his actions vital leadership during the war itself, as, in espousing the Arab cause, he attempted to follow in the steps of Voltaire and Gide in fighting for the underdog. Beauvoir's own radical thinking in taking the existential idea of the Other and applying it to gender relations was her great legacy. *The Second Sex,* bible of the Women's Movement, set in motion an unstoppable train, until her notions of equality, choice and self-determination became the common currency of many women's lives. How prescient she was in sweeping aside biological difference is only now becoming apparent, as pundits debate the crisis of masculinity and the demise of the Y chromosome.

In old age, Sartre and Beauvoir took to street politics. Their mutual devotion and interdependence over fifty-one years proved stronger than many a marriage. Whatever their mistakes, their courage was never in doubt. Human, flawed, gullible, yes; but they broke the mould of their century.

Carole Seymour-Jones,
London, December 2007

Part One

The Pursuit of Happiness

1905–38

1

Becoming

On ne naît pas femme; on le devient. One is not born a
woman, one becomes one.

Simone de Beauvoir, *The Second Sex*

JEAN-PAUL SARTRE TROTTED beside Simone de Beauvoir as she
strolled past the pond in Paris's Luxembourg Gardens, where a few
brave children were still sailing their boats. It was October 1929. Dead
leaves scudded across the surface of the water and snared the boats; a
pale sun lit up the stone statues of the queens of French history. But
Sartre's mind was not on the past but on the future. For the third time,
he pressed twenty-one-year-old Simone to marry him.

He was twenty-four, high time for a bourgeois graduate to marry; his
two best friends had already done so. And there were pecuniary
advantages to matrimony. He was doing his National Service at Saint-
Cyr and, if married, would qualify for an increase in pay.

Simone quickened her pace. For the third time, she refused. In her
eyes, marriage was a middle-class trap that deformed character and
stunted independence. '*Elle a dit "non"*,' recalls Sylvie Le Bon de
Beauvoir, her adopted daughter. 'She wanted to write, she didn't want
children; yet she needed Sartre.' Anxious not to lose the delectable
Mlle de Beauvoir, Sartre proposed an alternative: 'What we have,' he
said, 'is an *essential* love; but it's good if we both experience *contingent*
affairs.'

He had couched his proposal in philosophical terms cunningly designed to appeal to the most brilliant female student of her generation. The pact he offered was far more to her liking. Instantly Simone pledged herself to Jean-Paul, the only man she'd met who was her intellectual equal. The lifetime commitment that followed would prove more enduring than many a marriage. Bound together by their difficult childhoods, by the intellectual fireworks they created, and by a deep, visceral need which Beauvoir called a 'twinship', together they would light up their century. Their notorious contract would break the mould of respectable marriage in including the freedom to have affairs with other people while remaining committed to each other. It would last more than fifty years and become remarkably symbolic for several generations of people who followed them.

None of this was achieved without pain, whose concealment demanded the construction of a legend. The disparity between myth and a darker truth grew with the passing years, as the fame of the 'model couple' spread world-wide.

But Sartre never forgot his first impressions of Simone. 'I think she's beautiful,' he told Madeleine Gobeil in an interview for *American Vogue* in 1965. 'I have always found her beautiful, even though she was wearing a hideous little hat when I met her for the first time. I was dead set on getting to know her because she was beautiful, because she had then, and still has the kind of face which attracts me. The miracle of Simone de Beauvoir is that she has the intelligence of a man and the sensitivity of a woman. In other words, she is everything I could want.'

For Beauvoir too, despite disappointment on many levels, Sartre remained the object of her love. He 'corresponded exactly to the dream-companion I had longed for since I was fifteen', she wrote in *Memoirs of a Dutiful Daughter*. 'He was the double in whom I found all my burning aspiration raised to the pitch of incandescence.' That summer of '29, 'when I left him at the beginning of August, I knew that he would never go out of my life again'.

*

Stépha, the Polish governess, watched Simone de Beauvoir barge into the drawing-room. Everyone knew that the awkward twenty-year-old was Mademoiselle Lacoin's 'charity case', whose silly father had lost all his money and property. The Lacoins themselves were outrageously wealthy: they lived in the chic rue de Berri in Paris, and had an estate at Gagnepain in the Basque country. Madame Lacoin had taken pity on her daughter Zaza's friend and invited her to stay. How everyone had laughed when the girl arrived in lisle stockings and an old cotton summer frock, bleached by the sun. Zaza, of course, was in white tussore, with a pink sash. Stépha had heard that Mademoiselle Zaza had a dowry of 250,000 francs, a small fortune.

Poor Simone, thought Stépha:

> She didn't look very nice to me, although I am sure she thought she did, because she told me she had a new dress – awful, as I remember, very ill-fitting and a hideous colour. Her skin was not nice, her hair was sort of greasy-looking . . . She looked as if she had been neglected all her life . . . I knew many poor people among my student friends in Paris, and their poverty did not touch me as Simone's did.

On her return to Paris from Gagnepain, Stépha Awdykovicz attempted to take Simone's appearance in hand: 'Take off that hideous frock: I'm going to try one of my dresses on you – this green will suit you marvellously.' Simone was embarrassed to undress, knowing the state of her underclothes, but she allowed Stépha to pluck her eyebrows and clean her dirty nails with an orange-stick. With eye-liner, rouge and powder, her hair washed with ether, Simone was, if not transformed, improved. It was a flirtatious scene she used in a short story written in 1935, which carries undertones of sexuality:

> 'You have a lovely body,' she said. 'You are quite right not to wear a suspender belt.' She smiled archly. 'I don't wear one either,' she added. 'Feel.' She grasped my hand and pressed it to her belly . . . 'I know who you are like with those high little breasts and that slightly rounded stomach,' she said. 'It's the women Cranach painted. Not a regular beauty, but much better. A faultless body is . . . less touching.'

As a young student at the Sorbonne beginning to feel her way to freedom from her parents, but lacking in money and social graces, Simone was grateful to Stépha for taking her seriously and for showing her a protective friendship: 'From the very first I liked her so much,' said the governess. They met nearly every day for lunch, and Stépha brought Simone cakes and pastries, because she could afford only coffee and bread. She hugged and kissed Simone, who, coming from a family in which she received little physical contact from her parents, was astonished. In 1928 Stépha became the leader of a girl gang consisting of Simone, her sister Hélène, and Gégé Pardo, a working-class friend from Hélène's art school in Montparnasse, who went together on adventures in the bars of the *quartier*. Night-clubs, with their dim, orange lights, dancing bodies pressed close, their seductive odours of sweat, tobacco and cheap scent, exercised a powerful fascination for Simone; all around her, sex was the currency. Pimps lurked in the shadows, watching their women. Violence lurked just beneath the surface. In the Jockey, fitted out like a cowboy saloon, Hemingway and his friends drank whisky and listened to the lowlife *canaille* songs of Kiki, model and mistress of photographer Man Ray. The Monocle, on the boulevard Edgar-Quinet, a temple to Sapphic love, was ruled over by Lulu de Montparnasse. 'From the owner to the barmaid, from the waitresses to the hat-check girl, all the women were dressed as men,' remembered the photographer Brassaï. 'A tornado of virility had gusted through the place . . . changing women into boys, gangsters, policemen.' In black tuxedos, women danced breast to breast, their hair 'sacrificed on Sappho's altar'. The club was, said the photographer, the capital of Gomorrah.

Simone was by turns shocked and excited. Her feelings for Stépha grew warmer. 'I love Stépha as a man loves a woman,' she wrote in her secret journal on 31 December 1928. All the same, she was a dutiful Catholic girl. It was embarrassing to call on Stépha, who lived in a hotel in the place Saint-Sulpice, round the corner from the rue de Rennes, and find her being painted in the nude by her Spanish boyfriend, an artist named Fernando Gerassi. Clearly the couple enjoyed sexual relations. Simone put her hands up to her eyes: 'Physical love was . . . a tragic fall from grace, and I hadn't the courage to attempt it.'

La vie de Bohème both repelled and attracted her. Wandering down the boulevard Barbes, watching the whores and pimps, Simone began to lose her sense of horror at the sight of working women, and to feel instead 'a sort of envy'. There was an honesty and freedom about their lives which impressed her. She was surprised at her feelings:

There is within me I know not what yearning . . . maybe a monstrous lust – ever present, for noise, fighting, savage violence, and above all for the gutter. . . . I want life, the whole of life.

Yet it had all started so differently.

*

Beauvoir was born at four o'clock on the morning of 9 January 1908 in her parents' bedroom at 103 boulevard du Montparnasse. Twenty-one-year-old Françoise, the new mother, presented her first-born to her husband. Georges Bertrand de Beauvoir looked down into eyes as blue as a Delft plate, and chose names befitting a young girl of good family: Simone Lucie Ernestine Marie. She seemed destined for a life of privilege.

The Beauvoirs' elegant first-floor apartment overlooked the boulevard Raspail, a highly respectable bourgeois street on the Left Bank. The apartment itself was an oasis of upper-middle-class values: Françoise saw to that. The décor, apart from the white-enamelled master bedroom, was overwhelmingly red and black. 'The upholstery was of red moquette, the Renaissance dining room was red, the figured silk hangings over the stained-glass doors were red, and the velvet curtains in Papa's study, red also,' recalled Simone. Warm, womb-like, reassuring, the scarlet sofas and black pearwood furniture were as solid as her routine; every morning Louise, her nanny, dressed Simone, took the rags out of her hair and brushed her dark ringlets into a cascade of curls, telling her how lucky she was to have the unusual colouring of blue eyes and brown hair. At night Louise slept in the nursery.

Of Georges, Simone saw little. He left every morning for the law courts, briefcase under his arm, but when he came home in the evenings he would magic francs out of the end of his daughter's nose, and present his young wife with a bunch of Parma violets. In those early years the young couple would laugh and kiss, and disappear into the bedroom.

Two and a half years later a younger daughter was born, Hélène, blonde, compliant and pretty. Simone nicknamed her sister 'Poupette' or Little Doll. The family was complete, but already cracks were appearing in its fabric.

These were symbolized by their apartment which, like Janus, faced two ways. The corbelled wrought-iron balcony, on which Simone perched with a telescope spying on the passers-by, overlooked not only the smart boulevard Raspail but the legendary Carrefour Vavin, the crossroads at the raffish end of the boulevard du Montparnasse. In fact number 103 was next door to the coal depot from which blackened half-naked men emerged with sacks on their backs. To make matters worse, just two years after Simone's birth a rowdy new café opened underneath the apartment: La Rotonde. It was full of foreigners, 'wogs and pacifists', as her right-wing father called immigrant painters like Pablo Picasso, who would pay his bar bill with one of his canvases. At night the sound of music, of brawling customers, filtered upstairs: Russians smashed glasses, drunken Americans fell over.

And Georges de Beauvoir was not the aristocrat he had appeared when he first paid court to Françoise Brasseur, a rich banker's daughter. In the seventeenth century a certain Sébastien, Baron de Murat and Seigneur de Beauvoir, had been a king's councillor and superintendent of buildings at the château of Fontainebleau. He boasted a fine crest of a rampant golden lion on a silver field, under a golden fleur-de-lys. Another de Beauvoir lost his head during the Revolution, but there was no connection between any of these aristocrats and Georges. As Simone wrote with painful honesty: 'In the ranks of high society to which he laid claim for admittance, he found that he was a nobody; the "de" in de Beauvoir showed that he had a handle to his name, but the name was an obscure one, and did not automatically open for him the doors of the best clubs and the most aristocratic salons.' But even if he was not a lord, Georges de Beauvoir was determined to live like one.

Born on 25 June 1878, Georges was the grandson of a tax inspector, François-Narcisse Bertrand de Beauvoir, whose eldest son, Ernest-Narcisse, also a civil servant, married an heiress from Arras, Léontine Wartelle. The couple lived at 110 boulevard Saint-Germain, and Georges excelled at the élite Collège Stanislas until his mother died when he was thirteen. He became a dandy, spending his time with the actresses of the Comédie Française and taking up amateur dramatics.

Enrolling at the Faculty of Law, Georges could not be troubled to present the necessary thesis. Instead he took the job of secretary to a well-known lawyer, Alphonse Deville.

> He was contemptuous of successes which are obtained by the expense of hard work and effort. If you were 'born' to be someone, you automatically possessed all the essential qualities – wit, talent, charm and good breeding.

Acting gave him an entrée into the salons of the aristocracy, and legacies from his parents smoothed his path. While his elder brother, Gaston, made a living on the racetrack, Georges bought his way into high society.

By 1907 his legacies were dwindling. Georges could not be bothered to master briefs. His career stalled. It was time to find a rich wife.

At Houlgate, a fashionable seaside resort, a meeting was arranged between Georges and Françoise. He knew only that she was the daughter of Gustave Brasseur, Belgian founder of the Bank of the Meuse, named after the river that runs through Verdun, in western Lorraine. Françoise, tall, dark and musical, product of an opulent upbringing, had hoped to marry her first cousin, Charles Champigneulles, heir to a prosperous stained-glass business, but when whispers of corruption in the bank spread through Verdun, he vanished. Georges, fresh from Paris and unaware that Brasseur was on the verge of bankruptcy, was attracted by the promise of a fine *dot* or dowry to the reluctant, provincial brunette who had always played second fiddle to her blonde sister, Lili. Françoise, a devout Catholic educated at the prestigious Couvent des Oiseaux, to her surprise fell suddenly and passionately in love with the charming lawyer with a noble-sounding name, who offered her escape from an unhappy home life. Within months they were married.

But as Georges placed his honeymoon bets at the Nice racetrack, panic-stricken investors were withdrawing their money. In July 1909 the bank went into liquidation. Brasseur was sent to prison. On his release he fled to the slums around Montparnasse station, eventually moving with his wife and Lili into a flat in rue Denfert, on the east side of the local cemetery. Old friends ostracized them. Françoise was deeply affected. 'She believed herself to be dishonoured, to the point that she broke with all her relations in Verdun,' remembered Simone. 'The dowry promised to Papa was never paid.' Although Georges did not openly reproach his wife, she always felt to blame for the family's descent into comparative poverty.

Simone denied the impact of the scandal, protesting, 'I was very happy. My childhood was never affected by this drama,' but it had huge consequences. She often refused to eat. 'A spoonful for Mama, and another for Grandmama,' her mother coaxed her, but the child burst into tears at the sight of milk puddings and screamed at the oiliness of fat meat; tasting the clamminess of shellfish, she vomited. When her nanny, Louise, took her for a walk, Simone stood with her nose pressed to the windows of the confectioners, staring at the candied fruits and acid drops, and refused to go to the park. In desperation Françoise pounded sugared almonds in a mortar and added double cream for her sweet-toothed daughter, until Simone consented to dip her spoon into the mixture and finish the bowl. On the evenings when her parents entertained, and her mother took her seat at the grand piano, her profile, lit by crystal chandeliers, reflecting a myriad images in the gilt drawing-room mirrors, Simone hid behind the sofa. Biting thoughtfully into a candied apricot, she felt its exploding sweetness. Eating was both an exploration and an act of conquest.

Perhaps because of her lack of appetite, Simone grew slowly. But her small size hid a will of iron. Her paternal grandfather, Ernest-Narcisse de Beauvoir, who ruled over the estate of Meyrignac and 500 acres of chestnut groves in the Limousin, his elder son, Gaston, and wife Marguerite, his daughter, Hélène, and her husband, Maurice, in their neighbouring château, La Grillère, all doted on her. Aunt Lili, who lived close by with her parents, copied out in her neat convent script Simone's first story, written at the age of seven: 'L'Histoire de Jeannot Lapin' (The Story of Johnny Rabbit).

But the little girl flew into a rage if she could not have her way: 'I am given a red plum and I begin to peel it. "No," says Mama; and I throw myself howling on the ground.' In the Jardin du Luxembourg Simone's fury attracted the misguided sympathy of other mothers and nursemaids. 'Pauvre petite,' said one lady, offering her a sweet. 'Poor little thing.' All the thanks she got was a kick on the shins. In disgrace, Simone was locked in the broom cupboard, kicking and screaming, until bedtime. Her violence frightened her mother. Françoise scolded, but rarely smacked her. 'If you raise as much as a finger to Simone, she turns purple in the face,' she said despairingly. 'Simone is as stubborn as a mule,' agreed her father with more than a hint of pride.

No one told Simone and Poupette that their world was disintegrating: they only knew that their parents began to quarrel. Simone's tempers may have been partly due to the deteriorating domestic atmosphere, spiked with unspoken reproach, pursed lips, and the sight of Françoise bent anxiously over her black ledger book while her husband went out to the Café de Versailles, promising a win at cards to pay the bills. The child hid under her father's desk in his study, crouching on the red carpet with her favourite book, comforted by the neatness and order of the pens and blotters arrayed on the shining surface.

Françoise did not fit into Parisian society, although she did her best, joining her husband every summer to perform in the Casino at Divonne-les-Bains with a troupe of amateur actors. Behind her back, Georges's stylish friends laughed at her. 'She was provincial, unsophisticated; in this truly Parisian milieu, people smiled at her awkwardness,' wrote Beauvoir in A Very Easy Death, her memoir of her mother. Françoise was forced to endure mocking whispers and double-entendres when she entertained her husband's mistresses, for Georges was in the habit of sleeping with his friends' wives. Once she tearfully removed from his desk the photograph of his latest mistress, who often came to the house. 'You've hidden her photo,' Georges accused her. Françoise bent over her sewing: 'I never touched it.' Her rakish husband laughed and twirled his moustache.

At first Georges abided by Marcel Prévost's rule that 'one should treat a young wife with no less fervour than a mistress'. Simone never forgot the morning when, aged six or seven, she caught sight of her mother in a flimsy white nightdress, her bare feet gliding along the red carpet; the little girl was struck by her mother's sensual smile, connected in some mysterious way to the bedroom from which she had just emerged. In the evenings Françoise, a more distant, capricious figure than Simone's nanny, appeared in a dress of green tulle decorated with a single mauve flower, or, statuesque in black velvet glittering with jet, clasped her daughter in her soft, perfumed arms and kissed her goodnight. But as time went by, Françoise lost her freshness and Georges grew indifferent. From the age of thirty-five she was forced to sleep next to a man whom she loved, but who never touched her. Her personality changed; there were slaps, shouts, scenes, even in public. 'There's Monsieur and Madame fighting again,' said Louise. 'Françoise has a bitch of a temper,' Georges told his friends. The word went round that Georges's wife was neurotic, hysterical.

'I began to drown in the chaos that preceded creation,' wrote Simone. She loved her charming *boulevardier* father with romantic fervour, and took his side: 'I don't blame my father,' she wrote, drawing a conclusion from these parental rows that would stay with her for ever: *'Chez l'homme, l'habitude tue le désir.'* With men, habit kills desire.

To revive his sexual appetite, Georges turned to professionals. From the age of fifteen Simone would bump into Papa, smelling of alcohol, rolling home after a night in the Sphinx, Paris's most luxurious bordello, at eight o'clock in the morning. In the kitchen she would hear his mumbled excuses to Françoise that he'd been playing bridge, and listen as she pretended to believe him. The example of her parents, wrote Simone, 'was enough to convince me that middle-class marriage is against nature'.

The downward spiral of the Beauvoirs' marriage went hand in hand with their financial meltdown. Drafted into the army as a corporal in 1914, at thirty-eight Georges had a heart attack. On discharge he again became his father-in-law's dupe. Brasseur talked him into committing the last of his capital to a shoe factory, but it went bust in 1919. Georges's Russian stocks crashed, and he was reduced to selling space on financial newspapers. In October that year, when Simone was eleven, the family moved to a smaller, cheaper apartment at 71 rue de Rennes. They had joined the ranks of the newly poor, said Georges.

Françoise decided to manage without a servant. To do all the housework in an age when one cook-general was the absolute minimum among the middle classes was a shocking step for a woman brought up to balls and hunting parties in Verdun parkland. Her sisters-in-law, Marguerite and Hélène, her parents-in-law at Meyrignac, had both indoor and outdoor staff. Not far away, in rue le Goff, another precocious child named Jean-Paul Sartre, born three years earlier than Simone, had every whim met by three servants in addition to a devoted mother and grandparents.

'Je me sacrifie' became Françoise's mantra. But martyrdom bred resentment. She scrubbed away the sin that her husband brought into the flat, but she could not scrub away her fury. To Simone she became a devouring mouth, as she and Poupette hid from their mother's criailleries, her constant shouting, her sudden outbursts of rage. There was no question of Françoise going out to work; convention forbade it, and so she dedicated herself to nourishing the young lives in her charge. 'I've never been an egoist,' she justified herself to her elder daughter. 'I've lived for others.' But also, through others, noted Simone bitterly, of her possessive, dominating mother who allowed neither of her girls privacy or solitude.

One summer at La Grillère, when Simone was roasting crayfish with her cousins, Robert and Madeleine, five and three years older than herself, the figure of her mother, the only adult, loomed up: 'It's my right to eat with you,' she announced grimly. The teenagers were turned to stone, as surely as if they had been caught in the eye of the gorgon; but Françoise stayed, however unwelcome her presence. 'J'ai bien le droit' became a threat Simone dreaded, as her mother walked her to her private Catholic school, the Cours Adeline Désir on rue Jacob (abjuring her to look straight ahead and ignore the putains on the pavements or the winks and sweating torsos of the coalmen), sat in at classes, learnt Latin in order to help with Simone's homework and opened her letters. And for Françoise to be a good Catholic mother, it was necessary for Simone to be a dutiful daughter. Her morals were to be as pure as the white bedroom with the crucifix in the flat they had lost. Standards, as least, could be salvaged, if money could not. Over and over again Françoise told Simone that they were the same: dark-haired, difficult, unlike their sunny-tempered blonde sisters. Soon her elder daughter gave up her temper tantrums; she no longer vomited at the taste of shellfish, for shellfish had become a rare treat. Now she would be good, as good as she knew how.

There was no bathroom or running water in the new flat, which was on the fifth floor without a lift. In winter the apartment was icy cold and the family huddled round the solid-fuel stove in the study. Scrimping and saving, Françoise waged a constant battle to keep up appearances: 'At home, nothing was ever wasted: not a crust, not a wafer of soap, nor a twist of string,' recalled Simone. Free tickets, free meals, were greedily seized on. The girls wore their clothes until they were threadbare, and even after that. Françoise's hands were always busy, knitting, sewing, patching; even in the Métro she crocheted 'tatting' to edge the girls' petticoats. Idleness was a sin, work a duty.

One afternoon Simone was reluctantly helping in the kitchen:

[Mama] was washing the plates, and I was drying; through the window I could see the wall of the barracks, and other kitchens in which women were scrubbing out saucepans or peeling vegetables. Every day lunch and dinner; every day washing-up; all those hours, those endlessly recurring hours, all leading nowhere: how could I live like that? . . . No, I told myself, arranging a pile of plates in the cupboard; my life is going to lead somewhere.

It was a seminal moment that fired her fierce determination to escape. Simone's loathing for domestic drudgery recurs in a short story in which she paints herself as 'Marguerite', a Cinderella skivvy among the potato peelings. This child, impoverished emotionally as well as financially, lived in Beauvoir's heart for the rest of her life:

We lived on the fifth floor, and every evening after dinner it was my duty to carry down the dustbin. It was too small – for years Mama had been promising to buy another soon – and greasy paper, cabbage-stumps and potato peelings often spilled on the stairs; I pushed them back into the bin with my toe, though sometimes I had to deal with them by hand: even that was less revolting than the feel of the cold, greasy metal handle against one's fingers . . .

As she stood in the courtyard behind 71 rue de Rennes, heaping the rubbish on to the bins, while the yellow dust from the ashes blew back into her face, Simone calculated how to break free from the parents who had given her a man's job, taking out the rubbish, who complained that if only she had been a boy she could have gone to the Polytechnique, who said she had 'a man's brain' but still clung to the fantasy of a 'good' marriage for their daughter. Was it to become the son they wanted?

Poverty sharpened academic ambition. Simone began arriving at the school gates half an hour early, only to be teased for being a swot. In the classroom, she studied obsessively, covering every inch of paper in minute script until her teachers asked Françoise if her daughter had a 'mean streak'. The lesson that 'one must make use of everything, and of one's self, to the utmost' remained indelibly imprinted on her personality. She took extra courses in English, piano and catechism. Victory exalted, failure terrified.

The tiny room which Simone and Poupette shared had no space for a desk: 'Outside my bed, there wasn't a single corner I could call my own,' remembered Simone. 'I found it painful never to be on my own.' Doing her homework while her mother received female callers, Simone learnt to work to a constant background of voices. This became a habit, so that in the future she would rarely write in her own room but would prefer to work at a café table, the warmth from the patron's stove and the buzz of noise from customers providing a reassuring background to composition.

'My father was totally ruined,' Beauvoir remembered. But the more difficult Georges's life became, the more sorry his elder daughter felt for him. He had not forgotten how to *jouer la comédie*. When on the stage he played the part of a down-at-heel newspaper hack weighed down by money troubles and an extravagant wife, she was moved to tears. Her father's melancholy resignation added to his stature in her eyes, and she convinced herself that he possessed a superior character above money or success, which he had deliberately ignored. She was grateful to him for the outbursts of gaiety, the wild stories that transported her far from the dreariness of their flat. Only Georges, who had taught Simone to read and spell, who dictated Victor Hugo to her and read aloud the plays of Rostand, would answer her probing questions without condescension. He treated her as an equal. 'Papa used to say with pride: "Simone has a man's brain; she thinks like a man; she *is* a man."'

It was taken for granted that a man's brain was superior: the seat of reason and rigour, naturally qualifying him for public life. A woman's brain, weak organ of feeling and emotion, fitted her only for the private domain, where the best she could hope for was to become 'an angel of the hearth'. But it was frustrating to find that, despite her precocity, everyone still treated Simone like a girl. Only through the males of the family, her father and her cousin, Jacques Champigneulles, did tantalizing tales of the closed world of literature and politics enter the house. 'How I longed to explore that world!' she wrote wistfully, as she listened to them discussing Montaigne or La Rochefoucauld.

Georges and Jacques despised the Third Republic and prayed for the restoration of the monarchy. Georges did not actually subscribe to the royalist paper, L'Action française, but he had many friends among the Camelots du Roi, followers of Charles Maurras. He shared their opinion that there was no place in France for Jews like Dreyfus, whose guilt was as much a given to Georges as was the existence of God to her mother. As for his patriotism, 'It's my only religion,' the ultra-nationalist told Simone, who listened spellbound as her pagan father introduced her to the sorcery of words. Together they opened the stiff covers of the books Simone brought home from the lending library, and turned the crisp white pages. The devout child of the church who had made her first communion in a white dress, her head wreathed in roses, was absorbing forbidden ideas.

In vain Françoise snatched Claudine at School from Simone's hands and pinned together a whole chapter of Wells's War of the Worlds: her daughter was developing her own stratagems. She hid the novels of Colette under the mattress and selected English novels, which her mother considered good value as it took Simone longer to puzzle her way through them with the aid of a dictionary. Her first heroine was tomboy Jo March in Louisa Alcott's Little Women, also disappointed not to be born male. Like Simone and Poupette, the March sisters were poor and lived in a modest home. They were Protestants, obliged to read Pilgrim's Progress rather than The Imitation of Christ, but like the Beauvoir girls they were taught that a cultivated mind and true righteousness counted for more than money. How Simone felt for Jo and Meg when they had to go to a matinée in brown poplin frocks when all the other girls were dressed in silk; it was exactly her own predicament. Decked out in ill-fitting hand-me-downs from their cousins, Madeleine and Jeanne, Simone and Poupette had often turned pink with embarrassment at the parties given by their wealthy schoolfriends. The other little girls preened themselves in satin and taffeta; she and Poupette stood about awkwardly in their mud-coloured woollen frocks. Simone's greatest humiliation came on the day when, turned out by her mother in a skimpy pair of tights at the gymnastics class, where the other girls were dressed in pale blue jersey leotards with pleated skirts, she overheard Aunt Marguerite whispering: 'Simone looks like a monkey.'

I suddenly felt I was clumsy, ugly . . . a little monkey; that was certainly how those children must have looked upon me; they despised me; even worse, they ignored me. I was the helpless witness . . . of my own extinction.

Simone was thirteen. She was no longer pretty: her skin broke out in spots, and she developed nervous tics. Her father transferred his affections to Poupette. There was no help to be had from Françoise, who increasingly scorned the body and its fleshly desires, even neglecting basic hygiene. Tut-tutting with annoyance, she bound Simone's budding breasts tightly with bandages in order to fit her into her outgrown dress for a cousin's wedding. The photos confirmed what the ungainly adolescent already suspected: not only was she badly dressed, she was plain.

'*Ne gratte pas tes boutons.* Don't scratch your spots; don't twitch your nose,' said Georges. 'My poor daughter, how ugly you can be!'

2

The Frog Prince

I loathe my childhood and all that remains of it.
Jean-Paul Sartre, *Words*

FOR SIMONE DE BEAUVOIR the fear of being physically unattractive was one which, touching her briefly in childhood, receded as she emerged from 'the difficult age' and found, to her surprise, that she had no difficulty in attracting the attention of both sexes – although she never lost her reputation for being badly dressed. For Jean-Paul Sartre, the reverse process would prove true.

Sartre's first memories were of being a beautiful child. Chubby-cheeked, golden-haired, he stares out of early photographs with all the confidence of an adored son. 'I am pink and fair, with curls, I have full cheeks, and my expression is one of amiable deference to the established order; I pout my lips with hypocritical arrogance; I know what I'm worth.'

Born on 21 June 1905, he, like Beauvoir, had seemed set on a path of privilege. His father, Jean-Baptiste Sartre, was upwardly mobile. Sartre, from *sartor*, 'tailor' in the local dialect, is a peasant name from Périgord: small, dark men bound to the land, like Jean-Baptiste's slow-witted elder brother Joseph, who never strayed far from the family farm at Puifeybert, a hamlet not far from Thiviers, in the Dordogne. But Jean-Baptiste took after his father, Eymard, who studied medicine at Montpellier before becoming the only doctor in Thiviers; and although the boy dutifully accompanied Dr Sartre on his visits to his patients by horse-drawn cart, his ambitions soon reached far beyond the family house on the rue du Thon, which the doctor had bought after marrying a local heiress, Elodie Chavoix, the pharmacist's daughter. The son escaped to Paris and the École Polytechnique, nursery of France's military and political élite.

Jean-Baptiste was small, only five foot two, and he came from land-locked Périgord, but, unlike most ambitious Polytechniens, he dreamt of going away to sea. On 1 October 1897 he joined the French navy. It proved a dangerous choice. Service in Indochina led to the ruin of his health and disgust at French colonial wars. 'I'd have preferred a trip to Japan,' he wrote home. 'The Far Eastern campaign is a mess.' Two years later, he was sent back to France on convalescent leave. One day in Cherbourg a fellow ensign, Georges Schweitzer, introduced him to his sister, twenty-one-year-old Anne-Marie. Within a few weeks Jean-Baptiste had proposed marriage.

On May 5 1904, Jean-Baptiste Sartre and Anne-Marie Schweitzer were married in Paris. The bride, who stood a head taller than her husband, brought a dowry of 40,000 francs, which may have encouraged Jean-Baptiste in his decision to leave the navy. He requested six months' leave without pay, and moved into his wife's family flat on the rue de Siam, in the 16th *arrondissement* of Paris. Within months Anne-Marie was pregnant, but before she was delivered the navy again claimed the expectant father, who had failed to find another post. In May 1905 he reported as first officer on the destroyer *La Tourmente*, bound for Crete. Not until 5 November did illness bring him home to meet his newborn son.

'We trod the same earth for a while, that is all,' Jean-Paul wrote later of his father. Jean-Baptiste's reaction was more effusive: 'My little Paul is lovely,' he told his parents. 'He screams at the top of his lungs, roars with laughter, never cries. His eyes are curious, intelligent and very sweet . . . He is very precocious.' Less than a year later, on 17 September 1906, the father was dead of enterocolitis and TB. Just fifteen months after Jean-Paul's birth, Anne-Marie Sartre had become a widow.

The tall twenty-four-year-old, in her black weeds, returned to her parents' house in Meudon. 'Families naturally prefer widows to unmarried mothers, but only just,' Sartre recalled bitterly in 1963, when he wrote his autobiography, *Words*. Anne-Marie, the younger daughter of Chrétien-Charles Schweitzer, a teacher of German from Alsace, and his wife, Louise, had few skills to offer. She had been brought up to be bored, said her son: to sew, to play the piano, and to cultivate the traditional female virtues of quietness and submissiveness. Returning, dependent, with 'Poulou', her pet chicken, in her arms, she was deemed guilty. She had chosen a husband who had failed to support her. Nothing was said. Charles, who at sixty-four was about to retire, silently went back to work. But Anne-Marie knew that she was a burden. Humbly she kept house for her parents, acted as companion and maid to her mother, but she had again become a minor: a tarnished virgin. She had no income of her own; her clothes became threadbare; and when old friends asked her out to dinner, she had to promise to be back by ten o'clock. Her father, in his nightshirt, would patrol the bedroom, watch in hand. 'On the final stroke of ten, he would begin to roar,' his grandson remembered. Invitations grew rare.

Jean-Paul's view of his father's family may have been coloured by his mother's attitude towards them as she struggled to have the remnants of her dowry repaid. But he inherited more than he cared to acknowledge from the pocket-sized ensign with the enormous moustache whose photograph hung on the bedroom wall. Physically he and Jean-Baptiste were doubles. At five foot two and a half, the son was just half an inch taller than the father, although from his mother, rather than the balding officer, he inherited his thick, blond hair. And it was with his mother that he fell in love:

> I was shown a young giantess and told that she was my mother. On my own I should more likely have taken her for an elder sister . . . I loved her: but how could I respect her if no one else did? There were three bedrooms in our house, my grandfather's, my grandmother's, and the 'children's'. We were the 'children': both minors and both maintained . . . A young girl's bed had been put in *my* room. The young girl slept alone and woke chaste . . . I should marry her later on so as to look after her.

They were two does in a wood, playing with the Fairies. Two lost and incestuous children. 'My mother and I were the same age, and we never left each other's side. She used to call me her "attendant knight" and her little man.'

This idyll might have continued for ever, had it not been for Poulou's grandfather, Charles Schweitzer, a tall, white-bearded figure of great presence, who 'bore so close a resemblance to God the Father that he was often taken for him', his fearful grandson remembered. A Lutheran, Charles – or Karl – was the eldest of the five sons of the mayor of Pfaffenhofen, his brother Louis being the father of the most famous member of the family, Albert. In 1872, after the French defeat in the Franco-Prussian war, Karl chose French citizenship and married a Catholic, Louise Guillemin. But he still talked to his brothers in Alsatian dialect and taught his grandson to call his grandparents 'Karlémami'.

Strangely enough, for a teacher, Karl distrusted school for his grandson. Although his two grown-up sons, Georges and Emile, had been educated by Dominican friars, he decided Poulou was too precious – or precocious – to entrust to a *lycée*, and educated him at home. 'My young pupil – please forgive a doting grandfather – is naturally and prodigiously intelligent in everything,' he wrote to a friend, judging accurately that 'he is eloquent and combative'. Modelling himself on Victor Hugo, who had written a treatise on the art of being a grandpapa, he devoted himself to the infant prodigy. On one occasion only was Poulou enrolled at the Lycée Montaigne. Karl explained to the headmaster that his grandson's only fault was to be *too* advanced for his age; the cooperative headmaster placed Poulou with older boys, only for the deluded grandfather to be summoned to the school to be shown the result of his grandson's first dictation: an inky sheet, covered with blots, in which '*aime*' was spelt '*ême*', '*sauvage*' '*çovache*'. Poulou was barely up to the standard of the preparatory class. Anne-Marie burst into giggles when she saw her son's misspellings, but Karl quelled her with a terrible look. The next day he withdrew Poulou from school.

The only child was moulded by the expectations of three adults, Karl, his mother and his grandmother. 'Until the age of ten, I was alone between one old man and two women,' Sartre remembered. The booming voice of his grandfather, which even in middle age he still heard in his head like a harsh Jehovah ordering him to the writing table every morning, formed an austere Protestant conscience. Alone with the old man, Jean-Paul became Karl's *wunderkind*. The boy's first poems were written from his holiday home in Arachon to the headmaster still teaching his classes in Paris. Poulou knew that he could no more escape his daily duty, to pick up his pen and write, than the old teacher had done on the day when he picked up the chalk and returned to the classroom, to keep his destitute daughter and fatherless son. At that age, certain traits became fixed in Poulou. Even in 1939, when he was thirty-four and about to serve his country against the Nazi invaders, Simone de Beauvoir noted that when she knocked on Sartre's door to waken him in the morning, he answered her: 'Oui, ma petite maman' ['Yes, Mummy dearest'].

In 1911 the family moved back to Paris, to 1 rue Le Goff, near the boulevard Saint-Michel, and Karl opened a language school. It was only a stone's throw from the eastern entrance to the Luxembourg Gardens, and Anne-Marie took Poulou to the park every day. His small stature was becoming noticeable. Even at seven or eight, Anne-Marie still carried him: 'a shrimp that interested no one', wrote Sartre, bitter still at fifty-five.

Seeing her son leaning alone against a tree, guessing that 'I was in danger of seeing myself as a dwarf – which I am not quite', Anne-Marie feigned impatience. 'What are you waiting for?' she demanded. 'Ask them if they'll play with you.' Poulou shook his head. It was a point of honour not to ask. Anne-Marie advanced towards the ladies knitting on the iron seats. 'Shall I speak to their mothers?' 'No,' begged the little boy. She took his hand, and the two of them went from group to group, 'ever pleading and ever rejected'. 'I never got over it,' said Sartre.

Increasingly he consoled himself in his grandfather's library, on the sixth floor of the apartment, a temple where the study of the Humanities led to the Divine, as Karl explained to him. High up among the rooftops of Paris, Sartre would for the rest of his life prefer to breathe in the rarefied air of belles-lettres from a symbolic sixth floor. As he wrote, 'every man has his natural place . . . childhood decides everything'. Roaming the shelves, Poulou learnt long passages of *Madame Bovary* by heart, turned the fables of La Fontaine into alexandrines, and made his first attempts at writing stories, in violet ink, in an exercise book. The first one, called 'Pour un papillon' (For a Butterfly) was lifted from a comic his mother had bought him, but Poulou rejoiced at his plagiarism. Just by changing the names of the protagonists, touching up the lines, he had made the characters his own, and, sitting at his desk, furrowing his seven-year-old brow, he could pretend that he was *a writer*.

But Karl was becoming uneasy at the spoiling of his pretty grandson, pampered by the women of the house and endlessly photographed in a sailor suit, at his mother's knee, or in the prow of a ship. Anne-Marie amused herself by touching up these photos with coloured crayons. 'You're making a girl of him; I don't want my grandson to be a milksop,' said Karl, but Anne-Marie held out. 'I was to have the sex of angels,' remembered Sartre; 'indeterminate, but feminine around the edges.' Already he preferred the company of girls and had one or two special friends he called his 'fiancées'.

Like Lucien Fleurier, the boy in Sartre's short story, 'L'Enfance de Chef', who is treated as a doll by the grown-ups, he was unsure of his gender. Dressed up as an angel, Lucien feels that his sexuality can change at a moment's notice. When one of the gentlemen draws him between his knees and strokes his arm and asks, smiling: 'What's your name? Jacqueline, Lucienne . . . ?' Lucien turns red and says: 'My name is Lucien.'

> He was no longer sure about not being a little girl: a lot of people had kissed him and called him mademoiselle, everybody thought he was so charming with his gauze wings, his long blue robe, small bare arms and blond curls: he was afraid that the people would suddenly decide he wasn't a little boy any more; wouldn't let him take off his dress except to sleep . . . and when he wanted to wee-wee during the day, he'd have to lift up like Nanette and sit on his heels . . . Maybe it's happened already and I *am* a little girl; he felt so soft inside that it made him a little sick . . .

One day Karl could take no more. Poulou, at seven, was too old for golden curls. When his mother was out, the headmaster marched his grandson to the barber's, where the small boy watched as his curls slid down the white towel around his neck and dropped to the floor. He went home, shorn, but proud.

His mother's reaction was unexpected. She shut herself in the bedroom, weeping. Not only had her little girl been changed into a little boy, but his ugliness had been revealed. The white speck in his right eye, which was to blind it and make him squint, had worsened, and his sight was fading. Even Karl was disconcerted: 'He had gone out with his wonder child and brought back a toad.'

It was a defining moment for Poulou. No longer did the ladies crowd around him, laughing at his jokes, as they used to. Like Lucien, he lost his audience: 'He still went to the salon when Mama was having visitors, but since they had cut off his curls the grown-ups paid less attention to him . . . unless it was to point out a moral to him.'

Revealed as a boy, Poulou seemed hardly to exist.

The magnitude of the change is recorded in *Words*: 'I . . . discovered my ugliness – which was for a long time my negative principle, the quicklime in which the wonderful child was dissolved.' Pretty Poulou had become a toad, the horror from which other people recoiled. Like the Breton poet Tristan Corbière, who also caricatured himself as 'the toad', he felt an outcast: '*Il s'en va, froid, sous sa pierre* [he's going away, cold, beneath his stone].

'*Bonsoir, ce crapaud-là, c'est moi.*'

*

It was Anne-Marie who rescued her distraught son. She bought him a Punch and Judy theatre, and encouraged him to spend his pocket money on puppets. Deprived of the company of other children, Poulou invented imaginary companions. In the lavatory at rue Le Goff he made up plays, rehearsing until he was word-perfect. Then Maman and he set off, Poulou carrying the puppets and a towel, to the Luxembourg Gardens. In the 'English Garden', Poulou picks a chair, crouches down behind it, drapes the towel around its legs, and displays his glove puppets through the uprights of the back of the chair. The seat of the chair becomes his stage. He moves his actors, speaks their parts, as if for himself alone; but, within a quarter of an hour, the children break off their games, sit down on chairs, and listen to the free performance.

Once again, Poulou has girlfriends. There is Nicole, pretty and freckled, who becomes his new 'fiancée'. She is particularly dear to the diminutive, squinting boy because he has won her over by means of his 'contrivances'. Humbly, he recognizes that it is impossible for him to gain the affection of little girls except by his talents as an actor and story-teller. 'I should have hated anyone to love me for my looks or my physical charm,' he wrote. 'What was necessary was for them to be captivated by the charm of my . . . plays, my speeches, my poem, and to come to love me on that basis.' It was an important connection: art and love, one that became, said Sartre, the deepest element in his desire to write. If not through looks, then through words, he would seduce women.

In 1963, from the pedestal of fame, Sartre could deny that he had ever wanted to be loved for his looks. It was a courageous, mendacious statement. In fact he brooded over the burden of his ugliness, identifying miserably with the story of Cyrano de Bergerac, rejected by Roxane, writing his own version of 'Beauty and the Beast' and finding a grain of hope in discovering that it was in his guise of Beast that the monster first won Beauty's interest. She had recognized his greatness, as perhaps another Beauty would recognize Sartre's, if only he worked hard enough.

In the library, he was separated from the natural world. Unlike Beauvoir, he had no one to play croquet with on the lawn, or to dam streams; there was no bird-nesting with other boys, no games of conkers in the chestnut woods: 'Books were my birds and nests, my pets, my stable and my countryside; the library was the world trapped in a mirror.' But this did not prevent Poulou from setting off on his adventures, hero of the novels he wrote in bed in a black exercise book with red-edged pages, when he was 'lucky enough' to be ill, for he was a sickly child, or at his desk, scribbling secretly. He wrote for his own pleasure, feeling that

> I was born from writing: before that, there was only a reflection in a mirror. From my first novel, I knew that a child had entered the palace of mirrors. By writing, I existed, I escaped from the grown-ups; but I existed only to write, and if I said: me – that meant the me who wrote.

Once again, Anne-Marie encouraged him. One night, when Poulou leapt on to his bed in his nightshirt, she gave his shoulders a hard squeeze and said with a smile: 'My little fellow will write.' And when the German pupils came to dinner in the house, Karl would lay his hand on Jean-Paul's skull and say, articulating every syllable so as not to waste the opportunity of teaching French by the direct method: 'He's got the bump of literature.'

One day an illustration in a magazine caught Jean-Paul's eye. It showed a vast crowd massed on the quayside in New York, awaiting the arrival of Charles Dickens; as his ship could be seen drawing near, a thousand caps waved. Jean-Paul was impressed at such greatness. It became clear to him that authors were as much heroes as knights-errant, those men of steel who rescued fair maidens. Whatever their physical imperfections, their 'womanishness' even, writers' books were their deeds, which could win them as much fame as prowess with the sword. It was a comforting conclusion to stumble upon, that 'the mind can rise above abjection, can take responsibility for the body's miseries, dominate and suppress them: manifesting itself through the ill-favoured body, it can shine all the more brightly'.

In October 1914 Anne-Marie bought her son another stack of exercise books, with mauve covers featuring Joan of Arc. It was a sign of the times. Jean-Paul set about writing a new novel featuring a Private Perrin who captures the Kaiser. By his side were the comics, the cowboy stories, which he and his mother secretly bought together, for he had tired of the rows of classics in the rooftop library: he no longer wanted to be Corneille, but a writer of thrillers. The war years were the happiest years of Jean-Paul's childhood, when he and his mother were insepar-able and developed their own private language. But one morning, just as Anne-Marie was about to pay for some second-hand *Buffalo Bills* at a *bouquiniste* by the Seine, the stall holder spoke to Jean-Paul:

'You're spoilt, boy, you're spoilt.'

Poulou clasped his mother's hand more tightly. He was not used to being spoken to so familiarly. At that moment, he later recalled: 'I learnt to scent the male, to fear and loathe him.'

In October 1915, when Jean-Paul was ten years and three months old, his sequestration finally ended. Karl entered him at the junior Lycée Henri IV, his father's old school, as a dayboy. He came bottom of his first class, and an anxious Anne-Marie hurried to make an appointment with his teacher, Monsieur Ollivier, who promised to keep an eye on his new pupil. Soon Jean-Paul was getting better marks. To his surprise he found friends, other boys to play tag with in the place du Panthéon. One day the classroom door opened and a skinny new boy entered; he wore steel spectacles, a muffler, and the air of a chick susceptible to the cold. 'Name, profession of parent?' demanded the teacher.

'Paul-Yves Nizan, engineer's son,' came the reply. Jean-Paul stared at the new boy; behind the glasses perched on his aquiline nose, he too had a squint.

The two became inseparable. Jean-Paul thought his broken world mended. But the *drôle de famille*, or odd family, which had so long sheltered him from reality and left him feeling strangely lacking in substance for all its smothering love, was about to change again. It was 1917: Anne-Marie told her son that she had decided to accept the proposal of marriage made to her by a former classmate of his father's, M. Joseph Mancy.

3

Jacques

I comforted myself . . . by entertaining the idea of marriage: the day would come when, clad in white satin, in a blaze of candles and under great blasts of organ music, I would be changed once more into a queen.

Simone de Beauvoir, *Memoirs of a Dutiful Daughter*

FRANÇOISE'S CATHOLIC FAITH was her armour against the evil that she saw all around her, and she was determined that her daughter should be equally protected. To her delight, Simone seemed made in the maternal mould: she made her confession twice a week to old Abbé Martin, attended Mass three times a week, and read a chapter from *The Imitation of Christ* every morning. At school she often slipped into the chapel to pray between lessons. With the onset of puberty, her piety deepened. From the age of twelve she began to practise mortification of the flesh, scrubbing her skin with pumice stone until it bled, and whipping her body with the gold chain of her rosary. She knelt before the suffering Christ, gazing with the 'eyes of a lover . . . at his grave, tender, handsome face', and prayed ardently for mystical union with God. She went into annual retreat, sleeping on a stone floor; but the more fiercely she demanded apparitions and ecstasies, the more elusive the divine presence remained. Eventually Simone decided that it must be everyday life that separated her from the supernatural. The solution was simple: she would become a nun. Not a sister of charity, for Simone had no time for good works, but a white-cloaked mendicant: 'I will become a Carmelite,' she vowed, informing her parents that she would never marry.

Georges smiled, just as he did when her aunts enthused over the miracles at Lourdes: 'We'll have plenty of time to think about that when you're fifteen years old.' He knew his daughter better than she knew herself.

One day the Abbé gave Simone a ticking-off: she was disobedient, noisy, she answered back in class. Simone ran from the confessional never to return; was God a fussy old church-hen like the Abbé, with his swishing black skirts? She went to the church of Saint-Sulpice to find a new confessor, but no priest seemed the exact 'incarnation of God'. Her father told her that great writers shared his scepticism; only women went to church. As she ticked off the 'proofs' for God's existence, Simone dismissed the allegory of the clock and the clockmaker. But surely the voices of Joan of Arc were proof enough?

Her doubts grew as she and Françoise, equally imperious, battled for supremacy in the household. Georges always took his wife's side: 'Do as your mother says,' he told her. As she fervently identified with her atheist father, who denied her his love in favour of her more feminine sister, and rebelled against her 'spiritual' mother, Simone's mental conflict deepened. For so long she had felt 'necessary' to God, and 'to His glory'. How could she, who craved the Absolute, not be part of His plan? But, one day, leaning out of the window at Meyrignac, her grandfather's house outside Uzerche, she gazed at the starry sky and suddenly knew that she could not be a nun. 'I no longer believe in God,' I told myself. 'He had ceased to exist for me.' What remained was a mystical, pantheistic sense of nature that had its roots in her childhood experiences roaming at will through the wooded family estates. Henceforth Simone would find the transcendental in the mountains and forests of France, but not in front of an altar.

Her obsessional nature sought a new outlet. At her private school, the Cours Désir, in 1917, Simone met a new girl, Elizabeth Lacoin, known by her family as Zaza, whose wealthy family owned Gagnepain and would employ Stépha, the Polish governess. Zaza was the second of five daughters of a mother to whom she was passionately attached. The ten-year-old girl's body was scarred from burns, the result of an accident, but her thin, intelligent face and sharp mimicry of their teacher, Mademoiselle Bodet, made Simone resolve to know her. A vast social gulf separated the Lacoins, who belonged to the *bonne bourgeoisie* of the 16th *arrondissement*, from the shabby genteel Beauvoirs, and Simone determined on drastic action. Despite her mother's favourite saying, taken from Marcel Prévost: 'A girl has two friends: her mother and her needle', Simone was all fingers and thumbs when it came to sewing, but she made Zaza a raffia bag and lined it with red satin. When she presented it, Zaza blushed to the roots of her hair. Such behaviour was embarrassingly forward. Both girls stood looking at each other, unable to find word or gesture to express their heart-thumping emotions. The next day they met with their mothers. 'Now thank Madame de Beauvoir for all the trouble she has taken,' said Mme Lacoin in an attempt to pass off Simone's faux pas as polite behaviour. This remark confirmed Simone in her dislike for the self-assured matron with the perfect *maquillage* who contrasted so greatly with her own gauche parent.

The two girls became inseparable. To begin with, Simone was the follower rather than the leader, the dutiful daughter in thrall to the sophisticated Zaza, who introduced her new friend to the subversive maxims of La Rochefoucauld. At the Cours Désir, despite being affiliated to the Jesuits, the unqualified spinsters who taught the girls honoured Christian virtues above degrees. But when Georges proposed that Simone and Poupette should attend a *lycée*, Simone refused to be separated from Zaza. Instead she became an auto-didact, like the character in Sartre's *Nausea*, reading voraciously in both French and English.

Simone's sense of difference and isolation nourished a growing sense of uniqueness. Although her teachers criticized her French compositions for being stilted, in a friend's album, at the age of fifteen, she answered the question: 'What do you want to do in later life? with "to be a famous author" . . . I had set my heart on that profession, to the exclusion of everything else.' Like George Eliot, whose *Mill on the Floss* was her favourite novel, like Rosalind Lehmann, whose *Dusty Answer* she and Zaza both read, like Stendhal, Flaubert, and Alain Fournier, author of *Le Grand Meaulnes*, on whose moody hero her cousin Jacques modelled himself, she would be a novelist. It seemed the surest route to success. Zaza laughed at her friend's ambitions. Provocatively she declared, 'Bringing nine children into the world as Mama has done, is just as good as writing books.' Simone disagreed; babies and animals were repugnant to her: 'Maternity was something I couldn't entertain, and I was astounded whenever Zaza started cooing over new-born infants.' In the summer of 1926, at Meyrignac, she began 'a vast novel', whose heroine was to live through her own experiences and find herself in conflict with her environment. Halfway through, not knowing the outcome, she gave up.

Perhaps it was fortunate that Simone had no interest in babies for, as the Beauvoirs' poverty bit more deeply, bourgeois marriage was moving out of reach. This did not prevent Simone calculating her prospects. Was she quite definitely ugly? she asked Poupette. Might she grow up into a woman pretty enough to be loved? Accustomed to hearing their father declare that Simone was a man, Poupette did not understand the question; she loved her, Zaza did. What was she worrying about?

Simone's love for Zaza grew intensely physical. Photographs of the two show them sitting side by side, in identical white dresses, hands touching. The earnest, painstaking Simone was overwhelmed by a flood of feeling:

> I allowed myself to be uplifted by that wave of joy which went on mounting inside me as violent as fresh water falling from a cataract, as naked, beautiful, and bare as a granite cliff.

And when she watched exquisitely dressed Marguerite de Théricourt, daughter of one of the richest men in France, being driven to school in a chauffeured car, and stared at her soft, nude shoulders veiled by chiffon, Simone felt the same strange tightening of her throat.

The journal Simone kept from the age of seventeen reveals a green girl, 'unripe fruit', the term she would later use of her own virgin lesbian lovers, trembling on the verge of womanhood. 'I'm waiting for you,' she writes, of the imaginary lover who will awaken her to romance and passion. Her notebook is peppered with quotations from Claudel, Tagore, Bergson and Mauriac, expressing her longing: 'Est-ce que j'aime? Ai-je aimé? Je ne sais pas . . .' 'Am I in love? Have I been in love? I don't know.' From the age of twelve she had been conscious of physical desire, tossing and turning in bed, 'calling for a man's body to be pressed against my own, for a man's hand to stroke my flesh': her flannel nightdress had become a 'shirt of nettles'. When her cousin Titite became engaged, and openly expressed her impatience to be married to her 'ravishing' fiancé, Simone was full of sympathy. 'Are your studies all you want out of life?' asked Titite curiously. 'Don't you want anything more?' Simone shook her head; she dared not confess that her head was filled with thoughts of Titite's brother, Jacques Champigneulles, son of the perfidious Charles who had jilted Françoise. Titite would have laughed. Jacques generally ignored his cousin, apart from occasionally beating her at tennis. Mournfully Simone longed for the day when he would realize her true worth.

After Charles was killed in a motoring accident his wife, Aunt

Germaine, remarried and moved to Châteauvillain, to which, at the age of eight, Simone had been sent to spend a summer holiday with Jacques, also eight. 'With his rosy cheeks, his curly hair bright as freshly fallen horse-chestnuts, he was a very good-looking little boy,' Simone remembered forty years later. In Paris Jacques often invited her to visit him in the old house that also served as a factory for the manufacture of stained-glass windows. One day he presented Simone with a gift: a real stained-glass window, made of blue, red and white lozenges framed in lead, which he had made himself. On it, in black letters, were the words: 'For Simone.' 'I called Jacques "my fiancé",' she remembered. 'I took our engagement very seriously.'

Jacques often spent the evening with the Beauvoirs during term times at the Collège Stanislas where he was a pupil. Françoise, who had never forgotten his father, Charles, had a soft spot for his son and encouraged his visits. Simone began to fantasize that, like Maggie Tulliver, who proved irresistible to Stephen Guest in *The Mill on the Floss*, her brilliant mind would attract just such a dashing lover to her side. 'I should be in love,' she wrote, 'the day a man came along whose intelligence, culture and authority could bring me into subjection . . . I should not marry unless I met someone more accomplished than myself, yet my equal, my double.' Only such a man would allow her to 'fulfil her destiny as a woman'.

By 1926 Simone was developing into a young woman of remarkable intellectual gifts, but one who was confused as to which path to follow. Lying in the long grass at La Grillère that summer, working through an extensive reading list in French and English, she made notes to herself to 'finish Verlaine, read Mallarmé, Rimbaud . . . continue with Conrad, Joyce, Wilde, Whitman, Blake, Dostoevsky, Tolstoy . . .' while fretting that she was too intellectual. 'I can no longer change . . . Certainly I am very individual,' the eighteen-year-old wrote on 12 August, as she worried that she was turning into a *bas bleu*, a bluestocking: 'But is this incompatible with the disinterested love of others?'

The girl scribbling in her diary daydreams of becoming a wife: '*Un jour je me marierai,*' she writes hopefully on the 17th.

One day I'll get married. If it's not probable, it is at least possible . . . At any rate, it's the greatest happiness that I can meet in this life; I think it's the greatest happiness in life that any woman, or any man, can attain. When two beings love one another, marriage is, perhaps, a great and beautiful thing.

For three months in the Limousin, Simone mused over her future. Jacques, meanwhile, seized control of the factory from his uncle. He had grown into a striking young man: gold-flecked eyes under curly golden brown hair, a sensuous mouth and outwardly confident air made for an irresistible combination, especially when coupled with the inner vulnerability which Simone detected within this 'little lord'. She should have been more wary. When Jacques was twelve he had improvised a charade in which he took the part of a young man who refuses to marry a girl without a dowry. 'If I am to set up home,' he explained in this apologia for marriages of convenience, 'I must be able to guarantee my children sufficiently easy circumstances.'

The relationship between the cousins became the subject of heated debate. Françoise and the aunts discussed the match endlessly: 'What a catch it would be for a girl without a dowry if he were to marry me!' Grandfather Brasseur was firmly opposed. 'The name of Champigneulles is forever dishonoured,' declared the virtuous bankrupt sternly. 'No granddaughter of mine shall ever marry a Champigneulles.' Françoise and Simone took no notice. Simone dined frequently at Jacques's home, where Aunt Germaine and Titite welcomed her warmly. In the afternoons she often slipped in to see Jacques in the long gallery where, standing at his workbench in the dim coloured light filtered through the stained-glass windows, he would read aloud to her from the poems of Laforgue or Mallarmé, or the novels of Jacques Rivière. Sitting on the red velvet sofa, watching Jacques walk up and down, a cigarette dangling from his lips, Simone felt they were drawing closer. When she asked him to explain what he was reading, he replied with a quotation from Cocteau: 'It's like a railway accident: something you feel but can't explain in words.'

She imagined her dress: white satin, the thunder of the organ, all eyes upon her as she walked up the aisle. The greatest prize was the prospect of a home of her own. At La Grillère she built castles in the air: the Champigneulles' 'beautiful apartment with its thick pile carpets, the airy drawing-room, and the shadowy gallery were already my own hearth and home; I would read side by side with Jacques, and I would think of "the two of us", just as in former days I had thought of "the four of us"'.

It was Georges de Beauvoir who crushed his daughters' hopes: 'You girls will never marry; you have no dowries; you'll have to work for a living.' There was bitterness in his voice. In his daughters he saw the embodiment of his own failure, knowing, even as he flicked through a handbook on marriage for *Jeunes Filles sans Dots* (*Young Ladies without Dowries*), that no handy hints could repair the damage done.

For what purpose had Françoise taught her daughters the rules of good society, that a 'lady' ought not to show too much bosom, wear short skirts, dye her hair, have it bobbed, make up her face, or kiss her husband in the Métro? Now the girls were *déclassées*, barely clinging by their fingertips to the class into which they were born. That there was an abyss of poverty even below their own was revealed to Simone when Françoise took her to visit Louise, her old nurse, and new baby. The family lived in one room, a dark, squalid sixth-floor garret. Soon afterwards the baby died. 'I cried for hours,' recorded the shocked teenager.

But Simone's poverty, which bred in her a steely determination to better herself, was nevertheless a twist of fate with unexpected benefits. It allowed her opportunities denied to Zaza, whose wealthy family forbade her a future outside marriage. Geography also helped. Had Simone not lived in Paris, her choices would have been more limited. As she reached the end of her schooldays, Georges reluctantly accepted that she had to find a career: it was no longer the nineteenth century, when ladies down on their luck became governesses. He suggested the civil service, a traditional family choice for the Beauvoirs, saying resentfully: '*You*, at any rate, will have a pension.' But a new career more to Simone's liking had opened up since the passing of the Law Camille Sée, which gave girls access to state *lycées*. The law also created the new profession of female *lycée* teacher. Simone set her sights on the highest qualification, the fiercely competitive *agrégation* examination, which demanded two further years at university on top of a degree. But it was the key of the golden door. An *agrégé* had a job for life, and a pension. As a privileged civil servant, or *fonctionnaire*, he or she taught less and earned more than an ordinary teacher.

Simone's first taste of philosophy at the Cours Désir, where Zaza's father, an engineer, had insisted that his daughter and her friend learnt the 'boys' subjects of philosophy and mathematics, had inspired her. It seemed to her to 'go to essentials', especially when an article about a woman philosopher named Léontine Zanta caught her eye. Mademoiselle Zanta had taken her doctorate, one of the first two women in France to do so. Photographed in a grave and thoughtful posture, sitting at her desk, she lived with a young niece whom she had adopted. 'How I should love to have such flattering things written about *me*,' wrote Simone. The challenge of philosophy was all the greater because, in the words of a male reporter in 1914, 'it requires such strength of mind and such experience in handling ideas that it is considered a male prerogative'. Zanta, active in the French feminist movement in the 1920s and author of several novels, became Simone's real-life heroine.

'I wanted to be one of those pioneers,' wrote Simone. But the poor teaching at the Cours Désir meant that she had only scraped through the philosophy exam with eleven marks out of twenty. Her next step was made possible only as the result of historical change since World War I, which brought about the slow death of the dowry system. Economic necessity pushed Parisian women into the labour force, and many who demanded access to university education were going to the college for women at Sèvres, outside Paris, sister to the élite École Normale Supérieure, which was closed to their sex. But if his daughter was to be forced into the workplace, Georges wanted the best for her. Simone's destination was to be the Sorbonne, open to both sexes, where she could do her *licence* (degree), her teaching diploma and, finally, the *agrégation*. She was to be a prodigy, taking three *licences*, in literature, philosophy and mathematics.

In the autumn of 1925 Simone was luckier than she realized. 'By and large we have won the game,' she would write of the women of her generation in 1949, in *The Second Sex*. But had she been just a few years older she would have missed these opportunities. Only by the skin of her teeth did she sit university exams that until 1924 had been reserved for men. Even Léontine Zanta had never been an *agrégée* in philosophy, and by 1928 only seven women had succeeded in winning this coveted, 'masculine' qualification. Three years later the French state took another remarkable step forward in granting female teachers the same salaries as their male counterparts. The institutional barriers to Simone's success fell like dominoes just as she was starting out on her career, which is why she could write, with a startling lack of perception: 'My feminine status has been for me neither an embarrassment nor an alibi.'

As Simone stood outside the black gates of the Sorbonne under the great clock, staring up at the garlanded figures of gods and goddesses, and contemplating the stone figure of Auguste Comte in the cobbled square, where the pigeons fluttered among the wet trees, it might have occurred to her how far she had come from her little private school. Aware of her exceptional abilities, she asks herself, 'Am I proud?' on 16 September, as she waits for the new term to start at the Sorbonne. 'Yes, in the sense that I love myself passionately; that I'm interested in myself, and that I am sure that I want something, I mean I want to be a woman with a unique and interesting life.'

*

On 6 September 1926 the Beauvoirs returned from La Grillère. Jacques had failed his law exam, and Simone sent him a letter of commiseration. There was no reply, and back in the rue de Rennes apartment with its threadbare carpets, she waited anxiously. Her mother, tired of her weeping, forbade her to see Jacques. There were nights of 'solitude and anguish, *toujours en moi ce meme désir*'. She was a girl who wanted '*un grand amour*' without the means of realizing it. Humbly she wrote that it pleased her to love, without being loved in return. At last, on 20 October, Françoise relented. 'Maman thinks she's making me very happy sending me round to Jacques,' wrote a sulky Simone. But when they did meet, he simply handed her an envelope. '*Il m'a dit un merci si bref et chuchoté*,' she recorded, mystified by his hurried murmur of thanks. But Jacques's message, written in violet ink at the top of his reply, should have given her pause for thought: 'Is it any business of yours?'

'I only torture myself,' confided Simone to her diary, in a rare moment of self-knowledge. Miserably she copied out quotations from Oscar Wilde's *Intentions*: 'Action is the last refuge of he who only knows how to dream.' On 29 October she underlined her entry: 'It is only necessary to search for happiness.' 'Eight days without seeing you,' she sighed on 6 November. '*Pardon! A toi, Jacques . . . toi, je t'aime.*' 'It's so tiring to have this same hope for so long,' she sadly admitted.

Hearing rumours that he had a girl named Magda, she threw herself on the sofa and sobbed. There seemed to be a kind of conspiracy in the air: his family and hers regarded them as 'already practically engaged', and yet Jacques had never so much as kissed her. Dolefully Simone clung to the knowledge that Jacques found her attractive; had he not said to his mother, as Françoise repeated with a wry smile: 'Simone is very pretty; it's such a pity that Aunt Françoise dresses her so badly.'

Day after day Simone's pen races over the pages of her journal, the firm, sloping, at times illegible writing, with its heavy underlinings, tracing every twist and turn of her passion for her cousin. The contrast is dramatic between the feverish emotion of this adolescent diary, with its outpouring of love for Jacques, whose name – and Zaza's – peppers every paragraph, whose casual remarks provoke paroxyms of joy, whose rejection results in storms of misery, and the cool and measured tone of *Memoirs of a Dutiful Daughter*, a moral existential tale written in 1956, in which the author denies her desire. Beauvoir cannot resist recounting the story of her first love, but assures her readers that the feelings she has for Jacques are like that of a sister for an elder brother, a spiritual 'love for an angel' guide.

> The idea of marrying him revolted me . . . I wanted to run away . . . The thought of love shared between us chilled my heart . . . Jacques never once caused me the least physical disturbance or roused in me the faintest sexual desire.

When Jacques fails his exams for the second time and takes his first steps on the road to the alcoholism, he disqualifies himself from marriage to the implacably serious Simone, who from childhood wants 'everything in my life to be justified by a kind of absolute necessity'.

It was essential to deny Jacques's significance, for it would never do to let her readers know how close her gender had come to derailing her career before it had even begun. But had she been in possession of a dowry, Simone's 'becoming' would have taken a traditional form. The success story was never simple. Between seventeen and twenty-one, academic hopes and dreams of marriage struggled for dominance within her, and there is little doubt that, had he proposed, it was Jacques, at the time 'my destiny', whom she would have chosen. Simone was ambivalent, torn, as she believed all women to be. Divided, conflicted, unable 'to accept her femininity, nor transcend it', Simone wanted Jacques. She wanted to be a wife, rather than join the priesthood of learning.

4

~~~

La Rochelle

The mirror was a great help to me: I gave it the job of
teaching me that I was a monster.

Jean-Paul Sartre, *Words*

ANNE-MARIE INTRODUCED Poulou to his new stepfather in 1917. The
boy detested 'Uncle Jo' on sight. It made no difference: the timid
twelve-year-old had been tipped out of the nest. Mancy, a graduate of
the Polytechnique, was a man of substance. Formerly general manager
of the navy, and now director of the Delaunay-Belleville shipyard at La
Rochelle, he at once removed his new family from Paris to the
provinces and sent his stepson to the local *lycée*.

'I hate the provinces,' Sartre wrote in 1940. For the rest of his life
provincial France symbolized his expulsion from paradise. Ports,
whether La Rochelle or Le Havre, became places of horror where small-
town bourgeois life was at its most stifling and its most cruel. Anne-
Marie, on the other hand, through remarriage at the age of thirty-four,
regained status and security. Instead of the room shared with Poulou,
she had a luxurious house of her own on the avenue Carnot; instead of
economic dependence upon an ageing, autocratic father, she had
servants, new clothes and the prestige of being the wife of one of
the most important men in the city. Delighted to be part of the local
élite, she wasted no time in taking down from the bedroom wall
the photograph of the sickly ensign who had abandoned her so

inconsiderately, and replacing it with a portrait of her new husband. Never again, except in the mirror, would Poulou see the likeness of his diminutive father.

'One thing is certain, my mother did not marry my stepfather for love,' Jean-Paul assured his friend John Gérassi. 'Besides, he was not very pleasant. He was a tall, thin man, with a black moustache, a very uneven complexion, a very large nose, rather handsome eyes, black hair.' But the evidence of his ears told him otherwise. Into the character of Philippe, the sensitive young bourgeois who loves Rimbaud and loathes his stepfather, the General, in *Le Sursis* (*The Reprieve*), Sartre poured his own suffering:

Philippe awoke with a start – no – it wasn't the crow of a cock, it was a soft and feminine moan, ah-h-h-h; he thought at first that she was crying, but no, he was familiar with that sound, he had often listened to it, with his ear glued to the door, pale with rage and cold.

By turns perplexed, disgusted, Philippe listens.

Ah-h-h! How I love you . . . .' said the woman in a throaty voice. 'A-h-h . . . Oh . . . oh – oh!
    A silence followed. The dark-haired angel . . . lay upon her with the full weight of his body. She was crushed, satiated. Philippe sat up abruptly, a sneer on his lips and his heart distraught with jealousy.

In the novel, Philippe runs away. In real life, the stepson had no choice but to stay and witness his mother's growing love and gratitude to the forty-three-year-old husband who had given her back her self-respect. It was the beginning of Poulou's 'interior quarrel' with his adored Anne-Marie.

His jealousy of the second husband who nightly exercised his conjugal rights was the more acute because, as Sartre admitted, at thirteen or fourteen, 'I certainly did have a fairly sexual feeling for my mother.' During one of his many absences from school, he was operated on for mastoid trouble and Anne-Marie slept on a bed beside him in the nursing home: 'When I was going to sleep in the evening she undressed, and she probably showed herself to me half naked. I stayed awake with my eyes half closed so as to see her undressed though my eyelids.'

Poulou wished his mother would restrain herself, repress her late-blossoming sensuality. Maternal displays of emotion towards 'Uncle Jo' revolted him, he later confessed to Beauvoir: 'I found my mother's letting go very disagreeable.' He grieved for the all-encompassing intimacy he had shared with Anne-Marie during those magical, formative early years and now lost: an incestuous bond in which forbidden sexuality played a larger part than he claimed:

> What attracted me in this family link was not so much the temptation to love as the prohibition against making love; I liked incest, with its mixture of fire and ice, enjoyment and frustration, so long as it remained platonic.

And now the boy who thought of himself as a sort of 'aerial plant', a rare orchid drawing sustenance from books in the monastic seclusion of a sixth-floor library, found his face pushed up against the earthy realities of life in a provincial *lycée*. Often he lay bloody-nosed on the muddy cobbles, felled by the blows and taunts of his schoolmates. They laughed at his Parisian accent, at his elegant clothes, at his spectacles and at his small stature. The little prince who already believed he was a genius, who was working on his second novel, found himself barely mediocre in this harsh new world. This did not prevent his raising a hand in class to correct the prose of his new professor of French, Father Loosdregt, thus confirming his reputation as the school swot.

The three or four years Jean-Paul spent in La Rochelle were the unhappiest of his life, he later wrote in the preface to *Aden-Arabie*. At the *lycée* he attended, the brightest, Catholic boys had already been skimmed off by the Collège Fénelon, leaving behind tough Protestant lads, descendants of those Huguenot rebels who had challenged Richelieu and King Louis XIII in 1627. Jean-Paul was unprepared for the gratuitous violence he encountered. Fatherless sons, for many fathers had been lost on the Eastern Front, threatened their mothers. One boy drew a knife on *Maman*. Gang warfare was rife between the Protestant lads and the working-class apprentices. Poulou shuddered as he watched the boys rolling in the streets, saw the blood run. Beaten up, he learnt to take revenge. One afternoon, when she took her son on a shopping expedition after school, Anne-Marie was astonished, on leaving the shop, to find Jean-Paul fighting in the gutter with a hooligan. 'We rolled on the ground, hitting and kicking one another . . . I felt her hand plucking me from his embrace. We used to fight wholeheartedly.'

La Rochelle taught Sartre about violence, and it was a lesson he never forgot. 'I've never had tender relations with my friends since then,' he explained to Beauvoir. 'There's always ideas of violence between them or from them to me or from me to them.' It was not a lack of friendship, he said; he simply knew that 'violence was imperative in the relations between men'. The experience reinforced his distrust of the male and his affinity with women, but it was women who also drove home the realization of his ugliness. In his early days at the *lycée* he had tried to impress his classmates by saying that he had a mistress in Paris and that on Saturdays and Sundays they went to a hotel and made love. He even persuaded his mother's maid to write a letter: 'Dearest Jean-Paul . . .' Seeing that he was twelve and well below average height, this tall story was not believed. Sartre became the school scapegoat, left to wander the promenade alone.

At fourteen, longing to recapture the intimacy with girls that he had known as a child, he set his cap at Lisette Joirisse, the ship's chandler's pretty daughter. She was twelve. Often he watched her walking along the inner quay, and thought her very beautiful. He'd like to meet her, he confided to his classmates. Easy, he was told. Just go up to her on the promenade. She likes you. When he approached Lisette, she jumped on her bicycle and set off along the alleys. Sartre followed, and was soon left behind as her tinkling laughter vanished into the darkness of the cobbled streets. The next day he approached her again. As he drew close, she turned in his direction and asked loudly, in front of his friends: 'Who's this bum with one eye that says shit to the other?'

Sartre withdrew, mocking laughter ringing in his ears. Lisette's words plunged him into despair.

> I knew then that I was ugly. I had such a hint after my grandfather cut my curls and my mother cried. But now I was absolutely certain: I was really ugly.

If he was the whipping-boy at the *lycée*, at home Sartre hardly felt any less betrayed – not only by his mother, but by nature, which had made him vile. 'One is not born ugly, one becomes it.' He stared at his wall-eye in the mirror, the 'one thing that was always there . . . the squinting eye'. The mirror taught him that he was a monster, a Quasimodo. He could cut his hair, wash his face: 'The eye, the eye remained.' The eye failed to meet the eye of the observer, but looked away; it experienced life tangentially, and, so it seemed to Sartre, left his face an empty map. His sense of self, already precarious, was increasingly threatened in a familial situation in which he felt, even more than he had as a child, superfluous to existence. 'I had no true self,' he wrote. 'I found nothing within me except a surprising insipidity. Before my eyes, a jellyfish was striking against the glass of the aquarium.' The ghostly image of a soft and translucent sea-creature, fleeing into the shadows, represented his amorphous psyche. In rue Le Goff Sartre had felt himself to be a toy for the adults: an object, a lapdog. In La Rochelle he was simply in the way.

One precious link remained between himself and his mother: music, a potent source of pleasure to the Schweitzers. Jean-Paul had been taught the piano, but now his stepfather stopped these lessons. In the afternoons, however, when his mother played the grand piano in the drawing-room, the boy would sit beside her and listen. Anne-Marie played difficult pieces, Chopin, Schumann and Bach. She also had a trained voice and sang well. When she went upstairs to change for dinner, Jean-Paul would attempt to pick out the notes: 'At first I played with one finger, then with five, and then with ten.' He wanted to play four-handed with his mother, and for a little while he succeeded. The work was, he remembered, slow and difficult, but he was sensitive to rhythm. At fourteen, however, he gave up trying.

Mancy, meanwhile, decided to make a man of Poulou. Intent on training the boy as an engineer, he took over Charles Schweitzer's role as teacher and set his stepson to the sciences. He talked of physics and factories. The lessons often ended in slaps. Forced to sacrifice music to maths, the boy's unhappiness deepened. His marks plummeted.

Frustrated in so many other ways, Jean-Paul at first persisted with his writing. Up to the age of fourteen he showed his mother everything he wrote, and she used to say, 'Very pretty, very well imagined.' She never showed his stories to his stepfather, who was not interested:

> He knew I wrote, but he didn't give a damn about them . . . He took no notice. So he was perpetually the person I wrote against. All my life. The fact of writing was against him.

'Writing against' Joseph would become Sartre's lifelong motivation, the only way in which he could feel superior to his stepfather. But at the time his exile in La Rochelle paralysed him. Discouraged by the hostility of his schoolmates, who laughed out loud when he read them a few pages, he began to feel that far from being a world-famous celebrity like Dickens, a writer was simply 'a poor devil, unfortunate and damned'.

Yet it was an important time of transition. Sartre abandoned the cloak and dagger stories he had been writing about 'Captain

Pardaillon'. His next work was a sharply observed study of the owlish 'beak', 'Jésus la Chouette' (Jesus the Owl), his French master at the lycée, a 'pitiful character' who died in the course of the year he taught Sartre, but a kind one who asked the precocious school misfit back to his home. The novella demonstrated a new realism. The master, with his stained red beard, 'big hooked nose, sharp as an eagle's beak, his blood-red mouth, his yellow-orange complexion, and his short-sighted eyes hidden behind a gold-rimmed *lorgnon*', was tormented by the boys. 'He never did survive the ridicule. He killed himself two years later,' said Sartre. 'Jésus' was Sartre's first anti-hero. In the character of the fragile and timid but highly intelligent boy, the schoolboy writer retained his old tradition of a positive hero. In the martyrdom of 'Jésus', he voiced his own suffering.

The death of 'Jésus' in Jean-Paul's fiction echoed the equally dramatic death of God he experienced at age twelve when He 'tumbled down into the blue sky and vanished without explanation . . . He does not exist, I said to myself in polite astonishment, and I thought the matter was settled.' Sartre's religious upbringing had been confused, divided as it was between the milk-and-water Catholicism of his mother and grandmother, who took him to Mass at Saint-Sulpice chiefly to hear good music, believing 'in God just long enough to enjoy a toccata', as Poulou tartly noted, and Karl Schweitzer's earthy Lutheranism. The coarse jibes against the Pope and the Saints which Poulou had heard at Karl's dinner table, and which bore a marked resemblance to Luther's own obscene table talk, prejudiced him against Catholicism, and ultimately against Christianity. But God was not so easily forgotten. 'I grew up, a rank weed on the compost-heap of catholicity,' wrote Sartre in *Words*. His roots sucked up its juices and made his sap. The boy who was baptized a Catholic and once won a silver-paper medal for his essay on the Passion would remain a theologian à *rebours*, against the grain.

The third form was Jean-Paul's nadir. He had thrown down his pen, and was suffering 'the torments of unrequited love', not this time for a girl, but for two of his comrades: Pelletier and Bouteillier. Sartre denied that the attraction was homosexual, but the two older boys forced him to dance to their tune, and he made himself their lackey. He began stealing, helping himself to money from his mother's handbag in order to buy cakes and *babas* from the local pastry shop. Beginning with single francs, he moved on to notes, five francs here and two francs there. Unlike Mme de Beauvoir, Mme Mancy was wealthy enough not to count her money. By May 1918, therefore, her son had accumulated seventy francs, an enormous sum at that time. But one day Jean-Paul made the mistake of putting his jacket, which contained his hoard of notes and coins, over his legs to keep him warm as he lay ill in bed. 'What is all this money?' demanded Anne-Marie, as she picked up the jacket and heard the coins rattling about inside, ding, ding, ding. 'Just a joke,' stuttered Sartre. 'It's money I've taken from Cardino for a joke.' But no sooner had Sartre 'returned' the money to his classmate Cardino than the boy bought himself a huge flashlight, and Mme Cardino discovered the truth. A great scene ensued with Anne-Marie and M. Mancy in which fourteen-year-old Poulou received a severe smacking from his mother.

Karl and Louise Schweitzer hurried down from Paris to see their disgraced grandson. Poulou thought Karl would understand that he had had to steal to buy love. Instead, he never forgot the moment when the arthritic old man dropped a ten-centime piece on the floor of the chemist's shop. The boy hastened to pick it up, but Karl stopped him with his cane. 'Then he bent down, slowly and seemingly painfully – and I heard, or thought I heard, his bones crack – to pick up the coin himself, saying, "You have shown that you have no respect for money." '

A family conference took place. It was decided that Jean-Paul should return to Paris at the earliest opportunity. Although his schoolwork was barely average, Karl used his connections to procure him a boarding place at the senior Lycée Henri IV. At the age of sixteen, Sartre returned to the capital. It had been a lucky escape, but he never forgot that second betrayal by the two boys for whom he had stolen, and for whom he had fought on numerous occasions. It left him with a lasting sympathy for the thief and the underdog, and for all the *orphelins* of his generation, for it seemed to him that he had lost not only a father but a mother and was himself a loveless orphan.

*

It was a relief to return to the world of music, to swallow cherries in brandy during the interval at the *concerts rouges* in the rue de Seine with his grandfather once again, to plunge into the world of *belles-lettres* and breathe the literary ether of Karl's library. At the *lycée* Jean-Paul promptly joined the choir and sang at Sunday Mass. At weekends he played the piano, encouraged by his grandmother, Louise, returning to the pieces which once his mother had played to him when he was young: Chopin's *Ballades*, Franck's *Symphonic Variations*, the 'Fingal's Cave' overture. 'Like a voodoo drum, the piano would impose its rhythm on me,' he wrote.

It was a slow healing. Sartre had been deeply scarred by his experience at La Rochelle, and it left him estranged from Anne-Marie. In *Words*, the trauma is barely hinted at. The first version of his autobiography, begun in 1952, was more honest. He called it *Jean-sans-terre*, or 'John Lackland', a man without inheritance or possessions, which was what Sartre felt himself to be: a writer who owned nothing bar a pen and a pipe. Who as a child never had a home: 'Careful! We aren't at home!' his mother would whisper to him when he made a noise. 'We were never at home: either in the rue Le Goff or later on, when my mother remarried,' Sartre wrote bitterly. *Jean-sans-terre* was a savage indictment of his unstable childhood, and one that was never published. It was too 'ill-natured', said its author. Instead, he wrote *Les Mots*, his most polished, 'highly worked over' book. Like Beauvoir's *Memoirs*, it was full of secrets: even so, his pain was too great to continue the story after the age of twelve; to tell the truth would have wounded his mother too greatly. 'How could I continue?' he asked Gerassi.

> Anne-Marie was still alive. How could I blame her for not caring enough about me, for abandoning me, for choosing a shit [*un con*] over me? Yet that was the real reason I was so desperate to fit into that vile Protestant centre of La Rochelle . . .

Yet La Rochelle had been a life-changing metamorphosis. It was 'to my great misfortune then and to my great future good fortune', he wrote, with grim sarcasm, that he had become the 'whipping-boy' of the La Rochelle *lycée*. Dislocation and rejection put a chip of ice in his heart. The brutalized prince now resolved to be king. He took as his model the nineteenth-century comedy by Paul Verlaine, *Les Uns et les autres*, in which the leader of a band of handsome young men and pretty girls rules through strength of mind and charm. The future was going to be different. Jean-Paul would take revenge on all the *salauds*, bastards, who had humiliated him.

His first step was to renew his old friendship with Paul Nizan, with whom he shared a dormitory at the senior Lycée Henri IV. The two boys, united as much by their strabismus as by their literary ambitions, became the inseparable stars of the class; one tall and elegant, but from a working-class background, the other short and often scruffy, but inescapably a *bon bourgeois*. It was a fresh shock to Sartre, however, to find how far behind he had fallen intellectually. Nizan came to the rescue of the *petit provincial*, introducing him to modern literature in the form of Proust, André Gide and the popular playwright Giradoux. Sartre himself read voraciously, and he and his grandmother spent many hours discussing Dostoevsky. It was a mark of his rejection of Anne-Marie and his affection for Louise that when he began writing for the student *Revue sans titre*, he adopted her surname for his first *nom de plume*: Jacques Guillemin. Meanwhile, he worked at his Latin, Greek and philosophy. His reward was the *prix d'excellence* awarded to the best student in the class. He was now on the royal road to success, having qualified for entry to the famous Lycée Louis-le-Grand, founded in 1563, crammer for the university-level École Normale Supérieure, in its turn nursery for the supermen which Sartre and Nizan already imagined themselves to be.

The change in Jean-Paul's fortunes had been breathtaking. From the western fringes of France, he had stepped back into the heart of Paris, to the mythic streets that educated the future leaders of the nation before burying the greatest of them in the nearby Panthéon. Louis-le-Grand, on the corner of rue Saint-Jacques and the place du Panthéon, was only a short walk from Henri IV, itself on the corner of rue Clovis and the place du Panthéon, just up the road from the École Normale. Sartre's route home, through the Latin Quarter – so called because it was here that medieval students came to learn Latin when Paris's first university moved from the cloisters of Notre-Dame to the Left Bank – took him past the Panthéon, down the rue Soufflot, the road named after the architect of the mausoleum, to rue Le Goff. Sometimes he wandered into the great secular temple to the heroes of the Republic, where emblazoned on the altar, beneath the figure of Marianne, spirit of the revolution, was the motto: *Vivre libre ou mourir*, live freely or die. Descending into the crypt, he stood at the foot of the tombs of Victor Hugo and Émile Zola, and pondered: could he, little Jean-Paul, be as celebrated a novelist as Zola, as important a philosopher as Voltaire?

He paused before the floodlit marble statue of Voltaire, quill pen in his right hand and sheaf of papers in his left, casually knotted scarf thrown over his cloak, hailed as '*le Prince de l'Esprit*'. Opposite stood the tomb of Jean-Jacques Rousseau, '*Philosophe de la Nature*': two men whose works embodied the principles of the French Revolution. It was the first of these totemic figures that held his attention. Voltaire was responsible for the 'dechristianization' of France since the Enlightenment, which had infected Jean-Paul's own family. But Voltaire's work was only half done. The Church still retained its hold over men's souls. 'I *had* my tomb in the Père-Lachaise cemetery – perhaps even in the

Panthéon, my avenue in Paris, my squares and *places* in the provinces and abroad,' the schoolboy fantasized as, oblivious to the passing crowd, he dreamt of fame in the dim light of the crypt.

The teacher responsible for Jean-Paul's sudden interest in philosophy was already legendary: tiny, crippled Colonna d'Istria, smaller even than the pimply new pupil whom he began teaching in *khâgne*, the top sixth-form class. 'Read this,' he commanded, tossing the boys a book by Henri Bergson on consciousness. 'Your homework is to write an essay with the title "What will last?"' To Sartre it was a revelation. In Bergson he found his own psychological life described. '*J'en ai été saisi*,' he said. 'I was gripped by it.' He decided to study *la philo* at university, although as he later admitted, 'What I at that time called "philosophy" was actually "psychology".' His subject would be his own, troubled self. His desires were twofold: to interpret his interior life by examining *le vécu* or lived experience, and to become a novelist. Studying philo and becoming a teacher would, he calculated, help him understand character.

Sartre had made great progress, but he was still unhappy. It was gratifying to be one of a pair, so closely connected that their friends called them 'Nitre et Sarzan', but neither eighteen-year-old had a girlfriend. I 'spent all my time despairing about it', said Sartre. 'From that time on, the great thing for me was to love and be loved. Especially to be loved. I couldn't understand how that feeling, which used to seem so very cheap to me in my childhood, had become so rare and precious.' He wept over the symbolist poems of Jules Laforgue, lamenting the '*seul oreiller! mur familier!*' (single pillow, familiar wall) of the bedroom in which he, like other adolescent Pierrots, lived a single sex existence. Nizan was the first to strike lucky: Jean-Paul introduced him to the cousin with whom he was half in love, Annie Lannes, daughter of his Aunt Hélène in Thiviers. Annie was coming to Paris to study, and nothing could be more natural than to introduce her to Jean-Paul's best friend, to whom she was instantly attracted. Often Nizan, with whom he shared a room, would disappear for days at a time on romantic adventures, leaving his roommate distraught. Sartre expressed his sense of abandonment in a short story, 'The seed and the diving-suit', about their relationship:

It was more tempestuous than a love affair. I was tough, jealous, inconsiderate, like a maniacal lover. Lucelles, independent and sly, seized every opportunity to cheat on me . . . He had a crush on an Algerian Jew and then on a guy from Marseilles. On those occasions, for days he would try to avoid me. I couldn't stand it. Then, tired of strangers, he'd come crawling back. He would find me aggressive and irritable, even though, inwardly, I was choking on the tenderness I couldn't express.

The disconsolate teenager clung to a chance, prophetic remark made to him by a young woman named Mme Lebrun, when he was ten. She was the subject of his first sexual memory: 'I desired her as much as a child of ten can desire a woman: in other words, I'd have liked to see her bosom and touch her shoulders.' Like other of Anne-Marie's friends, Mme Lebrun had responded to the boy's interest, ruffling his hair and gratifying him with caresses. 'I'd like to know the boy when he's twenty,' she had remarked. 'I'm sure all the women will be crazy about him.'

Sartre did not have to wait so long. Tragically, at nineteen Annie died of tuberculosis, and her cousin attended her funeral in Thiviers. He wore a well-cut dark suit, black tie and hat. A photograph taken of Sartre with Paul Nizan in July 1925, on the terrace of the Luxembourg Gardens, shows that his perception of his own ugliness was perhaps exaggerated. Stylish, in a similar expensive suit, tie and starched Eton collar, a straw boater on his head, a cigarette at his lips, Sartre smiles into the lens; Nizan, beside him, in plus fours, has his hands in his pockets. He is without the malacca cane he often carries. Both young men wear horn-rimmed spectacles, and exude an air of privilege and confidence. They had just completed their first year at the École Normale. Sartre had more to offer than perhaps he realized.

Certainly he made an immediate impression on a distant cousin named Simone Jollivet, who was also at the funeral. Simone, a future actress with an interest in Nietzsche, was a pharmacist's daughter from Toulouse, Jean-Paul the grandson of a pharmacist's daughter, but both aspired to a writer's life. Jean-Paul explained that he was extremely ambitious: 'When I think of glory, I imagine a ballroom with gentlemen in evening clothes and ladies in low-cut dresses all raising their glasses to me.' Glory tempted him, he said, 'because I want to be far above ordinary people, whom I scorn'. But what really mattered was 'the urge to create, to construct . . . I cannot look at a sheet of blank paper without wanting to write something on it.' His other defining feature, he confessed, was cowardice.

Sartre's ugliness, Simone told him later, had a 'Mirabeau effect' on her; it was a powerful ugliness, like that of the eighteenth-century revolutionary, mixed as it was with charm and eloquence. Later she teased him about it.

'So how come you still love me?' I asked.
'You talk good,' she replied.
'What if I were uglier still?' I insisted.
'Then you'd have to talk all night,' she responded.

In the years to come, Sartre often did.

In the liberated Simone Jollivet, who frequently made nocturnal visits to the town brothel in the company of her gypsy maid, Zina, Sartre had found a willing partner. She agreed to run away with him. His sexual fantasies were about to come gloriously alive.

5

Zaza

Who could believe that I love her in this way with so
many tears, with such passionate being, with such
poignant sentiments?
Simone de Beauvoir, journal, 29 September 1928

FRANÇOISE DE BEAUVOIR was screaming like a banshee. It was three in
the morning on the boulevard du Montparnasse, but one by one the
neighbours put their heads out of their windows to watch as she leant
against Aunt Germaine's doorbell, shouting that Jacques had dishonoured her daughter. Aunt Germaine poked her head out of the
window. How dare Françoise make such accusations? 'Where is
Simone?' demanded the angry matron. 'I want her back this instant.'
Jacques came to the window, rubbing his eyes and protesting that he
had escorted his cousin home to to 71 rue de Rennes after taking her to
the cinema. 'You're lying!' bellowed Françoise, as Georges dragged her
home, her curses echoing down the street.

When Simone turned the key and crept up the stairs, she was greeted
with tears of rage. Soon she, too, was screaming at her parents as she
was forced to confess that Jacques and his friend Riquet Bresson had
taken her, not to the cinema, but to the Stryx, a bar of ill repute.

That night Jacques had invited Simone and her parents to dine
before leaving for his military service in Algeria in the autumn of 1928.
Two years had passed, in which she had embraced an ascetic regime in

order to accomplish her goals, coming second in the *certificat* in philosophy in the summer of 1927; Simone Weil, the clever daughter of a doctor, had come first. Third, trailing behind the two women, came Maurice Merleau-Ponty, a student at the École Normale. Beauvoir's was a phenomenal feat, achieved only at the cost of personal grooming. Frequently she forgot to wash, or even to brush her teeth. Without running water, washing her hair was a major project often left undone. But she had proved her brilliance, and surely Maggie had earned her Stephen.

And Françoise was vexed that her daughter was now twenty, and there was still no sign of a proposal. Reluctantly she agreed to allow Simone to go out with Jacques, unchaperoned, after dinner. What befell her next was fictionalized by Simone de Beauvoir in the story 'Marguerite', in *When Things of the Spirit Come First*, a collection of stories whose original title was borrowed, in the spirit of irony, from a work by Maritain, *Primauté du Spirituel* (*Primacy of the Spiritual*). She began writing these tales of women she had known in 1935, before she was thirty, her aim being to show 'the harm done by the religiosity that was in the air I breathed during my childhood and early youth' and 'my own conversion to the real world'. It was, she said, 'a beginner's piece of work'. But it was probably her shocking opinions, her explicit sexual content, more than any lack of skill, which prevented their being published before 1979. Beauvoir went so far as to suggest a connection between Catholic piety and masochism, making fun of the 'shameless appetite' of an aunt who asked her husband to whip her heartily at night. 'Marguerite', writes the author, is 'a satire on my youth. I give Marguerite my own childhood at the Cours Désir, and my own adolescent religious crisis . . . After this she falls into the pitfall of "the wonderful", as I did when I was influenced by my cousin Jacques . . . I wrote it with a fellow-feeling for the heroine.'

The new experiences and new ideas Jacques showed 'Marguerite' were an important aspect of the fascination he held for her. She longed to live in 'Denis's world – the real world I had never seen'. That evening she was wearing a mauve dress – Françoise liked 'cheerful' colours that did not show the dirt – a beige coat and a hat that came down over her eyes: 'I knew perfectly well that it looked horrible, but I didn't give a damn.' As the taxi drew up outside the Stryx, her eyes nearly popped out of her head. A convolvulus-blue sign glowed outside the half-open door, as 'Denis' pushed her through the orange haze into a room full of dancing couples:

Denis was wearing a long beige overcoat: between the lapels of his upturned collar his face seemed hard and closed: I kept my eyes fixed on him . . . He helped me climb on to one of the bar stools. 'What will you drink? A gin fizz?'

The barman set a glass full of yellow liquid in front of her. Marguerite sucked it through a straw, and her mouth filled with the taste of lemon. There were little American flags stuck in the mirror behind the bar, above the rows of bottles. Greta Garbo's smile, Maurice Chevalier's hat and Charlie Chaplin's boots made strange mosaics against the light brown walls. 'How you knock it back!' said Denis with amused admiration. 'Michel, fix another gin fizz for mademoiselle; we'll roll dice for it.'

A few days earlier Denis had been teasing Marguerite. She had been sitting at a table working on a Greek translation when he walked in. He sat down at the end of the table, and lit a cigarette. 'Don't you ever feel like tossing those books out of the window?' he asked abruptly. Marguerite gazed at him. 'What should I do then?' she said. He smiled, turning over a small coin in his pocket: 'Anything.'

'It is not by methodically searching for freedom, as you are now doing, that you will find it,' said Denis . . .

'Why shouldn't everything be absurd?' he went on with a kind of flippancy.

'Dying is as absurd as living, and once can just as well twiddle one's thumbs as fire a revolver in the street. You can do anything at all, once you do not hope for anything. And sometimes you come upon the miracle.'

'The miracle?'

'Yes, a genuinely gratuitous action, an unlikely combination of words and colours, a two-headed woman, anything at all. Sometimes, the absurd makes its appearance.'

The idea of the *acte gratuit*, an independent, purposeless act, which Simone read about when Jacques lent her the *Surrealist Manifesto*, excited her imagination. Surrealist notions, interpreted by Jacques, lent a new fervour to her resolution no longer to be 'a dreary little bourgeoise' to look at prostitutes not with repulsion but with admiration and envy and, when she read novels about obscene or sadistic acts, to see violence as way of filling the emptiness of the soul: part of 'man's eternal drama in search of the absolute'. To her revolt she brought the same intensity she had brought to the practice of Catholicism, and to her studies. When Simone walked into the Stryx, she was 'waiting for miracles'. After several dry martinis and gin fizzes she created one, smashing glasses on the floor. Miracles exploded. It was a perfect Surrealist 'happening'.

The next morning, red-eyed and nursing her first hangover, Simone met Jacques on the terrace of the Select, a bar frequented by homosexuals and drug addicts, and heard his account of her mother's scene outside his house. He had not treated Simone with disrespect, he told her: 'I have too much real regard for you to do that,' said Jacques, gazing tenderly into her eyes. As he gave her a lift in his car to the Sorbonne, he promised that they were not saying goodbye for ever. But as Simone mounted the steps of the library, her heart was heavy. She knew his true opinion of Françoise de Beauvoir, as hysterical and silly a woman as Mrs Bennet in Jane Austen's *Pride and Prejudice*, whose heavy-handed matchmaking and loud outbursts of temper similarly hampered her daughters' chances of marriage.

Like Jean-Paul Sartre, Simone began stealing from her mother's handbag: 'My mother used to count her pennies. It was not easy, but I managed anyway.' Determined to taste the poetry of the bars, she lied to Françoise that she was teaching working-class women in Belleville, a poor *quartier* of Paris in which Robert Garric, her literature professor at Neuilly, ran a social centre. This attempt to cross the class barrier failed, for Simone found that she had nothing in common with her pupils. A more regular source of income than pilfering from her mother's purse was the small salary she received from Mme Mercier for teaching psychology. This funded Simone's gin fizzes at Le Jockey, Paris's first night-club, which became her favourite watering-hole: she drank so much that she often vomited in the Métro. She put rouge on her cheeks, and refused to wash it off when her mother accused her of wearing Satan's cloven hoof-mark, and boxed her ears. Now Jacques had converted her to surrealism, his tales of food-fights between the movement's leaders, André Breton, Louis Aragon and Michel Leiris, and the novelist Rachilde and his supporters at the Closerie des Lilas, of fisticuffs at the ballet, delighted her. Violence, excess, eroticism, she would taste them all.

When 'Denis' disappeared to Algeria, another young man began paying attention to Beauvoir: Maurice Merleau-Ponty, whom she had beaten in last year's summer exams. Tall, thin and serious, he had the long pale face and heavy dark eyelashes of an aesthete. To Françoise's relief he lived in the fashionable 16th *arrondissement* and came from a good Catholic home. Unaware of her daughter's evening antics, Françoise now allowed her even more freedom.

Maurice (Jean Pradelle in the *Memoirs*) was the first man to lead Simone through the iron gates of the École Normale in the rue d'Ulm, the most famous of the Grandes Écoles which dominated French academia. For a female student from the Sorbonne, it was awe-inspiring to wander through the hallowed gardens and watch the carp in the fishpond, a relic of the time when the university had been a convent. But it was the Luxembourg Gardens that became the young philosophers' daily meeting place: like Beauvoir, Merleau-Ponty was engaged in the search for truth, which he believed would be revealed to him through the medium of philosophy. For a fortnight the two intellectuals hotly debated the topic, he accusing her of choosing despair while she attacked him for clutching at straws. 'You prefer the search for truth to truth itself,' protested Maurice. The truth for Maurice, his strong-willed opponent suspected, still resided in Catholicism. At the Normale he belonged to the conventional group known as *talas* (a contraction of *talapoin*, priest). Beauvoir's unbelief, however, was still 'as solid as a rock', and when she introduced Maurice to Zaza, it was clear that he had more in common with the devout Mademoiselle Lacoin than the little atheist Sorbonnarde.

In September 1928, it was Zaza who remained the focus of Beauvoir's passionate friendship. On her visit to Ganepain, the Lacoin family estate, it wasn't just Simone's clothes that caused raised eyebrows. Mme Lacoin's sniffs at the wild 'ruined girl' who had lost her faith as well as her dowry, the sniggers of Zaza's little sisters at the Plain Jane who had come to stay, were hard to bear. At the dinner table there were shocked murmurs from the gentlemen as Simone defended her atheism and justified Kant and free will. But to Zaza herself Simone grew closer during their moonlit walks in their nightgowns among the scented phlox. Although Zaza used the familiar '*tu*' to her other friends, Simone and she had remained '*vous*' to each other. Now this changed: on her return, Simone wrote Zaza a love letter, confiding to her journal on 24 September: 'I think of Zaza with infinite tenderness.' Five days later she received a letter from Zaza, '*bouleversée*' (overwhelmed) by Simone's letter declaring her love. 'She had no idea that I love her! But who could believe that I love her in this way with so many tears, with such passionate being, with such poignant sentiments? . . . I have too much to give. *Le-sais tu, toi?* Do you know it?'

Zaza responded with equal warmth. On Tuesday 1 October, Simone crossed the gardens of the Palais-Royale, near the Louvre, for a rendezvous with her beloved friend. The next day another billet-doux was waiting: 'I find a letter from Zaza, a Zaza who loves me,' she wrote in her journal: 'A Zaza whose tenderness brings such sweetness.' Soon she and Zaza were playing Saturday tennis in the Bois de Boulogne with Maurice and his friend Maurice de Gandillac, who also belonged to the same right-wing group at the École Normale as Merlean-Ponty and Robert Brasillach (who would be executed in 1945 as a Nazi collaborator).

In Zaza Simone had found her first 'double', or soulmate. She tried to copy her, cropping her dark hair. It was not a success, and nor was the home perm that Françoise subsequently attempted. While Zaza's angular body carried her expensive clothes well, the shorter Simone lacked grace. Nevertheless, Zaza, and Stépha too, sought Simone out daily, sitting on the end of her bed and bringing her books when she was ill.

Only four years older than Simone, but far more worldly wise, Stépha listened as Simone assured her that she was 'almost betrothed' to Jacques. Gently Stépha tried to make her see the impossibility of the marriage. Foolish Françoise had commissioned a portrait photograph of Simone, in the style used at the announcement of an engagement of marriage, showing her daughter gazing modestly down at her left hand; but there was no engagement ring on her finger, and when Jacques was presented with the photograph, he ignored it.

On 31 December, as she took stock of 1928, Simone bitterly recognized that for the last two years she had 'passionately desired the presence of Jacques'; now her ardour was 'better directed and less full of illusion'. 'The old despair is dead,' she wrote. *'Je ne le regrette pas.'* Leaving the festive streets for the silence of her room, 'I think of you, but quite calmly, with confidence in you . . . I have no need of you.' Midnight was about to sound. As the bells rang out the new year, she prayed for happiness for Zaza and Maurice, and *'Jacques, pour toi, le bonheur'*. She made a wish for herself too: *'L'amour et le bonheur*, love and happiness.'

*

When Simone Weil had met Simone, in her tawdry respectability, the young Communist had snapped at the girl with a 'de' in her name: 'It's easy to see you've never gone hungry!' In fact, Simone, bringing crusts from Françoise's kitchen to go with her café crème, was often hungry. Desperate to gain her independence, she decided to complete her degree in philosophy in April 1928, to write her thesis and to prepare for the postgraduate *agrégation* exam in the same year. In eighteen months, 'I would be free, and a new life would begin!' Such a feat by a female Sorbonnarde was considered impossible, for she would be competing against the men from the École Normale, who scooped nine out of ten *agrégé* places. Gloomily her friends predicted failure.

But Simone had come a long way from her first essay on Descartes. Her 'enormous' dissertation on the personality had impressed her lecturer. 'If I *have* got genius – as I sometimes believe; as I am sometimes *quite sure* – then it simply means that I recognize clearly my superior gifts,' she wrote complacently in her journal. Her philosophy dean, Léon Brunschwig, with Henri Bergson, the dominant figure in French idealist philosophy, advised her to write her thesis on Gottfried von Leibnitz's logical doctrine; at the same time she was working on a new novel. Her intensity scared her male friends. When she solemnly told Jacques that she intended to consecrate her life to a search for meaning, and that meanwhile she would base her standards on acts of love and free will indefinitely repeated, he laughed nervously. Sin was more fun, he protested: sin was a space yawning for God. She should try it.

Often that autumn Simone pushed open the doors of Sylvia Beach's bookshop, Shakespeare & Company, at 12 rue de l'Odéon, a home from home for Americans in Paris. Brave Miss Beach had published James Joyce's *Ulysses* in 1922, and made the first French translation of T.S. Eliot's 'Prufrock', *Le Navire d'argent*. Browsing among her shelves customers might bump into Ezra Pound, Ernest Hemingway, André Gide, one of the first subscribers, or even Joyce himself. Borrowing armfuls of books from Shakespeare & Co, as well as from that other intellectual pillar of Paris between the wars, Adrienne Monnier's bookshop and library, La Maison des Amis des Livres, in rue de l'Odéon, Simone was absorbing the ideas of modern novelists as fast as those of philosophers. She read Gide's hymn to personal freedom, *Fruits of the Earth*, which called on his readers to reject the family – his particular bête-noire – and to lose themselves in the slipstream of desire:

I hated the family, the home, and all places where men think they can find rest . . . each new thing must find us always and utterly detached . . . Families, I hate you . . .

The 'diabolical' Gide, as he was known, preached ardour and spontaneity: 'When you have read me, throw this book away – and go out.

I should like it to have made you want to get away . . . from your family, from your room, from your thought.' He defended homosexuality in *Corydon*, and took his friend Oscar Wilde's egotism to extreme lengths in *The Counterfeiters*, bestseller of 1926. Wilde, the model for the hedonist Ménalque of *Fruits of the Earth*, had written of Gide's book: 'The egotistic note is, of course, and always has been to me, the primal and ultimate note of modern art.' Now, in the mid-twenties, Gide declared he could not find a single sentence spoken by Christ which authorizes the family; his message was to jettison morality and to 'act without *judging* whether the deed is good or evil'. It was a heady manifesto, which excited Simone. '"Live dangerously. Refuse nothing," said Gide, Rivière, the surrealists and Jacques,' she wrote in her journal. But the red- and mauve-haired prostitutes, in their silk stockings and high heels, laughed at her in her sensible shoes when she pretended to be a hooker, and when one of her pick-ups put his hand on her knee, she pushed him violently away. She felt caged within prison walls, either those of the library or her room. Zaza was in love with Merleau-Ponty, Jacques was in Biskra, and she had nobody.

*

In Simone Jollivet, Sartre had found a real hooker. Over dinner after Annie's funeral, surrounded by stuffy Thiviers notables, he sought out the only other young person present, the tall, blonde daughter of one of Captain Frédérick Lannes's sisters. After coffee, he led her into a nearby wood. Shortly afterwards, the two cousins disappeared from Thiviers for four days and nights, and were only discovered and brought back by the combined exertions of the Sartre and Lannes families. Sartre returned a changed man: previously he had lost his virginity to a married woman from Thiviers who had sought him out at the École Normale, but the event had left him unmoved. With 'Toulouse', as he called her, after the town where she lived, he was in the hands of an uninhibited girl, who although only just twenty-one, was already a semi-professional; whose custom it was to receive her clients naked in her bedroom, her long blonde hair streaming down her back. Zina the gypsy, whom Jollivet had herself deflowered, assisted her. When the lighted window of Jollivet's bedroom over the chemist's shop of her father, Joseph Jollivet, was pushed open, her lovers knew it was time to call.

Sartre's mistake was to fall in love with this first Simone. He wanted a love 'serious as the rain'. She wanted a rich lover and an actor's life.

When Sartre, penniless as usual, took the train to Toulouse to see her again, he had to sleep on a park bench for four nights. When at last he was admitted to Jollivet's bed, he fell fast asleep. She woke him by reading Nietzsche's *Thus Spoke Zarathustra*, with the implication that he should will himself awake and act like a superman.

But sensuality had only limited appeal for Sartre. One of his most fundamental instincts was to instruct; like his Schweitzer grandfather, he was a born teacher, who addressed his correspondent as 'my student'. She was to trust him, to develop a positive mental attitude, and to develop her writing, 'so that you will not be Madame Bovary but an artist, with no regrets or melancholy . . . So do write, don't be afraid of words, you'll do them more harm than they'll do to you.' Soon Jollivet was complaining that his letters were 'little lectures'. Her replies dwindled to postcards bemoaning her inferiority and unhappiness in Toulouse. A 1926 card provoked from Sartre just 'one more little lecture on moral well-being', in which he again exhorted her to correct the fault of melancholy, as he had done: 'Until last year I was very melancholy because I was ugly and that made me suffer. I have absolutely rid myself of that, because it's a weakness.'

By dint of doing translations and borrowing, Sartre scraped together enough money to bring Jollivet to Paris for the student ball at the École Normale, where she created a sensation in a red dress. The following year one of her rich lovers paid for her return to Paris, where she saw the film *The Miracle of the Wolves* and fell in love with the actor and future theatre producer Charles Dullin. By 1928 Sartre's dominant image of Jollivet was of a woman behind a mask, a disguised prostitute: 'You look like Dorothée Reviers, who plays the prostitute in *Épaves vivantes* [*Living Wrecks*].' He even compares her to 'an old madam trying to squeeze out the last penny' with her false protestations of love: 'I don't like to hear you say you love me "passionately, *like La Marietta*", who was after all just a slut with a crush on Fabrice . . .'

The affair ended when Jollivet became, as she wished, Dullin's lover. Sartre transposed his defeat at the hands of Dullin into an unfinished novel, 'Une Défaite' (A Defeat), written between 1927 and 1928. He had, he said, 'mastered' his love for Jollivet, and turned it inwards. She became the inspiration for the character of Cosima Wagner, wife of Richard, while Sartre himself was teased for his own likeness to the fictional Friedrich Nietzsche, tutor to the Wagner daughters. The three, Richard, Cosima and Friedrich, form an incestuous trio, a theme which would recur both in Sartre's life and in his work. He also used his experiences of tutoring the son of Mme Morel, a wealthy Argentinian woman known as 'that lady', with whom his friend Pierre Guille was in love: 'See, you're just like that awful Frédéric,' Mme Morel was fond of taunting him, for 'Frédéric', like his creator, was a boxer who relished battering his opponents into submission. 'He loved the big body of that stooping athlete,' wrote Sartre. 'The sight of it made him shiver with ecstasy at the prospect of their future combats. The body was always there: he would have liked to rub against it as if it were a wall, but, particularly, he would have liked to fight with it, to clasp it with all his might and try to throw it down.'

In fact, Sartre had lost this particular battle, and on two fronts. His 'beautiful novel' was rejected by the publisher Gallimard, soon after Jollivet rejected his love. He, like Simone de Beauvoir, had experienced the humiliation of being treated as a 'charity case'. His physical defects, diminutive height, a wall eye, were less easily overcome than her lack of means. 'Do you want me to see me – yes or no?' he had demanded of the licentious first Simone: 'I can no longer accept . . . the charity of three days of intimacy a year.' So deep had been his need for 'warm and foolish tenderness' that he had been prepared to wander the streets of Toulouse, to wait upon Jollivet's pleasure, 'totally dazed' by the pain of knowing that his licentious 'porcelain girl' was upstairs entertaining another man.

At the beginning of the relationship he demanded of Jollivet: 'Tell me whether you prefer your Jean-Paul to this Percy Bysshe Shelley whom women adored – or whether you prefer Shelley. He was very handsome.' Now he had his answer.

From the love affair the spurned Jean-Paul learnt two lessons about women: that money and looks make the difference. He did not forget the former, although he could not change the latter. '*La laideur m'a été découverte par les femmes*' [My ugliness was revealed to me by women],' he later explained to Beauvoir. Jollivet's casual cruelty underlined his 'crime'of ugliness. It seemed as if his stepfather's prophecy, 'You'll never know how to please women', was coming true. Sartre's suffering was immense. It is possible that he even contemplated suicide. He continued – without foundation – to believe that 'Jésus', his owl-like schoolteacher, had killed himself because of his ugliness, which led his class to ridicule him. In *The Family Idiot*, his biography of Flaubert, Sartre describes little Marguerite, so hideous that she frightens people: condemned by the crowd for the 'crime' of ugliness, she is driven to suicide.

Sartre survived, somehow. He had become, he told Jollivet, 'hard, brittle, hobbled'. It was time to multiply his masks, for in the corridors of the Sorbonne he had noticed another Simone. Short, unlike Jollivet, of impeccable character and aristocratic background, unlike Jollivet, she was also beautiful and spirited. This time, resolved Jean-Paul, there would be no defeat.

6

Rivals: The Kobra and the Llama

> I love him profoundly – Oh! Llama si aimé, mon Prince
> de Llamas.
> > Simone de Beauvoir, journal, 10 September 1929

On 4 April 1929 a new name appeared in Simone de Beauvoir's journal. 'Noticed Maheu,' she wrote, after a day at the Bibliothèque Nationale. 'Really *sympathique*; clever!!' Two days later she again spotted the tall, blond, ruddy-faced student who, with Jean-Paul Sartre and Nizan, made up an exclusive and notorious 'gang of three' at the École, and he seemed just as charming and intelligent as the first time. They caught the bus together, as Maurice de Gandillac, already attracted to Simone, jealously noted. At home that night Simone carefully underlined Maheu's name with her fountain pen – always a sign of importance with the diarist.

A week later Simone gleefully recorded Gandillac's tight smile when he saw her holding hands with Maheu ('a singularly strong and tender man'). The future philosopher was already regretting having introduced her to the friend who was fast overtaking him in her affections. 'How I love you, men!' wrote Simone, revelling in her new-found popularity. On 23 April Maheu lent her his notes on Spinoza. The next day, for the first time, Simone underlined his full name: *René Maheu*. But when, early on the morning of 25 April, she hurried to the library again, ostensibly to work on her diploma, there was no sign of him. Instead it was Gandillac who stopped to speak to her, to Beauvoir's disappointment.

But Maheu had plans. 'Happily Maheu is sitting next to me; then he offers me lunch at a chic restaurant, Le Fleur de Lys,' scribbles Beauvoir, who has abandoned Leibnitz to write up her journal in the library. 'He speaks of his admiration for me.' Two vertical lines deeply scored into the margin of her notebook mark this entry, which precipitated a new development. Gandillac, seeing Beauvoir slipping away, declared his love for her, even hinting at marriage. 'I defended myself against Gandillac,' she wrote on 3 May. 'I like him very much – but my great happiness is *Maheu*.' It was Maheu's manner that appealed, his gestures, his deep laugh, the way he called her his 'young friend'. He was, sighed Beauvoir, '*bien masculin*'.

The rivalry between the two young men intensified. 'I am surrounded by men,' wrote Beauvoir happily. She and Maheu spent an evening together: 'Oh! I so enjoy being with him!' she confided to her diary on 5 May. The two were becoming inseparable, lunching together, walking openly together. Gandillac, however, would not be shaken off. 'Gandillac! What can we do with him?' demanded Beauvoir three days later. The next day, in the courtyard of the École Normale, Gandillac was looking at her with so much warmth, while Maheu wore 'a wicked smile'.

Gandillac had good reason to pursue his court, for he had one inestimable advantage over his rival: he was free, unlike Maheu, a married man with a wife in the country. Beauvoir's first entry on the subject is on 10 June, when she writes that, over lunch with Maheu, 'We discuss marriage, and he tells me about his . . . Only, he adds, a man ought not to stop being free', even if he is married. At first Beauvoir accepts this specious argument, recording only: 'How dear he is to me!'

Maheu's marriage seemed not to matter. Were they not, after all, only friends? But this Benedict did not resemble any of Simone's other friends. He was far more handsome than Merleau-Ponty, or even Jacques. 'The jutting jaw, the broad, liquid smile, the blue irises set in their lustrous corneas; his flesh, his bone structure, and his very skin made an indelible impression . . .' she wrote breathlessly. And Maheu 'had more than a face: he had an unmistakable body, too . . . How proud he was of the young red blood pulsing in his veins!' Watching him come striding towards her in the Luxembourg Gardens, Simone would look at his ears, transparent in the sun as sugar-candy, and know that 'I had beside me not an angel, but a real man. I was tired of saintliness and I was overjoyed that he should treat me . . . as a creature of the earth.'

Already Maheu had designated Simone as an 'earth woman', or Houmos, in the mythology invented by the *petits camarades* and inspired by Jean Cocteau's novel *Le Pontomak*. In Sartre's invented world, different classes were given new names: there were the intellectual, bohemian Eugenes, to which Socrates and, naturally, Maheu, Nizan and Sartre belonged, as opposed to the dull Mortimers. 'The Eugene tries to make of his life an original work of art,' explained Maheu. Sketching Eugene figures, and penning a poem, as they sat side by side in Brunschvig's lectures, the handsome student whispered to Simone that earthy women like her were those who 'have a destiny'. He had already sensed in her the sensuality at war with her Catholic upbringing. Other people took her seriously, but Maheu found her amusing. 'How fast you walk! I love that,' he said gaily. 'Your funny husky voice!' he remarked another day. 'Sartre and I are very much amused by it.' Simone discovered that she had a way of walking, a way of talking: it was something new. She began to take more trouble with her appearance, and Maheu rewarded her efforts with a compliment: 'That new hair-style, that collar, suits you very well.'

Disgust at Jacques's recent behaviour increased Simone's susceptibility to her new admirer. One evening in the Stryx, Riquet invited her to his table. At the bar was a dark girl swathed in silvery furs; her hair was black, her mouth a slash of scarlet in a pale face, her long legs in silk stockings seemed to go on for ever. This was Magda, Jacques's mistress, now discarded. 'Any news of Jacques?' she asks Riquet. 'Didn't he ask about me? *Ce type-là, il a foutu le camp il y a un an et il ne demande pas de nouvelles de moi?* The bastard fucks off – it's over a year ago now – and he doesn't even ask after me!' Simone spends the night sobbing over this 'sordid little liaison', which reveals the Jacques she idealizes as a young man-about-town who has lost his virginity to a working girl, of whom he is now anxious to rid himself.

The next morning, 9 May, Simone received a letter from her grandmother in the Limousin: her grandfather was dying. On the morning of the 14th she left Paris for the funeral, aware that the past was slipping away from her. Her grandfather's death seemed to signal the end of her childhood. '*Au revoir à Meyrignac*,' she wrote sadly in her journal, as the train steamed back to Paris.

Her return in mourning, on 23 May, caused a sensation. Suddenly she looked like the aristocrat she potentially was, as well as a beautiful woman, although one quite unaware of her beauty. Shrouded in the deepest black crêpe georgette, Simone stepped into the Sorbonne after her short, emotional absence; Sartre, Maheu and Pierre Guille were lounging on a window-sill in a corridor. Her slight stature, enormous blue eyes, brimming with tears in a pale oval face, and soft, dark hair, hidden under a black hat swathed in tulle, made an impression upon all three young men. But for Sartre it was a *coup de foudre*. He fell deeply in love.

Beauvoir too, noticed Sartre. 'Maheu is there, in the corridor, beside Sartre,' she records in her 'Journal of 1929'. But only Maheu says '*Bonjour*' to her, and clasps her hand. Since he has not yet formally introduced his friend, good manners do not permit Sartre to address Simone.

Beauvoir's entrance was heartstopping because she was, recalled Nizan's wife, Rirette:

> a very pretty girl with ravishing eyes, a pretty little nose. She was extremely pretty, and even that voice, that same voice she has now, rather curious and a little broken, somewhat harsh – that added to her attraction. I don't think I ever saw her then dressed in anything but black, probably because hers was a distinguished family and in those families someone was always dying and they were mourning all the time . . . She was a very serious girl, very intellectual, and these qualities and the black dress actually enhanced her glamour, her unselfconscious beauty.

'I think she's beautiful. I've always thought her beautiful,' Sartre later remembered. 'I was dead set on making her acquaintance.' But he was forced to wait for an introduction. In the Luxembourg Gardens he watched in frustration as Maheu walked the small figure in the neat cloche hat round the lake at lunchtime; on another occasion it was Beauvoir who did the watching, sitting on the terrace in the park ostentatiously reading Isadora Duncan's *My Life* as Maheu and Sartre strolled around the lake. By then she, too, was curious to know Sartre. She was sure that Maheu had seen her, but he refused to acknowledge her, as this would oblige him to introduce Sartre. Peering over the pages of her book, Simone felt a pang of irritation. 'When he's with Sartre he persists in regarding me as a stranger,' she recorded on 24 May. 'Maheu was . . . very jealous,' Sartre remembered. 'He kept her for himself. When we were together, he would not even nod to her for fear of then being forced to introduce her.'

But Maheu had underestimated his adversary. There were good reasons for Sartre's nickname, 'the Kobra'. His reputation for protest and subversion had grown during the four years he had spent at the

École. With the addition of a beard and the Légion d'Honneur, he had performed in the annual student revues as Gustave Lanson, the principal. His mimicry brought howls of laughter, but Sartre had a darker purpose. Lanson symbolized toxic authority, pedagogy, the old values of Charles Schweitzer. Venomous and subtle, Sartre hatched a scheme to bring him down. In 1927 Lindbergh flew across the Atlantic, arriving in Paris in May, and Sartre and his friends telephoned the press to say that the aviator was visiting the École Normale. The next morning a crowd of 500 had gathered. One of Sartre's fellow students, disguised as Lindbergh, paraded to the strains of the Marseillaise. All the evening papers carried the story, and Lanson was forced to resign. It was, said Sartre, 'a gorgeous practical joke'.

The joke backfired when, a year later, the authorities failed Sartre in the *agrégation* in philosophy, at which he had been expected to excel. Sartre, who allegedly tried to be too original in the exam, had to watch his rival Raymond Aron top the list, while he was banished to the outer darkness of Cité University, near the Porte d'Orléans, an establishment reserved for foreigners and provincial Frenchmen. 'I just could not believe he had flunked it,' wrote Simone, amazed at the failure of the man she had heard was a genius. To make matters worse, Sartre's recent engagement to a grocer's daughter from Lyon was broken off by her parents when they heard of his disgrace. Sartre's two close friends, Nizan and Maheu, were both already married, and he had been anxious to take the same conventional step. Now he was doubly rejected: 'I took a bottle and went off into a field, alone, and there I drank and wept.'

These setbacks, however, only made Sartre more determined. The woolly, charming 'Llama', as Maheu was nicknamed, would prove no match for the Kobra. The day after glimpsing Simone in the corridor, Sartre gave Maheu a drawing he had done for her. Entitled 'Leibnitz bathing with the Monads', it depicted monads, or 'units of being' described by Leibnitz as naked water nymphs, and was an implicitly erotic gift. 'Jean-Paul asked me to give you this,' muttered Maheu, reluctantly handing over the drawing.

Sartre's interest made Maheu, in turn, more possessive. At first he had addressed Simone as 'Mademoiselle'. It was a sign of their growing intimacy that, one day in the library, the Llama gave Simone the nickname she would bear for the rest of her life. Bending over her notepad, he wrote in large capital letters, 'BEAUVOIR = BEAVER. *Vous êtes un Castor.*' Henceforth she was Castor, the Beaver. Maheu chose the name, he said, not only because of the similarity between

Simone's surname and the English 'beaver', but because 'beavers like company and they have a constructive bent'. He might also have added that, like llamas, beavers have soft, silky coats, and, when tamed, like to be stroked.

They began to share secrets. 'We understood each other almost intinctively,' recalled Simone. Maheu had little time for religion, and when Simone proudly gave him her dissertation on 'The Personality' to read, he pulled a face as he handed it back. It smacked of Catholicism and romanticism, he told her. Time to put an end to all that. 'I am an individualist,' he told her abruptly. 'So am I,' agreed Beauvoir. A powerful chemistry was developing between them, which expressed itself in private jokes about philosophy and sex. One afternoon Gandillac approached Simone with a book in his hand and earnestly demanded to know whether Mlle de Beauvoir agreed with the opinion of Brochard that Aristotle's God would be able to experience sexual pleasure. It was all Simone could do not to burst out laughing at Gandillac's lugubrious expression, as Maheu cast him a droll look and replied: 'I should hope so, for His sake.'

As the written examination that would test the young philosophers drew closer, Maheu came to the Bibliothèque Nationale every day to see Simone. 'He's a man I like immensely,' she confided to her diary on 31 May, as they sat side by side in the dimness of the library. She struggled with her feelings for the attentive 'country boy', for his moral code worried her. A man need not limit himself, in respect of women, declared the Llama, but a woman, on the other hand, should remain a virgin until she married. 'Marry Jacques,' he counselled her. A woman who did not marry by eighteen would become a frustrated neurotic. Shocked to discover that Maheu's views were almost identical to her father's, Simone protested at these male double standards, which allowed men free love but denied it to women.

'Women should be as free as men to dispose of their virginity,' she argued. Maheu smiled. 'I find it impossible to respect any woman I've had,' he said 'Society only respects married women.'

Simone listened in confusion. She could not help comparing her own, painful situation with that of Zaza, who had fallen in love with Maurice Merleau-Ponty. Zaza, in a dress of pink silk and a little straw hat, had never looked so flushed with happiness as when sitting beside Maurice in a rowing-boat on the lake in the Bois de Boulogne. The Beaver's beloved Llama, however, would be returning to 'Madame Maheu' at Bagnoles-de-l'Orne the moment the exams were over.

The relationship between Eugenes and 'earthy' women is usually difficult, said Maheu, because they want 'to swallow everything up and the Eugene sets up a resistance'. 'Do you think I haven't already found out already?' asked Simone. She knew that in her own life she had a Eugene, one who could never belong to her; yet she longed to consummate their love.

As the relationship between Maheu and Simone grew more passionate, it seems almost certain that he did take Simone's virginity. Since the age of twelve, as Beauvoir relates in *Memoirs of a Dutiful Daughter*, she had been tormented by physical desire; aroused by Jacques, she had been frustrated in her hopes of marriage. In the *Memoirs*, Beauvoir plays down the importance of Sartre's precursors, but in her journals the disparity between what she wrote for public consumption and what really happened is very clear. The self-portrait she created in the *Memoirs* of a 'little, well-brought-up young lady' who came a virgin to Sartre demanded that she denied her sexual relationship with Maheu to her biographers. 'I never even kissed a man full on the mouth before I met Sartre,' she protested. Maheu 'would have liked to, but *never, never, never* did he try to seduce me . . . I was truly the dutiful daughter.' The journal tells a different story.

Between 15 April and 15 June, Simone de Beauvoir relates her seduction by Maheu. In her journal she describes 'the long desire, its slow approach', which built between them over these two months. In giving herself wholly to him, she risked losing Maheu's respect, as he warned her, but she wanted him enough to throw caution to the winds. His ardour, spiced by the sense that Sartre was waiting in the wings, spurred her to act out her bold creed of freedom, and sleep with her 'Prince of Llamas'. It appears that 15 June was the day on which she finally lost her virginity. On that day, she writes, finally, '*J'apprends la douceur d'être femme*, I learn the sweetness of being a woman.'

This sentence signals the fulfilment of the deep love she felt for Maheu. At last she was a real woman, and it was everything she had hoped for. Their love affair would last throughout that summer. 'I love him profoundly – Oh! *Llama si aimé, mon Prince de Llamas*,' Simone was writing as late as 10 September 1929. There is little doubt that a physical relationship continued intermittently – Maheu had to go home to his wife – although, almost from its first, tender consummation, it was bittersweet. As the months passed Simone, as she relates in her journal, is forced to face the fact that, once again, she has chosen someone unattainable.

Towards the end of his life Sartre grew careless about maintaining the fiction that Beauvoir was a virgin when he first met her. He admitted in 1971 to Tito Gerassi, son of Simone's friends Stépha and Fernando, that Maheu had been Castor's first lover, and this was the reason for his reluctance to introduce Sartre to her. 'Maheu was in love with her . . . And she was in love with Maheu; in fact he was her first lover, so she wasn't in a particular hurry to meet us.' Maheu himself, in a final telephone conversation with Gerassi in 1989, also insisted that he had been Beauvoir's first lover. 'Sartre was incredibly generous, and a genius,' he recalled. 'But Castor . . . What a heart! She was so authentic, so courageously rebellious, so genuine . . . And she was so distinctively attractive, her own genre, her own style, no woman has ever been like her . . . But they had to continue.'

In her memoirs Beauvoir denied that Maheu was her first lover. The construction of the legend required her to tamper with the truth. 'I saw love as a total engagement; therefore,' she protests unconvincingly, 'I was not in love with [Maheu].' But days before her death Maheu was still on Beauvoir's mind. In her final interview with her biographer Deirdre Bair, on 4 March 1986, she repeated that 'The people [who believed that she and Maheu were physically involved] are dreaming. It's all false.'

The issue remains controversial. Sylvie Le Bon, Beauvoir's partner and literary executor, has continued to defend Beauvoir's reputation. 'Gerassi is a liar,' Le Bon told me. 'Sartre said that Simone de Beauvoir was a virgin. She was attracted by Maheu, but she was "*une jeune fille*". Without a proposal of marriage, one doesn't go to bed with someone. *Cette histoire n'est pas possible*.' Le Bon agrees, however, that in 1944, at the liberation of Paris, Beauvoir and Maheu slept together. In that 'explosion of joy', their old passion reignited. It was unlikely to have been for the first time.

*

'*Bonne chance, Castor*,' whispered Maheu tenderly, as the pair took their seats in the library of the Sorbonne for the examination. Simone put a thermos of coffee and a box of butter biscuits on her desk. 'Your subject is "Liberty and Contingency",' announced the examiner. While other candidates stared at the ceiling, her pen flew over the pages.

The next day Maheu made a surprise appearance at 71 rue de Rennes: he was leaving to join his wife at Bagnoles-de-l'Orne. On his return, in ten days' time, he would be preparing for the oral philosophy exam with Sartre and Nizan, and he had a message to deliver: Sartre had expressed a wish to invite Mlle de Beauvoir to join them. He desired to make her acquaintance: could they meet one evening?

Aware that he had probably already failed the written exam, and desperate not to lose Simone, Maheu begged her not to meet his rival. He was afraid that Sartre would take advantage of his absence to 'monopolize' her. Simone agreed to send her sister Poupette in her place, with instructions to say that she had been called away suddenly to the country.

Courteously Sartre accepted his decoy's excuses, and escorted her to the cinema. He was not nearly as amusing as Maheu said, reported Poupette to her sister: 'That is pure invention.'

By Sunday, 7 July, Simone was feeling nervous. The prodigiously intelligent Sartre was expecting her at the university the next morning to discuss Leibnitz; anxiously she reread her notes on the philosopher.

I don't think I slept all the night before . . . I was terrified they would not find me brilliant enough but only a silly girl who knew very little and could not think . . .

7

The Summer of Love

I need Sartre; and I love Maheu.
> Simone de Beauvoir, journal, 8 August 1929

THE SUMMER OF 1929 was one of the hottest on record. The *marronniers*, the chestnut trees of Paris, had burst into flower early, and by May the scent of lilacs filled the walled garden of the École Normale, where the students sat idly by the fountain, the leaves of their books curling in the sunshine. In July the weather grew sultry: the pavements shimmered under a blue sky, and only the evening breeze blowing up from the Seine stirred the air. Parisians flocked to the cinema to see Al Jolson in *The Jazz Singer*, the first talking film, or danced to the intoxicating voice of the saxophone. On the boulevards tarts stood under the blue neon lights; Paris was alive, the throbbing rhythms of the Jazz Age expressing the sexuality of the city of dreams.

Simone tapped at the door of Jean-Paul Sartre's room. She was intrigued by his reputation: 'A terror, but absolutely brilliant.' She'd heard that he'd gone naked to the student ball, that he and his friend Pierre Guille had dropped water bombs from the roof of the École Normale on to the heads of the dinner-jacketed guests below, shouting, 'Thus pissed Zarathustra!' It was common knowledge that he had vomited drunkenly on to the feet of the principal of the Lycée Henri IV on passing his baccalauréat, and performed in drag in *La Belle Hélène*.

Sartre was courtesy itself when he opened the door. A slovenly dresser who disliked washing, he had made more effort than usual in honour of his guest. In his open-necked black shirt, he struck Simone as a man of the world as he greeted her formally and showed her to the only comfortable chair. His thick dark blond hair was parted on the left and carefully brushed. Behind round horn-rimmed glasses his eyes were intelligent, his lips full and sensitive, his nose straight. As one of his lovers later remembered, he had a noble forehead. Apprehensively Simone glanced about her, through the clouds of tobacco smoke, at the piles of books and overflowing ashtrays. Pinned up on the walls were Sartre's satirical drawings. She was too scared to speak. Sartre, smoking a pipe, nodded absently at her. Nizan, puffing on a cigarette, inspected her through pebble lenses.

Soon Leibnitz was forgotten. 'Something great has happened,' she recorded that night. '*Oh! Charme unimaginable.*' Dazzled by Sartre's eloquence, and his obvious interest in her, she for the first time underlined his name in her journal. For Sartre, too, the meeting was life-changing. That evening he made her a present of a Japanese print, which the Llama helped her carry home. '*Sartre et moi,*' she wrote, 'are working together now.'

The next day, 10 July, she arrived at Sartre's room to hear the Llama angrily protesting, 'No, this evening *I* am taking Mademoiselle de Beauvoir to the cinema,' and the 'Grand Duke' (Nizan) replying, 'Fine, fine,' while Sartre went, 'Go, then.' A joint expedition had been proposed, but Maheu would only allow Sartre to walk the Beaver and himself as far as place Denfert-Rochereau. That evening he looked sad. 'I'm happy to be going out with you, Castor,' he told her, conscious that their idyll was doomed. As they watched a film of the Tour de France, he talked morosely of his wife. '*Ah! Mon Llama,*' sighed Beauvoir to her diary.

On Friday, 12 July, Maheu and Beauvoir disappeared to his hotel room in rue Vanneau. At first the Llama sat in an armchair, telling her once again how happy he was to see her there. Then the couple moved to the bed, where Maheu proved 'tender', recorded Simone, and she was 'flooded with the sweetness of his presence'. Not even the reproachful photograph of the Llama's wife on the chimneypiece prevented her yielding to his skilful caresses. Afterwards, Beauvoir made a desultory attempt to look at Aristotle, but the lazy Llama waved the books away; it was too late to bother. Instead, he showed his Beaver Sartre's drawings of 'metaphysical animals', and nude Michelangelo prints, and told her stories.

All that month, Beauvoir wrestled with her feelings. On the 13th

Sartre expounded Rousseau's *Social Contract* to the group. Sometimes Simone attempted to argue with him. 'She's a sly puss!' exclaimed Maheu, as she made a point while Nizan studied his fingernails. 'Sartre always succeeded in turning the tables on me,' Beauvoir remembered, but she was impressed by his generosity, for he seemed to her to learn nothing from the sessions, although 'he would give of himself for hours without counting the cost'.

Her mind was still on '*mon Llama*'. He took her out to lunch after the session, and a spin in his car. '*Que nous sommes gais!*' she wrote. But on Bastille Day, 14 July, Maheu was finally forced to capitulate: Sartre might be allowed inside the lovers' private fortress. All four *petits camarades* had dinner together in an Alsatian restaurant and watched the fireworks from the lawn of the Cité Universitaire. As the last rockets exploded into the darkness, Sartre hailed a taxi and took the party to the Falstaff in the rue Montparnasse, where he kept Simone 'lushed up with cocktails' until two in the morning. The three gentlemen competed to entertain their new female friend. 'I was in seventh heaven,' recalled Simone. 'I thought Sartre was even more amusing than Maheu.'

Two days later Maheu announced that he would allow Sartre to be the Beaver's friend. By now he had no choice. At the Falstaff, Sartre was once again buying, and Beauvoir was impressed. 'Yet it's not him I love,' she confided to her diary. 'Le Llama! How I could suffer for that man! . . . I know how to suffer tonight. I'm nervous. I have a terrible sense of dependence on him.'

But Maheu could offer her no future, while Sartre was free. He was also generous. In time Sartre's munificence would become legendary. Anne-Marie could deny him nothing, and he always carried a fat roll of notes in his back pocket. In 1929 this was even thicker than usual, as his paternal grandmother had left him a legacy which he was in the process of spending. Sartre's profligacy would prove highly attractive to Simone after her penny-pinching upbringing.

And there was a gap in Sartre's life, which lent urgency to his courtship. His bond with Nizan had weakened after the latter's marriage in 1927. Sartre and Nizan had been so intimate that Sartre felt they had become a single being: '*Un seul être.*' It was an important coupledom which blotted out the fears and insecurity of '*l'homme seul*, man alone'. Now Nizan had Rirette, and Sartre longed, too, to find a woman with whom to recreate the incestuous union with Anne-Marie which formed his earliest pre-memory.

A pattern was quickly established: mornings working, followed by playtime. Simone joined the group scampering over the university rooftops and singing among the chimneypots. Sartre and Maheu composed a mocking motet based on Descartes: 'Concerning God, whether he exists'. In his pleasant tenor voice Sartre sang *Old Man River*, and other jazz hits and Negro spirituals. Riotous lunchtimes were followed by trips to the nearby funfair at the Porte d'Orléans, where they would play pinball or try their luck at the shooting gallery. One evening Simone went home hugging a pink vase she had won on the Wheel of Fortune.

As she listened to the *petits camarades'* mockery of Christian spirituality or *la vie intérieure*, the Beaver began to feel a sense of shame about her own lingering attachment to 'bourgeois humbug'. In Sartre's masterclass, the soul had no place. There was no other dimension: man stood alone, adrift in the universe.

The trio had refused to sit the examination in religious knowledge, preferring to adopt the ideas of Cocteau, who had declared, 'I explore the void.' 'If God does not exist and man dies,' said Sartre, repeating his favourite quotation from Dostoevsky, 'everything is permissible. One experience is as good as another; the important thing is simply to acquire as many as possible.' They would live by the surrealists' motto, trumpeted in their 1924 manifesto, to *épater les bourgeois*. And as Eugenes, was it not their duty to mock all universal moral systems? Exhilarated by Sartre's invitation to join him in that 'brutal adventure called life', Simone wrote in her diary on 25 July: '*Quel délicieux soir avec quel délicieux Sartre.*'

A few days later Simone ran to the Sorbonne to discover the results of the written *agrégation*. At the door she met Sartre. They had both passed, as had Nizan. Maheu had failed. 'From now on,' said Sartre to Castor: '*Je vous prends en main*, I'm going take you under my wing.' His remark was a challenge as much an offer of help, she thought: 'He was very pleased to have me all to himself.' With Maheu off the scene, his long deferred seduction of Simone could begin in earnest.

Within a fortnight, Sartre and Simone had become inseparable. They socialized with the Nizans, who lived in the rue Vavin with Rirette's parents. 'To do the old Deux Magots in the eye', they avoided the place Saint-Germain-des-Prés in favour of the Café de Flore. It was dark and dingy. Young writers published in the radical literary journal, the *Nouvelle Revue Française*, sprawled on red chairs and admired themselves in mahogany mirrors. They met up with Aron, also socialist in his sympathies, who was doing his military service in the Meteorological Corps, and Georges Politzer, a Communist. Often they chose to be alone. Sartre bought armfuls of second-hand books at the *bouquinistes* on the banks of the Seine. They drank gin fizzes and martinis in the Falstaff, and went to the cinema, where Sartre introduced Simone to Westerns. He talked of his heroes, Captain Pardaillon, Buffalo Bill and Nick Carter, the fictional New York detective. They listened to the records of Sophie Tucker and Jack Hylton. And, day by day, the precocious twenty-one-year-old fell further and further under Sartre's spell, as he talked to her about the subject which interested her above all others: herself.

Shyly Simone confided to Sartre her longing to be a novelist. 'Whatever happens, you must try to preserve what is best in you,' he urged: 'Your love of personal freedom, your passion for life, your determination to be a writer.' Apart from Zaza, no one before had encouraged her solitary ambition. But in Sartre she found a man who said, 'I can help you,' a man whose desire to write exhibited a 'frenzied passion' even greater than her own. 'He lived only to write,' she recorded. 'Books are fountains of light,' he said, 'In ruined libraries, they will survive man.' Simone was impressed. Maheu made notes on Spinoza, but Sartre wanted to *be* Spinoza – and Stendhal too.

Boldly the Kobra expounded his 'theory of contingency', a fashionable topic in the late twenties: there are two kinds of events in the world, those that are unavoidable, like gravity, parents, or your digestive system, and are necessary to existence; and those that are the result of luck or accident, like missing the bus and meeting the love of one's life on the next one. The second, contingency or randomness, had shaped Sartre: his father's death, his exam failure in 1928, his meeting with Simone. Gratuitous, arbitrary, unforeseen events had acted upon his personality, which he would spend the rest of his life decoding.

It seemed a gloomy philosophy. 'At the root of humanity, I can see only sadness and boredom,' wrote Sartre. Without God, the divine spark extinguished, Sartre felt bereft. He found some echo of his own feelings of loneliness and sadness in the work of the nineteenth-century Danish philosopher Søren Kierkegaard. Kierkegaard had identified the chasm in the human mind that is the absence of God and of any meaning, and had invented the phrase 'to be in dread of nothing'. It expressed the notion that man is terrified at the prospect of the emptiness, *le néant* or nothingness which lies ahead of him, of death without a hereafter. Kierkegaard is credited with setting the stage, and providing many of the ideas for existentialism, and certainly in 1929 Sartre's dread of nothingness came close to Kierkegaard's own psychological anguish.

The phrase 'to be in dread of nothing' had particular resonance for the young Frenchman because of its links to his childhood fears. As a child of seven Sartre had dreamt that he was on a train without a ticket. When the ticket collector came round he had no ticket to show, and no right to travel; this lack symbolized the fact that he had no right to existence. The dream became recurrent. The boy who looked in the mirror and saw only a jellyfish striking feebly at his own reflection still felt inadequate and afraid. The loss of his faith had taken away a crutch that might have helped him. Like Kierkegaard, 'the dread of nothing has entered into him', and had led to an even greater fear at the alarming possibilities of being free. 'Dread of nothing is linked to dread of freedom,' wrote Kierkegaard, who made the leap of faith back to Christianity. Sartre, on the other hand, without the guiding light of Catholicism, was spinning loose.

'We are as free as you like, but helpless,' he wrote in an early essay. 'Everything is too weak: all things carry the seeds of their own death.' Condemned to be free, we must take up our burden and create meaning in a meaningless world.

Beauvoir was impressed by Sartre's strenuously ethical attempt to formulate a new philosophy by which to live. He, in his turn, was delighted to find a disciple who was engaged in her own quest to find a substitute for Catholicism, but also brought with her habits of obedience learnt in her devout childhood. There was never any need to tick Castor off, as he had the first Simone.

One morning, however, beside the Medici fountain in the Luxembourg Gardens, Simone plucked up the courage to put forward her own thoughts. Despite accepting, like many modern thinkers and writers she was reading from Nietzsche to Dostoevsky, that 'God is dead', she still clung to her own system: a belief in the 'Absolute', a Goodness – or Godness – in the universe. Sartre listened in silence; then he quietly took her philosophy apart ('*il la mit en pièces*'). Still Simone resisted; *her* ideas allowed her to look upon her 'heart as the arbiter of good and evil'. For three hours she argued, before finally admitting defeat:

> I was simply not in his class . . . My reasoning was at fault and my ideas were in a muddle. I'm no longer sure *what* I think, nor whether I can be said to think at all . . .

Beauvoir's humiliation beside the Medici fountain was a critical event in the development of her relationship with Sartre. It was his moment of intellectual conquest. And as Sartre demolished God, he put himself in His place. Cut loose from the Jesus Christ she had worshipped so passionately in her early adolescence, Simone began to idealize Sartre with an equal fervour. She set him on a pedestal: a Magus figure, keeper of the secrets, magical guardian of the truth. In her memoirs she wrote: 'Je ne me demandai plus: que faire? Il y avait tout à faire. I no longer asked myself: what shall I do? There was everything to be done . . . to find the truth, tell it . . . to the world, perhaps to help change the world.'

But her journal demonstrates that the process of falling in love was far more gradual than she claimed in her *Memoirs,* which distort and fictionalize her first reactions to Sartre. 'I need Sartre,' Simone wrote on 8 August in her journal. 'And Maheu, I love him – I love what Sartre brings me – and what Maheu *is.*' But if she was still unsure whether Sartre was her 'twin soul', she had become convinced that, compared to his clique, her knowledge lacked depth: 'Their culture had a more solid grounding than mine . . . *Je n'étais ni l'unique, ni la première:* I wasn't the One and Only, but one among many, by no means first.' With this sentence, Beauvoir made her obeisance to Sartre.

The oral examination, to which the pair now submitted themselves, was the final hurdle in their university career. Of seventy-six candidates who had sat the written philosophy examination, only twenty-seven were allowed to present themselves at the orals, of whom thirteen passed. Women generally required four or five attempts, and Sartre himself, winner of the *prix d'excellence* at the École Normale, had failed once. Simone's supporters in the audience, Zaza, Stépha and Poupette, held their breath, therefore, as she stepped up before the adjudicators. Not only was she competing against the most brilliant young men of her generation, but against Simone Weil, who had been taught by Alain at the Lycée Henri IV like Sartre and Nizan, had beaten Beauvoir in the certificate in general philosophy in 1927, and had also studied at the École Normale from 1928.

Everyone knew that the teaching received by Beauvoir had been inferior, so when the results were published, they caused a sensation. She had triumphed, beating everyone except Sartre: he was ranked first, she second. At twenty-one, she was the youngest person ever to pass the *agrégation* in philosophy, and only the ninth woman. It was an extraordinary achievement.

The three-member jury had debated long. Beauvoir 'was rigorous, demanding, precise, very technical', recalled Gandillac, who was present. Sartre, on the other hand, noted the judges, 'shows a keen, rigorous and well-rounded, if not always dependable, intelligence'. But his 'extraordinarily poised' presentation on phenomenology, the sensational new movement in philosophy founded by Edmund Hüsserl, finally won the day, although the voting was divided, two to one. It had been difficult to decide who should be first, confessed Davy and Wahl, two of the examiners, 'For although Sartre demonstrated obvious qualities, great intelligence, a strong culture be it in some ways sketchy, everyone agreed that *she* was the true philosopher.'

Predictably, the educational establishment had awarded the crown to one of its own: Sartre, a male, a *normalien* and, at twenty-four, three years Castor's senior. For the rest of her life Simone de Beauvoir would consider herself second to Sartre.

8

A Month in the Country

> I'm only a desire for beauty, and outside of that: void,
> nothing.
>
> Jean-Paul Sartre, *War Diaries 1939–40*

ON 19 AUGUST Beauvoir caught the train to Uzerche. She was
returning to the Limousin, possibly for the last time. Meyrignac, which
had been so large a part of her childhood, had now passed to Uncle
Gaston. Her destination was the Château de la Grillère, ten miles from
Uzerche, where as a child she had spent idyllic summers with her
cousins Robert and Madeleine and their parents, Aunt Hélène,
Georges's elder sister, and her husband, fox-hunting Maurice de
Bisshop. But the penniless status of Simone's immediate family within
the rigid stratification of the bourgeoisie had been underlined two
summers ago, when she had played a set or two of tennis with a young
man at the château and his mother had sharply warned Françoise that
there was no question of her son marrying Simone, a girl without a
dowry. At dances, clothed ignominiously in her cousin's cast-off ball
dress, Simone hid behind a pillar, an awkward wallflower ignored by
the local squires. In her journal the words 'rejection' and 'exile'
repeatedly appear.

And yet nothing had changed. The green Limousin countryside was
timeless. In the turreted château the copper hunting-horns still hung in
the tiled hall, the stuffed foxes and buzzards adorned the walls of the

billiard room, Simone and Hélène still slept in four-poster beds, and the hens and guinea-fowl scratched in the yard outside the kitchen window as the sisters drank their steaming *café-au-lait* at breakfast. The kitchen was the room Simone loved the most: sparks flew from the cast-iron cooking range as she sat warming her feet at the great wooden table surrounded by shining pots and pans, dressers and cupboards piled high with porringers, *bains-marie*, stockpots and soup tureens decorated in bright paintbox colours. Across the corridor, in the dairy, patterned blocks of butter and round cheeses lay in ordered rows under white muslin, while in the cellar, among the bottles and barrels, huge hams, ropes of sausages, onions and mushrooms hung to dry in the still air.

Outside, the gardens, the fruit loft, the stables and the acres of chestnut groves were still her demesne. Early each morning she would rise and walk along the drive with a book in her hand, watching as pale rays of sunshine burnt away the morning mist. Later Poupette and Madeleine would join her on the croquet lawn, and afternoons would be spent hunting for mushrooms in the chestnut groves, or digging up anthills for eggs on which to feed the peacocks. On Sundays Aunt Hélène would order the carriage to take the ladies to Mass at nearby Saint-Germain-les-Belles. However, this holiday promised to be more eventful than was usual: both Maheu and Sartre had told Simone that they wished to pay her a visit.

It was high summer in the Limousin when Jean-Paul Sartre arrived on 21 August. He booked a room at the Hôtel de la Boule d'Or in Saint-Germain-les-Belles, and early the next morning set out on the half-hour walk across the fields to the château. Simone was still sitting over breakfast when Madeleine burst into the kitchen: she had found a young man in the grounds who was asking for her cousin. At once Simone ran out of the kitchen to meet him. She was excited at Jean-Paul's arrival – as was Madeleine – and anxious to keep her suitor to herself. Would Jean-Paul like to go for a walk? she asked. 'No,' replied Sartre. He was allergic to chlorophyll. All this lush green pasture exhausted him. How about tennis? He shook his head. Should she bring some books? No. He just wanted to talk. 'Very soon I realized,' wrote Simone, 'that even though we went on talking till Judgement Day, I would still find the time all too short.'

Sartre was impressed by the turreted château and all that it implied. Despite the scorn that he claimed to feel for the bourgeoisie, he was sensitive about his own peasant roots among the 'suspicious, ugly and for the most part dirty . . . yokels' of Thiviers, as well as his Alsatian heritage on his mother's side, with its inferiority complex vis-à-vis

France. Although Karl Schweitzer had thrown in his lot with the French in 1871, he often saw his grocer brother Auguste and other German-speaking relations in Gunsbach and Pfaffenhofen, and it was a bone of contention with him that the German teacher in most *lycées* was an Alsatian who had opted for France but, 'trapped between two nations, two languages', met only with hostility from his French colleagues. 'You will avenge me, Jean-Paul,' commanded Karl. 'Though the grandson of an Alsatian, I was a Frenchman of France,' recalled Sartre in 1964. 'In my person martyred Alsace would enter the École Normale Supérieure, take a degree brilliantly and become a prince: a teacher of literature.'

That summer Jean-Paul had done everything Karl had asked of him. He was the crown prince of the École Normale. Never had he felt more optimistic. It was a period, he would later recall, when he felt like 'a thousand Socrates'. His proud boast, copied from Hippias, was, 'I have never met any man who is my equal.' No doubt he expected that if he hovered nearby, Simone's parents would invite him to lunch at La Grillère. But no such invitation was forthcoming. Françoise, referring icily to her elder daughter's 'friend', expressed the opinion to her sister-in-law that he must surely be passing through on his way to another destination. When the gong sounded for luncheon, Simone was in a dilemma. She made it a point of honour never to help in any domestic capacity such as clearing the plates, and was therefore obliged to ask Madeleine to save some food for Sartre. This, Madeleine, who felt she was helping the hero and heroine of a romantic novel, was happy to do, hiding cheese and gingerbread for Sartre in an abandoned dovecote. Two days later Simone herself missed lunch and spent long hours in the cornfields with her suitor.

Opposition from Simone's parents only stiffened Jean-Paul's resolve. Every morning he appeared and waited for Castor. Every day he wore an 'aggressive' red shirt. The sight of her 'small, honest figure', as he described it in a love letter, inspired confidence; she was only an inch taller than he, unlike his mother. Simone, for her part, at first felt a little timid which, as she confessed to her journal, made her 'artificial'. But every morning she woke at seven o'clock, her heart beating with joy. 'Perfect' days followed: 'Now I accept without embarrassment the slightly disturbing sensation of being in his arms and feeling his power.'

In her journal, ten days after his departure, under the heading '*Sartre*', she would summarize what her new lover meant to her: 'The world finishes opening itself up – I'm learning that I have a destiny as a woman – with you whom I love. I'm learning what it is to think, what a great man is, what union means.' The last few months had witnessed 'the birth of Castor who for so long hesitated between an intellectual Mlle de Beauvoir and a passionate Mlle de Beauvoir'. That summer, the summer of love, innocence turned to experience.

Her response touched Sartre on the deepest level. Beauvoir, the toast of the university, the prettiest girl among all the students, was prepared to love him. She gave him the acceptance he craved when she kissed him. It was a mythic, maiden's kiss, offering transfiguration. The boy who believed he had become a toad when he lost his golden curls was reborn as the adored '*petit prince*' of his childhood. 'Women's company', which had revealed his defects, also enabled him 'to get rid of the burden of his ugliness'. My appetite for beauty, he said, 'wasn't really sensual, but more magical. I should have liked to eat beauty and incorporate it.'

For Simone, by contrast, earth woman, as Maheu described her, sexuality was at the heart of being, as 'necessary' as the pull of the tides or the march of the seasons. Intense and passionate, she wanted 'life . . . the whole of life'; to taste it in its totality. Awakened to physical intimacy by Maheu, she now had few reservations about taking her pleasure with a new lover.

Ever since adolescence, she had associated the green glades of the chestnut forests with sexual exploration. As a thirteen-year-old girl Simone had stolen away from her sister one hot afternoon to discover her own body, alone, lying propped against the broad trunk of a chestnut tree. She had brought a book of Balzac's stories with her, but as she had read these Rabelaisian tales of peasant life, of summer couplings in the countryside, the heavy volume had dropped from her hand. The glade was warm and private, silent except for the buzzing of bees. Her thoughts turned to her cousin Jacques. She glanced around. There was no sign of her uncle's gamekeeper. Simone pulled up her skirts:

> She peeled the bark from a small wooden stick and gently rubbed the sticky wand between her thighs: it disgusted her to touch her warm flesh with her fingers. The image of her mother flashed before her and she banished it with no feeling of shame; this was like another existence in which you no longer had parents, nor a future, nor even a name; there was the smell of the scrub, of pine needles . . . a sweet and mysterious sensation which transformed the whole of her body from her head to her feet into a piece of shivering silk . . .

The angelus sounded. Simone jumped to her feet.

The strength of her orgasm had left her trembling. So momentous was the experience that she described it in the first three pages of the first chapter of her first novel, *She Came to Stay*. (Her shocked publisher, Gaston Gallimard, cut the offending chapter). Long afterwards, Beauvoir continued to associate sex with nature, writing: 'The pleasures of love-making should be as unforeseen and as irresistible as the surge of the sea or a peach tree breaking into blossom.'

Alone now with Sartre, in the meadows and forests she had known since girlhood, Simone was ready for the same release. She had known '*cher Jean-Paul*', as she now described him in her diary, for barely six weeks, but already she recognized that they had a 'twin sign' on their brows. She gave herself to the vital, muscular 'little man' known as 'O.S.', 'Official Satyr', a play on his surname probably connected to his relationship with Simone Jollivet, who had given him a lampshade made of her purple lace-trimmed pants as a memento of their affair. Sartre did not rush Simone, for he found his greatest satisfaction in foreplay. '*J'étais plutôt un masturbateur de femmes qu'un coïteur*,' he would write in 1939 (I was a masturbator of women rather than a copulator).

Under the chestnut trees, Simone kissed her Pan. For both of them, the excitement of this pagan coupling *en plein air* was increased by the fear of discovery, the thrill of knowing that they were not only defying Simone's parents but flouting the rules of society. As they lay in the grass only a mile from the walls of the family château, they laughed wildly at the thought that Uncle Maurice might come riding by on horseback, or that Aunt Hélène might cease inspecting her pantry and witness her niece's antics. In surrendering herself to Sartre without even an engagement, Simone was destroying for ever her reputation as a respectable, if impoverished, young bourgeoise. But their Arcadian ecstasies were worth the risk to two student rebels seeking a confrontation with authority.

They did not have long to wait. Only four days after Sartre's arrival, the Beaver looked up to see the figures of her parents standing on the edge of the meadow. They walked towards the young couple. Under his yellowing straw boater, Georges de Beauvoir wore a resolute but embarrassed expression. Sartre jumped to his feet, 'the light of battle in his eye'. Georges, unconvinced by Simone's story that she and Sartre were working on a book on Marx, ordered him to leave the district. People were gossiping. His sister was hoping to find a husband for Madeleine, and Simone's scandalous behaviour was jeopardizing her cousin's reputation. Sartre refused: it was essential, he told M. de Beauvoir, that he and Simone continued studying together. Her parents retired, defeated. The next day the young couple found new hiding places, deeper in the forest. Sartre stayed on until 1 September, and Georges did not return to the attack.

It was a victory for youth. 'My mother and father no longer controlled my life,' Beauvoir wrote with a sense of wonderment. 'I was truly responsible for myself now. I could do as I pleased, there was nothing they could do to stop me.' Sartre, too, was emboldened by success. The next day, lying in the green light with Simone, flushed and compliant in his arms, he blurted out a proposal of marriage. It was not the first time he had brought the subject up; less than two weeks after first knowing Simone, while they were studying together, he had hinted at marriage. Now she simply laughed and said: 'Don't be silly!' She was amused by his proposal, which she did not at first take seriously. How could marriage be reconciled with his doctrine of freedom, with his plans to follow in his father's footsteps and travel East? But Sartre persisted for several days with his marriage plans, believing that it was the institution to which she objected rather than the suitor. He had fallen in love with Simone and wanted to steal her from Maheu. She was beautiful, intelligent and well bred, albeit dowryless. He had compromised her in front of her family and scandalized the neighbourhood, to their mutual satisfaction. Duty and honour now demanded that he make her his wife.

Simone blushed and thanked Jean-Paul; she was not ready to give him an answer. In fact, she suggested, he really ought to leave. Her cousin Robert was waiting to drive him to the station at Uzerche.

*

'Sartre corresponded exactly to the dream-companion I had longed for since I was fifteen: he was the double in whom I found all my burning aspiration raised to the pitch of incandescence,' Beauvoir wrote in a famous passage in her memoirs. 'I should always be able to share everything with him. When I left him at the beginning of August, I knew that he would never go out of my life.'

Yet on 4 September, just three days after waving Sartre goodbye, Simone de Beauvoir kept a secret rendezvous with René Maheu in Uzerche. This meeting was one of 'certain facts' which Beauvoir warned readers of *The Prime of Life*, the second volume of her memoirs, she had 'suppressed'. 'I have no intention of telling them everything,' she wrote in her Preface. 'There are many things which I firmly intend to leave in obscurity . . . though . . . I have at no point set down deliberate falsehoods.' Her defence was that she was not interested in 'spiteful gossip': but her meeting with Maheu was a turning point in her life.

It left her trembling and confused. Both her suitors had pursued her to the Limousin, and in her journal she compares them, her notes under 'Sartre's stay', and 'the Llama's stay' revealing her complicated feelings as she tries to make her choice. Her head was in conflict with her heart, which told her to choose Maheu: vividly Simone describes the rush of joy she feels at the sight of 'a Llama in a beige checked jacket, dirty and tired, sitting on his two suitcases at the train station'. The pair hurry to a hotel, where she has booked two rooms with a view over the River Vézère and is paying with money borrowed from Madeleine. The Llama kisses her hand as they go down to dinner, where Sartre is the main topic of conversation over a bottle of 1923 Chablis.

Beauvoir's agitation is evident in her hurried, barely legible handwriting, as she pours out her tale to her journal: the Llama's dear voice, as he says, *'Bonjour Castor'*, in his blue pyjamas the next morning; the scent of his eau de Cologne as they lie on the bed together and he tells her stories from Shakespeare; his arms around her as they drift together on a boat on the river. 'How tenderly I love him,' she writes of her Llama, *'gai – spirituel – tendre – et si familier déjà.'* But it is a hopeless love, for a man for whom she has no respect, as she tells herself over and over again. On 10 September, two days after Maheu has finally left, she repeats her doubts about 'My prince of Llamas'; his touches of vanity, his lack of generosity in talking about his wife:

Morally, I don't esteem him . . . *But* . . . I love him deeply – beloved Llama, my prince of Llamas . . . the most delicious, the most sure, the most tender of lovers.'

Her conflict torments her, despite her efforts at self-control – this time, there'd been 'nothing physical' with this 'sensual man'. On the one hand there is this 'trouble – passion inquiète'. On the other, with Sartre, 'a great man', as she already recognized him to be, there is 'passionate friendship, sure and calm'.

It is time to return to Paris. She is still uncertain, confides Beauvoir to her dear diary, about 'This love for Sartre which will go where it will . . .'

9

~~~

A 'Morganatic' Marriage

I was hoist with my own petard. The Beaver accepted
that freedom and kept it.

Jean-Paul Sartre, *War Diaries*, 1939

IN MID-SEPTEMBER Simone returned to Paris. For the first time in her
life, instead of making her reluctant way with her family to the grimy
flat at 71 rue de Rennes, she was to have a new home. Her widowed
grandmother Brasseur had decided to take in lodgers, and Simone had
waited many months for the room on which she had set her heart to fall
vacant: a spacious back bedroom, out of her grandmother's hearing, in
which to begin an independent life. Now the old lodger left; Françoise
accepted her daughter's argument that moving in with Grandmama,
who would be keeping an eye on her, was not like leaving home.
Georges agreed to pay for the furnishing of the room. Simone packed
up her belongings and moved into the fifth-floor flat on place Denfert-
Rochereau, a leafy square named after the general who had defeated the
Prussians at Belfort in 1871. It was only a few minutes' walk from her
mother, still in the heart of Montparnasse; but it was a room of her own.

From her balcony Simone could gaze out on the majestic, bronze
Lion of Belfort, sculpted by Bertholdi, which dominated the square,
and the plane trees which lined the street. Inside, in the high-ceilinged
room, she set about recreating an image she had stored in her mind
since she was twelve, when she had read a story about an English girl in

a magazine and stared wide-eyed at the coloured illustration of her room: 'There was a desk, and a divan, and shelves filled with books. Here, within those gaily painted walls, she read and worked and drank tea, with no one watching her – how envious I felt!' Like the girl in the picture, Simone would have an orange room: she papered the walls the colour of clementines, and added a divan to match. Her sister Poupette helped her varnish the unpainted furniture she had bought. To keep herself warm, Simone purchased a kerosene stove, whose evil stink she grew to love. It seemed to protect her solitude.

As long as Simone paid her rent, her grandmother Lucie did not bother her. Free to come and go as she pleased, Simone could read all night and sleep till midday. For lunch she had a bowl of borscht, for supper a cup of hot chocolate at La Coupole, strolling up the boulevard Raspail, past the cemetery, to the familiar cafés of her childhood. After the strain of cramming for the *agrégation*, she felt as if she were on holiday. Her workload was light. Despite now being fully qualified as a teacher of philosophy, Simone had decided not to apply for a full-time post because new teachers were sent to the provinces. For her, as for Sartre, Paris was 'the centre of the world', and to leave it would feel like exile. Instead she had found a part-time job teaching Latin to ten-year-olds at the Lycée Victor-Duruy. This gave her enough to live on, and was so easy that when she found herself in the staff room talking to senior mistresses, or to parents, the twenty-one-year-old teacher could hardly prevent herself laughing aloud. She opened the envelope containing her first salary cheque and felt as if she had played a practical joke on someone. Female teachers had financial parity with males, and even a part-time income seemed like a fortune to Simone after years of cheese-paring.

At last she could afford to dress as *she* wanted. Still in mourning for her grandfather, Simone had no wish to shock her family, so she bought a grey coat, with shoes and a neat toque hat to match. She visited the dressmaker and ordered two dresses to be made, one grey, the other black and white. Determined no longer to be clad in wool or cotton, the serviceable fabrics favoured by her mother, she selected rich, silky material, crêpe de Chine and *velours frappé*, crushed velvet. She was defiantly aware that her shiny new outfits and single pair of cheap evening shoes, worn at the heel from walking, were out of place in the corridors of the *lycée*, but she didn't care. Newly conscious of her own femininity, Simone bought vanishing cream, powder and a red lipstick and experimented before the mirror in her bedroom. Her confidence had revived dramatically. She, the ugly sister, the spotty brunette who had always believed herself inferior in looks to Poupette, was the object of male desire, her virginity joyfully disposed of. She was no longer a girl but a woman, she reminded herself, as she drew a cupid's bow on her lips and smiled at her reflection.

Sartre, by contrast, was fretting. He had not seen Castor since 1 September, and would not see her again until he returned to his grandparents' flat on rue Saint-Jacques in mid-October. In early November he would again have to leave Paris for the fort of Saint-Cyr, to begin his eighteen months' military service, already deferred four years. The 'wasteland' of his future stretched ahead, the subject of his 'terrified contemplation', and he was anxious about leaving his flirtatious girlfriend alone and underemployed in Paris. It was high time to marry. Two years had passed since Sartre had been best man to Nizan, who had married a young woman he had met at the first dance given by the École Normale, and Sartre had not forgotten the double defeat of 1928, when his fiancée's parents had broken off her engagement after he had failed his *agrégation*.

His worries deepened when heard that Maheu would be returning to Paris to retake his exams. The thorny problem of marriage was becoming more pressing.

Marriage was on Beauvoir's mind also. Remarkably, her journal shows that even after meeting Sartre she still harboured hopes regarding Jacques. The day after her return from Meyrignac, she rang the bell of his house in the boulevard de Montparnasse. Jacques was back from North Africa, and she wanted to see him. He seemed distant. 'I shall never marry him,' she wrote in her journal on 16 September. Nevertheless, she continued to go out to the Stryx with him, and to cling wistfully to hopes of a future together. Strangely enough, he always contrived to have Riquet and his friend Olga with him, so that they were never alone.

Both Sartre and Maheu were ready with advice. Beauvoir's thoughts 'swarm', to use a Sartrean term, over the pages of her journal, as she struggles to choose between the men in her life. Her anxious musings are matched by Sartre's dark warnings, as the date of Maheu's arrival draws near, about the dangers of extramarital sex. 'Sartre told me one day that I am too honest a Castor to have a love life outside marriage,' she writes on 18 September; 'but I am above all too honest a Castor to marry without love, as the Llama advises me.' Bravely she adds, 'I have no fear for the future – I have total confidence in Sartre.'

Three days later a letter arrives from Maheu, which throws her into confusion: '*Jean-Paul, comme il faut que je vous aime – comme il faut que j'ai confiance en vous.*' She *ought* to love Sartre, to trust Sartre, but, 'Oh! I don't know what I want any longer – I don't know.' On the 24th, '*Je t'aime, Jacques,*' sighs muddled, lovelorn Simone.

There is no doubt that one can love two men, she reflects – and 'so passionately', although which two seems to change daily. But as she hesitates between Jacques and Sartre, and the Llama she 'holds so dear', a bombshell falls. Simone has decided to entertain Jacques and his friends in the new room of which she is so proud. Poupette has helped her set out bottles of cognac and vermouth, and some little cakes. But of Jacques there is no sign: only their friend Olga arrives, alone, and the talk turns to his future:

'It will all depend on his wife,' said Olga; she heaved a sigh. 'Unfortunately I think she's the wrong one for him.' 'Who do you mean?' I asked. 'Odile Riaucourt. Didn't you know he's going to marry Lucien's sister?' 'No', I replied dumbfounded . . . Now I understood why I had never seen Jacques alone.

On his return from Africa, Jacques had gone to stay with his friend Lucien, whose sister had fallen in love with him; Jacques barely knew her, but she came with one important recommendation: a substantial dowry. He accepted.

That night Simone and Poupette tramped the streets, heartbroken at seeing Jacques revealed in his true colours as a 'calculating bourgeois'. Bitterly Simone asked herself whether it would have made a difference if she'd had a dowry. Would Jacques have married her? The fact of being dowryless seemed to affect her profoundly. Perhaps Jean-Paul had mentioned that his own mother, Anne-Marie, had brought a dowry of no less than 40,000 francs when she became Jean-Baptiste's bride. 'Marriage was impossible; I had no dowry,' Simone was still complaining to her biographer towards the end of her life.

But in the post-war world of 1929, old habits were breaking down. The lack of a dowry was no longer a valid excuse for not marrying. Simone's own aunt Marie-Thérèse, younger daughter of her ruined grandfather Brasseur, had, like Simone's mother Françoise, brought no dowry to her marriage, and her uncle Herbert had also married a woman without a dowry. This did not prevent Simone from boiling with fury at the hypocrisy of arranged marriages.

Her 'new life' began when Sartre knocked on her door. During his holiday with his mother and stepfather he had sent her daily letters 'of an extraordinary intelligence'. But Sartre had misjudged his moment if he expected her to accept him as husband material. The Beaver, still smarting at Jacques's 'betrayal', listened in silence as, walking side by side in the Luxembourg Gardens, her 'dear Jean-Paul' again raised the subject of matrimony. They should take advantage of the increased pay he would earn as a married soldier. For the third time he urged Simone to accept him.

She remained reluctant. Only two and a half months ago Sartre had roundly condemned marriage as a 'despicable bourgeois institution', his only concession being that, for a woman from Simone's background, it might be difficult to avoid. 'It seemed to me better to stake everything on love, and to hell with domesticity,' she declared boldly. She prized too highly her own freedom, so painfully wrested from her family, to want to give up a room of her own and her hard-earned pay packet. She, at least, would remain true to their ideals. How could Sartre desire such chains? Were they not like Kant's dove? Instead of holding the bird back, the resistance of the air supported its flight. Together they would fly. Or was Jean-Paul, as their Communist friend Politzer claimed, really a *petit bourgeois* at heart?

There was no way out of the hole that Sartre had dug himself. Previously he had explained to Simone that he 'was not inclined to be monogamous by nature', and that he believed a great man should keep himself free: 'I was hoist with my own petard. The Beaver accepted that freedom and kept it. It was 1929. I was foolish enough to be upset by it: instead of understanding the extraordinary luck I'd had, I fell into a sort of melancholy.'

The balance of power at that point lay with Beauvoir. To Sartre, suppliant, Beauvoir remained tantalizingly out of reach, the princess who refused the frog. Sylvie Le Bon confirms that Sartre proposed to Beauvoir, and she refused: 'She didn't want marriage . . . For her it was a trap, a social institution which deforms one's feelings and creates dependence. She saw this with her friends, and her mother.' As for Sartre: 'His real aim was to define himself, not by marriage, nor by prizes, but through his art.'

Unsure how to retrieve the situation, Sartre came up with an alternative. It was a key moment which Simone would enshrine in existentialist history, as Sartre defined the parameters of their relationship. The new pact of 'essential love' which allowed secondary affairs was intended to guarantee their 'reciprocal liberty', but it would become the template for an open relationship with unforeseen complications. The pact indicates Sartre's own fundamental ambivalence towards the idea of marriage, but in October 1929 it was chiefly designed to keep Simone 'under his wing'. He was deeply anxious about losing her, and may have sensed that she, rather than he, had not lost her taste for 'contingent' affairs, and the 'fleeting riches', as she described them, of encounters with other people.

One afternoon in the gardens of Les Tuileries, Sartre and Simone walked down as far as the Carrousel Gardens beside the Louvre. The autumn sunshine bathed the pink marble of the great Arc de Triomphe du Carrousel, emblem of Napoleon's victories. As the shadows lengthened, they sat down on a stone bench beneath the wall. In her memoirs she described the scene:

> There was a balustrade which served as a back-rest, a little way out from the wall; and in the cage-like space behind it a cat was miaowing. The poor thing was too big to get out; how had it ever got in?

A woman appeared with a paper bag full of scraps of meat, and began feeding the cat, stroking it tenderly all the time. At that moment Sartre turned to Simone and said: 'Let's sign a two-year lease.' She would stay in Paris for two years, and they would spend them together 'in the closest possible intimacy'. He drew Simone to him.

'Toi et moi, on ne fait qu'un.' We are one, you and I.

Simone took his face in her hands, and covered it with kisses. It smelt of pipe tobacco, and, endearingly, of the pâtisserie he had just eaten. 'We are one,' she repeated.

She squeezed his hand. It was the end of solitude.

Beauvoir puts the same words – 'We are one' – into the mouth of Pierre, the lover of the heroine, Françoise, in her first novel, *She Came to Stay*. 'Françoise' (her mother's name) is, she explained, a largely autobiographical creation, 'endowed with my own experiences', and the author puts Françoise into a similar position to her own when she and Sartre formed their bond. Beauvoir's memoirs are her most fictive works, but in her fiction she was free to tell the truth about how she felt:

> She had allowed Pierre to share her sovereign position, and now they both stood together at the centre of a world which it was her compelling mission to explore and reveal.

At the beginning of the relationship, there is perfect love. 'I am a faithful woman,' Françoise tells him between kisses. 'There's no need to talk of faithfulness or unfaithfulness between us,' says Pierre airily. 'We are one.' '*Aucun malentendu n'était possible avec Pierre.*' No misunderstanding was possible with Pierre.

No misunderstanding seemed possible either between Sartre and Simone. Now that she had permitted Sartre 'to share her sovereign position', there was to be no question during the two-year lease of their actually taking advantage of those 'freedoms', which in theory they had the right to enjoy, Beauvoir later claimed. 'We intended to give ourselves wholly and without reservation to this new relationship of ours.' Sartre offered a second agreement: 'We would never lie to one another.' Their life together would be one of total transparency. 'The thought that Sartre was now an open book to me, as easily read as my own mind, had a most relaxing effect on me,' wrote Simone. If she felt a flicker of disquiet, she quickly stifled it.

The pact, including as it did both the necessary and the contingent, might have struck the couple as over-ambitious, but Simone, for her part, felt full of confidence. 'I have never met anyone in the whole of my life who was so well equipped for happiness as I was, or who laboured so stubbornly to achieve it,' she wrote in 1960. 'I was able to cherish the hope of turning my life into a model experience.' The date, 14 October 1929, became the 'wedding anniversary' of the future model couple of the counter-culture. 'It's a morganatic marriage,' the pair said, a strange term to choose for their union since it was not between a man of royal rank and a woman of lower rank, nor was it even a marriage.

On occasions they pretended to be 'Monsieur and Madame M. Organatique', a civil servant and his wife, who dined at the Brasserie Demeroy, where Sartre indulged his love for Alsatian beer and sauerkraut; at other times they drank American cocktails, Bronxes, Sidecars or Martinis, at La Coupole, metamorphosing into an American millionaire and his wife, 'Mr and Mrs Morgan Hattick'. Sartre recited ballads, epigrams, fables, and sang lyrics of his own composition to the tunes of Offenbach. The next day, nursing a hangover, he would sink into sudden melancholy and Simone decided he looked like an old sea elephant. 'Mr and Mrs Morgan Hattick' enjoyed the pleasures of the idle rich for a few hours, explained Simone, because they believed that by parodying their lifestyle they were simply confirming their own contempt for high society. Only Politzer furiously attacked his old friend for his failure to rise above the beliefs – and behaviour – of his class.

As the first frosts arrived, Sartre and Simone huddled one evening round the stinking kerosene stove in her room, munching bread and *foie gras*. Sartre's money had nearly run out, but Simone had bought a bottle of cognac. She poured out two glasses. Sartre was still resentful; he was not engaged to Simone, and he was not looking forward to the 'stupidity' of military life. He begged her to change her mind. Did he smell dishonesty in the evil-smelling room? But Simone was obdurate.

On 3 November Sartre boarded the train for Saint-Cyr, where he was to train as a meteorologist under his old friend Raymond Aron, a sergeant-instructor. His pride was wounded. Like the mewing cat, he had to make do with scraps. Confined to barracks for the first fortnight, he brooded darkly. As Simone would learn to her cost, he would never forget her rejection.

*

'By the time I met [Sartre] again, in October, I had . . . jettisoned all past attachments, and now threw myself unreservedly into the development of this new relationship,' wrote Beauvoir in *The Prime of Life*. Reality was very different. On 24 October, at 11 a.m., the Llama arrived on Simone's doorstep. 'It's the Llama's stay, Stépha's arrival, and the beginning of Sartre's service,' recorded Simone in her journal. Four days later she and Maheu spent the afternoon together:

> How gay he is, how full of spirit, of charm, of tenderness – how happy I am to have him here, in my bedroom . . . this enchanted room . . . How I love him!

He called her 'My little Beaver', his arms clasped tightly around her body as they lay together on the divan. Their tenderness for each other was painful, because she would have to wait so long to see him again, and then it would be with his wife. 'I love him so much,' confided Simone to her journal. Maheu visited her again on the 28th, and the next day she and Zaza met him at Mme Morel's.

Three weeks earlier Beauvoir had told herself that she must not lie about her feelings, even if it made Sartre unhappy. 'I *cannot* lie to him,' she wrote in her journal of 2 October. But if Sartre was to be privileged with transparency, Maheu was to be the victim of duplicity. Still deeply attached to the man who had, as she put it, 'taught her the sweetness of being a woman', Beauvoir played down the significance of her relationship with the absent Sartre and continued to lead her Llama on.

*

Zaza's hoped-for betrothal to Maurice Merleau-Ponty seemed no nearer. Simone could not understand why he did not propose, and nor, at first, could Zaza. Simone identified with her friend's unhappiness. Only much later would she discover that Zaza's parents had taken the first step towards her marriage by hiring a private detective to investigate Maurice's background, a common practice among bourgeois families. The Lacoins were scandalized to discover that he was in fact the product of an illicit liaison of his mother's. M. Lacoin informed Zaza and Merleau-Ponty of this fact, and the unhappy young man withdrew from the match. The secret was kept from Simone, although it explains the mysterious phrase in Zaza's last letter to her referring to the 'sins of the parents'.

Simone only knew that Zaza was ill and strained. Around 11 November Zaza called unannounced upon Maurice's mother. White-faced, with a feverish flush to her cheeks, she demanded unsteadily: 'Do you hate me, Madame?' Mme Merleau-Ponty tried to calm her down, but shortly afterwards Zaza collapsed and was rushed, suffering from either meningitis or encephalitis, to a clinic at Saint-Cloud.

Zaza's mother sat by her bedside. Both families had now removed their objections to the marriage, but it was too late, wrote Simone:

'N'ayez-pas de chagrin, maman cherie,' dit-elle. 'Dans toutes les familles il y a du déchet: c'est moi le déchet.' [Don't cry for me, Mama darling; in every family there is an outcast; I am the outcast in ours.]

This is one of the most significant events in Simone's memoirs, marking the moment of her final, conscious rejection of family and class. Four days later, on 25 November, Zaza was dead, the scapegoat murdered, in Simone's eyes, by the bourgeoisie and their hideous conventions. 'It was through Zaza that I discovered how odious the bourgeoisie really was,' she wrote forty-three years later, the pain still as fresh as in 1929:

I should have turned against the bourgeoisie in any case; but I should not have felt the falseness of their attitude towards things of the spirit, their stifling conformity, their arrogance and their oppressive tyranny – I should not have felt it in my heart nor paid for it with my tears. For me, Zaza's murder by her environment, her milieu, was an overwhelming, unforgettable experience.

As Simone stared at Zaza in her coffin, the corpse seemed to reproach her. Together they had struggled against the 'revolting fate' which lay ahead of them; now Simone believed that Zaza had paid for her friend's liberty with her life.

'I wept and felt my heart would break.' Simone de Beauvoir had loved Zaza, and would spend the rest of her life looking for a substitute for her. Had it not been for the death of Zaza, it is possible that Beauvoir might have agreed to marry Sartre. She had had no objection to marriage for Zaza. Now, as she mourned her, she cut it out of the equation for herself. The scapegoat's sacrifice was not to be in vain: Beauvoir's task was to dedicate herself to living freely, in Zaza's memory.

After Zaza's death Simone was too grief-stricken to continue her journal. '*Jacques est marié et Zaza est morte* [Jacques is married and Zaza is dead],' her diary ends. 'Zaza, my friend, my darling . . . I need you so much.'

10

On Her Paris Honeymoon

To love is to relinquish everything for the benefit of a
master . . . Woman must become a passive thing, a
promise of submission.

Simone de Beauvoir, *The Second Sex*

'I BELONG TO you, body and soul,' wrote Simone to her 'dear Jean-Paul'
on Sunday night, 3 November 1929. 'I can love other beings, suffer for
them, be sorry when the Llama leaves, but I belong to you, body and
soul, this soul that *you have filled*, with a violence in the face of which I
am helpless.' Her little soldier, 'full of desire', had made love to his
passionate girlfriend before he left for Saint-Cyr in his blue uniform,
beret and puttees: 'I am a woman of flesh with a heart of flesh,' recorded
Simone after he left.

She had chosen *la vie contingente*, and it made her profoundly happy,
as she reminded herself frequently in her journal. She had made an
existential choice 'to embrace all experience and to bear witness
concerning it'. Contingent life meant grabbing life by the throat, thrill-
seeking, fantasy and play.

The playboy or 'baladin' from Synge's *Playboy of the Western World*
was at the heart of Sartre's private mythology, which he now shared
with Beauvoir. She loved his 'Playboy soul', she responded. Life was a
game, already lost, said Sartre: 'I have never wished to be serious – I felt
too free.' The man who at twenty wrote a long poem entitled *Peter Pan*,

about the boy who didn't want to grow up, had adopted Schiller's phrase: 'Man is fully a man only when he plays.'

Beauvoir's diary reveals a romantic, feminine woman with a lust for life, adventure and heightened sensation, who responded eagerly to this message; every line in the autumn of 1929 expresses her incredulous joy at the connection she feels to her new lover. But beneath his playful exterior, Sartre was full of purpose. His second aim, now hers too, was as immodest as the first: to 'recreate Man' through the agency of their work. After reading Freud's *Interpretation of Dreams*, they both rejected the notion of the unconscious, which they believed eradicates free will, and put their trust in the Cartesian *cogito*. Life would bend itself to their will and, with the arrogance of youth, they already believed that, by virtue of contingency, *it* had chosen *them*.

It was a golden period. Simone revelled in her autonomy and control over her own life. Sartre and she continued to spend his legacy on pleasure and to ignore events in the wider world. Politics seemed irrelevant. The French Left was convinced that peace was assured. The Nazis in Germany appeared only a fringe movement. As for the Wall Street crash of 1929 – which had abruptly emptied Le Jockey of Americans – this merely served to confirm the couple's assumption that capitalism had had its day. Soon colonialism would 'fold up,' wrote Simone, as Gandhi's campaign in India was proving. It was only a question of waiting for socialism to usher in an age of equality.

Sometimes she visited Saint-Cyr by train, but Sartre's duties, measuring wind speed and direction, were undemanding, and he was often able to visit her in Paris. Snatched hours with him were all the sweeter for their brevity. On Saturday 9 November, Simone waited impatiently for her 'beloved Jean-Paul': 'Then *he* arrives – oh!' At the Falstaff they kiss and pet, until it is time for her little soldier to leave for the station and she cries miserably: '*Oh! Quel amour!*' 'Never in the world was there a man like you,' she writes on 13 December. On Christmas day he is '*Mon unique Baladin*', by January her 'beloved little man' whom she 'adores without reserve', her 'little husband': 'I knew that no harm could ever come to me from him – unless he were to die before I died.'

'She's on her Paris honeymoon,' said Georges de Beauvoir sourly, as Simone began to cut her ties with her family. 'I wanted to relax a bit, to sink back into happiness, into Sartre's love,' she recalled in the 1980s. So complete was her trust in him that 'he supplied me with the sort of absolute, unfailing security that I had once from my parents, or God'.

But a problem was becoming apparent. Sartre is not a 'sensual man', like Maheu, Simone confides to her diary, as she tries to convince herself that 'With Sartre, who is not sensual, the harmony of our bodies has a meaning which makes our love more beautiful.' Her demanding sexuality required an equally passionate lover, and it is clear from her entries that she was missing the overwhelming sense of physical compatibility she had experienced with Maheu, and still making comparisons between the two men. 'Liquidating her past', as she puts it, is difficult.

The death of Zaza was a watershed. 'You've cried enough now,' Simone tells herself firmly in mid-December, as she mourns her. Zaza's 'murder' by the hated bourgeoisie was highly significant in persuading Simone to commit herself to Sartre, whose anarchic, rebellious ideas attracted her even more powerfully now that she had vowed to 'live freely' in memory of her dead friend. It was an important factor in the final break with Maheu which followed, for the lusty Llama was still on the scene. In her journal Simone wrote coyly that, at twenty-two, she was a young woman who needed male branches for support. Sartre, yes, was an especially big branch, but she was not quite ready to let go of Maheu, whose wife, she recorded complacently, was 'very jealous'.

By the new year, however, the Llama, teaching out of town in Coutances, realized that Simone was deceiving him. On Monday, 5 January 1930, he sent her a hurt note, apologizing for disturbing her in the midst of her 'tender and picturesque memories' of Sartre, but demanding to see her on Wednesday, or take her to lunch on Thursday:

I take the liberty of insisting – insofar as I have any right to do so – that I see you . . . It is possible that I shall never see you again. For you'd better understand that I've had my fill of the pretty situation that now exists, as a result of that September of yours and the two months of lying which followed it, and that I deserve something better than the crumbs – relations continued out of our charity 'because I am unhappy' – that you both offer with such elegance.

He was too unhappy to be able to take a final decision: 'I shall postpone this, *I promise you* (and my promises I keep), until Wednesday.'

Simone was annoyed by the reproaches of an unfaithful husband: 'I shall assure him, of course, that neither you nor I is prolonging our relations with him out of pity,' she wrote to Sartre. 'I see it as mere jealousy of the most disagreeable kind.'

But it was not easy to make the final break with her beloved boyfriend. On Thursday, 8 January 1930, Simone waited in all day for Maheu, who failed to turn up. She was deluding herself in thinking that so intense a relationship could be lightly severed. That night she wrote in her journal that she felt 'stupidly' upset as she caught the train to Saint-Cyr: 'What is this sadness in my body, my flesh?' she demanded miserably. Frustrated by the fact that there was no private place where she could enjoy sexual relations with Sartre, with whom she could only dine at the local brasserie, Simone was tormented by her 'strong, immense – and ever present' physical urges.

In January Sartre moved to the meteorological station at Saint-Symphorien, near Tours, to continue his training, and was no longer able to come up to Paris in the evenings. The couple were separated for days and weeks at a time, and on their Sundays in Tours were too shy to go brazenly to a hotel bedroom in broad daylight. Nor did Simone like to plan love-making, which she held should be spontaneous and as irresistible as the surge of the sea. But her body had its own whims: 'Their violence overrode all my defences . . . I was forced to admit a truth which I had been doing my best to conceal ever since adolescence: my physical appetites were greater than I wanted them to be.'

In the night train from Tours to Paris the touch of an anonymous hand along her leg aroused feelings of shattering intensity. Beauvoir was ashamed to confess this to Sartre, despite their code of truth-telling. Her body became a tyrannical master. She was mortified to discover that the mind, far from existing in isolation from the body, is compromised by it: 'Humanity does *not* subsist in the calm light of the Good; men suffer the dumb, futile, cruel agonies of defenceless beasts.'

Her strict upbringing had taught her to associate sex with sin, to speak of physical desire as a 'hidden disease rotting the marrow in my very bones'. Under her healthy exterior, she wore a poisoned shirt. Even in the morning Métro, still numb with sleep, she stared at her fellow travellers wondering if they, too, were racked with desire. At night her 'obsession', as she describes it, roused itself again. 'Thousands of ants would crawl across my lips.' 'I am feeble, I am cowardly,' she wrote guiltily in the new journal she had begun.

Simone's body had become a stumbling block between her and Sartre. As the months passed, their sexual differences grew. She wanted to experience the intense sexual excitement that she wrote of much later in *The Second Sex*, in which she makes a disparaging comparison between male desire, 'keen but localized', which, according to her, 'leaves a man quite in possession of himself', and the overwhelming feelings of 'a woman of ardent temperament', who, 'on the contrary, really loses her mind'. 'Woman's sex feeling extends towards infinity,' wrote Beauvoir; 'she longs to melt with him into one.'

She wanted to be brought to the heights of ecstasy, preferably every time, to feel a sense of annihilation and surrender. Beauvoir believed that unless a woman remained 'pure passivity, open, a utensil . . . she breaks the spell that brings on her enjoyment . . . She fails to reach the climax of pleasure.'

Sometimes that summer Sartre was as masterful as she desired. On 9 June she was still 'passionately happy' remembering their Sundays in Tours or on the banks of the Loire, 'our conversations, a tenderness dear to my heart, our embraces so dear to my body', but her 'carnal suffering [de souffrances toutes charnelles]' leaves her impatient to see him again. Nor has she, after all, cut her ties with Maheu, writing excitedly on 10 June: 'LLAMA back!'

*

Sartre was bewildered by the sexual demands made of him, which he found impossible to meet. 'I should perhaps have been saved if nature had endowed me with sensuality, but I am cold,' he wrote. Even at the age of twenty-five, sexual intercourse brought little satisfaction: 'The whole thing seemed to me a scandal of unreasonable proportion.' It was an act he engaged in because it was expected of a man, rather than for pleasure, although performing presented no difficulty in itself:

> So as I was reasonably well equipped, my erection was quick and easy, and I often made love, but without very great pleasure. *Juste un petit plaisir à la fin, mais assez médiocre.* Just a little pleasure at the end, but pretty feeble. I should have been quite happy in bed with a naked woman, caressing and kissing her, but without going as far as the sexual act.

The obligation to make love came from the woman, from outside, not from within Sartre. It was with an air of puzzlement that he wrote: 'The act seemed to me required and that was why, in my relations with women, things had to end that way.' Uncomfortable with his own body, he found it difficult to understand how anyone else could gain pleasure from it. Obliged to repeat an act which he did not greatly enjoy, and which still left him with strange feelings of emptiness, it seems likely that it was the actual conquest of the woman which began to interest him. Sartre would, in future, want above all else to sleep with virgins, to be the first to take the prize.

Quite soon, Beauvoir sensed Sartre's chilly detachment from the act of love. As she later explained to her American lover Nelson Algren, '[Sartre] is a warm, lively man everywhere, but not in bed.' Sartre's sexual problems may be responsible for many of the negative views of heterosexuality she later expressed. Her much criticized statement in *The Second Sex* that 'the first penetration is always a rape' probably had its roots in her early experience of Sartre's 'violence'. The sad lines recalling love-making that disappoints speak of a personal memory in which a woman:

> feels an unexpected pain in her sexual parts; her dreams vanish, her excitement fades, and love assumes the aspect of a surgical operation.

The feeling of being a patient on an operating table would be remarked on by another future lover of Sartre, Bianca Bienenfeld. He himself admitted that his self-control amounted to 'almost a slight touch of sadism. Since in the end the other person was yielded up and I was not.'

*

But if his body was cold, his mind was on fire. Barely had Sartre stepped out of the train at the Gare d'Austerlitz before he was telling Beauvoir: 'I've got a new theory.' 'Except when he's asleep, Sartre *thinks* all the time!' observed Maheu. Sartre agreed in 1951 that he often had a hundred projects in his head; he 'lived to write', as Beauvoir repeatedly emphasized.

In 1930 Sartre was deeply influenced by the Dutch philosopher Spinoza, from whose *Ethics* he took two main ideas: that of the transformation of existence, an 'existential conversion', and that of salvation. Sartre was preoccupied with the idea of morality. 'To be moral,' he wrote, 'was to me tantamount to achieving one's salvation . . . not in the Christian sense of the word, but in the Stoic sense: to impress a total modification upon one's nature.' Writing that he wanted to be 'really good', Sartre believed that in this way he would deserve the 'fine life' of a great writer: 'It was *in order to achieve the finest life* that I'd be moral.'

Yet it was hard to reconcile ideas of moral transformation with

Sartre's other anarchic instinct for freedom, and his observation of the part that chance played in human lives. He rejected the idea of duty, which he associated with his stepfather. 'I have always wanted my freedom to be above morality,' he wrote in 1939. In the real world, there was something 'harsh, immoral and naked, that didn't give a fig for parents or teachers'.

Simone's confidence shrank as she listened to Sartre bubble with ideas. His imagination soared. Already, he was writing 'The Legend of the Truth' while training at Saint-Symphorien, exploring the idea of the solitary intellectual, 'l'homme seul', who has access to Spinozist salvation. By contrast, when Beauvoir went to see a female magazine editor with a view to becoming a journalist, she was told that in order to make a start in journalism you have to have ideas to contribute. 'Do you have any ideas?' asked the editor. No, I didn't. They advised her to stick to teaching.

*

'You used to be full of little ideas, Castor,' said Sartre. He could hardly believe his eyes. Simone was turning into a housewife, like Rirette Nizan, with whom she often went to the cinema. After losing her job at the lycée, where she had found it difficult to keep order, her life had become aimless. 'I must try to write,' the diarist told herself, but as she sat in her room staring at a sheet of blank paper, she realized that she had no idea what to write *about*. '*Ma petite épouse morganatique*,' wrote Sartre encouragingly, in an undated letter of 1930, to his little, morganatic wife. 'I've read the description of your first chapter. If its style is as simple as the style in your letter – no more, no less – it will be excellent.'

'The little man told me that I must work,' recorded Beauvoir on 20 October. 'He's right.' But it was far more tempting to go for a spin in the car with Sartre's friend Pierre Guille, her 'guardian angel'. He was a Protestant, with peasant connections, who loved the countryside and *la vie rustique*. When she went into one of her 'trances', as Sartre called them, at the sight of a river or forest, Guille understood. Sartre, on the other hand, explained that landscape did not make him *feel* anything.

Meanwhile, Simone was feeling jealous. Her 'little man' was again seeing Simone Jollivet, or 'Toulouse', as he called her. The beautiful, licentious actress was holding Roman orgies in her cellar and boasting that she was in communication with the Devil, Nietzsche and Emily Brontë. Even Maheu attended dressed as a Roman emperor. In Paris her name was on posters in the Métro, now that she had become a celebrity at the Atelier Theatre and drama school founded by Dullin. When she invited her old lover to rehearsals, Sartre was spellbound as he watched the director develop his avant-garde techniques; backstage, he discovered a new world which fascinated him. It suited him so well that he 'went to bed with [Jollivet] once in a while'.

The actress invited Simone to call on her at her apartment in the rue Gabrielle, near the Atelier. Toulouse received her rival in a scarlet dress glittering with jewels, her blonde hair falling over her shoulders, and discoursed eloquently on Japanese Noh drama. Simone was disconcerted: Toulouse was more educated than she had expected. The Beaver had not lost her own taste for low life, visiting dance halls with a young butcher's assistant, and even risking bumping into her father emerging from a bedroom at the Sphinx bordello at 31 boulevard Edgar-Quinet, where 1,000 bottles of champagne were consumed each night. But she had been horrified to learn that Toulouse picked up young men on the street and brought them back to the apartment for her pleasure.

Increasingly, Simone's journal betrays her anxiety at her loss of identity. Sartre treats her as a '*petite fille*', a little girl. Her indolence and passivity disappoints him. 'When you think in terms of *problems*, you aren't thinking at all,' he chides her. Writing a 'factum', a philosophical analysis, he hopes to spur her interest. His factum will be 'in arid, obscure prose, of no interest whatever to my Beaver, but it might just amuse Mademoiselle Simone Bertrand de Beauvoir, the brilliant academic'. But Simone is deaf to Sartre's efforts. In February 1931 she accepts an invitation from Guille, whose training has finished before Sartre's, to go on a tour of France with him.

Two days before the pair leaves, Maheu shows up. He has a fortnight in Paris, without his wife, and wants to spend it with Simone. He issues an ultimatum: if she goes off with Guille, he will never see her again.

'I can't let Pierre down,' protests the Beaver.

'*Pourquoi pas?* Why not?'

'"No I can't," I said. Upon which he broke off with me.'

On their way to the South of France, Pierre and Simone stop at Lyon to see Simone's cousin, Sirmione, who has married a medical student. Seeing her unmarried cousin travelling alone with a strange man, Sirmione and her husband present Simone with a 'Grenoble nut' over dessert. Inside the nutshell she finds a condom.

Simone is shocked. But condoms are a necessity. As she later confessed, on that holiday she slept with Guille. If Sartre had expected her to remain faithful to him after breaking with Maheu, he was to be disappointed. 'She profited very early from the pact,' confirms Sylvie Le Bon.

*

'It's not in some retreat that we will discover ourselves,' wrote Sartre. 'It's on the road, in the town, in the midst of the crowd, a thing amongst things, a man amongst men.' It was August, and he and Simone wanted to go travelling. Money was short. He had nearly run through the 80,000 francs of his legacy in a year, an extraordinary achievement, given that the salary of a *professeur agrégé* was 2,500 francs a month, and Sartre's inheritance therefore represented more than he could expect to earn in two and a half years as a teacher.

The artist Fernando Gerassi, Stépha's husband, who was living in Madrid, invited the couple to stay with him. Determined not to behave like tourists, they intended to follow in the steps of Valéry and Gide and discover the secrets of foreign cities. 'To reveal secrets, all means are good,' wrote Sartre. Sensation, taste and smell were as important as looking at cathedrals. Because Gide had said in *Pretexts* that you hold all Spain in your mouth when you drink a cup of Spanish hot chocolate, Simone forced down innumerable treacly cups of the stuff.

She held on tightly to her *Guide Bleu*; she 'wanted to see everything'. Sartre, on the other hand, was content to sit in a square, smoking his pipe, soaking up the atmosphere. On their mission to escape *la peau de touriste*, they allowed Fernando to take them to a bull-fight, ending up by spending every Sunday at the *corrida*, and learning Spanish expressions which they wove into their secret language. But Fernando, inspiration for Gomez in *Les Chemins de la liberté* [*The Roads to Freedom*], was shocked to see how little interest they took in politics, beyond registering that Spain had become a republic in April. For all their ambitions to 'recreate man', 'public affairs bored us', said Beauvoir. Sartre held the view that a writer should live his life in stages. Youth should be devoted to the 'production of works', to literature. Only at fifty did one 'dabble in politics', like Zola at the time of the Dreyfus affair, or Gide, in later life visiting the USSR.

Self-absorbed and self-sufficient, Sartre and Beauvoir would make their annual summer holiday central to their lives together over the next fifty years. They would continue to live by the academic calendar, departing in July, and starting their 'new year' in October. It was a time of renewal, in which shared new experiences bound them closer together. One of the more appealing aspects of existentialism, as they developed it, was that it was *un invitation à voyager*, a journey of self-discovery. 'On the road, in the town, in the midst of the crowd', they explored the world and their place in it.

*

Sartre was distraught. He had failed to get the post of lecturer in Japan, on which he had set his heart. Instead the authorities were offering him a post in Le Havre, where the last teacher of *la philo* had suffered a nervous breakdown. To Simone's relief, Sartre accepted. She no longer had to face the prospect of a major separation, but, on the other hand, she felt a different kind of panic when she heard that she had been assigned to a *lycée* in far away Marseilles, 500 miles from Paris.

Alarmed by her tears, Sartre offered marriage for the last time. 'If we got married, we would have the advantages of a double post, and in the long run such a formality would not seriously affect our way of life.' Yes, they were anarchists, whose purpose it was to live *against* society; but it was stupid to martyr themselves for a principle.

Simone disagreed.

> I didn't feel like it very much, and I knew that he felt like it even less, since to be a professor . . . was bad enough, but to be married . . . And since there was no question of having children – not that I didn't toy with the idea at eighteen or nineteen, when I contemplated a bourgeois marriage. I didn't reject the idea a priori, but with the life I expected to lead, having to earn my living and writing, there would be no place for children.

'A child would not have strengthened the bonds that united Sartre and me,' she added. 'He was sufficient both for himself and for me. I too was self-sufficient.' The truth was that Beauvoir had no maternal inclination: 'It was simply not my natural lot in life, and by remaining childless I was fulfilling my proper function.' She and Sartre, however, did renew their pact until the distant age of thirty.

To remain single was a courageous decision for a woman in 1931, when *vieilles filles*, old maids, were pitied and despised. 'She made her free choice, to live against convention, against her parents,' recalled Sylvie Le Bon: 'To live authentically, to prove something.' The Beaver was to be 'her own project'.

11

Marooned in Mudtown

I *was* Roquentin; I used him to show, without complacency, the texture of my life.

Jean-Paul Sartre, *Words*

THE SEAGULLS WERE screeching over the harbour. Sartre and Simone sat side by side in their usual seaside café in Le Havre, Les Mouettes, staring morosely out to sea. It was November 1934, Sartre's third year as a teacher in the port. In this famous scene recalled by Simone in her memoirs, the couple were complaining about the monotony of their lives. The waves were grey, and so was the sky. The wind rattled the doors of the café.

'Nothing new will ever happen to us,' said Sartre.

Simone nodded.

'We are living a constructed life. Our friendships are settled – Guille, that lady, Poupette, Gégé. Our own relationship, as we have constructed it, is a permanent, *directed* love.'

'Yes,' agreed Simone.

'We have been moderate for too long. We need immoderation.'

Simone set down her cup. She was becoming irritated at Sartre's depression. 'I mustn't miss my train.'

As they left the building and walked along the seafront, Sartre bent down and picked up a pebble. He turned it over in his fingers, feeling its roundness, its smoothness. He was about to hurl it into the sea when an overwhelming sense of disgust swept over him. He dropped the stone.

'Whatever are you doing?' demanded Simone. '*Dépêchez-vous*, hurry up.'

Sartre's disgust at the touch of the pebble was the first intimation of the nausea which would become the central theme and title of his most successful novel, *La Nausée*. He would make it a decisive moment for his character, Antoine Roquentin, who finds it unbearable to touch such objects. 'How unpleasant it was!' exclaims Roquentin, of the nausea he feels. 'Yes, that's it . . . a sort of nausea of the hands.'

Sartre's sojourn in Le Havre, crucible for *Nausea*, was equally decisive for his writing career and future fame. He and Simone, however, had done everything possible to avoid becoming provincial schoolteachers. Knowing that she couldn't follow Sartre to Japan, Simone had planned to work in Budapest or Morocco, but her plans, like his, had come to nothing. Instead of sailing to the Land of the Rising Sun, he had been forced to disembark in Le Havre, a chilly Normandy port which reminded him of his schooldays in La Rochelle. For a man who, like his hero Captain Pardaillon, longed for adventures, it was a cruel blow.

Simone hoped that getting his first teaching post might help her Peter Pan grow up; instead it pitchforked him into misery. Sartre had never been alone before. Now, at the beginning of October 1931, he found himself in town, where no one knew him and he knew no one. When Beauvoir caught the train to Marseilles that month, he rented a room in the seedy Hôtel Printania, frequented by commercial travellers, near the station, and began work at the Lycée Le Havre.

The days dragged. His *ennui* was intolerable. On Tuesday, 9 October, he wrote to Beauvoir, he went back to bed after lunch, and fell asleep. When he awoke he wandered along avenue Foch to a public park, found a chair and sat down to look at a tree. For twenty minutes he contemplated it. A fine tree, Sartre told the Beaver. For the first time, 'I understood . . . what a tree is.' Unfortunately, though, he was not sure what kind of tree. 'You'll tell me,' he wrote, making a little sketch of a twig with six or seven leaves so that Simone could identify it: 'I await your reply.'

Morosely he compared his situation to that of Paul Nizan. Like Jean-Paul, it had never been Nizan's first choice to become a teacher. He, too, wanted to mark the thought of his time by his work, and had just published *Aden-Arabie* after a long trip to Aden, Egypt and Ethiopia. He was fast making a name for himself as a Communist activist, and contributing to the literary review *Bifur*, where he was able to help his old friend by persuading the editor to publish the preface to Sartre's *Legend of the Truth*. Sartre felt resentful that the manuscript had been 'eviscerated' by Nizan, who, like Aron, judged it 'obscure' when it should have been lucid. And in October the book itself was turned down by Éditions d'Europe. Disconsolately, Sartre stuffed it into a drawer. The style was stiff and artificial, and he was forced to admit to himself that it was not much good.

Consoling himself by remembering that the playwright Racine had been living a petty-bourgeois life when he wrote *Phèdre*, Sartre again threw himself frenziedly into writing. He began a pamphlet 'On Contingency', but Simone was worried that this new 'factum', or philosophical analysis, was just as dry as the last one. In an important intervention, she insisted that Sartre turn it into fiction, adding a touch of the suspense they both enjoyed in detective stories. He agreed. Simone found that she was very good at putting herself in the reader's place, and she became a meticulous and severe critic, taking Sartre to task for using too many adjectives and similes. 'He invariably took my advice,' she remembered. She had become his *petit juge*, his little judge.

The leaf he had drawn, said Simone, was from a *marronnier*, a chestnut tree like the ones in the Luxembourg Gardens. Sartre returned to the tree, exhausting an 'arsenal of comparisons' in the style of Virginia Woolf. The evolution of the novel at the hands of James Joyce and Woolf had impressed him, especially their 'particular new technique: the interior monologue', which he commended to his students in a lecture given at the municipal library. *To the Lighthouse* had been published four years earlier. *The Waves* was received with acclaim in the same month, October 1931, in which Sartre noticed the tree whose 'pointless proliferation' would come to symbolize contingency for him. But six years' hard labour lay ahead before he was able to master experimental techniques.

For the time being, his novel was entitled 'Melancholia', after the 1514 engraving by Dürer, to which Sartre was particularly attached, showing a young woman slumped in depression. Sartre's hero was a certain Antoine Roquentin, who lived alone in 'Bouville', Mudtown, researching the life of an eighteenth-century nobleman, the Marquis of Rollebon. 'I live alone, absolutely alone. I never speak to anyone, never; I get nothing, I give nothing,' writes Roquentin in his journal, displaying the same isolation as his creator.

'Why is it that Antoine Roquentin and Mathieu [the hero of *Roads to Freedom*], who *are me*, are indeed so gloomy? – whereas, Heavens! Life for me isn't all that bad?' Sartre asked himself in March 1940, during the Phoney War. 'I think it's because they're homunculi.' Like the little men he writes about, Sartre feels 'cosmic sadness'. 'In all our thoughts and all our feelings, there's an element of terrible sadness,' he writes, confessing that his characters, stripped of his own obsessive passion for writing, his pride and faith in his destiny, 'are myself beheaded'. His anti-heroes feel a deeper gloom than humans in general: the 'sadness filled with reproach and bitterness of Homunculus in his jar. They know themselves to be unviable, sustained by artificial feeding . . .'

Deep down Sartre sometimes also felt trapped in his jar, for the sensation of being unviable and artificial was one he had experienced since childhood, when he had thought of himself as having aerial roots in the eyrie of his grandfather's library. Nevertheless, he soon began making friends with his pupils, for he was an inspirational teacher. 'We would watch this little man enter the room, hands in his pockets and no hat on, very rare for our school,' remembered one student. 'He also smoked a pipe – also quite unusual. He immediately started talking, off the top of his head, without notes, sitting on his desk – we had never seen anything like it.' In his open-necked black shirt and sports jacket, Sartre, who was only eight or nine years older than his students, presented himself as their friend and equal. He allowed them to smoke in class, to take off their jackets and ties, and instead of teaching them from the front of the classroom, insisted that the students made oral presentations – at the time a startling innovation. The young 'prof' boxed and drank with his pupils. Jacques-Laurent Bost, the engagingly handsome younger son of the *lycée*'s Protestant chaplain, remembered: 'Everyone called him *Le père Sartre* precisely because they trusted him, they liked him, they admired him like a father. He was small, ugly and friendly. Some of us boxed with him, and he would fight hard but explode with genuine, good-natured laughter if we knocked him down . . .'

But Troupe Matthews, an American pupil living in Le Havre, objected to Sartre's favouritism: 'Sartre was very elitist . . . He was not open to all his students, just the chosen few . . . they tended to be Protestant as well . . . Sartre believed in the Protestant ethic: those who work hard deserve to be recompensed . . . I was scared of him, and so were most of my classmates . . . In 1931, Sartre terrified me.' Selected pupils who, like 'Little Bost', so-called because he was younger brother to Pierre Bost, the novelist, admired their teacher and shared his

Protestantism, became part of his inner coterie, given special coaching and taken to the cinema.

The next summer, on 12 July, it falls to Sartre, as the youngest teacher, to give a lecture to the parents at the annual summer prize-giving. His reputation has preceded him: the brilliant Normalien from Paris, who came first in the examinations. Expectantly the good bourgeois of Le Havre file into the hall. Sartre walks on to the platform in his black academic robe and a yellow cloak trimmed with three rows of white ermine; he is careful not to trip, for the robe is too long for him. He is only twenty-six, and feels alienated from the assembly of principals and parents. Le Havre is a town of rigid class division, in which the upper-middle class live in houses on the cliffs, the Coteau Vert, the *nouveaux riches* in the town, on the boulevard Maritime, and the working class down by the docks; Sartre has deliberately chosen to settle among the brothels and drunken sailors, and takes malicious delight in teaching his teenage friends a bawdy soldiers' song:

> *Traîne tes coquilles par terre,*
> *Prend ta pine à la main mon copain.*
> *Nous partons en guerre*
> *A la chasse aux putains.*

('Drag your balls on the ground, take your cock in your hand, mate. We're marching off to war, looking for a whore.')

The crime of the bourgeoisie is that they are unreflective, therefore inauthentic. His rage at the unkind fate which has washed him up in Le Havre is expended on the rows of faces before him, the 'fat, pale crowd' whose haughty expressions remind him of the provincial élite in La Rochelle. *Salauds! Bastards!* It is his punishment, he tells his audience, to speak to them: but even a scapegoat has the right to choose his subject. Tonight, he is going to take advantage of his rights: he is going to talk about the movies:

> The motion picture is an art which . . . reflects civilization in our time. Who else will teach you about the beauty of the world . . . about speed, machines, industry?

In fact, for Sartre, films have particular significance. Sitting in the back row of a picture-house, watching the 'flicks', he understood for the first time the meaning of contingency. When the lights went up he realized that universal order was replaced with chaos. The randomness of the streets replaced the narrative of the movie. Ever since, he has become a film buff. This year alone, he and the Beaver have seen Mickey Mouse, Popeye the Sailor Man, Betty Boop, Rouben Mamoulian's *Dr Jekyll*, René Clair's *A Nous la liberté*, and Pabst's *Threepenny Opera*. 'Go to the movies often,' he exhorts his audience. 'But do it preferably during bad weather; first, enjoy your vacation.'

The second prize day in Le Havre the following July caused even more of a sensation. The rebellious teacher, supported on the platform by two colleagues, was too drunk to speak, and made a hasty exit through the emergency exit, where he could be heard vomiting. A rumour ran round the hall that his condition was due to having spent the previous night in a local brothel with his students.

Sartre might have been sacked, but for the fact that his results were exemplary. He cared little about his scurrilous reputation, for, apart from Bonnafé, the French teacher, and Isoré, who taught English, with whom he boxed at the gym, he remained isolated. His spare time was spent in his favourite café, the Guillaume Tell, where he would settle himself on the red velvet seats, half-hidden from prying eyes by the tall pot plants, eat a plate of sauerkraut at noon, drink a glass of beer, and write undisturbed. Later he moved on to the Café de la Grande Poste, wandering down the rue de Galions past the green and red windmills of the brothels, or watched the dockers unloading cargo. Around him swirled the life of the port, anonymous, noisy, mechanical and violent. The smell of the sea, of ships and seaweed, of tar and fish, filled his nostrils. The sound of jazz filled his ears, in the cafés and in his hotel room, for his American pupil had lent him jazz and blues records to play on his phonograph. Sartre listened to songs which echoed his own forlorn mood: '*Dans la tristesse et la nuit qui revient/Je reste seule isolée sans soutien*,' sang Damia. ('As sadness and night returns, I'm alone, helpless and lonely.')

He hoped to find comfort in this clamorous, restless milieu. In *Nausea* Roquentin is a strange character fond of picking up chestnuts, old rags, and especially pieces of paper. He closes his hand over them and feels like putting them in his mouth like a child; his former girlfriend, Anny – a name Sartre took from his dead cousin Annie – with whom he once shared 'perfect moments', used to scold him over his habit of scavenging dirty paper, which she suspected was soiled with excrement. In Mudville one day, Roquentin sees a piece of paper lying beside a puddle. He is about to pick up this fresh, tender pulp and roll it into a ball in his fingers: 'I couldn't do it.'

It is the second time the Nausea has visited him. 'Objects ought not to *touch*, since they are not alive,' he reasons. 'But they touch me, it's unbearable.' Now he remembers how he felt the other day on the seashore when he was holding the pebble. 'A curious horror overcame him.' He dropped the stone and ran way.

The Nausea pursues him. Objects terrify him: the glass of beer before him in the café, the patron's braces, even his own face, as he gazes in the mirror, hearing his aunt's voice telling him as she used to when he was small: 'If you look at yourself too long, you'll see a monkey in there.' And now he is far below the monkey, he is on the edge of the vegetable world, a polyp. His eyes 'are glassy, soft, blind and red-rimmed; anyone would think they are fish-scales . . . I have no friends: is that why my flesh is so naked?'

In the local art gallery Roquentin sees the smug faces of the bourgeoisie, admiring the pictures. Their faces are *éclatant de droit* – blazing with right. Satisfied with their wealth, position and families, borne up by a consciousness of their virtues, they imagine their lives have a 'real, *given* meaning', while his Nausea – 'it grabs you from behind and then you drift in a tepid sea of time' – grows at the sight of the solid citizens who see their importance reflected by the painter's skill. The philosopher Iris Murdoch understood Roquentin's 'special sense of the bad faith of these attempts to clothe the nakedness of existence with such trimmings of meaning'.

Even in his favourite café there is no escape. 'Things are bad! Things are very bad: I've got it, that filthy thing, the Nausea.' He is filled with a kind of sweetish disgust, *une espèce d'écoeurement douceâtre*, as the Nausea seizes him, the room spins, and he wants to vomit. He gasps his request to the waitress. Will she play him something on the gramophone, the one he likes: '*Some of These Days*'? Madeleine winds the handle and Sartre recognizes the old rag-time tune from the first bars. The American soldiers used to whistle it in 1917 in the streets of La Rochelle. It must date from before the war. As he hears the voice of the black singer, he begins to warm up, to feel happy:

> Some of these days
> You'll miss me honey.

He's '*in the music*'. His body hardens, the Nausea vanishes.

A *roquentin*, the name Sartre gives to his hero, is, according to the nineteenth-century Larousse dictionary, an old song made up of fragments of other songs: a song of bizarre effect, with abrupt changes of rhythm, full of comic surprises. It is, perhaps, Sartre's justification for the presentation of the novel in fragments, part journal, part pastiche and borrowings from other works; but the name 'Roquentin', bestowed on the shadowy, broken figure of the narrator, is also, surely, symbolic of the breakdown of meaning which Sartre himself experienced at Le Havre.

In 1945 he described existentialism as 'the attempt to draw all the consequences from a position of consistent atheism'. *Nausea*, which appeared seven years earlier in 1938, is his first and most brilliant attempt to describe a world without belief, godless, random and absurd. As Sartre explained more than once, in his *War Diaries*, and in his autobiography, *Words*, 'I *was* Roquentin,' and he used his hero to show the texture of his life. That texture, says Roquentin, is 'a comedy! All these people sitting there, looking serious, eating . . . Here we sit, all of us, eating and drinking to preserve our precious existence and really there is nothing, nothing, absolutely no reason for existing.' Nausea rolls over Roquentin when he realizes that he is as useless as the *salauds*. A *voyageur sans billet*, he is still on the train without a ticket. Life is a black comedy in which he tells himself that he is free; yet he lives like a *salaud*.

Roquentin's past is as unsubstantial as his personality. The reader suspects his journeys never happened, despite being told that he has spent six years travelling. 'A spy from the world of nothingness', he hoards his boxes of postcards, the sticky views of Algiers, Aden, Angkor, of Meknès, Moscow and Saigon, which the Autodidact respectfully inspects. In 1931 Sartre still believed in 'the magic of adventures', as he expressed it in an early story, 'L'Ange du morbide'. He thought that the only authentic voyage is that from which you return totally transformed, and he wove his travels with the Beaver into *Nausea*. Roquentin's postcards were Sartre's postcards, sent from Morocco, London and Naples, Roquentin's dreams Sartre's dreams. But holidays were hardly likely to satisfy the homunculus in his jar: already he knew *la nausée des fins de voyages*, the sickness, the disillusion of journey's end.

*

When, for her part, in October 1931 Simone de Beauvoir had caught the Bordeaux–Marseilles express, she had stepped out into the sunshine of Provence. Pausing at the top of the station steps, she looked out on sun-warmed tiles, distant hills and an azure sky. It was a pivotal moment in her life.

Simone dumped her case at the left luggage office, and began to walk down the station steps, one by one. She saw a card in a nearby window, 'Room to Let', and through the window a large table on which she could work. The rates were reasonable and she decided to take the room. Two hours later she had arranged her timetable with the head-mistress of the Lycée Montgrand in Marseilles. It was only necessary to teach for fourteen hours a week, and she had Thursdays and Sundays off.

Like Sartre, Simone set herself to explore her city of exile. Unlike him, she fell in love with it. Threading her way through the dark, sunken streets of the Old Port, and sitting in the public gardens and peaceful little squares, she inhaled the sea-wind of the Mediterranean mixed with the smell of decaying autumn leaves. On her first Thursday morning she caught the bus to Cassis, and trudged along the copper-coloured cliffs to La Ciotat. Soon hiking became more than a habit; it became a mania. Simone made it her rule to be out of the house by dawn on her free days, and never to return before nightfall. Avoiding the hiking groups to which the other teachers belonged, and scorning the appropriate gear of rucksacks and studded boots, she took to the hills in a dress and espadrilles with a few bananas and rolls in a basket. To begin with she walked for five or six hours, but soon she was breasting the mountains on twenty-five-mile hikes, climbing every peak in the area – Gardaban, Mont Aurélien and the Pilon du Roi – and clambering down every gully.

It became a matter of pride to push her body to extreme limits. When Poupette came to stay in November – funded by Sartre – Simone abandoned her, feverish and with a temperature, in a village hospice, and ploughed on alone through the snow in her espadrilles. Her obsessive desire was to 'see *everything*', every field and thicket, every abbey and château, in Provence.

Eventually the snows melted. One spring day Simone came across almond trees in blossom for the first time. The sight stunned her. 'I looked for a revelation from each successive hilltop or valley, and always the beauty of the landscape surpassed both my memories and my expectations.' Lost in the Lubéron, in a mountain ravine, she felt the moment belonged to her and to no one else. Early in the morning she strode into sleeping villages, and watched the dawn come up alone. On empty hillsides she slept at midday with the scent of broom and pine around her; no Wordsworth had a more mystical relationship to landscape than did Beauvoir.

She was a natural risk-taker. Ignoring the warnings of the other teachers, whom she dismissed as nervous spinsters, she hitched lifts. In her memoir, *Prime of Life*, Beauvoir shrugged off her encounters with men on the road. She did not want to frighten her mother. But she didn't forget 'fighting off a large man in a truck who believes he has the right to rape you, then beats you up before he throws you into a ditch because you kicked him where it hurts'. But she survived this ordeal, and another dangerous encounter when two young men picked her up in their car and began driving her to a lonely hilltop; threatening to jump out of the moving car, she persuaded them to release her.

Her independence thrilled her. Modelling herself on Katherine Mansfield's idea of the 'solitary woman', which Beauvoir found intensely romantic, burying herself in Mansfield's *Journal, Letters,* and short stories, Simone, too, felt self-sufficient. She had found a new equilibrium; perhaps as a result of her obsessive exercise, she no longer endured sexual frustration: 'I had subdued my rebellious body, and was physically at peace once more,' she wrote. 'This clean break put far less strain on me than a continual see-sawing between solitude and companionship.'

Writing suddenly filled Beauvoir with elation. Sitting, like Sartre, alone in cafés – her favourite being the Café Cintra, down by the Old Port – she at first set herself exercises in describing her surroundings, hoping to improve her technique, but abandoned them to plunge into a new novel. Once again, her subject matter was Zaza, renamed 'Anne', and her tragic death. The novel bothered her, and she struggled with dialogue. Meeting Sartre at Christmas, and on other illicit trips when she pretended to her school that she was sick, they pored over each other's work. He at least, she was convinced, 'was writing the book he had been fumbling towards for so long; and this time he would bring it off'. Her own apprenticeship would be longer.

Like Sartre, Beauvoir was popular with her pupils. Although she hardly looked any older than the girls she was teaching, she had none of her previous problems with discipline. In her second term, she invited controversy by introducing her class to Proust and Gide, who were then considered very daring, particularly in the provinces. Several parents complained, but the headmistress accepted Beauvoir's explanations and the matter went no further.

Simone had begun to relax. Sometimes she went so far as to come into school in a short, white tennis dress, which showed off her wiry figure, instead of the sweater and skirt which were *de rigueur*. And that spring, 1932, she was approached by Madame Tourmelin, the English teacher, a plump thirty-five-year-old with chestnut hair, whose husband was in a sanatorium with TB. The two women began going for walks together. Mme Tourmelin invited Simone to move into her maid's room, which she had converted into a studio. They spent a weekend away visiting an abbey near Arles. Evenings were spent eating grilled perch and drinking the local Cassis wine, and practising their English, Mme Tourmelin tut-tutting at Simone's dreadful accent. But one night when they arrived back at the apartment,

> She seized me in her arms. '*Ah! Jetons les masques!* Come on, let's drop this pretence,' she gasped, and kissed me passionately. Then she burst out about how she had fallen in love with me at first sight, and it was high time to have done with all this hypocrisy, and would I – she begged me – spend the night with her?

Simone muttered that in the morning they'd feel embarrassed. 'Must I kneel at your feet?' cried Mme Tourmelin. 'No, no, no!' screamed Simone, fleeing to her room. The next morning the English teacher explained that she had been joking. All the same, it was with considerable relief that Simone heard that her request for a post in northern France had been granted. Her new destination was Rouen, only an hour and a half from Paris, and an hour by train from Sartre.

12

The Little Russian

She felt Xavière's beautiful warm breasts against hers,
she inhaled her sweet breath. Was this desire?
Simone de Beauvoir, *She Came to Stay*

WHEN SIMONE DE BEAUVOIR arrived in Rouen in October 1932 to take
up her post at the Lycée Jeanne d'Arc, she at first barely noticed the
pallid, sullen face of the seventeen-year-old Russian emigrée sitting at
the back of the class. Olga Kosackiewicz, born in Kiev, half Ukrainian,
was not one of the bright girls who attracted their teacher's attention.
Nicknamed by her classmates '*la petite Russe*', the daughter of a White
Russian who had married his family's French governess, she was silent
and unhappy. But within six months the little Russian would ignite a
passion in Beauvoir as strong as that she had felt for any man.

Olga was the catalyst who set Beauvoir's imagination free and
inspired her first published novel, *L'Invitée* (*She Came to Stay*). Muse
and model, she was fictionalized by Beauvoir as 'Xavière' and by Sartre
as 'Ivich' in his trilogy *Les Chemins de la liberté* (*Roads to Freedom*).
Described by Simone as the '*perle noire*', the black pearl, whose 'pearly
cheeks' she wants to cover with kisses, the girl became a priceless jewel
in the eyes of her teacher, one soon coveted by Sartre too. So
powerfully did Olga inhabit the minds of first Beauvoir, and then
Sartre, that she inspired four books and at least one play, *Huis Clos* (*No
Exit*).

But to begin with Olga belongs to Beauvoir, whose pupil she is. The emotions she arouses leap from the pages of *She Came to Stay*. One evening 'Françoise' takes 'Xavière' to a night-club. The Russian is dancing, her head thrown back in ecstasy. 'Françoise', who doesn't dance, is sitting, watching. The smoke and the jazz remind her of her Montparnasse youth. She clasps the glass of whisky on the zinc table, but doesn't drink. Her gaze is fixed on Xavière, whose blue pleated dress fits revealingly over her slim, rounded schoolgirl body. She's supple and feminine. Her pale, fragile face is framed by sleek, white-blonde hair: the Little Russian, Françoise's possession.

Xavière's mind is small, hostile, stubborn. She is touchy and proud, remembering how in the old days, in Russia, her aristocratic father used to take her hunting at six o'clock in the morning. Now she is *déracinée*, uprooted. Fresh, young, androgynous, like a child, she has a small boy's head, which becomes that of a 'fond, ingenuous girl'.

The evening is nearly over. The teacher is planning to bring her protégée to Paris. She pats the warm hand that lies trustingly in hers. '*Vous verrez, vous aurez une belle petite existence toute dorée.* You see, you'll have a beautiful golden little life.'

'Oh I do want to come,' said Xavière. She sank with all her weight against Françoise's shoulder; for some time they remained motionless, leaning against each other. Xavière's hair brushed against Françoise's cheek. Their fingers remained intertwined.

'*Je suis triste de vous quitter.* It makes me sad to leave you,' said Françoise.

'So it does me,' said Xavière softly.

'My dear little Xavière,' murmured Françoise. Xavière looked at her with eyes shining, parted lips, yielding, abandoned; she had surrendered herself completely. Henceforth Françoise would lead her through life.

'I shall make her happy,' she decided with conviction.

*

For the first six months in Rouen, however, Simone had plenty to occupy her. She took a room in the Hôtel La Rochefoucauld, near the station. The hotel had an added merit for its new occupant. It was filthy, with only one bathroom, but for the Beaver, who had never set much store by personal cleanliness, no palace could have suited her better. Her year of independence in Marseilles had intensified her desire to 'live against' her mother, Françoise, and choosing the Rochefoucauld was the next step in her rebellion against the 'revolting fate' of bourgeois domesticity, which she often felt she had only missed by a hair's breadth. There was no need to cook or wash or clean. There was no need even to bother with a man underfoot, although she was glad to meet Sartre in nearby Le Havre. She was young, single and free.

At the *lycée* Simone met a colleague recommended to her by Nizan: Colette Audry, a young Communist friend of Simone Weil. Colette had dark, cropped hair and lived near the station like Simone, in a room whose walls were lined with the works of Marx and Rosa Luxembourg. She belonged to a Trotskyite splinter group interested in Freudian psychoanalysis, and, after some initial hesitation, became a close friend to the 'slim unknown' in the staff room, whom she had at first dismissed as 'excessively well brought up', until Simone's rapid, husky way of speaking convinced Audry that she was not as conventional as she appeared. Ignored by the other members of staff, Simone spent her lunch hour in the grubby, faded Brasserie Paul, where she corrected homework and wrote. Since the food was bad, and the service worse, no one bothered her. It became her *querencia*, in bull-ring parlance a place where you could feel completely safe. It was a 'defence against the provincial wilderness', for Simone disliked the Normandy landscape, which she found insipid, rainy and over-civilized, and gave up walking.

Her first action in Rouen was to buy herself a season ticket, in order to spend every possible moment with Sartre. She had finally broken with the Llama, and these were some of the happiest months in her life, to which she would refer with nostalgia in 1939: 'I'm not afraid of anything. I'm tangled up with Sartre once again, alone with him as in the days of Le Havre and Rouen before Kos . . . I'm happy.' Neither of them had any responsibilities apart from their work as high school teachers of philosophy, work that captivated Beauvoir more than Sartre. With no children, no homes, no political interests, they lived removed from reality:

We had a profession, which we pursued in the correct manner, but which did not detach us from *l'univers des mots*, the world of words . . . As Sartre said to me one day, we had a genuine sense of the truth . . . though this was a step in the right direction, it did not in any way imply that we possessed *a true sense of reality*.

Insulated from the workaday world in their verbal universe, Beauvoir and Sartre developed a private language together, of *querencias* and *erlebnissen*, emotions. Sartre is Castor's '*cher amour*', her dear love, her '*cher petit être*', her dear little being, '*mon doux petit mari*', her sweet little husband. They still used the formal '*vous*' to each other, but in his letters Sartre signalled their special relationship by the phrase '*vous autres*', in French the second person plural, 'you' or, roughly, 'all of you'. Used to Beauvoir alone, it was further refined as '*vous autre*', to heighten their intimacy.

As they juggled with words, Sartre and Beauvoir strengthened their intellectual and emotional bonds, reading each other's manuscripts, parrying ideas, and exchanging gossip about their friends. Their sense of oneness is powerfully expressed in *She Came to Stay*, in which Sartre was the inspiration for the character of Pierre Labrousse, a theatrical producer, and the lover of Françoise. She has to tell him everything; if she fails to do so, if uncomfortable thoughts are brushed aside or repressed, 'this allowed a shameful subterranean vegetation to grow up under the surface of true existence, where she felt utterly alone and in danger of suffocation'.

Sartre is the gardener hacking a way through Beauvoir's thoughts with his mental machete, clearing her personal wilderness of the jungle which threatens to throttle her.

> Little by little she had resolved everything: she no longer knew aloneness, but *elle était purifiée de ces grouillements confus*, she had rid herself of those chaotic subterranean tendrils. Every moment of her life she had entrusted to him, and he gave it back to her clear, polished, completed, and they became moments of their shared life.

This is perhaps Beauvoir's most honest confession of how 'necessary' Sartre's love was to her security, and how profound her need was for the rule of transparency, which preserved her psychological equilibrium. But she served the same purpose for him. The commitment to 'telling everything' intensified the complicity between the couple during that first, important, year in Rouen, and was at the kernel of their relationship.

Its nature and intensity became increasingly obvious to outsiders. Colette Audry, who had been introduced to Sartre, noticed that:

> [Beauvoir's] influence on him was just as great as his on her; that a boy like Sartre (because he *was* just a boy then) who had such

analytic power, both destructive and polemical, within himself was all the same taken by this girl – devoted, enraptured, tied, bound to her; that he, and I know it was he, insisted not only on establishing, but then also keeping her in, this famous contract with him.

Colette sometimes felt envious of the couple's symbiosis:

> Theirs was a new kind of relationship, and I had never seen anything like it. I cannot describe what it was like to be present when those two were together. It was so intense that sometimes it made others who saw it sad not to have it.

The writer Olivier Todd, who was to marry Nizan's daughter, was similarly struck by the 'matchless complicity' between the two.

> They seemed to think simultaneously even when they seemed to be mistaken. They were like some odd relay runners of ideas who did not need to pass the baton to continue the relay. They got in step, and followed one another in a way I have never seen any other couple in the world do. Those Siamese twins could be a little bit frightening . . . Simone de Beauvoir was even able to finish Sartre's sentences and vice versa. There was even a kind of mimetism in their rasping voices . . . How touching was their way of addressing each other by 'vous' even in public . . .

The 'twin sign on our foreheads', first recognized by Beauvoir in 1929, had developed into a 'twinship' which, despite being non-biological, writes psychiatrist Ricardo Ainslie, can form 'part of the psychological reality governing the twin's life, and thus, over time, it becomes part of the twin's personality organization'. Two are more powerful than one as the incestuous couple mirror each other's thoughts and acts. Beauvoir recognized as much when she wrote to Sartre on 7 November 1939: 'We are truly one person, you and I, and that's a fantastic power.'

Within this shared, cerebral universe, Beauvoir was happy. But at times she felt 'imprisoned by happiness'. Although, like her mother, she possessed that *optimisme de commande*, which had allowed Françoise de Beauvoir to deny her husband's adultery, the physical side of her relationship with Sartre was increasingly imperfect. 'Pierre', in Beauvoir's novel *L'Invitée*, admits that he is not 'a great sensualist . . .

The truth is that I enjoy the early stages [of an affair]'. '*Il y a un élan passioné qui lui manque*, there's no surge of passion in him,' another of Sartre's lovers, Bianca Bienenfield, would complain in 1939. By 1932 the twenty-four-year-old Beauvoir also craved in vain the warmth she missed with Sartre.

In a short story, 'Marcelle', she created the figure of Denis Charval, whose cold brutality humiliates his wife on her wedding night.

> In a jet of passion she bit Denis' shoulder. He started; his hands gripped her body harder and he nibbled the quivering flesh. Marcelle clung to him ecstatically, drunk with shame. 'I'm his thing, his slave,' she murmured to herself . . . He turned her on her belly and made her kneel. 'Stay like that . . . It's more fun.'

In Beauvoir's description, Denis relishes Marcelle's 'ignominy'; he keeps her in this 'degrading posture' like an executioner forcing her 'to dance under the whip'. Sadly she perceives 'that life always fell short of dreams'.

The poverty of Beauvoir's sexual life created a space which the admiration of her pupils began to fill. In class she was creating a sensation. She made light work of teaching, never preparing lessons, for philosophy, which she had so recently studied, was still fresh in her head. She simply sat on a desk and began talking so fast in her deep smoker's voice that the slower girls found it impossible to take notes. She was, remembered one student, 'incredibly dazzling'. In 1932 Beauvoir was young enough almost to be mistaken for one of the older girls, but her authority dominated the room. For more than one she became their *flamme* or crush. 'She was beautiful, she was young, she wore make-up, she had a vivacious air,' recalled Olga Kosackiewicz, trying to analyse Beauvoir's attraction. Accustomed to lined, middle-aged teachers with their hair in a bun, Beauvoir was certainly a novelty, and the girls began vying for her attention.

Meanwhile a film about a schoolgirl who falls in love with her teacher was attracting a cult following. *Mädchen in Uniform* (*Girls in Uniform*), set in a Prussian school, premiered in Berlin on 27 November 1931 and was soon playing in Paris – with subtitles by Colette – to full houses. The novel of the film became a bestseller, following Colette's Claudine series – *Claudine at School, Claudine in Paris*, which Beauvoir had read as a teenager – along with *Mademoiselle Dax* by Farrère, a book about the sexual awakening of a young middle-class girl. *Olivia* by Dorothy Strachey Bussy, sister of Lytton Strachey and wife of French painter Simon Bussy, was also becoming an underground classic of female pedagogical paedophilia. In this thinly disguised account of Dorothy Strachey's own schooldays near Fontainebleau, stern 'Miss Julie', reading Racine aloud, 'lights the flame' that begins to burn in the young Olivia's heart.

In the Rouen classroom, it was not until the end of the second term that Simone de Beauvoir noticed Olga Kosackiewicz. The highest marks, she announced, had been gained by *'la petite Russe'*. It was astonishing. Only a few days before the girl had burst into tears at her teacher's desk, unable to finish her essay; only when Simone took her for a stroll by the river and bought her a drink at a brasserie did her spirits lift.

The Little Russian talked of God and Baudelaire. Simone was enchanted. Although as far as she was concerned, '[Olga] was still a child', a bud of a girl, she began inviting her to lunch weekly at the Brassserie Paul, and even took her to the Opéra Russe to see *Boris Godunov*. Coached by Simone, Olga passed her bac with flying colours. Although she had wanted to be a dancer at twelve, her parents, who lived in Laigle, a Norman town west of Rouen, decided that she should study medicine. In October 1934 she returned to Rouen and took a room in town.

'At first it was Olga who wanted the relationship and brought it into being,' claimed Beauvoir disingenuously in her memoirs. 'It could not have been otherwise.' Olga was 'anti practically everything, while I,' wrote the teacher, 'slid through life with the ease of a swimming fish'.

In fact Simone, nine years older than the withdrawn, uncertain emigrée, took the initiative. Wooing rather than wooed, her own rebellion found its echo in Olga's. Both rejected bourgeois mores. And the attraction which pubescent girls held for Beauvoir is made clear in her letters to her young pupil, whose childlike nature and slender body she emphasizes in *Prime of Life*. There was no need to call her 'Mademoiselle' any longer, wrote Beauvoir in her first letter to Olga in July 1934, written while holidaying with Sartre in Germany:

> You are much too close to me for this formal word to be suitable any longer . . . I'm deeply attached to you, but did not know to what extent until you left. I miss you, almost painfully. Not only are you one of the most admirable people I know but you are one of those people who enrich the existence of those around them, and who leave a big emptiness behind them.

Olga, who found letter writing difficult, tore up her letters to Beauvoir, to her disappointment. She begged Olga to write to her: 'I want you to know that there is not one of your facial expressions, not one of your feelings, and not one incident in your life that I do not care about . . . Naturally [I] would love to get long and detailed letters.' Already Beauvoir was planning the next term with Olga: 'We'll go for long walks, and we will see each other very often.'

'[Olga's] feelings towards me quickly reached a burning intensity, the full implications of which I took some time to appreciate,' wrote Beauvoir. Olga's future psychological development suggests that she may already have suffered a childhood loss of innocence that predisposed her to enter, or even seek out, a same-sex relationship with an older woman that had the potential to become abusive. But Simone's feelings were 'burning' too.

*

Ennui had been rolling over Sartre like fog coming in from the Channel, despite Castor's occasional visits. He sensed that in Rouen she was having a better time than he was, trapped in Le Havre; and his recent, annual holiday with his mother, Anne-Marie, and his stepfather, Mancy, had opened up old wounds. Morosely he brooded over the life of the poet Baudelaire, whose biography he would write, and whose early history is uncannily like his own. Like Sartre, Charles Baudelaire lost his father young. Like Sartre, Baudelaire

> felt himself united body and soul to his mother in a sort of primitive and mystical involvement; he lost himself in the sweet warmth of their reciprocal love; there was only one home, one family, one incestuous couple.

In his biography, Sartre quoted Baudelaire's letter to his mother: '*Tu étais à la fois une idole et un camarade*, you were both an idol and a friend.' Wholly absorbed by the mother goddess who appeared to him 'to exist both by necessity and by right', the son felt that his existence, too, was *justified* (Sartre's italics).

Like Anne-Marie, Baudelaire's mother had remarried, and the young poet felt the same sense of outrage and abandon as the young philosopher. Remarriage was the unforgivable sin: 'When you have a son like me, you don't remarry,' Baudelaire wrote curtly to his mother. His old life had gone out like the tide, leaving him naked and alone.

His overpowering feeling was of solitude: 'Already he feels this isolation is his *destiny*,' writes Sartre with emotion.

Cut off from humankind, walled up by choice, Baudelaire becomes a pariah: *le merle blanc devenu aveugle*, the white blackbird who's gone blind, a description which seems to fit the author of the biography as well as his subject. When Baudelaire writes: *'Je suis un autre*, I am an Other', it is Sartre's voice we hear, full of pain and despair, as he quotes Baudelaire's furious letter to his parents:

> you've chased me away, you've rejected me . . . You've condemned me to a separate existence . . . *Je suis un autre*. Other than all you who make me suffer. You can persecute my flesh, but not my 'otherness'.

The son feels he has been skinned, stripped, like Marsyas, the Phrygian flute player, whose punishment for challenging the god Apollo to a contest of skill was to be flayed alive. It is no coincidence that in *L'Invitée* Françoise is reading a script about Marsyas which Pierre has given her. Beauvoir, like Bienenfeld after her, senses the 'otherness', the despair of Sartre, who like Baudelaire 'prefers himself to everybody, because everybody abandons him', and has made his heroic, Stoic choice to situate himself above the earth, to dwell in his own 'pure consciousness'.

The damage Anne-Marie had done to him could never be undone. Or could it? Was he eternally cursed, like Baudelaire? Like the homunculus to whom Sartre compared Baudelaire and himself, to his friend Paul Nizan, it seemed so; the little man thrashed against the walls of his jar, as unhappy as the *poète maudit*.

Nizan worried about his old friend's depression. He satirized him as 'Lange', a miserable, anarchical high school teacher, in his second novel, *The Trojan Horse*. The name 'Lange', 'angel' in French, was taken from Sartre's story 'L'Ange du morbide', published in *La Revue sans titre* in 1923. It reveals how Sartre at thirty appeared to others during those gloomy Le Havre years in which he toiled over his 'Factum on Contingency', as it went through three successive versions, three changes of title, evolving under the influence of his trips abroad and his relationships, in particular with Olga, until finally bursting upon the world in 1938.

Lange has come out of the École Normale – 'which was in itself reason enough for his colleagues to hate him', writes Nizan. 'He had reached the extreme limit where culture merges with exhaustion in the no man's land of solitude and death . . . *Il attendait la mort* [He was waiting for death].' Scornfully Nizan, a militant Communist, compares the vigour of the Communist hero, Bloyé, with the lassitude of Lange, who remarks:

> 'When I think about it, Bloyé, your activity seems extraordinarily absurd to me. What do you want to do?'
> 'To change the world,' said Boyé.

But politics, and the Communist cause, bored Sartre and Beauvoir. One day a docker sat at the next-door table in one of their favourite cafés in Rouen, the Café Victor. He was 'decently dressed', recalled Beauvoir, in his blue smock, but the manager ejected him. The incident, sign of class segregation at a time when the working class was suffering spectacularly during the Great Depression, prompted Sartre to wonder whether they should join those working for the Revolution. He was 'vaguely tempted', but the two comfortably-off civil servants, despite professing sympathy for the proletarian struggle, decided: 'It was not *our* struggle . . . We had our own tasks to fulfil, and they were not compatible with joining the Party.'

Nizan wanted to warn Sartre of the dangers of remaining aloof from politics. He failed. Sartre knew that writing required every atom of his energy, whatever the cost; he had made his choice as an artist and an individual to set himself against convention and community:

> It was [Lange's] fate to be alone in the town, to walk among stones as paralysed as himself, which had no more communication between themselves than he had with others. He was a man alone, really alone, like *un îlot desert*, a desert island.

Exasperated at 'Lange's' scorn for the people, Nizan condemned his old *camarade* for being obsessed with ideas and systems. 'Systems are like boxes, those mazes used for experiments with rats, guinea pigs; in the end the rat always finds the centre of the maze . . .' Sartre, said Nizan, was a rat in a trap.

*

In fact Sartre was down at the public park, looking at the chestnut tree. Its root plunged into the ground just under his bench. He no longer remembered that it was a root, for words had disappeared, and with them the meaning of things. His head bowed, he stared at the black, knotty mass. The bark, black and blistered, looked like boiled leather; he could hear the sound of water in the fountain, smell a green, putrid smell. At that moment 'Un événement m'est arrivé, something happened to me.' Existence suddenly unveiled itself in front of his eyes; he saw that it was 'the very stuff of things'. Sartre's revelation is that there is no middle way between non-existence and nature's awesome, swooning abundance. 'What exists at all must exist to this point: to the point of mouldering, of bulging, of obscenity. In another world, circles and melodies retain their pure and rigid contours. But existence is a degeneration.'

'How long did that spell last?' asked Sartre. 'I *was* the root of the chestnut tree.' He had learnt that to exist 'is simply *to be there*'.

It was only when Sartre stopped thinking, and listened to his intuition, that he was able to experience the world about him. But the bounty of nature, which for others was proof of God, was for Sartre a confirmation that the 'essential thing' was contingency: 'I mean that, by definition, existence is not necessity.' It is simply being. People had tried to overcome this contingency by inventing a necessary, causal being, but no 'necessary being' could explain existence:

> Contingency is not an illusion . . . It is absolute, and consequently perfect gratuitousness. Everything is gratuitous, this park, this town, and myself. When you realize that, it turns your stomach over and you start floating about . . .

Existence is a gift; but it is also nauseating, obscene. The natural world threatens loss of control, like the writhing roots at the temple of Angkor Wat. Sartre was afraid of the green spaces outside the town, of the vegetation which might at any moment strangle and destroy man-made structures. Civilization was precarious, temporary, endangered. 'When the town dies,' he wrote, 'the Vegetation will invade it, it will clamber over the stones, it will grip them, search them . . . It will bind the holes and hang its green paws everywhere.'

Even corralled in the public park, the chestnut tree is barely tolerable. Sartre, who had turned to the piano for comfort in the upside-down world of La Rochelle, reached out again to music for its promise of order and harmony.

He returns to the café. Madeleine winds the gramophone, and the notes of 'Rendez-vous les Cheminots' float in the air. They bear him away to another world. In the circle of the melody is necessity and rigour: the notes *are*. His beating heart grows calm. In the voice of the blues singer he hears the meaning of the melody, and its message: he must be like her, and suffer in rhythm. *Il faut souffrir en mesure.* In the purity of his loneliness he will create his masterpiece.

13

Berlin

Les Juifs, ça n'existe pas. There's no such thing as Jews.
Simone de Beauvoir, *Prime of Life*

ARRIVING IN BERLIN in the autumn of 1933 to meet the writer Christopher Isherwood, John Lehmann, publisher at the Hogarth Press, was immediately struck by the huge pictures of Hitler, illuminated by candles, displayed in the windows of middle-class districts. The crude likenesses of the Führer, row upon row of them, were 'like altars dedicated to some primitive, irrational demon-cult'. On 27 February the Reichstag had burnt down, the result, claimed Hitler, of a Communist plot, and he consolidated his power as Chancellor with the Enabling Act in March. An orgy of Jew-baiting began in the press, and 'sickening stories' circulated of atrocities committed against those who had been arrested. Boy-bars were raided. Perturbed by the ominous atmosphere, Isherwood would pack up his papers the following April and leave.

That same autumn, 1933, Jean-Paul Sartre arrived in Berlin. His comfortable bedroom in the French Institute looked out over immaculate lawns, and he was able to contemplate a tree which, although unlike his 'old friend in Le Havre . . . helped keep the memory of that chestnut alive'. He placed his new copy of Heidegger's *Sein und Zeit* on the antique desk, and breathed a sigh of relief. He had, at last, escaped 'Mudville'.

He owed his arrival in the German capital to his old friend and rival Raymond Aron, who had introduced him to a new and inspirational influence in philosophy, phenomenology. One weekend the previous year Sartre, Simone and Aron had been sitting in the Bec de Gaz in the rue Montparnasse, drinking apricot cocktails – a *spécialité de la maison* – when Aron, who was studying the work of the founder of phenomenology, Edmund Hüsserl, in Berlin, pointed at his glass and said: 'You see, *mon petit camarade*, if you are a phenomenologist, you can talk about this cocktail and make philosophy out of it!' Sartre went white with emotion. Aron had put his finger on what Sartre was trying to achieve, to describe objects or phenomena just as he saw and touched them, and to 'extract philosophy from the process'. Overcome with excitement, Sartre rushed to a bookshop in the boulevard Saint-Michel and bought the latest book on Hüsserl by the French author Levinas. In his haste he began reading as he walked, his heart missing a beat when he came across the entry: 'Contingency'. Had Hüsserl got there before him? But there were only a few scattered references to Sartre's obsession. Deciding not to waste a minute before beginning his own study of the great German philosopher, Sartre at once applied to the French Institute for a place in the coming year. Aron, meanwhile, took over from him at the Lycée Le Havre.

As for Isherwood, it was the Berlin of Sally Bowles that appealed to Sartre, and he wasted no time in looking for a woman to help him discover it. In the game of seduction, handicapped by his looks, 'I counted on my power of speech alone. I can still recall the trouble in which I found myself in Berlin. I'd set off determined to experience the love of German women, but I soon realized I didn't know enough German to converse. Stripped of my weapon, I was left feeling quite idiotic and dared attempt nothing – I had to fall back on a French woman.'

He duly sought out pretty Marie Ville, the wife of a philology teacher, as a suitable target. Together they went to night-clubs, watched live sex acts, and drank deep in the beer halls of the capital. Marie, whom Beauvoir called 'Marie Girard' in *The Prime of Life*, responded to Sartre's seductive ritual, which he compared to a bull-fight. He did not want the woman to yield at the first 'placing of the banderillos'. Like the bull, she had to resist. Her 'collapse . . . had to be *deserved*: in other words, occur at the end of the play, at the very moment when the curtain falls'.

Marie was prepared to play the game, refusing as he gently insisted, each day winning a little more ground. 'I was less keen on the woman than on the play-acting she gave me an opportunity for . . . Possessing her counted for less than the prospects of possession.' The sexual relations which resulted – the 'terminal event' which he compared to the killing of the bull – were unfortunately inevitable: 'Most of the time we have no choice,' Sartre complained to Gerassi. 'To be close to a woman demands that a love relationship be established, and most women find love incomplete without sex.' In his *War Diaries* he later confessed: 'A strong sensual passion – if some woman had conceived one for me – would have totally disconcerted and shocked me.' It was the drama of courtship which fascinated him, played out to a female audience:

> There's one half of humanity that hardly exists for me. The other half – well, there's no denying it, the other half is my sole and constant concern. I take pleasure only in the company of women; I feel respect, tenderness and friendship only for women . . . *J'aime les femmes à la folie*.

It was not only women's company, but their conversation which attracted Sartre.

> I prefer to talk to a woman about the tiniest things than about philosophy . . . It's because those are the tiny things which exist for me; and any woman, even the stupidest, talks about them as I like to talk about them myself: I *get on* with women.

Chattering about 'tiny things' with Marie, Sartre was blind to the unfolding Nazi terror around him. Although, in his Gidean quest to understand the city, he spent whole days in the dingy bars around the Alexanderplatz, and knew enough German to stumble through the newspapers, Sartre ignored the Nuremberg Congress and the November plebiscite which finally gave Hitler control. Goebbels's rabid anti-Semitic speeches went over his head. When, however, he passed the Brownshirts in the street, on their way to beat up Jews in the public squares, he experienced, said Beauvoir, the same 'unpleasant feeling' he had first felt in Venice, where the Brownshirts had struck him as more sinister than Mussolini's Blackshirts.

*

Nor did Simone de Beauvoir herself feel cause for concern in Rouen. Jews seemed completely assimilated into French society. Their friend

Fernando Gerassi, born in Constantinople, was descended from Sephardic Jews expelled from Spain, but this was of no consequence. When Olga, who had joined a group of Rumanian and Polish Jews and heard stories of the anti-Semitism which had driven them out of their own countries, asked Beauvoir one day: 'What does it *really* mean to be a Jew?' her teacher replied with absolute certainty: '*Rien. Les Juifs, ça n'existe pas. Il n'y a que des hommes.* [Nothing at all. There are no such things as Jews; there are only human beings].' The next day Olga marched into the room of a Polish violinist and announced: 'My friends, none of you exist! My philosophy teacher has told me so!'

Nor did Simone change her mind when she visited Sartre in Berlin in February 1934. It was icily cold, but warm inside the cosy restaurants, where the couple tucked into the German food they both enjoyed: red cabbage and smoked pork. Berlin 'did not look as if it were crushed under a dictatorship', wrote Simone; 'the streets were cheerful and animated'. Together they drank beer in the huge beer-halls, like the Vaterland, where people embraced each other as they rocked to and fro, singing loudly to a brass band. 'That,' Sartre explained to her, 'is *Stimmung* [harmony].' Simone met her first transvestite, in veil, silk stockings and high-heeled shoes, and visited some 'villainous' night-clubs.

Back at the French Institute, the students, like the majority of the French Left, believed that Nazism would collapse at any minute. The Germans were simply suffering from collective hysteria: anti-Semitism was, surely, '*trop stupide*' to be taken seriously. At the Institute there was a tall, good-looking Jewish student whom the Germans took for an Aryan, while a small, dark Corsican was assumed to be a Jew, much to the amusement of the French *pensionnaires*. Even when the Austrian Chancellor Dolfuss savagely crushed a socialist uprising, Sartre and Simone refused to take notice. They would not themselves put their shoulders to the wheel of history, said Beauvoir, but they did want to believe that it was turning in the right direction: 'Otherwise we would have had too many problems to rethink.'

Sartre was still in Germany on 30 June, the 'night of the long knives', when Hitler's SS murdered Röhm, leader of the Brownshirts. Simone had returned for a summer tour of Germany and Austria with Sartre. On a boat up the Elbe they fell into conversation with a German veteran of World War I:

'If there's another war, we shall not be defeated this time,' said the former sergeant. 'We shall retrieve our honour.'

'There is no need for war,' replied Sartre. 'We all ought to want peace.'

'Honour comes first,' said the German. 'First we must retrieve our honour.'

At Nuremberg thousands of swastikas fluttered from the windows, and Simone shivered as she remembered the photographs she had seen of marching, saluting Nazis: 'A whole people hypnotized.' She and Sartre hurried away to Austria, where 'the atmosphere seemed lighter', until they saw people fighting for the newspapers and learnt that Dolfuss had been assassinated. Was Nazism less of a 'straw fire' than the Communists claimed? Quickly she repressed the thought.

Soberly they pressed on to Oberammergau for the Passion Play. Sharing a meal of potatoes with a local tailor and his family, and a couple from Munich, Sartre found himself the target of suspicious eyes. 'You speak extremely good German,' said the Austrians, adding disapprovingly: 'You haven't the least trace of an accent.' The teacher had been taken for a spy.

In 1971 Sartre defended his gullibility. According to him, his German was weak, too weak to understand the situation, and Aron had misled him:

> Despite all the efforts by my grandfather to teach me German, I did not speak it well at all, and reading it was an effort . . . After the night of the long knives, I understood that something brutal had taken place, but there was no one in the streets, and no one knew anything for sure. We were dependent on the French left, and it did not seem very apprehensive. Aron, who was still a socialist then, told me that Hitler and his horde could not possibly last another year.

Sartre protested that at the time he still believed in 'the special status of the writer. My job may have been to denounce fascism, but in my writing, at my desk. And if you read *Nausea* carefully, you'll see that I did, within of course the context of the time, and of my political consciousness, which was *petit bourgeois*, individualistic and democratic.' Describing the ruling class, and the 'potential rebels, the marginals, crushed by that class', was, he claimed, the beginning of his political awareness.

In July 1934, having just spent nine months in Berlin, Sartre was in fact in a better position to judge the political situation than Raymond Aron, who had been in Le Havre, substituting for Sartre. But Sartre's optimism remained unshakeable: Beauvoir correctly ascertained his blinkered attitude, which she, and many Europeans, shared, when she wrote: 'The true condition of the world *had* to be peace.' After France's suffering in the Great War, the war to end all wars, many of Sartre's generation of *orphelins* ignored the gathering storm-clouds.

*

Simone remained even more aloof from politics than Sartre. She had been shocked to discover that Sartre was in the throes of an affair with Marie, the Moon woman. It was the first time in their 'morganatic' marriage that her 'sweet little husband' had been unfaithful to her, apart from the occasional slip-up with Simone Jollivet. Somehow she had assumed that he would remain monogamous, true to their contract of 'essential love', despite her own dalliance with Pierre Guille, which he appeared not to mind.

Simone was disconcerted when she met Marie, a woman who smoked and dreamt away her days and was as much Castor's opposite as it was possible to be. Marie was attractive and graceful. 'I met her and liked her; there was no feeling of jealousy on my part,' claimed Simone in *The Prime of Life*. Possibly not, but she may have toyed with thoughts of revenge. Sartre had emphasized that they must on no account permit themselves to experience jealousy, with its dangerous potential to destabilize their pact. They had agreed to allow lovers on the side: had she not herself already taken advantage of this option? It was vital to keep a tight rein on emotions. In 1973, Sartre described the rules:

> I was always free, Castor was free, we were always free to pursue any desire that we felt was important to us. To have such freedom, we had to suppress or overcome any possessiveness, any tendency to be jealous. In other words, passion. To be free, you cannot be passionate.

But passion was at the core of Beauvoir's personality, and Sartre too, ostensibly the cold-blooded 'Kobra', would prove capable of violent emotion. Attractive in theory, the vaunted 'freedom' of the pact presented many pitfalls. 'Jealousy is far from being an emotion of which I am incapable, or which I underrate,' wrote Beauvoir in 1960, speaking from bitter experience. She was hurt by Sartre's fling, although in her memoirs, she denied this to her readers:

This affair neither took me by surprise nor upset any notions I had formed concerning our joint lives, since right from the outset Sartre had warned me that he was liable to embark on such adventures. I had accepted the principle, and now had no difficulty in accepting the fact.

Yet it was hard to accept that Sartre preferred Marie to herself. Marie, aimless and uneducated, who shut herself away in her room for weeks on end, and had not 'the slightest notion of what the purpose of her existence on this earth might be'. Marie, whom they nicknamed the 'Lunar Woman' because she lived in 'a private fog'. But with her slow smile and pensive manner, Marie was neither demanding nor challenging. She offered the traditional feminine virtue of submission to the male exhibited by Anne-Marie. She cherished Sartre's battered ego.

Beauvoir, on the other hand, possessed 'masculine' qualities: ambition, tenacity of purpose, intellectual rigour. Significantly, it was to other men that Sartre compared her: 'I've had three "intimate friends",' he wrote, 'and each corresponded to a specific period of my life: Nizan-Guille-Castor (because Castor was *also* my friend and is still). What friendship brought me, much more than affection . . . was a federated world . . . And that world was constantly renovated by incessant invention. At the same time each of us strengthened the other and the result was a *couple* of considerable power.'

If Sartre's nights were spent with Marie, his days were spent writing at his desk. There he truly existed. His most powerful memories of Berlin would not be of either Marie, or the Nazis, but of the philosopher Hüsserl, formerly dean at Freiburg University, who 'gripped' him for four years: 'I saw everything through the perspectives of his philosophy . . . I was "Hüsserlian" and longed to remain so.' Sartre found Hüsserl instantly accessible because his 'brilliant, *scholarly* synthesis' developed Cartesian ideas of consciousness, which Sartre had already absorbed in Descartes's *Meditations*. Descartes had, in Hüsserl's eyes, made a 'tabula rasa of all previous beliefs and accepted sciences', and Hüsserl had continued this path by developing, in phenomenology, a way of describing immediate experiences and how they are processed by the mind. He put a new emphasis on intuition. The phenomenologist suspends or 'brackets off' his judgement in order to purify a phenomenon of interpretation. In this way Hüsserl distinguished between thinking and perception, and explored awareness. Arguing that 'all consciousness is consciousness *of* something', a doctrine he called 'intentionality', and attempting to 'bracket off' the 'pure phenomenon' from the 'I' who sees it, he went on to claim that a transcendental Ego 'stood behind' consciousness. In the 1920s he even suggested that if the world were destroyed pure consciousness would remain – an idea which appealed to science-fiction writers.

But Sartre had a problem. It seemed to him that phenomenology was evolving towards idealism, which he rejected. Tussling with Hüsserl during the long German winter, the 'disciple' wrote against his 'master' in his first philosophical essay, *The Transcendence of the Ego*, in which he challenged the contention that 'the Ego is an "inhabitant" of consciousness'. Instead, said Sartre:

> The Ego is neither formally nor materially *in* consciousness: it is outside, *in the world*. It is a being of the world, like the Ego of another.

Sartre's interest in Hüsserl originated with Karl Jaspers, the Heidelberg phenomenologist who believed that human existence was characterized by the clash between the individual's presence in the world and his desire for transcendence. Sartre's denial of transcendence was a crucial, logical step for a thinker who began with the 'death of God'. It was an austere train of thought, born of his Protestant background, and one that attempted to go back to first principles. Cartesian dualism, the subject-object dichotomy, would, in his philosophy, be firmly grounded in the here-and-now of observable phenomena. Sartre summed up his belief by saying: 'Every consciousness is consciousness of the world, first and foremost.'

Reading Levinas on Hüsserl had initially excited Sartre because of its rejection of rationalism, which he considered failed to do justice to the 'immediacy of living'. Phenomenology restored man to his place in the world, with his anguish, his passion and his revolt. It concerned itself with human activity in concrete situations, with existing, and had, therefore, the potential to become an 'existentialism'. It also gave the young philosopher a powerful tool, as he delved into the psyche (the title of the 'big book', *La Psyché*, Sartre began and abandoned in 1937) in his quest to understand the imagination and emotions.

Under the influence of his master Hüsserl, in whom Sartre may have felt a particular interest because he had converted from Judaism to Protestantism, Sartre recast 'Melancholia' from a phenomenological perspective. In describing Roquentin's encounters with the world of Mudtown, Sartre expressed in fiction the ideas he was developing formally in his essay, using words as a painter uses a brush. It was a satisfying time, which became more so in the spring of 1934 as the dormouse awoke to the 'little adventure' of a love relationship with Marie. As for *Being and Time*, the book by Martin Heidegger, Hüsserl's former student and successor at Freiburg, Sartre fully intended to read it after Easter, but found the language too difficult: after fifty pages he gave up.

*

'Didn't you meet anyone?' asked Beauvoir's handsome friend, Marc Zuorro, on her return from Berlin. 'No little *encounters?*'

The Beaver shook her head, and Marc looked at her pityingly. An old friend of Sartre's from the Cité Universitaire, a French Algerian and homosexual, who inspired Sartre to create the gay character 'Daniel' in *Roads to Freedom*, he was tall and striking, with 'burning' dark eyes in an amber complexion. He reminded the Beaver both of a Greek statue and of an El Greco portrait, kept a blond boy in his apartment, and made a welcome confidant. Marc was training to be an opera-singer, and regarded teaching as the day job until he was discovered. While Sartre was away, he often escorted Simone in Paris. One evening at the Closerie des Lilas, his eye swept over the customers: '*Tous ces petits-bourgeois minables!* All these pathetic bourgeois people!' he exclaimed. 'How can you possibly put up with such an existence?' One day, declared Marc, he would have an enormous white car and take care to splash mud all over the middle classes. Beauvoir agreed. The bourgeoisie were contemptible. In the meantime, they exchanged the latest gossip: Pierre Guille and Madame Morel were probably no longer sleeping together; Poupette probably *was* sleeping with one of Sartre's former students, Lionel de Roulet; Gégé Pardo had married her art teacher.

But despite Marc's questions, Simone retained a discreet silence about her own private life. In Sartre's absence, she had renewed relations with Guille, her last lover, whose elegant presence at the Gare Saint-Lazare, where he often met Simone on her trips to Paris, had given rise to the rumour that she was the mistress of a wealthy senator, much to the horror of her pupils' parents. Her reputation as a rebel had grown at the *lycée*. After Marshal Pétain made a speech in December 1933 on the sanctity of the family, a circular was sent round to teachers asking them to play their part in propaganda to raise the birth rate. Beauvoir taught her girls that women were not exclusively intended for bringing children into the world, and was reported to the Departmental Commission for Natal Increase and Child Care as an 'unworthy teacher' undermining family values. Guille helped her compose a reply protesting her innocence, and the inspector sent down from Paris backed her up. It was a close shave.

'If I needed advice, it was to him I turned . . . He occupied a most important place in my life.' That summer, while Sartre was on his annual holiday with his parents, she went camping with Guille in Corsica, where they could sleep out under the stars and wake to the scent of the *maquis*, the Mediterranean scrub. Of that holiday her memories were *rouges, dorés et bleus*, red, golden and blue.

Her most important 'adventure', however, was closer to home. In Rouen '*la petite Russe*' was responding to her advances, and Beauvoir, her pride wounded by Sartre's affair with Marie, took advantage of his absence to explore her own sexuality. Eager to see whither her interest in same-sex love, first aroused by Zaza, would lead her, Beauvoir was undoubtedly bi-curious: and in Olga she found a precocious partner. The girl was unhappy at medical school. It was hard, she explained, after having been educated at the Institute for Young Ladies of the Nobility in Russia, to find oneself among a mass of medical students. Her parents had filled her heads, and that of her sister Wanda, with tales of old Czarist Russia, and taught them to despise traditional French bourgeois virtues of hard work and order. Olga, yearning to return to her mythic past, betrays all the attitudes of a decayed aristocrat: 'Is it absolutely necessary for me to do something?' she asks haughtily in *She Came to Stay*, when 'Françoise' suggests that she might train as a beautician or model, or learn to type.

Defiant, wilful, capricious, Olga began cutting classes. She moved out of the boarding house for young ladies in which her mother had placed her, and began sharing a bedsit with a Polish girl. On nights out with her Jewish friends, Zionists and Communists, she would often drink and dance until she passed out. She shared with Beauvoir a hatred of bourgeois convention, and soon the two were inseparable. When Beauvoir had gone out with Sartre in Le Havre, he had on occasion refused to take her into a hotel because she had holes in her stockings, but for Olga he made an effort. For Olga, Simone experimented with her appearance. She put combs in her hair, and wore dresses 'ablaze with vivid embroidery'. When the young woman took her dancing, she dressed up. 'I only remember you,' says Xavière in the night-club. 'You were wearing a long tight black skirt, a lamé blouse and a silver net in your hair. You were so beautiful!'

It amused Olga, when they entered a night-club, to give the impression that they were a lesbian couple: '[Xavière] had not let go of Françoise's arm, for she did not dislike having people take them for a couple when they entered the place: it was the kind of provocation which gave her amusement.'

The relationship became more intimate. Instead of watching, 'Françoise' began to join in the dance. Olga held her tight, smiling with assurance. She liked attracting attention. Simone smiled back. Dancing made her head spin. She inhaled Olga's scent, of tea, honey and flesh. She felt her arm in the small of her back. What did she desire? Her lips against hers? Her body surrendered in her arms?

> She could think of nothing. It was only a confused need to keep for ever this lover's face turned towards hers, and to be able to say with passion: 'She is mine.'
> 'You danced extremely well,' said Xavière as they reached their table.

Simone was attracting other female suitors; she declined the offer of sex with Jollivet, who had also become an intimate friend. On her last visit, Jollivet had welcomed her in a black velvet dress with a bouquet of black flowers stuck in her belt, and announced: 'I want to seduce you.' Simone laughed and refused; but she accepted invitations to spend the weekend with Jollivet and Dullin at their pink-washed farmhouse at Ferrolles, near Crécy-en-Brie.

It was Olga's need for Simone which touched her so deeply. Alienated from her past, confused and insecure, Olga had come to depend upon, and finally to idolize her former teacher. For the first time, Simone felt the pleasure of giving: 'The smiles that I provoked on her countenance from time to time gave me a deep joy . . . I savoured the special charm of her features and gestures, her voice, her speech, and her special way of talking.' Ultimately the relationship became a sexual one, although, according to Sylvie Le Bon, physical relations took place 'très peu', very infrequently. Nevertheless, it seemed to Simone that she had found another Zaza.

14

Bewitched

> We fell, the Beaver and I, beneath the intoxicating spell
> of that naked, instant consciousness, which seemed only
> to feel, with violence and purity.
>
> Jean-Paul Sartre, *War Diaries*

'WHAT ARE YOU doing these days?' Nizan had enquired politely of Beauvoir, when he came to visit her and Sartre in their provincial exile one day in 1933.

'Working on my novel,' she replied.

'Oh? You mean – you made up the plot?'

Beauvoir was annoyed that Nizan doubted her creative abilities. Even the German refugee who came to teach her his language three times a week eyed the pages piling up on her desk with alarm. 'Normally,' he told her, 'people begin with short stories. When you've mastered technique, then it's time to tackle a novel.' Beauvoir smiled scornfully. She was taking Stendhal as her model. The book was to have a grand romantic sweep. Once again, her heroine was Zaza, rechristened Anne, and the story of her revolt against her *milieu* – essentially Beauvoir's own story – was set in the Limousin. She showed the first chapter to Sartre and Guille, who both gave their approval, and pressed on to the end. Her hero, 'Pierre Labrousse', was an actor-manager, like Dullin. But before she had even reached the dénouement, Beauvoir recognized that her second novel was also worthless.

After two years she abandoned it. Still she ached to express in fiction her own urgent problem: how to reconcile her desire for independence with her passionate longing for love.

Disheartened, Beauvoir turned to America for inspiration: Hemingway, Faulkner and John Dos Passos, whose *42nd Parallel* with its new technique of simultaneity intrigued Sartre. He and Beauvoir also liked Lytton Strachey's satire on Victorian pomposity, *Eminent Victorians*, and Céline's *Journey to the End of Night*, with its attack on war and colonialism. Dutifully they learnt whole passages of the book by heart and resolved to give up the 'marmoreal phrases' of classic French authors like Gide, Alain and Valéry. Sartre finally abandoned the pretentious style of *The Legend of the Truth*, and took Hemingway's *Fifty Grand* and *The Sun Also Rises* as the basis of the new 'rules' which he and Beauvoir decided to follow. Even Proust and Joyce seemed out of date:

> Hemingway's lovers were in love all the time, body and soul: actions, emotions and words were equally permeated with sexuality, and when they gave themselves to desire, to pleasure, it bound them together in their totality.

They dreamt of America, the promised land, their heads filled with a whirling montage of cowboys and cops, of skyscrapers and automobiles, of broken rhythms and silk-sheathed legs, as they played the records of Sophie Tucker and watched their favourite stars at the movies: Greta Garbo, Marlene Dietrich and Joan Crawford, as well as Mae West in *Lady Lou* and *I'm No Angel*. New York seemed to Sartre the artistic capital of the world. In *Nausea* he imagines an American songwriter 'with thick black eyebrows, who is suffocating with heat, on the twentieth floor of a New York skyscraper . . . He is sitting in shirt-sleeves at his piano; he has the taste of smoke in his mouth, and, vaguely, a ghost of a tune in his head. "Some of these days" . . . The moist hand picks up the pencil on the piano. "Some of these days, you'll miss me honey" . . . That's how it was born. It was the worn body of that Jew with coal-black eyebrows which it chose to give it birth . . . When I hear the song and I think it was that fellow who made it, I find his suffering and his sweat . . . moving.'

Antoine Roquentin listens to the record one more time. 'She sings. That makes two people who are saved: the Jew and the Negress . . . So you can justify your existence? Just a little.'

It is this glimpse of creation in a Manhattan loft that inspires

Roquentin to dream of writing a story which will be 'beautiful and hard as steel, and make people ashamed of their existence'. Salvation through art, Sartre's youthful ambition, seems more possible in the New World, with its size and freedom. The four notes of the saxophone, the silver screen, symbolize the art of the future. Already Sartre identifies with persecuted and dispossessed races, with Jews and American blacks, and the pain he hears in their music, just as he identified with the notion of the artist as an outsider, misunderstood by the mindless majority. The more he distances himself from classic French authors, the more he begins to see America as his spiritual home.

But he could not approve of its politics. Beauvoir and Sartre condemned the USA for its 'odious' capitalist oppression and racist lynchings. Like many European intellectuals they sympathized with Soviet Russia, especially when, in the early thirties, the influential writer André Gide announced his admiration for Communism, which the Left assumed would bring about the collapse of capitalism. Gide, preoccupied with the problem of personal freedom, looked towards the USSR for a system that would permit the artist to flourish. 'To free oneself is nothing; it's being free that is hard,' says his character Michel in *L'Immoraliste*. In his 1930 journal Gide had written:

> The only drama that interests me, and that I should always be willing to depict anew, is the debate of the individual with whatever keeps him from being authentic, with whatever is opposed to his integrity, to his integration. Most often the obstacle is within him.

By August 1934 Gide was writing enthusiastically to the Congress of Soviet Writers praising 'the Communist ideal [whose] task it is today to establish, in literature and art, a Communist individualism', and trustingly explaining that, 'Each artist is necessarily an individualist, however strong . . . his attachment to the Party.'

Socialist paradise, maybe, but Beauvoir found it hard to muster much enthusiasm for the literature of the USSR. She struggled with Mikhail Sholokhov's *And Quiet Flows the Don*, but failed to finish it. 'Thus, paradoxically, we were attracted by America, though we condemned its regime,' she wrote, 'while the USSR, the scene of a social experiment which we wholeheartedly admired, nevertheless left us quite cold.'

*

The couple preferred to pore over *Détective*, a murder-mystery magazine which reported the crimes rocking France: the Papin sisters, who had murdered their middle-class employers, Falcou, who burnt his mistress alive, and many others who demonstrated *l'infracassable noyau de nuit*, the indestructible heart of darkness, which, according to Breton, the surrealists, and even Freud, existed within us all. Breathlessly they followed the trial of Falcou, which took place in Rouen, eager to read of abnormal happenings behind lace curtains. Ever since he was young, Sartre had devoured *roman policiers*, but now he and Beauvoir studied crimes in real life, eager to learn all they could about the extreme and the aberrant.

During these years of apprenticeship, Sartre continued to hammer out his ideas. In London, at Easter 1933, the couple had had their first serious tiff in a grubby restaurant near Euston station. The absence of Parisian cafés, about which they had both complained bitterly after a bun in a Lyons Corner House, added heat to the argument. Beauvoir was astonished by the conventions of English life: women appeared in tea gowns at breakfast, men really *did* wear bowler hats and carry umbrellas. In his usual quest to see the *quartiers populeux*, Sartre dragged the Beaver down to the docks at Greenwich, while refusing to visit the British Museum or Oxford colleges. While she followed in the footsteps of Dickens and Shakespeare, he surveyed the unemployed and planned a visit to Birmingham. It was with ill grace, after a lonely afternoon before the statues in the Museum, that she sat down to an 'insipid, synthetic' English meal at the station café. A rift was developing. For Beauvoir, who believed their harmony was foreordained, repeating to herself, '*On ne fait qu'un*, we are as one,' it was horrifying to find that Sartre refused to bend to her wishes.

'*Je croyais à la verité*, I believed in the truth,' wrote Beauvoir. The question was how to discover it? Their usual method was for Sartre to propose a theory and Simone to criticize it, until they agreed on a revised version of the original. But in London, as Sartre's flights of fancy grew wilder, as he compared English cooking to the empiricism of Locke, and struggled to fit Britain into his embryonic schema, something snapped in the Beaver. His passion for generalization irritated her, as did his blind faith in phenomenology. His hypothesis was, she told him sternly, 'inadequate, tendentious, and based upon unsound principles'. After only twelve days in London, how could he glibly sum up the country? Reality was more than mere words: it was, she asserted, something inexplicable, impenetrable, whose mystery needed to be acknowledged. Sartre's riposte was sharp: for anyone whose task was to find a pattern in the world it was necessary to do more than merely observe and react; he must grasp the meaning of phenomena, '*et le fixer dans les phrases*, pin it down in words'.

Beauvoir gave way, just as she had done before at the Medici Fountain. Silently she repressed her doubts that, having rejected idealism, realism, even Freud, they had no system by which to synthesize their knowledge of people. Inspired by Jaspers, Sartre was proposing the idea of *mauvaise foi*, bad faith or self-deception: behaviour that people blamed on the unconscious mind, but which he thought was 'a lie to oneself'. Like Heidegger, he believed that lying is part of the human condition for *Mitsein*, the 'being-with' others in the world. Sartre went further, arguing that the liar must make a 'project of the lie' and completely comprehend the lie and the truth that he is altering: 'There is myself and there is myself in the eyes of the Other, that is, the deceiver and the deceived.' What changes everything with 'bad faith', he adds, is that 'it is from myself that I am hiding the truth'.

Sartre gives the example of a woman who goes out with a man for the first time; halfway through the evening he takes her hand. To leave the hand there is to consent to flirt; to withdraw it is to break the harmony of the moment. Her aim is to postpone a decision, and so she leaves her hand 'between the warm hands of her companion – neither consenting nor resisting – a thing. We shall say that this woman is in bad faith.'

Again, Beauvoir agreed. Her task, a congenial one, would be to help Sartre expose hypocrisy, which they considered a particularly unpleasant characteristic of the bourgeoisie. 'We rejoiced,' wrote Beauvoir, 'every time we discovered a new form of deception.' There was no unconscious or Freudian id; nor did the body count for anything. Even when Sartre was writhing with renal colic, he denied his pain to the doctor. When Beauvoir gave way to tears, she was simply being weak, he told her sternly.

On his return to France from Berlin in the late summer of 1934, Sartre gave her his new 'phenomenological' version of *Nausea* to read. There were still too many adjectives, but the Beaver had to admit that the book worked. Sartre had, indeed, seized Le Havre, *dans sa verité*, in its truth. Nevertheless, the quarrel in London marked a significant split between them: 'I put life first, in the here-and-now, while for Sartre writing came first.'

By October Beauvoir, in Rouen, was suffering from writer's block. She was not in the mood to attempt a new novel, nor, surprisingly, did she feel capable of tackling a philosophical subject, even though Sartre had lent her Hüsserl in the original German, and had been impressed by her quick grasp of his arguments. Her excuse was that she did not have an original mind:

> I did not regard myself as a philosopher. I was well aware that the ease with which I penetrated to the heart of a text stemmed, precisely, from my lack of originality.

Only an élite few were capable of getting results from that 'venture into lunacy' which creating a new philosophical system constituted. 'Women,' remarked Beauvoir, in a patriarchal aside, 'are not by nature prone to obsessions of this type.' She remained deeply imbued with the idea that only men such as Sartre, with his patience and audacity, could become philosophers.

Instead Beauvoir continued her self-imposed programme of study. By concentrating on the 'novelty and richness' of phenomenology, which led her to feel that she was at last drawing close to that elusive 'truth' they were both seeking, and indeed, moving on before Sartre to Heidegger, she was training herself to become the perfect editor. Nothing could have pleased Sartre more. The Beaver, with her quick, precise mind, would iron out the illogicalities in his own creative insights. She would even save him the trouble of reading Heidegger, the sorcerer's apprentice who in 1933 disowned his Jewish mentor and joined the Nazis.

*

Behind the cool prose of Beauvoir's second volume of memoirs, *The Prime of Life*, lies another story. Bewitched by Olga, the 'little witch' Ivich of Sartre's *Age of Reason*, Beauvoir had chosen love over literature. Olga despised application. In her incarnation as Xavière, she sneers at Françoise when she sits down at a certain hour to write, rather than waiting for inspiration, and mocks her self-discipline:

> How can anyone submit to living according to a plan, with time-tables and homework, as if they were still at boarding school? I'd rather be a failure!

Writers seemed no different from civil servants to her, putting in the hours at their desks. And when Xavière meets Elisabeth, a painter, in *She Came to Stay*, her reaction is the same:

'An effort is not a pretty thing to see. And when the effort miscarries, well then,' she sneered, 'it's ludicrous.'

'It's the same in every art,' said Elisabeth curtly. 'Beautiful things are not easily created. The more precious they are, the more work they require. You'll see.'

But Olga won't see. 'I'm not an intellectual,' she says proudly. Her values are those of youth: to live in the moment. She has an aristocratic disdain for bourgeois penny-pinching. When careful Mathieu in *The Age of Reason* counts his francs before deciding to push the boat out and buy Ivich a bottle of Krug, the only champagne she drinks, her reaction is to upend the bottle into the ice bucket and laugh in his face.

Olga stopped Beauvoir writing for a whole year. Her pallor, the blonde curls on a pale broad forehead, the high Slav cheekbones and slanted green eyes, signal an 'ethereal transparency', but her nose and mouth are 'extremely sensual'. Her face changes with her moods; at night it seems 'not to be composed of flesh, but rather of ecstasy'. She pushes the twenty-eight-year-old Simone to defy Sartre's relentless emphasis on the cerebral; like the young Simone, she flirts with the idea of prostitution, and enters cafés dressed as a prostitute.

The motif of prostitution reoccurs in *L'Invitée*, as in Beauvoir's memoirs. Olga and Simone are watching an Arab belly dancer in a night-club. As they cuddle up on the woollen cushions, watching the girl's undulating hips and stomach muscles ripple to the rhythm of the tambourine, 'Françoise' remarks: 'In the red-light district of Fez, I saw them dance naked; but that was a bit too anatomical.'

'I could perhaps try to be a prostitute,' replies Xavière, 'but I'm not experienced enough yet.'

Françoise laughs: 'That's a hard profession.'

Xavière roots through her bag. 'I've made a little sketch of you.'

The drawing is of a woman who looks like Françoise, leaning against a bar with her elbows on the counter. Her cheeks are green, her dress yellow. Underneath Xavière has written in large, purple lettering: 'The Road to Ruin'.

With hindsight, for she wrote the book during the war years, this is how Beauvoir may have viewed the beginning of her relationship with Olga, but the flirtatious dialogue of *L'Invitée* captures the heady excitement of those early days when she felt that she and the Russian refugee were Hemingway lovers for whom nothing was base. Olga was not simply a new toy; she assuaged Beauvoir's feelings of confusion, for by 1934 she was less sure of her future. 'What were we really, really?' she asks, of herself and the other teachers, like Colette and another teacher, Simone Labourdin, whom Marco would torment by allowing her to sleep in his bed without satisfying her frustrated caresses: 'No husband, no children, no home, social polish, and twenty-six years old?' Without Sartre as her 'guarantee', facing the failure of her writing hopes, trapped in the provinces, Beauvoir felt *dépaysé*, disoriented. At least, that was her excuse for what followed.

*

Sartre, on the other hand, was miserable, more *dépaysé* than Beauvoir had ever seen him. After a brief taste of freedom in Berlin, the door of his Norman prison slammed shut again in September 1934: 'I was recaptured by Le Havre and my life as a teacher – perhaps even more bitterly.' He had returned fatter – and balder – as the Beaver noticed with a shriek when they were walking together in the Tarn, and he suspected that, as his hair dropped out, his opportunities dwindled. Grimly he recalled at twenty-two noting in his diary a dictum from the Swiss author Töpffer: 'Whoever is not famous at twenty-eight must renounce glory for ever.' Now he was thirty, and quite unknown.

Paul Nizan, by contrast, was already something of a celebrity. A member of the Party for three years, he had recently returned from a year in the USSR, where he had attended the Congress of Revolutionary Writers with Malraux, Aragon and Jean-Richard Bloch. He arrived in Rouen, expensively dressed with a fine new umbrella over his arm, and regaled his old friends with tales of Russian banquets where vodka flowed like a river and caviar was piled high. 'It was a most corrupting period for me,' said the Communist, holding forth about the comforts of *wagon-lits* and magnificent Soviet hotels, and implying, with his accounts of contented peasants, that this luxury trickled down to the general populace. He talked about a new writer, an anarchist called Olesha, saying, 'Sartre *is* Olesha,' and wetting the appetites of the provincial teachers to see the USSR. But when Nizan talked of death, an obsession he shared with Beauvoir, he was forced to admit that Communism made no difference: in Russia, as in France, one died alone.

Marooned in Mudville, Sartre's only consolation during the long winter months was that Henri Delacroix, his former professor and an editor at the publisher Felix Alcan, commissioned him to write a book based on his prize-winning thesis, 'The Imagination in Psychological Life'. Abandoning Roquentin, Sartre returned to psychology, working at fever pitch as he researched the meaning of dreams and dream-imagery. He was studying chronaxia (the minimum time it took for a current to flow to excite nerve tissue), as part of a phenomenological probe into intentional awareness and the mind's capacity for conceiving nothing (*néantisation*), in order to establish whether, as Frantz Brentano claimed, consciousness is always consciousness *of* an object. By the end of the winter, he was exhausted.

In February 1935 an old Normalien friend, a psychiatrist named Daniel Lagache working at Sainte-Anne's hospital in Paris, proposed to Sartre that he be injected with mescaline, a new drug used in experimental psychology. There would be no danger. The drug would induce hallucinations, a useful experience for the author's research. The worst that could happen was that Sartre might 'behave rather oddly' for a few hours afterwards.

On the appointed day Sartre presented himself at the hospital. A few hours later he telephoned the Beaver. His voice was thick and muffled. He had been fighting with devil-fish. Half an hour later, when he arrived to meet Beauvoir and Mme Morel, he described how he had lain down in a dark room to receive the injection, whereupon objects metamorphosed into creatures, umbrellas became vultures, shoes turned into skeletons. Out of the corner of his eyes he saw great crabs and grimacing lobsters. In the train going home with Beauvoir he was listless and surly, disturbed by the orang-utan hanging from the ceiling.

Over the next few days Sartre sank into a severe depression. Lobsters pursued him, houses leered at him with grinning eyes, clocks turned into owls. Running by the docks, he stared at the black water, wondering what lay beneath it. 'A monster? A huge carapace, half embedded in the mud? A dozen pairs of claws slowly furrow the slime.' One afternoon, as he and the Beaver walked along the left bank of the Seine, he turned to her in terror: 'I know what the matter with me is,' he said. 'I'm on the verge of a chronic hallucinatory psychosis. In ten years I shall be completely mad.' Beauvoir tried to comfort him. 'Your only madness,' she told him, 'is believing that you're mad.' 'You'll see,' replied Sartre gloomily.

At the *vernissage* of Fernando Gerassi's paintings in Paris, Sartre sat in a corner, ignoring everyone. The Beaver took him to Mme Morel's doctor, who prescribed belladonna, an atropine stimulant, morning and evening. Somehow Sartre dragged himself back to the classroom, although by now his hatred of *les salauds* had become an obsession. Alone in his room, the crustaceans swarmed about him. He became scared of his own company, and begged Little Bost not to leave him.

Beauvoir, busy teaching in Rouen, grew impatient with Sartre and the passive way in which he accepted his condition. She ascribed it to his fear of growing up, of accepting that he had reached manhood, or the 'age of reason'. The doctors had told her that mescaline alone was not responsible for his breakdown, which had deep emotional roots. From her point of view, Sartre's collapse was treachery: 'Psychology was not my strong suit,' she wrote briskly. 'He had no right to indulge such whims when they threatened the fabric of our joint existence.'

Colette Audry, who had had a brief affair with Sartre, was also, so Beauvoir thought, 'indulging' in depression. Both seemed to her narcissistic and self-pitying. We would meet and ask each other 'about our respective madnesses. Until one day when Castor suddenly stopped on the sidewalk, slammed down her foot and shouted: "I've had enough. I see no one but nuts. I'm the only one who isn't mad. I too want to be crazy!" We all laughed: from then on, I was half-cured,' said Colette.

But in Le Havre, Sartre was still hallucinating. Exasperated, Castor sent her Peter Pan a substitute nurse, who had time on her hands: *la petite Russe*.

In March 1935, when Olga became his *infirmière*, Sartre craved excess. Life, which he had visualized as a tapestry-frame to be embroidered with bright threads, had become a soggy grey blanket. Massaging his head in front of the mirror, 'balding became the tangible sign for me of growing old . . . I felt as old as the hills.' His ant-like toil had brought little reward; Delacroix had rejected the second part of his book on the imagination, of which he was most proud. His confidence was at rock bottom.

From the beginning Olga laid down her terms. She was not to be touched. She was too beautiful, too blue-blooded for the likes of Sartre. 'I loathe being touched,' says Ivich in *The Age of Reason* when its protagonist, Mathieu, the philosophy teacher, takes her to a Gauguin exhibition and timidly tries to take her arm. Although Mathieu should not be mistaken for a portrait of the author, for Sartre considered him a negative model who used his freedom irresponsibly, he and Beauvoir borrowed freely from life. The boy who was likened to a toad was able to draw on his own painful experiences in creating character: '[Mathieu] liked to show her fine pictures, fine films, and fine things generally, because he was himself so unattractive.' While Ivich looks at the paintings, he stands beside her, 'ugly, persistent, and forgotten', admiring her fair curls pulled over her low forehead, which she calls 'my Kalmuck forehead', and her pale, girlish sensual face, 'like a moon between clouds'. He stares at her long tapering nails, brightly lacquered in the Chinese manner: 'Indeed, these awkward, fragile adornments made it plain that Ivich could have no use for her ten fingers.' Humbly he trots behind her, admiring her slender shoulders and straight round neck.

'I loathe being touched,' repeats Ivich. '"I have a horror of people who are not conscious of their bodies." Mathieu was conscious of his body, but rather as though it were a large and embarrassing parcel.'

The more Olga insisted on distance, the more Sartre craved union with this unattainable, voluptuous being:

> I was at the nadir at the time of my madness and my passion for O. . . . I entered a world that was blacker, but less insipid. As for O., my passion for her burned away my workaday impurities like a Bunsen-flame. I grew thin as a rake, and distraught . . . and then we fell, the Beaver and I, beneath the intoxicating spell of that naked, instant consciousness . . . I placed her so high then that, for the first time in my life, I felt myself humble and disarmed before someone, felt that I wanted to learn . . . Because of this passion, I began to have doubts about salvation through art. Art seemed pretty pointless faced with that cruel, violent, naked purity.

As Olga's face mutated from innocence to sensuality, so her moods fluctuated from rages even more dramatic than Simone's to dreamy, childlike states. Her wild, wilful character had an irresistible attraction for Sartre, who had already made one failed attempt, through drugs, to escape an intolerable situation.

In July 1935 Olga failed her medical preliminaries, and refused to resit. Her exasperated parents decided to bring her home, and discussed sending her away to a new boarding school. In the face of this crisis, Sartre and Beauvoir hatched a plot. They proposed taking Olga under their wing, just as Sartre had originally done with Simone, offering to coach her for a philosophy diploma. Beauvoir visited Victor and Marthe Kosackiewicz at their sawmill in Laigle, on a mission to persuade them to allow Sartre and herself to take charge of their daughter. Their consent was necessary, as Olga was still a minor. Beauvoir was so nervous that she arrived half a day early. The Kosackiewiczs, whose business was floundering, and who despaired of Olga, entertained the teacher to 'a Russian dinner' and innocently agreed to her terms. They were grateful, if a little bewildered, by Beauvoir's offer to support Olga, and even more surprised at her claims that she could turn their feckless daughter into a model student.

'I do not understand how, at twenty, she can accept the beautiful gift you want to give her,' wrote Marthe in August. 'I would have liked her to show more independence.' A detailed timetable was drawn up. But Olga never wrote so much as the first line of her first essay. After Christmas the philosophy lessons became history.

As a lady of leisure, however, which Olga felt to be her birthright, she blossomed. Her helplessness captivated Sartre and Beauvoir; her spontaneity banished their boredom: 'By her *maladresse à vivre*, her inability to cope with life, she claimed our help,' wrote Beauvoir. 'In return she freshened up a world we already found stale.'

Olga's intimacy with Beauvoir, which probably dated from September 1934, when she first took a room in Rouen, moved on to another, more debauched level when she joined her teacher in the notorious Hôtel du Petit Mouton. Simone had moved to the hotel, a favourite of Olga's Polish friends, on her recommendation, and from October 1935 paid for Olga's room also. Simone adored the picturesque three-storey Norman building situated in an alley off the rue de la République, with its exposed beams and leaded windows. It was divided into two parts with separate entrances. One side was for regular guests, mostly young couples whose nightly love-making, interspersed with beatings, Beauvoir could hear through the paper-thin walls; the other side was a bordello. The establishment was presided over by a fat old madam who lived in private quarters in the middle. That October, Zuorro, also appointed to a post in Rouen, joined the two women at Le Petit Mouton; he chose to move into the brothel.

The gay troika that ensued was a merry one. For Beauvoir, who had not lost her taste for the gutter, Le Petit Mouton, with its tarts and pimps and fist fights, provided endless entertainment. She had often resented sacrificing her adolescence to academic toil; now Olga enabled her to live out all her fantasies. The hotel was even more squalid than the Rochefoucauld. In bed, after a hasty supper of ham eaten from its greaseproof paper wrapper, Beauvoir would wake to the sound of rustling as mice dragged the wrapper from the waste-paper basket into which she had tossed it. At night she felt tiny paws pass over her face, although during the evening, when Simone and Olga played chess and drank cherry brandy, the rodents remained behind the wainscoting – not that the pair would have noticed. So drunk was Olga one evening that she rolled down the stairs and spent the night asleep at the bottom, until one of the tenants kicked her awake.

Marc was soon thoroughly at home. When not joking with the

patronne, or entertaining young men, he would invite Simone and Olga up to his room to listen to records, or to the studio to hear him practise arias. Sometimes he and Olga went out together; they made a striking couple, he dark, she fair, as they strode down the street holding, on a short leash, Marc's wolfound. On one occasion Marc seized Olga by the waist and began dancing in the road, singing lustily as they whirled past a group of onlookers; suddenly the teacher noticed one of his pupils, accompanied by his parents, staring at him. '*Merde!*' exclaimed Marc; but he kept tight hold of Olga. '*Tant pis*, keep going,' he whispered, and he and the little Russian continued to waltz down the street.

Sometimes Marc pretended that Olga was his sister. Once the couple lured a captain up to her room and plied him with whisky, tipping their own glasses on to the bed; the plan was that Marc would disappear, leaving the captain alone with the pretty 'sister', whom he would attempt to rape. She would scream, Marc would return and demand money with menaces. But the plan miscarried and Marc was forced to sob that poverty obliged him to pimp for his sister. Sometimes the gay trio would jump aboard a boat, where Marc talked his way into the crews' quarters and brought the most attractive crew member back to Le Petit Mouton. In dockside bars they drank cassis and ate apricot ices, while Marc hummed Bach or Beethoven. Beauvoir had never felt more alive, as her feelings for Olga reached new heights of intensity and, in the privacy of a hotel peopled by transient lovers, she found the freedom to express them.

Sartre was feeling left out. He took every opportunity to join Simone and Olga in Rouen. Olga took him to the Café Victor to hear the gypsy fiddler or the all-female orchestra. Down at the Cintra Bar they took turns to play poker dice, and, in Colette Audry's absence, the two teachers and their young protégée decamped to her flat, where Beauvoir cooked spaghetti and listened to jazz records as Sartre made up impromptu plays for Olga. When they ran out of money, Beauvoir pawned the gold brooch her grandmother had given her, as well as Colette's gramophone. Sartre, too, was resurrecting student life.

As he watched Olga flirting with Marc, Sartre's attraction to his pretty *infirmière* grew. He exerted himself to entertain her. During the long afternoons in the cafés of Rouen, he told Olga stories and sang to her, watching as she sat, gracefully twirling her tall glass of *crème de menthe frappé* and smoking a cigarette. The smell of her hair reached his nostrils, with its particular odour of cake and vanilla-flavoured sugar from the egg yolks she used to wash it:

A violent and undefined desire had taken possession of him: a desire to *be* for one instant that distracted consciousness so pervaded by its own odour, to feel those long slender arms from within, to feel, at the hollow of the elbow, the skin of the forearm clinging like a lip to the skin of the arm, to feel that body and all the indiscreet little kisses it so ceaselessly imprinted on itself.

No longer did he desire to be one with Simone; he wanted only to merge into oneness with his little witch.

Olga's company worked its magic. The lobsters receded, leaving behind a 'vast empty beach . . . all ready to be filled with new obsessional fantasies'. Sartre began to study Olga's every twitch and blink, in order to discover whether she loved him. 'He wisely refrained from overwhelming her with endless questions and theories, though,' wrote Beauvoir bitterly, 'he was not so considerate with me.' Had he scored against Marc? Did Olga prefer him? Sartre became determined to usurp Marc's place as head of the gang at Le Petit Mouton, and to conquer her, although, claimed Beauvoir unconvincingly, the climax he desired had no physical dimension.

The couple spent every waking moment discussing Olga. Their friends were amazed at the power she had over them. 'She became Rimbaud, Antigone, every *enfant terrible* that ever lived, a dark angel judging us from her diamond-bright heaven,' said Beauvoir. 'But she was powerless to prevent herself being devoured.' Finally, Sartre demanded that they form a threesome. Simone felt rising panic: everything for which she had fought and struggled was threatened, but, reluctantly, she agreed.

Henceforth their first priority would be 'to build a future for her and for us: instead of a couple, from now on we would be a trio'.

15

The Trio

Each conscience seeks the death of the Other.

Hegel, epigraph to *L'Invitée*, 1943

THE SPLIT HAD become a chasm. Sartre's infatuation for Olga was dividing him from Simone. And Olga, her black pearl, was no longer hers; the Kobra was stealing her away, with no thought for the Beaver's misery and pain. The jealousy Simone de Beauvoir felt was murderous.

The pact of '29, the basis of her very existence, was under threat. It was Olga who was 'necessary', Simone who was pushed to the contingent margin. Waves of anger washed over her, and she, for so long the stable one in the relationship, began to doubt her own hold on reason.

A recurrent fear was that she was turning into her mother, Françoise, with her shrieks and *criailleries*. It is no coincidence that Beauvoir chose her mother's name for the protagonist in *L'Invitée*, the story of a girl, called Xavière, whom the Olympian couple, Pierre Labrousse, producer of *Julius Caesar*, and his girlfriend, Françoise, invite into their shared life only for her to destroy it: 'The anguish that suddenly overcame her was so violent that she wanted to scream. It was as if the world had suddenly become a void . . . Pierre and Françoise's love did not exist. There was nothing but an infinite accumulation of meaningless moments, nothing but a chaotic seething of flesh and thought whose termination was death.'

Thoughts of ageing and death preoccupied her. Her head was swollen 'with water and the night, it became enormous, and so heavy that it pulled her towards the abyss: sleep or death or madness – a bottomless pit into which she would disappear for ever'. Desolately she compared herself to Olga, in her blue dress or her new red and white striped blouse, the smooth folds of her hair framing her face, smiling at Sartre in a café; Beauvoir stood outside on the pavement, exiled, an outcast not only from Paris, but from the Sartrean world they had created together. She was only nine years older than Olga, but it seemed a lifetime; she was drawing nearer to forty, the threshold of old age. Forty is the age at which women lose the freshness of youth, thinks Françoise, surveying the actresses around her at a party: they may keep their figures, or even the firm outline of their faces, but it is an embalmed youth:

> They were ageing underneath, they would go on ageing for a long time before the glaze cracked; and then one day, suddenly, this flawless shell, grown thin as tissue paper, would crumble into dust. Then the effigy of an old woman would emerge, complete in every detail, with wrinkles, large brown moles, swollen veins, and knotted fingers.

Beauvoir's relationship with Olga had given her the illusion that she, too, was young. Like Sartre, the adult world aroused loathing in her; rather than compromise with it, he had taken acid and had a mental breakdown, while as for Simone: 'I frequently told myself, weeping, that growing older meant falling into decay.' The cult of youth, with its emphasis on freedom and revolt, would remain with them all their lives; for now, staying up all night with Olga, sharing glimmering, iridescent *nuits blanches* with their Lucy in the sky with diamonds, their black angel in her *ciel de diamant*, drinking, dancing, refusing to eat, rejecting any restraint or responsibility, allowed the couple to fool themselves that they too, were still adolescents, rather than the civil servants they had 'shamefacedly' become. Together they created a myth around Olga, drinking from her elixir of youth and beauty as they spent alternate, competing evenings with her. In the Easter holidays they took her to Paris, to the Dôme and the Viking, to see Charlie Chaplin in his first talkie, *Modern Times*; they introduced her to Simone Jollivet, who said that she was a child of Lucifer; Poupette began painting her portrait. And all the time the pressure on Olga grew. The 'silken cocoon' of words and smiles the couple wove around her seemed at times to show that the trio was 'a dazzling success'. But she was caught in its silver threads. That Easter, Olga began to self-harm.

*

Teetering on the edge of the abyss, Beauvoir found consolation in work. After a year off, she had finally taken the advice of her German teacher and begun writing short stories. Katherine Mansfield remained her model, as she did for Sartre who, on a cruise to Norway with his mother and stepfather in July 1935, had decided to write 'short stories of a similar kind to those of K. Mansfield', by which he meant escaping the traditional logic of the form in order to show life's 'motley chaos'. He was still excited by Maurice Barrès's idea that cities held signs and secrets: Roquentin before the public garden was, he said, like himself before a Neapolitan alleyway: 'things were making signs to him and it was necessary to decipher them'. It was the secret meaning of objects that he wanted to capture, but he lost the first story he wrote in Norway, 'The Midnight Sun', when it dropped out of the pocket of his jacket during his walking holiday in the Tarn with the Beaver. His second, 'Dépaysement' (Disorientation), about a visit to a Naples brothel, would reveal his feelings about the titillating nature of girl-on-girl sex as foreplay for the waiting male, a prelude to heterosexual union. 'It didn't come off at all,' said Sartre of his story; nor, so far, had his attempts to seduce Olga, who, to his annoyance, after his gratifying experience with the Lunar Woman, was putting up a determined resistance.

Eventually Sartre gave up his original aim, finding that the 'inherent logic' of the short story genre led him to write the classically shaped 'Le Mur' and 'La Chambre'. Beauvoir, too, was writing rapidly. In the spring of 1936 the trio often took off on a Sunday to Saint-Adrien, at the foot of the chalk cliffs beside the Seine. There they discovered the Aero Bar, so named because it was in a field beside an aerodrome, where at night people danced *en plein* air under strings of coloured lights hung from the trees. We 'behaved as if we were twenty again', recalled Simone. While Sartre intensified his courtship of Olga, Simone hid her irritation by taking herself off into a corner to work on stories of her own adolescence, ironically entitled *Primauté du spirituel* (*When Things of the Spirit Come First*). She was tired of phenomenological tricks, of trying to find the exact words to describe the taste of cassis, or the curve of a cheek, tired of playing gooseberry to

Sartre and Olga, over whom he now demanded exclusivity. 'I therefore determined not to allow Olga too important a place in my life, since I could not cope with the disorder she had sown there . . . *Je l'aimais de tout mon coeur*, I loved her with all my heart . . . but the truth was not in her. Nor had I any intention of yielding up to her the sovereign position that *I* had always occupied, in the very centre of the universe.'

Her tactics didn't work. Beauvoir could not bear to be at odds with Sartre: 'My need to agree with him on all subjects was so great that I could not see Olga through any eyes but his.' 'Ivich' had cast her spell, and the Beaver could only watch in despair as her lover fought her for the little witch's favours, and usurped her place in Olga's heart. For the first time since she had discovered in Sartre her intellectual double, Beauvoir had the terrifying experience of feeling that she was the Other. But what could she do? She had agreed with Sartre that '*les rapports humains sont perpétuellement à inventer*', that human relationships are to be constantly reinvented, that no particular kind is a priori especially privileged or beyond the pale. And she herself had fallen in love with Olga's 'authenticity', that quality they both considered the essential virtue. Beauvoir could no longer fight. One of the saddest lines in *L'Invitée* is when Françoise concedes victory: 'Henceforth, Xavière belonged to Pierre.' As for their own love, it has become a tomb full of dust and ashes, an 'old corpse' dragging at their heels.

In 1960 Beauvoir would contend that she had distorted the character of Olga in her novel by adding a streak of 'sly and indomitable egotism' in order to justify Françoise's murder of Xavière in the final pages, an ending which the author later regretted, as it was lambasted by the critics. 'When I created Xavière, all I kept of Olga – and even that I darkened in tone – was the myth we had created around her,' she wrote. But murder was in Beauvoir's heart. She hated this new coquettish Olga who flirted outrageously with Sartre, and she hated Sartre even more for preferring Olga to herself. It was he who had created the trio, he who deserved the blame; the rift between them began to poison the very air Beauvoir breathed as, like a capricious child, Olga quarrelled with Sartre, made up, cut Simone dead, kissed her, hugged her, begged her forgiveness.

To both Simone and Olga, Sartre had become a snake, insinuating himself between the two women. 'He's a real little asp, hissing and poisonous,' says Xavière to Françoise. When he tells Xavière that she is in love with him, she is scared. 'I'm afraid,' she says, but Françoise reassures her: 'Pierre is a little snake, but his hiss is worse than his bite, and besides, we'll tame him . . .' The frisson between the two women undoubtedly titillated Sartre. Significantly, in 'Dépaysement', which the Kobra wrote in the summer of 1936, when the hothouse atmosphere of the trio was at its most stifling, the protagonist, Audry, asks to see a lesbian *tableau vivant* when he visits a Neapolitan brothel. Audry, like Sartre a tourist in Italy, is excited when Renato, his guide, offers him eight beautiful women who will replicate 'the positions of Pompeii' for a hundred francs.

'That's too much.'

'You can ask for four or even just two.'

'Two will be enough. How much for two?'

'Let's see . . . forty francs.'

'Still too much.'

'Well, you could pay thirty,' says Renato. 'I'll tell *la patronne* that you're a student. She'll show you eight women, and you can choose the two most beautiful.'

They stop at the door of the brothel, and Audry hands over ten francs, which Renato promptly puts in his pocket before ringing the bell inside and disappearing inside to negotiate with the madam.

The positions of Pompeii, thinks Audry dreamily, are something to seen. They must be like *la mère Poulard*'s omelette at Mont Saint-Michel, a speciality of Neapolitan brothels.

'Twenty francs,' says Renato, interrupting Audry's reverie. 'She says it's not much, she's not happy. But I said that you were a student. *Vous pouvez monter.*'

Alone with the old Sicilian procuress, Audry waits patiently. 'Eight women,' he repeats to himself, 'eight women are going to come in and I shall choose the two most beautiful.' But only two women appear. Renato has lied to him.

The first woman is not too bad, but the second is old and fat, with a blemished skin: 'She can't be far off fifty.' Audry stares at her enormous breasts straining against a black satin bra, and her naked belly.

Arms folded, he watches as the prostitutes listlessly perform with an ivory dildo.

'*You speak English?*' asks the younger one.

'*No,*' replies Audry.

He adds, '*Ich spreche Deutsch.*'

'*Deutsch, nein, nein,*' says the fat woman, as her hips move rhythmically back and forth.

The young woman presses her stomach in Audry's face.

'*Lécher, lécher,* lick, lick,' she says.

Embarrassed, Audry grabs hold of a leg.

'Tongue, tongue,' she repeats. 'Lick.'

Finally, shutting his eyes, Audry forces himself to lick the oiled and perfumed skin. The two women sit on each side of him on the banquette. 'They want to undress me,' he thinks, shivering with embarrassment, but, as they twist their arms round his necks and shake their tambourines under his nose, he realizes that it is money they want.

The Sicilian madam stands up abruptly.

'*Voulez-vous monter avec Mademoiselle?*'

'*Non*,' says Audry, fleeing.

'How was it?' asks Renato.

'*Très beau*,' says Audry.

Sartre had discovered the delights of voyeurism.

*

The stakes were raised when another player entered the game. Jacques-Laurent Bost, Sartre's pupil at Le Havre, had grown into a tall, strikingly handsome young man, with a charming smile and thick, black hair that flopped over his face. He had become the unhappy teacher's intimate friend and companion, and, perforce, had seen much of Olga. He had also caught the attention of Beauvoir, who never forgot her first meeting with him.

> He was nineteen years old, with a dazzling smile and a most princely ease of bearing . . . He too, in his way, personified youth for us. He possessed the casual grace of youth, so casual that it bordered on insolence . . . He was both quick-witted and droll . . . Bost had made conquests everywhere in Rouen. Marco devoured him with his eyes. Olga stayed out with him all one night; they drank a whole bottle of Cinzano as a special treat and woke up at dawn to find themselves lying in the gutter . . .

Beauvoir, too, found herself eating Little Bost with her eyes:

> The moment he pushed through the door of the Métropole, with that half-bashful, half-aggressive air, I felt myself drawn to him.

That afternoon Sartre went off with Olga, and Beauvoir went for a walk with Bost, who entertained her with stories of his professor's fits of anger in class. These, he suspected, were not mere expressions of frustration at life at the chalkface so much as the outbursts of a man suddenly shocked into consciousness of life's absurdity. Sartre would walk into the classroom 'with a nauseated expression', Bost remembered, 'chew his nails and, every now and then, glare at his pupils and, after a silence of forty-five seconds, would roar: "All these faces, and not one single glimmer of intelligence!"' Most of the class were terrified, but Bost could barely stifle his laughter.

Like Olga, Bost was exploited by the couple in their fiction. Featuring as 'Gerbert' in *She Came to Stay*, he was also the model, as Beauvoir acknowledged, for Boris in Sartre's *Age of Reason*: 'Sartre painted and russianized a portrait of "Little Bost" at least as he appeared to us at the time.' Neither she nor Sartre had a high opinion of Bost's intelligence, however. While he was constructing 'tireless spotlights' with the Beaver in 1929, Sartre recalled in 1940, he was dreaming of another man, who'd be 'handsome, hesitant, obscure, slow and upright in his thoughts', but with a silent, spontaneous grace. 'I saw him, for some reason, as a worker and hobo in the Eastern USA', who had the capacity to boil with obscure rages, or faint with tenderness. 'My American worker (who resembled Gary Gooper) could do and feel all that.' Sartre pictured his hobo sitting on a railway embankment, waiting for a cattle-truck, tired and dusty – 'and I should have liked to be *him*. I even invented, with the Beaver, a charming little character called *Petit Crâne*, Little Head-high . . . I finally encountered Little Head-high: to wit, Little Bost.'

Beauvoir was even more impressed with this French Gary Gooper than Sartre, although later she, too, wrote witheringly about his limited intelligence: 'He did not possess an original mind, and in any case, he was so afraid of saying something stupid, as he put it, that even if an idea did pass through his head he made every effort to conceal the fact.' Jacques Bost, younger brother of the novelist Pierre Bost, youngest of the ten children born to the Pastor and his wife, and his mother's favourite, was insecure, and did not get on with his father. Like Olga, he exhibited a 'narcissistic fragility', and was overwhelmed by the authority and brilliance of the two professors, the 'royal couple', as Bost dubbed them. The two vulnerable teenagers were drawn to each other; although Olga would later fake her age on her marriage certificate, giving her date of birth as 6 November 1917, instead of 6 November 1915, in order to appear younger than Bost, who was born on 6 May, 1916, she was in fact five months the elder.

After a year, Sartre was finding Olga's stubborn resistance to him intolerable. His desire for her 'nymph-like' body, the 'nymph-like character' of a young girl, as he and the Beaver described it, in a phrase borrowed from the preface to Hope Mirrlees's novel *The Counterplot*, grew more frenzied. Sitting at the Café Victor in Rouen, Olga, who found the tubby, balding teacher unattractive, although she enjoyed his largesse, continued to hold him at bay: a man's body is 'too highly spiced, too rich, too strong-tasting to be capable of being desired immediately', she explained. 'The charm of a woman or young boy is disclosed at once, whereas long familiarity and particular attention is needed before a man's is revealed.' Sartre understood, or thought he did: 'I've always thought, when taking delight in kissing fresh, tender lips, of the singular impression my own must be making – all rough and smelling of tobacco.' But as the months went by, Olga began to run out of excuses.

The tension rose when Beauvoir received news that in October 1936, despite her scandalous record at Rouen, the authorities would be transferring her – and Marc – to a new post in Paris. Sartre was offered a job in Lyon, preparing pupils for the École Normale entrance exam, but Lyon was far away, and he was afraid that the new position would be regarded as a promotion and that he would face another lengthy exile. Instead, he accepted a *baccalauréat* class in Laon, only 150 kilometres north-east of Paris, in the hope of returning to the capital the following year.

The ambivalence of Beauvoir's feelings towards Olga, accomplice and foe, grew increasingly profound. She veered between love and hate. Although she felt 'shut out' by Olga's 'spite', totally dispossessed, floating in the void, her throat so tight she couldn't swallow, although she dreaded Olga tagging along with her and Sartre on their travels, and wrote that when she thought of the trio as a long-term project, '*J'étais terrifiée,*' she was nevertheless determined to bring the girl to Paris. She and Sartre would continue to support her, and help her train as an actress. The idea intrigued Olga, unlike Beauvoir's previous suggestions for employment as a secretary or beautician, although her contempt for the idea of any sort of effort continued undiminished. In *L'Invitée*, Xavière has a new ally when she laughs at Françoise, conscientiously working on her short stories:

> 'It seems queer to sit down every day at one's desk and write line after line of sentences,' said Xavière. 'I admit that people should write, of course,' she added quickly. 'There's something voluptuous about words. But only when the spirit moves you.'

When Françoise tries to justify herself, Pierre smiles maliciously. His smile is aimed at Françoise as well as at Xavière, and his disloyalty is shocking.

> Xavière never batted an eyelash. 'It becomes home-work,' she said and she laughed indulgently. 'But then, that's the way you do things, you turn everything into a duty.'

Beauvoir was deeply wounded. Sartre and Olga were in triumphant collusion against her; they considered her severe and dutiful. They were making her into an object, the despised Other.

But Olga was in a dilemma. Her contempt for work of any kind meant that she had become a 'a charity case', parasitic upon the couple and their money. The trio was unstable and mutable, its balance of power ever shifting as Olga, the 'guest' in the relationship, began, in turn, to find herself as powerless before the implacable duo as a butterfly pinned to a board. They had abused the teacher/pupil relationship and annexed her to themselves. Now they held out seductive promises of a glittering career on the stage: 'You can rely on us,' Pierre tells Xavière. 'We have enough will-power for three.' '*Hélas*,' says Xavière, smiling. 'You've a frightening amount.' Sitting opposite the two of them, she feels confused at the 'twins' complicity: 'You both have so many ideas in common,' says Xavière. 'I'm never sure which of you is speaking, or to whom to reply.'

'It was an awful experience for Olga,' remembered Colette Audry. 'They made her the invited one, the third one in their relationship, and she had to spend most of her time defending herself. The major complicity was between them, and they required that she bend to their wishes. The poor girl was too young to know how to defend herself really.' Beauvoir also later acknowledged that culpability lay with herself and Sartre: '[Olga's] role was . . . that of a child – a child up against an adult couple united by an unfailing complicity.' But Beauvoir, too, felt helpless; they had set in motion a machine which was running out of control.

*

Insulated from the outside world, Sartre and Beauvoir barely noticed political developments in France. Nizan's angry message to his *petit camarade* in *Le Cheval de Troie* that he should join the struggle of the Left fell on deaf ears. Remembering Sartre's distaste for the masses when they had been at L'École and felt themselves to be supermen superior to the common crowd, Nizan made Lange – his fictional portrait of Sartre – the critical spectator of an anti-fascist meeting in the place du Théâtre in Villefranche: 'The crowd was moving, it had a heart, a life: he scorned it, but at the same time he felt envious of it, and he hated it for being enviable.' In the novel 'Lange' finally becomes a fascist, an unjust conclusion to draw from Sartre's detachment. 'I was well aware that the *salauds* were in power, everywhere, and that we risked being engulfed in a vicious fascism,' he later claimed. Maybe. Yet Nizan had grounds for calling Sartre a traitor. In 1936, during the demonstrations on behalf of the Popular Front, the united Left, Sartre, despite rejoicing in its victory, did not descend from *le trottoir*. Nor did he vote. On the night of 3 May he and Beauvoir stood in a square in Rouen listening to the loudspeakers announcing the results. Sartre, recalled Beauvoir, shrugged his shoulders contemptuously at the political aspirations of left-wing intellectuals. The Communists might have increased their parliamentary representation from nine to seventy-three deputies, but as far as he was concerned, speeches, manifestos, propaganda, were all a waste of time. Nor did Beauvoir have any regrets over the fact that, as a woman, she could not vote. Even had she been able, she would never have bothered to go to the polls.

There were widespread strikes in France that year, and Beauvoir recorded proudly that she and Sartre gave all they could to the collections for picketing workers. But when Jacques Bost urged them to join him at the celebrations for Bastille Day, 14 July, they refused. There was no need to watch the marching masses. Mussolini had invaded Ethiopia in October 1935, Hitler had occupied the Rhineland in March 1936, and in France itself there were street battles between Croix de Feu fascists and left-wing militants, but Sartre and Beauvoir believed they could count on the Popular Front to 'save the peace'. Nor did they feel cause for concern over reports that, on 13 July, General Franco had landed in Spain. The Spanish Popular Front had won a landslide victory for the Republic the previous March, and the defeat of the rebels seemed assured.

It was with a sigh of relief that, in July, the Beaver saw Olga go home to her parents in Laigle. She had failed even to sit her teacher's diploma. In the final weeks of the school year, she and Sartre had quarrelled and had stopped seeing each other. Beauvoir's heart had lifted, as she and Olga re-established their old intimacy and once again spent their evenings with Marc, 'slumming' it down at the docks with the sailors and staying up till four in the morning. Olga spoke fluent

English, and the two women got into conversation with a Norwegian who asked their names.

'*Elle s'appelle Castor*,' said Olga, pointing at the Beaver.

'Then you must be Pollux,' exclaimed the sailor. Henceforth whenever he saw them he ran up shouting, '*Voilà Castor et Pollux!*'

The reconciliation between the two women had been achieved at Sartre's expense, and the Kobra was hissing and angry; Beauvoir, on the other hand, was shaky but calm. There was no chance of Olga 'tagging along' on holiday with them, and Sartre was taking her to Rome.

*

To see Naples was the aim of this, their second visit to Mussolini's Italy. Poupette had not liked the city, writing: 'Naples: just big, filthy houses. But filth alone is not enough.' 'And the good Beaver and I honestly had to agree that, generally speaking, filth is not enough,' wrote Sartre to Olga, in a monumental, thirty-six-page letter, which showed that Beauvoir's sense of relief was ill-founded. Physically present with her, her companion's mind was, nevertheless, on the little Russian, and it was his passion for Olga which provoked this extraordinary, *séduisant* portrait of Naples in its 'swarthy, gilded filth'. Overwhelmed by the pagan promiscuity of the city, where life on the street presented a panorama of naked urchins, nursing mothers, families eating and sleeping under rows of washing hanging between candy-pink houses, the whole permeated by 'nauseating odours', Sartre could barely believe the beauty of the men in their white linen suits, or of the plump women, 'much fatter than the Romans, with hair black as night, thick, bestial lips, and a look of brutish sensuality'. Beauvoir was also entranced. 'The Beaver was in heaven,' Sartre told Olga. 'She wanted to follow each little street, and I was hard at my map trying to keep a set direction for our walk.' He felt responsible, for 'We take turns as tour leaders, and it was my turn in Naples.' But he did not get lost. Instead, he tasted his first pizza, although the Beaver demanded spaghetti. In *Dépaysement*, Audry, the French tourist, presses his nose against the window of the pâtisserie Caflisch. Like Proust, he finds that, '*un gâteau, c'est plein de sens*', a cake is full of meaning. Spanish cakes crumble into dust when you bite them, Arabic cakes are as greasy as an oil lamp, German cakes remind him of shaving cream, but Italian cakes are enchanting, porcelain miniatures which melt in the mouth.

Pompeii, however, disappointed the eager tourist in his quest to find the 'real Rome' behind the classical stereotype. The frescoes of gods and goddesses seemed only tired symbols of a dead civilization. But a day or two later, Sartre managed to give Simone the slip. As she departed, guidebook in hand, to view Amalfi, Ravello and Sorrento, he remained in Naples, determined finally to penetrate the city's secrets. Alone that night, he fell into conversation with two Neapolitans who promised to show him, in real life, the 'positions of love' he had seen in the Villa of Mysteries. The gullible tourist believed them; Pompeii had retained a greater hold over Sartre than he knew, despite the night of bathos which ensued. When 'Audry' emerges into the street, Renato, his guide, places his mandoline on his knees, and begins to sing:

> *Tutta Napule . . .*
> *Tutta Napule . . .*

Sartre had found his new *querencia*.

*

It is September 1936, and Beauvoir has taken a room in the Royal Bretagne hotel on the rue de la Gaîté, the street of theatres on the west side of Montparnasse cemetery. It's not an attractive room, but she doesn't give a fig, for now all Paris is hers again, with its beloved, familiar streets, squares and cafés. She's hugging herself with joy, confident that, while she's alone in Paris with Olga and Sartre is banished to Laon, the trio will die a death.

Like Beauvoir, who is teaching at the Lycée Molière in the suburb of Passy, Marc has a new teaching job in Paris, at the Lycée Louis-le-Grand; he has moved into a slightly more expensive hotel a few hundred metres from the Beaver, at the end of rue Delambre, on the north side of the cemetery. Only the boulevard Edgar-Quinet separates the two friends. Little Bost, meanwhile, studying at the Sorbonne for his teacher's diploma, is renting a room from his brother, Pierre, who has an apartment on the place Saint-Germain-des-Prés, right beside the venerable church of that name, and opposite the Deux Magots, on the west of the square. Next door, on boulevard Saint-Germain, is the Café de Flore. But it is the Dôme, at 108 boulevard du Montparnasse, on the street where she had lived as a child, which Beauvoir and Sartre now make their headquarters. Every morning, unless she has to go to the *lycée*, Simone strolls up rue Delambre to breakfast there, moving into one of the booths at the far end of the café to begin writing, encouraged by the murmur of conversation in foreign tongues – for many refugees come to the café – to make the first marks on the blank sheet of paper before her.

It was unthinkable to 'abandon' Olga in Laigle, wrote Simone in *The Prime of Life*. Olga agreed. When her parents forbade her to join Beauvoir, she defied them, jumping on the train to Paris and moving into the Royal Bretagne with her former teacher; but there was no longer any pretence at taking lessons. Olga began working as a waitress in a café-cum-bookshop on the boulevard Saint-Michel. Castor had already rejected the idea of finding a flat of her own, preferring to *jouer a la bohème* in a hotel; now her Pollux had joined her. Their love bloomed: in the evenings the two women visited Le Sélect, where they held hands among the crop-haired lesbians, who sported ties and monocles.

Sartre's fury at his exclusion can only be imagined. He was the only member of the 'family', as the group of students whom the couple had gathered around them came to be known, not to be in Paris. Twice a week Castor crossed the Seine to meet Sartre's train from Laon, an hour from Paris, at the Gare du Nord, but it was no substitute for living in the capital. His mental state had become agitated, the Beaver noticed, towards the end of their stay in Italy; in Venice they had decided to stay up all night, wandering beside the canals and through the silent piazzas, but the *nuit blanche* was not a success. All through the night a lobster followed Sartre.

Alone in Laon, he again reworked 'Melancholia'. More of an outsider than ever, he was deprived anew of the 'collective life' which alone alleviated his anxiety. In May 1971 Sartre explained his powerful need to live in a group, with

> Friends, comrades, in situations where I could be myself and a stranger simultaneously, where each of us had a voice, hence an identity, but where decisions were collective, made by the group, six, eight, ten individuals whose individual will fused into the collective will . . . In such circumstances, anxiety-ridden folk, like me, for I was always anxious, become less so.

School, the École, the French Institute, had made him an insider. There he experienced the male comradeship for which even the most intimate relationship with a woman was no real substitute: even the 'life-long relationship with Castor, which was much more precious to me than my past, rather vague relationships with ten or so comrades . . . wasn't the same thing'. Making friends with his students in Le Havre had allowed him to experience a new 'collectivity' – 'which is probably why I hung out with them so much'. Robbed even of this succour, 'I could no longer count on a life without the terrible weight of existence staring me in the face.' Never had Sartre, prisoner of the classroom, felt more like Roquentin, who returns from six years in the Far East only to experience a startling epiphany: *le voyage est inutile*. Travel is a waste of time. Six years of travel have been the big sleep, *six ans de sommeil*. The curling photos Roquentin retrieves from his shoe box to show the Autodidact all look the same. *C'est tout pareil*. He might as well tear them up, or throw them in the fire. Swaying with nausea, his head spinning, ready to vomit at *la viscosité*, the slimeyness and stickiness of existence which sucks you in and traps you in holes, in voids, in quick-sands, Roquentin is paralysed with terror. He can go neither forwards nor backwards. As Sartre confided to his interviewer, the lobsters 'represented both fear of the future and loss of the past'. His rite of passage to manhood was proving as agonizing as walking on coals.

Nizan finally took pity on 'Lange' and sent the third draft of the manuscript to his friend Gaston Gallimard's publishing firm, where it was passed on to a reader. The report was negative. Sartre received a note from Jean Paulhan rejecting the book; it was his second rejection by Gallimard, who had turned down 'The Legend of the Truth' in 1930. Never had the crouching figure in Dürer's engraving so accurately represented Sartre's mood of despair. Melancholia represented more than four years' work, and both Sartre and Beauvoir considered that it succeeded as a metaphysical novel; but now their friends began to be influenced by its rejection. Mme Morel and Guille began to hint that the book was, perhaps, 'a little tedious, and clumsily written'. Depressed even further by their poor opinion of his ability, Sartre decided not to submit the book elsewhere.

His unbalanced, disoriented mood may have been responsible for the venom with which Sartre pursued Olga in the autumn of 1936. In turn titillated and humiliated by women, he was intent on bringing her to bed. Into Melancholia he wrote a rape scene which Gaston Gallimard later cut. He also pruned all references to Roquentin's erection; 'a pair of small grey balls' became 'a pair of small grey erasers'. But of the depth of the author's frustration there is no doubt.

Beauvoir, who had hoped that Paris would provide a way out of the 'labyrinth' in which Rouen had imprisoned them, was shocked to see his obsession with Olga burst out even more floridly than before. She puts these words into the mouth of Pierre:

'To make her love me is to dominate her, to enter into her world and there conquer in accordance with her own values.' He smiled. 'You know this is the kind of victory for which I have an insane need.'

'I know,' said Françoise.

Olga was the first to crack. She had responded to Sartre's letters from Italy, and hesitantly agreed to see him again. So feverish was his need for her that, as well as strolling down the boulevards by day, Sartre again began spending *nuits blanches* with Olga, walking the streets till dawn. He persuaded her to visit him in Laon, and introduced her to Pernod. She began to drink heavily. But, although she accepted francs from Sartre, she would not keep her side of the implicit bargain; she still refused him sex.

Even Sartre had had enough of verbal seduction. He demanded submission, and Olga had to find another way of showing it. Trapped in a situation in which she felt powerless, Olga began burning her pain away. Self-harm is common in women prisoners and among rape victims, and Olga, who may have been violated by Beauvoir, knew Sartre was tempted to take her by force: his rape fantasy had already been expressed in fiction, which is why she had to walk the streets till she dropped. To burn her flesh was Olga's way of punishing herself and numbing her mental pain. Blotting out her feelings of worthlessness and anger, physical pain brought a sense of relief; it was also a means of avoiding conflict, as she turned her anger upon her own body instead of expressing it verbally. In *Cutting it Out: A Journey through Psychotherapy and Self-Harm*, Carolyn Smith writes about feeling 'wobbly and alone' in London. 'That's when I progressed to razors. I wanted to bleed everything out. My thoughts were often self-rubbishing.' Olga, alone in Paris apart from 'the family', also often felt like rubbish.

The scene Beauvoir paints in *L'Invitée* of Olga's first act of masochism reflects actual events, as she confirms in her memoirs:

Françoise could not help taking a surreptitious glance at Xavière: she gave a gasp of amazement. Xavière was no longer watching, her head was lowered. In her right hand she held a half-smoked cigarette which she was slowly moving towards her left hand. Françoise barely repressed a scream. Xavière was pressing the glowing brand against her skin with a bitter smile curling her lips. *C'était . . . un sourire de folle*, it was the smile of a mad woman . . .

the voluptuous, tortured smile of a woman possessed by a secret pleasure.

Pierre and Françoise watch Xavière: both are speechless.

With her lips rounded coquettishly and affectedly Xavière was gently blowing on the burnt skin which covered her burn. When she had blown away this little protective layer, she once more pressed the glowing end of her cigarette against the open wound. Françoise flinched. Not only did her flesh rise up in revolt, but the wound had injured her more deeply and irrevocably to the very depths of her being . . .
    'That's idiotic,' she said. 'You will burn yourself to the bone.'
    'It doesn't hurt,' said Xavière.

The burn is large and deep, but Xavière swears that she can't feel anything: 'A burn is voluptuous,' she tells her audience.

In Sartre's *The Age of Reason*, Ivich's self-harm is presented differently. It is a violation of the flesh, not the sexual union Sartre demanded, but a substitute cutting and mingling of bodily fluids, in which Mathieu, the 'thinking reed', who can't get drunk and doesn't know how to let himself go, opens out like a wound and finally *feels* his existence in their shared pain. It is Ivich who goes first: in the night-club Lola the dancer, Boris's girlfriend, is snorting her 'dose', two pinches of cocaine. The moment is 'like a little diamond', hanging in space. 'I am eternal,' says Ivich, taking hold of Boris's claspknife and bending the blade against the table. Suddenly her neighbour shrieks:

Mathieu looked hurriedly at Ivich's hands. She was holding the knife in her right hand, and slashing at the palm of her left hand. The flesh was laid open from the ball of the thumb to the root of the little finger, and the blood was oozing slowly from the wound.
    'Ivich!' cried Mathieu. 'Your poor hand!'

He takes the knife from her: '*Vous êtes folle*, you're crazy,' he says, urging her to come along to the lavatory and have her hand bandaged, but Ivich is enjoying herself. Cutting is an agreeable sensation. Her hand feels 'like a pat of butter'. 'It's my blood,' she says, 'I like seeing my blood.' But when Mathieu tries to restrain her, she shakes herself free, laughing savagely: 'You've dared to touch me again . . . I ought to have guessed that you would find that too much for you. You are shocked that anyone should enjoy the sight of their own blood.'

Now Mathieu is pale with rage. 'Too much for me? *Mais non, Ivich, je trouve ça charmant,*' he says, jabbing the knife into his hand, where it remains, sticking upright, embedded in his flesh. A moment later, Ivich applies the palm of her left hand to Mathieu's wounded palm, with a sticky, smacking sound.

'That's the mingling of blood,' she says.

The pain stings; Mathieu feels that a mouth is opening in his hand. 'You're almost handsome,' says Ivich.

Olga is a deep cutter. She slashes her palm from her thumb to her little finger, and burns her arm 'to the bone', a significant sign that she had sustained profound psychological damage in early life, even that she wanted to end her life. 'The deeper the cut, the more serious the act of parasuicide,' writes psychiatrist Jonathan Pimm. For Olga to mutilate herself to this extent – and there is no reason to disbelieve Sartre and Beauvoir's accounts – suggests that she may have already been disturbed when Beauvoir began teaching her. It begs the question, did Beauvoir, and subsequently Sartre, pick Kosackiewicz because she was already damaged, as they themselves were? Was it in answer to a mutual need that they found each other?

The three accounts of Olga's self-harm, in *The Prime of Life*, *The Age of Reason*, and *She Came to Stay*, are remarkably similar in depicting Olga as mad. In Beauvoir's memoir, she is 'positively maniacal', just like Xavière with her maniacal grin, *'ce rictus maniaque'*. Sartre's Ivich also has a *'visage maniaque et réjoui'*, a wild, ecstatic face, like the patients of French psychiatrist Jean-Martin Charcot, who identified a disorder he named *manie sans délire*, mania without delirium, in which the patient is manic without manic-depression or psychosis, and today would be described as suffering from personality disorder.

Condemned as crazy, *une folle*, it is Xavière, not Françoise who is on the road to ruin. Inhaling ether was a popular form of inebriation in the thirties, and the next step for Xavière. She begins by drenching a handkerchief with ether, and sniffing the fumes. 'Be careful,' Françoise warns, 'or you'll end up a dope fiend or wreck yourself completely.' But Xavière has found a way out of her prison: stuffing a piece of cotton wool saturated with ether up her nose renders her 'practically unconscious for hours'.

Through the release of self-harm, Olga also regained control. She began to reassert herself. Already, she had slept with Marc Zuorro, to Sartre's chagrin. 'Sartre was already jealous of me whenever my closeness with Olga excluded him, but when Zuorro moved into the picture he went really wild,' Simone told Fernando's son, Tito Gerassi. Marc's true nature revealed itself, however, when he dropped Olga and conceived a desire for Bost, who was mystified and embarrassed by Marc's passion for him; one night, returning to his room, Marc heard sounds within. He peered through the keyhole, only to espy Olga and Bost locked in an embrace. They had fallen in love.

Marc was distraught, and refused to sleep alone. Sartre and Beauvoir took him on a winter sports holiday with them to Chamonix, where his hysterical sobs kept them awake at night. Back in Paris, in January 1937, Beauvoir began to feel permanently exhausted; Sartre was talking of the trio as a five-year project, and it was she who could see no escape. They were caught up in a *dance macabre*, in which she was the whirling dervish. Sartre rested up in Laon, Olga spent all day in bed, but Simone was burning out. If wishes were deeds, Olga would die. Instead, every night, a night-club; every morning, the *lycée*, counting the hours, sixteen hours until Simone could sleep again. In February, chatting to Bost in Le Sélect, she felt a shiver run through her; the next day she collapsed at a dinner party and Sartre called a doctor, who prescribed mustard plasters. For two days Poupette, Olga and Mme Morel nursed Simone as she lay in bed, drenched with sweat. When she moved, a pain shot through her left side. A nurse came to wet-cup her, but her fever did not abate. Mme Morel called an ambulance to take her to the clinic at Saint-Cloud. Two male nurses carried Simone downstairs on a stretcher: she was dangerously ill with pleurisy.

16

✦

Notoriety

Why do you write such unseemly things? Mon petit
enfant, *try to regain a little purity*.
　　　　　　　　　　　Mme Mancy to Jean-Paul Sartre

'Now you seem like a young girl again, and I want to write you a
courting letter,' wrote Sartre in April 1937 to Beauvoir, convalescing
in the South of France. 'Of course, my little grumbler, you will say it's
the ingenuously good husband in me trying to make the conjugal
relationship attractive.' 'Things are still idyllic despite the distance
between us,' he wrote guiltily, a day or two later. 'I love you, my darling
Beaver . . . I kiss your gaunt little cheeks, my love.'

Beauvoir had nearly died of jealousy. Her collapsed lung necessitated
missing a whole term of teaching. In the clinic her mother and her
friends sat anxiously by her bed as her fever raged, waiting to see if
her second lung would fail. The doctors had no means of checking the
infection. When they tried to X-ray her lungs, to see the extent of
the damage, she found standing so painful that she nearly fainted. But
gradually Beauvoir's hands, which had been constantly clenched due to
tension, opened. 'Someone had taken charge of me . . . the trio, with all
its upsets and obsessions, had become so burdensome to me in the end
that exile seemed restful by comparison.'

At Easter Beauvoir was allowed out of hospital, and moved into a
comfortable room in Marc's hotel. She was still bedridden, and

depended on Sartre to bring her the *plat du jour* from the nearby Coupole for lunch every day. Seeing Sartre tripping along, taking care not to spill the sauce from the dish he carried from the largest brasserie in Paris, a miracle of Art Deco with its tall, green pillars crowned with paintings of women and dancers, and already a favourite of the 'family', revived Beauvoir's spirits. In the evening she munched ham and fruit; but still she could not walk without feeling dizzy. When the holidays ended, and Sartre had to return to Laon, Marc and Bost decided, one warm day, to take Castor on her first outing. Supported on both sides, half-walking, half-carried, she managed to reach the Luxembourg Gardens where, overwhelmed by the unaccustomed sunlight and fresh air, she lost her balance and nearly fell.

Her doctor prescribed a three-week rest cure in the Midi. Arriving at Toulon, Beauvoir inhaled the scent of fish and mimosas. She caught the slow train snaking along the coast to Bormes-les-Mimosas, where she put up at the best hotel. Across the village square she could see the distant sea and the Iles d'Hyères. It was, she wrote, 'a glorious resurrection'. As in Marseilles, it was the mountains that drew her back, and soon she was gorging herself on *crème de marron*, the speciality of a region whose chestnut groves reminded her of her childhood. Ignoring her doctor's orders not to take 'fatiguing exercise', she climbed the Monts des Maures and strode along the clifftop paths on a little peninsula she had discovered, named Saint-Tropez. She sat on the red rocks of the Estérel massif and read Orwell's *Animal Farm*; she climbed to the summit of Mont Vinaigre, and sunbathed under the mimosas in the Tanneron valley. And, finally, she regained her strength.

Sartre's letters followed her wherever she went. Retrieving them from village post offices, Beauvoir sensed his remorse. He had tested the pact and pushed Beauvoir over the edge; clinging on by her fingertips, she had only just avoided annihilation in that dark abyss she always sensed close to her. Nearly losing her had frightened Sartre, and the almost daily letters he and Beauvoir exchanged read like a renewal of vows. They were 'two consciousnesses melded into one, floating . . . between earth and sky, and two little robot bodies', he told her. The pact was all the stronger for its mended fracture.

Sartre never had succeeded in wearing down Olga's resistance, as the Beaver reminded him many years later, when they discussed his jealousy of Zuorro: 'I didn't much care if there was another man in an affair with a given woman,' said Sartre. 'The essential was that I should come first. But the idea of a triangle in which there was me and another better-established man – that was a situation that I couldn't bear.'

'You were given a bad time by Olga,' Beauvoir reminded him, with relish.

'By Olga, yes.'

'Have you sometimes been rebuffed by women? Were there women you would have liked to have certain relations with – women you have not had?'

'Yes, like everything else.'

'There was Olga.'

'Ah, yes.'

News came of faraway places. For the first time Beauvoir felt personally involved in politics when she heard from Fernando, who had left to fight for the Republicans in the Spanish Civil War, that Franco's troops were bombarding Madrid. In April came the massacre at Guernica. Fernando, who would end the war as a general, told her that lack of arms was the trouble, and Beauvoir felt indignant at the policy of non-intervention practised by the French and the British. The war came closer still when Bost took it into his head to volunteer, and talked of illegally crossing the Spanish border, which had been closed since February. Sartre was in a quandary: he believed in individual freedom, but he did not want to be responsible for Bost's death. He sent the student to Nizan, who sent him to André Malraux, who served as a pilot with the Republican forces. Malraux asked two questions: 'Have you done your military service? Can you use a machine gun?' – with negative answers. The Republic needed trained men, not raw recruits, wrote Beauvoir; had not Simone Weil, who had crossed the frontier demanding to be given a gun, been put in the kitchens? But Bost's experiences were not wasted: they formed the basis for Sartre's story 'The Wall', which he wrote in the first months of 1937.

Beauvoir had no desire to emulate Weil. Although her own and Sartre's political impotence were brought home to her when she contemplated the war, illness reinforced her sense of detachment: 'Being powerless to fight the world's evils, I asked nothing better than to forget them.' Similarly, when she heard that André Gide had performed a sudden volte-face over the USSR, retracting his former support for the regime after his visit there in 1936, she airily dismissed his report, Retour de l'URSS, which caused a sensation in 1937. 'Gide had been too quick to develop a passion for the USSR, too quick to back out, for us to take Retour de l'URSS seriously,' she wrote in 1960. Certainly, Gide had been in a hurry to publish his condemnation of the Soviet system: his honeymoon with it had been brief, and he wanted the world to know the reason for his disillusion. On the plane taking him to Moscow, he had been horrified to learn of the sudden death of the novelist Maxim Gorky, Stalin's fallen favourite, who had recently warned his master that when the great French writer arrived, he would tell him the truth about the repressive regime. Gorky's convenient death on 18 June 1936 instantly aroused Gide's suspicions; subsequently secret policeman Yagoda and Gorky's family doctors would plead guilty to having poisoned the ailing novelist. On his arrival in Moscow, Gide agreed to deliver the eulogy at Gorky's funeral, but he refused to see Nikolai Bukharin, who had demanded an interview in order to vet the eulogy. It took only twenty-four hours for Gide's antennae to pick up the dark truth of Stalinism.

But Gide's revelations scandalized liberal intellectuals. Before leaving for the USSR he had declared: 'I believe that the value of a writer is linked to the revolutionary force that drives him . . . In our form of society, a great writer or a great artist is essentially nonconformist. He swims against the tide.' Now Gide was ahead of his time. He had the courage to stand against the intellectual fashion of his day. Having seen at first hand the lack of personal liberty in the Stalinist Utopia, he warned the French Communist Party against its errors. In his *Retouches à mon Retour de l'URSS* he repeated his criticisms; but Beauvoir and Sartre, as her pejorative comments show, saw Gide's recantation as proof of a flip-flop mentality. Condemning his behaviour, they ignored news of the show trials taking place in Moscow, even though the Communist Nizan was 'deeply disconcerted' at the direction of events. Like many British intellectuals, they believed, as Nizan had written: 'We in the West live in a society where greatness consists in saying no.' They would continue to swim with the Stalinist tide, although they demonstrated no interest in themselves visiting a country which 'left them cold'.

A letter arrived from Sartre which made Beauvoir cry with joy. 'Mon cher amour, my dear love, here's some news which will doubtless make you happy,' he wrote from the Hôtel de Paris & de la Poste at Laon on 30 April 1937. 'Le factum est pris et j'aurai un contrat. The factum is taken and I shall have a contract.' Delirious with joy, he copied out word for word for her to see the letter he had received from Brice Parain demanding cuts but saying, in a postcript, that at a Gallimard editorial conference they'd decided to accept the book. It was a seminal moment, as Beauvoir recognized. Across the top of the letter, she wrote: 'La Nausée acceptée.'

It had taken some strenuous networking. In March Sartre had written to Jollivet: 'Dear Toulouse, the note to Gallimard produced the anticipated effect.' Dullin had written to his old friend Gaston Gallimard asking him to reconsider 'Melancholia', and Pierre Bost, a reader at Gallimard, had also put in a good word with his boss after Jacques-Laurent had appealed to his elder brother to help his friend Sartre get published. Together, they made the difference. 'Enquire of Pierre Bost if this author has talent,' an earlier reader had scribbled doubtfully on his report. Pierre's answer came in the affirmative. Little Bost even dictated Sartre's humble letter to Jean Paulhan, editor of the distinguished literary journal *La Nouvelle Revue Française,* thanking him for agreeing to a meeting, and begging to submit his short stories. Sartre's typescript, which had languished so long in the slush pile, arrived on Gaston's desk. He read it and liked it. His only criticism was of the title, and it was he who suggested an alternative: *Nausea.*

Breathlessly Sartre conveyed to the Beaver the details of his interview with Parain. Leaving Bost at a café, 'I made my magnificent entry. There were seven guys already waiting up in the outer office . . . I gave my name to an amiable sort of woman who sat at a table answering several telephones. She picked up one of them and announced me. I was told to wait . . . I sat down in one corner on a little kitchen chair, and waited. I saw Brice Parain go past; he gave me a vague glance, but didn't appear to recognize me. I began to reread "The Wall" – partly to pass the time, and also, just a little to reassure myself . . . Then a dapper little man arrived . . . It was Jules Romains – yes, it really *was* he, don't worry, and not just someone rather like him.' Sartre remained forgotten in his corner until the receptionist returned and asked the waiting men for a light. No one could oblige. 'What, four men and not a match between them?' she demanded. Sartre raised his head. She glanced in his direction and said hesitantly: 'Well, five.' Then she asked him what he was doing there.

'I want to see M. Parent – I mean, Paulhan.'

'Well, go on up then,' she said.

The insignificant writer climbed two storeys to Jean Paulhan's office. His luck was about to change. Paulhan, tall, swarthy, with a greying moustache, at once ushered Sartre into his private office. His voice was caressing. He apologized for the mistake; the initial rejection of *Nausea* had come about because he had understood that it was submitted to the NRF, for which it was far too long. 'But it's an admirable bit of work . . . Do you know Kafka? . . . Kafka is the only modern writer who comes to mind when I considered this work of yours.' Sartre sat gingerly on the edge of a leather chair. He could hardly believe his ears. But although flattered by Paulhan's good opinion of 'Melancholia' (as he still called it to the Beaver), he was anxious to know whether Paulhan liked his short stories.

He need not have worried. The editor announced that he was giving one to another review, *Mesure*, and keeping one for the *NRF*.

> I said: 'They're a bit . . . er . . . outspoken. I deal with what might be described as, hmm, sexual problems.'
> He smiled with an indulgent air. 'We at the *NRF* are prepared to publish anything.'

Next Sartre was taken to meet Brice Parain, who was all cordiality, addressing him as '*tu*' from the start. 'There's only one Sartre, after all,' he said, telling the astounded author that he had read the first thirty pages of *Nausea*, and thought: 'Here's a character drawn like something out of Dostoevsky.' Roquentin reminded him of Dostoevsky's underground man, outside society and therefore bound to undergo extraordinary experiences. He'd loved the nausea motif, loved the looking-glass scene when Roquentin sees himself in a mirror . . . 'Revise the book if you can,' he asked Sartre, but if that was too difficult, they would publish anyway. *Gallimard can't not take it*. 'Let's go for a drink.'

Stumbling out of Gallimard's, barely able to believe the turnaround in his fortunes, Sartre decided to play a trick on Little Bost, who was waiting for him. He walked into the café and threw the manuscript of 'Melancholia' on the table.

> 'Rejected,' I told him, in a pathetic voice . . .
> 'Oh *no*!' he exclaimed. 'But why?'
> 'They found it dull and boring.'

Bost was dumbfounded, until Sartre told him the truth, to the student's utter delight. Refilling Bost's glass, Sartre left for his celebratory drink with his editor.

'At the precise moment when I was at the nadir – so miserable that on several occasions I contemplated death with indifference; feeling, old, fallen, finished . . . everything began to smile on me,' wrote Sartre. 'All of a sudden I felt full of tremendous, intense youthfulness; I was happy and found my life beautiful. Not that it was anything of the "great man's life", but it was *my* life . . . And this time life won out over art.' His nausea, like his self-pity, vanished overnight.

'I know a life is soft and doughy, unjustifiable and contingent, but that's unimportant,' he added. What was important was that it was

. The infant Simone
de Beauvoir, with,
l to r, her father,
Georges de Beauvoir,
her grandfather, her
mother, Françoise,
her aunt and her
uncle Gaston,
Meyrignac, 1908

2. Hélène and Simone
de Beauvoir, aged
three and five, in the
garden at Meyrignac

3. 'Poulou' and his
mother, Anne-Marie

4. The de Beauvoir
family leave la
Grillère for
Meyrignac: father,
mother, cousins
and servants, 1911

5. The Schweitzer family at Pfaffenhoffen, Alsace: l to r, Sartre's grandfather, Charles Schweitzer, his mother, Anne-Marie, his uncle, Emile Schweitzer, with eight year old 'Poulou' shorn of his curls, his uncle and aunt Beidermann, and his grandmother, Louise Schweitzer

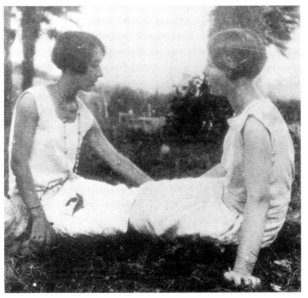

6. Elisabeth Lacoin ('Zaza') and Simone de Beauvoir

7. Simone de Beauvoir at the Lycée Jeanne d'Arc at Rouen, 1932;
Olga is in the second row, second from the right

8. 'La petite russe':
Olga Kosackiewicz in 1939

9. Bianca Bienenfeld c. 1938

10. Simone de Beauvoir, Paris 1938

11. Simone de Beauvoir and Nathalie Sorokine in front of the statue of Balzac in the Boulevard Raspail

12. Caricature of her teacher by Nathalie Sorokine

13. Beauvoir and Bianca Bienenfeld at the Lycée Molière, Paris

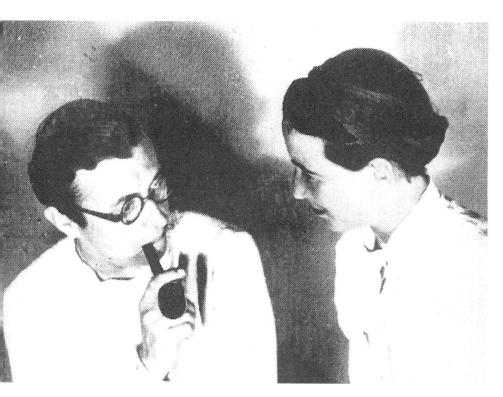

14. Sartre and Castor on holiday
in Juan-les-Pins, a few weeks before
the outbreak of war, 1939

15. Jean-Paul Sartre, called up
September 1939, in Alsace

16. Jacques-Laurent ('Little') Bost, in the infantry, November, 1939

17. 'Castor de guerre': 'You look like a lesbian, a cocaine-addict and a fakir, because of your turban,' replied Bost when Beauvoir sent him this photo of herself in 1939

18. Marie-Olivier [Wanda Kosackiewicz] and Francois Périer in *Les Mains Sales* [*Dirty Hands*]

19. At the Café de Flore, 1943, l to r: Raymond Bussières, Maurice Baquet, Marianne Hardy, Annette Poivre, Jean-Paul Sartre

20. Simone de Beauvoir at the Café de Flore, November 1945

21. Nazi officers at La Shéhérazade, a favourite nightclub during the Occupation

22. Albert Camus, editor of *Combat* from 1944-47, at the Deux Magots, 1945

23. Performing Picasso's farce, Le Désir attrapé par la queue, 16 June 1944, Paris: left to right: Jacques Lacan, Cécile Eluard, Pierre Reverdy, Louise Leiris, Zanie de Campan, Pablo Picasso, Valentine Hugo, Simone de Beauvoir; front row, Jean-Paul Sartre, Albert Camus, Michel Leiris, Jean Aubier

happening to him: 'Every event is *my* event.' Since his existence was justified in the eyes of the Other, the Kobra himself felt sure of his existence; someone had handed him a ticket. He had, suddenly, slid out of his jar and joined the human race.

*

Two other events contributed to Sartre's transformation, a process that he compared to sloughing off a snakeskin and starting a new life. He'd heard that he was at last to have a teaching post in Paris; and, as he put it cryptically in his *War Diaries*: 'I met T.' 'T' stood for 'Tania', the name given to Wanda Kosackiewicz, Olga's younger sister, who was born, also in Kiev, in 1917, and left Russia with her family in the White Russian exodus following the Bolshevik Revolution. In his letters to Beauvoir, Sartre calls her 'T.P. Zazoulich', '*toute petite*', the youngest Zazoulich, the name given to the Kosackiewicz sisters in the correspondence. Olga, '*la petite*', had been since January the acknowledged girlfriend of Bost, although Sartre dedicated *Le Mur* (*The Wall*) to her and continued to meet her as frequently as possible in Paris, when he could afford to finance her visits. 'Z. [Olga] was strange and sweet,' he wrote to Beauvoir on 26 April. She didn't hate him; she had become 'the faded garter of a woman once deeply loved'. His interest in her virginal little sister led to awkwardness between them, and Sartre tried to clear the air. Can I talk to you frankly, he asked. 'Why, yes, Kobra.' I'm embarrassed, because I can't talk to you about Wanda. Olga agreed that she too felt uncomfortable. Did the Kobra know of her mother's marriage plans for Wanda, she asked demurely. But Wanda had only told Sartre that her mother was planning something. The agitated suitor accused Olga of being disloyal and making him quarrel with Wanda. 'There are times, Kobra, when you're completely mad,' replied Olga calmly.

Wanda, twelve years younger than Sartre, plumper, quieter and less attractive than Olga, shared a superficial resemblance to her lively elder sister, but promised to be more malleable. Your letter was very short, Sartre reproached his 'darling Beaver', but Wanda's was long 'and very appealing. That girl seems to have a lazy but considerable intelligence, because each of her letters shows progress over the previous ones.' 'I just wish I could be there beside you, so handsome in your little blue pyjamas, and kiss you with all my strength,' responded Beauvoir. 'I love you so passionately.' 'And I love you passionately too,' Sartre reassured his 'crazy Beaver . . . wheezy Beaver', who was walking

'20 kilometres a day,' who only weighed forty-nine kilos and wouldn't be a 'choice morsel' if she didn't eat up. But all his tenderness could not hide the fact that his frustrated lust was now redirected towards the silent, virginal youngest Kosackiewicz; as for the Beaver, he joked to Bost: 'You terrorize me and you're a woman of steel.'

*

By the time Simone de Beauvoir returned to Paris in May, Gallimard's acceptance of *Nausea* had already changed Sartre's status relative to hers. In July 1937 the publication of *The Wall* in the *NRF*, followed by *Nausea*, dedicated to the Beaver, the following April, brought about a paradigm shift. Jean-Paul Sartre burst upon the literary scene, the new *enfant terrible* of French letters, and was hailed as a genius. The reviews were universally laudatory. Roquentin's heart swelled with pride when he heard that Gide himself, after reading *The Wall*, had asked Paulhan: 'Who is this new Jean-Paul? I think we can expect a great deal from him. As for his short story, it's a masterpiece.' 'One of the most striking literary débuts of our times'; 'A singular and vigorous mind' – Albert Camus. 'A real philosophical novel'; 'flawless style'; 'rare talent'; 'With his meditation on existence, Sartre brings a new theme into our literature.' In the space of a year Sartre was accepted into literary Paris, *The Wall* was compared to Malraux's *The Human Condition*, and *Nausea* was being spoken of for the prestigious Prix Goncourt.

There were few dissenting voices in this chorus of praise. One of the most vocal was Sartre's stepfather, Joseph Mancy. The story which caused offence was 'The Childhood of a Leader', a vicious attack upon the fascist Right and Charles Maurras's Action Française. Lucien Fleurier, a young bourgeois, is seduced by the *camelots'* anti-Semitism, expressed in their hatred of Leon Blum, Jewish Prime Minister of the first Popular Front government which fell apart in 1938. Lucien beats up up a Jew in the street and he decides to join the movement: '"I'll grow a moustache," he decided.' But it was the sexual details, 'Lucien's' unnatural love for his mother, whom he watches soap herself on her bidet through the bathroom keyhole, and, to cap it all, the gripping account of his homosexual seduction at the hands of a surrealist named Bergère, which disgusted M. Mancy. 'You are Rimbaud,' Bergère tells the handsome youth, handing him a spliff, 'an anal', 'an angel-faced little tart'. As a prisoner of the Oedipus complex he has no choice but to become a pederast.

'My little one, Uncle Jo has asked me to return your book – he has read "The Childhood of a Leader" and he is outraged,' wrote a distressed Anne-Marie to her son in February 1939. She couldn't judge the story herself, because she hadn't read it, 'But why do you write such unseemly things? If he speaks to you on Thursday, be very nice . . . My little one, *try to regain a little purity.*'

Sartre laughed harshly. 'A family is a real pile of shit,' he had written furiously to Beauvoir while on a cruise with his mother and stepfather in 1934, and nothing had happened to make him change his mind. He still thought of himself as an *orphelin*, son of a dead father and a mother lost to him on her remarriage, and now he had proved he had no need of his false family, the stepfather he was still obliged to call Uncle Jo, but heartily detested. 'Writing against' Mancy had brought him fame, and when the older man sent back the book, Sartre tossed it in the waste-paper basket.

His uneasy, strangely dependent, relationship with his mother continued, however. She paid for his haircuts, bought him a 'superb' suede coat (225 francs), and gave him an allowance of ten francs a day. In September 1937, while Beauvoir was away on holiday in Strasbourg with Olga, he was eating as often as possible at his mother's . 'It's not always fun but it's food.' When he started teaching at the Lycée Pasteur at Neuilly, just outside Paris, she offered him lunch daily, which he was tempted to accept, but for his stepfather, who 'bawls me out continually'. Sartre was, as usual, financially embarrassed, still owing money to his Laon hotel. His cheques were bouncing, and he had to suggest sending Olga home to Laigle. The ten francs his mother gave him every morning were carefully eked out: tobacco, matches: 5 francs; 2 Métros: 40 cents; the rest drinks, one beer, one coffee. 'Try to borrow 200 from your parents,' he begged the Beaver. 'We haven't one sou between us.'

Had Mme Mancy read 'Intimacy', the short story in *The Wall*, which did most to give her son a reputation for obscenity, she might have rescinded her invitation. Sartre's intention in all five stories, he said in 1967, was to show that 'Nobody wants to look Existence in the face.' In 'Intimacy' an unfaithful wife remains bound to her impotent husband: she is living in 'bad faith'. 'Lola lies to herself'; at first she views her situation through a 'light mist', but suddenly, the mist evaporates: 'She knows that she's lying to herself . . . Every flight comes up against a Wall; to flee Existence is still to exist.' Vivid, modern, pornographic, Sartre's stories were viewed by readers as a revelation of his own loose-living Bohemian lifestyle, although critics saw in Roquentin the Romantic image of the writer as a tormented genius.

*

Under a Greek sun, Beauvoir grew strong again. In July 1937 she and Sartre bought tickets on the *Cairo City*, Marseilles to Piraeus, fourth class, sleeping on deck in hired deckchairs. They were not alone. Little Bost came too, as 'technical expert', with a small Primus stove, which soon gave up the ghost. In 1960 Beauvoir wrote lyrically about their passage through the Cyclades: the blood-red cliffs dropping into the blue sea at Santorini, nights *à la belle étoile* on the hotel roof, Delphi, surpassing in beauty anywhere else on earth, the hike through purple hills to Olympia, Sartre, rucksack on his back, with his straw hat and stick, Beauvoir with their picnic in a cardboard box under her arm. She 'bathed' in splendour so intense that she felt her heart would burst.

Sartre, however, did not find Greece altogether a paradise, as his long letters to Wanda attest. His attention was fixed on the *postes restantes*, where he searched in vain for a reply from *'la toute petite'*. Frustrated by Wanda's silence, he nevertheless kept writing: 'I'd like to talk a little to you about yourself. But since you're mute, I shall continue to speak to you about myself. These aren't letters I'm sending you, but a travel journal.' Over 150 pages survive of Sartre's *journal de voyage*; he remained a bourgeois tourist against whom Athenian children, much to Beauvoir's dismay, threw stones.

Trapped in their tub of a boat, the *Cairo City*, Sartre studies the passengers and decides: 'Innocence is not a state, it's a role.' A little later he would write *Huis Clos* (*No Exit*), for Wanda. In Athens he decides: *'Les Grecs sont des peigne-culs*, the Greeks are arselickers.' At Delphi the wasps drive him mad, he can't stand retsina: it's *infame*, foul. At Olympia he's eaten alive by mosquitoes, unlike the Beaver, who has sensibly coated her face and hands in Vaseline and is turning them into Boy Scouts. Finally, 'apoplectic under his straw hat', Sartre goes on strike and refuses to climb Mount Taygetus. It's only nine and a half hours up, protests his intrepid companion, but Sartre values his skin too highly to go on. In the end, even the Beaver reluctantly admits that, in a temperature of 105, they're in danger of dying of sunstroke.

It's only in Salonika, where they run out of money, that Sartre begins to appreciate the antique. A good way of understanding a country is to be forced to stay there until you're sick of it, he tells Wanda, as he and the Beaver wait for Bost, who has returned to France, to wire their salaries to them. They're down to a loaf of bread, a pot of jam and a bunch of onions, and still the money draft hasn't arrived. Resourceful as ever, the Beaver insists on full board at a local hotel, where they live on credit for six days until the money comes through. 'Now we can see the Meteora,' exclaims the indefatigable tourist. At the prospect of a fourteen-hour train journey, Sartre again digs in his heels, leaving the Beaver weeping tears of rage on the boat back to Marseilles.

'I'm delighted,' Sartre writes to Wanda on 26 August 1937, on the boat going to Salonika. 'I find that this end of the year is going to be absolutely brilliant for me. It's certain that *Mr Roquentin* will be published, and in Paris.' The gap between him and Beauvoir is widening. Sartre already receives fan letters from readers; Beauvoir remains an unknown: Caesar's wife. She has finished her short stories and, despite negative comments from friends who have read them – Lionel de Roulet judges the characters 'obscure . . . artificial . . . conventional', and even Sartre agrees that Anne, the fictional Zaza, 'does seem the weak point in your factum', submits them to Gallimard, who turns them down. In October a second publisher, Grasset, rejects them, the reader reporting that *La Primauté du spirituel* lacks originality.

What was to be done? 'I showed you my stories,' recalled Beauvoir, 'and you found them pretty bad.'

'Actually, they weren't much good,' said Sartre. 'You didn't know how to write dialogue. They weren't very natural.'

'We had a conversation in the Dome which struck me enormously. You said, "Look, why don't you put *yourself* into your writing? You're more interesting than all these Renées and Lisas."'

'Screw up your courage,' said Sartre. *Mettez-vous dedans.* But the idea frightened Castor because she felt that if she gave herself so profoundly to literature it would become something very serious, like love, life, death . . . 'I hesitated for a long time before I did it.'

*

Beauvoir's heart is sinking into her boots. Wanda has promised, in her 'little voice, rough and appealing', to come to Paris on 15 September. 'You'll stay in my hotel and we'll never be apart,' says Sartre. He has already chosen the hotel, Hôtel Mistral in rue Cels, between Montparnasse cemetery and the avenue du Maine, into which he and the Beaver both move in the autumn of 1937. In her memoirs, Beauvoir would put the best possible gloss on events: 'Sartre lived on the floor above me; thus we had all the advantages of a shared life, without any of its inconveniences.' But it was not only she who was sharing that life. There was a new guest in the relationship: Wanda, *la muette*, the dumb one, now just twenty. Beauvoir, woman of steel, could handle the situation. 'Harmony between two individuals is never a *donnée*; it must be worked for continually,' she wrote grimly. No one would best Caesar's wife.

'We were all like snakes, mesmerized. We did what they wanted because, no matter what, we were so thrilled by their attention, so privileged to have it,' Olga later recalled. Wanda, like Olga and Bost, had joined the 'family' and would remain infantilized for the rest of her life.

Just occasionally a member of the group sensed danger: the danger of surrendering his will to the couple, of becoming a small planet in the Sartrean solar system. Zuorro was unusual in fighting the gravitational pull. On 5 May, after attending Dullin's rehearsals of *Julius Caesar*, he explained awkwardly to Sartre that he wanted to see less of him and Beauvoir, wondering aloud if 'the pleasure one enjoys with such strong personalities isn't sterilizing'. 'When someone is in your world,' said Marc, 'it's impossible to get out.'

His departure left a vacuum. Awakened to the pleasure of same-sex love, Beauvoir looked for a substitute for Olga. In the front row of the Lycée Molière was another pretty, fragile, immigrant girl who worshipped her teacher.

17

⌒

Breaking the Rules

Bienenfeld arrived, pretty and charming. She told me
that she would never love anyone as much as me . . . she
had the air of a superb Jewess.
    Simone de Beauvoir to Jacques-Laurent Bost, 1938

IT SEEMED AS if the template already hammered out would fit again.
Bianca Bienenfeld, skinny and pale, with flame-coloured hair, had also
suffered dislocation in her early life. Her father, a Polish Jew, had
qualified as a doctor in Vienna before bringing his family to Paris in
1922 and becoming a prosperous dealer in oriental pearls. Poverty and
her mother's illness marked her childhood but by the time she was ten
she was living in an apartment in the smart 16th *arrondissement*. At the
Lycée Molière Bianca longed to become a concert pianist. 'Maman
didn't want me to,' recalled Bianca. 'But I cried, I screamed . . . *J'amais
beaucoup la musique.*' Her dramatic temperament brooked no denial,
and her parents, Esther and David, gave in. But after two years at the
Conservatoire, her hopes faded; she returned to the *lycée* and devoted
her energies to catching up. Clever, nervous and ambitious, Bianca,
born in Lublin in April 1921, was sixteen when, in September 1937,
Simone de Beauvoir walked into her classroom.

'We were all thrilled at having a beautiful young woman as a
teacher,' recalled Bianca. She was deeply impressed by the beauty of
Beauvoir's 'sculpted, perfectly proportioned face, with its classic profile

and pronounced cheekbones. The intelligence in her luminous blue eyes struck us right from the start,' although the schoolgirl also noticed that her teacher was nervous, picking at a spot on the back of her hand until it bled, and walking abruptly. 'She was all energy and no calm.' Her voice was 'broken, hoarse, rather unpleasant', her slight figure devoid of curves, her movements a little clumsy. And Bianca, 'always very well-dressed by Maman', was amused to learn that Beauvoir's mother, who used to knit her jumpers in Rouen, still made their teacher's clothes, tight ill-fitting suits, in order to save money. When she became intimate with Beauvoir, she was horrified to discover that she wore dicky shirt fronts, held in place by a piece of elastic round the bust, under her jackets. As for her thin, light brown hair, which she wore in two, smooth coils on top of her head, the teacher often added a false braid to plump up her home-styled coiffure.

Bienenfeld's scorn for Beauvoir's penny-pinching stratagems came later, when she wrote her story of betrayal in *Mémoires d'une jeune fille dérangée* (*Memoirs of an Deranged, or Upset Daughter*), a play upon the title of Beauvoir's own memoir. But when Bianca first sat in Beauvoir's class, she, like the other 'élite girls', fell under the spell of the charismatic teacher. It was not only Beauvoir's bold, brilliant, incisive mind, her effortless grasp of philosophical topics, as she raced through Descartes, Hüsserl, the Epicureans, Stoic logic, Kantian morality, and tore Freud apart, leaving the slower pupils hopelessly begging, 'Please speak more slowly, Mademoiselle!' but her new ideas which startled, shocked and excited her class of bourgeois girls.

By January 1938, her thirtieth birthday, Simone de Beauvoir had developed a surer sense of style. She was also discovering her own power. 'She was tremendously dynamic and attractive,' remembers Sarah Hirschmann, another of her pupils.

With her we were in a completely new world. She came in with no notes, just a cigarette. Wearing purple and heavy make-up, red lipstick. Her voice was deep and raucous from smoking, like Marlene Dietrich. Beauvoir didn't talk to us about the history of philosophy, but about existentialism. She told us to think about what reality was . . . to think about something outside your mind, but we couldn't. She told us how fascinated she was by people in the street, how we should observe their behaviour. 'Did that man have a parting in his hair?' she'd ask. 'I don't remember,' I'd say. She was trying to get us to really look at the Other. We became involved in a process of thought, instead of just learning from books and spouting them out again. 'Don't get married,' she said. 'If you do, be sure not to have children.' For some of us this was very attractive.

One day Beauvoir asked the girls to describe an emotional experience, Bienenfeld put up her hand, and described how she had frightened off a burglar at her parents' home. For the first time, the teacher noticed the shy Jewish girl. That term, Bianca was top of the class. In March 1938 she wrote Mlle de Beauvoir an earnest fan letter, and was astonished to receive a reply within the hour by *pneu*, the express blue notes sent by pneumatic tube and hand delivery. 'I expected to wait several days,' said Bianca. Her teacher proposed a meeting at the Brasserie Lumina near the rue de Rennes, where her mother lived.

Bianca arrived in her school uniform, a beige tabard or pinafore with her name, 'Bianca Bienenfeld', embroidered across the front by her mother. Her blouse was also beige, her belt pulled tight. Beauvoir was delighted with her. She offered to begin meeting Bianca privately out of school. 'I floated on a cloud of happiness,' recalled the schoolgirl.

Simone's physical presence entranced Bianca also, because it reflected her determined personality: 'She was like a ship's prow, speeding through the waves, a prow made of solid, brilliant, unchangeable stone.' Beauvoir seemed an unstoppable force in motion. One day Bianca asked her why she was always in a hurry. '*La vie est courte*,' replied Beauvoir. In class it was always *vite, vite, vite*, recalled Bianca.

But it was Bianca who was in a hurry that spring. Waking up on Sunday mornings, she would sprint to the Métro at Passy, the nearest stop to her family home, and count the minutes until she arrived at Edgar-Quinet. Then she would run all the way down the rue de la Gaîté to the seedy Hôtel Mistral on rue Cels, a tiny street near rue Froideaux, to find Beauvoir. Teacher and pupil, arm in arm, would spend the day strolling through the flea market, exploring Montmartre, and exchanging confidences. On one occasion Bianca persuaded Simone to make a nostalgic journey to Suresnes, to visit the château of her uncle Jacques, founder of Maison Bienenfeld pearls. The château was ruined, its owner having lost his fortune in the 1929 stock market crash, and in a deserted bedroom Bianca told Simone about her wandering childhood, and how Uncle Jacques had saved her family from the death at the hand of the Nazis which would probably have awaited them, had they stayed in Poland. In her turn, Simone told Bianca about her attachment to Zaza; how she had fought the prejudices of her milieu to win the right to advanced study; how she had met Maheu, Nizan and Sartre. 'The one who was the ugliest, the filthiest, but also the nicest and the most supremely intelligent was Sartre.' Bianca knew at once that he was *l'amour de sa vie*, the love of her life.

Simone explained the basis of their relationship: no marriage, and certainly no children – they're too demanding. They were free to live their own lives and have their own sexual adventures; their only promise was to tell each other everything. Absolute freedom and complete openness. '*Programme ambitieux!*' concluded Bianca. At the time Beauvoir maintained the 'official' theory of the pact, hiding any signs of jealousy or anxiety. Beauvoir talked about Olga; 'she was very taken with Olga', recalled Bianca, sensing also Beauvoir's fear of losing Sartre. Eight or nine years after the pact, she barely slept with him: '*Elle était frustrée,*' she was frustrated. 'Sartre was a very poor lover. He took little pleasure in love-making . . . He didn't want your body, he wasn't natural, he only wanted to conquer women.'

Bianca's passionate attachment to her teacher, whom she now called Simone, became stronger by the day. After she had taken her *bachot*, Simone proposed a walking holiday together in the Morvan. Together they hiked through the mountainous countryside, covering twenty kilometres a day, rucksacks on their backs. One evening they arrived exhausted at an inn and asked for a room. The innkeeper showed them to a sparsely furnished room with a double bed; when they enquired about the bathroom, she pointed to the garden. After an omelette and a piece of bread, the pair went to bed. Until then their relationship had been close, but not physical. That night, it became so. 'She was a little embarrassed at first,' remembered Bianca. 'She wasn't completely naked. Me, I didn't mind. She had . . . no shame afterwards.' Five days later they arrived at a comfortable hotel in Vézelay, and spruced themselves up. Simone complimented Bianca on her *tailleur de toile de lin rose*, her pink linen suit. On the bus back to Paris they held hands, which seemed to shock the passengers.

*

Seduction was in the air that summer. On 14 July Simone de Beauvoir took the train from Paris to Bourg Saint-Maurice to meet Jacques-Laurent Bost, with whom she would spend ten days on holiday in the Alps. 'I found Bost already tanned and looking very nice in his yellow pullover,' she wrote to Sartre the next day.

Her letter crossed with Sartre's own, smug account of his sexual triumph with Colette Gibert, a drama student at Dullin's Théâtre de l'Atelier. Sartre had so far had no more luck with Wanda than with her sister: despite hopefully pushing fifty-franc notes under the sisters' door, 'la toute petite' remained sulky and distant. His nerves were jangled, Sartre complained, his passion turned to ice since the 'Olga affair', but Colette suddenly stirred his reptilian blood. Possibly the fact that his old philosophical rival, Maurice Merleau-Ponty, Beauvoir's friend from Sorbonne days, was in love with her acted as a stimulus; certainly the fact that Simone had disappeared into the mountains with Olga's boyfriend did so.

'I kissed that fiery girl, who pumped my tongue with the force of a vacuum cleaner (it still hurts),' Sartre wrote to Beauvoir on 14 July. Colette's aunt, like Merleau-Ponty himself, had warned the girl against Sartre, saying that he lived with Simone de Beauvoir as husband and wife, so she was nervous when she met Sartre for drinks at Les Deux Magots. He, however, smoking his favourite Boyard cigarettes, and wearing either his black turtleneck pullover, or his white shirt – he appeared to have only two outfits – was excited by Colette Gibert's reputation: 'Don't try for the agrégation, your gifts lie more in bed,' Jean Wahl, another philosopher attracted to the dark, exotic drama student, had leered at her.

Sartre and Gibert move on to the Dôme, where he takes her hand. 'I've got a taste for you,' he says. 'You've unleashed my rough side, which is rare, since I'm rather thin-blooded . . . I have three days to give you – let's make the most of them.' This tough approach works better than Merleau-Ponty's protestations of love, and Sartre gets to bed at five the next morning.

Friday: 'Catastrophe!' The Merloponte, as Sartre calls him, demands a meeting, at which he makes it plain that he considers his rival a bastard. A painful conversation with Colette follows, in which Sartre tells her that he is in love with her, but there is no place in his life for her. On Saturday he takes her to the Falstaff, and then back to his room.

Except for sleeping with her, I did *everything* . . . It's the first time I've slept with a brunette, actually *black-haired*, Provencale as the devil, full of odours and curiously hairy, with . . . a very white body, much whiter than mine. She has teardrop buttocks . . . Very lovely legs, a muscular and absolutely flat stomach, not the shadow of a breast, and, all in all, a supple, charming body. A tongue like a kazoo, which unreels endlessly and reaches in to caress your tonsils . . . On the whole, I'm happy as an undertaker's assistant.

The music from the open-air orchestras on the avenue du Maine creates a bond between them more powerful than any talk of love, says Sartre. 'I mean an auditory bond . . . They were playing "Some of These Days" under my windows.'

Colette demands to sleep in his arms. 'I'm jealous of Simone de Beauvoir,' she tells him. 'I've always wanted to be with some guy the way you are with Simone de Beauvoir.'

The two 'beautiful and tragic nights' pass in a flash. Sartre has hardly slept. 'I'm barely holding on,' he writes to Beauvoir, as he puts Colette on a train. The girl has begun to love him passionately: 'She wanted to give me her virginity. I'm not quite sure if I took it or not . . .' In any case, says Sartre, reverting to his usual opinion of sexual intercourse, 'it seemed like a profoundly difficult and disagreeable task'.

Beauvoir receives Sartre's account of his passionate nights with Gibert with apparent equanimity. She has been greatly entertained, she assures him on 22 July: 'You're very sweet to have told me the whole story in such detail, my love.' Sartre is sticking to the kiss-and-tell rule of the pact, which over time Beauvoir will find increasingly painful.

Alone together in the mountains, Beauvoir and Jacques Bost have been sharing a single sleeping bag after an accident in which, sliding down some rocks, she slits open her hand. The cut is deep, blood spurts everywhere, and her solicitous companion insists on taking her to the doctor, who bandages her up. That night they sleep in a 'charming' barn, with views over Chamonix. By 27 July Beauvoir has her own news to announce, with vengeful nonchalance: 'I slept with Little Bost three days ago. It was I who propositioned him, of course. Both of us had been wanting it.'

It was a rainy evening in Tignes when they were again sheltering in a barn, their faces inches apart. Beauvoir laughs softly. 'Why are you laughing?' asks Bost. 'I was trying to picture your expression if I propositioned you.' He confesses that he had wanted to kiss her, but didn't dare. When he finally does so, Beauvoir tells him she has always been attracted to him, and Bost, in his turn, says that he's loved her for ages. 'We spend idyllic days, and nights of passion,' writes Beauvoir. 'Goodbye, dear little being . . . Your Beaver.'

It was better than tit-for-tat, for Sartre was already unsettled by Colette's sensuality, to Merleau-Ponty's bewilderment. 'Why on earth don't you sleep with her?' he demanded: she was ready and willing.

Earnestly the two philosophers discussed Sartre's relationship with Beauvoir: 'I told him that it was for keeps, and on a level where we wouldn't worry ourselves about our little spring fevers.' As Sartre left to meet Colette again, he muttered, like one charged with a difficult task, 'I'll do the best I can . . . I'll screw Gibert – if I have to.'

In fact, Sartre was thinking about his forthcoming visit to Morocco with Beauvoir rather than the eager Provençal virgin. 'I love you, my good little Beaver,' he wrote tenderly. But Beauvoir had embarked on a relationship which would prove deeper and more enduring than a mere spring fever.

18

In the Shadow of War

> I didn't want to admit that war was imminent, or even possible.
>
> Simone de Beauvoir, *The Prime of Life*

'I WAS DRUNK with joy,' wrote Simone de Beauvoir to Jacques Bost after they parted, picturing her lover, his rucksack on his back, striding along the path under the same blue sky which shone over her that summer. She was dizzy with happiness, recalling how she had lain in his arms, whispering sweet nothings to him as he slept peacefully beside her. All I wanted at the beginning was that you would let me love you, she said; five days later he had left her with a 'totally transfigured life. *Je me sens heureuse d'une violence folle.* I kiss your cheeks, your beautiful eyelids, your cracked lips. I love you.'

In twenty-one-year-old Bost, Simone had found someone who could accept the passion she offered and respond to it fully. Someone who rejoiced in the body as she did, without reservation or inhibition: 'I still feel we are fused together,' she wrote. It was a revelation, after the years with Sartre, for whom the body was a fleshly prison from which, like St Augustine, he sought release. Simone had had no qualms in propositioning Bost, any more than she had done in sleeping with Guille, Olga or Bianca, for she believed that human relationships have to be perpetually re-invented. But daring to love each other was difficult and dangerous:

both had other, non-negotiable ties, Bost to Olga, and Beauvoir to Sartre.

Beauvoir knew that Sartre deserved an explanation, and she gave it to him on the boat going to Morocco. Embarking from Marseilles on 31 July, she was astonished to find Sartre treated like a celebrity. 'Sartre! It's the great Sartre!' exclaimed the officials, under orders from the director of the steamship company, an old classmate of Sartre's from La Rochelle, when the new *enfant terrible* of French letters presented his passport. It was a taste of things to come. Sartre was led at once to the captain. The couple were ushered into a vast outside cabin with two private bathrooms with running water. 'We live like kings,' wrote Beauvoir to Bost, as she ate her way through ten courses, gnocchi, risotto, steak, pigeons, finishing with strawberry ice cream. It was a contrast to their last poverty-stricken trip on the *Cairo City*, and she felt 'almost immoral'.

Sartre and she discussed Beauvoir's new liaison at length. Sartre said that he wasn't astonished, although he hadn't been expecting it, but how the devil did she think she'd find time to see Bost? 'I don't know, but I will, in abundance,' Beauvoir promised her lover, as she lay curled on her bunk reading Sartre's latest short story and the boat steamed on towards Tangier. She felt melancholy: her place beside Bost in the tent was empty, he was sitting alone in front of his slices of sausage. Would there be a letter waiting for her at Casablanca? She heard the tenderness in his voice, heard him say, 'You poor bitch,' with that funny, sideways look . . .

Bost had understood her predicament: bound to Sartre, her intellectual twin, but unrealized as a woman. His sympathy for her had released a flood of emotion, which bound her to him as tightly as physical passion. In the daily letters which followed Bost from Morocco, from Mazagan, Fez and Meknes, one theme dominates: the life-changing nature of their love. On 3 August, for the first time, she addresses him as '*tu*', something she had never done to Sartre: *Je t'aime avec violence. Je pense que personne ne peut savoir, pas même toi, comme l'amour que j'ai pour toi, l'amour que tu m'as donné, ont transfiguré ma vie.* To *tutoyer* Sartre was unthinkable: Castor retained ingrained bourgeois habits, spurning the intimacy of '*tu*', but that vestigial 'vous' was a sign that she had never felt for him the same hunger that she now felt for Jacques Bost. And Sartre's own cool reasonableness over the situation expressed itself in a conversation he had with Beauvoir in an Arab restaurant over a banquet of 'pastilla', galette stuffed with pigeon and almond pâté, followed by chickpea tagine, whole chickens swimming in oil with olives and baked lemons, and a leg of lamb which they tore apart with their fingers.

What would Bost say about this pastilla, asks Sartre.

Castor: He'd say he didn't like it, but he'd eat it all.

Sartre: I really like Little Bost.

Castor: So do I.

Apparently Beauvoir has nothing to fear from Sartre, who holds fast to that part of the pact which forbids jealousy. He may already know that nothing will move Beauvoir, as fixed in her path as a comet; she has been sending her letters 'into the void', but on 6 August, for the first time, the other voice breaks its silence. Bost, too, wants Castor beside him in the tent. He, too, loves her madly. He lies awake thinking of their last five days together. He wants to kiss the frown line on her brow, over and over, until it disappears. He is lost in love for her, he overflows with happiness.

But if Sartre's response was lukewarm, making no real objection to incestuously incorporating further into the 'family' Little Bost, already treated as a surrogate son, and accustomed to accompanying his 'parents' on holiday, both Castor and Bost knew that Olga Kosackiewicz's reaction would be very different, were she to discover the truth. Kos, the Cossack, as Castor always refers to her in her letters to Bost, must never find out. To prevent her suffering, Castor and Bost must live out their love clandestinely. It was a heavy price to pay. They were obliged to lie and deceive: with heavy hearts they guarded their secret. '*Des remords, pas de regrets*, remorse, but no regrets,' became their motto, and their moral choice.

This life of deceit broke Sartre and Beauvoir's own rules of openness and authenticity. Ironically, just as 'Intimacy', Sartre's tale of a fictional wife, Lulu, who lives in bad faith between her husband and her lover, was published, and attracting attention to a fundamental tenet of existentialism, Beauvoir herself was tormented by pangs of 'primal jealousy' and fell into the trap of *mauvaise foi*.

Another consequence of the secret nature of the affair was the injustice suffered by Bost himself, whose real place in Beauvoir's life went unacknowledged in her memoirs. She warns readers of *The Prime of Life* that 'there are many things which I firmly intend to leave in obscurity'. 'Without doubt,' writes Sylvie Le Bon, editor of the letters between Beauvoir and her secret lover, 'her silence over her liaison with Bost is the most substantial omission. How many journeys on foot, which she claimed to make alone, were really made with him, like the trip to Corsica in July 1937?' Beauvoir dedicated her greatest work, *The*

Second Sex, to Bost, a significant sign of his importance in her life. Bost was intimately present, from 1938 to 1986, discreet, warmly attentive, unfailingly kind, showing solidarity in her darkest hours, totally honest. 'He had a horror of pushing himself forward, unlike others,' writes Le Bon. 'It is time that justice be done to him.'

As well as the injustice done to Bost, in airbrushing him out of her life Beauvoir also did herself an injustice. Her lopsided account in *The Prime of Life*, and her subsequent memoirs, has led many readers to conclude that she was Sartre's victim: 'A poor sacrifice!' In reality, while Sartre was playing away with his women, Beauvoir was comforting herself with the handsome pastor's son, whose 'dazzling smile, and princely bearing' had touched her heart as early as 1935.

*

Bicycling through Provence, Bost received a letter from Beauvoir dated 25 August 1938. It brought alarming news. Madame Bienenfeld had read one of Beauvoir's 'passionate' letters to her daughter, Bianca, and was beside herself with fury. She accused Beauvoir of being '*une vieille dame de moeurs speciales*', an old maid with special tastes. The row would blow over, wrote Beauvoir hopefully: she had other problems. As usual, she and Sartre were running out of money. They had only 150 francs left and were forced to go without dinner as they waited for a further supply of *le fric* from Mme Mancy. After visiting the Roman remains at Volubilis, Sartre accepted an invitation to smoke *kif* for the first time and was feeling remarkably cheerful, despite the fact that they now had only eleven sous left. There had been difficulties when Sartre was in charge, and they got lost in the labyrinthine back streets behind the souk at Fez; Beauvoir was afraid that their guide was going to rob them: 'But now I've put matters in order with a firm hand.' As Sartre lay in bed, ill with a liver attack, awaiting his mother's money draft of 100 francs, the Beaver busied herself organizing a walking tour of the Atlas Mountains, equipped with maps, guides and provisions. Gamely Sartre followed her over the lonely paths, sleeping in rest huts below the Berber villages, before the couple caught the long-distance bus to the south. They were the only Europeans apart from the driver, and the disease and poverty of the region appalled them. At Ouarzazate they watched their hotelier hand out boiled rice to the tiny, spectral figures of blind children, their sight destroyed by trachoma. Many were dying of typhoid, others deformed: a great weight lifted from our hearts, wrote Beauvoir, when we finally left this 'southern hell'. But, for the first time, they had stepped outside the skin of the tourist.

They returned in September to the Munich crisis. The Beaver, joked Sartre, only read the fashion pages of the newspapers, and was still taking an ostrich-like attitude to politics. 'I refused to admit that war was even possible, let alone imminent,' she recalled in 1960. But it was difficult to ignore the martyrdom of Spain, where French and British neutrality made defeat inevitable in the summer of '38. Images of violence, of rape, torture and sadomasochism, had dominated the Surrealist exhibition in January, and Picasso's *Guernica* forced Parisians to confront Spain's despair. '*Salauds de Français!* (French scum!)' snarled Fernando, when he returned on leave to Paris at the end of August, seeming to include his old friends in his attack.

On 13 September the Beaver was still waiting in Marseilles for the arrival of Kos. Promising to telegraph for her if the situation deteriorated, Sartre left for Paris as Chamberlain flew to Berchtesgaden to meet Hitler. 'Perhaps this is the place, my darling Beaver, to slip in some information about the current situation,' wrote Sartre, who blamed the French Prime Minister, Édouard Deladier, for the policy of appeasement which gave the Sudetenland to Hitler.

> The backing down is coming from the French. It is at Deladier's request that Chamberlain left for Berchtesgaden, and from that moment on doubtless Deladier was ready for any concessions . . . The democrats have lost all hope of making Hitler retreat. It is a true victory of fascism . . . the conflict is no doubt put off for several years. There, my darling Beaver, you have the picture.

'Bouþou' (Fernando) was leaving for Spain, in despair at the retreat of the Great Powers: 'We parted with real emotion.'

Beauvoir barely absorbed Sartre's lesson in current affairs. Her first thought was for Bost, beginning his two-year National Service in the French army. As a second-class infantryman, his life would be in danger in the event of war. 'O my beloved, it's terrible to think that war is possible, that we're going to be separated after such a short time together – I'm tormented by regrets for all the time we've lost,' she wrote on 21 September. On the 26th the couple were reunited in Paris. 'Bost was convinced that he would soon be off to the front, and he thought it very much on the cards that he would lose his life there,' recalled Beauvoir in *The Prime of Life*. But on 30 September, after signing the Munich Agreement, Deladier and Chamberlain returned to their respective capitals, proclaiming 'Peace with honour'. General mobilization was averted – for the time being. Beauvoir snatched a bare month with her young lover before he rejoined his unit at Amiens on 3 November.

*

'I retain only a misty recollection of this entire year. Nor can I remember anything of outstanding interest in my private life,' wrote Beauvoir untruthfully in her memoirs, although she admitted to feeling depressed. Nearly 1,000 pages of letters between the two lovers testify to her torment at Bost's absence. After a final goodbye on the avenue du Maine when, choked with tears, she watched his departing figure give her a final, tender smile before vanishing – it was Kos who had the privilege of accompanying him to the station – it was to Bianca that the Beaver turned for comfort. Bianca was too pretty to be allowed to meet Bost: 'I saw him, but I was not introduced to him,' remembers Bianca. 'Simone kept her other friends separate from me.' But, her throat constricted, 'paralysed all over', Beauvoir found solace in two hours of abstract conversation with 'Bienenfeld . . . bien sympathique comme toujours.'

Studying philosophy at the Sorbonne, where she met three of Sartre's past students, Jean Kanapa, Raoul Lévy and her future husband, Bernard Lamblin, Bianca, 'voluble, flirtatious, brilliant', was able to offer Beauvoir an intellectual rapport she had never found with Olga. Both Kanapa and Lévy were attracted to the vivacious red-haired student, but found themselves rejected on the grounds of her affair with her former teacher. Only three days after Bost's departure, after teaching her 'un peu de phénoménologie', Beauvoir took Bianca to her room for 'an exchange of passionate kisses'. As with Olga, 'un peu de philo', a little philosophy, was the entrée; the main course followed in the bedroom.

On 21 November Beauvoir was again running into Bianca's arms for a 'philosophical conversation . . . mingled with passionate embraces'. Bianca had poured out her heart in a long letter expressing her affection for Beauvoir. 'I loved her very much,' wrote Beauvoir. Bianca's admiration comforted her, not only for Bost's absence, but also for Sartre's growing preoccupation with Wanda. In July he had finally taken Colette Gibert's virginity, and continued a desultory affair with her. Although Wanda allegedly displayed the 'mental faculties of a dragonfly', she had enough intelligence to keep Sartre dangling.

'I played the whore and addressed her tenderly,' he told Beauvoir, but Wanda would allow him only a peck on the mouth. Her excuse was that she was not sensual. When Sartre tipped her back on the bed and kissed her, she dashed to the bathroom to vomit, behaviour he attributed to her having mixed her drinks, white rum with sherry. She tantalized him, in her 'angelic little jacket', with her hair down, until he could take no more. Meeting her at the Dôme a few hours later, 'I froze her out, abruptly dropping my game and declaring that we were through unless she became more loving with me.' Wanda promised to think about it. They moved on to another café at the Palais-Royal, where she demurely explained that she derived complete physical pleasure merely from contact and a few kisses.

Sartre's appearance was no doubt a deterrent – Wanda was soon complaining that he was giving her spots, as he had so many himself – but his increasing wealth and prestige were proving a greater draw. In the same month, July 1938, Jean Paulhan had hired him as a columnist on the *NRF* for 350 to 400 francs a month, and Gallimard had proposed *Nausea* for the Prix Goncourt. By September leading critics had caught 'the scent of a masterpiece'. Editors had 'stables', prizes were 'races', and his novel was a favourite, Sartre wrote proudly to the unpublished Beaver. That autumn his confidence soared. Robustly he rebutted Paulhan's criticisms of 'The Childhood of a Leader'. *Nausea* defined existence. The five stories describe the possible escapes from it, and the failure of each. In his new novel, *The Age of Reason*, he will offer the possibility of moral life at the core of existence and with no escape. Tired of the 'bundle of garbage' from readers, letters accusing him of being a morbid pornographer – smutty magazines were even printing extracts from 'Intimacy' with banner headlines 'By the author of *Nausea*' – he will show them that he is precisely the opposite.

The professional gulf between Sartre and Beauvoir was growing. In the Dôme they read each other's first chapters, and found them 'well written', Beauvoir confided to Bost on 8 November. She continued eagerly working on the second chapter of *L'Invitée*, settling down at a little table at the back of the café, but when Sartre read the manuscript he handed it back as useless. 'He's read my second chapter, I've got to start again at the beginning,' she wrote, adding stoutly, 'It will be good.' Beauvoir needed all her self-belief. When she sent Brice Parain the first 100 pages of the novel, typed out by Poupette, about the early life of 'Françoise', her own alter ego, he too returned it, brusquely remarking that it did not even reach the standard of her rejected stories. Sartre agreed. Beauvoir decided to jettison her heroine's past: she would start with the trio, and progress to the murder of Xavière. Sartre still found the plot two-dimensional, and made a suggestion. To prove her love for Pierre/Sartre, Françoise should give something up. What would convince the reader? mused the apprentice author. The answer came in a flash: Bost, named Gerbert in the novel. Tempted by his youth and charm, the heroine would at first renounce them. Only later, when he had won Xavière's love, would she fall into his arms, and take her revenge. Writing the scene in which her fictional self turns on the gas tap beside the sleeping Xavière, Beauvoir's 'throat was as tight as though I had the burden of a real murder on my shoulders'.

Sartre's advice worked, bringing Beauvoir's writing finally to life, but it indicates that he cared more than he admitted about her affair with Bost. Not only in fiction was it Bost's green eyes, a lock of his hair, the smell of his cheeks, for which 'Françoise' longed, shedding tears of 'pure joy' at the prospect of seeing him again at Saint-Lazare station. 'Spend the greatest possible time with me,' she implored him, as his first leave drew near. 'Can't you tell Kos that you're arriving later than you are? I want to meet you at the station and pass the first moments with you.'

Seeing Bost was a shock. Beauvoir wrote about one of their meetings at the Café Rey on avenue du Maine:

> Françoise drew aside the hangings over the door. Gerbert was sitting near the mechanical piano with a glass of *marc* in front of him. He had put his forage cap on the table. His hair was cut short, and he looked ridiculously young in his khaki uniform.
> . . . She took his hand and their fingers intertwined.

Bost, who had hopes of becoming a reporter after graduating at the Sorbonne, loathed the *ennui* of army life. Holed up in his barracks with peasants from Normandy and Picardy, 'congenital idiots' who passed their time throwing their sabots at each other, forced to salute and square-bash, he had made the mistake on the first day of letting the NCOs see that he understood how to break down a gun faster than the other recruits, and at once found himself put in charge of three men. Four days later the lieutenant in charge of the company summoned Bost into his presence, and enquired whether he would like to become an officer. 'I declined politely.' The officer exploded with rage: as a member of the élite, Bost had a duty to 'serve', that is, to command the yokels. Insolently the young recruit replied that, in his opinion, stripes put a barrier between officer and victim. Pale with fury, the lieutenant informed Bost that, whether he liked it or not, he would be made a lance-corporal. Bost refused: he had already concluded that the army leaders were 'totally incapable', and a 'nameless chaos' reigned. As for the officers, tall, thin and elegant in their fine uniforms, smoking, playing cards and manicuring their nails, 'I hate them with a violent hatred. They're a pile of shit.' The anarchist views Bost had learnt at the knees of Sartre and Beauvoir were setting him on a collision course with the authorities.

Reading Bost's letters plunged Beauvoir into 'black despair'. She instantly identified with his youthful rebellion. On 24 November she and Sartre quarrelled violently, probably over Bost. 'I went into the lavatory, where I cried a little.' In a taxi she broke down completely, reproaching Sartre with his luck in being free to work. Sartre told her that she was 'odious', as she sobbed and laughed hysterically for two hours, waking the next morning with a blinding headache. Two days later she was still 'delirious' with melancholy, 'at the bottom of an abyss', and an exasperated Sartre told her that he no longer loved her. 'Try hard to see me . . . I love you passionately,' she begged Bost. But Bost also wanted to see Kos, who had caught the attention of Dullin and been given a small role in a play, although he was embarrassed to say so. 'You make me afraid,' the young soldier told his ruthless paramour, who had spluttered with rage when Kos showed her a photo of Bost in uniform.

Jealousy was in the air, and in December Marc Zuorro passed on the latest gossip to the Beaver: Bost had been seen at the Alma café with an older woman. On leave the young soldier was responding to Castor's ardour. 'I adore your new coiffure,' said Zuorro two months later, staring suspiciously at the glowing, almost unrecognizable woman in front of him, who had just made Bost 'as happy as a king', on his Sunday leave. It looked as if Beauvoir's secret was about to come out.

*

At this point Bianca's relationship with Beauvoir took a new turn. Bianca asked the Beaver to help her study Sartre's *The Psychology of Imagination*. The Beaver hesitated a bit and replied, 'Why don't you ask Sartre yourself? He works at the Café Mousquetaires on avenue du Maine, quite near here.' Upon arriving at the café, Bianca caught sight of a man sitting near the front window, writing. He greeted her warmly. He was wearing 'a sort of faded blue T-shirt of questionable cleanliness. On his ill-favoured face was a constellation of blackheads,' but he answered her questions kindly.

That Christmas Bianca went skiing near Megève, where Sartre and Beauvoir, registered as 'M. and Mme Sartre', were also staying at the Hôtel les Primevères. Skiing down from her youth hostel halfway up Mont d'Arbois, Bianca met up with Sartre and Beauvoir. On 26 December Sartre joined the two women for dinner. That night Bianca, rolled in a duvet, slept in the bath off Sartre and Beauvoir's bedroom. The next night Sartre discoursed on Spinoza to Bianca, after which she lay down on the bed and began to free associate. Sartre, who relished the role of psychoanalyst, paid close attention. Once again, Bianca slept in the bath, and shared Sartre and Beauvoir's morning ski lesson.

Bianca was just seventeen, Sartre thirty-three, but from that moment he wooed her assiduously. It was a cold winter, and the *prof de philo* wore a beige, fake fur coat: she called him her 'bear', and he called her his 'bee', a play on Bienenfeld. Bianca was flattered, although 'I was not so strongly attached to him as I was to Simone de Beauvoir. Sartre was very ugly, with his dead eye. He was small, but with a big tummy.' Nevertheless, after a few weeks she agreed to consummate the relationship. It proved an experience she never forgot: as they approached the Hôtel Mistral, Sartre remarked smugly: 'The hotel chambermaid will be really surprised, because I already took a girl's virginity yesterday.'

Inside, Sartre undressed and washed his dirty feet in the basin. Shyly Bianca asked for the curtains to be drawn, but her companion refused, saying that what they were going to do should be done in broad daylight. When she at last stood before him, embarrassed, naked, but still wearing her pearl necklace, he laughed at the 'bourgeois' ornament. The gentle, generous man she knew had disappeared: 'It was as if he wanted to brutalize something in me (but also in him), and was driven by a destructive impulse.' 'He wanted to brutalize the ugliness in himself. He had no sensuality. It was because of his ugliness that he had such need of women, a need to prove himself. He lived in his head, not in his body.' This cold, sadistic Sartre behaved as if 'he were a doctor, preparing for an operation, and I had only to let myself be taken'. When his first attempt to take Bianca's virginity failed – he managed the deed a few days later – she was subjected to a lecture on the anatomy of lovemaking.

With hindsight, Bianca came to believe that Beauvoir had been instrumental in setting up her initial meeting with Sartre in order to meet his need for romantic conquests. In November Sartre had finally broken off with Colette Gibert, and Beauvoir may have considered Bianca a useful substitute, whom she could control more easily than Wanda. 'I now think that she not only accepted Sartre's attraction to very young women, but also introduced him to some of them,' wrote Bianca. 'I think that he was already starting to distance himself from her, at least sexually, and that she was therefore creating other, vicarious ties to him.' Beauvoir was perfecting her method: breaking in her pupils through lesbian seduction before procuring them for Sartre. Bianca even came to question whether Beauvoir's lesbian affairs were posturing with a purpose, rather than the product of genuine attraction. 'She liked new adventures. Homosexuality was part of her bourgeois rebellion.' Certainly the letters which passed between Beauvoir and Sartre, detailing the grooming and betrayal of their pupils, demonstrated that words could be as titillating as acts and that building complicity through the sexual colonization of their pupils ensured the survival – with an exciting new twist – of their joint pact of sexual freedom.

At the heart of Beauvoir's intention was her need to stay in control. Never again would she allow another Olga to steal Sartre from her. 'Simone was the princess,' recalled Bianca. 'Her sister obeyed her like a slave . . . I lost my head in asking for parity with her. I committed an act of sacrilege against the queen.'

*

Unaware of the dangerous ground on which she was treading, on 18 January Bianca showed Beauvoir a passionate letter she had written to Sartre suggesting 'complete communism within this new trio'. Physical relations had restarted between Bianca and Beauvoir, to their mutual satisfaction, and despite Bianca's complaints that Sartre lacked passion, 'she loves him very much', recorded Beauvoir. Sartre's love letters to his 'dear little Polak' that summer were full of promises for a common future: '*Our* future is *your* future,' he assured her. 'There is no difference – the Beaver lives in a world in which you are everywhere and always present . . . I love you passionately.' A few days later he wrote again: 'I want to stress that the Beaver loves you as much as you could wish . . . You know how you always say that Simone is perfect. Well, this is the moment to believe it and wait.'

At the beginning of July Bianca had been operated on for an ovarian cyst at a clinic in Annecy, where Sartre visited her, to the annoyance of Bianca's mother. In August he wrote to tell her how appealing she looked in her photos, especially 'the big one where you're nude. Who took it? Your father, of course.' Bianca's father, concerned at the weight she had lost, had photographed her naked, and Sartre wanted a copy.

What he did not tell Bianca that July, although he could not resist a triumphant blow-by-blow account for the Beaver, was that Wanda, jealous of her new rival, had finally agreed to sleep with him. No sooner had the deed been done in a hotel in Aigues-Mortes than Sartre rushed round the corner to a café to report his conquest to Beauvoir. It was a cruel letter, in which not only did he dwell on how 'very nice' it was sleeping with Wanda, 'which happens to me morning and evening', between which Wanda, naked under her coat, went shopping in the market, but on the emotion they shared: 'All is perfect love, gazing into one another's eyes, holding hands. She's really charming, even touching.' He'd had to tear up all the Beaver's letters – 'even those you wanted me to keep' – as he and Wanda shared a room and she would find them while he was asleep. Nor could he express his feelings for the Beaver on paper, as Wanda could read his writing upside down.

Sartre had taken his revenge on Beauvoir for her affair with Bost. It was simply rubbing salt in the wound to assure her that he preferred the life of the mind to 'the nothingness of the flesh'. Beauvoir began to fear that Wanda might usurp her role as *maîtresse en titre*, official mistress, with all the benefits that accrued to that position. After the publication of *Le Mur* in February, hailed by Albert Camus in *Alger républicain* as the work of a 'great writer' whose obscenity reached a greatness comparable to 'the obscenity of Shakespeare', and Sartre's sensational attack upon François Mauriac in the *NRF* in the same month, in which he accused a respected Catholic writer twenty years older than him and a pillar of the Académie Française of failure as a novelist ('God is not an artist; nor is M. Mauriac'), his star rose to even giddier heights. He was widely acclaimed as a critic of the Left, as well as the novelist of nihilism and lucidity. 'We lead completely separate lives,' Beauvoir complained miserably on 17 February, as Sartre described his latest publicity photos, in full colour, looking 'genial and sympathetic', to be shown on a magic lantern. His days were spent presenting literary prizes, attending literary salons. 'We fucked off,' wrote Beauvoir angrily, after one such evening, tired of watching her famous companion, seated in a throne-like chair, graciously receiving compliments.

Competing with both celebrity and polygamy was hard. Beauvoir often found herself kicking her heels at the Dôme or the Café de Flore as she waited for Sartre. He still wanted to make time for his 'fragile little iron-willed' Beaver. When she read aloud to him the latest 'immense' chapter from her novel, he was encouraging. 'The plot moves extremely well,' was his verdict. Brice Parain might publish her. Beauvoir, who had written 120 pages, set herself a deadline of July

1940. Waiting to meet Bost at Amiens, she had begun reading Heidegger, and that spring she and Sartre worked together on the German text. But often she felt like an outsider, listening second-hand to tales of dinner parties with Sylvia Beach and Adrienne Monnier to which she was not invited.

Bost, on the other hand, needed her love more and more. Punished for his insolence, he was confined to barracks 'like a rat in a hole', ill, drunk, 'tortured' at not being able to see Beauvoir. In March he was posted to the Ardennes. 'It breaks my heart' that you are so unhappy, Beauvoir assured her 'cher fantôme', her dear phantom. Few in Paris suspected that she had a secret, male lover, for she often made a point of dressing like a piège à loup, a 'wolf-trap', the 'family' name for a homosexual. At the lycée she wore a jacket and tie, and was shunned by the other teachers, who saw her as a dangerous influence upon young female minds, especially since another young Russian pupil, Nathalie Sorokine, had developed a violent crush on her. In the Dôme a crop-haired lesbian in a mackintosh touched Beauvoir's arm and enquired if she was all alone. Blushing, Beauvoir said she was waiting for Kos. 'Le Castor, c'est un homme, the Beaver is a man,' declared Wanda, watching her sister dance with Beauvoir at the Bal Nègre in rue Blomet, the Harlem of Paris, although Wanda herself was no slouch in suggesting a threesome with herself, Sartre, and Marcel Mouloudji, a sixteen-year-old Algerian film star whom Olga had met at the Atelier. Even Bost had his doubts when his girlfriend regaled him with stories of her afternoons in bed with Bienenfeld, drinking champagne and giving themselves up to 'guilty embraces'.

With Bianca, who could afford the latest fashions, Beauvoir presented a different, more feminine face to the world, wearing a chic little black hat with a veil, with black or yellow shirtwaisters and high heels. 'I'm as pretty as an aster in spring,' she boasted, as she kept a June rendezvous with Bianca, 'toute belle', with her mass of red hair falling over her forehead like a Toulouse-Lautrec painting, in a little blue dress with a violet coat. After a sumptuous lunch at La Coupole, accompanied by a bottle of champagne nature, followed by an iced coffee at the Flore, the pair tripped back to the Mistral, up the stairs past Sartre writing in his room, before collapsing giggling on the bed. There they kissed; Beauvoir had long ago shed her inhibitions about undressing completely.

Unsure of where she sat on the sexuality spectrum, and anxious to reassure Bost, Beauvoir wrote on 4 June: 'In the end I think I'm not really piège [gay], because sensually it hardly touches me; but it's charming and I adore being in bed in the afternoon when the sun's shining outside.'

How could she call gay sex *charming*? demanded her enraged lover. 'I find that frighteningly obscene.' She was treating Bienenfeld like an object, as well as behaving like a shrew towards Kos. Simone apologized; she had not used the word in a 'libertine' sense, but only meant to imply that Bienenfeld herself was 'charming'.

> I have only *one* sensual life, and that's with you, and for me that's something infinitely precious, and solemn and important and passionate; I would not be unfaithful to you . . . I don't want any other life, I am totally committed to you . . . With Sartre I also have physical relations, but very infrequently, and mainly to show affection, I don't quite know how to put it, but I'm not involved because he's not involved himself.

Bost's conscience was troubling him as he struggled to love two women. He apologized to Beauvoir: 'You're not *une mégère tracassière*, a nagging shrew. But please burn all my letters,' he begged Beauvoir on 21 August: *'Je ne regrette rien.'* Yet he felt 'vile and deceitful', 'profoundly guilty' about Kos. Beauvoir, too, regretted nothing, *rien de rien*, although she felt both jealous and guilty:

> *J'ai une espèce de remords sans regrets*, I have a kind of remorse without regrets which yesterday night almost turned to anguish and gave me lots of nightmares – but, thank heaven, for my morality as much as for the repose of my soul, I no longer have the vague impulses of jealousy which I've sometimes had formerly . . . I love you in the love which you have for her . . . That for me is the only correct attitude. I love you – with a demanding, greedy, love, certainly – but also with a disinterested love.

Despite their mutual protestations of remorse, however, the lovers lied brazenly to Kos in order to spend a summer holiday together in Marseilles. In the last days of peace, they clung to happiness. 'I saw the little blue flowers on the mountain and my heart turned over,' wrote Beauvoir, remembering the gentians Bost had picked for her in the Alps. 'Do you remember?'

'Don't lose heart,' wrote Sartre, still full of optimism on 31 August 1939 from Mme Morel's villa in Juan-les-Pins, to Bianca, still alone in Annecy. 'It's impossible that Hitler is thinking of starting a war, given the mental state of the German population. It's bluff.' Sartre's mind was on the swimming lessons he was giving the Beaver, every evening at seven o'clock, when he would hold her by the chin and lavish advice as she struggled to stay afloat in the warm water. There were seven in the house party, and Zuorro was flirting with the waiters in the Cannes restaurants. August drifted by in a dream; afterwards Sartre would remember how calm and happy Beauvoir seemed, as they sat on the green marble terrace of the villa, listening to the music from the casino floating over the water. The band were playing: 'Bei mir bist du schön', 'our song', as he reminded Bianca.

On 1 September Beauvoir was eating her breakfast at the Dôme when a boy shouted: 'They've declared war on Poland.' The headline screamed 'WAR' in *Paris-Midi*, and Beauvoir ran up the road as fast as her legs could carry her to find Sartre. The signature of the Nazi-Soviet Pact on 23 August had extinguished Bost's final hopes of averting a conflict, for he kept a closer grip on reality than his old master. 'This time it's serious,' he had written sombrely, as his regiment, the 51st Infantry, waited to move up to the front. The men were being handed out identity discs with which to identify their bodies in the event of death. 'Everything is ready.'

'There will be a peace and an *afterward*,' Sartre reassured Bianca, already scared for the fate of her family, on 2 September, the day before France and Britain declared war on Germany. 'I will come back to you. I'm in no danger, I'm the faithful type.' Notices announcing general mobilization had been pasted up all over Paris, and, despite his blind eye, Sartre was called up.

At three o'clock in the morning he and Beauvoir began making their way to the Gare de l'Est, Sartre in an old blue suit and carrying two food bags over his shoulder. The city was dark as they walked side by side through the silent streets. Slowly the sky grew pink. There was time for one last cup of coffee. Sartre repeated that the war wouldn't last long, that as a meteorologist he wouldn't be in any danger. At the barrier they kissed goodbye, and he boarded the train for Nancy to join his unit behind the Maginot Line.

Walking home, Beauvoir noticed that workmen were blacking out the windows of the Dôme with thick, blue curtains. 'In 1939,' she wrote, 'History took hold of me and never let go.'

Part Two

The Dark Years

1939–44

19

Women in Love

I feel abandoned by God and by men.
Simone de Beauvoir to Jacques-Laurent Bost,
9 October 1939

ON THE TRAIN to Nancy, Sartre read Kafka's *The Trial*, and he would experience the Phoney War which lay ahead as Kafkaesque: a time in which the men felt they were either on manoeuvres, or a country holiday. For Sartre himself, service in the meteorological section of an artillery HQ in Sector 108, just behind the front in Alsace, was the equivalent of a writers' retreat. Never was he so productive as in the army, which gave him the leisure to write a novel in four months, fifteen notebooks of his War Journal, which would form the basis of *Being and Nothingness*, and hundreds of letters, a million and a half words up to the end of his captivity in March 1941. He worked so hard that his vision grew fuzzy, and he feared for his sight: but, buoyed up by the camaraderie of his unit, eating and drinking like a king – he commonly breakfasted on *foie gras* and red wine – Sartre plunged into a pro-ject or *Vorwurf*, which he characterized as the will leaping into the future. This journey of self-examination would change him from individualist to humanist.

His initial embarrassment over army life, finding himself '*absurde et tout petit*' in overlarge fatigues, soon faded away. Private Sartre rolled up his trouser legs, swapped his beret for a kepi, and prepared to muck in.

Another small, bespectacled intellectual named Corporal Pierre came looking for him, and introduced the other two men in his section: Muller, fat and fortyish, and dark, curly-haired Pieterkovsky, who shortened his name to Pieter to disguise his Jewish origins in case he was captured by the Nazis. 'That Jew, Pieter, is invaluable,' Sartre was writing to Beauvoir on 5 September. 'It's thanks to him that we're billeted with the priest and eat at the house of an old retired cook . . . A strange solidarity is developing amongst us.' The cook's 'excellent meals' included fricassee of rabbit, chicken with cream sauce, and immense plum pies, after which the men would stroll through the village for a coffee and brandy at a local café. At night Pieter and Muller shared one mattress, Jean Pierre and Sartre the other. Woken by Pieter and Muller's snores ('I've never had so much desire to pee'), Sartre would rise and relieve himself out of the window into the street. Cheek by jowl with his fellow soldiers, he was happy 'hemmed in by the human, big guys who shit, wash themselves, snore and smell of man'.

Well fed by the sexton's wife, the men were putting on weight. The locals began to resent the fact that the soldiers were not at the front: 'Eat up. That way you'll die fat,' said the cook as she dumped some badly cooked potatoes on Pierre's plate. So large was Muller's 'elephant-seal behind' that the group could hardly fit on the bench opposite the priest's house as they sat in the warm night air, listening to a guy down the road singing 'J'attendrai', in a pleasant tenor voice. 'All we needed was mandolins,' Sartre told the Beaver. They didn't talk much: their camaraderie was anonymous. Each of them was distanced from the others by his whole life, like the spray of a bursting shell, explained Sartre: 'Pardon this first philosophico-military joke.' But as the September days passed he found himself sharing a pipe and a chat with Muller before getting down to his letter to Wanda.

Meteorological measurement provided a pleasant diversion. On 14 September Corporal Pierre and Sartre went into town to pick up a tank of hydrogen, as well as tobacco and sweets, and the next day let off their first balloon. Having taken over an hour to install the theodolite on true north, they were mortified to lose sight of the balloon, but at the second attempt they were able to take their first reading to work out the 'ballistic wind'. A few days later they realized that the balloons were leaking and rotten, and the colonel ordered a halt to save hydrogen while they waited for the new ones to arrive. Sartre was able to devote himself entirely to André Gide's *Journal* of 1914, which Beauvoir had sent him, and his novel, which was moving 'like clockwork'. Even so, there was time to give the colonel philosophy lessons, at his request, to 'round out his general culture'. Unlike Bost and the ordinary *poilous* in khaki, the meteorologists wore air-force blue; they were afforded officer privileges, seats on the 'reserved' bus, from which they could look down on the columns of dark shapes, the light infantry, cigarettes glowing red as they marched. 'We are respected, on familiar terms with the sergeants, exempted from fatigue duty, calm, specialists in all accepted meanings of the word,' wrote Sartre complacently. In return they recycled the rotten balloons, cutting them up to make tobacco pouches for officers.

'Would you send me . . . a strong black notebook – thick but not too tall nor too wide, ruled in squares of course,' wrote Sartre to Beauvoir on 12 September. The smells of the Alsatian countryside, which reminded him of his childhood, the German-style taverns, hearty meals with mugs of kirsch, after which he slept 'like a god', his new experiences as a 'being-for-the-war', made him eager to record his thoughts; two days later he bought a leather notebook himself. From the beginning his *carnets de la drôle de guerre*, notebooks from a Phoney War, were, like Gide's *Journal*, intended for publication: 'Whoever reads [my little black notebook] after my death – for you will publish it only posthumously – will think I was an evil character unless you accompany it with benevolent and explanatory annotations. In short, morally I'm a bit disoriented.' The temptation of evil to a being 'abandoned in the world to discover its own goals' was on his mind. 'If God is dead, everything is permitted', the Dostoevsky quotation on which he often ruminated, led him to consider his options. 'Will' now appeared to him as inherently the will to change a given situation: Heidegger's being-in-the-world becomes a 'being-for-changing-the-world . . . The primary structure of will is to be a transcendence that posits a possibility in the future, beyond any currently given state of the world.' But in escaping from itself through action, will meets many possibilities: in his notebook Sartre misquotes Medea: '*Video meliora proboque, deteriora sequor*' ('I see the Good and approve it, I follow Evil').

A bare fortnight after mobilization, Sartre had developed a military air. The proprietor of a local bookshop asked him: 'Was it quiet last night for you at the front?' 'All quiet,' replied the writer. 'I'd just read it in the papers,' he confessed to Beauvoir. For all his short stature, his personality and intelligence commanded authority, and the other three men in the unit began to defer to him. By October Sartre was calling them his 'acolytes' or 'Assistants', from Kafka's *The Castle*, and complaining to the Beaver that they stuck to him like leeches. But the wily Kobra also used them, habitually sending Pieter to seek out a *querencia* in a local hotel or schoolroom. Even the captain was persuaded to leave Sartre the hot water in his bath.

Sartre's first thoughts were for Beauvoir's safety. Parisians expected a *blitzkrieg*, similar to that endured by the Spanish during the Civil War. 'They say here that London has been bombed. If that's true, Paris will be next,' wrote Sartre on 4 September, entreating her to leave if the situation deteriorated. His urged his 'dear little wife' to go down to the air-raid shelters when she heard the alerts. How was she managing now that their 'little *querencia* at the Café de Flore' was closed? He was deeply touched by a letter in which she wrote that if the worst were to happen to him, she would no longer live. 'I felt a profound peace . . . It would be the ultimate cleansing, as though the two ends of the severed worm were annihilated.' In the long run, however, he'd want her to go on with her own life even though, without him, she'd be in an absurd world.

Separation intensified Sartre's love. 'I've never felt so intently that you are me . . . I love you so, my darling Beaver,' he wrote eight days after they parted. She was 'solider than Paris', which could be destroyed, she was solider than anything: 'You are my whole life, which I will find again on my return.' As the uneventful weeks of *la guerre fantôme* passed, his anxiety diminished and his gratitude grew for Beauvoir's long, newsy letters and parcels of tobacco and detective stories, in contrast to Wanda's silence: 'If the war were to last three years, as the English think (but I do not) I won't ever see her again: she'll be dead, crazy, or gone off with some other guy.'

In this time of insecurity the Beaver's loyalty shone like a beacon. She had worried that she was being ousted: now he reassured her. 'We two are one . . . This phantom war . . . answers the question that was tormenting you: my love, you are not "one thing in my life" – not even the most important – because my life no longer belongs to me, because I don't even regret it, and because you are always *me*.'

Sartre considered October 6 as a day of celebration, and he wanted to send her a flower petal, except that there was only manure. When she received his letter, it would be exactly ten years since they had been married morganatically: 'My dearest love, I immediately renew the lease for ten years, fervently hoping I'll be there next October to ratify our renewal out loud. My dearest, you're the most perfect, the most intelligent, the best, the most passionate. You are the little paragon . . .' She was 'his conscience, his witness', and he would gladly cut off his finger to see her for five minutes.

But when the news came that Sartre was to receive his salary while mobilized, his first reaction was to ask Beauvoir to cash it and '*have the two Zazouliches come to Paris*'. She was to give Olga and Wanda the bulk of his salary, so that all his 'little family' would be provided for.

As the months passed, Sartre cherished his intellectual solitude more and more. He grew a 'necklace' beard in the fashion of Stendhal. Like the monk he had sometimes wished to be, he examined his soul, writing: 'On the occasion of some great event, when one is in the process of changing one's life like a snake sloughing its skin, one can look at that dead skin – that brittle snake-image one is leaving behind – and take one's bearings.' The spitting cobra had found an opportunity for metamorphosis. Isolated from his women, a strange peace descended upon him.

*

Beauvoir was crying like a fountain. On 3 September the headline in *Paris-Soir*: LA GUERRE EST DÉCLARÉE, although expected, shocked her to the core. The war was real: Bost might die. The odds against his survival were one in four. If he were wounded she needed to know, and she wrote immediately to Sartre to say that she would tell Kos that she'd given Bost her address, as Sartre wished to be informed of any bad news.

Terrified of sleeping alone, Beauvoir ran to the Boubou, and asked if she might stay at his studio. Fernando Gerassi, who was back in Paris, made up a bed for her. He had shared a walking holiday with her that summer, and they had slept together in 1937. Now she turned to him for comfort.

'I have the impression that *I* no longer exist,' she wrote to Bost. Only her two men existed: Sartre and Bost, and the dangers they faced. Send me a photo, she begged Bost, I want one so much. If anything bad happened to him, she would never know happiness again. Beauvoir did not, however, make the same offer to Bost as to Sartre, to kill herself if he died.

The next day Beauvoir reported to the Lycée Molière, where the headmistress measured her for her gas-mask. She left with the putty-coloured cylinder slung over her shoulder; most of the Métro stations were closed, and in the blackout gloom the violet and blue headlights of the cars lit up the prostitutes, carrying gas-masks as they patrolled the streets. Beauvoir hurried to her friend Gégé's flat, at 116 rue d'Assas, by the Luxembourg Gardens, but Gégé had been quarrelling with her husband, Pardo, and was sobbing on the bed. 'I'm scared, I'm scared,' she mumbled, trembling all over. 'I flung myself down beside her and have become such a *piège*, and so used to these situations,' wrote Beauvoir to Sartre, 'that I petted her with tender little whispers . . . and came within a ace of saying, "My darling" – it was hilarious.' This time she restrained herself. The next night she and Gégé and Pardo were awoken by the wail of sirens at 4 a.m.; people were running for the shelters, and there was talk of poison gas, but the Pardos decided it was a false alarm and they all went back to bed. At seven the all-clear sounded. Leaning out of the window, Beauvoir watched women in flowered dressing-gowns emerge from the shelter.

The Flore crowd had migrated to the Deux Magots on the place Saint-Germain-des-Prés, and Beauvoir, too, returned to the familiar Montparnasse square. On 8 September she passed an afternoon reading Gide's *Journal*, comparing 1914 with the present, as she watched men fill sandbags in the quiet sunlight. A few hours later, on place Edgar-Quinet, she stared miserably up at the grey barrage balloons floating against a red-streaked sky. Her world was disintegrating; that night she felt so lonely, and got so drunk on red wine, that she nearly slept with a Hungarian she picked up at the Dôme. 'God knows, he repels me,' she told Sartre, but in the evenings she would 'do anything' in order to blot out the moment.

It was a blessed relief to find a note from Olga saying that she was back at the Hôtel Mistral. Lighting a candle, for the electricity was down, Beauvoir stumbled from room to room till she found her. They talked till three in the morning. 'Kos is a magnificent resource,' she told Sartre, overjoyed to find a link with her past. It was the 'tiny memories' which tore at her heart, as she and Kos strolled through Montmartre. A few days later they decided to become real 'women on the home front': after packing up a parcel of books and tobacco for Bost, they bought blue powder paint, which Kos mixed with water and Gégé's Ambre Solaire and daubed on to the windows. When she had finished, the flat looked like a mausoleum, for not a ray of light penetrated. When the Pardos left Paris, Kos and the Beaver moved in.

On 11 September Beauvoir wrote her first 'official' letter to Bost, in which she copied out Sartre's letter to her, signing off formally: '*Salut bien . . . S. de Beauvoir*'. It amused her to deceive Kos as she wrote her own letter to her soldier boyfriend. Kos had let slip that her relations with Bost were not 'essential' to her, which fortified Beauvoir's determination to assert her own love for him. Bost's regiment was on the move from its secret location behind the Maginot Line, but the men were kept in ignorance of their destination as hundreds of lorries, camouflaged with branches, rolled forward in the darkness. It seemed a case of *jouer la comédie*, acting a part, said Bost, who could barely believe that the war was real. But they were moving up the line; three days later Bost reported that he was not far from Sartre.

The French mood was optimistic. The section leaders told the infantrymen that German tanks could easily be immobilized, and that their air force was inferior to that of the French: most of it had already been knocked out by fighter planes. 'I don't know if it's true,' wrote Bost doubtfully. 'It's putting the wind up us a bit, because . . . we're the ones who will attack the Siegfried Line.' But – even though their equipment included 1870s muskets – he counted on coming out of the war alive, telling the Beaver that although he thought her life was worse than his, she was to write no more sad letters: '*Je voudrais que vous soyez tranquille pour moi*, I want you to stay calm for me.'

Beauvoir tried to do as she was told. 'Read with confidence: this is a happy letter,' she headed a reply to her '*cher fantôme*' on 20 September from Quimper, in Brittany. She had decided to leave Paris after having a panic attack in the Métro, overcome by feelings that she was simply an anonymous face in the crowd, 'drowned in the war'. Her heart was thumping in her chest: she was a rootless being without a home, without her men. Disobeying Bost's repeated pleas to burn his letters, she packed them away in a locked trunk and, distrusting Kos's prying eyes, sent her home to Laigle with the lie that the proprietor of the Hôtel Mistral would not allow her to stay in Beauvoir's room.

A visit to Simone Jollivet at Crécy-en-Brie did little to lift her spirits. Dullin, who had heard that the Russians had entered Poland on 17 September, talked about the heroic fate of the light infantry in wartime and reduced her to tears. 'I'm almost convinced that I shan't see [Bost] again,' she wrote to Sartre. As the train carried her westwards to Brittany, her thoughts returned to death. Privileging happiness had been her way of grasping the world in peacetime, but it no longer seemed relevant: 'I didn't feel it was painful to be a consciousness withdrawn from happiness and unhappiness, and I understood how one can be detached painlessly too from even the will to live i.e. to accept the idea of dying.' Before the war she and Sartre had revelled in their detached, 'existential' attitude to fascism. Now, like Sartre, she was absorbed into a tragic collective history.

In 1939 Beauvoir believed that men were superior to women. In the society into which she had been born, men and women were divided into two 'embattled castes'. Shaped by patriarchal society, it was as a woman of her time that she reacted to events. In *The Second Sex* her revolutionary thesis is that 'femininity is neither a natural nor an innate entity, but rather a condition brought about by society, on the basis of certain physiological characteristics', but, despite perceiving the importance of nurture, she continued to hold many traditional ideas: that women have a greater need for stability than men, that they do not have the 'temper' to be explorers, to question the 'fundamental premises of society' or to 'organize and control the world'. Therefore, she explained, 'it suited me to live with a man whom I regarded as my superior. My ambitions . . . were timid.'

In a man's world Beauvoir had remained an old-fashioned woman, deferring to Sartre as her intellectual 'superior', even though her own intelligence had qualified her to be materially self-sufficient. Spared economic dependence, the 'curse' of womanhood, and trumpeting her creed that 'to earn one's living . . . is the only way to achieve securely based inner independence', for ten years she had found it easy enough, so she claimed, to ignore her own femininity and to live as a surrogate man. She had revelled in 'male' freedoms, at work and at play. Now Beauvoir was forced to confront her own solitude, and was astonished to find that she reacted as a woman. Bereft of Sartre and Bost, she felt 'completely mutilated'. It was a revelation. In this crisis, it was to women she turned. They would be instruments of her own metamorphosis.

At Quimper, Bianca, in a little blue suit, was waiting to meet the Beaver on the platform. She was trembling and on the verge of tears after a scene with her mother, who was vehemently opposed to Beauvoir's relationship with her daughter. Madame Bienenfeld had found a letter from Beauvoir, and was threatening to write denouncing the teacher to the ministry of education. 'She's lying,' Beauvoir informed Bost. Her letters were 'passionate' but not 'compromising'. Scornfully she checked into the down-at-heel Hôtel de l'Épée, which reminded her of the notorious Petit Mouton in Rouen, and met up with Bianca for crêpes and cider. The weather was hot, and teacher and student strolled beside the river. The next day they set out on a seven-hour hike, past the grey Breton farmhouses garlanded in white roses, but the local women in their tall white headdresses took Beauvoir for a spy, and muttered in Breton as she passed.

Mme Bienenfeld wrote to her husband that Beauvoir was a '*sale bonne femme qui court après les petites filles,* a dirty old woman who runs after little girls'. Hysterical scenes continued, as she forbade Bianca's daily rendezvous. 'B. arrived this morning with her face white from crying, with rings under her eyes, looking devastated; her mother seems to be slowly going mad,' wrote Beauvoir to Bost on Friday 22 September.

Mme Bienenfeld's fears were not without foundation. Although Beauvoir now omitted any mention of lesbian sex from her letters to Bost, she did not practise the same self-censorship in writing to Sartre. After getting off the coach from Concarneau, Beauvoir had taken Bianca up to her hotel room, where 'we petted one another a bit – as much as possible actually – but I was as cold as a log. I think I'm totally frigid.'

There was a reason for her coldness. The day before, Bianca had demanded an equal share of Sartre's leave, which she calculated as six days in six months' time. 'You will let me spend three days with him, won't you? That'll be three days left for you.' Beauvoir felt herself trembling with anger. She wanted Sartre all to herself, and hated the idea that they would have to hide from Bianca like criminals.

On Monday Mme Bienenfeld removed her daughter to the safety of a college in Rennes. Beauvoir was left alone in Quimper, gazing wistfully at the handsome Canadian soldiers who reminded her of Little Bost.

*

At Angers, where she spent a few days with Mme Morel at La Pouèze, Beauvoir found a new idea forming in her mind. She had heard that some wives had managed to get to the front to see their husbands. 'Do find out about this,' she demanded of Sartre. 'After all, you're only in the rear.' Sartre was not enthusiastic. The women she'd heard about must be 'legitimate spouses', and officers' wives into the bargain, but he suggested that perhaps Colette Audry's brother-in-law, a general, could help get her a pass.

At La Pouèze, Beauvoir dreamt of Sartre coming to her bed in the little white garment he wore at night. He was her little Poulpiquet, a demon in Breton legend. She reproached herself for never having been 'nice enough' to him. Now she no longer had 'tender feelings' for Bost, she promised. Her love for Sartre had laid everything waste, like a tornado: 'We had so much happiness, passion never had any opportunity to be volcanic – but I always knew it could produce earthquakes in me.' By 6 October she had taken to wearing his clothes, putting on his smart little white jacket, which suited her splendidly, and wearing it with a green scarf, a green turban and a black belt, when she went 'dolled up to the nines' to collect his salary from his *lycée*, as well as her own at the Lycée Camille See, with which the Molière was amalgamated during the war. She had begun wearing a turban in order to save the cost of hairdressers that winter, telling Bost: 'I already have turbans in mauve, yellow, green – and I want them in every colour.'

Probably Beauvoir's turbans were a fashion statement rather than an economy, for, after having her nails manicured in her favourite shade, 'heather', she decided to take a taxi to collect their joint salaries of 6,700 francs. This vast sum allowed her to summon the Kos sisters to Paris on 15 October, allocate them 1,500 francs and pay back 1,000 each to Mme Morel and M. Bienenfeld, whose wife was 'clamouring' for his money (the debt was 5,000 francs). Despite moaning that, *hélas*, Poupette was coming to Paris, Beauvoir also paid the costs of her stay, her own rent of 2,000 francs, 500 francs to Sartre, and allowed herself just 50 francs a day, as she had to save up for her tax bill of 3,000 francs. 'I have the most wonderful luck to have money and not depend on anyone,' she wrote with a surge of elation. Money didn't prevent tragedy or horror, but it meant that she was free.

Paris was calm, the mood among civilians as insouciant as among the soldiers. At the Coupole, when the Beaver ordered a '*demi-Munich*' beer, the waiter laughed and said: 'Better wait until we're past the Siegfried Line.' But still she found herself crying all evening on 7 October, as she thought of the 'pure miracle' of the love between her and Bost, of the tender, passionate nights they had shared. Bost had seen his 'shadow on guard', and the Beaver felt the same strange sense of depersonalization or *dédoublement*, of watching events happen to herself. She was woman eternal, wiping her ravaged face, in the same 'classical and predictable way' that women had done through the centuries. She was Eurydice, he Orpheus whom she would only meet again in the 'kingdom of shades'. Bost, more prosaically, was annoyed that she had not given him any other address but Gégé's, where he was afraid Kos would see his letters to Castor, but he assured her that she was a good *marraine de guerre*, godmother of war. Their correspondence was 'as precious as the devil'.

Just when Beauvoir was feeling that her future was a 'black hole,' she found a new shoulder to cry on. Nathalie Sorokine, another former pupil with a crush on Castor, returned to Paris. She and Beauvoir went for a walk, and when Sorokine slipped her arm through her teacher's and squeezed it tight, Beauvoir was momentarily lost for words. She felt that she was becoming more and more attached to the girl: a pattern was repeating itself, she confessed to Bost.

C'est gênant . . . d'être à la fois une proie et un séducteur . . . It's annoying to be in this role, one which I've already had with Bianca, and with Kos, when she was very little, of being both prey and seducer – a seducer, not that I engage in seduction, but because my partner displays the reserve, the caprice, the mystery and the moods which she would display to a seducer – and besides, it's she who chases me and behaves in a loving way.

To Sartre she expressed herself even more bluntly: 'I feel a bit like some clumsy seducer confronted with a young virgin, as mysterious as all virgins are. Only the seducer at least has a clear mission, which is to seduce and, as it were, pierce the mystery. Whereas, in my case, I'm simultaneously the prey. It's a dreadful, awkward situation, and one exclusively confined to gays [*pièges*].'

The next day, 10 October, Beauvoir moved out of Gégé's to the Hôtel Danemark, 21 rue Vavin, a stone's throw from her childhood home at the Carrefour Vavin. Her room was small, but spartan surroundings were no deterrent to love. Sorokine, like her predecessors, was an immigrant who needed Beauvoir's help. Without an identity card, she was unable to register at the Sorbonne. As before, the girl's mother initially felt gratitude for the teacher's help, particularly so, in this case, as the family were poor. Beauvoir decided to pull strings with Colette Audry to get Sorokine into the university, and pay her fees. A few days later the student declared her love for the older woman: '*Je vous aime tellement*, I love you so much,' cried Nathalie, shedding tears and muttering in Russian as she and Beauvoir exchanged passionate kisses.

As usual, Beauvoir titillated Sartre with intimate details omitted in her letters to Bost: Nathalie 'pulled me on to the bed, then – amid sobs – into her arms and towards her mouth; finally, after about an hour, she even drew my hand to specific parts of her body . . . *elle fait absolument "fruit vert"*, she is the very image of "unripe fruit".' To Sartre, Beauvoir emphasizes Sorokine's virginity, her awkward, adolescent movements, and the danger of her becoming a nuisance like Bianca. The Beaver assures him that in bed, as with Bianca, she is as cold as a log; indeed, by the end of the war she'll have become an asexual being.

The truth was very different. The log was melting. In Nathalie Beauvoir had found someone whose temperament was as fiery and wilful as her own. Nathalie had stolen the 'intimate journal' which Beauvoir, like Sartre, had begun writing in imitation of Gide, and she exploded in fury when she discovered the web of relationships described in its pages. 'It's so unfair! I'm only the fifth in your life,' stormed Nathalie, collapsing into sobs and sulking for a full ten minutes. When Beauvoir began stroking her, the teenager kissed her on the mouth. In a long letter to Bost, Beauvoir confessed how moved she was by Nathalie's declaration of love, how she had tried to express her own warm feelings without promising too much. 'This girl has a strength of passion which moves me: her whole body trembles, and she almost suffocates me, she holds me so tight.' Her beautiful, unhappy face upsets Beauvoir. 'I like her very much, I esteem her, she's really sweet . . .' As Bost had already discovered, with mingled horror and admiration, the Beaver was *le plus grand menteur du monde*, the greatest liar in the world'.

Soon Beauvoir was recounting with satisfaction that Nathalie had become 'a little tamed animal'. Most importantly, for Beauvoir's paedophile tastes, she was a 'nymph', whose childish ways spurred the teacher to take the initiative when they went up to Sorokine's room at her home in Saint-Cloud.

> I was very tender with Sorokine . . . telling her sweet nothings. And for the first time with me she was absolutely melting and happy and abandoned . . . There was a charming, childlike complicity . . . She was really precious to me yesterday evening, with her tartan hair-ribbons, her teddy-bear in her arms, and her serious face . . . It's a damn nuisance for the future, because I won't ever be able to dump her now.

In the Sapphic nest in Hôtel du Danemark, Simone and Nathalie embraced so ardently that Kos, in the next-door room, grew suspicious. By now they were meeting three times a week, for the usual formula of Kant and kisses. Nathalie, 'wild and tender', touched Beauvoir more deeply than any of her previous female lovers. At the *lycée*, her lesbian persona was common knowledge: 'When I am sixty, there will be plenty of "suicides of passion",' she boasted to Bost. Although she complained to her men that the company of women, the only available company in wartime, was 'pathetic', and her scorn for many of the women in her life is a constant theme in her letters to Sartre (Poupette is *moche*, ugly, her clothes hideous, Wanda is fat with broken veins, Bianca is jealous), when she sent Bost her photo in a turban he replied that it had made him laugh till he cried because 'You look like a lesbian, a coke-addict, and a fakir too.' By 10 November Beauvoir had also renewed relations with Bianca: 'The strength of that girl's passion is incredible,' Beauvoir wrote dismissively to Sartre. 'Sensually I was more involved than usual, with the vague, boorish idea that I should at least "profit" from her body . . . There was a hint of depravity which I can't quite explain . . .'

In a moment of self-analysis, Beauvoir recognized that although she was 'very lucky' to be 'an intellectual', whose mind was always at work, 'I am physiologically a *bon vivant*.' Like her father, she liked food and sex. In a manner historically more male than female, she objectified her prey.

*

Sartre had found a new best friend in Corporal Jean Pierre, with whom he was as happy as he had once been with Nizan. He was alarmed by the Beaver's plans to 'visit my sister Emma', a coded expression, designed to deceive the censors, for her intended clandestine visit to Sartre. Nothing could stand in Castor's way. She faked appendicitis to get a sick note from the doctor and bribed the concierge at Gégé's flat fifty francs for a residence certificate. *'You're not allowed to know my address,'* wrote Sartre uncomfortably, but by dint of 'close reading' she might learn it. On 15 October he composed a careful letter about 'Emma's' friends. The first letter of each name spelt out his location: BRUMATH. A fortnight later he sent her a sketch map of 'Quimper' (Brumath), and advised 'Emma' to book a room at the Auberge du Cerf.

Sartre professed to long to hold his 'slim turbanned Hindu' in his arms again, but he was more anxious about Wanda, who was being pursued by Roger Blin, an actor at the Atelier. *The Age of Reason* vividly portrays the sense of reluctant duty that ties Mathieu to his mistress, Marcelle, in a relationship as stale and old as any bourgeois marriage. Marcelle, whose voice is 'curt and masculine', whose face with its brown skin and bluish, veined rings below her eyes makes him think: 'Good Lord, she's getting old,' Marcelle, his mistress of seven years, is pregnant.

'*Merde!*' said Mathieu.

And he thought: 'She ought to have told me at least three weeks ago.'

' . . . What's to be done?' said Marcelle.

'Well, I suppose one gets rid of it, *non?*'

Mathieu, who like his creator is thirty-four, finds the idea of pregnancy abhorrent. It interferes with Freedom, his 'secret garden'. He sets to work to find the money for the abortionist. There is no time to lose, 'for the blister was expanding, at that very moment; it was making obscure efforts to emerge, to extricate itself from darkness, and growing into something like *that*, a little, pallid, flabby object that clung to the world and sucked its sap'. He detests the 'tiny human creature, conscious, furtive, deceitful and pathetic'. He stares down at Marcelle, sleeping peacefully: 'But the pustule deep within her did not sleep, it had no time to sleep: it found nourishment and grew . . . I must find the money in forty-eight hours.'

Fortunately for Sartre, Beauvoir was no more enthusiastic about maternity than he. When Mme Morel had urged him to give the Beaver a child, offering to bring it up, she had declined. It was Olga who was pregnant after a casual affair, and whose abortion provided material for both Sartre and Beauvoir's fiction. But the mood of *The Age of Reason* is of weariness for the ageing Marcelle, of desire for 'tragic, voluptuous' Ivich, a composite of the Kossacks, Olga and Wanda. It was to the latter that Sartre would dedicate his novel.

Beauvoir's arrival in Brumath on 1 November acted on Sartre like a 'time bomb'. 'I can hardly endure even the Beaver,' he wrote in his notebook, remembering how, in Paris, while she waited for him in one café he used to dive into another and 'quickly gulp down a coffee and croissants, in order to remain for a moment still wrapped up in myself and last night's dreams'. Perhaps in Brumath he did the same thing, for when Beauvoir, dressed like a true Parisian in yellow turban, high heels and earrings, sat expectantly the next morning in the Taverne du Cerf waiting for Sartre, no one arrived. She sent a cryptic note to 'Private Sartre', saying that his pipe was waiting for him in the tavern, and eventually spotted her reluctant lover coming down the street: 'He's grown a horrible scrubby beard which makes him look simply awful.' She communicated her disapproval, and at eleven o'clock he returned, clean-shaven.

It seems that Beauvoir penetrated Sartre's shell. 'We were so intent on love that I forgot to take the money,' he wrote afterwards, recalling 'your presence, all alone and totally naked, the little expressions that cross your face, the tender smiles, your little arms round my neck'. Had she felt 'how deeply I love you and what you mean to me? Oh my darling Beaver, I would like you to feel my love as much as I feel yours.' Passing her off as his fiancé, Sartre found them a room together at the Boeuf Noir, where they spent five days, often huddling together under the duvet like Hansel and Gretel in the 'glacial' temperature. While he was away making meteorological observations, Beauvoir stayed in bed reading his novel and notebooks. It was a mark of Sartre's trust that he allowed her to criticize the character of Marcelle, although he felt bound to end his autobiographical musings at the point at which he met Wanda, for fear of giving offence. His girlfriend was already 'crazy with rage' at the news of the Beaver's visit.

For his part, Sartre read Beauvoir's journal and advised her to engage in the same Proustian self-analysis as himself. At first Beauvoir agreed: 'I shall soon be thirty-two, and feel myself a mature woman – but what *sort* of woman? I wish I knew. For instance, in what ways am I typically "feminine", and in what ways not?' On reflection she decided to finish her novel first.

In the Brumath taverns, among 'thick, comfortable voices, tobacco smoke, warmth, and the smell of sauerkraut', the military world thrilled Beauvoir. Surrounded by *chasseurs* in their berets with red pompoms, hearing the clink of metal, the tramp of boots, watching horses and camouflaged trucks moving up to the line, eating black pudding and potatoes opposite Sartre in his blue uniform, she felt a sense of exultation: 'I'm on holiday again, alone with Sartre.' 'This will be a war without any real fighting,' he explained: 'A modern war.' People expected it to be over by Christmas. On the last night, under a starry sky, he walked her to the station yard. On the midnight express to Paris, a soldier began stroking Simone's feet. When she demurred, he told her that this was the first contact that he'd had with a woman for twelve weeks. She drank a mug of *marc* and let him squeeze her ankles.

Beauvoir the adventurer, small, tough and fearless, would have made a keener soldier than Sartre. She longed to be in a foxhole with her man, throwing grenades at the Germans. Had it been possible, she would have joined up. Failing this, the next best thing was to visit Little Bost, even nearer the front than Sartre. His letters were far more exciting than Sartre's: Bost was holed up in a barn, while planes whistled overhead. 'À *nos trous!* To our holes!' came the cry at the sound of shots.

'I've absolutely decided to come and see "your sister", by December 1st at the latest,' wrote Beauvoir peremptorily to Bost. 'I don't know if this will please you, *mais tant pis*, too bad . . . I have such a burning desire for you.'

Bost was horrified. Beauvoir's tales of how she had been taken for a prostitute at the Taverne au Cerf ('You could make a fortune here'), of how she felt like a queen while the sex-starved soldier caressed her feet, had the opposite effect to that which she intended. 'I don't want you to come here,' replied Bost on 4 November. There were no hotels, not even a single road; even the officers' wives were turned away. Colossal rats ran round their quarters, and he had the fever; the men were so short of food that they were making mayonnaise with machine oil.

Beauvoir's longing for *la vie de soldat* was so intense that she took no notice. No one would be able to identify her because they weren't married, she argued. This time she had mistaken her man: Bost had grown up in the army and, despite his lowly rank, was treated as an officer by the men. He, like Sartre, had found a new friend, Amsellem, and a new nickname: Jacquot. He ordered Beauvoir, 'shrewish bitch', to stay away; she was *'un peu trop sur la bouche'*, too pushy, too mouthy. Yet he loved her, and promised that he would lie to Kos that he was spending his leave at Taverny, so that Beauvoir should be the first to meet her soldier-hero in his uniform.

In Paris, surrounded by her 'regiment of women', Beauvoir, too, was growing up. Separated from Sartre, the dominant twin, she was writing feverishly, valuing the 'fertile apprenticeship' of solitude. Sartre had been shocked by her October account of an orgy with Marie Girard, the 'lunar woman', her friend Youki, Blanche Picard and Thérèse, a friend of the celebrated artists' model Kiki of Montparnasse, who personified the permissive society of Paris in the 1920s and 30s: 'Everyone was on heat, or pretended to be . . . Blanche has been a whole month without a screw, she's hysterical.' At 4 a.m., after a drunken sing-song, Beauvoir brought Marie, who claimed to be in love with her, and a 'handsome blond fellow' back to her room for what appears to have been three-in-a-bed sex. It was her way of blotting out thoughts of death, and she returned for another orgy on 10 December. 'Sartre says I have sickened him with stories of Youki and the lunar woman,' she wrote gleefully to Bost. 'It's due to his moral meditations, I think, that he's turning again to saintliness.'

Dancing had resumed in the Paris night-clubs, where the strippers wore Union Jack G-strings. At the reopened Flore, Beauvoir spotted the young Simone Signoret in her black beret, but kept her distance. Despite sleeping regularly with Bianca, it was Sorokine, 'bare-legged, with heavy shoes on her feet, a red ribbon in her lovely blonde hair, and the look of a tiny little girl who'd grown too fast', who attracted her. 'Normally it's only women who find me pretty,' Beauvoir confided to Sartre, after conducting a survey on the subject among her male friends, and discovering that Mouloudji considered her angular and brusque. Nathalie, however, found her beautiful and alluring; she offered her teacher entry into her 'self-enclosed little girl's world', just as once Kos had done. On 14 December Simone suggested 'complete relations'.

20

⌒

The Turn of the Screw

My charming vermin are beginning to devour me again.
Simone de Beauvoir to Jean-Paul Sartre, January 1940

ON 24 DECEMBER 1939 Jacques-Laurent Bost moved up to the front.
His *trou* was one metre wide. The men were 'drunk as donkeys', and
their officers treated them like dogs. The propaganda leaflets dropped
by the Germans lay mired in the mud:

> The leaves fall, we shall fall like them
> The leaves die, because God wills it so
> But we, we shall die because the English will it so
> By next spring, no one will remember either dead leaves
> or slain *poilus*, life will pass over our graves.

In the comfort of the Chalet-Hôtel Idéal-Sport at Megève, where she
had gone skiing with the eighteen-year-old Jean Kanapa, a friend of
Bianca's, Beauvoir felt a pang of conscience. Were her generation the
guilty generation, responsible by reason of their passivity for the war? In
her journal she wrote tenderly: 'Never have I esteemed [Bost] so greatly;
he is more and more intelligent, and he has character. I feel a
tremendous affection for him – as he is now, dirty and muddy and
brutish – and when I think back to what he was, to his gentleness, his
beauty, his tenderness, it belongs to a far-off past – as if I really *lived with*

him *en soldat.*' The 'dread' she felt over his fate deepened as she read *Prelude to Verdun,* and wondered if history would repeat itself.

In the icy cold, Bost hunkered down in his foxhole under the boom of the cannon and strict orders not to shoot even if he saw a German. Sartre, by contrast, was seated at the piano singing 'Toreador' to the colonel, who poured the first glass of champagne for his favourite tenor. 'Well, Sartre,' boomed the colonel, as they drank Christmas toasts. 'Haven't you found anything yet for your novel in this Phoney War?'

'*Eh non, mon colonel.*'

'Oh, I'm sure you will find something, you'll know how to do it, eh?'

Beauvoir returned from the slopes to her 'charming vermin', Kos, Bianca, Poupette and Nathalie, who were squabbling more than usual. They worshipped their queen 'blindly', wrote Beauvoir with satisfaction. She ruled her court with a rod of iron, allocating her time according to a rigid schedule. This was a constant source of friction, as Sorokine jockeyed with Bianca for more of Beauvoir's attention, and Bianca complained at having only two evenings with Beauvoir instead of five like Kos. Nathalie's star was in the ascendant. In January the crunch came as Sartre's leave drew near. 'Devoured' by her women, jealous of the 'burdensome' Bianca's relationship with Sartre, Beauvoir decided it was time for the axe to fall.

As she fell in love with Nathalie, Beauvoir had fallen out of love with Bianca. It was not convenient, but she couldn't help herself. Her friends saw the signs: '[Beauvoir] loves Sorokine as passionately as if she were a man,' observed one.

To some extent Sapphic sex was opportunistic sex, in a Paris all but empty of men. Beauvoir craved the connection which Nathalie offered her, and which she was sexually fluid enough to find at different times in her life with either men or women. She moved with ease along the sexuality spectrum, defying labels, and often discovering that personality mattered to her as much as gender. The relationship with Nathalie also, however, reveals Beauvoir at her most predatory, and cannot be separated from her ruthless dismissal of Bianca, whose demands for 'an exact tripartite division' of the threesome with Sartre had become a bone of contention.

The previous November the student had asked for an equal share of Sartre's expected leave, five or six days of ten. Beauvoir had flushed with anger: 'Threesomes won't be so agreeable, during so short a time,' she replied. 'You've no sense for threesomes any more!' said Bianca in surprise. Shutting herself in the lavatory to read Sartre's letters in peace, Beauvoir decided that, after Brumath, she could no longer bear to share him. The next day, 12 November, there was another 'big scene', when Bianca explained that she expected to 'cut our lives into thirds', for example spending one month of the holidays with Beauvoir, one with Sartre, and leaving Beauvoir and Sartre only one together. Beauvoir exploded at the prospect of giving up the three months of summer she was accustomed to spending with Sartre. 'You love me less than Sartre,' Bianca accused her. 'I love you just as much,' said Beauvoir, 'but I have more need of Sartre.' Her last ten years with Sartre had not been 'idyllic', she explained; there had been separations, difficulties of every kind. As a result she was 'situated differently' from Bianca; she was old and Bianca was young, and had more years of happiness ahead; her relations with Sartre no longer had the 'youth and ardour' of those with Bianca, so this had to be compensated for by their duration. It was the argument of the older wife against the younger mistress, and, sobbing, Bianca agreed that she'd lost 'respect' for Beauvoir's relations with Sartre, which she had once seen as forming the base of the triangle. On the other hand, argued the redhead sharply, she had to take advantage of Sartre *before* he grew too old.

Beauvoir smelt danger. This time she would put a stop to the repeating pattern. She wrote to Sartre that, as she had explained to Bianca, 'those ten years of common life have given me rights over you of a kind that no one else can have – that you thought you *owed* yourself first to me'. On 17 December Beauvoir advised him to 'stop the affair . . . It would take a lot of toughness . . . Diminish the passion in your letters, say a cool farewell.' But she kept Bianca in the dark, and continued sexual relations with her, stumbling away from Bianca's bed the very next morning like a 'satisfied man'.

Bost was horrified by Beauvoir's treatment of Bianca, for whose position, which in some respects echoed his own, he had a great deal of sympathy. Beauvoir's anti-Semitic jibes at Bianca 'wailing on the wall of Sion' since the start of the war, her hypocritical complaints about being Bianca's 'prey' during 'nights of passion . . . when I was detached enough to feel a cad', her outrage at Bianca's demands, led him to blame her for leading the girl on:

I think that in these matters you (Sartre and you) always lack foresight and you give so much to people and let them hope for so much that the attitude they almost always end having towards you is one that you have provoked. Honestly, you look as if you're picking holes in people who have ceased to please you . . . They feel duped.

It was a fair comment. Beauvoir acknowledged that Bienenfeld in part irritated her because she was a caricature of herself, the girl's nerves and hysterics mirroring her own agitation. What Beauvoir remained curiously blind to was Bianca's well-founded fear of the future as a Jewish woman, and it is pertinent to question whether the extreme anti-Semitic opinions with which Beauvoir's father bombarded her as a child were now resurrected in her mind. '[Bienenfeld]'s prophesying doom like a Cassandra (what's new) and hesitating between the concentration camp and suicide, with a preference for suicide,' sneered Beauvoir on 10 March 1940. Only a year later the decree of 21 March 1941 revoked their nationality from French Jews. Bianca's aunt Cécile was deported to Auschwitz on 11 February 1943; her grandfather died in the train before it reached the camp.

In November Beauvoir had complained to Sartre of being 'sickened by passion' with Bienenfeld – 'like *foie gras*, and poor quality into the bargain'. A few weeks later she confessed to 'frigidity' with Bianca: 'the first time I'd ever felt a real hatred of sleeping with a woman I don't love'. Apparently Bienenfeld's technique was at fault, her caresses 'clumsy'. Why is it women rather than men who are clumsy in 'localized caresses (Kos, R and Védrine have put me through equal tortures),' demanded Beauvoir. She found her answer in Gide, who said that it was because women put themselves in your place, but it's always *themselves* they put there, whereas a man is unable to make this substitution, so he 'theorizes the other person directly and honestly.' Two days later she wrote that she was tempted 'to let passion flower' with Nathalie.

On 5 January Beauvoir finally seduced Nathalie:

I asked her if she wanted us to have complete relations . . . She answered: 'As you like' . . . She started punching the wall, twisting about nervously and half-sobbing into the pillows. Then I told her that for my part I certainly did want more complete relations . . . 'We mustn't be hypocritical,' she moaned. So then I began to undress her a bit, and she said: 'Turn off the light, please' . . . A moment later she asked me with the greatest politeness: 'How about you, would you mind undressing?' I took off my blouse . . . We undressed and got into bed. I caressed her – intimately . . . She was paralysed by shyness . . . She couldn't be more of a virgin . . . As for me, I was charmed by her . . . She left me at midnight, with money for a taxi and quite radiant.

A week later Beauvoir slept with Bianca. Her physical revulsion for the girl had grown. 'Her body had a pungent faecal odour which made things pretty unpleasant . . .' she wrote to Sartre. Only four days earlier she had raised with Sartre the question of the 'Jews of France', agreeing that one would have a greater sense of solidarity with them than the persecuted Jews of Germany, since the idea of being 'situated' necessarily also included frontiers. But in her *Journal de Guerre* she wrote 'sentences so terrible' about Bianca, '*pathétique*' because she felt afraid, that over sixty years later Bianca found herself unable to forget them. It could have been Georges de Beauvoir, supporter of *Action Française*, anxious to 'rid France of the Jews, whom he held responsible for the ills that had befallen the country', who accused Bianca of an obsession with 'making a profit' in a shockingly stereotypical representation of the young student as a Fagin figure. Beauvoir's journal entry of 10 December 1939 reads: 'She weeps before a wailing wall that she diligently builds with her own hands, that she builds often to protect the positive wealth she bitterly seeks to defend. Something like the old Jewish usurer who weeps with pity for the client he has driven to suicide.'

On 14 January Beauvoir again had full sexual relations with Sorokine, whom she found 'so perfect and charming . . . I've a very keen taste for her body.' Nervously Sorokine asked if she and Beauvoir were criminals, and if they'd be put in prison if they were discovered. Beauvoir told her no. On the next occasion, on the 24th, Sorokine 'grew languid and melting till I was obliged to ravish her . . . I was in turmoil when she left and still am.' Nathalie, shyly hiding her face behind a curtain of straight, blonde hair, excited Simone more and more: '*Elle me plaît physiquement de plus en plus . . .*' she recorded in her War Journal.

*

On 4 February Sartre, 'surely the dirtiest soldier in France', in his frayed greatcoat, big boots and filthy uniform, arrived at the Gare de l'Est, to be met by Beauvoir. She had been so afraid of missing him that, two days beforehand, she had waited for hours in the station café, feeling that his leave was simply a myth. Only when his mother brought over a suitcase of his clothes did his arrival seem imminent, and she felt tears of joy pricking her eyes. Now the small, plump figure stood smiling before her. She hurried him away to the Hôtel Mistral, where Sartre changed into mufti. Shaken by Wanda's affair, he had agreed to devote most of his leave to the Beaver. 'Never have I felt so forcefully that our lives have no meaning outside of our love, and that nothing changes that, neither separations, nor passions, nor the war,' he had written: 'You said that this was a victory for our morality, but it is just as much a victory for our love.' He assured her that 'this war has bromized my infamous desire for flirtations that you used to see. As I say, there is no one but you.'

Beauvoir had been to some trouble over her appearance, buying herself a new blue pullover. 'Everyone finds me beautiful,' she recorded in her journal. Everyone but Sartre, who preferred Wanda's womanly curves. On the first night of his leave, despite the excitement of being together 'on the sly' (Sartre having lied to Wanda that he was arriving later), and dinner and drinks *chez Rey*, when they retired to bed at midnight Sartre simply expounded his theories for an hour. 'They're precious to me, but very familiar,' wrote a disappointed Simone in her journal. All the same, with Sartre's head on the pillow beside her, her insomnia disappeared.

Together they reclaimed the boulevards and their beloved cafés: 'How united we feel in Paris,' wrote Beauvoir as, side by side, she read his war notebooks and he her novel. Over dinner at the Brasserie Lipp, Sartre paid her 'a heap of compliments' over the book. On Wednesday, 7 February, Beauvoir felt happier than she had done for months: 'Sartre is here, Bost is nearly here, my year's work has been really good. Paris is beautiful . . .' It was a moment of prolonged joy. After seeing James Stewart in *Mr Smith Goes to Washington*, the twins strolled up the Champs Élysées to the opera, talking non-stop about simultaneity, *la conscience d'autrui*, the consciousness of the Other – which preoccupied the Beaver – and Sartre's topic of the moment, authenticity. If their bodies were not entwined, their minds were. The next day, over coffee *chez Rey*, the Three Musketeers café in Avenue du Maine, the great moment came when Sartre almost finished her novel and she finished his. Not only was *The Age of Reason* 'a work of *great beauty*', better than Stendhal or Dostoevsky, Beauvoir assured Sartre, but she now saw with clarity that she, too, was '*une profiteuse de guerre*', a war which had finally given her the opportunity to write a novel worthy of publication.

But Beauvoir had another object also in mind. Like the Marquise de Meurteuil, she knew when it was time to end a dangerous liaison. She persuaded Sartre that he must end the trio with Bianca. The notion of 'authenticity', borrowed from Martin Heidegger, was to be their justification.

The previous Thursday Beauvoir had related 'words of wisdom' to

Bianca 'justifying to her . . . her inauthenticity'. 'Authenticity', with its mystical associations of blood and race, was the buzzword of the time, the goal towards which Sartre believed he was striving in 1939 and 1940, but it is doubtful whether at that period he understood the term in the sense intended by Heidegger. Phenomenology was a style or movement first, rather than a philosophy, as Maurice Merleau-Ponty emphasizes in *La Phénoménologie de la perception*. The German philosopher's notoriously difficult *Sein und Zeit* had been translated into French by Henri Corbin, and although Sartre would later fudge his dates and claim that he had read it in the original before the war, it is unlikely that he found the time to do so. Only after his conversations with the priest Marius Perrin in the Stalag did he request a copy of the book in German. In November and December 1939, Sartre was still using the term *réalité humaine*, which is simply the rendering chosen by Corbin for Heidegger's central concept of *Dasein*, or man. 'Heidegger rightly signalled that the world is "that whereby human reality discloses to itself what it is",' Sartre writes on 24 November, in a long notebook entry which finds him puzzling over what it means to be

A being thrown into the world. It is the world which frees consciousness dressed by its own dreams – by its total freedom. Will characterises the human condition, as the necessity for a being abandoned in the world to discover its own goals.

In his flawed reading of Heidegger, Sartre made 'human reality' the subject of *Sein und Zeit*, whereas its true subject is '*Existenz*', Existence, the 'ecstasy' of being. The translation *réalité humaine* continued to lead to misunderstanding: on 5 February 1939 Beauvoir recorded that Sartre outlined to her Heidegger's ideas on death, 'but I must find out more'. Five days later she was excited by the 'revelation that Sartre made to me yesterday evening on Heidegger and "the existential"'. Clearly, at this stage, Sartre was the teacher, Beauvoir the disciple. Nine months later, in a letter thanking the Beaver for the 'scrumptious' halva she had sent him, Sartre was congratulating himself on the fact that phenomenology had allowed Merleau-Ponty, the Beaver and himself to escape the old Cartesian mind-body dualism in which their former teacher, Brunschvieg, was still stuck. Yet, groping for comprehension, Sartre did understand the essentials of what Heidegger offered. Intuitively he sensed that the great phenomenologist had 'dared, in the postwar period, to pull philosophy down from the heavens to earth, to speak to us of ourselves', of such simple things as existence, being, death and nothingness, with 'freshness and incomparable power' in a 'liberating, destructive catharsis'. For Sartre, deeply troubled by his loss of faith, schooled on Kierkegaard's image of man as a lonely, anguished individual, and influenced by Bergson's idea of movement, of an *élan vital* which carries humankind forward, Heidegger seemed to offer answers to the mystery of being, if only he could find the key to understand him.

Certainly Sartre had by now stumbled on the famous paragraph 10 of *Sein und Zeit* in which Heidegger argues that 'fundamental ontology' finds itself in a paradoxical situation between 'being' and 'not being able to be', but that 'not being' weighs more heavily on man that 'being'. We are 'beings-for-death' who must accept our finitude, and only in cultivating a resolute attitude (*Entschlossenheit*) towards death can we become genuinely 'authentic'. Knowing that we are creatures who will die spurs us to act now, to create rather than to procrastinate. On 27 November Sartre continued to meditate on authenticity: 'I can see clearly how this authenticity I'm aiming at differs from Gidean purity. Purity is an entirely subjective quality . . . But authenticity . . . can only be understood in terms of the human condition, that condition of a being thrown into a situation. Authenticity is a duty that comes to us from outside and inside at once, because our "inside" is an outside . . .'

He was going round in circles. On 9 January 1940, Sartre realized his failure to come up with original ideas for the 'truly atheist philosophy' which was his goal. He wrote a mournful letter to Beauvoir expressing his disillusion:

> I have reread my five notebooks, and they don't please me nearly as much as I had expected. I find them a little vague, too discreet, even the clearest ideas are little more than rehashings of Heidegger's: in the end, all I have done since September . . . is only a long elaboration of the ten pages he devoted to the question of historicity.

Fortunately for Sartre, Beauvoir's own mind was, as her examiners had realized in 1929, razor sharp. She had caught up and overtaken Sartre. Her long sessions of concentrated study of Heidegger's German text in the library had born fruit, and she had incorporated many philosophical ideas into *L'Invitée*. 'It takes me far too long to understand things . . . It takes me a lot longer, for instance, than it does the Beaver here,' admitted Sartre in interview in 1972. 'The Beaver is much faster than I am. I'm more like a snail.' Now it was her turn to provide the revelation. Reading the Beaver's metaphysical novel in at least eight sessions between 5 and 15 February, Sartre saw that, slicing through Heidegger's dense language, she had developed her own ideas on individual consciousness, on things, on nothingness and time, which she presented in a literary form intelligible to him. Despite the brief nature of his leave, and the need to meet Brice Parain and Dullin, as well as seeing Wanda, Sartre devoted hours to reading the pages of manuscript, 150, 200, 250 pages, which had accumulated on Beauvoir's desk as she set herself to prove to her father that she was not, as he taunted her, a *fruit sec* who would never bring forth a book; nor was she Sartre's inferior as a novelist and a thinker.

Sartre's heart beat with excitement as he raced through *She Came to Stay*, and striking images lodged in his memory: a woman in a night-club, her bare arm lying inert on the table while a man's hand stroked it: 'It lay there, forgotten, ignored, the man's hand was stroking a piece of flesh that no longer belonged to anyone.' The woman has allowed her arm to become a mere thing that she pretends is no longer connected to herself: it is an illustration of bad faith which would become one of most famous scenes in *Being and Nothingness*. Similarly Xavière experiences her body as her own, and as an object when she touches her eyelashes. 'It's extraordinary, the impression it makes on you to touch your eyelashes,' said Xavière. 'You touch yourself without touching yourself. It's as if you touched yourself from some way away.' Sartre used the example of touching oneself to begin his discussion of the body and its modes of being in *Being and Nothingness*.

Significantly, it is through Beauvoir's concept of the Look that she illustrates her theory of the Other. When I perceive someone looking at me, I experience myself as the other's object, and hence a conscious being. The Look makes me an object of the other's hate, indifference, love or desire. 'Looking' is a threat, a source of alienation. Beauvoir saw clearly that people relate to each other either through mutual respect, as equal subjectivities, or by means of a relationship in which one is the object, the other the dominating subject. The theory of the Other, so important for the understanding of the mechanism of social oppression which inspired the women's liberation movement, would be developed formally in *The Ethics of Ambiguity* and *The Second Sex*, but had its first airing in *She Came to Stay*. The Look inspired Sartre too: the man looking through a keyhole in *Being and Nothingness* would become the most memorable example of his philosophy. 'We start with the first revelation of the Other as a *look*,' he writes, in his explanation of how people seek to enslave each other. 'The Other's look fashions my body in its nakedness . . . The Other holds a secret – the secret of what I am.'

Sartre had discovered a 'mother lode' of ideas for *Being and Nothingness*, which he began writing five months later. Although both books were published in 1943, Sartre read Beauvoir's before beginning his own. She had written to him on 17 January: 'I think you'll really heap me with praises when you read my 250 pages (for there'll be at least 250).' Her journal shows that he read her last chapter before leaving.

On his first day back in the army, Sartre recorded his debt to Beauvoir: 'The Beaver has taught me something new.' For 1,000 words he transcribed Beauvoir's ideas about unrealizable situations. The next day he plagiarized her ideas about time which, tongue-in-cheek, Beauvoir had put into the mouth of the Sartre figure, Pierre, in her novel. Sartre began modestly:

I feel strangely bashful about embarking on a study of temporality. Time has always struck me as a philosophical headache . . . And behold, I now glimpse a theory of time! . . . I feel like a kid.

But as quickly as he glimpsed it, his theory evaporated in woolly, long-winded prose: 'Time is the opaque limit of consciousness. It is moreover, an indiscernible opacity in a total translucidity . . .' He would need many more tutorials with Beauvoir in the Café Flore before he was ready to present existentialism to the world.

Although Sartre acknowledged his debt to the Beaver in his war diary, he did not do so in *Being and Nothingness*. Like the boy who stole from his mother's purse in La Rochelle, he claimed ownership of her ideas. To Beauvoir this never mattered. ' "You both have so many ideas in common," said Xavière, "I'm never sure which of you is speaking or to whom to reply." ' But the legend that Beauvoir was Sartre's disciple deserves to be turned on its head: he was merely the conduit for their shared endeavour.

*

'It struck me as rotten, thinking of the blow that was about to fall on her head,' wrote Beauvoir guiltily on 16 February. While Sartre was seeing Wanda, Beauvoir had taken Bianca to an Alsatian restaurant on the Boulevard St Michel, where they discussed authenticity and Bianca, 'so passionately admiring of theories she doesn't understand', irritated her more than ever. Despite Sartre's (and Beauvoir's) claims of solidarity with French Jews, he agreed to drop Bianca on a 'whim' of authenticity. Like Pieter, also 'inauthentic', the Jew remained the Other. 'I am more and more convinced that in order to achieve authenticity, something has to snap,' he had written, fretting that he himself was not, as Wanda informed him, 'authentic'.

But when Sartre wrote curtly to Bianca ending their relationship, Beauvoir reproached him: 'My love, you really did go too far with Bienenfeld. A bit more consideration was needed.' She met up with Bianca, hurt but beautiful in a dark red dress with a black hat and veil, angry that Sartre hadn't even bothered to give her an explanation. 'She knows there's a lie somewhere . . . she's not without her suspicions even with respect to me,' wrote Beauvoir anxiously. On 4 March her soul-searching continued: 'I blamed us – myself as much as you, actually – in the past, in the future, in the absolute: the way we treat people. I felt it was unacceptable that we'd managed to make her suffer so much.'

Did Beauvoir realize that she was abandoning Bianca to persecution? In 2005, Bianca was generous in her own judgement on Beauvoir:

> *La guerre était un catastrophe pour Simone de Beauvoir.* She was hurt by the war, which threatened her most important relationships, with Bost and with Sartre. She was jealous and she was afraid, afraid that Sartre was too attached to me . . . Bost was the pretext. She was very attached to Bost. She said, 'Men are better than women at making love.' She was not lesbian. She liked adventures, but her great love affairs were with men.

*

On the afternoon of Friday, 16 February, the day after Sartre's departure, Beauvoir was teaching sociology at the *lycée* when a maid knocked at the door: a M. Bost was waiting in the parlour below. Beauvoir's hands began to tremble, her cheeks grew scarlet, she felt a lump in her throat, but she had to finish class. Finally she was able to run downstairs, where she found Bost, alone in the room, tall and handsome in khaki. Looking into his green eyes, she knew nothing had changed between them.

He took her arm. The sky was blue, the snowy streets sparkling in the sunshine, as they strolled towards the Bastille. Beauvoir telephoned Kos, to give her their prepared lie: Poupette had just arrived, so Beauvoir had to cancel their meeting. Excuses made, Beauvoir and Bost enjoyed a leisurely dinner before taking a taxi to pick up her overnight bag and going on to the warm, luxurious Hôtel Oriental on place Denfert-Rochereau. In the taxi Bost kissed Beauvoir, and she was 'bouleversée', overwhelmed at the touch of his lips again. 'I can't believe that six months separate me from his kisses,' she wrote in her journal. 'It's a great joy to me to feel important, profoundly important, in Bost's life.'

A night of love-making in the overheated room left Beauvoir tired and 'feverish'. She lay silently in Bost's arms, savouring his closeness after the 'tender and passionate' hours they had spent together, before going downstairs for the petit déjeuner. Afterwards, while she went to meet Kos, waiting morosely in a nearby hotel, unaware that her supposed boyfriend was actually in Paris, Bost lurked in a café reading The Age of Reason. At soon as she could, Beauvoir joined him. As they sat side by side, while jazz crackled over the radio, Beauvoir was so moved by 'his precious, miraculous and fragile presence' that she almost burst into tears. As Bost talked of the war, the future, his regret and hopes, Beauvoir thought that she had never known a union like the one she had with him, and her tears welled up afresh.

The next day, while Bost was lunching with his brother Pierre, Beauvoir wrote to Sartre. The slow-burning rivalry between the two men had come to a head; more than once Beauvoir had teased Sartre that she read Bost's letters before his, that they were longer, funnier, more affectionate. Now she sent Sartre a thunderbolt:

> There's one thing of which I'm now sure, which is that Bost forms part of my future in an absolutely certain – even essential – way. I felt such 'remorse' because of him, that I want a postwar existence with him – and partly for him . . . He has been beyond all that I hoped for . . . I honestly felt there was no comparison between the ways in which he cares for Kos or for me – and felt, too, how I was essential to him.

It was a letter which threatened their pact, and Sartre retaliated swiftly. On 28 February he wrote to tell her that Wanda, for whom he felt a rekindled passion since his leave, was making a fuss about the Beaver's place in his life. 'There's something ignoble about my relations with Wanda. It's ignoble that I should be obliged to tell her that I no longer love you, ignoble that I should feel I have to write to her: "I'd trample the whole world underfoot (even the Beaver . . .)" but . . . whoever wants the ends must want the means.'

Beauvoir was upset by his tit-for-tat letter, especially the 'unpleasant' sentence to Wanda: 'I'd trample the whole world underfoot', but, conscious of her own betrayal, she took it on the chin, politely thanking Sartre for the 'eleventh year of happiness' he had given her. Her mind was on Bost, for whom she was certain that she was no longer *'une* histoire . . . un peu *accidentale'*, a casual love affair. At last she sensed that he wanted the relationship as much as she had always done. The war, with its message of life's transience, lent their secret love-making a new intensity, as they coupled in the Hôtel Porc-Lion in the Latin Quarter before moving on the next day to Montmartre. Of Kos, they spoke little.

Beauvoir's journal ends with her last glimpse of Bost and his dazzling smile. Poupette, bad-tempered at being used to provide an alibi, had arrived at the station. 'I feel neither jealousy nor remorse, I definitely want this affair . . .' writes Beauvoir on 21 February, determined to snatch happiness while she can. Her resolve, like Sartre's, to 'live against' convention, to live freely and passionately, making up her own rules, was, in her eyes, as ethical a code of conduct as that of any bourgeois *salaud*, and she would live it as strenuously and courageously as she was able.

Her next step would test her courage to the limits. In March Beauvoir finally achieved her aim of visiting Bost at the front. Her dream was no longer to share *la vie de soldat*, but to spend 'ten days of conjugal life' together. The domestic idyll she visualized, one which she had never sought with Sartre, was arranged by Bost, who rented a lodging near Nettancourt (Meuse), where he was stationed.

On Sunday, 17 March, Beauvoir took the train east to Vitry-le-François, ninety-two kilometres from Verdun. Monday found her installed in Charmont in a room with a huge bed, a tiny dressing-table, and a large, round table on which she spread out her books and papers. Next door was a kitchen and dining-room, with a cooking stove. 'Emma' (Bost) did the shopping. When he arrived with a bottle of Moulin à Vent, and his pockets stuffed full of rillettes, eggs and sardines, Beauvoir made a 'merry lunch', while he cut wood and lit a roaring fire. When Bost went back on duty, Beauvoir wandered out for a walk, her *Pléiade* Shakespeare under her arm. She was dozing by a lake, when two soldiers approached and demanded to see her papers. On hearing that she was 'visiting her aunt', the commandant cut her short: 'No point in lying – you came here to see a soldier.'

Bost was hauled before the lieutenant, with whom he had a brief exchange:

'This morning, when I met you, I asked where you'd been, and you told me: "To post a letter." Was that true?'

'No, sir.'

'You'd just been seeing her?'

'Yes, sir . . . She's not the first woman to come here, sir.'

'No, but she's the first to get herself caught.'

The next day Beauvoir was taken away in a military vehicle to the captain of gendarmes. She allowed her eyes to brim with tears. This time it was the captain's turn to be slightly apologetic: on searching her room they had found Sartre's notebooks, which they had taken for Communist tracts until they realized that the writing was in French, not German. All smiles, the captain stamped Beauvoir's pass, and she was allowed to move to another lodging in Nettancourt. That night, the 21st, she and Bost cooked four steaks in the warm, bright kitchen, and ate two each. A cat purred on Beauvoir's lap, and outside in the courtyard chickens scratched in the dirt.

It was too good to last. On 23 May Bost was seriously wounded, and evacuated to a field hospital near Beaune. It took the German army only six weeks to bring about the death of the whore (*la gueuse*), as the Republic was known to its enemies. Hitler, who had sworn to enter Paris on 15 June, kept his word.

21

~~~

Occupation

We've lost the war. They gave it us to do something
with, and we've lost it.

Mathieu, in *Iron in the Soul* (1949)

'THE REIGN OF EVIL' began, wrote Sartre, when the Germans entered
Paris on 14 June 1940, their camouflaged lorries rolling down the
boulevard Saint-Michel as blond gods with eyes 'like glacier lakes',
narrow waists and impossibly long muscular legs tossed packets of
English cigarettes to silent Frenchmen. The date of the fall of Paris was
engraved on Sartre's heart, like Calais on Mary Tudor's. He begins *La
Mort dans l'âme* with the date and time, *Saturday, 15 June 1940, 9.0 am*,
when the news reaches New York, and the shame of the French nation
is announced to the world on the radio. For Sartre, defeat means death
in the soul, peace without glory: angrily he contrasts the 'horrible little
khaki soldiers, those champions of Man and the Citizen', who ran like
rabbits in the face of the advancing Nazis, with the grave 'angels of
hate' who represent 'the victory of contempt, of violence and bad faith'.
Daniel, the homosexual character in *Roads to Freedom*, voices feelings
shared by other Parisians when the fair-haired German soldier standing
upright on a tank with 'impassive face and sparkling eyes' breaks into a
smile as he reaches into the pocket of his breeches for a packet of
cigarettes:

An intolerable, a delicious thrill mounted in him from thighs to head: there was a mist before his eyes: his breath was coming in pants. To himself he said: 'Just like butter! – they are going through Paris like a knife through butter!' Other faces passed before his dimmed vision, more and more of them, each as beautiful as the last. They have come here with intent to do evil: today the Reign of Evil begins. What joy! He longed to be a woman so he might load them with flowers . . .

Once, France had held the moral high ground. Defeated, she had lost it, and Mathieu, Sartre's cowardly anti-hero, knows the reception he and his fellow soldiers will get from their women when they return, hanging their heads. 'I should worry! . . . Nice sort of welcome *we're* going to get when we turn up at home! – Oh, lots and lots of con-gratulations!' While many of France's women were preparing for horizontal collaboration with the enemy (it is estimated that the Germans fathered between 50,000 and 70,000 children during the Occupation), her men, too, had lost faith in old ideals. To Sartre, like many of his countrymen, the 'new Judges' with their 'New Law' would prove devilishly attractive.

'Why do Evil?' the character Catherine asks of Goetz in Sartre's play, *The Devil and the Good Lord*.

'Because the Good has already been done.'

'Who's done it?'

'God the Father. As for me, I invent.'

In the murky period that followed, there was to be plenty of room for invention.

*

It was 16 June. Sartre and his unit were falling back, to Hagenau, at the furthest limit of north-eastern France, to Breschwillers and then to Padoux. They were among Alsatians, some of whom were for 'the other side', and argued with the French soldiers. The Germans were coming closer. 'One evening we heard guns firing on a village that was about six miles away,' Sartre told Beauvoir later. 'We could see it fairly well along the flat road, and we knew that the Germans would arrive in the course of the next day . . . Our little village was being shelled; another, which was going to be taken in its turn, was waiting.'

Trapped in their village, the people could only wait. Sartre went to bed. The French soldiers had been abandoned by their officers, who had walked into the forest with a white flag. 'We, the privates and sergeants, stayed together; we went to sleep, and the next morning we heard voices, shots, cries. I dressed quickly; I knew that it meant I was going to be taken prisoner.' It seemed to Sartre that he was acting a scene from a film: none of this could be real. A gun was firing at the church, where some soldiers were holding out. 'They were certainly not people belonging to us, because we had no notion of resisting – in any case, we did not possess the means of doing so. Under the Germans' rifles I crossed the square to go from where I was to where they were.'

Corporal Pierre, a socialist, recalled that at the moment he was taken prisoner, an Alsatian threw himself into the arms of a German, crying: 'Ah, vous voilà enfin! You've come at last!' Turning away in disgust, he found himself among an 'immense troop' of men, who were marched to the gendarmerie barracks at Haxo de Baccarat and left without food to sleep on the floor.

It was 21 June, Sartre's thirty-fifth birthday. He had been taken prisoner a few hours before the armistice, proposed by Marshal Pétain, veteran hero of Verdun, 'as the necessary condition of the survival of eternal France'. Winston Churchill, arriving at Tours, declared capital of France since the fall of Paris, for a meeting of the Supreme Allied War Council, had in vain urged the French Premier Paul Reynaud to continue the fight; the Germans were shelling Tours, which burnt for three days. At Saumur, military cadets made a gallant last stand. In London, on 18 June, General de Gaulle, broadcasting on the BBC, told his fellow countrymen that although the battle of France was lost, the war was not over:

> Crushed by superior mechanical force today, we can conquer in the future by virtue of a superior mechanical force. There lies the destiny of the world . . . Whatever happens, the flame of French resistance must not be extinguished and will not be extinguished.

Sartre, at heart a pacifist, expected peace to follow the armistice. 'It's unthinkable that they'll take us to Germany,' he told Pierre. 'The war'll be over soon.' Pieterkowsky, terrified of deportation, clung to the same belief. But Churchill had made his 'finest hour' speech, declaring that there be no surrender, only 'blood, sweat, toil and tears . . . the battle of Britain was about to begin'. On 3 July the Royal Navy sank the French fleet at Oran, and Pétain broke off relations with Britain.

Imprisoned with 14,000 other soldiers at Baccarat, between Strasbourg and Nancy, Sartre slowly absorbed the shock of defeat.

'What ifs' ran through his mind: what if the Parisians had held out for two and a half years, as the Spanish had done in Madrid? What if the God in whom he didn't believe was punishing the French for betraying the Spanish? What if he, Sartre, had acted like a hero, instead of meekly giving himself up? In *Iron in the Soul*, he wrote the version he would have liked to play out in real life: Mathieu, the fictional Sartre, chooses a rifle. The war is lost, but he has made his decision: 'I shall save my honour!' Kneeling behind the parapet of the church tower, like the soldiers he had seen in Padoux, he brings his rifle to his shoulder and fires. A German lies dead in the dust.

> Mathieu turned to Chasseriau.
> 'I rather think we're giving Jerry a bit of a headache!' he said excitedly . . . Mathieu looked at the dead soldier and laughed. For years he had tried, in vain, to act. One after another, his intended actions had been stolen from him . . . But no one had stolen this! He had pressed a trigger, and, for once, something had happened, something definite . . . *His* dead man, *his* handiwork, something to mark *his* passage on the earth. A longing came over him to do some more killing: it was fun, it was easy. He would have liked to plunge Germany into mourning . . .
> Mathieu went on firing. He fired. He was cleansed. He was all-powerful. He was free.

Instead, Sartre burnt with impotent fury. His anger was directed at the officers, who had made them 'the army of defeat'. Divisional Headquarters Staff, twenty officers in all, had walked off into the night, the old general leaning on the colonel's arm, their servants carrying their valises, laughing subalterns bringing up the rear. For Sartre, like Bost, '*la connerie militaire passe des bornes*, military bullshit knows no bounds'. And because 'our officers have left us in the lurch . . . We are the scapegoats, we are the conquered, the cowards, the vermin, the scum of the earth: we have lost the war: we are ugly and we are guilty, and no one, no one in the whole world, likes us . . . "We're pariahs." '

For two months Sartre brooded in the Haxo barracks. Pierre noticed that he showed a new spirit of solidarity with the men. The conditions of captivity encouraged his dislike of washing, which had already given him the nickname of 'the man with black gloves' because his hands, *les mains sales*, 'were black with dirt up to his elbows'. Spending twelve hours a day writing during the Phoney War, Sartre would refuse to cross the road and spend ten *sous* on a bath. Now, in Haxo, he turned to the mobile library for diversion and read Jules Verne's *Around the World in Eighty Days*.

The barracks was right beside the railway, but Sartre continued to believe that he would soon be freed. Had not the Alsatians been released following the annexation of Alsace and Lorraine to Germany? Had not a notice been pinned up, signed by the commandant: 'The prisoners in the Camp at Baccarat will remain in France'? 'I thought . . . one day, when the Germans had settled down, they would let us out and send us home,' Sartre later told Beauvoir. On 24 August, therefore, when he and his friends were loaded into a freight train, they remained at first optimistic, believing that it was taking them to Nancy, to Châlons, to Paris even.

The men smile, thinking of freedom, of their wives and children, of being home in time for the lavender-picking. As it approaches the points the train slows down and the men hold their breath: left for Châlons, right for Trèves, 'in Bocheland'. The rails leap into view under the wheels, two parallel flashes of light show for a moment and then vanish, over to their left. 'Bloody hell.' A young soldier throws himself out of the wagon; there is the sound of gunfire. The boy's body jerks and is still. Beneath his head, the rails are black with blood.

*

In Paris, Beauvoir's ear is glued to the radio. The invasion of Holland and Belgium: Poupette leaves France for Portugal, where Lionel de Roulet is living. Premier Paul Reynaud announces that only a miracle can save France: Dunkirk. 'Perhaps Hitler had not been bluffing after all?' thinks Beauvoir. 4 June: bombs fall on Paris; Olga and Wanda obey their parents' orders to leave the capital. 9 June: Beauvoir remains at her teaching post because she has to invigilate an exam the next day.

There was only one idea in her head: 'Not to be cut off from Sartre, not to be caught like a rat in occupied Paris.' And only one person to whom she could turn for help: Bianca, even though it was not long since the April day of Sartre's second leave when, at Bianca's request, he and Beauvoir had met the student face to face in the place du Trocadéro to confirm her 'dismissal'. Bianca, distraught that Sartre, who had so recently professed love for her in his letters, now stood before her awkward and distant, could not hold back her tears: it 'was like a second slap in the face'. But the couple were implacable: 'A like-mindedness strengthened their attachment, despite their very different natures,' recalled Bianca. 'They seemed to be a stone slab with two faces, a sort of Janus figure.' Afterwards, she continued to see Beauvoir, whom she had always preferred.

On the morning of 9 June, Bianca sent Beauvoir a note saying that she and her father were planning to leave Paris that night for Quimper: he'd heard from a friend at GHQ that the Germans were by-passing the Maginot Line and would be in Paris within days. Realizing that Sartre would be taken prisoner, Beauvoir had a fit of hysterics: 'As far as I was concerned, it was the most awful moment in the whole course of the war.' Bianca calmed her down. 'I asked Papa if we could take the Beaver with us, since she had no one to leave with. He hesitated a long time because of his well-founded animosity and mistrust towards my friend, but, either because he felt sorry for her or was incapable of resisting my request, he agreed.' To keep up their spirits, the two women sat drinking at the Flore until four in the morning; at seven Beauvoir took a taxi to the Lycée Camille See, where her headmistress told her that she was released from her duties as the school was being evacuated to Nantes. Everyone was leaving. Cars choked the boulevards, inching their way past the deserted cafés and shuttered shops. Beauvoir and Bianca were startled to see horse-drawn wagons, piled high with hay, on which perched peasants, children, old folk, pots and pans, rolling along the boulevard St Michel. They were crossing the city from the Porte de la Chapelle in the north to the Porte d'Orléans in the south, intent on escaping the advancing army. On the terrace of the luxurious Café Mahieu, at the end of rue Soufflot, the two women waited for M. Bienenfeld's car. Hours passed. Bianca was sobbing, and tears welled up in Simone's eyes as she craned her neck to catch sight of her rescuer.

M. Bienenfeld's vehicle finally arrived, and Simone and Bianca jumped in. Outside Chartres, an alert forced them to stop. In a detail in her *Journal de Guerre*, but omitted from *The Prime of Life*, Beauvoir noted that M. Bienenfeld was clutching a 'precious cloth containing all the pearls from his business'. The pearl dealer was shortly to serve as the model for 'Monsieur Birnenschatz', the prosperous Jewish merchant in Sartre's *The Reprieve*, whose daughter 'Ella' (the name of Bianca's sister) bears a resemblance to Bianca, a woman who has 'made herself' by her life in Paris into a Frenchwoman. 'Would you take Ella for a Jewess if you met her in the street?' asks Birnenschatz. 'I'm French myself. Do you feel like a Jew? . . . But what is a Jew? It's a man whom other men take for a Jew.'

Sartre had encapsulated the predicament of the French Jews, who felt themselves French, who had fought for France, and who believed that the French state would offer them a protection not afforded to foreign Jews. But in arguing in *Anti-Semite and Jew* that a Jew is, in the words of Benny Lévy, 'an invention of the anti-Semite', he seemed to many people to deny Jewish history and thought, while his surprisingly hostile caricatures of Jews in his fiction were emblematic of the anti-Semitism widely prevalent in France, which found extreme expression in the exhibition *The Jew and France*. Scapegoats for the sins of the Third Republic, responsible, in the eyes of many Frenchmen, for the shame of defeat, Jews, rather than the smiling occupiers, became the target of hate.

On the way Beauvoir and Bianca quarrelled. Distressed by the plight of the refugees, anxious for Sartre's life, Beauvoir kept repeating: 'Why don't they stop all this? Why don't they call an armistice? What good is all this slaughter?' Bianca was irritated by her 'feeble pacifism, inspired only by personal considerations . . . the Beaver was childishly selfish'. At Laval they parted, Beauvoir taking a train to Mme Morel at La Pouèze, where she stayed for the next eighteen days.

Rumours of German atrocities, based on stories of World War I, had gone ahead of the advancing troops. When Beauvoir and Mme Morel heard that the enemy had reached Le Mans, they hid in the villa. Every door in the village was bolted, every shutter barred. It was said that the Germans would cut off the hands of all the little boys. Beauvoir stood behind a window, peering through the slats at the deserted road, bathed in sunshine. Suddenly the window opposite was broken: 'A guttural voice [was] barking out some words . . . and they were all upon us – all very tall and blond, with pink complexions.' The column goosestepped through the village, followed by horses, tanks, trucks, artillery and field kitchens.

Contrary to expectation, the Germans behaved with exemplary politeness. They did not cut off children's hands, but paid for their drinks and provisions. Two soldiers assured Beauvoir of their friendly feelings towards the French: 'It was the English and the Jews who had brought us to this sorry pass.' Beauvoir passed the time reading detective stories and listening to Pétain on the radio: 'It is with a heavy heart that I tell you today that we must give up the struggle.' Relieved that 'the shedding of French blood would cease at last – how absurd and ghastly these so-called rearguard actions were, in which men died to maintain a pale shadow of resistance!' – she scanned the terms of the armistice for news of the prisoners of war, and resolved to return to Paris in case Sartre had made his way there.

Marooned in Le Mans, after the Dutch couple she was with had run out of petrol, Beauvoir was hungry. Food was running short; reluctantly she forced down a hunk of salty black bread as she sat on the side of the road, scanning the laden cars for a lift. No one had room for her. At last a German truck hove into view, and she sprinted forward and climbed in, only to find that the smell of petrol and the motion made her throw up over her fellow passengers. At Mantes the Germans, in their well-pressed uniforms, laughed as they clicked their heels and pressed cigarettes, chocolate and champagne on the rabble of refugees. Beauvoir refused; but she could not help noticing that the victors had 'gorgeous' red roses pinned on their grey uniforms.

In Paris, a 'lunar silence' reigned. Happening across her father in a café, Beauvoir shared a beer and a sandwich with him. Sartre would remain a POW for the duration, starving on a diet of 'dead dog', remarked Georges sourly, now that Occupied France, the northern two-thirds of the country, had been 'assimilated' into Germany. Her mother told her to hurry home, because of the curfew, and to set her watch to German time, for Paris and her suburbs were renamed GrossParis, the German metropolis of Occupied France. Signs were going up in German to guide the soldiers of the Wehrmacht. Over the Sénat in the Luxembourg Gardens, the swastika flew. Beauvoir felt 'utter despair'.

When she went round for a meal with her parents, they could give her only soup and macaroni. 'I haven't had a good square meal for days,' Beauvoir recorded miserably. At the Palais Royal she could find no mention of Sartre on the lists of prisoners, which only covered the Parisian area. 'I know only too well that all life is nothing but a brief reprieve from death,' she wrote in her journal. But at least she had work, for she had been taken on at the Lycée Duruy, and a ticket for the Bibliothèque Nationale, where she decided to study Hegel each day from 2 to 5 p.m. And, wobbling her way through the back streets behind rue Vavin, Beauvoir learnt to ride a stolen bicycle, under Sorokine's instruction, and to explore the suburbs on wheels.

'I misconstrued the meaning of Pétain's words,' wrote Beauvoir in *The Prime of Life*, in an attempt to provide some extenuation for her initial welcome for the armistice, which she claimed to have at first believed to be 'a purely military capitulation'. By 10 July there could be no mistake: 300 kilometres away, in the spa town of Vichy, the parliament of the Third Republic convened for the last time in the casino, and voted full powers to Philippe Pétain, 'saviour' of France.

In the countries defeated by the Nazis, no other significant political figure like Pétain participated in collaboration. Scandinavia witnessed two extremes; on the one hand, a hitherto minor figure, Vidkun

Quisling betrayed Norway and became a puppet ruler, on the other, King Christian of Denmark took the honourable course of refusing collaboration. But on 30 October 1940 Pétain said: 'It is with honour and to maintain ten-century-old French unity in the framework of the new European order that I embark today on a path of collaboration . . . Follow me: keep your faith in eternal France.'

The country had staked its future on 'the new European order', or Nazi victory, which was seen as only a matter of time. Rallying to Pétain seemed the least worst choice, as it avoided direct rule by a German gauleiter. In theory the Vichy government remained sovereign in both the Occupied and Free Zones, but in practice it was cut off from occupied France, where the French civil administration was obliged to do business with the German military administration. The 'softly, softly' approach of their conquerors would seduce the French into closer and closer co-operation, as they saw opportunities for profit and pleasure proliferate.

At last, on 11 July, word came from Sartre. He was alive. It was only a pencilled note, but it was enough: 'I have high hopes of seeing you again soon, and everything is fine with me . . . I love you with all my might.' 'I breathe a little easier now,' recorded Beauvoir. Bost, too, was far away in hospital at Carpentras, near Avignon, although she hitchhiked all the way to Taverny to beg the *pastoresse*, his mother, for news of her son. '*Bewohnt*', inhabited, said the notice on the door, but no one was home; disappointed, Beauvoir thumbed a lift back to Paris. This time, when a German soldier offered her a bar of chocolate, she accepted.

She could not help her men, but the 'children' of her 'family' needed her. Kos was pregnant by a new lover, Niko Papatakis, a good-looking half-Greek, half-Ethiopian whom she had met at the Flore and the Bal Nègre. Bost knew nothing of the short-lived affair, which was now over, and Sartre and Beauvoir kept Kos's secret. It was a 'purely physical affair', Wanda told Sartre in mitigation, an excuse that racked up his anxiety that she might copy her sister's example while he was away; in May he had offered to marry Wanda in order to get three days' leave. 'I don't imagine that it will be very nice for you,' he wrote to Beauvoir, in a masterly understatement of her probable reaction. 'Though it's purely symbolic, it does make me look committed up to my ears . . . But I've told you that my mind's made up: I want to do everything I can for W. from now on.' Marriage leaves, however, were not forthcoming in the midst of war, and Sartre was obliged to shelve his plans. Meanwhile, Papatakis was not told that Kos was pregnant, for she wanted an abortion, illegal in Vichy France. As soon as the trains were running, on 18 July, she came to Paris so that Beauvoir, who had moved into her grandmother's empty flat in rue Denfert-Rochereau, could help her.

The abortion, even more difficult to arrange than usual in occupied Paris, left an indelible impression on Beauvoir, reinforcing her abhorrence of pregnancy and childbirth. She may have gone at first to a doctor like Dr Waldmann, 'the dirty Jew' in *The Age of Reason*, who 'wouldn't budge' on his fee of 4,000 francs, but in both the fictional accounts of abortion by Sartre and Beauvoir the pregnant woman ends up with a backstreet abortionist, of the kind to which most women in Kos's predicament were forced to turn. To both writers a baby is the worm in the apple, destroying their 'secret garden' of freedom. 'Mathieu was barring its passage,' writes Sartre. 'There was a tiny human creature, conscious, furtive, deceitful and pathetic . . . and a pin would pierce it and explode it like a toy balloon.' Children are 'greedy little devils . . . all their senses are mouths'. They suck the sap of the world, parasitic, 'sullen, passionate, sinister'.

Beauvoir, however, focuses on the mother, and what is happening to her body. Hélène's lover is '*un sale type*, a dirty beast who had slipped his hand up her dress. He had hurt her: she is going to suffer, and she is a child.' Jean, her former boyfriend in *The Blood of Others*, is reluctant to help, as Beauvoir was probably reluctant. 'Someone has to lend her a room,' says Hélène's friend, as perhaps Wanda said to Beauvoir. It is a late abortion; they have wasted a lot of time trying to find an abortionist. 'Jean' lets 'Hélène' in. Under her blue dress, beneath her childish skin, 'was that thing which she fed with her blood'. Beauvoir has made up a fire and put clean sheets on her bed. Soon the girl is lying on the bed in a white nightdress scalloped in red, like a schoolgirl's nightdress: there is 'that thing in her womb, and the night was a great dangerous black desert which we had to cross without any help'.

Beauvoir, whose descriptions of the female body in *The Second Sex* are markedly negative, who saw the body, with its cycles of menstruation and pregnancy, as an obstacle to woman's free choice and self-fulfilment, was alarmed at being left alone with Kos and her pain.

'Oh! *dit-elle*. 'Oh! *J'ai trop mal*.' 'Oh,' she said. 'Oh, it hurts too much.'

She was clinging to my hand as if it were a lifeline . . . I could see nothing but her haggard eyes and the little turned-up nose in the middle of a sheet-white face. 'Be brave. It will stop. It will all be over.' I repeated those words endlessly. Without ceasing, the pain tore her belly, it stopped for an instant and then pierced her again relentlessly . . . The whites of Hélène's eyes were showing. Sometimes I felt that a sharp scream was going to break from her lips and I put the palm of my hand over her mouth.

For pain relief, Beauvoir has a bottle of ether. She takes a pad of cotton wool, pours a few drops on it and holds it to the girl's nostrils. Twelve hours have passed, and Kos no longer seems to recognize her. When Beauvoir summons the abortionist for help, the old woman at first refuses to come out:

I looked at her anxiously. *Une avorteuse*. An abortionist . . . She was dressed in black, and had fair hair, flabby pink-and-white cheeks and an orange mouth; her eyes were the eyes of a very old woman, blinking and bleary. Could she see properly? Under the paint, I was aware of the badly washed flesh . . . She lifted the sheet and I turned away . . .
'Where's my bag? It's dreadful to grow old: I can't see an inch in front of my nose.'

At last she finds her scissors, and Beauvoir is too frightened to tell her to pass them through a flame.
The abortionist does her work. Soon she is holding a basin, and her arms are red with blood.

'*Allez vider cette cuvette*. Go and empty that basin.'
Hélène was lying flat on her back, with her eyes closed . . . Under her legs was an oilcloth covered with bloody rags. I took the basin. I went across the landing and opened the lavatory door. I emptied the basin and pulled the plug. When I went back into the room, the old woman was washing the red rags in the sink.

The heroine of one of Katharine Mansfield's stories, quoted by Beauvoir in *The Second Sex*, says 'coldly, "I don't like babies": Linda was broken, made weak, her courage was gone, through childbearing. And what made it doubly hard to bear was, she did not love her children . . .' To Beauvoir, a mother 'is almost always a discontented woman'.
She had warned Kos not to get pregnant, but Kos had rebelled against Beauvoir's domination. 'I'm not a little dog,' says the woman in *The Blood of Others* when her abortion is over, reproaching her helper for talking so much about respecting people's liberty but 'making

decisions for me and treating me like a thing'. If she prefers to be unhappy, to take unsuitable lovers, it is for her to choose. But being party to an illegal abortion, which nearly went wrong, may have been more harrowing for Beauvoir than for Kos. It was to prove a pivotal experience in her journey towards feminism.

22

Stalag

I shall bend my knee to no one.
Jean-Paul Sartre, *Bariona or the Son of Thunder*,
December 1940

'I CAN PICTURE you so well, with a shaven head, saying "*Ja*" with a nice smile just as you used to in Berlin, as blond and Germanic in appearance as the Germans guarding you, and finding satisfaction – I'm sure – in speaking with your purest accent,' wrote Beauvoir to Sartre on 11 July 1940, the day she heard that he had been taken to Stalag XII D. The Beaver's intuition was right: she knew her Kobra. Soon after arriving at the transit camp perched on top of Mount Kemmel, overlooking Trier or Trèves, Germany's oldest city, on the Luxembourg border, Sartre set about arranging matters to his advantage.

From the beginning, he liked the situation of the camp, on top of a mountain, like an eagle's nest looking down on the world. 'To be a prisoner on top of a mountain, what a paradox! Everything lies at our feet: the red roads of the Palatinate, the flat, sinuous glint of the Moselle, and the nation of our conquerors.' The Stalag held more than 7,600 prisoners during the first months of Sartre's internment, a fraction of the 1.75 million French prisoners of war transported to the vast prison camp which Germany had become. It was a shock to find himself finally face to face with the enemy, but, crammed into a dormitory with thirty men, including Poles and Czechs, who showed little respect for the defeated French 'rabbits', Sartre soon proved himself a survivor. A sharp kick in the bum from a German sentry who threatened him with a bayonet, slaps and blows from the adjutant, only increased his feeling of solidarity with his fellow Frenchmen. 'In a strange way, but in one which marked me, I became acquainted with a society . . . of defeated men who were fed by an army that held them prisoner . . . I was a second-class soldier and I learned how to obey spiteful orders and to understand what a hostile army amounted to. Like everybody else, I had contacts with the Germans, either to obey them or sometimes to listen to their stupid, boastful conversations . . . I had been reshaped, you might say, by the prison camp. We lived in a crowd, perpetually touching one another . . .' Released, Sartre said wistfully that he was astonished at how far apart people sat from each other in Parisian cafés. 'In the stalag, I rediscovered a form of collective life I had not experienced since the École Normale – in other words, I was happy.'

A thief named Braco, 'an ugly, filthy little man, with sparkling, intelligent eyes . . . who is here under a false name and spends his time stealing, pillaging, bartering, and, all in all, working very hard to amass a small fortune', taught Sartre all he needed to know about the black market. 'If we place our orders eight days in advance with him, he usually gets us what we've asked for,' wrote Sartre of Braco, who supplied him with tobacco. The writer also took up his boxing gloves again in a bout with a young printer, but he was unfit and the match ended in a draw. 'Which I found disappointing, because Pardaillon did not have drawn matches.' Deep in his heart, Sartre, who always feared he was a coward, longed to be a hero; all his life he would oscillate between cowardice and courage. Now the violence endemic to the camp reminded him, not without a certain masochistic pleasure, of his street-fighting schooldays in La Rochelle. '[The Germans] can beat us all they want, but in the end we'll fuck them over,' he wrote belligerently in 1982, recalling how his army experiences had changed and politicized him.

Like Braco, Sartre was small, ugly, filthy, and covered with lice. The majority of the prisoners felt that it was a matter of pride to keep themselves clean, and objected to his going round looking like *un clochard*, a tramp. Disgusted that Sartre's straw palliasse was crawling with lice, his neighbours poured insecticide over it as he slept. Certain of the prisoners remember how, when it was cold, Sartre picked the lice off himself, put them on the stove, and listened to them pop as they roasted. One day, exasperated at his squalor, they dragged him by force to the shower, where he struggled and shouted under the cold water: 'Stop, gentlemen! *Messieurs, ne faîtes pas ça!*'

'I'd been repulsively dirty, by choice and semi-mysticism, I was repugnant,' explained Sartre to Beauvoir in a letter of 29 July. But, shamed by meeting 'a kid from the Flore', a teacher at the École Normale who recognized him, and asked incredulously if he was related to the writer, Sartre decided to shave and wash: 'It created quite a stir in the courtyard . . . Now I'm washing every day.'

It was time to find a more comfortable billet. A new friend among the camp 'aristocracy', an officer named Captain Bourdin, arranged for Sartre to work as an interpreter in the infirmary, where he was given a bedroom shared with two other prisoners, and a table, chair and wardrobe. Three months later he was reclassified as an 'artist', and moved into the artists' hut with musicians and actors who were paid to put on twice-monthly Sunday shows for the prisoners at the little camp theatre. The walls of the hut were hung with guitars, banjos, flutes and trumpets, and there was a piano on which the Belgians played swing. Sartre relished acting in comic farces, as he had at the École Normale, and even writing plays, although his early efforts were not presented. But despite finding the artists 'very appealing', he soon gravitated towards more congenial company, the priests who filled the role of camp intellectuals: Abbé Marius Perrin, head of the barracks, a Jesuit named Paul Feller, Abbé Henri Leroy, a Basque abbé named Etchegoyen, and a Dominican, Père Boisselet. Sartre and Perrin became close friends. Long conversations on theology took place, and Sartre took the role of adjudicator between the Dominican and the Jesuit on the subject of the Immaculate Conception: 'I ruled against Pius IX.' On Tuesdays he gave lectures to his 'disciples', as he called them. He joined the choir and, under a priestly baton, began practising carols and the Pilgrims' Chorus from *Tannhäuser*.

Father Espitallier, a professor of rhetoric at Lyons, persuaded Sartre to reread Bossuet's *Sermons*. 'It is quite advantageous to have faith,' he told him one day. Sartre removed his old pipe from his mouth. 'What do you mean, "to have faith"?' he demanded. 'Do you own faith the way I own this pipe? Or do you mean that faith entertains, with you, its owner, some sort of magical relationship? Wouldn't you rather say that, by becoming a believer, you assume a fundamental attitude?' Espitallier thanked Sartre for this 'lesson in spirituality'. Moments later he confided to another priest his impression of Sartre's uniqueness: he is 'a being like no one else, a kind of prophet'.

Perrin and Etchegoyen had friends among the Benedictines at the monastery of St Matthias at Trier, who provided the priests – and Sartre – with special food and Moselle wines. One of the brothers also procured a copy of *Sein und Zeit*, which Sartre had requested. He at once began translating from the German for Perrin, who was interested in phenomenology, tutoring him in the philosophy of Heidegger, Rector of Freiburg until 1934, and an early supporter of Nazism.

One day Oberleutnant Arndt, Camp Kommandant, came looking for Sartre. He was absent. 'Is this the Sartre who was in Berlin in 1933?' he asked. Sartre had let slip that he had studied at the French Institute in Berlin, and that he was an admirer of Heidegger. When he finally met the Kommandant, did Sartre reply, '*Ja, mein Herr,*' as Beauvoir anticipated? Certainly his ostentatious interest in German culture counted in his favour when he asked permission to stage a mystery play at Christmas.

Sartre had found a dog-eared copy of *The Satin Slipper*, a play by the celebrated Catholic playwright Paul Claudel, lying around in the artists' hut, and it stirred his interest in writing a play. Claudel, whose anti-Protestant dramas had been popular before the war, would later prove a rival to Sartre. But in 1940, Sartre was the novice, Claudel the established playwright: more than once he wrote to Beauvoir asking her to send him copies of Claudel via the American Red Cross.

'I want you to know that I am writing my first serious play, and putting all of me into it . . . and it's about the Nativity,' wrote Sartre. 'Have no fear, my sweet,' he added, he wouldn't convert to Catholicism. 'But take it from me, I really do have a talent as a playwright . . . After this, I will write plays.' The play was *Bariona, or the Son of Thunder*, the story of a village chief who rebels against the Roman occupiers of Palestine. Set in a village near Bethlehem, on 24 December, the subject had been chosen, said Sartre, to appeal to both believers and unbelievers at Christmas time. To the audience of prisoners the play presented a covert call to resistance, although the message may not have been as clear as the playwright hoped, wrapped as it was in Christian mythology. 'The Germans didn't understand [it],' said Sartre. 'They just saw it as a Christmas play. But the French prisoners got the point.' 'I must be free, free. Free against God and for God, free against myself and for myself,' cries Bariona, as he plots to kill the Christ child in order to save the villagers from submission to their conquerors. Sartre played Balthazar, the black magus who argues that yes, it's true that God can do nothing against human liberty, *mais quoi donc?* So what? 'A new freedom will soar to Heaven like a column of granite . . . *Jette-toi vers le ciel et alors tu seras libre . . . tout étonné d'exister dans le plein coeur de Dieu, dans le royaume de Dieu qui est au Ciel et aussi sur la terre.* [Hurl yourself towards heaven and you will be free . . . Astonished to exist in the bosom of God, in the kingdom of God which is in Heaven as it is on earth.]' The God-shaped hole which still existed in the atheist playwright is evident in a text which reveals his own internal debates about faith, and his nostalgia for the religion of his mother and grandmother; it is not surprising that at least one confused prisoner converted to Catholicism after hearing the play and seeing its author hurry off to midnight Mass.

Acting as well as writing and directing, Sartre, master of revels, for the first time experienced the spine-tingling thrill of holding an audience of thousands spellbound. It was a life-changing experience: the beginning of a long love affair with the stage. Gazing across the footlights at the silent mass of his *confrères*: 'I realized what the theatre ought to be: a great, collective, religious phenomenon . . . a theatre of myths.'

He had glimpsed the next step in his 'destiny'. 'There are moments when it seems to me, as it does to you, maniacal and obstinate to be writing [my novel] while men are dying like flies in the North and when the destiny of all Europe is at stake, but what can I do?' Sartre had asked Beauvoir on 27 May, as France fell around him. 'Besides, it's *my* destiny, my specific individual destiny, and no big, collective bogeyman should make me renounce my destiny.' Nothing would make him renounce his fundamental project of writing, but captivity had raised his consciousness. By now he had heard the news that his old friend Paul Nizan had been killed at the front on 6 May, only days before Bost had been wounded and most of his regiment wiped out. It was a bitter blow, which roused in Sartre a new sense of outrage and responsibility.

'Till the war, I had never done anything: I used to juggle harmless ideas in front of a bunch of kids,' Sartre confided to Perrin during one of their morning chats around the stove. After Christmas his sense of mission crystallized. During the Phoney War he had decided to plunge into the 'soufflé' of politics: 'I shall follow no one and those who want to follow me can follow me.' 'Sartre does not like what is happening in France, but he is reserved about de Gaulle,' noted Perrin in his journal in early 1941. 'He has no liking for any regime: that of the fascists horrifies him: power in the hands of the *salauds* . . . He has decided to leave his ivory tower and plunge into the fray.' To the priests, who watched in fascination as Sartre picked lice off his jumper as he talked, he expressed his disillusion with contemporary politics: 'It is impossible to join a party: they are all rotten, including the communists.' The only solution was to start a new one, 'the party of freedom'.

On one of the open letterforms from Sartre which had to run the gauntlet of the censor, Beauvoir received the message that 'Poulou' would soon be going to Paris. 'My sweet, be patient and confident.' Soon her little chicken would see her 'little smile again', her 'little old cheeks', and would squeeze her 'frail little body' in his arms. Beauvoir had written that she was lonely and solitary, and her 'sad . . . dear little letters' had upset Sartre. In one of many tender replies stressing the depth and permanence of their relationship, he wrote: 'Keep in mind that I love you, that I haven't changed at all, and that we are together in everything, my little one.' Guiltily he confessed that, despite the hard winter, he wasn't cold at all: 'I've often thought, my poor little one, that you were much colder than me.' The prisoners had as much coal as they needed and, 'adopted by the priests', he was stuffed with food. 'I lack for nothing.'

Sartre was too comfortable, too involved in writing *Being and Nothingness*, which the censors had returned to him, to wish to make an abortive escape attempt at a time when the Germans appeared invincible. Twice he was offered the opportunity to escape and refused. At last Abbé Perrin came up with a foolproof idea: Sartre could be repatriated without risk by adding to his medical papers, in red ink, a note that he had a strabismus which affected his sense of direction. When an order came from the Abwehr to liberate 'incurables', Sartre requested a medical examination. 'It was a childish falsification which wouldn't deceive anyone,' claimed Jean Pierre, his fellow meteorologist, although Sartre, blind in one eye, was never fit for active service.

But when he came up before the board, composed of four Germans, the fourth officer, after a perfunctory glance at the prisoner's dossier, agreed to his repatriation. Many whispered that it was Sartre's reward for *Bariona*, which had enabled his captors to show that the prisoners, far from being oppressed, were royally entertained.

23

~⌐

The New Order

Never were we more free than under the German
occupation.

Jean-Paul Sartre

SEPTEMBER 1940. RATIONING was introduced: 350g of bread a day, 300g
of meat a week, 500g of sugar and 200g of butter a month for every
French adult between twenty-one and seventy. Although more
generous than British rations, which were fixed at only 4oz (113g) of
butter and 12oz (340g) of sugar a month in January 1940, it was the
beginning of austerity. Parisians were hungrier than the rural French. At
Beauvoir's parents' table, she sat down to a plate of swedes, or rutabagas,
fed exclusively to cattle before the war, and Jerusalem artichokes.
Drinking her ersatz coffee in the Dôme, she watched morosely as the
Blitzmädchen, German women auxiliary helpers known as 'grey mice',
put out bread and jam on their tables and handed over a packet of real
tea to the waiter. 'Ils nous prennent tout [They're grabbing everything]'
said bewildered Parisians, as the shops and markets emptied. Up to
three-quarters of French produce was siphoned off to Germany, and
Parisians turned to Système D, or Do-It-Yourself, a barter system by
which a plumber mended someone's drains in exchange for a chicken,
which he used to pay his doctor's bill. A black market sprang up for the
wealthy. Deprived of cosmetics, French women followed Colette's
advice to put turnip juice on their faces to prevent wrinkles.

The winter of 1940–41 was even colder and snowier than the previous one. The British blockade of the ports led to a shortage of coal, and Beauvoir's room was not heated. At night she crept between icy sheets wearing ski trousers and a sweater. In the 'dismal' streets, there were no cars and the few buses ran on gas, so that bicycles had become the main means of transport. Many Métro stations were still barricaded.

After the 'car crash' of defeat, as the vilified Léon Blum described it, humiliation was heaped on humiliation for the French nation. On 24 October 1940 Pétain met Hitler at Montoire and shook hands with him. The photo went round the world, sending the message of French collaboration with the Nazi Reich. Following the signature of the armistice, which, in a spirit of revenge, the Führer had insisted took place in the same railway carriage at Compiègne in which German generals had surrendered to the French at the end of World War I, he entered Paris on 23 June 1940. There he ordered the destruction of several statues, including that of Edith Cavell, the British nurse shot by the Germans in 1915. At the Opéra, where Hitler's party, guided by Colonel Hans Speidel, chief of staff to the military governor, arrived soon after dawn on Sunday, the janitor, known as Glouglou, received him. As requested, he switched on the stage lighting – but, so the story went, with dignity refused a tip.

Would the tale of the janitor's symbolic resistance inspire others? On 11 November, anniversary of Armistice Day 1918, Radio London called on the Parisian population to put flowers on the tomb of the Unknown Soldier under the Arc de Triomphe. Defying German orders, thousands of students demonstrated in the streets with their professors, singing the Marseillaise and wearing tricolour cockades. The French police treated the demonstrators with brutality, arresting 140. The University of Paris was closed, its Rector, Roussy, sacked. Beauvoir, however, took no part in the protest: 'I knew none of these young people who had openly said No to Nazism. All I could see around me were people as helpless as myself.'

Her passivity was typical: *chacun pour soi*, each man for himself, became the motto of the majority, as loyalties shrank to self, friends and family. Most of the bourgeoisie thought that the armistice had preserved intact the honour of France, that Pétain would serve as a 'shield' against the Occupiers, and that Blum was to blame for defeat. Animosity towards the British after the loss of 1,600 French sailors at Mers-el-Kebir fuelled a 'desire to get along with the victors at any price', to embrace Hitler's New Order. Returning to the Lycée Camille

See for the autumn term, Beauvoir was asked to sign a document swearing that she was neither a Freemason nor a Jew. Despite claiming in her memoirs that she found this 'repugnant', that Pétain aroused her 'active personal loathing', she did so. 'No one refused to do so. *Il n'y avait aucun moyen de faire autrement.* There was no possible alternative.' She needed the work.

Every month, Vichy persecution of the Jews ratcheted up a notch. From the end of July onwards notices saying 'Out of Bounds to Jews' had begun appearing in shop windows, and Vichy Radio screamed its denunciation of Jews and Bolsheviks. Pétain repealed the law forbidding anti-Semitic propaganda, rowdy anti-Jewish demonstrations filled the streets in Vichy, Marseilles, Lyon and the Champs Élysées, and factories began firing Jewish workers. On 3 October 1940 a German edict ordered all Jews to declare themselves to their employers, and on the 19th Vichy published its own *statut des Israëlites*, forbidding Jews from holding public office.

In her memoirs Beauvoir states that in 1940 she found this persecution 'terrifying'. 'I wished that there was someone with whom I could share my fear, and more particularly, my rage.' She claimed to have felt empathy for Bianca as the noose tightened around her family, writing that in 1939 'I had foreseen, with a twinge of private shame, that her life was destined to be very different from mine.' Beauvoir's journal and letters of the time, however, exhibit a very different tone, displaying the same indifference towards Jews, even French Jews such as Bianca, as the majority. Dismissive, cutting comments sprinkle the pages of Beauvoir's letters to Sartre as a frantic Bianca tries to find a way of escape through marriage to a non-Jew. At the Flore, writes Beauvoir on 31 December 1940, 'I spotted Bienenfeld – who now permanently has quivering nostrils, difficulty in breathing, and anguish of spirit. Her father was conferring with M. Lamblin: she knows she's getting married in a fortnight, but doesn't know to whom – Lamblin or the American? It's a pitiful situation, yet one with which I can summon up no sympathy.'

Awareness of others' feelings had always posed a problem for Beauvoir: 'The misfortune of others can't be imagined, still less fully understood,' she recorded in her War Journal on 2 July 1940. Only much later, in 1950, when she herself felt threatened, would understanding flood over her, and remorse for the suffering of her Jewish lover belatedly prick her conscience.

It was those Jews who obeyed orders, like Bianca's father, David, dutifully registering as a Jew in the fear that if he did not do so he would be 'accused of wrongdoing', who courted most risk. In June 1941, getting out of the Métro a stop early, he narrowly missed being picked up by the police and fled to Villard-de-Lans, near Grenoble in the Free Zone, with his wife and daughter Ella, leaving Bianca and her new husband, Bernard Lamblin, in Paris. The decree of 21 March 1941 had revoked French nationality from French Jews like the Bienenfelds and made them stateless, but with her marriage to Bernard, Bianca regained it. Defiant, resourceful, she hid out in the city and refused to wear the six-pointed yellow star, embroidered with the word 'Juif', which Jews in France, like those in Germany and Poland, were ordered to wear from 29 May 1942.

Collaborators like Robert Brassillach found it distasteful to see how many Jews inhabited the streets of Paris. 'The yellow star may make some Catholics shudder but . . . it renews the most strictly Christian tradition,' he wrote in the fascist paper *Je Suis Partout*. Every Paris paper approved of the new law. *Paris-Midi*, for example, wrote on 8 June: 'The abundance of Jews on the Paris pavements has opened the eyes of the most blind.'

'You really shouldn't walk around like that! It's very dangerous, very risky!' Simone Signoret, then a young Jewish film extra whose real name was Simone Kaminker, cautioned Bianca when she met her in the street, not wearing a star on her coat. Signoret also refused to wear her star. '*Tais-toi!* Be quiet!' Bianca ran away. Her yellow stars, the three issued by the authorities to each Jew, were hidden at the bottom of her drawer.

Beauvoir saw that rebellious Bohemians had found the best way of buying life. 'Optimism remained so obstinately rooted in French heads that a certain number of Jews, particularly small folk without adequate resources, naïvely supposed that by observing the regulations they would escape the worst of what was happening. In fact, few of those identifiable by the yellow star survived. Others, equally ingenuous, thought they could flout all the decrees with impunity. I never saw anyone wearing a star in Montparnasse or Saint-Germain-des-Prés.' Even when, from 15 July, Jews were forbidden to enter public buildings, like restaurants or cinemas, Jewish singers and dancers like Sonia Mossé or Simone Signoret 'turned up at the Flore and chattered away until closing time'. Signoret told the people at Pathé, where she was playing in *Boléro* with Arletty, that she had 'forgotten' her work permit, which was issued by the propaganda staff of the German army to prove that its holder was Aryan. But soon the censors spotted her in another film, and she was fired. A new danger was spreading: denunciation. The occupiers paid 100 francs to informers, and many French people were happy to oblige.

By the end of 1940 Beauvoir, like Sartre, had abandoned Bianca Bienenfeld. It was a 'double execution' for the terrified young woman. '*J'ai porté toute ma vie le poids de cet abandon* [I carried the weight of that abandonment my entire life].' She was, in the words of Jean Kanapa, cast out of the Holy Existentialist family. Into the vacuum stepped Nathalie Sorokine, whose position within the Sartrean nest was strengthened without the awkward cuckoo.

Nathalie had laid siege to Beauvoir on her return to Paris, intent on moving into her grandmother's flat in rue Denfert-Rochereau with her. But Beauvoir, tormented over Bost's fate, was nervous and irritable, and at first quarrels punctuated her ambivalent relationship with Nathalie. 'I break things, I tremble, my voice becomes toneless – and once I almost slapped her,' she confessed to Sartre in July 1940. Nathalie was undeterred; when the curfew approached and the teacher warned the girl to leave, she refused. Reluctantly Beauvoir let her stay the night. Two days later Mme Sorokine threw her daughter out, saying her teacher could keep her; this Beauvoir agreed to do for three months, paying Nathalie 500 francs a month. The flat became the base for Nathalie's bicycle-stealing scam, although Beauvoir refused to act as her accomplice. Otherwise the pair shared a rickety lifestyle. Nathalie cooked up rice or potatoes for Beauvoir, whose black rages often escalated into violence:

> When I tried to shake [Nathalie], she pummelled me with her fists. I nevertheless dragged her as far as the door . . . I frankly hated her. She wanted to talk, but I refused angrily and threw her a mattress, a pillow and some blankets – so that she could make herself comfortable on the floor.

The next day the women made up. Days later Nathalie was pinching Beauvoir so hard that the blood came, and Beauvoir was responding with a slap. Despite vowing not to let Nathalie 'tyrannize' her, Beauvoir again bore 'complaints, blows, clinches and threats', before throwing Sorokine out. The next day, inevitably, was one of reconciliation. Girl on girl action continued, and despite Nathalie's jealousy of Olga, by October Simone de Beauvoir described her relationship with Nathalie as 'idyllic'.

Bost's return to Paris in the autumn restored Beauvoir's equilibrium. After a fortnight's holiday in Montpellier, they settled into a routine in

Paris, where Bost had a 'cushy' job as a teaching supervisor at a school in rue Denfert. He was still seeing Olga, but he and Castor lunched together every day as well as spending Saturday nights à deux. 'It's still all roses with Bost, Olga and Sorokine,' wrote Beauvoir to Sartre on 29 November. But intellectually she was isolated; despite her charming toyboy, she missed Sartre's darting intellect. A second Christmas passed without him, and on New Year's Day 1941, she mused: 'I couldn't get on better with Bost – yet how alone I always am in his company!'

Her mind was on her novel and its prospects. Visiting Brice Parain at the Nouvelle revue française, she learnt that being published under the Occupation meant running the gauntlet of the German censor. Parain himself had refused to edit the NRF, and the fascist writer Drieu La Rochelle was taking over. Parain spoke of the 'Otto lists' of books which the Germans had ordered be destroyed: Freud, Thomas Mann, Paul Nizan, de Gaulle, and soon Raymond Aron, too, were all prohibited, although, signicantly, Sartre was not. As she sat in the Dôme, redrafting her final pages of L'Invitée, Beauvoir became impatient for Sartre's return. 'My heart's breaking all the time as I work. My little one, I feel like weeping all the time these days. I love you so, with such a yearning for your face and your affection . . . It's *you* I miss, your smiles, the little nape of your neck that I remember so well.' Towards the end of January, 'seared by grief', she stopped writing: she was troubled by constant nightmares that he no longer loved her, and was often 'literally fighting for breath'. Even Hegel no longer comforted her. Instead Beauvoir turned back to Kierkegaard, to the certainty of 'J'existe', and to thoughts of the Absolute.

*

Sartre was taken to Drancy, the prison camp run by the SS at the gates of Paris, and released. It was towards the end of March that Beauvoir found a note in her pigeonhole at the Hôtel du Danemark: 'I'm at the Three Musketeers.' He had been in Paris for two weeks without telling her. An undated letter suggests that he had run straight into the arms of Wanda, for whom he had become 'a beloved cat or Pekinese . . . I feel great tenderness towards her.' With Wanda, one of those 'dark, drowning women' for whom he felt a 'magical attraction', Sartre filled the gap left by the loss of his camp comrades.

'Sartre completely baffled me,' wrote Simone de Beauvoir, when she met him again. Each felt the other was speaking a different language.

Having told her about his 'escape', as Beauvoir persisted in calling the ruse by which Perrin had faked Sartre's medical papers, he took her severely to task for her behaviour. 'What *did* disorientate me rather was the stringency of his moral standards.' What was she buying on the black market? he demanded. 'A little tea.' It was too much. She had been wrong to sign the paper stating that she was neither a Freemason nor a Jew. Sartre, who was fundamentally anti-fascist, had returned 'armoured with principles', and was shocked that Beauvoir shared the widely prevalent attitude of *l'attentisme*, or wait-and-see. London was being bombed. It looked as if Hitler was about to invade England. Just being alive in Paris implied 'some sort of compromise', protested the Beaver. He had best accommodate himself to the Fritzes, like everyone else.

To the couple's initial horror, their old friends Dullin and Simone Jollivet had already decided to align themselves wholly with the winning side. As early as July 1940 Jollivet, a triumphant Valkyrie in a long white dress with her blonde hair in a burnous, had boasted to Beauvoir that the moment had come for the flowering of her genius. Now, dining with Beauvoir in spring 1941, at the grillroom of the Théâtre de Paris, she declared that, since Nazism was in the ascendant, 'We should rally to it.' Dullin, whom she held 'in the palm of her hand', planned to produce two plays she had adapted. Beauvoir was shocked, and left the table. Sartre, too, was 'completely disgusted' by the news of Jollivet and Dullin's opportunism.

In April 1941 Sartre believed that the 'Reign of Evil', as he put it in *Iron in the Soul*, had begun with the Occupation. He had learnt at the feet of his Lutheran grandfather, Karl, that sometimes it was the Devil's turn. Hegel had taught him that the 'tourniquet of history', which Sartre visualized as a spiral rather than a dialectic, was a motor in human events, although later he would condemn that 'misunderstood Heglianism' which makes of History a god to which people must submit. 'Take the point of view of History,' he wrote, 'and you will see how this humiliation, this defeat, these death camps, these tortured resistance fighters, these German soldiers in the streets of Paris, this fascist, senile Marshal on Radio Vichy, the whole of this unworthy, hateful present, will suddenly seem normal and, therefore, acceptable to you.' But in 1941 he did accept something very close to Hegelian determinism: Contingency, which had been malign enough to make Sartre ugly, which had brought an ugly regime to rule over France, and which implied the notion of Evil, *Le Mal*, within creation.

Despite his physical frailty, Sartre was eager to do battle with the Evil One. On their first evening together, Beauvoir was amazed to be told that he had not returned to Paris to enjoy the 'sweets of freedom . . . but to *act*'. He would start a resistance movement. The first meeting was held in Beauvoir's room in the Hôtel Mistral, to which she and Sartre returned. Their freedom-fighters were philosophy students, past and present, Marxist and non-Marxist: Maurice Merleau-Ponty, who had formed his own group, Sous la Botte (Under the Boot), from his students at the École Normale, Jean-Toussaint Desanti and his wife, Dominique, François Cuzin, Simone Debout and Yvonne Picart. Sartre, for his part, had invited the 'family', Bost and Olga, Wanda, plus Jean Pouillon, Jean Kanapa and Raoul Levy. It was a time of '*camaraderie joyeuse*' recalls Dominique Desanti. Her husband and Bost were all for making bombs, *boîtes à sardines*, plastic explosives, and throwing grenades. The Beaver herself volunteered to 'smash in' Robert Brasillach's face, when they learnt that he would be among the French collabo writers taking the train to Weimar. However, the group, which Sartre named 'Socialism and Liberty', recognized that their talents were best suited to information-gathering and writing clandestine pamphlets. 'If we accept the Vichy regime, then we are not men,' declared Sartre. 'No compromise is possible with the collaborators.'

Beauvoir was doubtful of success: the group was so amateur that Bost walked through the streets carrying a duplicating machine, and Sartre's meetings with Jean Cavaillès, leader of another nascent group, later shot for his part in the Resistance, took place in the Closerie des Lilas or the Luxembourg Gardens, where they could be overheard. Jean Pouillon lost his briefcase, which held the names of all their comrades as well as a stash of pamphlets. Fortunately, it turned up in the lost property office. On another occasion the physicist Georges Chazelas was printing pamphlets at the house of the writer François Coppée when the Gestapo hammered on the door. They had come to seize Coppée's books. Chazelas had a lucky escape, but on 15 June 1941, pasting up posters calling for new recruits for acts of sabotage on the walls of the medical school, he was arrested and sent to prison for six months.

By the summer Sartre's group had grown to fifty in number, and he was keen to travel to the Free Zone to recruit Gide and Malraux. But ever since the Kobra's return from the Stalag rumours about his 'escape' had been circulating. The French Communist Party (PCF) remained suspicious of him, putting it about that Drieu la Rochelle or even the Nazi Heidegger had fixed his release. The Communists already linked

Sartre with Paul Nizan, condemned as a traitor after his resignation from the Party following the Nazi-Soviet Pact. Now they said Sartre was an *agent provocateur*, a German spy, and the story spread like wildfire.

People watched and waited to see whether Sartre would live up to his promise of 'no compromise'. Instead, he rapidly demonstrated his ability to navigate the treacherous reefs of Occupied France, trimming his sails to the prevailing winds. The serpentine cunning that had already marked his career would never be more in evidence than during *les années noires*, the dark years, in which he penetrated the structures of power and influence and positioned himself ideally for the Liberation. The emptiness of his words was revealed after Easter 1941, when he returned to teach at the Lycée Pasteur at Neuilly. As Beauvoir recorded, Sartre 'adapted to these new conditions', but far faster than she admitted. He met Georges Davy, the Inspector General of Education, whom he had known since he had served as a member of the 1929 *agrégation* jury, and struck a deal with him. If Sartre would teach for two more terms in the suburbs, he could have promotion to the fashionable Lycée Condorcet in the autumn, and become *professeur de khâgne*, taking the top class for entrance to the École Normale. Sartre was still reluctant to put his signature to the oath that he was not a Freemason or a Jew, although the pragmatic Beauvoir argued that 'I should sign so I could have a job and money to do what I wanted to do, which was to set up a resistance group.' Did he sign? It seems so. It is likely that Sartre lied when he told his biographer that Davy was a 'a secret Resistant', who waved him through with a nod and a wink.

*

Sartre and Beauvoir had no intention of allowing the Occupation to stand in the way of their usual summer holiday. Their mission to meet André Gide, the grand old man of letters who had famously asked before the war, 'Who is this Jean-Paul?' added an extra dimension to their plans to make the forbidden crossing into the Free Zone in the south.

Sorokine gave them two of her stolen bicycles, which she camouflaged in the courtyard off Picasso's studio, and Sartre sent them on ahead by train to a priest in Roanne. At the border at Montceau-les-Mines, a local woman guided them across the fields and woods at night until they reached an inn, where they spent an uncomfortable night on mattresses shared with six other people. But the next morning Beauvoir was elated. They had evaded the Germans. Soon she and Sartre were freewheeling along the roads which bore them south, camping out at night after dinner in a local bistro. At Bourg Sartre got his demobilization papers, and the couple pressed on to the Ardèche. Stopping at the house of Pierre Kahn, a former student of Cavaillès, they enjoyed a delicious lunch, with the novelty of fresh bilberries for dessert. Food was more plentiful in the Free Zone, and, as the first cypresses and olive trees appeared, and the scent of heather was replaced by that of lavender, Beauvoir had never felt more carefree: 'In one sense the war makes every moment I live so precious; never have I felt things so violently, so profoundly, as now.'

At Marseilles their mood changed. Sartre met the socialist Daniel Mayer, and asked him if he had any special task for his group, but Mayer could only suggest sending a letter to Léon Blum on his birthday. Sartre left, disappointed. It had been a test for Sartre, who had no political track record, said Mayer later. The next name on Sartre's list was Gide, with an indecipherable address scrawled beside it. Caloris? Vallauris? Finally they found Gide's house at Cabris, but only his daughter Catherine was in. Bicycling into Grasse, Beauvoir had a puncture and stopped beside a fountain, while Sartre tracked down the octogenarian author in a café. Gide was as cagey as Mayer had been. Sartre told him they were meeting André Malraux the following day. 'Well,' remarked Gide as they parted, 'I hope you find him in a good mood – un *bon* Malraux, eh?' The future resistance fighter gave them lunch, but no encouragement. Comfortably situated in his villa near Saint-Jean-Cap-Ferrat, Malraux said dryly that he was depending on Russian tanks and American planes to win the war.

Crossing over the Alpes Maritimes on the way to Colette Audry's house in Grenoble, Simone made the mistake of drinking too much white wine in the hot sunshine. Bowling downhill, she felt a little dizzy. When two other cyclists blocked the road, she swerved and skidded towards a precipice: 'So this is death.' When she recovered consciousness, she had lost a tooth and her face was scraped and swollen. For Beauvoir, the 'business of dying' suddenly seemed easy. 'Death is *nothing*.' She had exorcized her fears. When her father had died in July, at his own wish unattended by any priest, she had been impressed by the peaceful way he 'returned to nothingness'. Her own accident underlined the ease of that transition.

*

'*The* biographical question' on Sartre is, according to one biographer: 'What did you do in the war?' In accepting his new post at the Lycée Condorcet in October 1941, Sartre made a controversial move. He stepped into the shoes of a sacked Jewish teacher, Henri Dreyfus-le-Foyer, great-nephew of Captain Alfred Dreyfus of the Dreyfus Affair. Dreyfus, 'a young and brilliant *professeur de khâgne* in 1941', was dismissed when the first Vichy anti-Semitic law was applied. 'Who's going to replace him? Jean-Paul Sartre,' recalled one of Dreyfus's pupils.

In Sartre's defence, it is alleged that he did not succeed immediately to Dreyfus's job, but that a temporary teacher, Ferdinand Alquié, was appointed for the academic year 1940–41. Did Sartre know that he was both legitimizing and profiting from Vichy racial laws when he took the plum job at Condorcet, which demanded only nine hours of teaching a week, and allowed him time to fulfil his 'destiny' as a writer? Condorcet was a tempting post which brought Sartre level with Beauvoir, herself a *professeur de khâgne* teaching for only eight hours a week. But to take it was to betray his principles.

The facts incriminate Sartre. Although Alquié worked as a temp (*à titre provisoire*) from the end of January until October, it was Sartre who followed Dreyfus as permanent *professeur*, and there is little doubt that he was aware of the fact. According to André Burguière, a pupil of M. Dreyfus, the teacher remarked openly: 'I've been sacked by Vichy; Sartre's taking over from me.' Dreyfus's family recall his saying that Sartre, not Alquié, was his successor. And, unless he failed to read his contract, Sartre could not have avoided the knowledge that he was replacing Dreyfus: the name of a teacher's predecessor was invariably stated on his letter of appointment.

No teacher could have been unaware of the flight of the Jews. It was the event of 1940–41 in schools and universities. The anti-Semitic laws meant 1,111 jobs in education suddenly became vacant. Jean Wahl, Bianca's professor, was also relieved of his post, as was Claude Lévi-Strauss. Sartre, as well as Beauvoir, who notes in her memoirs that she dined with Wahl, knew of the suffering of the victims of Vichy. But it was easier to look away, to avoid the embarrassment and unease felt by non-Jews when they came face to face with Jews wearing the yellow star. In order not to make them Jews by virtue of 'the look', wrote Sartre, he avoided a meeting. It was, he said, 'the supreme mark of friendship to appear not to know'.

Sartre did not need Dreyfus's job; he could have stayed at the Lycée Pasteur. Careerist to the bone, it was his hunger for fame which led him to step over Dreyfus, who disappeared to the Free Zone where he became a medical orderly in the Resistance. Famously, Sartre would write:

> I hold Flaubert and Goncourt responsible for the repression which followed the Commune because they didn't write a line to prevent it.

Equally, Sartre never wrote a line to oppose the laws of Vichy or their implementation; instead he took advantage of them.

24

Supping with the Devil

You know what it means to be a coward . . . Yes, you
know what evil *costs* . . . I made my choice deliberately.
A man is what he wills himself to be.

Jean-Paul Sartre, *Huis Clos*

THE DANGER OF war lent a new urgency to sex. The Occupation
created a new need to feather the Sartrean nest, as the 'family' became
more dependent on its 'parents' and more tightly knit. Sexually
colonized by Sartre and Beauvoir, conditioned to be helpless, its chicks
were a growing financial drain. Wanda, said Sartre, was his 'child', as
Olga was the Beaver's. Little Bost, who disliked regular work, was
increasingly infantilized. Polygamous relationships within the family
tightened the bonds between them.

New consenting triangles had arisen with the return of Sartre. He
had quickly re-established his position as pasha within the harem by
sleeping with Nathalie Sorokine, who also slept with Bost. Beauvoir
continued her lesbian relationship with Sorokine, even though the
tall Russian blonde had found a new boyfriend, Jean-Pierre Bourla, an
ex-pupil of Sartre's from the Lycée Pasteur. Olga's relationship with
Bost continued to limp along, despite his sexual tie to Beauvoir,
with whom he spent every Saturday night at the Hôtel Poirier in
place Emile Goudeau in Montmartre, far away from the prying eyes
of Montparnasse and Saint-Germain-des-Pres. Simone has been

described as 'the senior wife in a harem', but, as Caesar's wife, one half of the imperial couple, she was powerful in her own right. Financially independent, she dispersed her income as she pleased. Nor was she a sexual discard suffering at the hands of a pocket Don Juan, for her bisexuality put her in a strong position, in which she took her pleasure with both Bost and Sorokine.

'I've never known how to lead either my sexual or my emotional life properly; I most deeply and sincerely feel like a grubby bastard. A really small-time bastard at that, a sort of sadistic university type and civil-service Don Juan – disgusting,' Sartre had written only eighteen months ago. 'That has got to change. I've got to swear off (1) vulgar little affairs . . . (2) big affairs undertaken lightly.' But his remorseful promises to end his career as an 'old rake' came to nothing. On the contrary, as his fame grew so did the number of groupies pursuing him, and the potential for a deeper complicity with Beauvoir. When Sartre related to her his seduction of the Provençal drama student, Marie Gibert, or his penetration of Bianca or Nathalie, Beauvoir, who also preferred virgins, was able to assume the masculine role in her imagination, using Sartre as a sex-toy. It was as if she slept with Sartre's mistress by interposing his body. Similarly, her own accounts of her conquests allowed Sartre to assume his femininity. Sartre had admitted in February 1940 that 'the power of our physical relationship is fading slightly', and Beauvoir had confided to her journal her fear that, like the couple in Cocteau's *Monstres Sacrés*, their love might be jeopardized by the temptations of youth. Now the oxygen of youth kept it alive.

In pasha mode, Sartre resolved to put Wanda on the stage: 'I have decided to have her give up painting, which she hates, and have her do theatre work.' But it was Wanda's sister, Olga, who first came to Sartre demanding that he make her a star. In July 1941 Olga played a small part for well-known actor-director Jean-Louis Barrault in his production of Aeschylus's *The Suppliants*. During rehearsals one day she and her friend, also called Olga, asked Barrault how to win a bigger role. 'Find an author and get him to write a play for you,' came the reply. Nervously Olga went to Sartre: 'After what I've done to him, he'll never, never give me a role,' she said to her friend, who was known as Olga La Brune. But Sartre was always generous to his intimates; confident that Barrault would put on his play, he began writing *Les Mouches* (*The Flies*) for Olga.

By October 'Socialism and Liberty' had collapsed, its members melting away to join the Communist Party, which became the driving force in the Resistance after Hitler's invasion of Russia in June 1941.

Many of Sartre's group were disillusioned by the philosophical seminars in the Flore. Now they left for the Free Zone. Sartre, in his teddy-bear coat, continued to hug the stove and write. His play, said Beauvoir, 'represented the one form of resistance still open to him'.

But while still nominally the head of a resistance group, Sartre had already decided to sleep with the enemy. Jean Paulhan at Gallimard introduced him to René Delange, editor of Comoedia, a collaborationist weekly. Amused to see certain writers, like Sartre, buzzing like flies round a lamp to which their ambition attracted them, Paulhan, who spied for the Resistance, received writers and journalists on Fridays at Gallimard's offices. Sartre, keen to advance his literary career, brushed aside awkward knowledge: Comoedia's Paris edition would be submitted to the German Propaganda-Staffel, the censorship commission headed by Sonderführer Gerhard Heller. All editors were obliged to accept the suppression of any passage deemed harmful to German interests; all Jewish writers were, of course, proscribed. Delange was delighted to find how many of the Parisian intelligentsia were prepared to collaborate with him, including Sartre, who offered to write a weekly column. Jean Guéhenno, a writer who refused to publish during the années noires, wrote of his fellows: 'Incapable of living a long time hidden, he would sell his soul in order to have his name appear. A few months of silence, of disappearance – he can't stand it.'

On 21 June 1941 the first edition of Comoedia appeared, with Sartre's name among the contributors as author of an article on Melville's Moby Dick. 'We have come to an agreement over a precise programme concerning Franco-German intellectual collaboration of which Comoedia will be the tribune,' wrote Delange to the German Institute in Paris. Sartre realized that the journal was less independent than he had thought. At the Liberation he would claim never to have written for Delange, informing the tribunal investigating the Comoedia dossier that he had asked the editor if he would be free to write what he thought, and Delange had assured him that he would be 'completely independent'. 'Nevertheless,' Sartre assured Judge Zoussmann, 'I decided . . . to abstain from all collaboration. I did this not because I distrusted Comoedia, but because the principle of abstention allowed no exception to be made.'

The truth was very different. Sartre's relationship with René Delange would grow closer. As late as February 1944 he gave the editor his 'Hommage à Jean Giraudoux,' on the death of the playwright who was the most powerful influence on Les Mouches.

*

On 9 November 1940 a fresh-faced, thirty-one-year-old German linguist named Gerhard Heller marched into the offices of the Propaganda-Staffel at 52 avenue des Champs Élysées. Heller later claimed to be an anti-Nazi, but he held the rank of Lieutenant in the Wehrmacht. His superior, Dr Kaiser, wasted no time in explaining to him the purpose of the German propaganda machine in Paris: 'To present the new Germany to the French and lead them into collaboration with her.'

Gerhard – 'mon cher Gérard' to his new French friends – posed as the protector of French literature. After Kaiser was recalled to Berlin in December, all doors were open to him. Even the greatest intellectuals courted Heller's favour, not only overt collaborators like Drieu la Rochelle or Jean Cocteau, but others like the publisher Gaston Gallimard. In November 1940 Gallimard wrote to Jean Luchaire, a Nazi collaborator and journalist, that his publishing house was concentrating 'on collaborating' with Kaiser. The letter would sully Gallimard's reputation after the war; he obeyed the rules laid down by the German ambassador, Otto Abetz, whose 'Otto list' demanded the destruction not only of all books by Jewish authors but also those which 'poisoned French public opinion', sacrificing authors like the Resistant André Malraux, the Communist Louis Aragon, and the Jew André Maurois. Yet Gallimard also paid monthly allowances to several such authors. Attacked by the collabo press, he was playing the game of survival for Maison Gallimard.

Jean Paulhan, arrested in 1941 and released at the instigation of Drieu la Rochelle, was Gaston's éminence grise. Late that year Paulhan met Heller, and invited the smiling young censor to an Arab meal. Over the conspiratorial lunches that followed, it occurred to Heller that Paulhan was also playing le double jeu, at times hostile, at other times favourable, to the new NRF edited by Drieu. If the German Occupation was going to last fifty, 100 years, then the NRF was 'necessary . . . who knows, courageous', wrote Paulhan on 16 December 1940 to the Nazi collaborator Marcel Jouhandeau. At the same time he warned writers like Raymond Queneau and Malraux not to write for it. From Heller's point of view, it was a question of 'preserving the tone and the appearance of freedom . . . under this cover the divers collaborators . . . can play their games'.

Undoubtedly Paulhan rumbled the German censor. 'Haven't you seen that he's bait?' demanded Giradoux, who dined with Heller and

Delange while at the same time sending back intelligence on clandestine newspapers to his son, Jean-Pierre, who had joined General de Gaulle in London. Heller himself realized that he was viewed as Machiavellian, luring French intellectuals into collaboration rather than making martyrs by repression. Others saw the 'ring of protection' Heller drew round Maison Gallimard and believed that Heller was 'the agent of Gallimard, and Paulhan's secretary'. But the censor's declared aim remained to build 'the new Europe' run by Germany. Under his control, French writers practised self-censorship. In no other defeated country did cultural life flourish as it did in France. The number of new books published soared, the theatre provided circuses for the populace, and the Germans could point to the complicity of French intellectuals and artists with the same satisfaction that they took in *la collaboration horizontale* of French women with German soldiers.

Sartre, too, took the bait. No doubt in his own mind he was playing the same delicate, dangerous game as Gaston Gallimard, or François Mauriac, who dedicated a copy of his latest novel, *La Pharisienne*, to Heller '*avec ma gratitude*'. Certainly the ubiquitous Heller, dressed as usual *en civil*, attended rehearsals of *Les Mouches* at the Théâtre de la Cité, formerly known as the Théâtre Sarah Bernhardt until the Nazis aryanized its Jewish name. He records that he sat close to Sartre and Beauvoir in the Flore, which he visited twice a week, but never introduced himself. 'I judged the approach dangerous for them and for me.' The Flore, unknown to Beauvoir and Sartre, was kept under surveillance by German agents. Heller facilitated the acceptance of the play by the German authorities, writing in his report that it had nothing to do with the Resistance. Sartre had been courageous, said Heller in his memoirs. The censor had understood at once that it was not only Clytemnestra whom Electra and Orestes had in their sights.

Barrault had reneged on his promise to present *The Flies*, and Sartre was enraged. The director was saying that Olga was Sartre's mistress, whom he wished to push. 'Olga has never been and never will be my mistress,' Sartre wrote in an angry letter of 9 July 1942, protesting that it was her talent only that he wished to serve. He guessed that the real reason was that the great Paul Claudel had offered Barrault his own play, *Le Soulier de Satin* (*The Satin Slipper*). It was enough to make Barrault drop the *débutant* play by an untested playwright.

When Charles Dullin stepped into the breach, offering to put on the play himself, it was too tempting an offer to refuse. Sartre took another step along the slippery path towards intellectual collaboration. 'It wasn't difficult to get my first play put on because I knew Dullin,' he admitted after the war. It was Dullin who had interceded with Gaston Gallimard to take *Nausea*, Dullin, judged *deutschfreundlich*, friendly to the Germans, by the *Propaganda-Abteilung*, who now launched Sartre's career as a playwright. Conveniently forgetting how 'disgusted' he had professed to be in July 1940 by Jollivet's pro-Nazi stance, he followed '*le vieux renard*', the old fox, wherever he led. Dullin submitted a list of his actors to the censor, swearing that they were all Aryans. Sartre also sent his text to the censor, having ensured that, as Heller put it, 'nothing anti-German' remained. Had its call to resistance been as clear as Sartre claimed, the play would never have received the swastika seal of approval.

On the first night, 3 June 1943, there was a magnificent buffet for the company and their friends. Champagne flowed as the many Nazis present, in uniform and civvies, including Sonderführer Baumann, from the Theater-Kulturgruppe, which had ranked Dullin's Théatre de la Cité fifth out of forty-four theatres in terms of collaboration, drank to the success of the play. Sartre himself was observed by Marc Bénard, an old friend from Stalag days who had painted the scenery for *Bariona*, politely returning the German toasts and 'raising his glass in their honour'.

The playwright had already given a publicity interview to *Comoedia* on 24 April. Even so, its critic, Roland Purnal, savaged *The Flies*, calling the play a 'travesty of the *Oresteia*'; Olga, under the stage name Olga Dominique, won kinder notices as Electra. Artistically the play, with its archaic masks and didactic rhetoric, was a failure, although a lone voice of praise came from Alfred Buesche, the German critic in the *Pariser Zeitung*, organ of the Propaganda office. In Sartre's retelling of the Orestes–Electra story, Orestes, son of Agamemnon, sees his city covered with flies, symbolizing his guilt for having acquiesced in his father's murder. The curse under which Orestes lies in Aeschylus's original drama leaves him no choice but to avenge Agamemnon by killing the usurper, Agisthos, as well as his own mother, Clytemnestra. But at the heart of Sartre's interpretation lies his belief that we are 'condemned to be free': 'I *am* my liberty,' says Orestes, a man who freely decides to do his duty and commit an act of murder against the usurpers. Sartre's message to the students in his audience was that, like Orestes, resistance fighters can kill without remorse.

His timing, as so often, was superb. On 21 October 1941 the *Feldkommandant* of Nantes had been shot by the Resistance, and acts of sabotage against the Vichy regime were increasing as the turn of the tide became increasingly obvious to the French following the fall of

Stalingrad in January 1943. V-signs were chalked up on the walls of buildings in Paris, despite Allied bombing of the Renault works in the suburb of Boulogne-Billancourt, where tanks for the Wehrmacht were made, on 3 March 1942. Sartre's call to arms was, he later explained, directed against the Vichy regime of *mea culpa*, guilt and breast-beating for the fall of France. It was time for France to take back her liberty. It was also Sartre's message to himself to step outside the world of the imagination and become real.

'The man who wanted to become a playwright and put his friends on the stage had been less anxious about the Jews than his career and his intimates,' would be the verdict of Michel Contat, himself a Sartrean, in 1985. Contat saw clearly that Sartre was an *arriviste sous la botte*, under the German boot. Even Sartre's crony, the former surrealist writer Michel Leiris, perceived only a general call to liberty in *The Flies*, and waited six months before endorsing it in the clandestine paper *Les Lettres françaises*. Later he came to realize that Sartre had run none of the risks to which he later laid claim. But, far away in Berlin, the message of revolt reached Goebbels, to whom it was reported as a 'lone voice of defiance'. Clothed in allegory, Sartre had smuggled his appeal to murder the murderers under the noses of the Germans. As a 'writer who resisted and not a resistant who wrote', it was the best the Kobra could do.

*

Our hotel rooms were not heated . . . so I always worked in cafés. During the war, Castor and I worked on the first floor of the Flore, she at one end, I at the other, so we wouldn't be tempted to talk. We wrote from 9:00 to 1:00, went to Castor's room to eat whatever she had scrounged up the night before, or whatever our friends, who ate with us, brought along, then back to the Flore to write some more, from 4:00 to 8:00 or 9:00.

Castor had moved to a room with a kitchen attached in the Hôtel Mistral, and had borrowed a saucepan, casseroles and crockery from Poupette's studio. From the winter of 1941–42 she cooked all the meals for the family herself, with the help of Bost, whose reputation rested on his boiled beef with vegetables, known as *boeuf mode*, and veal blanquette. The combined salaries of Beauvoir and Sartre, 7,000 francs, no longer stretched to restaurant meals for the family, which had been swollen by the addition of the Spanish Jew, Bourla. 'I had little natural liking for domestic chores,' recalled Beauvoir, but soon 'the alchemy of cooking' became her new obsession. It would last three years: her days were often spent queuing, in search of turnips and beetroots. The first meal she prepared was 'turnip sauerkraut', over which she poured a tin of soup. Sartre, who wasn't fussy, ate it without complaining. Beauvoir didn't let him see her wash the maggots off the rotting rabbit carcasses and pieces of meat which Mme Morel sent up from the country: they were an important source of protein. Nathalie and Bost helped the Beaver sort the maggoty butter beans from the sound ones, or pick mouse droppings from a packet of pasta or oatmeal, while Sartre, who missed his cigarettes, searched the gutters and banquettes of the Three Musketeers for dog-ends to stuff into his pipe.

Beauvoir used her dead father's clothing coupons to have a dress and coat made, which she kept for best. Like most women, she began wearing trousers, with wooden-soled clogs. For many months after losing her tooth on the way to Grenoble, she had a suppurating boil on her chin; one day she squeezed it hard. Something white protruded from the flesh, like one of those Surrealist nightmares in which cheeks sprout eyes. Simone squeezed harder; out slid the tooth which had been embedded for weeks in her chin.

In the winter of 1942–43 the family's hardships increased. Beauvoir returned to Paris after spending the summer in the Free Zone, where food had become so scarce that she, Sartre and Bost, lived on mouldy bread and sucked ice to stave off hunger. She had lost over sixteen pounds, and her room at the Hôtel Mistral had been let. With difficulty she found another hotel, the squalid Hôtel d'Aubusson in rue Dauphine, near the Pont Neuf. She hired a handcart and climbed between the shafts to haul her few belongings across Paris. Her new room was cold and dirty, with peeling walls and a single naked bulb. The kitchen also served as the lavatory. Outside on the stone staircase, a child wept. Inside her room his mother, a prostitute, entertained her clients, emerging every so often to cuff the sobbing boy.

Rats and mice were breeding prolifically, and one day Beauvoir found that they had gnawed through her cupboard and ripped open her packets of lentils and dried peas. The squalor was no longer delightfully bohemian as it had been at the Hôtel du Petit Mouton. In the candlelight the rodents scuttled over the floor and frightened her with their boldness. Sartre and Wanda also moved into the hotel, although Wanda refused Beauvoir entry to the room she shared with Sartre. But Nathalie and Bourla were there too, and every night the matriarch went up to their room and kissed her 'children' goodnight.

In the Flore, on the boulevard Saint-Germain, there were acetylene lamps and warmth. It became their *querencia*, wrote Beauvoir. 'I tried to arrive as soon as the doors were opened, in order to get the best and warmest table, right beside the stove-pipe. I loved the moment when Boubal, a blue apron tied round him, came bustling into the still-empty café.' Picasso and Dora Marr, with her dog on a lead, sat at one marble-topped table, the poet Jacques Prévert at another. Maloudji wrote a novel. The sculptor Giacometti sketched. The entire family retreated to 'this warm, well-lit snug retreat, with its charming blue-and-red wallpaper . . . its members, according to our principles of behaviour, scattered in every corner of the room'. Sartre and Wanda would be in one corner, Olga and Beauvoir in another, but only Sartre and Beauvoir returned there every night. 'When they die,' remarked Bourla, 'you'll have to dig them a grave under the floor.'

As their pens scratched over the paper, Beauvoir and Sartre barely noticed when Bianca fled to the Vercors, when Yvonne Picard was arrested, or Sonia Mossé. Sonia's last request, for some silk stockings, came from Drancy, before she disappeared. There is no mention in *The Prime of Life* of the round-up on 16 July 1942 of nearly 13,000 Jews, including over 4,000 children, who were herded into the Vélodrome d'Hiver stadium in Paris by the French police before being sent to Auschwitz. Only the torture and execution of their red-headed Communist friend Politzer in May pierced the couple's self-absorption.

As the Jews were deported and the Communists joined the Resistance, the intellectual élite dwindled. The lack of competition offered unprecedented opportunities to the remaining writers. 'Never were we more free than during the Occupation,' wrote Sartre in 1944.

> We had lost all our rights, first and foremost the right to speak; we were openly insulted daily, and we had to remain silent . . . Since the Nazi poison was seeping into our very thoughts, each accurate thought was a victory; since an all-powerful police was trying to coerce us into silence, each word became as precious as a declaration of principle; since we were hunted, each gesture had the weight of a commitment. The often frightful circumstances of our struggle enabled us finally to live, undisguised and fully revealed, that awful, unbearable situation that we call the human condition.

Although in the élite Flore, where, wrote the novelist Boris Vian, 'people were cheerful and created the atmosphere of a club from which it would have been embarrassing to be left out', conditions were rather better than Sartre painted them, there is no doubt that repression made him phenomenally productive. His virtuosity and creativity were unparalleled. He was thirty-eight, Beauvoir thirty-five, and the fame they had both craved for so long was about to burst upon them in a shower of glory.

The year 1943 was when Beauvoir's world changed. It started badly. Nathalie's mother brought a complaint to the educational authorities against Beauvoir of 'corrupting a minor'. Nineteen-year-old Nathalie, whom Beauvoir had known since 1938, when she was at the Lycée Moliere, had certainly been seduced by her teacher, and her interest in her pupil was paedophile in nature. Mme Sorokine had spent two years compiling her report, in which she claimed that Beauvoir had also seduced Nathalie and then acted as procurer, handing her over to her male lovers, Sartre and Bost.

Mme Sorokine alleged that her daughter was not by any means Beauvoir's first victim; before her there had been Olga and Bianca, whom she had groomed and seduced before passing them on to Sartre. The 'vile trade' was not always successful; Olga had persistently refused Sartre, although he had been successful in seducing her younger sister, Wanda.

Despite intensive investigations, the authorities were unable to make the charge stick. Beauvoir admitted that Nathalie had developed an 'exalted admiration' towards her, as was often the case with her pupils, but denied that she had responded in any way. Sartre had been her lover for six years, but was now simply a friend. She had never had sexual relations with Bost, and nor had Nathalie.

Sartre stated that Mademoiselle de Beauvoir had never had unnatural tendencies towards women. Bost swore that he was merely Beauvoir's friend, nor had he received money from her. Olga denied that her former teacher had made unusual advances to her or procured her for any man. Carefully coached in their replies, all the members of the family, including Nathalie, stuck to their stories. Even Wanda professed herself outraged at these scandalous allegations against Beauvoir.

In her memoirs Beauvoir claims that Mme Sorokine was motivated by revenge, because Beauvoir refused her request to break up Nathalie's relationship with Bourla. But Mme Sorokine's first complaint against her daughter's teacher dated back as far as 27 November 1941. On 3 April 1942 Rector Gidel, President of the University Council, recommended Beauvoir's exclusion from teaching. Although the case against could not be proven, the Pétainist rector objected to her private life as an unmarried woman living with Jean-Paul Sartre. She was also condemned for teaching two gay authors, Gide and Proust. Sartre was himself incriminated on the basis of his 'pathological and erotic' short stories in *The Wall*. The Rector's conclusion was that both teachers were unfit to teach 'at a time when France aspires to the restoration of moral and family values'. In the eyes of Vichy, with its motto of '*Travail, Famille, Patrie*' (Work, Family, Fatherland), not only Beauvoir but Sartre had sinned. In June 1943 Beauvoir was dismissed.

The loss of her income was a crisis for the family. 'I can't remember how I managed to wangle a job as a features editor on the national radio network,' wrote Beauvoir disingenously in her memoirs. She claimed to be obeying the unwritten rules of the writers in the Occupied Zone: 'No one was to write for any journal or magazine in the Occupied Zone, nor to broadcast from Radio Paris . . . [Although] it was permissible to work for the press in the Free Zone and to speak on Radio Vichy.' But, like Sartre, she had long ago become accustomed to breaking rules. A word from the Kobra to the collaborationist René Delange was all it took: 'Delange, who is definitely a pearl, told me this morning that he is going to find something for you,' wrote Sartre in the summer of 1943. '12 radio sketches, one a month . . . 10 minutes, for which you would be paid 1,500 to 2,000 francs . . . It would take you all of four hours a month. I enthusiastically accepted for you!'

Beauvoir made programmes, innocuous in themselves, about medieval French festivals with Pierre Bost, Little Bost's elder brother. But following the Allied invasion of North Africa on 8 November 1942, the Germans had occupied the Free Zone, and Vichy Radio had been swallowed up into *la Radiodiffusion Nationale*, National Radio based in Paris. It was now part of the German propaganda machine under the control of Pierre Laval, Prime Minister since April that year. As Laval agreed to meet Himmler's deportation quota for Jews – 100,000 from France – Beauvoir stepped into the heart of collaboration, into studios thronged by Germans in well-cut uniform or civvies, like Heller. Did she flirt and socialize, as she did with Albert Camus, whom she propositioned soon after meeting him with Sartre at the first night of *Les Mouches*?

'I had become, overnight, a real writer. I could not contain my joy,' said Beauvoir, when she read the first review of *L'Invitée* in *Comoedia*. Feeling at last that she was 'fulfilling the promises I made to myself at fifteen', she was ecstatic at the publication of her novel in August 1943, and to find herself greeted as a literary celebrity on her return to Paris.

Gallimard printed 23,000 copies. To most readers the story of the threesome was a lightly disguised autobiography, which earned for Beauvoir the same reputation for obscenity that *The Wall* had brought Sartre. It was a window into Bohemia, into the wicked world of writers, all in love with each other if not at the same time. 'I'm reading Beauvoir's book, *L'Invitée*, which everyone's talking about,' recorded Jean Cocteau, playwright and collaborator, in his journal: 'She's a bitch who recounts the lives of dogs, who gnaw at bones, who take turns to piss on the same lamp post, who bite and sniff each other's bottoms . . .' Nevertheless, he wrote a polite letter of congratulation to the author. Favourably reviewed in the pro-Nazi press, *Je suis partout* and *La Gerbe*, the book sold well and was submitted for the Prix de Goncourt. As Cocteau quipped, '*Vive la paix honteuse!* Long live the shameful peace!'

By contrast Sartre's 700-page *Being and Nothingness* passed almost unnoticed when it was published in June. As it weighed exactly one kilo, it would prove useful for weighing vegetables, joked another former surrealist, Raymond Queneau: 'All the grocers who sell flour or potatoes by weight will be obliged to have a volume in their stores.' More pessimistic than *The Flies*, in his greatest philosophical work Sartre pleaded for the almost limitless nature of human freedom. 'Anyone who is an existentialist must adopt the view that men are free, and their freedom extends further than they will have thought,' writes Mary Warnock. 'Essentially they are free to choose their morality, their attitudes towards God, their approach to death and love.' But the freedom of the human individual to create meaning in a world itself meaningless is closely connected to his alienation. The inescapable human consciousness ('*le pour-soi*') is Sartre's tragic theme. Separated by the world of things by a gap or Nothingness, unable to flee the curse of self-awareness, the consciousness longs for the hardness and solidity of stone (the *en-soi*, or physical object). Consciousness, imagination, freedom itself are all brought into being by *Le Néant*, the Nothingness which 'lies at the heart' of Beings-for-themselves. It was a peculiarly Sartrean problem, for the author lived in his own head more than most people, and wrestled with his lifelong need to translate awareness into true being, to live authentically instead of going 'limp as laundry', like Lola in *Intimacy*, when presented with a course of action. Like Lola, Sartre felt that he lived in bad faith. To conquer the inferiority complex born of his ugliness he constantly seduced pretty women, and surrounded himself with younger men who idolized him. He wanted to be authentic like Castor, whom he considered effortlessly authentic and true. But he remained trapped in Nothingness and emptiness.

The ontology Sartre created offered no escape from the burden and anguish of freedom. In his fascinated description of concrete reality, the physical properties of the world, in particular viscosity, the reader senses Sartre's fear of the all-engulfing, mindless 'It-Itself' which threatens the fragile human: the 'sticky death of the For-itself in the In-itself'. The seven-year-old child, caught out without a ticket on a train, still struggles with his own right to existence.

Metaphysical despair is expressed also in Sartre's belief that conflict characterizes human relationships: love and desire give way to sado-masochism. Hate lies at the heart of things. And what difference is there between sitting in your room drunk or leading your people to glory, asks Mathieu in *The Age of Reason*, because man and his freedom are useless. Human beings can never become 'the *Ens causa sui*, which religions call God . . . We lose ourselves in vain. Man is a useless passion.'

As to *Being and Nothingness*, Sartre left a tantalizing footnote on page 412 promising an ethical theory in the future. It was never to come. Clues lie in his assumption of an 'emptiness' or lack within human beings, which they must be free to fill as they please; ontology itself cannot formulate a morality. But since it is the nature of human individuals to perceive values in the world, values 'spring up round them like partridges'. Once man has recognized that he himself is the source of all values, he can choose to value whatever he pleases: to reject society and convention and embrace the taboo.

The question of how and why human beings should behave morally when there is no God was one to which Sartre continually returned. At the Condorcet Dostoevsky's statement, 'If God does not exist then anything is permissible,' was a favourite essay topic. Beauvoir, who thrashed out Sartre's ideas with him and, at the very least, edited his text, began her own 'moral period', writing *The Ethics of Ambiguity*. As to *Being and Nothingness*, she observed crisply, 'There will be a few boring passages, but there are also a few spicy ones: one concerns all holes in general, and the other focuses on the anus and love Italian style.' Conscious of his debt to her, the author dedicated the book 'To the Beaver'. There was no other acknowledgement of her part in its genesis.

June 1943, the month of *Les Mouches* and *Being and Nothingness*, and the month in which the Allies landed in Sicily and the French Resistance leader, Jean Moulin, was tortured and killed, was also the month in which, said Beauvoir, one day at the theatre 'a dark-skinned young man came up and introduced himself: it was Albert Camus'. The twenty-nine-year-old author of *The Outsider*, the literary sensation of the previous year, and a philosophical essay, *The Myth of Sisyphus*, was everything that the squat, wall-eyed manikin was not: tall, dark, olive-skinned, and dazzlingly attractive to women. Marooned in France by the Allied landing in North Africa, Camus had left behind his colonial, working-class background in Algeria, as well as his wife, and was about to take Paris by storm. Sartre, who had already recognized the younger writer as a philosopher of the absurd like himself, felt a sudden *coup de coeur*.

'We were like two dogs circling a bone,' said Beauvoir. 'The bone was Sartre, and we both wanted it.' Although Sartre was 'the strongest heterosexual' Beauvoir knew, and had 'without a doubt not one trace of homosexuality in his disposition', his intense 'infatuation' with Camus frightened her. The handsome *pied noir*, a Frenchman born in Algeria, was easy in his skin, unlike Sartre, but he was also vulnerable, ill with chronic tuberculosis. Within days the two men were drinking together at the Brasserie Lipp, and chasing women together, although Sartre had to try harder than his new friend. 'Why are you going to so much trouble?' asked Camus, as Sartre showed off to a pretty girl. Sartre replied, 'Have you taken a look at my face?'

Sartre immediately invited Camus to play the part of Garcin in *Huis Clos* (*No Exit*), and to direct the play which he had written in just two weeks while staying at Mme Morel's in September. In one sense *No Exit* is Sartre's defiant response to Beauvoir's dismissal, his way of saying, '*Merde à l'Alma Mater*,' piss off to the University and the Establishment. In his portrayal of hell, a reworking of the threesome with Olga and Beauvoir, in which 'each of us will act as torturer of the two others', Inès is a lesbian who desires Estelle, an abortionist, and Garcin is simply a coward. That summer, in July 1943, Vichy had guillotined an abortionist, an execution to which Beauvoir refers in *The Prime of Life*. Memories of Olga's abortion were still fresh in her mind and in that of Sartre, and in *No Exit*, with its message that 'Hell is other people', Sartre was presenting in a modern and easily understood form the same ideas about masters and slaves buried in *Being and Nothingness*.

Camus accepted. He was as ambitious as Sartre, having already agreed to cut a chapter on the Jewish Kafka from *The Myth of Sisyphus* the German censor, and was eager to follow the older man's lead. Sartre's own growing fame had brought important new connections: Michel Leiris was a wealthy bourgeois, whose art dealer father-in-law had helped launch Picasso, and through Leiris Sartre met other intellectuals and artists such as Queneau, Georges Bataille, Jacques Lacan, Maurois, Picasso and Dora Marr. Most valuable was an introduction to the Comité Nationale des Écrivains (CNE), a clandestine, predominantly Communist group of writers. The CNE had at first refused to have anything to do with Sartre, whom they considered tainted by his repatriation at the hands of the Germans, but after the death of their founder, Jacques Decours, they invited him to join. From January 1943 Sartre attended their meetings, and began writing for *Les Lettres françaises*, organ of the CNE. His attack on the pro-Nazi Drieu La Rochelle came out in April 1943. After the war Sartre claimed that the CNE had agreed to the production of his plays, but he had already announced the production of *Les Mouches* in *Paris-Midi* on 17 September 1942, months before joining the committee. In 1943 Sartre's personal Mr Fix-it, Delange, after finding jobs for Beauvoir and his own mistress, Barbara Lange, on the radio, also arranged for the author to write screenplays for Pathé. Soon the 'dirty money' was flowing in. 'I wanted the dough,' Sartre told Beauvoir that summer, after writing *The Chips Are Down*. '37,000 francs, I hope . . . Well anyway, the screenplay is taken, don't worry: you'll need no work at all next year, we'll be on easy street.'

Rehearsals for *No Exit* took place in Beauvoir's room in the Hôtel Louisiane on the rue de Seine, to which she and Sartre moved in October 1943, together with her 'kids', Nathalie and Bourla, as well as Mouloudji and his wife Lola. The cast of three also rehearsed at the home of Olga 'La Brune' Barbézat, whose wealthy husband, Marc, was paying for the production, the vehicle for her launch and that of Wanda. At other times Wanda and Camus ran through their lines together at the down-at-heel Hôtel Chaplin, where she lived with Olga and Bost. Wanda, who had used the casting couch to her advantage, sleeping with Sartre as the quickest route to the role of her dreams, as Estelle in *Huis Clos*, now moved on to the star. Garcin is a Don Juan figure, reflecting Sartre's own private life, but Camus in role was a more wickedly attractive figure to Wanda than the playwright, to whom she complained crossly, 'With nobody in the whole world do I feel so bored as with you.' Sartre had put up with Wanda's tantrums and tears, her drug-taking (she was addicted to amphetamines), he had paid her bills, he had written a play for her, but it was Camus, self-confident and aloof, a man who kept his own counsel and refused to join the 'family', but at whose feet women fell, who seduced her.

Sartre was deeply hurt when he found out early in 1944. 'What was she thinking about, to go running after Camus?' he asked the Beaver. 'What did she want from him? Wasn't I so much better? And so nice? She should watch out.' In February Olga Barbézat was arrested in a Gestapo sweep at the home of a member of the Resistance. Camus, committed also to the Resistance since writing in July 1943 his first 'letter to a German friend', a moral justification of the French struggle against their conquerors, withdrew from the production of *No Exit*. Sartre took his revenge on Wanda, replacing her and the rest of the cast with professional actors. Never again would he feel the same way about her.

*

The upward path of Beauvoir's life continued serenely, despite the bloody repression around her. Since entering public life, and becoming *une metteuse en ondes* (radio producer), she had discarded her turban. She wore 'an elaborate high coiffure', and a dress 'in a beautiful electric blue', designed by Mme Morel and made at La Pouèze, as she waited to hear whether she had won the Prix Goncourt. 'The idea that I might become the centre of vast publicity I found both terrifying and attractive,' recorded Beauvoir. The prize went to Marius Grout; but she had finished her second novel, and was working on a third.

In her spacious room at the Hôtel Louisiane, which had a kitchen attached, and which Beauvoir called 'the apartment of my dreams', she began giving dinner parties. Bost helped with the cooking, and Zette Leiris, who had access to the black market, provided the meat. 'I would offer my guests bowls of green beans and heaped dishes of beef stew, and I always took care to have plenty of wine . . . I had never "entertained" before, and enjoyed the new experience,' recorded Beauvoir. 'The quality's not exactly brilliant,' said Camus, 'but the quantity is just right.' Her world had opened out, reaching beyond the incestuous and greedy family to a crowd of new friends. When Picasso and Dora came to dinner, she made 'something really special': a salad of whortleberries and blackcurrants. Beauvoir no longer queued, but went out with her friends to restaurants, which were divided into four classes. For 250 francs a reasonable meal could be had at a second- or third-class restaurant; she could afford to boycott the fourth-class, where rutabagas and artichokes were on the menu. Sartre continued to lunch with his mother, who kept a bourgeois table, thanks to the black market, at her elegant apartment, 23 avenue de Lamballe, at Passy, and sent her maid to stand in the queues.

Sartre could have made another choice. His potential rivals, like Vladimir Jankélévich or Raymond Aron, who worked on a Resistance paper in London, had left Paris and chosen to dedicate themselves to the struggle against the Occupiers. The poet René Char wrote nothing once he became a Resistant. Some refused to publish with Gallimard because it accommodated itself to the Germans. Others kept an honourable silence, or published only with small clandestine publishers like Éditions de Minuit. But 'very few intellectuals didn't publish during the Occupation', recalled Olivier Todd, who had married the daughter of Paul Nizan. 'Paris had two sides during the Occupation,' remembered another aristocratic witness. 'There were those who struggled, the poor, and then there was high society. It was fun and crazy. What wild and crazy times we had back then!'

The new power couple, Sartre/Beauvoir, took care to avoid the compromising salons of Florence Gould, the American hostess at whose 'Thursdays' the Nazis officers Heller and Captain Ernst Jünger mixed with openly pro-Nazi writers like Jean Cocteau or Marcel Jouhandeau. Instead Sartre accepted Camus's invitation to join the jury of the Pléiade Prize, set up by Gallimard, where Camus was a reader. Sartre persuaded the jury to award the prize to Maloudji for his novel *Enrico*, and his win was celebrated at a 'gay' lunch party at the Hoggar restaurant.

Unperturbed by the progress of the war, Beauvoir and Bost took their usual skiing holiday in January 1944, at Morzine, without Sartre. Beauvoir, busy working on her parallel turns, was surprised when the Maquis ransacked the ski shop where she had her skis waxed, demanding contributions to the Resistance. A gulf was opening in French society between Pétainists and the increasing numbers who had changed their minds about the Occupiers. Young men refused to be sent to Germany under Laval's notorious *relève* scheme, by which one prisoner of war was released in exchange for three workers. Over 1,400,000 skilled Frenchmen were already working in German factories under the Service du Travail Obligatoire (STO), forced labour service, and many now ran away to join the Maquis. Fascists, on the other hand, joined the Waffen SS French Division and the French Gestapo. As Allied bombers dropped their cargoes on French cities, as the Milice, the feared paramilitary arm of Vichy, dealt out summary justice to the *maquisards*, and the sight of pitiful trainloads of Jews from all over France leaving for the east spurred more and more French people to help the regime's victims, Sartre and Beauvoir amused themselves at a party given by Michel and Zette Leiris in their magnificent apartment at 9 Quai des Grands-Augustins.

It was fiesta time, laughed Beauvoir. She was wearing a red angora jumper and blue pearls, and Pablo Picasso complimented her on her appearance. The rest of the guests had gone home, and it was too late for the curfew. 'Stay the night,' proposes Leiris.

Sartre moves to the piano, and runs his hands over the keys. '*J'ai vendu mon âme au diable*,' he sings in his light tenor voice. 'I've sold my soul to the devil.' He smiles into Beauvoir's eyes: 'I've sold my soul to the devil.'

25

Liberation

Paris liberated! Liberated by itself, by its own people with the help of the armies of France, with the help of the whole of France, of fighting France, of the one and true France, of eternal France.

General de Gaulle, 25 August 1944

CROUCHING OVER HER radio in the Hôtel Louisane, Beauvoir was listening to the BBC. It was February 1944: 'The Allied air forces had conquered the skies. Cologne, the Rhineland, Hamburg and Berlin were all devastated. On the Eastern Front the Germans were retreating.' In Italy there was stalemate at Monte Cassino. 'The RAF was preparing for D-Day by stepping up its raids on French targets, pounding at factories, ports and railheads. Nantes was razed to the ground, and the Paris suburbs hard hit.' As the Resistance blew up German trucks and trains, Beauvoir paused under the arches of the Métro to stare at photographs of condemned *franc-tireurs* (guerrillas), plastered up on the walls. Twenty-two were shot on 4 March. 'How soon I would forget them,' she reflected sadly.

All over Europe German armies were falling back, but in France alone they continued to give an impression of strength. It was the ferocity of desperation. Since the French police had come under the direct control of the High Commander of the SS and German Police, Höherer SS und Polizeiführer General Karl-Albrecht Oberg, in May

1942, instead of the German army, a terror had been unleashed. General Heinrich von Stülpnagel, the troubled Kommandant von Gross-Paris, who by May 1944 was privy to a plot to kill Hitler, shut himself up in the Hôtel Majestic and allowed Oberg to carry out his excesses with the help of René Bousquet, Secretary General of French Police. Bousquet, intent on preserving the autonomy of the French police by doing the Gestapo's dirty work, hurried to his task of bureaucratic murder, ably assisted by Louis Darquier de Pellepoix, head of the Commissariat Général aux Questions Juives. Eighteen months earlier, in June 1942, Adolf Eichmann had visited Paris to discuss the speeding up of the Final Solution, and informed Theo Dannecker, his SS subordinate, of 'the objective of deporting all French Jews as soon as possible. Pressure needs to be put on Vichy and the pace of deportations accelerated to three transports a week.' It was Pierre Laval who proposed to Dannecker that the French-born children of foreign Jews should be included. 'The representatives of the French police expressed the wish several times to see the children also deported to the Reich,' read the minutes of a Franco-German conference of 17 July 1942, held during the *Grand Rafle* (Round-up) at the Vel d'Hiv, in the presence of Bousquet and Laval.

In the summer of 1942 some 20,000 Jews were interned in French concentration camps in the unoccupied zone, but by December 1943 even Laval and Bousquet's efforts seemed too lukewarm to the Gestapo. Pétain, who had never planned to turn Vichy anti-Semitism into genocide, forbade the extension to the unoccupied zone of the yellow star, and even after the total occupation of 11 November 1942 the rule was not applied. Laval began to be seen as an insolent 'fox', dragging his heels: Jews can't be handed over 'as in a supermarket, as many as you want for the same price', he warned Oberg. In 1944 thousands of French people sheltered Jews from deportation, but, as some 300,000 joined the Resistance, another 45,000 volunteered for the Milice, the paramilitary arm of Vichy. France will become a 'moat of blood', warned Bousquet, as the blackshirted, fascist vigilantes of the Milice and the 'outlaw' Maquis prepared to shoot it out in the last days of the Occupation.

Beauvoir, like her fellow countrymen, dazed by the speed of the fall of France, had long continued to believe in the invincibility of the Wehrmacht. She had judged that the Occupation would last twenty years, but in 1944, even as Pétain continued to hope for an orderly transition of power to de Gaulle, the illusion finally faded. It was not easy for Parisians to ignore Drancy, on their doorstep, as even third-generation French Jews, who wore their iron cross next to their yellow star, disappeared within its gates. From 1943 the concentration camp was run by a German, Hauptsturmführer Alois Brünner, reflecting the importance of the Final Solution to the Nazis in the final paroxysms of the regime. The goods trains full of Jews, a thousand at a time, left from the Gare d'Austerlitz, where Claude Mauriac, son of the novelist, caught sight of 'the white faces of children' at the narrow openings of the cattle trucks. It was the crying of the children, which could be heard in the streets outside the Vel d'Hiv, which struck Ernst Jünger: 'Not for a single moment can I forget how I am surrounded by wretched people, human beings in the depth of torment,' he recorded in his diary. In the countryside, people watched as the trains, with their human burdens, swept past:

I saw a train pass. In front, a car containing French police and German soldiers. Then came cattle cars, sealed. The thin arms of the children clasped the grating. A hand waved outside like a leaf in a storm. When the trains slowed down, voices cried, 'Mama!' And nothing answered except the squeaking of springs . . . The truth: stars worn on breasts, children torn from their mothers, men shot every day . . . The truth is censored. We must cry it from the rooftops.

In February 1944 the surrealist poet Max Jacob was arrested and taken to Drancy. 'Well, this time it is myself,' he wrote to Jean Cocteau. *'Je t'embrasse.'* Cocteau and Sacha Guitry, the actor and dramatist who interceded for many Jews, petitioned Abetz on Jacob's behalf, but the old poet died in Drancy. Twelve days later, Beauvoir's 'kid', Jean-Pierre Bourla, who had always refused to wear his star, was arrested. Bourla, a friend of both Cocteau and Jacob, had been staying the night with his father, Alfred. At five in the morning the Germans rang the bell and took both men to Drancy. M. Bourla's girlfriend bribed a German named Felix, who promised to save father and son: the price was three and a half million francs. When Nathalie received a message on a scrap of paper from Bourla, saying that he was still alive, her spirits rose. She was told that Drancy was empty, as the transports had left, but that Felix had arranged for the Bourlas to stay behind.

That afternoon spring flowers were blooming as Beauvoir and Nathalie took the train to the concentration camp. 'We walked up to the barbed wire,' recalled Beauvoir in her memoirs. Through field glasses she could make out 'two distant figures gesturing to us'. One of them pulled off his beret, exposing his shaven scalp, and waved 'joyfully'. Was it Bourla? The two women thought so. Reassured, they returned home, believing Felix's story that the Bourlas would be transferred to a camp for American prisoners of war. It took days of questioning before the German said: 'They were both killed some time ago.'

In fact both men were deported from Drancy to Auschwitz on 13 April 1944, in convoy seventy-one, and died in the gas chambers. Beauvoir never tried to find out what happened to Bourla, although she claimed in her memoirs to know 'moments of convulsive agony and tears' after his death. It made no difference whether one died at nineteen or eighty, said Sartre, but reading Bourla's last note: 'I am not dead. We are only separated,' Beauvoir felt differently. '*Ce néant m'égarait.* This nothingness terrified me.'

*

Sartre, eight years older than Camus, had begun by being the elder brother in the relationship. 'I'm more intelligent than you, huh?' he once drunkenly told Camus. 'More intelligent!' Camus nodded obligingly. As a young journalist in Algeria he had hailed the 'greatness and truth' of Sartre, who 'brings us to nothingness, but also to lucidity', although there was a sting in the tail of his review of *Nausea*: the author had 'both lavished and squandered' his 'remarkable fictional gifts'. Sartre had himself recognized, in Camus's grim description of life in *The Outsider*: 'Getting up, tram, fours hours of work, meal, sleep and Monday, Tuesday, Wednesday, Thursday, Friday, Saturday . . .' a 'hopeless lucidity' like his own, but he, too, had dealt a stinging rebuke: 'Camus shows off a bit by quoting . . . Jaspers, Heidegger and Kierkegaard, whom, by the way, he does not always seem to have quite understood.' From the beginning of their friendship, Sartre regarded Camus as a lightweight philosopher; Camus regarded Sartre as a failed novelist, but in literary Paris it was Jean-Paul who could pull rank over the washerwoman's son from Algiers.

If Camus's education at the University of Algiers was, however, in Sartre's eyes vastly inferior to his own at the great École Normale, the younger man's newspaper experience was far more solid. Expelled from the Communist Party as a Trotskyite in 1937 because he disagreed with its lack of support for Arab nationalism, Camus had become a crusading journalist on *Alger républicain* under its editor, Pascal Pia, and, at only twenty-six, editor of its sister paper, *Le Soir républicain*. Months after arriving in Paris, Camus was approached by Pia and asked to edit *Combat*, an underground paper sponsored by the Combat movement. In March 1944 he succeeded Pia as editor-in-chief, but putting out the smudged single sheet, with its cross of Lorraine cut across the 'C' on the masthead and its defiant declaration that it had 'only one leader: de Gaulle. Only one combat: for our freedoms', was dangerous work.

'Camus and his young friends worked with guns at the ready, all the iron doors closed, a little scared because at any moment German soldiers could come and it would have been a bad mess,' recalled Beauvoir. 'The whole building was a hive of tremendous chaos and tremendous gaiety, from top to bottom.' Camus was given false papers and an identity card under the name of 'Albert Mathé' by the National Resistance Committee Director, Claude Bourdet, at the end of 1943; shortly afterwards Bourdet was arrested and sent to Buchenwald, and Camus received a second alias, 'Bauchard'. Almost all active members of the Resistance had false papers, but Sartre never had any. Jacqueline Bernard, a fellow journalist on the paper, was given the codename 'Augur', before her arrest. The printer who produced the paper, André Bollier, guessing the fate that awaited him in the camps, committed suicide just before the Germans arrested him. One day, waiting in line with his girlfriend Maria Casarès to be searched by French and German police, Camus handed her the design for the masthead of *Combat*. Afraid that she too would be searched, Maria swallowed it.

Camus was always modest about his Resistance activities. 'I never touched a gun,' he said. His contribution was 'derisory next to that of some of my comrades who were real combatants'. But writing anti-Nazi articles in Paris, or using his office at Gallimard on the rue Sébastien-Bottin as a mailbox, was an act of sabotage as much as derailing a train, and Camus risked his life. In March 1944 he wrote a bold call to *engagement* or commitment to the Resistance, under the pseudonym Bauchard: 'To Total War, Total Resistance'. His aim was to touch the consciences of those whose excuse was 'this doesn't concern me', his argument that every enemy action and every Resistance reprisal concerns 'all of us. For all French people today are linked by the enemy in such a way that one person's gesture creates the spirit of resistance in everyone else, and distraction or indifference in only one person leads to the death of ten others.'

In the April edition of *Combat* Camus attacked the Milice, the French militia who were more hated than the Gestapo. In May he described the massacre at Ascq. In his *Letters to a German Friend* the former pacifist passionately argued the moral case for resistance: unlike the Occupiers, who used violence with 'dirty hands', *maquisards* had 'clean hands'. The symbolic power of *Combat* and other underground papers like *Libération* or *Franc-Tireur* was enormous. As the voice of the United Resistance Movements it gave its readers the latest news on Maquis successes: the December 1943 issue announced 310 Maquis 'attacks, sabotages and executions'. And with its slogan, 'If you are brave, you will join the Maquis,' it acted as a recruiting agent for the movement.

In Camus, as he had once done in Nizan, Sartre, puny and cowardly, saw the man of action he longed to be, and immortalized in print as Brunet in *The Roads to Freedom*. In Camus he saw a man living the commitment to the Resistance which he could only watch from the sidelines, ruing the failure of 'Socialism and Liberty'. Camus represented an ideal-type for Sartre, his 'flash and dazzle', as Beauvoir described it, blinding the little man still trapped in his head, struggling with theories and systems. Like a jilted lover, Sartre recalled in 1952 what Camus had meant to him during the war: 'You gave yourself unreservedly to the Resistance. You lived through a fight which was austere, without glory or fanfare. Its dangers were hardly exalting; and worse, you took the risk of being degraded and vilified.'

In 1952 Sartre for a second or two acknowledged the truth. Camus was the authentic fighter for the Resistance that Sartre was not. Generally, Sartre, and Beauvoir, glued together by their lies, colluded on an official version of events in which Sartre claimed parity with Camus. 'Like us,' wrote Beauvoir, 'he had moved from individualism to a committed attitude; we knew, though he never mentioned the fact, that he had important and responsible duties in the Combat movement.' 'Like us' was as false as Sartre's testimony that 'I became a member of [Camus's] Resistance group shortly before the Liberation; I met people I didn't know who together with Camus were seeing what the Resistance could do in this last stage of the war.'

In fact, Sartre and Beauvoir came to one meeting of the newspaper, at which Sartre offered his services 'even for stories about dogs run over in the street', according to Jacqueline Bernard. 'Sartre's resistance, in my opinion, was nil,' says Olivier Todd. But, as the Normandy landings drew near, as maps chalked up on the walls of Paris showed the 'snail' of the Allied armies crawling towards Rome, Sartre woke up to the fact that it was high time to change.

*

'In the Catalan, rue des Grands-Augustins, juicy chateaubriand steaks were grilled to perfection,' recalled the writer Hervé le Boterf. 'At Picasso's table were sometimes grouped Éluard, Desnos, Braque, Leiris, Sartre, Simone de Beauvoir, and Albert Camus.' With the right money and connections, one could still eat *foie gras* canapés washed down with champagne, although President Laval jokingly asked his guests to bring their bread coupons with them when they lunched with him at the Café de Paris. In the most famous brothel of Occupied Paris, One Two Two, on the rue de Provence, the madam, Fabienne Jamet, boasted that she was able to keep her girls well supplied with food and champagne thanks to her underworld contacts. The febrile, decadent atmosphere of the capital heightened as Allied victory approached and spring turned to summer in 1944. At the Leirises' 'fiestas', where alcohol and free love were on offer, Sartre bonded more closely with Camus.

'We became a sort of secret fraternity, performing its rites away from the world's common gaze,' recalled Beauvoir. Between March and June, in George Bataille's apartment in Paris, in Bost's mother's house at Taverny, in Simone Jollivet and Dullin's huge apartment on the rue de la Tour-Auvergne, the 'nocturnal fetes in honour of young love' took place. For Beauvoir, these orgiastic revels blotted out thoughts of death, of the arrest of her friend Yuki Desnos's husband, Robert, of the deaths of Kahn, Cavaillès and Bourla, of the 1,300 people burnt alive at Oradour: 'Beneath the lively wine-flown raptures there is always a faint taste of death, but for one resplendent moment death is reduced to nothingness.'

> We let rip on the food and drink . . . We found ourselves eating and drinking all we could put away. Casual love-making played a very small part in these revels. It was, primarily, drink which aided our break with the daily humdrum round . . . We constituted a sort of carnival, with its mountebanks, its confidence-men, its clowns, and its parades. Dora Marr used to mime a bullfighting-act; Sartre conducted an orchestra from the bottom of a cupboard . . . Camus and Lemarchand played military marches on saucepan lids . . . We put on records and danced; some of us, such as Olga, Wanda and Camus, very well; others less expertly. Filled with the joy of living, I regained my old conviction that life both can and ought to be a real pleasure.

The fiestas continued till dawn. On at least one occasion Camus disappeared to a bedroom with Wanda. On another it was Bost who began making love to an Algerian actress, until Olga had hysterics. In April Camus had a narrow shave at the Hôtel Chaplain, when he was in bed with Wanda one morning and there came a hammering on the door: 'Monsieur Sartre, you're wanted on the phone,' shouted the manager. Camus jumped out of bed, said Bost, and took at least an hour to recover.

Beauvoir, one of those who danced 'less expertly', was also attracted to Camus, whom Sartre, with bitter self-knowledge, admitted was his 'absolute opposite, handsome, elegant, a rationalist'. Her memoirs are carefully constructed, but the frequency with which Camus's name crops up, and her lacerating comments, betray her hurt feelings. 'Beauvoir wanted to have an affair with him. He refused,' recalls Olivier Todd. Later Camus laughed about the *bas bleu* (bluestocking) to Arthur Koestler: 'Imagine what she might say on the pillow afterwards. How awful – such a chatterbox, a total bluestocking, unbearable!' After Camus turned her down, she hated him, said Todd.

On the night of 5 June 1944 Sartre and Beauvoir invited their friends to Dullin's apartment. Camus brought along Maria Casarès, the actress who was performing in his play, *The Misunderstanding*. She was wearing a striking Rochas dress with violet and mauve stripes, her dark hair was pulled back off her face, and she laughed frequently, revealing 'fine white teeth'. 'She was a very attractive woman,' wrote Beauvoir, her own teeth gritted. This time Camus ignored Wanda, but danced the *paso doble* with a drunken Simone Jollivet. As dawn broke, Beauvoir and Sartre caught the first Métro of the morning, staggered across the place de Rennes towards the rue de Seine, and fell into bed. Five hours later the radio woke Beauvoir up: the Allies had landed on the Normandy beaches.

As the 'flight of the Fritzes' drew closer, Sartre and Beauvoir worked feverishly to have a body of work ready for the peace. Five days after Operation Overlord, *No Exit* opened to rave reviews. Sartre had given the play to professional actors, and his dark and desperate vision of hell in a Second Empire drawing-room spoke to the trapped inhabitants of the capital, in which betrayal had become an everyday event. 'I asked myself how one could put three people together and never let one of them get away and how to keep together to the end, as if for eternity,' recalled Sartre. 'Thereupon it occurred to me to put them in hell and make each of them the others' torturer.' Critics saluted him as 'the lion of his generation', and compared him to Dostoevsky and Edgar Allen Poe. As Sartre put into literature the passion he could not put into life, Beauvoir was herself writing against the clock. In July she finished her own play, *Useless Mouths*, about how, in time of siege, a city's defenders would sacrifice the 'useless mouths' of women, children and old people.

The 'secret fraternity' performed one of its most well-known rites on 16 June, when a farce written by Picasso, *Désir attrapé par la queue* (*Desire Caught by the Tail*), was staged in the painter's studio at 7 rue des Grands-Augustins. Camus directed, Sartre played Round End, Leiris Big Foot, and Simone de Beauvoir had a small role as the Cousin. The rehearsed reading was captured on camera by Brassaï, the photographer of underground Paris who was fascinated by the 'night people [who] belong to the world of pleasure, of love, vice, crime, drugs. A secret, suspicious world, closed to the uninitiated.' Brassaï had taken time out from photographing the inmates of Paris's bordellos and opium dens, which he considered represented the city at its most alive and authentic, to snap a group of artists who shared some of the same values. His favourite writers, Stendhal, Dostoevsky and Nietzsche, said Brassaï, were infatuated with outlaws who lived outside the conventions. 'They admired their pride, their strength, their courage, their disdain for death.' Dostoevsky worshipped 'real criminals', added Brassaï. 'Thieves, murderers, convicts – his own prison companions. These criminals, cast out by society, became his mentors, their doctrine of life . . . became his ideal. Dostoevsky consciously adopted the convicts' code: to live life according to one's own passions, to create one's own laws!' Sartre felt a similar pull towards 'low places and shady young men', and his rejection of middle-class rules, his fascination with the thief Jean Genet, and his art all bear comparison with Dostoevsky's convict code.

The iconic photograph of Sartre and Camus squatting on the floor, side by side, Sartre small, tense, bespectacled, wall eyed, and Camus, broad-shouldered, handsome in his sharply cut suit, his black hair slicked off his face like a gangster's, indicates their intimacy. No wonder Castor was jealous. 'How we loved you then,' wrote Sartre in 1952, remembering the early days of their friendship.

On 11 July Camus and Casarès, who was acting as a courier, went to a meeting with Jacqueline Bernard. She never showed up. An informer had denounced their Resistance group. Arrested by the Gestapo, she managed to telephone Camus to warn him before being sent to Ravensbrück. Afraid that under torture she would reveal his name, and perhaps those of Sartre and Beauvoir, Camus warned his friends to move. Days later Camus and Casarès were stopped by German and French police, and he was searched; watching her lover with his hands up, Maria thought that if the Germans tortured him in front of her, she would talk. The couple, together with Pierre and Michel Gallimard, went into hiding in a safe house in Verdolet, sixty kilometres from Paris. Sartre and Beauvoir moved in with the Leirises for a few days, before fleeing to Neuilly-sous-Clermont, a village on the Oise, seventy kilometres north of Paris.

It was as good as a summer holiday. Beauvoir and Sartre found a little inn-cum-grocer's, centre of the local black market, where they rented an attic room. Sartre slept in the single bed, Beauvoir on a straw mattress on the floor. They ate rabbits and chickens, went for walks in the afternoons up country lanes frothing with larkspur and cow-parsley; placidly Beauvoir wrote under a tree in the garden, as RAF planes streaked overhead, strafing German convoys. From their visitors, Bost, Olga and the Leirises, the couple learnt that in the Vercors, the mountainous area south of Grenoble, the Maquis uprising had been crushed by the Germans on 23 July. Villages had been burnt to the ground, peasants slaughtered. Did Beauvoir know that Bianca was cooking for the Resistance fighters, that her husband, Bernard, was a telephone operator? She makes no mention of it in her memoirs, although Sartre, on the other hand, boasted to his landlord that he was on the run from the Germans, who wanted to shoot him as a member of the Resistance.

A month passed. On 11 August the radio announced that the Americans were on the outskirts of Chartres. 'We hastily packed up and mounted our bicycles,' recalled Beauvoir; they pedalled furiously in the sunshine: 'We had no wish to miss the actual Liberation.' In Paris, for safety's sake, they moved into a different hotel, the Welcome, down the road from the Louisiane, on the corner of the boulevard Saint-Germain. When they met up with Camus at the Flore, he told them that the Resistance leaders were in agreement on one point: 'Paris should liberate itself.' But what form would the uprising take?

Already services were being cut off, electricity, gas and the Métro. In the Hôtel Chaplain, Bost stuffed old newspapers into a stove and tried to cook noodles. Nervously the group waited to see whether the Germans would blow the city up; there was talk of underground mines planted round the nearby Sénat, which meant Beauvoir and her friends would catch the blast. But on 18 August, 'I saw trucks crammed with troops and packing cases moving along the Boulevard Saint-Michel, making for the North. Everyone stopped to watch. "They're pulling out!" people whispered.' Leclerc's army was at the gates of Paris.

When Beauvoir awoke the next morning, she checked the flagpole at the Sénat: the swastika was still flying. Moments later a German detachment emerged, let off a volley of machine-gun fire into the crowd, and marched off down the boulevard. That day the uprising began. The FFI, Forces Françaises de l'Intérieur, had fired on a German convoy, reported Beauvoir. Twenty-four hours later, with General Leclerc only three miles away, tricolour flags were at every window. FFI snipers hid behind the balustrades along the *quais*, and Beauvoir watched, fascinated, from the window of the Leirises' apartment, as a German truck passed by 'with two flaxen-haired young soldiers in it, sitting bolt upright, tommy-guns at the ready'. She stifled the impulse to shout a warning. 'A burst of fire ripped out, and they fell.'

As the collabo journalists fled, Camus occupied the editorial offices of *Paris-Soir* on the rue Réamur. On 21 August, in the middle of the insurrection, the first open issue of *Combat* was published. Bent double, Beauvoir and Sartre ran across the bridge to the right bank of the Seine, past armed guards, to the office in which Camus was exultantly writing his editorial, with the new slogan: 'From Resistance to Revolution.' At this key juncture, he gave Sartre a golden opportunity to win credibility as a resistant, asking him to write a descriptive report on the Liberation.

Strangely enough, Sartre passed up this opportunity. After a cursory tour of the barricades, he remained detached from events, asking Beauvoir to write up the account. The first article, 'Walking around Paris during the Insurrection' appeared under Sartre's byline, blazoned across the front page of the issue of 28 August. Yet Beauvoir told her American lover Nelson Algren three years later that 'we wrote reports about what was happening and brought them to Camus'. In the 1980s she confided to a biographer that it was she who had written the famous *Combat* articles because Sartre was 'too busy'.

On the evening of 24 August, the French Division of the American and Allied forces, commanded by General Leclerc, reached the Hôtel de Ville. General Eisenhower, commander of the Allied armies, had been persuaded by General de Gaulle to abandon his original plan to swing round Paris, to avoid fighting in the capital, and to allow Leclerc to lead the parade. 'The guns fired; all the bells of Paris began to peal, and every house was lit up,' wrote Beauvoir. In the street the crowd joined hands and danced around bonfires. The next morning she was up at six, running up the boulevard Raspail to watch Leclerc's columns march proudly up the avenue d'Orléans. Feverish with excitement at the sight of the soldiers, whether the FFI – she had met one friend, rifle slung over his soldier and red kerchief knotted at his neck, who looked 'splendid' – or the Americans, at whose uniforms she stared with 'incredulous eyes', she felt 'the most poignant joy I had ever experienced'. She and Olga saw the tricolour rise again over the Eiffel Tower, watched women who only weeks before had been kissing the soldiers of the Wehrmacht clinging to the necks of Americans, and cheered de Gaulle from the steps of the Arc de Triomphe as he marched down the Champs Élysées. At last the Republic, whose rebirth had been proclaimed in the Vercors on 3 July and brutally crushed by the Waffen-SS, lived again.

*

Sartre's reaction was less euphoric. Asked by Camus to help guard the Comédie-Française, with other members of the Resistance theatre group, the Comité National du Théâtre (CNT), he strolled across Paris and promptly fell asleep in the theatre. Camus found him snoozing in the stalls and woke him up, laughing: 'You have turned your theatre seat in the direction of history!' At every turn, Sartre rejected the chance to play a real part in the Resistance. This was because it was, in his opinion, relatively unimportant. Observing events dispassionately, he kept that splinter of ice in his heart which Graham Greene considered essential for the novelist. With his cold writer's eye Sartre wrote:

> The Resistance was only an individual's solution and we always knew that: without it the English would have won the war, with its help they would have lost it anyway if they were supposed to lose it. In our eyes it had above all a symbolic value; and that is why many resisters were filled with despair: they were always symbols. A symbolic rebellion in a symbolic city: only the torture was real.

Sartre may have recognized that if General von Choltitz, commander of the German army in Paris, had not disobeyed Hitler's order to destroy the city and, instead of defending it, signed the surrender on 25 August 1944, the Liberation would not have been achieved with so little loss of life. Von Choltitz's reluctance to engage his troops encouraged Colonel Rol-Tanguy, Communist leader of the FFI, to put out the slogan: 'Chacun son boche' (To each his Boche), and his men to respond to it. Sartre saw the scale of the uprising. In Paris, about 900 FFI and nearly 600 civilians were killed; in Warsaw, by contrast, 30,000 Poles died in the armed insurrection to liberate the city.

But within a month Sartre would collaborate in the making of a Gaullist myth – that Paris had liberated itself – and link himself personally to the brave *maquisards*.

Part Three

Écrivains Engagés

1945–56

26

Retribution and Remorse

We were to provide the post-war era with its ideology.
Simone de Beauvoir

'C'EST FINI, C'EST FINI,' it's all over, repeated Simone de Beauvoir incredulously to herself, as Patrick Walberg, an American army friend of the Leirises, drove her round Paris in his jeep. It was the first time for years that she had been in a car. On the pavements gum-chewing Yankee soldiers with wide smiles and teeth 'white as children's' ambled by, singing, whistling, laughing. To Beauvoir they were 'freedom incarnate: our own and that we were about to spread . . . throughout the world . . . This victory was to efface our old defeats.' The jackboot had been lifted, and the French *coq* could now crow his defiance at the hated occupiers, whom by March 1945 the army of the Provisional Government had finally pushed forward of the Maginot Line.

Sartre's perception of the Americans was more hostile. To him they were invaders, like the Germans: 'The arrival of the American army in France seemed to many people, including myself, like a tyranny.' Within days of the Liberation, he was writing 'The Republic of Silence', in which he not only made his provocative and paradoxical statement that 'Never were we more free than under the Germans', asserting that freedom is always a choice, that, even under the fiercest oppression, each one of us can remain free and authentic by choosing a position in a given situation, in the face of death, but also, with one audacious stroke of the pen, claimed a connection to the Resistance for the whole, suffering French nation. 'On nous déportait en masse,' he wrote. 'We were deported en masse, because we were workers, because we were Jews, because we were political prisoners.' 'I'm not speaking here of the élite among us who were true Resistants,' he went on, 'but of all those Frenchmen who, at every hour of the day or night, for four years, said, "Non."'

The silence and solidarity of the many, claimed Sartre, had been essential to the success of the few. 'Each of us – and what Frenchman was not at some time or another during this period in this position? – who had some knowledge of the resistance operations was led to ask himself the agonizing question: "If they torture me, will I hold out?"' . . . and we were alone, without a single helping hand anywhere.'

By a dazzling sleight of hand, Sartre connected to the passive majority, the attentistes, who had sat on the fence and now wanted to align themselves with the winners – to those active members of the Resistance who numbered only a small minority within the population, at most three per cent. In Paris, during four years of Occupation, only 28,000 people, 0.5 per cent of the population, were resisters. But, reading Sartre's article, the pusillanimous majority could identify with Resistance leaders like the heroic Jean Moulin, who had died under torture at the hands of Gestapo chief Klaus Barbie, the 'butcher' of Lyons, in June 1943, or Marie-Madeleine Méric, the head of 'Noah's Ark', the only resistance network to be led by a woman, and feel a warm glow of pride and vindication.

Remarkably, Sartre, who had played no effective part in the Resistance, became its principal spokesman within a month of Liberation. Camus was awarded the Resistance medal in 1946, an honour Sartre never merited, but it was Sartre who within two years was being described in the USA as 'fearless and active in the Underground'.

How did Sartre manage it? How was he able to put a different gloss on his 'Resistance from the Café Flore', as Aron ironically called it – although others argued that being a journalist for the Free French in London was even less dangerous than staying in Paris – and become a major interpreter of the movement and of the Occupation? In 'The Republic of Silence' Sartre made no claim to have been one of the 'real resisters', only 'a writer who resisted'. He knew how little he had done compared to Camus. In his heart he remained the cowardly Mathieu of Roads to Freedom, or Garcin, the deserter in No Exit. However, his ability to feel the pulse of the public, his consummate skill as a self-publicist, allowed him to shape the two dominant myths of 1944: that Paris had liberated itself without the help of the Allies, and that the whole nation, *la nation résistante*, had shaken off the Nazi yoke 'without a single helping hand'. As de Gaulle declared Vichy illegitimate, and stated that the Republic had never ceased to exist, thus establishing an unbroken line between his defiant rallying call to '*la France libre*' on BBC radio on 28 June 1940, and the Liberation, Sartre played his own part in creating the culture of blame which followed hard on the heels of post-Liberation euphoria.

Sartre's byline was everywhere, in *Les Lettres françaises*, in *La France libre*, the Free French journal published in London by his old friend Raymond Aron, in *Combat*, over the seven articles on the Liberation written by Beauvoir, who was amused at a deception which contributed to the couple's joint fame. Camus, by contrast, was published anonymously in the American collection of 1947 which trumpeted Sartre's name as a resistance hero to his eager public. Within three weeks of Liberation Sartre's name was up in lights again: *Huis Clos* reopened at the Vieux-Colombier theatre. Sartre gave the first two novels of *Roads to Freedom* to Gallimard, and Beauvoir, who had been writing equally industriously, handed Gaston the manuscript of *The Blood of Others* and began negotiating the production of *Useless Mouths*.

A savage purge of collaborators had begun even before the Liberation. Summary executions were carried out by the FFI. Collaborators known to work for the German police were sent small black coffins, their homes and offices daubed with swastikas. Over 20,000 women accused of having German lovers were publicly humiliated, their hair shorn, their heads shaven, as, naked, they were paraded before jeering crowds intent on reasserting French male dominance. The retribution of *l'épuration*, the purge, was seen as essential to a new beginning, and both de Gaulle and Georges Bidault, Christian Democrat leader of the Conseil National de la Résistance (CNR), in the Charter of March 1944, vowed to punish all collaborators. Martyred Marianne had to revenge herself on all those who had betrayed the Republic before she could look to the future.

Beauvoir congratulated herself on the fact that she and Sartre had ended up in the Resistance camp. It had been a good war. They were on the right side, with friends in high places. It was only a year since Sartre had overcome Communist smears that he had bought his release from the Stalag by acting as an informer for the Germans, and had been invited to join the Communist-sponsored Comité National des Ecrivains (CNE, the National Committee of Writers) by Claude

Morgan, editor of *Les Lettres françaises*. 'But,' said Sartre, 'your people call me a traitor.' He showed Morgan a Communist pamphlet, a blacklist on which his name appeared between Chateaubriant and Montherlant.' Morgan responded, 'Not my people, idiots. I'll fix that.'

Morgan had been as good as his word, and the petit-bourgeois writer had become friendly with the Communists. In 1944 the French Communist Party (PCF) had immense prestige as the 'party of 75,000 *fusillés*', those shot dead by the Germans, and the major part it had played in the Resistance lent it a quasi-mystical aura. As thousands flocked to claim that they had been resisters, thousands more joined the PCF, which had 380,000 members by January 1945. Sartre did not himself join the Party, but, like many intellectuals, was powerfully drawn to its virile image as the party of change, the party of the working class, whose victory was destined by that reified Marxist force, 'History'. Sartre's romantic idealization of the working class, with whom he had brushed shoulders in the Stalag, played an important role in his decision to become a *compagnon de route*, a fellow traveller. But friendship with the Communist-led Resistance also linked him closely to the movers and shakers of 1944. 'We could count on many important figures in the press and the radio as close friends,' recalled Beauvoir with satisfaction. 'Politics had become a family matter, and we expected to have a hand in it . . . We were writers, and it was our job to address ourselves to other men . . . It was our turn to carry the torch.'

It fell to members of the Resistance to define collaboration, in particular the National Committee of Writers and *Les Lettres françaises*, which demanded a radical purification of intellectuals. Vengeance became the prerogative of Aragon, Eluard, Benda, Vercors, Sartre, Beauvoir, Claude Morgan, and others on the CNE. A committee was set up to purify publishing, inevitably composed of publishers who had willy-nilly followed the orders of the Nazi *Propagandastaffel*. A convenient division was agreed between public and private: all social relations with Germans, in cafés, bars or theatres, were excused. This included, for example, Sartre's convivial mixing with the Germans who filled the stalls at *The Flies*, or Beauvoir's work for Vichy Radio. 'The less they themselves had resisted,' writes Oliver Todd, 'the more certain people wanted to punish others for having collaborated.' He was thinking of 'mischievous spirits, like Jean-Paul Sartre'.

Soon quarrels arose. Jean Paulhan and François Mauriac, both recognized resistance activists, preached forgiveness. Paulhan resigned from the editorial committee of *Les Lettres françaises* after a list of 100 expelled writers was published; he also left the CNE, as did Camus. 'I am too uncomfortable to express myself in an atmosphere where the spirit of objectivity is taken as spiteful criticism and where simple moral independence is poorly tolerated,' Camus told Paulhan. But Sartre was under attack by the Communist paper *Action* for being influenced by the Nazi philosopher Heidegger; his name, with that of Camus, had appeared in May 1944 in another Communist tract denouncing certain people pretending to be in the Resistance and the underground. He took a hard line.

In January 1945 Robert Brasillach, the fascist editor of *Je suis partout*, was tried for collaboration. His was one of several trials of writers and broadcasters dubbed the 'Academy of Collaboration' by one of their number, Lucien Rebatet, the fascist author of *The Debris*. On 19 January Brasillach was sentenced to death. Fifty-nine artists and intellectuals signed a petition asking de Gaulle to pardon him, including the painter Maurice Vlaminck and the writers Paul Valéry, Paul Claudel, Jean Anouilh, Jean Cocteau, Colette, Jean Paulhan and François Mauriac. Although the last two were Resistance activists, others were noted collaborators.

The novelist Marcel Aymé, himself a former collaborator, wrote to ask Camus to add his name to the petition. It was not an easy decision for Camus. His friend, the poet and resistance fighter René Leynaud, had been arrested and shot just before the Liberation. 'Until our last moment we will refuse a godly charity that cheats men of their justice,' wrote the atheist Camus in January 1945 in defiance of Mauriac, who was still advocating Christian pardons for collaborators. But, although their moral consciences arose from opposing positions, Camus, like Mauriac, felt unable to condone the death penalty.

'You have given me a bad night's sleep,' he wrote to Aymé. 'Finally, I have sent the signature that you asked for today . . . I have always been horrified by death sentences and I decided, as an individual at least, that I could not participate in one, even by abstention . . . That's all, and it's a scruple which I imagine will make Brasillach's friends laugh a lot.' Although Camus reminded Aymé that Leynaud and two or three other friends had been 'mutilated and slaughtered by Brasillach's friends, while his newspaper . . . encouraged [collaboration]', he asked the novelist to tell Brasillach that he was not 'a man of hatred'. But should he be pardoned, Camus would never shake his hand.

Sartre and Beauvoir also remembered the deaths of friends, Politzer, Cavaillès, Yvonne Picard, Bourla, and the poet Robert Desnos. They refused to sign. 'I did not want to hear the voices of people who had consented to the death of millions of Jews and Resistance members,' wrote Beauvoir. 'I did not want to find their name in any publication side by side with my own. We had said: "We shall not forget"; I was not forgetting that.' Under Brasillach's editorship, the staff of *Je suis partout* had denounced people and urged Vichy to enforce the wearing of the yellow star. 'It was with these friends, dead or alive, that I felt solidarity; if I lifted a finger to help Brasillach, then it would have been their right to spit in my face . . . There are words as murderous as gas chambers.'

Nevertheless, when Beauvoir fought to get a seat in the press gallery at Brasillach's trial, the procedure upset her. It transformed the executioner into a victim and gave his condemnation the appearance of inhumanity. On the way out of the Palais de Justice, she met some Communist friends and told them about her distress. 'You should have stayed at home then,' they replied dryly.

The labyrinths of collaboration guilt and innocence were not easily separated. 'The Vichy regime,' writes historian Robert Paxton, 'had made many Frenchmen accomplices in acts and policies that they would not normally have condoned.' The finger of justice began to point uncomfortably close to Sartre himself when both Gaston Gallimard and René Delange, editor of *Comoedia*, were questioned during the purge of intellectuals. Sartre gave evidence in both their favour. 'Any blame against Gallimard would also be attached to Aragon, Paulhan, Camus, Valéry and myself, in brief all the writers who took part in the intellectual resistance and who were published by him,' he admitted. In any event, Gaston had just agreed to finance his new review, *Les Temps modernes*. 'I'm just a poor paper dealer,' pleaded the publisher, who was spared, although another 'paper dealer', Robert Denoël, the publisher of Hitler, Céline and Rebatet, was murdered in the street in December that year.

Sartre also denied the close association he had continued to have with Delange throughout the Occupation. Delange got off, but the playwright Jean Cocteau, with whom Sartre had strolled by the Seine in June 1944, was less fortunate. Like Sartre, Cocteau had written for *Comoedia*, in 1942 enthusiastically reviewing the exhibition of heroic male figures by Arno Brekker, Hitler's favourite sculptor. But when Cocteau was accused of collaboration, Sartre laughed: '*Il avait mal mené sa barque* (he had steered his boat badly').

Sartre's name does not appear in Henri Noguères's definitive history of the Resistance because he was never a resister. But in later years Sartre created a false history, writing that he had 'taken an active part in the Resistance on the barricades of Paris'. By then he probably believed it.

*

Immediately after the Liberation, the Gestapo's torture chambers in Paris were discovered. The execution posts to which victims were tied, the Fort de Vincennes, where hostages were put before firing squads and thrown into ditches, the mass graves, all became known. Newspapers reported the annihilation of Warsaw. 'A ravaged world,' recorded Beauvoir. 'One's new delight in life gave way to shame at having survived.'

Bianca Lamblin's return from the Vercors dealt her a further shock. Bianca had had a breakdown. She began psychotherapy and got in touch again with Beauvoir. 'I'm upset about [Bianca],' wrote Beauvoir to Sartre late Thursday night, 13 December 1945, after taking the distraught woman out for a meal.

> We stayed talking . . . till midnight. She moved me – and filled me with remorse – because she's suffering from an intense and dreadful attack of neurasthenia, and it's our fault I think. It's the very indirect, but profound, after-shock of the business between her and us. She's the only person to whom we've really done harm, but we have harmed her . . . She weeps all the time – she wept three times during dinner . . . She's terribly unhappy, and extremely lucid without her lucidity getting her anywhere. At times, she really looked quite mad.

Beauvoir hoped that Sartre would feel equally sympathetic towards Bianca, but the tone of her letter suggests that she doubted it. 'You're dozing at Wanda's side,' she wrote resignedly. Beauvoir herself had been shaken by the photos of the concentration camps, by the reports brought back by Jacques-Laurent Bost, whom Camus had sent as a special correspondent for *Combat* to Dachau. 'Above the gas chamber door there is the inscription, "Shower",' wrote Bost. Face to face with the shaking, weeping Bianca, Beauvoir remembered how she had laughed at the Jewish girl's fears and called her a foolish Cassandra. 'It's important to see a lot of her, and I'm going to try, because I'm filled with remorse,' she told Sartre.

The Devil, to whom Sartre joked he had sold his soul when he became a 'war profiteer', giving the title 'Lucifer' originally to *The Age of Reason*, had revealed depths of darkness beyond his imagining. Sartre had been seduced by the Romantic idea of 'evil' portrayed in Baudelaire's *Les Fleurs du Mal*, a glamorous lifestyle choice to *épater le bourgeois*: the war had shown both the danger and naïveté of his vision. Bianca, tormented by the death of her family in Auschwitz, cast adrift by Beauvoir and Sartre, her 'mythical parents', in Lacan's analysis, now gripped so tightly by anguish that 'I was pinned to a corner of my bed, unable to get up, refusing to wash or do my hair', was living evidence of damage done. Beauvoir, who may have begun at this point to wonder whether Bianca was her only victim, invited her to begin 'a new friendship, which I could count on but which would, of course, have none of the passion of our former relationship'. From 1945, Beauvoir took Bianca out once a month for forty years.

'After the war she was full of remorse over Bianca,' recalls Sylvie Le Bon. Bianca demanded love, she imposed herself on others, says Le Bon. 'But Simone de Beauvoir was very hard on herself morally, very strict.' Sartre had interpreted Dostoevsky's remark that if God does not exist, then everything is permitted, as a licence to make up a new morality sanctioned by man alone. But for Beauvoir, and perhaps for Sartre too, doing away with the remission of sins was a frightening consequence of atheism. 'If God exists, everything *is* permitted, because He pardons,' argues Le Bon. If God was dead, who would pardon Simone?

Beauvoir had entered her 'moral period' in 1943, when she wrote 'Pyrrhus and Cinéas', a philosophical essay which she hoped would serve as the foundation for the system of ethics promised by Sartre at the end of *Being and Nothingness*. The war had shaken her old faith in individual consciousness and taught her that human beings do not exist alone, in a bubble, but in reciprocal relations with others.

> This then is my position in regard to other men: men are free, and I am flung into the world amid these alien liberties. I have need of others for once I have passed my own goal my actions would recoil on themselves inert, useless, were they not carried by new projects towards a new future.

For Beauvoir it was a new opening out to the world. She began to develop the idea of establishing 'an order of precedence' of different ethical situations, and to study her friends' 'historical moments'. Concerned to draw up guidelines to moral choice, in the context of individual capacity and situation, her aim was 'to set freedom free'. In *The Ethics of Ambiguity* in 1946 she continued to take up the challenge to 'base a morality on *Being and Nothingness*', although later she berated herself for perceived failure. 'Simone said that *The Ethics of Ambiguity* was for me,' recalls Bianca, as Beauvoir, conscious of her former girl-friend's own place in history, showered her with presents and struggled with her own ambiguous feelings.

Bianca did not, however, renew her relationship with Sartre. On the contrary, she was deeply hurt by his remarks in 'The Republic of Silence' that 'on *nous* déportait en masse, they deported *us* en masse . . . as Jews'. In April 1945 the first survivors of the concentration camps had returned to France. Known as 'racial deportees', the skeletal figures who stumbled half-alive from the returning trains were an embarrass-ment to Parisians, and their stories were greeted with indifference and incomprehension. Politician Simone Veil, née Jacob, survivor of Ravensbrück, said that she felt forced into silence. Only after the Marcel Ophuls film *The Sorrow and the Pity* (1971) began the recovery of Jewish memory of the Occupation, a period frozen in myth for thirty years, did Bianca herself feel able to voice her anger that the word '*nous* [us]' had been 'usurped by someone who had been neither an active Resistant nor Jewish'.

*

The winter of 1944–45 is one of hardship and food shortages. Coal, gas and electricity are in short supply. Sartre wears an old lumber jacket, and Beauvoir shivers in a rabbit coat as she treads the cobbled Montparnasse streets in wooden-soled shoes. During the 'fiestas' of the previous summer, she had put her dark hair up with a false piece heightening the crown, a 'Castilian' style which gave her a dignified and serious air, but as the weather grows colder she stuffs it into a grubby turban. When she smiles, her missing tooth is 'quite visible, and I didn't even think about having a false one put in: what was the point? In any case, I was old, I was thirty-six.'

At the end of June 1944, Sartre has given up teaching at the Lycée Condorcet. He and Beauvoir are both full-time writers. She depends on him financially, for Sartre's earnings from the cinema, as a Pathé screenwriter, and from the theatre are generous. 'I have so often advised women to be independent and said that independence begins in the purse, that I feel I must explain this attitude,' writes Beauvoir in 1963. She justifies it by arguing that if she wished, she could always go back to teaching: there is no need to prove her 'material autonomy'. Instead she devotes herself to researching her new novel, *All Men Are Mortal*.

Nathalie Sorokine, meanwhile, is playing a new game called Hunt-the-American. She sits alone on the terrace of the Café de la Paix, or along the Champs Élysées, and waits for a GI to pick her up. 'Hey, blondie,' the Americans call, as they stroll down the boulevards. Nathalie, having made her choice, accepts a drink, a ride in a jeep, a dinner; later she returns to the hotel she shares with Beauvoir, laden with tea, Camels, instant coffee and tins of Spam. One of her admirers is Ernest Hemingway's younger brother.

'Would you and Sartre like to meet Hemingway?' asks Sorokine one evening. 'Of course!' says Beauvoir. Hemingway, in Paris as a war correspondent, invites Sartre and Beauvoir to the Ritz. She has never before been inside the hotel and is impressed by the spacious bedroom and brass bedstead, but even more so by its occupant. Hemingway is lying on the bed in his pyjamas, his eyes shielded by a green eyeshade; several bottles of whisky are within reach on the bedside table. He grabs Sartre by the lapels and hugs him: 'You're a general!' he says, squeezing him. 'Me, I'm only a captain; you're a general!' Hemingway is bursting with vitality; a bleary-eyed Sartre finally leaves at three in the morning, but Beauvoir stays till dawn.

In the months before the Liberation, Camus and Sartre have planned two joint projects, an 'encyclopaedia of ethics' and a new literary review. The first is stillborn, but in September 1944 Sartre forms an editorial committee for *Les Temps modernes* or 'Modern Times', the name taken from a Chaplin film. Camus is too busy with *Combat* to be a member, and Malraux refuses; an odd group of Raymond Aron, Michel Leiris, Merleau-Ponty, Albert Ollivier (from *Combat*) and Jean Paulhan join the board. But in November, before the first issue can be produced, Camus has a new proposition for Sartre. The USA has invited a dozen French reporters to the States to report on the American war effort.

'I've never seen Sartre so elated as the day Camus offered him the job of representing *Combat*,' writes Beauvoir. She had always dreamed that she and Sartre would make their first flight together. Instead, on 12 January 1945, he alone boards a military plane bound for the New World.

27

Dolorès

Do you realize, I've slept with Napoleon!
Dolorès Vanetti Ehrenreich

ONE OF SARTRE'S last acts before leaving Paris had been to give a lecture on the 'American approach' to the novel. Despite not speaking a word of English – Beauvoir had painstakingly translated pages from John Dos Passos's trilogy *Big Money* for him – it was a subject on which Sartre felt himself to be an expert. His love affair with America had begun as a boy, when his mother had bought him cowboy comics, and had grown with his passion for jazz, movies, and writers like Faulkner and Dos Passos – as well as Proust, Joyce and Virginia Woolf – who tried 'each in his own way, to distort time'.

But when the quintessentially French philosopher stepped out of the military plane at New York's La Guardia airport on 12 January, after a bruising two-day journey, America felt stranger than he had ever imagined. He was no Dickens arriving to cheering crowds at the docks; instead the airport limo took him to the Plaza hotel, off Fifth Avenue at Central Park South. Through the window he peered at lights like red and green boiled sweets. He was in a city which both astonished and frightened him: 'I didn't know that, for the newly arrived European, there was a "New York sickness", like sea-sickness, air-sickness, or mountain sickness.'

The next day was a Sunday, a deserted Sunday. Sartre found himself at the corner of 58th Street and Fifth Avenue.

I walked for a long time under the icy sky . . . I was looking for New York and I couldn't find it. The further I progressed along an avenue . . . the further the city seemed to retreat before me, like a ghost town.' 'For the first few days I was lost. My eyes were not accustomed to the skyscrapers . . .' 'This chequerboard is New York. The streets look so much alike that they have not been named. They have merely been given registration numbers, like soldiers.

Around him were houses the colour of 'dried blood'. In vain he looked for *quartiers, cafés, terrasses*: 'The American street is a piece of highway . . . It does not stimulate one to walk. Ours are oblique and twisting, full of bends and secrets.'

Disorientated, he stared about him: 'It all shone and was full of lighted shops . . . open, lighted shops, with people working in them – they were barber shops – at eleven at night. You could have your hair cut or shampooed or get a shave at eleven at night.' Under the shadow of the *gratte-ciels*, skyscrapers, the New York which had seized Roquentin's imagination, the New York of 'Some of These Days', eluded him: he was, as in Le Havre, alone, *un homme seul*, in a city which hugged its secrets.

To their American hosts, the eight French journalists were in need of more than a wash and brush-up. Sartre, in his dirty lumber jacket and scuffed shoes, stood out like a sore thumb in the lobby of the Plaza, where, on that first evening, women in designer dresses on the arms of well-groomed men in dinner jackets brushed heedlessly past him in the revolving door. 'They didn't realize there was a war on,' recalled Sartre, struck by American wealth: he could barely believe the 'wonderful' breakfasts, the muffins and orange juice and real coffee. On Monday the Office of War Information (OWI) wasted no time in giving the hacks from war-torn Europe a makeover. Sartre was sent shopping for jackets, striped trousers and a tailor-made suit. Days later he moved to the vast Waldorf-Astoria, on Park Avenue, where, in the barber shop in the basement, he was shaved, pummelled and shorn before being delivered to the offices of the War Department for the first of many interviews.

If he was ever to discover America, Sartre needed a woman. In Dolorès Vanetti, a petite mixed-race (Italian and Ethiopian) radio journalist, formerly an actress in Montparnasse, he found her. Vanetti presented the popular *show féminin* on the Voice of America French broadcasts during the war, and was separating from her American doctor husband, Ehrenreich. Vivacious and attractive, with a classically oval face which strangely resembled Beauvoir's, she answered Sartre's need for a pretty woman who wouldn't bore him. 'First of all, there is the physical element. There are of course ugly women, but I prefer those who are pretty,' he explained in an interview for the documentary *Sartre by Himself*. 'Then, there is the fact that they're oppresssed, so they seldom bore you with shop talk . . . I enjoy being with a woman because I'm bored out of my mind when I have to converse in the realm of ideas.'

Vanetti knew better than to talk about ideas. When Camus came to New York the following year, she explained that Americans do not like ideas, although he didn't believe this French cliché: 'That's what they say, but I doubt it.' Speaking both French and American slang, fresh, spontaneous and cultured, a published poet – but no *bas bleu* like Beauvoir – she instantly appealed to Jean-Paul. 'In front of my office there was a long line of French journalists waiting to enter the recording studio,' she recalled. 'At the very end of the line there was this little gentleman, the last and the smallest. At some point he knocked against something and dropped his pipe, then he picked it up and that's when we started talking. I don't remember what we said to each other, but whatever it was, once it was said he asked me whether we could see each other again.'

At first Dolorès had no idea who Sartre was. She confused his name with that of a sculptor, Raoul del Sartre, whom she had once known. But the OWI soon put her right. Sartre, author of *The Wall*, a leader of the CNE, had, according to *Atlantic Monthly*, which had published 'The Republic of Silence' in translation, 'devoted himself to underground activities with sublime courage, organizing illegal publications [and] representing the most brilliant tendencies of postwar French literature'. Sartre put his usual technique of seduction into practice, making Dolorès feel that she was the most important woman in the world. Within two days he had slept with her. 'Dolorès gave me America,' recalled Sartre in 1974.

But Dolorès was not quick enough to prevent Sartre making his first gaffe. Representing both *Le Figaro* and *Combat*, the first piece he filed for *Figaro* on 22 January documented, with a certain malice, the wartime infighting between French supporters of Pétain and de Gaulle in America. Sartre alleged that American big business and the State Department had bankrolled *Pour la victoire*, a newspaper that he claimed had harmed the French cause. It was a sensitive subject. The

USA had recognized the 1940 Pétain government until the Allied invasion of North Africa in 1942, when de Gaulle became head of the Provisional Government of France. Roosevelt had continued to mistrust de Gaulle, whom he refused to receive at the White House until July 1944. Sartre's story was at once picked up by the *New York Times* Paris correspondent, and he was accused of undermining Franco-American friendship. There was talk of sending him back to France, and the journalist hurried to make his apologies to the editor of *The Times*: 'I have never lost sight of the fact that I am a guest in the United States.' Sartre promised that the criticisms he had made, and would continue to make of the USA, stemmed from 'a spirit of deep friendship' for 'the greatest of all free countries'.

It had been a close shave. He had been invited in order to report on the American war effort, but, as he told Beauvoir, '*L'effort de guerre de l'Amérique, moi, je m'en foutais. C'était l'Amérique que je voulais voir.*' He didn't give a fuck about the American war effort. It was America he wanted to see.

Under the close surveillance of the FBI, Sartre got his wish. In a specially charted military plane, a B-29 bomber, the French journalists spent eight weeks touring the USA and visiting factories, dams, schools, universities and army bases. 'We'll have seen more steel and aluminium than human beings,' complained Sartre. But in Hollywood he met up again with Rirette Nizan, who told him of her distress that her dead husband was being vilified by the PCF. In New York he caught up with Stépha and Fernando Gerassi, who introduced him to the sculptor Alexander Calder, and a host of French expatriates, including Claude Lévi-Strauss and the surrealist leader, André Breton. Dolorès took him to the Russian Tea Rooms, where they spotted Garbo and Stravinsky. The tour culminated in a meeting with President Roosevelt at the White House on 10 March.

'As he shakes our hands, I look at his brown earthy face, so very American,' writes Sartre. 'What is immediately striking is the deeply human charm of this long face, at once delicate and hard, the eyes gleaming with intelligence . . . He smiles at us, he speaks to us in his low, slow voice.' The President tells the Frenchman that he loves their country, which he bicycled through in his youth. Sartre and his colleagues duly repeat these assurances of Franco-American cordiality. Five weeks later Roosevelt dies at just sixty-three.

But it was not idle curiosity which had brought Sartre to the land of Buffalo Bill and Nick Carter. He had come to test out his new theory of *engagement* or commitment on American audiences. His first lecture in New York caused a sensation. Ostensibly a paean of praise to Camus, whose friendship, whose writing and whose example unquestionably inspired Sartre to become politically engaged, it was a masterpiece of self-promotion. 'The Resistance taught that literature is no fancy activity independent of politics,' was how American *Vogue* reported him. Dismissing the writing of the *avant-guerre*, Sartre praised the new writers 'who issued from the Resistance and represent the future'. The best of them was Albert Camus, now thirty years old:

> In publishing a great many clandestine articles, frequently under dangerous circumstances to fortify the people against the Germans or to keep up their courage, they have gotten into the habit of thinking that writing is an act; and they have acquired a taste for action . . . In the underground press, every line that was written put the life of the writer and of the printer in danger . . . The written word has regained its power.

Their participation in the Resistance had taught these writers 'that the freedom to write, like freedom itself, must be defended by arms under certain circumstances'. That is why, Sartre told his rapt audience, 'everybody in France today speaks of *littérature engagée*, "committed literature"'.

Swiftly Sartre introduced his listeners to Camus's books, to his themes of absurdity and revolt in *The Outsider* and *The Myth of Sisyphus*: 'I draw from the absurd three consequences which are my revolt, my freedom and my passion.' Promoting them as wartime writing, Sartre put again to his audience the question he had often posed himself: 'Would I talk if I were tortured?' He discussed Camus's latest novel, *The Plague*, which he had read in mansucript, and in which the plague which attacks Oran, in Algeria, is a metaphor for the German Occupation, Dr Rieux, the doctor hero, a man who 'defies Evil [and] affirms against all odds the rule of the human spirit'. By association, Sartre's own pre-war fiction became heroic work prefiguring the Resistance spirit. His 'intellectual resistance', the plays and novels he wrote under the Occupation, whose aim had been the promotion of 'the Self and its literary career', were recast as underground writing which had put his life in danger.

It was a bravura performance, whose ripples reached as far as Paris. Immediately afterwards, Sartre wrote his stirring manifesto on *engagement*, commitment, which would introduce his new journal.

Since the writer has no means of escape, we want him to embrace his time tightly; it is his unique chance: it made himself for him and he is made for it . . . We do not want to miss anything in our time. There may be some more beautiful, but this one is our own. We have only *this* life to live, in the middle of *this* war, of *this* revolution perhaps.

'Every word has consequences. Every silence, too,' he abjured his readers. In words for which he would later be held to account, he wrote: 'I hold Flaubert and Goncourt responsible for the repression which followed the Commune because they did not write one line to prevent it.' Contrasting Voltaire, Zola and Gide, each of whom 'measured his responsibility as a writer', Sartre declared that 'The Occupation taught us ours . . . Since we act on our time by our very existence, we decide that this action will be deliberate.'

He had, as it were, assimilated Camus to himself and, in his imagination, become the Algerian *pied noir*, hero of the Resistance, the swashbuckling Captain Pardaillon of his childish dreams.

*

Sartre's whistle-stop tour of the USA had awakened his consciousness to another aspect of American life that would profoundly affect his writing. In Maryland, the northernmost slave state, he and his group were travelling by Pullman from Baltimore to Philadelphia when two black army officers entered the restaurant car where they were eating dinner, and asked for a table. The maître d' abruptly refused them. Aware that this incident upset the French party, their interpreter interceded with the maître d'. After some negotiation, the two officers were seated at the back of the car, but a pink curtain was drawn between them and the rest of the diners.

'There is no negro problem in the United Sates, there is only a white problem,' the black American writer Richard Wright will tell Sartre when they meet in Paris. Wright's autobiographical novel, *Black Boy*, published in March 1945 while Sartre is in the USA, charts his experiences of racism in allegedly liberal Greenwich Village, but already Sartre's own encounters with segregation in the South have horrified him.

In this land of freedom and equality, there live thirteen million untouchables. They wait on your table, they polish your shoes, they operate your elevator, they carry your suitcase, but they have nothing to do with you, nor you with them . . . They know they are third-class citizens. They are Negroes. Do not call them 'niggers'.

Sartre channels his outrage into one of his most powerful plays, *The Respectful Prostitute*, in which Lizzie, a prostitute, hides a black man falsely accused of rape from the lynch mob. Its scorching lines convey his incredulity at a society in which the senator's son, Fred, can say: 'I have five coloured servants. When they call me to the phone, they wipe it off before they hand it to me,' or 'They caught a nigger. It wasn't the right one. But they lynched him just the same.'

His barely concealed distaste for American 'conformism', as he perceives it, also surfaces in several of the thirty-two articles Sartre writes during his four months in America: 'Like everybody else, I had heard of the famous American "melting pot" that transforms, at different temperatures, Poles, Italians and Finns into United States citizens. But I did not quite know what the term really meant.' Then he meets a man whose 'good French' is sprinkled with 'Americanisms and barbarisms'. Sartre feels a chill run through him when he learns that the guy is in fact French: an 'Ovidian metamorphosis' has occurred. The man's face still retains that 'intelligence which makes a French face recognizable anywhere. But he will soon be a tree or a rock.'

The deepest source of Sartre's antagonism lay in his feeling that Americans did not appreciate Europe's suffering or the extent of Nazi atrocities. On all sides he met cheerful optimists. When one well-meaning American vouched the opinion that war could be abolished for ever, Sartre said soberly: 'I believe in the existence of evil and he does not . . . Men can be wholly bad.'

'Do you think that there are two Germanys?' an American doctor asked him. 'I replied that I didn't.'

Heavily handicapped by his inability to speak the language, although he did learn to ask for a 'Scotch on the rocks', Sartre barely gave the USA a chance. '*Ça ne vous gênait pas trop de ne pas savoir l'anglais?* It didn't worry you too much, not speaking English?' Beauvoir asked him. No, said Sartre, he only saw those Americans who spoke French. 'The others dropped me, naturally.'

Almost entirely reliant on French exiles for company, Sartre drew closer still to Dolorès. He was tired of 'drowning women', like Wanda, with her temper tantrums, her neediness and her infidelity. Dolorès had a career of her own, but she was feminine, pretty, and available. Sartre was in love. He left the USA promising to return.

*

Sartre's absence worried Beauvoir intensely. There was no civilian mail service between the USA and France, and the only news she had came from reading his articles. She knew no more than any member of the public. But Camus, who was having difficulty in readjusting to married life with his wife Francine, and often sought sanctuary in the Café de Flore with Beauvoir, took pity on her. 'Whenever you asked Camus for a favour, he would do it so readily that you never hesitated to ask for another, and never in vain,' she recalled, remembering how he took on all their young friends who wanted to work on *Combat*. 'Opening the paper in the morning was almost like opening our mail.' When Camus learnt that Beauvoir's sister Hélène, who had married Lionel de Roulet and spent the war in Portugal, had invited her to stay, and that she was to lecture to the French Institute in Lisbon, he asked her, too, to represent his paper. Beauvoir's status as official correspondent speeded up the necessary government permission.

On 27 February 1945 Beauvoir crossed the border into Spain. It was the first time for six years that she had left France, and sixteen years since she had last visited Spain. The abundance of food stunned her and, like Sartre, she felt 'a furious solidarity with the poverty of France'. 'Look, she has no stockings!' people whispered as she walked past. 'It was true,' wrote Beauvoir bitterly: 'We were poor: we had no stockings, no oranges, and our money was worthless.'

In Madrid she feasted on raisins, brioches, prawns, olives, pastries, fried eggs, milk chocolate; she drank wine and real coffee. But when she arrived in Lisbon, Poupette was horrified at her sister's appearance: 'What are those clogs you're wearing?' she asked, staring down at Simone's feet, and immediately took her shopping. Intoxicated by the opulence of the shops, Simone went on a retail 'debauch', buying a completely new wardrobe: silk stockings, three pairs of shoes, new underwear, dresses, skirts, blouses, jumpers, a white jacket and a fur coat. In her new finery she went to a cocktail party at the Institute; but this did not prevent her disturbing her audiences – for Portugal had sympathized with Hitler – with accounts of prison camps, torture and executions.

When she returned in April, laden with fifty kilos of food, Sartre was still away. Beauvoir's articles on Portugal, which she wrote under the pseudonym 'Daniel Secrétan', in order not to compromise Lionel, offended the propaganda service. Pascal Pia, who was editing *Combat* while Camus was in North Africa, ended the series. Sartre, meanwhile, had written to his confidant, Camus, that he was 'smitten' by Dolorès, although the brief notes he sent Beauvoir did not allow her to guess the depth of his new infatuation: he had abandoned the official tour and joined Dolorès' in her Manhattan apartment.

Beauvoir's first reaction was to find solace with married men. Her old flame, René Maheu, had returned to Paris, and that spring the Beaver and the Llama wandered together through the forest of Chantilly holding hands. Together they celebrated VE Day. Maheu, who was teaching philosophy in Morocco and had fallen in love with one of his students, for whom he was waiting in Paris, took the opportunity to sleep with Beauvoir. Their love-making was all the sweeter for having no future: when in September *The Blood of Others* was published, she inscribed his copy: 'To my very dear Llama, in memory of spring 1945, very confidentially, S de Beauvoir.'

She began a new 'contingent' affair with Michel Vitold, the producer of her play *Useless Mouths*, which was in rehearsal at the Vieux Colombier theatre at the time. Vitold, with his eight-day-old stubble, and wearing a bright Portuguese shirt given him by Beauvoir, comforted the thirty-seven-year-old writer on a bicycling holiday in the Auvergne in July. Tall and fit, he was an 'ace cyclist', who pushed her up the hills, swam and sunbathed with her, and camped out under the stars, as once she had done with Bost. They slept together in a 'double bed – *honi soit qui mal y pense* [evil be to him who evil thinks]', she coyly told Sartre, who was on holiday with his mother in the Midi. But Beauvoir's real feelings for her 'twin' are transparent: 'I'd so like to spend a long while alone with you.'

Sartre returned from the States at the end of May. Beauvoir's alarm grew as he began pulling strings to find a job in an American university, although she played down his new relationship in the third volume of her memoirs, *Force of Circumstance*, which conceals many sexual truths:

He had met a young woman . . . half-separated from her husband and, despite her brilliant position in the world, not very satisfied with her life; they had been very much attracted to each other. When told about my existence she had decided that when he went back to France they should forget each other; his feelings for her were too strong for him to accept this.

These lines barely hint at the magnitude of the emotional crisis that was building in Beauvoir's life. In Dolorès, whom she calls 'M' in her memoirs, she had a far more formidable rival than the lightweight young actresses who had previously threatened her position. Beauvoir's intellectual dominance was absolute: she was the queen who parcelled out her time to her 'little family', the 'clock in the refrigerator', as Sorokine called her, a published writer and Sartre's partner on *Les Temps modernes*. But 'M' also had a 'brilliant position' in the media: the golden-skinned radio presenter was a fresher, less demanding version of Beauvoir, her dark hair piled up on her head, her intelligent eyes and her slim little body all reminding Sartre of the woman with whom he had shared fifteen years of his life. Bost, Beauvoir's long-term lover, who had just returned from New York, had also had sex with Vanetti and couldn't stop talking about it, until the anguish in the Beaver's face brought home to him his lack of tact.

Nor was 'M' the only new woman in Sartre's life. While he had been in America, his stepfather, Joseph Mancy, had died; Mme Mancy, considerate of her son's well-being, kept the news from him until his return to France. 'Poulou' at once rushed to his widowed mother's side. His financial success enabled him to buy Anne-Marie a spacious apartment at 42 rue Bonaparte, overlooking the place Saint-Germain-des-Prés. The son moved in with his sixty-three-year-old mother, overjoyed at the opportunity to re-create the incestuous intimacy of his childhood so cruelly interrupted by Mancy. In so far as he was able, Sartre rewound the tape: in the place of honour in the salon was the upright piano on which the 'little chick' had played as a boy. Once again four hands ran over the keys together, as Jean-Paul and Anne-Marie played Beethoven sonatas together. The son had the best room, which was turned into a study, and a bedroom with a balcony overlooking Les Deux Magots. Eugénie, the maid from Alsace, washed and ironed his shirts. Anne-Marie slept in a little room at the back, as did the maid. Soon a secretary, Jean Cau, joined the household. 'This is my third marriage,' said Madame Mancy happily.

When Cau, a former student of Sartre's, climbed the four flights of stairs to the flat at ten in the morning, he would often find Sartre just rising from the narrow divan bed in his study. On the wall was the writer's favourite engraving, Dürer's Melancolia. Opening the door, you could cut the atmosphere with a knife. Cau felt his stomach rise at the smell of tobacco and sweat, as Sartre greeted him, unshaven and unkempt, in a dirty dressing-gown, clutching a thermos of stewed tea. At other times Cau's arrival interrupted the family concert, as Poulou played the piano with '*ma petite maman*', who was '*très belle*, tall, elegant . . . with fine bearing and slim ankles, bright blue eyes and a clear, musical voice'. Unless Sartre spent the night away from home, he and his mother breakfasted together, and sometimes lunched also at a tiny, doll-sized table. Sartre behaved like 'a docile child', Cau recalled. 'Strange. Sweet and strange.' The man who wanted to be the architect of his own creation, absolute master of his freedom, had such a mother!

Ignoring the Beaver, despite his long absence, forty-year-old Poulou took his *petite maman* away on holiday. In her memoirs Beauvoir took up the story of 'M' again:

> At present their attachment was mutual, and they envisaged spending two or three months together every year. So be it: separations held no terror for me. But he evoked the weeks he had spent with her in New York with such gaiety that I grew uneasy; . . . suddenly I wondered if M was more important to him than I was; my heart's old armour of optimism fell away; anything could happen to me. In a relationship which has lasted for fifteen years, how much is a matter of mere habit? . . . I understood [Sartre] better than I used to, and for that reason I found him more opaque; there were great differences between us; this did not disturb me, quite the contrary, but him?

Sartre could talk of nothing but his new love. 'According to his accounts, M shared completely all his reactions, his emotions; his irritations, his desires . . . Perhaps this indicated a harmony between them at a depth – at the very source of life, at the wellspring where its very rhythm is established – at which Sartre and I did not meet, and perhaps that harmony was more important to him than our understanding.'

Was he going to leave her? The question tormented Beauvoir. 'I wanted to free my heart of its uncertainty,' she wrote. 'When a dangerous question is burning our lips we choose a particularly unsuitable moment to ask it.' As they were leaving her room to have lunch with the playwright Armand Salacrou and his wife, Beauvoir asked Sartre: 'Frankly, who means the most to you, M or me?'

'M means an enormous amount to me, but I am with you.'

'His answer took my breath away. I took it to mean: "I am respecting our pact, don't ask more of me than that."' Such a reply, she wrote, put their whole future in question. At lunch, she could barely shake hands, smile, eat. Sartre watched her uneasily.

In 1972, still wounded by the affair, Beauvoir hid Dolorès's identity and significance in *Force of Circumstance*. Sartre reacted with anger, confessed Beauvoir to her biographer ten years later: 'I didn't want people to know anything about her so I called her "M". Sartre wanted me to write about her, but I said no. He said I was being dishonest. I said they were my memoirs. He said they were about him as well . . . I knew . . . that she was hostile to me.'

But in October 1945 it was impossible to hide Dolorès's existence. Sartre made a very public declaration of his love when he dedicated the whole of the first issue of *Les Temps modernes* 'to a certain Dolorès'. It was a cruel cut to Beauvoir, who had been left with the responsibility of launching the literary review while he was away in the USA. It was she who had gone cap in hand to Soustelle, the Minister of Information, begging for a quota of paper, and worked with Merleau-Ponty and Leiris planning its contents.

With the launch of *Les Temps modernes*, with its clarion call for a committed literature, the 'Existentialist offensive', as Beauvoir termed it, went global. Already, in September, the first two volumes of Sartre's *Roads to Freedom* had been published on the same day. Beauvoir's *The Blood of Others*, immediately labelled a 'Resistance novel' as well as an 'Existentialist novel', came out the same month and received 'floods of compliments'. Her play *Useless Mouths*, starring Olga Kosackiewicz, opened at the Théâtre des Carrefours. The label 'existentialist' was attached to any work by the couple. During the summer Sartre had still refused to allow the adjective to be applied to him. 'My philosophy is a philosophy of existence; I don't know what Existentialism is,' he maintained irritably. Only two years ago the writer Jean Grenier had enquired of Castor in the Flore: 'What about you, madame? *Êtes-vous existentialiste?* Are *you* an existentialist?' and the question had embarrassed her, for she didn't understand what the word meant. Now, in the autumn of 1945, they had given in: The couple used the epithet everyone applied to them to build their brand as Sartre and Notre Dame de Sartre, or *la grande Sartreuse*.

The public image Sartre had constructed in the USA was his stepping-stone to celebrity. 'Napoleon', as Dolorès described him to Camus, fought his way through a mob of fainting women and cheering students on 29 October to give his lecture 'Is Existentialism a Humanism?'. An hour late, he began speaking. 'We are alone without excuses,' he told his rapt, sweating audience. 'That is what I mean when I say that man is condemned to be free.' Anxious to demonstrate that existentialism was not anti-humanist, not based on 'disgust for humanity' as reported in the *New Yorker*, he hammered home the message of *action* and optimism by which existentialist man defined himself. The next day the press fell over itself to praise Sartre's 'grit', his 'courage', and his personal magnetism. The event became part of the Sartre legend when Boris Vian, in his novel *L'Écume des jours*, described a certain Jean-Sol Partre, author of *Vomit*, fighting his way to the stage with an axe while his fans crawled out of the sewers.

But as the media storm broke over the Beaver, the fame for which she and the Kobra had struggled together since 1929 suddenly lost its lustre. Sartre informed her that on 15 December he would be returning by Liberty Ship to America.

'Every woman in love recognizes herself in Hans Andersen's little mermaid who exchanged her fishtail for a woman's legs for love, and then found herself walking on needles and burning coals,' wrote Beauvoir in *The Second Sex*. 'Every woman' included herself: like the little mermaid, who gave up her soul for her prince, she walked on coals when Sartre left her to spend Christmas with Dolorès.

28

~~~

The Abyss

Death suddenly appeared to me. I wrung my hands, I
wept, and banged my head against the wall.
                              Simone de Beauvoir, *The Prime of Life*

CELEBRITY WAS TURNING to sensation. The Communists accused
Sartre of being a 'false prophet' and a 'gravedigger'. Jean Cocteau's book
Vies, with its punning alternative title *Vits* (penises) inside the jacket,
colloquially known as Cocteau's book of cocks, heightened existentialism's reputation for licentiousness. Mme Mancy, who had signed a
paper asking for the Légion d'Honneur for her son, to Sartre's
annoyance – he refused the decoration – was tricked by a tabloid
journalist into giving *Samedi-Soir* photos of the writer as a baby and a
teenager. They appeared on the back page, next to a vicious article.
'Existentialists', it claimed, were troglodytes, cellar rats, who hid out in
the Tabou and danced the jitterbug; they were the 'enemy within', who
corrupted French youth. The diabolical Sartre, who had written a song
for Juliette Gréco, 'Hell is all my habit now', was a monster of depravity
who advocated abortion and atheism, while Beauvoir, fallen daughter
of the Catholic Church, practised free love and three-in-a-bed sex.
    The hysteria whipped up by the mud-slinging weekly destroyed
Beauvoir's privacy in Paris. In the Flore, people whispered and pointed
at her. Instead, she drank in the gilded basement bar of the Pont Royal,
balancing her notepad on the casks used as tables. Camus, in flight from

fatherhood now that his wife Francine had had twins, often joined her. One evening in December they dined together at the Brasserie Lipp, before going on to the Pont Royal; at closing time he bought a bottle of champagne which they took back to her room at the Louisiane and drank till three in the morning. 'I spent a marvellous evening with Camus,' Beauvoir wrote to Sartre. 'It bowled me over that he should be so affectionate and that we should be so intimate and talk so easily.' She was in the mood for a new love affair with the tall, brooding journalist, whose bawdy, cynical conversation amused her. They drank hard together, although it was usually Camus who ended up on the pavement in the small hours, meditating on love: 'You have to choose. Love either lasts or it goes up in flames.' Emboldened, Beauvoir asked him to go skiing with her in February, but Camus declined both bed and the slopes of Mont d'Arbois.

Bost was also proving a reluctant lover. 'He doesn't have the impression he's got any real place in a life where you are,' she told Sartre. Bost had thrown away letters he had written to Beauvoir on the boat to America, feeling that they were 'pointless', and was increasingly 'crushed' by his life with Kos, who was ill with TB. Beauvoir's 'little family' was melting away: Nathalie (Natasha) Sorokine, who had married a GI, Ivan Moffatt, was pregnant and sailing to the States in February. From the Chalet Idéal-Sport in Megève, two days after Christmas, Beauvoir wrote miserably to Sartre:

> Six years ago I was writing to you from here and it was wartime. It seems strange to remember that. In a sense, it seems much longer to me than six years. I feel somehow beyond all that, as though in a second life. I no longer recognize either myself or the old world. Yet there are the memories – the memories with yourself, in that former life. But they have a strange effect, rather harrowing, because they're so little related to the present.

She ended with a familiar, desperate plea: '*On ne fait qu'un*, you and I are one.' But never had the pact on which her happiness rested revealed more clearly its shaky foundations. Sartre, of whom she had written in 1929, that he 'was not cut out for monogamy', was finding that notoriety made women fall at his feet.

Her first plane trip, once eagerly anticipated with Sartre, was taken alone in January when she flew to Tunis to lecture. On a lone expedition to the Roman ruins at Dougga, she narrowly escaped being raped by an Arab. On her return a letter from Sartre awaited her: '*Tué,* killed by passion and lectures', he was delaying his departure, and would not be home until 15 March 15. 'Dolorès's love for me scares me,' he wrote ominously. 'In other respects she is absolutely charming and we never get mad at each other.' Dolorès was 'a poor and charming creature, really the best that I know after you', he repeated, cruelly stressing the sexual rapport he had lost with Beauvoir: 'Her passion literally scares me, particularly since that's not my strong suit . . .' His account of his daily routine with Dolorès in New York, which he now claimed to know as well as Paris, has an easy, domestic ring. It scared Beauvoir. For two and a half months Sartre has lived with Dolorès; she calls him her 'prisoner'. At weekends they barely go out. 'Here life is sweet and uneventful,' he taunts Beauvoir.

Sartre once told Olivier Todd that he lied to all his women, 'particularly to the Beaver', and he was lying now. Although claiming he wanted to come home, to Dolorès he promised marriage: 'He told me,' said Vanetti, ' "Come on, we'll get married, and that's that," without even considering that I was already married. And he really wanted to accept the offer of his friend at Columbia and stay in New York with me for two years. But I was not sure that, with his language problems, he'd really like to live in New York.'

When Don Juan finally returned, he promptly went down with mumps. While he worried about the effect that the disease might have on his virility, Beauvoir slipped back into her familiar role of protector to her famous consort. While Sartre lay in bed, swathed in bandages and wearing a pointed nightcap, Beauvoir, as so often in times of crisis, began a diary again. It reveals 'la poussière, the dust' of her life to her readers. At the end of The Prime of Life she had explained that in 1939, when 'in an agony of loneliness', because Sartre was called up, 'literature had become as essential to me as the very air I breathed. I am not suggesting that it constitutes a remedy against absolute despair; but I had not been reduced to such extremities.' Now, threatened even more dramatically by loss of love, feeling that her life had become 'alien', she turned to her journal to sustain her. Her personal writing, the diaries – edited before being included in her memoirs – and her letters, fulfilled a vital function, enabling her to express and manage her distress. They became her confessional:

At those times when my life has been hard for me, jotting words down on paper – even if no one is to read what I have written – has given me the same comfort that prayer gives a believer.

On Sunday 5 May 1946, Beauvoir's flat, devitalized prose tells its tale:

> There are sometimes days when I feel like those dabfish which have used all their energy spawning and get washed up on to the rocks, dying and draining. Felt like that this morning. Had bad dreams, which left a sort of chill around my heart.

She is suffering from a 'strange anxiety . . . This evening everything was somehow tainted with horror: for example, the woman's hand I saw, all the bones showed so clearly, fingering its way through blond hair: the hair was a plant, with a *root* in the scalp.'

Beauvoir's heightened sensations spoke to her of the skull beneath the skin, of death, which had become an obsession since the war, a time when the world wore 'the mocking, illusory mask of Nothingness'. She needed to write in order

> to exorcize death with words . . . Death closed over me . . . At the end of the road I would meet death, that dream of death which I take, every time, for the final truth, letting myself slip with a sort of glad abandon into the abyss of the Void while a voice cries: 'This time it is forever, there will be no awakening.'

Her bed frightened her. She was sure that she would die in her bed. But inside her 'writer's skin', she kept death at bay: 'I have written the beginning of the book which is my last and greatest recourse against death.'

Non-being itself, 'the banal image of a black ruled line . . . and after it nothing but a blank page', held associated fears: old age – when the black line grew inexorably closer – the decay of the flesh, the 'peril of loneliness and separation'. To these negatives she opposed positives: being, love, unity, plenitude. These polarities run through all her writing, private and public. The depressive themes, which surface regularly, and with great poignancy, in Beauvoir's personal writing, also break through the control she sought to impose on her published work. Her pain and anguish take on a life of their own as they dominate *All Men Are Mortal*, her least successful novel – dedicated to Sartre – and *The Ethics of Ambiguity* – dedicated to Bianca – both of which she describes as a 'protracted wandering' around the central theme of death.

Both works were written in the shadow of Sartre's affair with

Dolorès, and in the context of Beauvoir's terror that he would abandon her. She tried to comfort herself with the physical act of writing, with the familiar feel of her cigarette and fountain pen in her fingers, with the sight of the paper covered with green ink lying on her desk, with the thick fug of smoke in her room, but even her diary began to fail in its therapeutic role. On 13 May she reread it: 'Already it evokes nothing for me. And why should one hope that these words would be different from any others, that they should have the magic power of retaining life within themselves and resuscitating the past? No. For myself the last fifteen days are already merely sentences written down, nothing more.' Even language no longer performed its healing function.

In Count Fosca, hero of *All Men Are Mortal*, Beauvoir created a Faustian figure 'cursed by immortality', whose licence to commit evil allows him to rule the world. When she began the book in 1943, she felt that 'I always "had something to say"', but by 1946 her desire to show existentialist man continually reinventing himself across the centuries, perhaps inspired by Virginia Woolf's *Orlando*, failed to translate into realistic characterization or dialogue. Awkward and didactic, *All Men Are Mortal*, like *Useless Mouths*, met with hostile reviews. But in the actress Regina's fear of the metamorphosis of death, the reader feels Beauvoir's own: when Fosca leaves her, Regina becomes, like the mermaid who loses her soul and turns to sea foam when she loses her prince's love, 'a fleck of foam . . . she let out the first scream'.

The Ethics of Ambiguity was a bold attempt to supply the system of ethics promised by Sartre at the end of *Being and Nothingness*, in which he famously declares that man is 'a useless passion'. Often accused of operating in a moral vacuum, existentialism, with its emphasis on 'human existence making values spring up in the world' – like partridges, said Sartre – is, in Beauvoir's eyes, profoundly moral. The 'ambiguity' or paradox of life, that we are born to die, which underlies the cult of existence, is irrefutable, insists Beauvoir, who took as her epigraph a quotation from Montaigne: 'The continuous work of our life is to build death.' The game is already lost. But existentialism exalts the human individual as the creator of meaning in a world itself meaningless, and she was troubled by the criticism that the popular, new, atheist cult allowed man 'to make himself God,' enclosing him in a solipsistic, 'sterile anguish'. Her turgid prose fails to convince the reader, who senses her unease at Sartre's remark that 'Man makes himself man in order to be God, and selfness . . . can appear to be an egoism.' 'No Man really is God,' writes Beauvoir in *The Second Sex* when she analyses *l'amoureuse*, the woman in love who puts her man on a pedestal and treats him as a 'deified man'. In accepting total dependence, she writes with painful self-knowledge, 'Woman creates a hell for herself.'

Like Sartre, Beauvoir contends that existentialism is optimistic: the journey of a being-in-the-world is an 'engaged freedom, that surging of the for-itself which is immediately given for others'. Man exists only by transcending himself, and in order to exist authentically he 'will understand that it is not a question of being right in the eyes of a God, but in his own eyes'. Christians may claim that Sartrean philosophy is a licence to repudiate ethics. Not so, argues Beauvoir. Mankind bears the responsibility for a world 'which is not the work of a strange power, but of himself'. And since there is no God to pardon, 'man's faults are inexpiable'. There is a particularly puritan strain of severity in Sartre's insistence that man must save himself, and if he fails there is no meaningful God, no absolution of sins, no rest with the angels. For Beauvoir, forced to deny and sublimate her own passionate spirituality, living, as Camus put it, 'Life without appeal', was hard. Giacometti's sculpture of an agonized figure stretching out its hands to the void, *Mains tenants le vide*, expressed the hopelessness she felt.

The *Ethics* originated in a lecture that Beauvoir gave to a group of Catholic students in February 1945. Afterwards one of the students urged her to write a morality based on *Being and Nothingness*. Camus, too, asked her for 'an essay on action', and the warm reception given to *Pyrrhus et Cinéas*, which she had written for Grenier after he had asked if she was an existentialist, encouraged Beauvoir to return to philosophy. Afterwards, however, *The Ethics* became, of all her books, the one which 'irritated' her the most. 'I was in error when I thought I could define a morality independent of social context,' she wrote in 1963. But her polemical essay was more than a defence of existentialism: it was a step on her own road to self-discovery, an important prelude to *The Second Sex*.

During the war, wrote Beauvoir at the end of *Prime of Life*, 'The earth turned and revealed another of its faces to me.' Confronted with violence, horror, injustice, she was forced for the first time to engage with reality, to accept that her consciousness was not 'sovereign', but subject to greater forces. 'Down the stream of Time, History bore its vast jumble of incurable ills . . . [Yet] History was not my enemy.' Imperious, brilliant, rebellious, and often angry, it was a difficult lesson for her to learn, but she insisted that she would never again succumb to *le délire schizophrénique*, that

> schizophrenic delirium by which for years I had contrived to bend the universe to serve my will . . . I no longer pretended that I could escape my own human condition . . . I was ready to submit.

At last she had discovered that she impinged on other people's destinies, and had to face up to the responsibility which this implied. But her stoic assertion that in 1945 she found 'happiness' again was false. In her 'second life' the problem of the Other (*autrui*) was proving more intractable than ever.

Beauvoir's friends were concerned about her. She was turning to alcohol to blot out her pain, drinking steadily and silently until she frequently dissolved into tears. One night when Bost and Sartre were cheerfully exchanging gossip about Dolorès over dinner, ignoring Beauvoir sitting at the table, she again began to weep into her wine, humiliated by the 'shameless' way in which they talked about New York in front of her. Mme Mancy was publicly questioning Sartre's friends who had returned from New York about a possible marriage, even asking Rirette Nizan: 'What about this Dolorès, do you think she is right for Poulou?'

New friends provided diversion, of a sort. Standing in a cinema queue in the Champs Élysées the previous autumn, Beauvoir had begun talking to her neighbour, a tall, elegant blonde woman, whose face was as ugly as it was passionate. This was Violette Leduc, a lesbian who soon became devoted to Beauvoir. The author helped her new friend have her memoirs published by Gallimard, and introduced her to Jean Genet and another new aquaintance, Nathalie Sarraute, an ex-Resistant and the author of *Tropisms*. But Leduc and Sarraute soon fell out, and Beauvoir mistrusted Sarraute, who remained closer to Sartre than to herself.

The jazz trumpeter Boris Vian, whom Beauvoir also met by chance, this time in the bar of the Pont-Royal, lifted her spirits a little. Vian, who played in a *zazou* band, was another Gallimard author; he invited Beauvoir to a party in March, where she drank 'manfully' till dawn, sitting in the kitchen with her host discussing the novel. 'We talked on and the dawn came too quickly,' recalled Beauvoir. She found him full of kindness; but when Sartre returned he reasserted his authority by seducing Michèle, Vian's wife, whose long, silky blonde hair and pretty *retroussé* nose caught his fancy.

Beauvoir's self-esteem would sink even lower after an encounter with Arthur Koestler, a Hungarian Jew whose arrival in Paris ignited the rivalry already smouldering between Sartre and Camus.

*

Since his return from America, Sartre's reputation and riches had left Camus standing. His production was phenomenal: amphetamines or 'speed', in the form of tubes of orthedrine, fuelled the *machine à écrire*, the writing machine. His engine room was the study at rue Bonaparte, into which 'Napoleon' moved in October 1946. There he wrote for six hours a day, while Cau, his secretary, took calls, wrote cheques, and managed his diary. In the street photographers chased Sartre, and *Samedi-Soir* printed scurrilous 'revelations' that he had lured young women up to his room at the Hôtel Louisiane on the pretext of smelling a Camembert. At the theatre his name was again up in lights in November 1946 with the production of *Morts sans Sépulture* (*Men Without Shadows*), his play about Resistance heroes tortured by Milicien terrorists. The play dominated the theatrical season of 1946: once again Sartre had scored a first among playwrights in rendering homage to Resistance heroism. In the same year *Anti-Semite and Jew*, which continued the story of the making of the fascist, Lucien, in 'The Childhood of a Leader', was translated into English. *Nausea* was already in a dozen languages.

Camus was irritated by Sartre's celebrity status, and concerned to separate himself from his rival. 'I am not an existentialist,' he explained. 'Camus is not an existentialist,' confirmed Sartre. But the younger writer's anger was not based on envy so much as his sense of injustice. Sartre was commandeering the Resistance as a topic, writing with the authority of a former militant, which, in the public mind, he had become. The Grand Guignol spectacle of torture on stage, with Sartre's mistress Wanda, under the stage name Marie-Ollivier, playing Lucie, and Beauvoir's fling Michel Vitold as Henri, caused a scandal. Sartre's play outshone that of a real hero, the playwright Armand Salacrou, who had remained silent under the Occupation, but whose play *Les Nuits de la Colère* (*Angry Nights*) lost the battle in the Sartre–Salacrou duel of '46.

Vladimir Jankélévitch, a Jewish philosophy teacher who was sacked under Vichy and became a *maquisard*, accused Sartre's vaunted *engagement* after the war of being *une sorte de compensation maladive*, a kind of feeble compensation for his failure to act concretely during the war. Sartre, he said, failed in his 'duty as a man' when he stepped into Dreyfus-le-Foyer's shoes at the Lycée Condorcet. No one listened. When Julien Benda, author of *The Treason of the Clerks*, gave a lecture on the same night as Sartre, it was to an empty room. Sartre expressed postmodern despair, after a war that had exposed the optimism of the Enlightenment and nineteenth-century belief in man's perfectibility as a hideous delusion. The Sartre phenomenon was unassailable.

Arthur Koestler arrived in Paris in October on a wave of fame also. Even Mme Mancy was reading his *Darkness At Noon*, a vivid exposé of the Moscow trials: the book was supposedly based on the transcript of the evidence of Bukharin, one of the 'old guard' slaughtered by Stalin. Koestler, who had British citizenship after resigning from the Communist Party in 1938 in disgust at Stalin's show trials and escaping to London from a French camp during World War II, was already an adviser to the British Ministry of Information. His conversion to the defence of Western civilization, as the post-war world shattered into two hostile blocs, was genuine. As Winston Churchill made his 'Iron Curtain' speech in Fulton, Missouri, in March 1946, Camus, under the influence of Koestler, was making the equation between Marxism and murder. Disillusioned by the failure of his hopes to move 'from Resistance to Revolution', and the disintegration of the Resistance movement, beaten by the PCF with quotations from Lenin and accusations of being a *petit bourgeois* counter-revolutionary, Camus felt 'instant comradeship' with Koestler when he descended on the Parisian literary scene with his English lover, Mamaine.

From their first meeting, Camus and Koestler began using the informal '*tu*' to one another. Beauvoir was soon doing so also: she was attracted to the 'tumultous newcomer [who] burst into our group', although she criticized his 'poor Marxist education.' She had told Sartre how 'stunningly attractive' she was in January that year, but he had not responded. Now wife-swapping was in the air; Camus had fallen in love with Mamaine, a fragile, graceful blonde. On the night of 31 October 1946 Beauvoir and Sartre, Camus, Francine, Koestler and Mamaine had dinner together at an Algerian restaurant and went on to an intimate dance hall in the rue des Gravilliers. 'Saw the charming spectacle of [Koestler] squeezing the Beaver against him (she who I believe had practically never danced in her life) around the dance floor,' noted Mamaine in her diary, 'while Sartre (for whom ditto) squeezed Mrs Camus against himself.'

Koestler imperiously invited the party to follow him to the Schéhérazade, a favourite night-club of the Germans under the

Occupation, where he ordered Russian *hors d'oeuvre*, vodka and champagne. Sartre was due the next day to deliver a lecture, as yet unwritten, on 'The Writer's Responsibility', under the aegis of UNESCO, but he began to get drunk, and Beauvoir to weep into her glass. Camus leaned forward and whispered to Mamaine that he had been attracted to her since first he had set eyes on her. 'It doesn't bother Arthur if I flirt with men,' replied Mamaine, 'so long as it isn't serious.' 'You're the type of girl one could fall in love with,' responded Camus.

Beauvoir was also making declarations of love to her host. Arthur replied, 'It's impossible to be friends when you don't agree politically.' Two weeks later there would be a nasty quarrel when Camus attacked Maurice Merleau-Ponty for his defence of the Moscow trials in his review of Koestler's latest book, *The Yogi and the Commissar*. Sartre and Beauvoir would take Merleau-Ponty's side. Camus would walk out, slamming the door. The rift would last till March 1947. But now alcohol broke down barriers. At some point Sartre went back to rue Bonaparte and, after two hours' sleep, rose, crunched several of the innocuous-looking corydrane tablets which he always kept on his desk, and wrote his talk. Koestler and the Beaver left to have sex.

For Beauvoir, it became a night of date-rape. Koestler brutalized and humiliated her. It seems that at the last minute she changed her mind, but he refused to accept her 'No'. In Beauvoir's novel *The Mandarins*, the heroine, Anne Dubreuilh, is subjected to violence by Victor Scriassine:

> 'You don't want to!' he was saying. 'You don't want to! *Tête de mule!* You stubborn mule.' *Il me frappa légèrement au menton.* He struck me lightly on the chin; I was too weary to escape into anger. I began to tremble. A beating fist; thousands of fists . . . 'Violence is everywhere,' I thought, I trembled and tears began running down my cheeks.

Scriassine orders her to open her eyes. He keeps the light on. Anne is embarrassed: 'I no longer had the belly of a young girl.' There is a look of hate in his eyes. Afraid, she tells him that she has never had a better night.

> 'Never? Not even with younger men? You're not lying to me, are you?'
> The words had lied for me . . . 'Never.'
> He crushed me ardently against him. 'All right?'

To get it over with, Anne is willing to sigh and moan. She fakes an orgasm.

Beauvoir confessed to her American lover Nelson Algren that she had a one-night stand with Koestler in 1946. 'I hate challenge, chiefly in sexual business; so it never happened any more,' she told Nelson. '[Koestler] was a hell of a raper,' said Labour politician Richard Crossman. But Scriassine may have been a composite character: his voice, encouraging like that of 'a doctor', reminds the reader of Sartre, in his surgical violation of the virginal Bianca. Sartre, who remembered his grandfather, Dr Sartre, the only doctor in Thiviers, visiting his patients in his cart, would refer to his own visits to his 'women' as his 'medical rounds'. The disappointment Beauvoir felt in her sexual relationship with Sartre may have fed into this portrait of a brutal sexual encounter.

*

Not only did Sartre talk non-stop about Dolorès, he had discreetly added vivacious Michèle Vian, wife of Boris, to his harem; Beauvoir had nobody. Sartre's alarm grew at her depressed mood. He asked Philippe Soupault, an old surrealist friend, if he could wangle an invitation for the Beaver to America next year. At the Flore, a meeting was arranged. Soupault was concerned at Beauvoir's 'fragility', but asked if she wanted to visit America. 'Of course I want to go . . . I'm bursting to go,' replied an unsuspecting Beauvoir.

The Beaver needed a new wardrobe for the trip. Genet complained that she dressed far too simply, and one day Simone Berrieau, the producer of Men Without Shadows, said to her: 'You don't dress as well as you should!' 'I was a person who received invitations,' wrote Beauvoir, astonished at her new fame; but still she did not attend salons, and never owned an evening dress, finding the 'uniform' of the bourgeoisie as repugnant as their rituals. All the same, in Geneva on a Swiss lecture tour with Sartre, the couple were placed on twin thrones 'like a Catholic king and his queen'. Press conferences were bedlam, attended by 'swarms' of journalists, mostly hostile. Over 1,000 people came to Sartre's first lecture. In Zurich, where No Exit was being performed, as Sartre prepared to face his audience, he stripped off his overcoat like a boxer entering a ring.

Beauvoir had to prepare herself for similar ordeals; she bought a green tussore silk dress, some leather shoes, a suitcase and a Swiss watch. As the date of her departure grew nearer, she decided she needed a special dress for America; the cost of the knitted model she selected, 25,000 francs, made her pause. Sartre was wealthy beyond his wildest dreams, and reckless with his money, giving away most of it to his friends, or to people who wrote him begging letters. Beauvoir tried to compensate for his extravagance by cheese-paring; but this dress tempted her. 'It's my first concession,' she told Sartre, bursting into tears. 'Buy it,' said Sartre, pulling out the roll of notes he always carried in his back pocket. Guiltily Beauvoir packed the dress in her new leather suitcase. Against the wardrobe hung the rabbit fur which would be her protection against a New England winter.

One of her last acts before leaving France was to go on a solitary walking tour in the Dolomites. For three weeks she paced the valleys and peaks, scrambling over scree as she hiked between mountain huts, alone in the silence. She drove her body hard, seeking in nature a forgetting and a peace which eluded her with men.

*

'*Que vous avez l'air farouche!* How wild you look!' exclaimed Giacometti, when he bumped into Beauvoir in the Deux Magots, gazing into space. There was a blank sheet of paper in front of her. She had nothing to say. Like the little mermaid, she had lost her voice.

'It's because I want to write, but I don't know what about.'

'*Écrivez n'importe quoi,*' said the sculptor. This can mean both 'anything', and 'any nonsense'. The ambiguity could not have escaped Beauvoir. In fact she wanted to write about herself, and was pondering the question, 'What has it meant to me to be a woman?' It was one she quickly dismissed.

> 'For me,' I said to Sartre, 'you might almost say it just hasn't counted.'
>
> 'All the same, you weren't brought up in the same way as a boy would have been; you should look into it further.'

Beauvoir began looking. It was a revelation: 'This world was a masculine world, my childhood had been nourished by myths forged by men.'

29

Nelson, My Sweet Crocodile

I am your wife as you are my husband.
Simone de Beauvoir to Nelson Algren, 4 June 1947

ON 24 JANUARY 1947 Beauvoir touched down at La Guardia, leaving Sartre behind in Paris. She was, wrote Mary McCarthy, 'the leading French *femme savante* . . . In her own eyes, this trip had something fabulous about it, of a balloonist's expedition or a descent in a diving bell . . . To Mlle de Beauvoir, America was, very simply, movieland – she came to verify for herself the existence of violence, drugstore stools, boy-meets-girl, that she had seen depicted on the screen.'

But by 1947 America stood for more than movieland: Americans were liberators:

> I was prepared to love America. It was the homeland of capitalism, yes, but it had helped save Europe from fascism; the atomic bomb assured it world leadership and freed it from all fear.

Convinced that the American 'nation had a clear and serene awareness of its responsibilities', by which she meant the assumption that, having freed Europe, the Americans would go back in to their box, Beauvoir found that 'the reality was a great shock to me'. She had arrived in New York on the eve of President Truman's March speech calling on the American people to intervene on behalf of 'free peoples'. As the

Truman Doctrine, followed by the Marshall Plan in June, signalled the opening of the Cold War, Andrei Zhdanov in Belgrade called on the Soviet Cominform (the former Comintern) and the world intelligentsia to respond to the 'imperialist' challenge. The ideological chasm which opened up between West and East would draw writers and artists into the *kulturkampf*, dividing old friends and creating new enemies.

Like Sartre before her, Beauvoir set off eagerly on a journey of exploration from her hotel on Forty-fourth Street and Eighth Avenue, and found herself feeling like a 'ghost'. The pace of life was different from Europe's: she was disconcerted to discover that she could not linger in the bars and write. 'It's not customary here to do work in places where people drink . . . As soon as my glass is empty, the waiter comes over to inquire; if I don't empty it fast enough, he prowls around me.' Nervously ordering whisky, because meeting Hemingway had convinced her that all Americans drank Scotch, she squirmed on her bar stool: 'It seems wiser to leave before the fourth glass.'

Unlike Sartre, Beauvoir was determined to avoid the French 'colony' and meet Americans; she wanted to practise her self-taught English, learnt from reading English novels as a child; but when she did so, she found her hosts arrogant and condescending. At a party given for her by a journalist on *Vogue*, writers from the anti-Communist *Partisan Review* upbraided Beauvoir over the *Temps modernes* review by Merleau-Ponty of Koestler's *The Yogi and the Commissar* which had triggered the fight with Camus. Now, confused by too many Martinis and her difficulty understanding English, Beauvoir was stung by the virulence of the attack upon her. 'It seems my statements are worthy of a Soviet agent . . . The "red terror" is growing.' When a young intellectual reminded her that 'it isn't the Russians who send you food; America created UNRRA [the United Nations Relief and Rehabilitation Administration]', Beauvoir exploded. If even 'left-wing' journalists were so proud of the tins of condensed milk their government sent the starving French, she wasn't at all surprised at the tone of condescension in the press towards frozen, broke Europe. Americans were all imperialists. Even the literature she liked was apparently an insult to the country's intelligentsia, who dismissed her heroes, Hemingway, Dos Passos and Steinbeck, as unworthy of study. In the basement restaurant, hot, sweating and embarrassed, Beauvoir argues fiercely with her hosts. It is an inauspicious beginning.

The *Partisan Review* journalists, who had looked forward to the visit by *La Grande Sartreuse*, the second most important existentialist, found her equally patronizing. 'It is hard to say whether her literary or political opinions were more arrogant,' wrote editor William Phillips. McCarthy tittered at Beauvoir's appearance – the blue woollen dress, rarely changed, which carried with it a whiff of body odour, the single pair of leather high heels and sensible Swiss blouses. The two women disliked one another at sight: McCarthy was 'the beautiful, cold novelist who has already devoured three husbands and many lovers in the course of a cleverly managed career', wrote Beauvoir in *America Day by Day*.

McCarthy, domesticated and well bred, a writer who 'felt the command to prepare and serve a first course at dinner ought to be put in the Bill of Rights', personified, for Beauvoir, those aspects of American womanhood which most horrified her. With the return of the GIs, the same backlash against women in the workplace was in force as in Britain, where the 'back to the home' movement sent female factory workers scurrying back to the kitchen and the mythic joys of the vacuum cleaner and twin-tub washing machine. In 1947 *Modern Woman: The Lost Sex*, by Ferdinand Lundberg and Dr Marynia F. Farnham, an excoriating attack on Mary Woollstonecraft's *The Vindication of the Rights of Woman* and the emancipation of women from the home, was a best seller in the US.

On 7 February Beauvoir catches her first train from Grand Central Station. The shock of '*café au lait* served in cardboard cups!' is as nothing compared to the shock of Vassar, the first women's university at which she lectures. The girls' appearance astonishes her:

> How pretty they look! Up close, their faces are not so special. But their hair is beautiful, like in shampoo advertisements, and their features are heightened by makeup as heavy as a woman of thirty would wear. Whatever nature lovers might say, this mixture of freshness and artifice, those heavy painted lips half-opened over dazzling youthful teeth, the smiling eyes of a sixteen-year-old beneath long mascaraed lashes seem quite attractive to me.

Beauvoir is intrigued by the students' 'uniform' of jeans rolled above the ankle, with a brightly coloured man's shirt worn hanging outside and knotted carelessly in front. 'The jeans must be worn and dirty. If need be, they roll them in the dust.' The girls 'dressed like boys, made up like streetwalkers', knit as they sit in the audience. Their lecturer dislikes the clicking needles. 'Knitting,' she concludes censoriously, 'is an anticipation of marriage and maternity.'

On the train back to New York, she studies the college girls more closely. This time they seem even more of an alien species, dressed like their mothers in flowered hats, furs and high-heeled shoes. 'Jeans or mink – two uniforms.' American women, writes Beauvoir, do not dress for comfort, for themselves, but to display their social status and to catch a husband: 'These women who keenly defend their independence on every occasion and so easily become aggressive towards men, nevertheless dress for men . . . the truth is that the garb of European woman is much less servile.' She detects a spirit of 'rancour' between the sexes, an incipient sex war: 'the relation between the sexes is a struggle . . . men and women don't like each other'. Although 'in general the battle [for feminism] has been won', American woman, a phrase Beauvoir once considered synonymous with 'free woman', is uncomfortable in the masculine world to which she has only recently been admitted as an equal. In women's magazines Beauvoir devours long articles on catching a man. In a bachelor flat in New York, entertained by two thirty-year-old spinsters, she feels a 'conspicuous absence'. One complains of loneliness, the other says that she wants a husband 'with all her heart'. To their guest, both seem 'obsessed by that empty place on their ring finger'. Bereft of the respect afforded unmarried women in France – even though Frenchwomen only won the vote in 1947 – for American women, despite their rights, there is only one career: marriage.

Beauvoir's comparison between her situation and that of American women played a major part in the genesis of *The Second Sex*. The epiphany she had first experienced when Sartre pointed out that her own experience was unusual, even unique, was reinforced by the revelation that was America. She finally understood her difference: she was a pioneer, as she had wished to be, in the mould of Leontine Zanta. Professionally qualified, refusing marriage and domesticity, childless by choice, living like a man and internalizing masculine values, taking her sexual pleasure where she pleased, her life bore no relation to that of an American housewife, who had no servants but was still a slave to standards Beauvoir considered ridiculously high. Betty Friedan, the first desperate housewife, would chronicle a lifestyle that brought her to the brink of suicide in 1963, in *The Feminine Mystique*:

It was a strange stirring of dissatisfaction, a yearning that women suffered in the middle of the twentieth century in the United States. Each suburban wife struggled with it alone. As she made the beds, shopped for groceries, matched slip cover material, ate peanut butter sandwiches, chauffeured Cub Scouts and Brownies, lay beside her husband at night, she was afraid to ask even of herself the silent question: 'Is this all?'

Before writing *The Second Sex*, Beauvoir had never felt penalized by being a woman: 'Far from suffering from my femininity, I have, on the contrary, from the age of twenty on, accumulated the advantages of both sexes; after *She Came to Stay* those around me treated me both as a writer, their peer in the masculine world, and as a woman.' In America this gratifying combination of masculine and feminine privileges was even more marked: 'At the parties I went to, the wives all got together and talked to each other while I talked to the men, who nevertheless behaved towards me with greater courtesy than they did towards the members of their own sex.'

That curiosity, the 'dependent woman', had been outside her ken. Beauvoir's friends had been single, artists, teachers and actresses, like Stépha, Colette Audry, Simone Jollivet and the Kos sisters. Only during the war had she met married women over forty, like Zette Leiris. 'Because I was a good listener – they told me a great deal.' It had set her thinking about the 'feminine condition'. Now, observing 'rich, spoiled' Southern belles in Virginia, wearing 'those ladylike outfits I can't stand – a raw-silk dress decorated with a scarf and a crocodile-skin belt', and hearing about their plans to find a husband, or listening to a young mother in Rochester explain that with two children to raise 'a woman has no time to lead an intellectual life', her ideas about the sources of women's oppression sprang into dazzling life.

*

The hostility which Beauvoir expressed towards American women had a personal dimension: her furious jealousy of Dolorès Vanetti. When Beauvoir writes grimly, 'I wanted to have a good look at [America],' she meant she wanted to have a good look at the other woman. In New York she demanded that Stépha Gerassi arrange a meeting. Stépha was reluctant but, fearful of another of Beauvoir's crying fits, she telephoned Vanetti, who at first refused. 'She probably said yes because she could feel the terror in my voice over the telephone,' said Stépha. 'I was afraid of what Castor would do if Dolorès said no, and maybe she could sense it.'

Beauvoir and the Gerassi family, Fernando, Stépha and John, were sitting in the Menemsha bar when 'a stunningly beautiful, very tiny mulatto woman' walked in. 'I am Dolorès,' she announced, before sitting down opposite Beauvoir. Nervously Stépha said how much she envied Dolorès her forthcoming trip to France. It was not a tactful remark: the radio presenter was about to cross the Atlantic in the opposite direction, to Paris and Sartre. She planned to remain until Beauvoir's return. Castor flushed angrily as she stared into her glass of whisky, unable to meet her rival's eyes. Ira Woolfert, an editor on *Partisan Review*, chatted in English to Dolorès; Beauvoir did not speak. Dolorès finished her glass of wine, stood up and shook hands all round. As she clasped Beauvoir's hand, the two women exchanged farewells in French. 'She had the prettiest smile,' admitted Beauvoir.

Stépha was surprised by Beauvoir's reaction afterwards. 'It was as if this woman was her obsession, but then once she saw her, well, that's that and it was all over. Castor was so businesslike that at first she worried me. She was too cold and detached . . . Sometimes she made me mad, my good girlfriend, Castor, but at other times I had to admit that she was a smart one, she knew how to take care of herself. Maybe that was one of those times.'

Revenge is a dish best served cold, so they say, and Beauvoir was cold as ice. Bent on revenge for Sartre's betrayal, she set out to have her own tit-for-tat affair. Her first tactic was to see Dolorès again, and impress on her Beauvoir's own place in Sartre's life. 'Dolorès was as dainty as a little Annamite idol and truly charming to me,' she wrote to Sartre. 'I'd quite like to know what she is actually thinking.' Dolorès was nervous, voluble and 'crazy', said her rival, as Beauvoir kept her drinking whisky till three in the morning. The next day, she demanded lunch, and again Dolorès chatted nervously, embarrassed by Beauvoir's piercing blue eyes and intimidating silences. 'I like her a lot, and was very happy because I understood your feelings,' wrote Beauvoir silkily to Sartre.

On her return from Vassar, Beauvoir was invited to dinner by Mary Guggenheim, also at the *Partisan Review*, who was so disconcerted by her guest's machine-gun questioning on the 'condition of women' in America that she retreated to the kitchen for two hours to make a *zabaglione*. It curdled, and she threw it away; when she returned, Guggenheim asked Beauvoir where she was going next. 'Chicago.' 'I said, "Maybe you'd like to look up this good friend of mine who's a writer."' She gave Beauvoir, who carefully noted it down, the name of one of her lovers: Nelson Algren.

The next day Guggenheim sent Algren a note warning him that the French novelist was on her way. The acclaimed author of *Never Come Morning* was not impressed by Mary's account of the existentialist craze sweeping France, or her stories of *la grande Sartreuse*. 'That Simone de

Boudoir sounds real chi-chi and I'm sure J-P Sartre, whoever he may be, is real lucky,' he replied sarcastically. 'I bet she says, J-P honey, bite my little titties. And J-P, the hog, chews her tits clean off.'

When, however, Beauvoir arrived in Chicago on 21 February with thirty-six hours to spare, she nearly failed to make contact. With images of Ann Bancroft in *Chicago Nights* in her mind – for McCarthy was right, America was still movieland to Beauvoir – she was determined to get 'a taste of Chicago at night'.

> I pick up the telephone and ask for Mr NA [Nelson Algren]. A surly voice answers, 'You have the wrong number.' To be sure, I look it up in my phone book; it must be my pronunciation. I dial again. I've hardly opened my mouth when the voice repeats, this time with irritation, 'Wrong number.' He hangs up.

Algren, who speaks no French, nor will he ever learn it, cannot understand a word Beauvoir says. 'Somebody hollered into the phone, screeched something, and I hung up . . . I got back to the stove, the phone rang again and I got that same hoarse screech and I did this three times.'

Beauvoir eats a 'melancholy supper' alone in a drugstore. But, remembering how New York only opened up for her when she found the right guides, she tries Algren again. Again he hangs up. This time, Beauvoir asks the telephone operator to try the number for her. 'Please be patient and stay on the line for a moment . . .' says the operator in a reassuring accent. Success. Algren agrees to meet her in the lobby in half an hour.

Clutching a book to identify herself, Beauvoir awaits her date. It was 'as if I were going to an interview arranged by a marriage bureau'. When Algren, at thirty-eight a year younger than Beauvoir, walks in, communication in person is no easier than it was on the phone. Sitting next to him in the bar, Beauvoir finds that 'I lose half his sentences.' He also is barely able to penetrate her pronounced French accent, or understand her broken English, as she enthuses over the 'thrillings' (thrillers) she has seen at the movies. But language is unimportant. He finds her attractive. 'Mlle de Beauvoir,' the *New Yorker* had reported, is 'the prettiest Existentialist you ever saw; also eager, gentle, modest and as pleased as a Midwesterner with the two weeks she spent in New York.' A 'complicity immediately sprang up between us', Beauvoir confesses. The description she has been given of him, unstable, moody, neurotic, inclines her in his favour. Tall, fair, good-looking behind his wire-rimmed glasses, a Midwesterner of Swedish-Jewish stock (his father Americanized the name Abraham), he has already done time in gaol for stealing a typewriter, and written two published novels. He offers to show her Chicago's underworld; to Beauvoir, repelled by American luxury, he could not have made a better offer.

'I introduced her to stick up men, pimps, baggage thieves, whores and heroin addicts,' recalled Algren. 'I knew many such that year. I took her on a tour of the County Jail and showed her the electric chair.' A petite brunette, the type Algren favoured, Beauvoir intrigued him with her 'furious curiosity' to know and understand the world. 'Simone de Beauvoir's eyes were lit by a light-blue intelligence,' he wrote. 'She was possessed by something like total apprehension.'

On West Madison Avenue, Chicago's Bowery, Nelson and Simone – the American will never call her Castor – walk into a bar. Chicago's flotsam and jetsam inhabit it; cripples and prostitutes dance. Madness and ecstasy. 'It is beautiful,' says Beauvoir. The remark pleases Algren, because it seems typically French. 'With us,' he says, 'beautiful and ugly, grotesque and tragic, and also good and evil – each has its place. Americans don't like to think that these extremes can mingle.' Satisfied that this place fascinates her, he says: 'I'm going to show you something even better.'

Better means his apartment in Wabansia Avenue, in the Polish section of Chicago. Algren lives in a 'hovel', with no bathroom or fridge, and takes showers in the YMCA. In *The Mandarins* Beauvoir describes the moment when Anne, trapped in a sexless marriage with Robert Dubreuilh, is taken by Lewis Brogan to his apartment. Embarrassed by the dirty sheets, he goes to fetch clean linen; when he returns, 'Anne' is already naked in bed.

'I'm very comfortable,' I said, pulling the warm sheet up to my chin, that sheet in which he had slept the night before. He moved away, came back again.

'Anne!'

The way he said it moved me deeply. He threw himself on me and for the first time I spoke his name. 'Lewis!'

'Anne! I'm so happy!'

He was naked. I was naked, and felt no constraint; he couldn't hurt me by looking at me, for he didn't judge me, didn't compare me. From head to toe, his hands were learning my body by heart. Again I said: 'I like your hands.'

'Do you like them?'

'All evening, I've been wondering if I'd feel them on my body.'
'You'll feel them all night long,' he said.

Suddenly, he was no longer either awkward or modest. His desire transformed me. I who for so long had been without taste, without form, again possessed breasts, a belly, a sex, flesh; I was as nourishing as bread, as fragrant as the earth. It was so miraculous that I didn't think of measuring my time or my pleasure; I know only that before we fell asleep I could hear the gentle chirpings of dawn.

Je possédais de nouveau des seins, un ventre, un sexe, une chair; j'étais nourrissante comme le pain, odorante comme la terre. Algren had awakened Beauvoir to love and sensuality. It would be the most passionate relationship of her life.

*

Beauvoir smells coffee. She opens her eyes and smiles when she sees her blue woollen dress enfolded in Algren's grey jacket. Reclaimed by the French consulate for lunch and a tour of the city, she persuades her hosts to drive her back to the Polish quarter, and to 1523 West Wabansia Avenue, with its rows of wooden shacks, its steaming trashcans and flapping newspapers. The dark stretch limo deposits Mlle de Beauvoir outside Algren's 'hovel', and she runs into his arms.

'My impetuosity thrilled him,' remembered Beauvoir. Algren had made love to her the previous night, 'initially because he wanted to comfort me, then because it was passion'. He did so again, responding to Beauvoir's vulnerability under the carapace of confidence: mutual desire reignited the spark between them. For her part, Beauvoir sensed the loneliness and neediness in Algren. His German-Jewish mother, Goldie, had beaten him as a child, and he found it hard to trust women.

A promiscuous man, according to his friend the actor Ted Liss, 'Nelson liked one-night stands – there was no commitment. Nelson went through people – they used him, he used them, and that was all right . . . It was a process of survival – saving energy for friendships that you want for your art.' His marriage was in tatters, and he had drifted from one dead-end job to another, working as a 'pin boy' picking up skittles in bowling alleys, before finally publishing *Never Come Morning*.

The romance of poverty was part of the American's appeal. Simone found it 'refreshing' after the 'heavy scent of dollars' in big hotels. He was a Bohemian, a rebel, who, like herself, had 'lived against' society and suffered for his art: 'He's more or less a communist, of course,' she told Sartre. Born in Detroit on 28 March 1909, and brought to Chicago as a three-year-old, Algren had barely left the working-class neighbourhood in which he had spent most of his life, apart from army service. He was, Beauvoir noted admiringly, 'an authentic native', who had lived 'a classic American writer's life'. The new lovers spent the rest of the afternoon cruising the bars, drinking vodka and discussing gangsters.

'Before going to sleep I have to tell you that I really liked the book very much [Algren's collection of short stories, *The Neon Wilderness*], and I have thought I liked you very much,' wrote Beauvoir in her first letter to Algren from the train to California. 'I did not like to say goodbye, perhaps not to see you again in my whole life.'

He, meanwhile, had discovered Beauvoir's reputation after reading an article about her in the *New Yorker*. Still glowing from her visit, within a week he found Mary Guggenheim, who had fallen in love with him in 1946 and was already regretting her hospitable impulse to divulge her lover's name, on his Wabansia doorstep. Twenty-four-year-old Mary had impetuously given up her job and apartment to move, uninvited, to Chicago. Nelson slept with the young woman, toured the same lowlife dives as he had with Simone, but soon lost his temper. 'Get your douche-bag out of my house,' he ordered her. 'Nelson constantly got angry with women,' remembered Liss. 'He was a bit of a misogynist.' Mary left, and Algren wrote to entreat Simone, his 'little Gauloise', to return to Chicago. He had been awarded a thousand dollars from the American Academy and Institute of Arts and Letters. Suddenly, everything was going his way.

*

Reunited in Los Angeles with Natasha Sorokine Moffatt and her husband, Ivan, now a scriptwriter in Hollywood, Beauvoir exchanged the cold winds of Chicago for an intense blue sky, blue sea and the odour of eucalyptus. Ivan was touched by her 'ardour and the vitality of her face and those marvellous blue eyes and lovely smile and laughter', although his plans to make a film of *All Men Are Mortal* fell through. With Natasha as her driver, Beauvoir continued her lecture tour at the University of California at Berkeley, at Mills College, at Westwood, and other universities. With Natasha she toured Arizona, New Mexico and the South.

In New York Beauvoir had already grown close to the black writer Richard Wright, his wife Ellen, a white American from Brooklyn, and their small daughter. An outing with Richard and Ellen to the Savoy, a dance hall, had given her her first taste of racism. Ellen had already told her how, when she walked with her little girl in Greenwich Village, she heard 'unpleasant comments'. Now, men dart hostile looks at Wright, a black man with two white women. Taxi drivers deliberately refuse to stop for them. Beauvoir who, disdaining all advice, had walked alone into the centre of Harlem that morning, and felt that 'because I'm white, whatever I think and say and do, this curse [of racism] weighs on me as well', climbs the stairs at the dance hall with a light heart. Wright's friendship, his presence at her side, 'is a kind of absolution'.

In the South Beauvoir falls in love with New Orleans, where, in the Old Quarter, she hears the best jazz of her trip. But, as in Harlem, individual incidents impress the reality of racism upon her. In Texas,

> Everywhere we go, there's the smell of hatred in the air – the arrogant hatred of whites, the silent hatred of blacks . . . American niceness has no place here. In the crowded line outside the bus, the blacks are jostled. 'You aren't going to let that negress get on in front of you,' a woman says to a man in a voice trembling with fury.

In the Greyhound bus, a pregnant black woman faints. 'Everyone jeers – these women are always making trouble.' Beauvoir and Natasha dare not give up their seats in front, for the whole bus would oppose it. When the bus reaches town, the two Frenchwomen try to help the fainting woman, but she is afraid and stumbles away. The 'great tragedy of the South pursues us like an obsession'.

*

Nelson's letters were waiting for Beauvoir in New York, entreating her to return to Chicago. On 24 April she wrote from Philadelphia that this would be difficult, as she had only two more weeks left in the USA, and more lectures to give. Could Nelson come to New York? Her thoughts were turning to Sartre, whom she missed more and more. In long, twice-weekly letters she poured out her longing to see him again. 'I love you, you're my life,' she told him on 9 March. 'I depend entirely upon you,' she wrote four days later. 'We are as one.' A month later she booked her flight home for 10 May, and asked Sartre to keep the first fortnight free just for her: 'I mean seeing just you and Bost and nobody else.' Beauvoir was afraid of leaving 'the perpetual party' which was New York, a city she had come to adore.

On 8 May the bombshell dropped. A cable arrived from Sartre asking her to postpone her return for ten days: Beauvoir realized that his Josephine, Dolorès, who was reigning in Paris in her stead, was refusing to leave her Napoleon. The usurper had dethroned Castor.

'I had . . . a dreadful "breakdown", which kept me in tears all day,' replied Beauvoir. 'Shattered', insomniac, 'not eating, and drinking like a fish', she sought oblivion by trying pot for the first time in her life. Bernard Wolfe, a former secretary of Trotsky's, now working as an editor, took her to smoke marijuana in the apartment of a 'marvellous black dancer, with a party of homosexuals and lesbians. They were all "high", as they say, and I was told that with one cigarette I would be too . . .' But Beauvoir smoked six joints, without anything happening, and in fury downed more than half a bottle of whisky. 'I wanted to walk about on the arm of a man who, temporarily, would be mine.' She called a married man in New York, one of two with whom she'd had 'a couple of flings', but he didn't want to lie to his wife. On Saturday she flew to Chicago to join Nelson.

'We shall never have to wake up, because it was not a dream; it is a wonderful true story which is only just beginning.' In the three days Beauvoir spent with Nelson, in which they barely left their 'little home' in Wabansia Avenue, or the bed in which she experienced her first 'complete orgasm', she fell deeply in love. Sartre's venomous rejection and Bost's neglect – 'the little bastard' hadn't written her a single letter – enabled her finally to let go of past ties and give herself wholly to the American. Only when Beauvoir became an abandoned Ariadne was she able to experience true passion. Only when she stepped out from under Sartre's shadow was she freed to write her masterpiece, *The Second Sex*.

Before they left Chicago, Nelson gave Beauvoir a silver ring. It was Mexican, of no great value, but she slipped it on, glad to cover the 'empty place' on her ring finger, and wore it for the rest of her life. She persuaded him to fly back to New York with her and they spent the final days of her visit closeted in the Brevoort Hotel, in Greenwich Village. They shared, she wrote, 'the intoxication of a deep under-standing'. Sometimes he was blunt and rude; he was also 'virility incarnate'. Sartre had loved her mind, but Nelson validated Simone as a woman. She, to whom it had always mattered to be regarded as

Sartre's intellectual equal, now welcomed the 'profound self-abandonment' of the act of love. 'Woman,' wrote Simone tremulously, 'bathes in a passive languor; with closed eyes, anonymous, lost, she feels as if borne by waves, swept away in a storm, shrouded in darkness; darkness of the flesh, of the womb, of the grave. Annihilated, she becomes one with the Whole, her ego is abolished . . . her body is no longer an object: it is a hymn, a flame.' From that moment she called him her 'beloved husband', herself a 'loving wife'. Simone, Nelson's 'garrulous little frog', loved her 'sweet crocodile'.

Years later she recalled of Nelson: 'He possessed the rarest of all gifts, which I should call goodness if the word had not been so abused; let me say that he really cared about people.' But Beauvoir did not play fair with her infatuated lover: she told him nothing of Dolorès, nor of her own mixed motives. Weeping against the window of the plane carrying her home, Beauvoir opened the book Nelson had given her and read through tears a poem he had written on the flyleaf:

> I send this book with you
> That it may pass
> Where you shall pass
> Down the murmurous evening light
> Of storied streets
> In your own France
> Simone, I send this poem there, too
> That part of me may go with you.

Part Four

False Gods

1952–68

The Party's lines were sharply defined. Its tactics were determined by the principle that the end justifies the means – all means, without exception.

Arthur Koestler, *Darkness at Noon*

30

Breaking Point

An anti-Communist is a dog . . . After ten years of ruminating, I had come to the breaking point . . . In the language of the Church, this was my conversion.

Jean-Paul Sartre, July 1952

WHEN *les jeux sont faits*, the chips are down, and the game is over, it is by deeds alone than men are judged: this idea haunted Sartre as, with an eye over his shoulder at that 'mocking oracle called History', he wrote the screenplay of *In the Mesh*. Was he to remain locked in mutual bad faith, like Garcin and Estelle in *No Exit*, or was he finally going to seize his freedom and act? For ten years he 'ruminated' over action, or praxis, his leftward path towards the Communist Party as tortuous as the prose in which he examined his motives and morality.

People were sneering at Sartre's notion of a *littérature engagée*. 'The worst artists are the most committed,' an old critic complained. 'Look at the Soviet painters.' An American journalist accused him of being haunted by Flaubert, who had not committed. At Yaddo, Truman Capote queried whether 'the existentialism of Camus and Sartre was, from a Marxist point of view, a cop-out, a new *trahison des clercs*, or an unexpected shot in the arm for wavering political faith'. But in *What is Literature?*, a series of articles in *Les Temps modernes* in 1947, Sartre vigorously defended the 'committed' writer, arguing that although all writers deal with meanings, the 'empire of signs' is prose, by which the writer discloses the world to the reader. Words are 'loaded pistols', he wrote, and the writer must fire them at targets. The Communists remained his chief target as he declared: 'The politics of Stalinist Communism is incompatible in France with the honest practice of the literary craft.'

Poverty was biting deeper. In June 1947 the French bread ration was reduced to 200 grams, lower even than during the Occupation. The Renault workers went on strike and the French Communist Party was ejected from the government. The break-up of French political unity was largely determined by the Cold War and, as Maurice Thorez, General Secretary of the PCF, rejected the Marshall Plan and opposed the colonial war in Indochina, where the French were fighting Ho Chi-minh, Sartre began to find points of agreement. Increasingly defining himself *against* Camus and Koestler, he retreated from asserting pure, ontological freedom and began to justify the use of violence. 'Former communists,' he wrote meaningfully, 'would like to make us see Soviet Russia as enemy number one . . . they would like us to devote all our time to stigmatizing its extortion and its violence.' Stalin's 'machinations', claimed Sartre, were dictated by a desire to protect the Revolution. Violence was a 'setback', but an inevitable one in 'a universe of violence'. He had taken a dangerous step towards accepting that the end justifies the means.

In 1947 Sartre published *Baudelaire*, dedicated to Jean Genet. Critics suggested that the author was projecting his own experiences on to his biographical subject, although they congratulated Sartre on not succumbing to the same temptations as the *poète maudit* who, at seven or eight (crucial ages in Sartre's existential psychoanalysis), chose to reject the world. Hating his stepfather, General Aupick – as Sartre himself had hated Mancy – Baudelaire had proclaimed 'art for art's sake'. Sartre, on the other hand, proposed art to modify the world, and had founded *Les Temps Modernes*, through whose pages the journalist might become an agent of liberation. Savagely attacking the Romantic myth of the poet doomed to solitude and misery because of his artistic nature, he struggled to prove that he had escaped the Nausea, that he existed, that, through his acts, he was realizing his human nature.

But Sartre protested too much. For all his biographical subjects, Baudelaire, Genet and Flaubert, it was the fault of the mothers. Adjusting the facts to suit his thesis that eight is the critical age for a boy, Sartre would argue in *Saint Genet* that Genet's abandonment by his mother (in fact at eight months, not eight years) made him a thief – as Anne-Marie's remarriage had made a thief of Poulou. As a crusading journalist, Sartre convinced himself that he had avoided damage by mothers: but his incestuous relationship with 'ma petite maman' remained the enduring back story of his life. He had lost his illusions, like his golden curls, but he remained trapped under the mesh, in the gluey quicksands of existence.

At La Pouèze, at Christmas, Sartre started writing *Dirty Hands*. The play, based on the murder of Trotsky with an ice-pick in 1940, became anathema to the Communist Party. For all Sartre's claims that the proletariat should be the subject of committed literature, it was another play about middle-class dilemmas. Hugo Barine, like Garcin, like Baudelaire, is tormented by a self-defeating 'corrosive lucidity', and dare not assume his freedom. Hamlet-like, he hesitates over the act of political murder. Set against the backdrop of World War II, in 'Illyria' (Hungary), an occupied country, the play resonated with questions of political morality for an audience disturbed by the Communist coup d'état in Czechoslovakia in February 1948, just two months before *Les Mains Sales* opened.

As Sartre, too, dithered Hamlet-like on the road to Communism, Camus threw down the gauntlet. 'Terror is legitimitized only if we assent to the principle: "the end justifies the means",' he wrote in *Neither Victims nor Executioners* in *Combat*. 'In the Marxist perspective, a hundred thousand corpses are nothing if they are the price of the happiness of hundreds of millions of men.' In his notebook he put it even more starkly. Sketching out the dialogue for a farce, 'L'Impromptu des philosophes', about M. Néant, Mr Nothingness, a pedlar of ideas who ends up in a lunatic asylum, he wrote:

'You're a Marxist now?'
'Yes.'
'Then you'll be a murderer.'
'I have already been one.'
'I too. But I don't want to be any more.'

Camus and Sartre were changing places. Camus, a disillusioned ex-Communist, dreamt of a utopian world without violence. Wrestling with his conscience, with the problem of 'dirty hands' in the *realpolitik* of the Cold War, Sartre, on the other hand, agonized over his ethical choices. As he wrote feverishly, crammed corydrane tablets into his mouth and drew on yet another Boyard, he began to find Dolorès an increasing irritation.

*

On 18 May Beauvoir flew into Paris. To her consternation, Dolorès was still in situ; before getting on the boat to France, she had written frankly to Sartre: 'I am coming determined to do everything I can to make you ask me to stay.' Now she insisted on prolonging her visit until July.

Beauvoir fled, abandoning Paris to her rival. The city was 'dull, dark and dead', she told Algren, as dead as her heart, which ached for him. On 21 May she moved out to a little blue and yellow inn at Saint-Lambert, a village south-west of Paris. It was only a mile from Port-Royal-des-Champs, the famous monastery where Pascal once lived and Racine was educated. Re-immersion in French culture stirred her to raise a question which troubled her in her letters to Nelson: 'I deeply regret your not being able to read French books. Why do not you try to learn?' She suggested he write ten lines of French in each of his letters to her, and she would correct them. But when Nelson did so, he received a ticking-off. Simone was not proud of him: 'The version was all wrong, and you did not do the half of it . . . You are not a smart pupil at all.' Soon he gave up.

But as Beauvoir wrote, kissing was better than writing, and it was kissing she missed. Returning to a *mariage blanc*, a sexless 'marriage' with Sartre, underlined her sacrifice. 'I feel unhappy,' she wrote to Nelson. 'Let me cry a little. It would be so fine to cry in your arms. I cry because I do not cry in your arms . . . What is to be done when there is this dreadful Atlantic Ocean between you and the man you love?'

Coming back was too hard. She could barely do it. *Chavirée*, in a state of nervous collapse, for two months Simone hid out in the suburbs, isolated from her friends:

> [I experienced] an anxiety that bordered on mental aberration. To calm myself, I began to take orthedrine. For the moment it allowed me to regain my balance; but I imagine that this expedient was not entirely unconnected with the anxiety attacks I suffered from at that time . . . accompanied by a physical panic that my greatest fits of despair, even when enhanced by alcohol, had never produced . . . Suddenly I was becoming a stone, and the steel was splitting it. *C'est l'enfer*: that is hell.

Concerned at her emotional state, as she twisted the ring on her finger, abandoned her notes on women and mooned over the 'potboiler' she was writing on America, Sartre joined the Beaver for the fortnight he had promised her. Together they walked along the grassy paths once trodden by Jean Racine. On certain evenings Sartre would go into Paris to meet Dolorès; when he did not do so there would be dramatic telephone calls. When he returned to Paris, Dolorès let him know that she was not prepared to compromise: she wanted marriage, total commitment from Sartre, and refused his offer to be set up in a flat as a mistress. 'She was the only woman who frightened me,' wrote Beauvoir. 'She frightened me because she was hostile.'

Dolorès refused to accept the pact between Sartre and Beauvoir: 'To maintain through all deviations from the main path a "certain fidelity".' 'I have been faithful to thee, Cynara, in my fashion' was still their mantra. 'Complete fidelity' is a 'mutilation', wrote Beauvoir, determined to have as many adventures on the side as any man; but the dangers inherent in the pact, that one partner might prefer a new love to the old, and the other partner feel betrayed, had brought it to breaking point. 'In place of two free persons, a victim and torturer confront each other,' wrote Beauvoir.

To her credit, Vanetti refused to become Sartre's compliant victim. When he put her back on the boat at Le Havre, she told him that she would come back either never or for good. As he waved her goodbye, Sartre brooded remorsefully. The Sartrean family, eager to maintain the status quo, had closed ranks round Beauvoir, and behaved, said Vanetti, with 'incredible cruelty' towards her. She described the 'will power and implacable harshness' of the family, once Sartre had made it clear that he only wanted her in a compartment of his life, like his other mistresses. Sartre was a sex addict: even on the Liberty boat going out to see Dolorès, he had seduced another woman. His women had to fit into his life, as the Beaver so comfortably did, stoking the engine and oiling the wheels of the Sartrean machine. Castor had slipped back into the old pattern, spending nights in her 'toothpaste pink room' at the Hôtel de la Louisiane, lunching with Sartre at rue Bonaparte, reading submissions to their review in the afternoon, visiting the studio to watch a screening of *The Chips Are Down*, sharing a trip to London. But in Scandinavia the tension between them was tangible. 'I wondered in terror if we had become strangers to one another,' wrote Beauvoir: she and Sartre had nothing to say to each other. Abandoning him to Wanda, she went on a solo walking tour of Corsica. There she made the decision to return to Nelson.

He was suffering too. 'I did not think that I could ever miss anyone so badly,' he wrote to her in July. 'If I were to hold you now I should cry with pain and happiness.' Algren was ready to propose. Divorced from his wife in 1945, after seven years of marriage, he was free to respond to Simone's pleas to 'take me in your arms and kiss me and make me your wife once more'. She no longer had sexual relations with Sartre, so he hoped she would consent to staying permanently in their 'Wabansia nest', 'cooking his pot roast and maybe washing his socks in the kitchen sink'. He was waiting for her to return to America before asking her formally: but on 23 July he received a letter from Simone which shook him. 'Nelson, I love you,' she wrote. 'But do I deserve your love if I do not give you my life? I tried to explain to you I cannot give my life to you. Do you understand it? Are you not resentful about it? . . . I just know that whatever happens, I could never give everything to you and I just feel bad about it.'

Beauvoir's honesty was hard for Nelson to comprehend. He replied that he understood completely. Just because one could not give up one's life, it did not mean that one did not love deeply: they would love much more than many married couples. But he had missed her meaning. In one of her most insightful pieces of self-analysis, Beauvoir explained that she wanted to live life on her own terms:

> You see, it has never been very easy for me to live, though I am always very happy – maybe because I want so much to be happy. I like so much to live and hate the idea of dying one day. And then I am awfully greedy; I want everything from life, I want to be a woman and to be a man, to have friends and to have loneliness, to work much and to write good books, to travel and enjoy myself, to be selfish and to be unselfish . . . You see, it is difficult to get all which I want. And then when I do not succeed, I get mad with anger.

It was a credo which allowed Algren only a peripheral role; how small a one, he would not at first appreciate.

*

On 11 September Nelson's 'Wabansia wife' flew into Chicago, after a turbulent journey from Shannon in which an engine failed and, as the plane landed in the Azores, a tyre burst. Beauvoir had asked Nelson to get in Southern Comfort, ham and jam, and he was waiting anxiously in the apartment for her. 'When I think of seeing you, of feeling you, I become all dizzy in my head,' Beavoir had written fondly, and the reunion was as loving as they both expected. Nelson had been training regularly in the boxing ring 'to keep his figure in shape the way Simone liked it', his friend, the photographer Art Shay, remembered. But once again Algren asked her to stay with him for good, and she explained that this was impossible. He did so many things for her, 'so quietly and tenderly', he brought her to the heights of love in a way Sartre never had, he shared with her the manuscript of his new novel, *The Man with the Golden Arm*, he bought her armfuls of white flowers, he drank and he laughed with her, but it was not enough: politics and culture were dividing them. In the US the Communist purge was spreading, and Algren's liberal friends in the media were losing their jobs. In Chicago his 'outlaw' cronies ignored Beauvoir.

And she was finding Wabansia Avenue, which cost only $10 a month to rent, a little too primitive even for her taste; it was all right for Nelson to push the washing-up to one side to wash his hair, but she was desperate for a proper bath. Nelson asked Shay to help, and the photographer drove Simone to a friend's apartment. 'For some reason, she'd left the bathroom door open,' recalled Shay, who was waiting in the adjoining room, and couldn't resist snapping her. 'She smiled when she heard the clip of the Leica, and went on fixing her hair.' On 23 September Beauvoir flew home, having given her lover just ten days.

In Paris she and Sartre and their friends, Bonafé, Merleau-Ponty and Pontalis, were about to launch their own radio show, the *Temps modernes* hour. Here in France, she explained to Algren, ideas were important: 'The reason I do not stay in Chicago is just this need I have always felt in me to work and to give my life a meaning by working . . . You want to write books . . . I want it too.' But next spring they planned to spend several months together exploring the Mississippi. 'O my love, try not to get married before the spring,' wrote Simone, who knew how lonely he was. 'I love you so much . . . my crocodile, my own Nelson.' 'Please, please, don't take the phoney blonde in our nest,' she implored him. 'She would drink *my* whisky, eat *my* rum-cake, sleep in *my* bed and maybe sleep with *my* husband . . .'

*

The radio show created a furore. Within two broadcasts it was taken off air. The day after de Gaulle's new political party, the Rassemblement du Peuple Français (RPF) had won a landslide victory in the municipal elections, Sartre and his colleagues compared the General to Pétain and Hitler. The duel with the Gaullists led Sartre to break with his old friend Raymond Aron. In the fervent belief that a Third Way was possible for socialists, he founded a new party, the Rassemblement Démocratique Révolutionnaire (RDR), with David Rousset, a socialist and former Trotskyite, who was the author of several books on the concentration camps. Sartre clung to the idea that the revolutionary message of the Resistance could be revived in a neutralist movement which rejected the Cold War and gave Europe a role as an independent peacemaker. 'M. Jean-Paul Sartre has denounced the fatalism which sees war between the two blocs as inevitable,' reported *Combat* in March 1948.

Sartre put his own funds, 300,000 francs, at the disposal of the RDR. For the first time he stepped into the political arena, sharing a platform with Rousset and Georges Altman of *Franc-Tireur* at mass meetings at the Salle Wagram on 19 March, and again at the Salle Pleyel in December. With Camus, Breton, the American Richard Wright and Carlo Levi, he addressed more than 4,000 people: but Aron's criticism of 'revolutionary romanticism' among the RDR leaders had more than a ring of truth. Whatever his fantasies, Sartre was no Lenin. As Rousset said, Sartre lived in a bubble. Nor was he any closer to the Soviets. Alexander Fadeyev, head of the Union of Soviet Writers, in Paris for the Cominform-inspired peace conference on 20 April 1949, described him as 'a jackal with a fountain pen'. Fadayev and the novelist Ilya Ehrenbourg, who had spied for the Soviets in Spain in the 1930s, as Koestler had probably also done, were among the Soviet deputation, bent on a much-needed public relations exercise. Tightening their stranglehold on Eastern Europe, the Russians were blockading Berlin. The peace rally, for which Picasso designed his famous dove, was boycotted by Sartre.

In Paris the January trial of the Russian defector Viktor Kravchenko, author of *I Chose Freedom*, which became, in Beauvoir's words, 'a trial of the USSR', revealed beyond doubt the existence of the Soviet labour camps. In *Les Temps modernes*, in January 1950, Merleau-Ponty and Sartre finally admitted that the gulags existed, but they continued to argue that the USSR was 'broadly on the side of the forces that are fighting against the familiar forms of exploitation'. The camps were a provisional stage in the revolution: 'We have the same values as a Communist,' affirmed Merleau-Ponty ambiguously.

And now Sartre had grown suspicious of Rousset, who had gone to America in search of RDR funding. Rousset agreed to take Marshall Plan 'candy' to put on a counter-conference, the International Day of Resistance to Dictatorship and War, on 30 April 1949. Beauvoir advised Sartre not to attend: Sidney Hook, an academic whom she had met in New York and knew as a 'frenzied anti-Communist', was speaking at the peace conference. Beauvoir had smelt a rat, although she did not know that Hook, a former Marxist, had close links as a 'consultant' to the newly created CIA (Central Intelligence Agency), which from 1949 used Marshall Plan funds to service its Cold War espionage and covert action. In October, Sartre defected from the RDR, which collapsed.

'Splitting up of the RDR. Hard blow,' wrote Sartre in his notebook. 'Fresh and definitive apprenticeship to realism. One cannot create a movement.' The pope of existentialism's dogmas had turned out to have little link with reality, and the isolation of his position was proving hard to bear. In an explosion of alcohol and emotion, he had broken with Koestler. During his 1948 lecture tour of the United States, the Hungarian had also been approached by the CIA: William Donovan, one of its chief architects, asked for his help in countering the Communist 'peace' offensive. 'Discussed need for psychological warfare,' noted Koestler in his journal. An important early adviser to the British government's Information Research Department (IRD), set up by Foreign Secretary Ernest Bevin in February 1948 to put forward 'a rival ideology to Communism', Koestler used his pre-war experience in the Soviet propaganda machine to help the West. Having convinced the Americans and British of the need to recruit intellectuals from the non-Communist Left, he became the moving spirit in *The God that Failed*, a collection of essays by André Gide, Richard Wright, Stephen Spender and others critical of Stalinism.

Like Sartre, Koestler believed in engagement, but unlike Sartre he was prepared to work within existing power structures. When he came out as a Gaullist, Sartre was horrified. One night Koestler invited Sartre, Beauvoir and Camus to go out with him and Mamaine to a Russian night-club, where the party drank heavily. Sartre was flirting with Mamaine when, shouting, 'No friendship without political agreement,' Koestler threw a glass at him, which smashed against the wall. As they stumbled out of the night-club, Koestler hit Camus, who threw a punch back at him before collapsing into vodka-fuelled tears. 'He was my friend! And he hit me!' moaned Camus.

When Koestler returned to Paris and ran into Sartre again, he suggested another meeting. The little man took out his notebook, studied it and changed his mind. 'We have nothing more to say to each other,' he said as he put the diary away.

Swimming in the murky waters of politics, Sartre was struggling to keep his head above water. His need for his 'old wife' had never been greater. Watching her pack for a four-month stay with Algren, his fear grew that she might leave him for good. The balance of power was changing. In an important, unpublished letter dated by Castor May 1948, Sartre poured out his love, promising that he would not leave her for Dolorès. 'My sweet little one,' he wrote, explaining that he was bored with his usual form of address, 'Mon charmant Castor', which had become conventional. His *'erlebnisse'*, 'emotions' in their secret language, were all over the place:

> *Mon Dieu*, how wonderful it is to write to someone you truly love
> . . . No exaggeration: I'm good with you, I mean it. No dramas, no
> trembling voice. *La verité est que vous me manquez*, the truth is that
> I miss you and that I couldn't live very long without you. Three
> months is okay . . . four at a pinch . . . If you didn't exist, instead
> of being a normal sort of guy, I'd be romantically mourning my
> solitude. And your little face. Full of integrity; how it pleases me
> . . . I don't want you to come back, I know that you're happy, but
> I feel rubbish without you and my *real* love has nowhere to go . . .
> You are the only person whom I love *as I am*, without faking, with
> nothingness, with thoughtless mistakes, but the way we want to be
> in our morality: with *consciousness* of everything and acceptance.
> It's certainly through you that I shall be saved . . . *Nous autres deux
> c'est bien.*

Sartre had plenty to apologize over. An American journalist named Sally Swing had approached him at the Cannes Film Festival. She was only twenty-four, but Sartre began a new affair with her, which he complained wore him out sexually. It was the one respect in which 'she kills me. I very punctiliously do as I'm told, but finally it becomes mere conscientiousness, doesn't it, it's boring.' Swing remained in Paris to cover the visit of Princess Elizabeth, and saw him every night: 'Invariably . . . I mount and submit.' But she was only a *'bon camarade'*, insisted Sartre, 'sweet and reasonable . . . She's *really* trying to see our affair as only a two-month fling . . . I would easily get bored with her if she wasn't so *very* nice.'

The Americans were pressing him to leave Castor: *'Plaque Simone et vis avec Dolorès,* drop Simone and live with Dolorès. I went white with rage, as you know I do sometimes and I said: "All you get through blackmail it to turn me against you all . . . If you don't want Dolorès to suffer a lot, shut up *parce que j'en ai plein le cul*, I'm fucked off with it all.'

Sartre was seeing another American woman by the name of Claude Day, with whom he went out on the Thursday after Beauvoir left.

> She'd lost her lighter in the Harris bar. Naturally it was gold and had cost 300 dollars . . . I *hate* people who poison your evening because they've lost something . . . The conversation revolved around two subjects: D and the lighter. She urged me to leave you, said that D would leave Teddy [her husband] on these terms. As I politely refused this bargain, she regarded me with a suspicious air and made this remark from grand classical comedy: 'What is there, really, between Simone and you?' That was *the first time* I went white with anger. *Elles me font chier.* They're a heap of shit, all of them, Claude, Jacqueline, and even Dolorès at times. I have never hidden the fact that I'm deeply fond of you (lied only over the *nature* of my feelings . . .) and that I shall *not* leave you. I am not a puppet . . . Not me.

Sartre went back to Day's flat, where she did her best to seduce him ('naked breasts, kimono, abandon . . .'). In the small hours he assured her that he loved Dolorès, 'because *la Claude* is not only an official, she's a spy'.

The news that Sartre was digging his heels in had already reached Dolorès, who changed her mind about coming to France in Beauvoir's absence. Anxious not to leave Sartre alone too long, Beauvoir decided to cut her visit to Algren by half.

In Chicago she funked telling Nelson that she was returning after only two months. The right moment never seemed to come. He had been so confident of their relationship, fondly sending her a list of 'frog commandments' in December: to have no other crocodiles but him, never to make light of him, to be a faithful frog and covet nothing but him. He had slept with no other woman, since meeting her, despite her insistence that he should not deprive himself of pleasure. The loner had surrendered to love. When Beauvoir wrote: 'The frog would give everything belonging to her to her crocodile (including life if it is was *really* necessary),' he had believed her. They had originally planned to spend as much as six months together retracing the steps of Mark Twain in a riverboat. He hoped she would never go home.

Now, steaming down the Mississippi, exploring the Yucatán, Simone let the days drift by. Her boyfriend had never been more attentive and loving, nor had their bodies been so in harmony, as they travelled lazily through Mexico. Finally, on the bus to Morelia, Nelson's 'frog wife' blurted out: 'I have to be back in Paris on 14 July.'

'Oh, all right,' said Nelson.

But when Beauvoir went shopping for embroidered blouses in the market, Algren walked out on her. At Taxco, among the silver mines, as she picked out some jewellery, he muttered crossly: 'After two days I'd be letting off a revolver in the streets just to make something happen.'

'Nelson *very bad*,' she recorded in their joint diary.

Abandoning their tour, the couple flew to New York. Beauvoir plied Algren with questions: 'Why are you spoiling everything? Don't you care for me as much as you did?'

'No,' he said. 'It's not the same any more.'

Their hotel room in the Village was burning hot. Beauvoir sucked on raspberry ice cream; Algren was sunk in a sullen mood. 'I can leave tomorrow,' she offered.

He turned a tormented face towards her: 'I'm ready to marry you this moment.'

At last Beauvoir realized the extent of his pain. When she flew home, she didn't know if it was the end of the affair.

On her return, she discovered that Dolorès had relented. Sobbing down the telephone, she had begged Sartre to spend a month with her in the South of France. He agreed. Beauvoir at once cabled Algren asking if she could return. 'No,' he replied. 'Too much work.'

*

Camus was watching Sartre's movements with horror. Like Gide, who after visiting Africa in 1925 became aware of colonial exploitation, so Sartre's visit to America in 1945 had raised his consciousness of racism. Like Gide in 1935, Sartre in 1950 was abandoning individualism in order to champion the underdog. The Cold War had closed off the possibility of the third way, and left no room for manoeuvre. Camus famously said that he did not learn about freedom from Marx: 'I learnt it from poverty.' Sartre, on the other hand, who had never been poor, learnt from the poverty of the blacks that you can't make an omelette without breaking eggs. Freedom would have to be subordinated to 'realism', violence and the gulag. For Camus, this signified betrayal, although to Sartre it seemed that his old friend had fled politics for morality.

In June 1948 Camus was reconciled with Maria Casarès, now a

famous actress, who left her latest lover, the actor Jean Servais, to go back to him. While they had been estranged, Sartre, unable to resist the line of women willing to climb on to the casting couch, probably slept with her. Casarès played the female lead, Hilda, in *Le Diable et le Bon Dieu* (*The Devil and the Good Lord*), in June 1951, her name billed above Wanda's on the posters. Certainly there was a 'personal episode' that Camus found 'disagreeable'. Was this, asked Beauvoir, 'the business of the woman you'd had an affair with yourself?' Although Sartre did not openly confess, he implied that Casarès had showed Camus letters from Sartre. Was it pay back for Camus's seduction of Wanda?

As the atmosphere between them soured, Sartre and Camus gave up their weekly lunch in 1949. But when North Korea invaded the South in 1950, and people began to panic about a possible Soviet invasion of France, Camus's concern for his old friend remained. 'The day the Russians march into Paris,' said Francine Camus, 'I shall kill myself and my two children.'

'Have you thought what you will do when the Russians get here?' Camus asked Sartre.

'I shall never fight the proletariat.'

'You mustn't make a mystique out of the proletariat,' retorted Camus.

'We felt a great distance between us,' recalled Simone. 'Yet it was with real warmth that he urged Sartre: "You must leave. If you stay . . . they'll cart you off to a camp and you'll die."' Sartre flatly refused to leave France, although Algren, convinced that General MacArthur was about to unleash World War III, invited Sartre and Beauvoir to stay at his new house on Lake Michigan. It was out of the question: the arms race was escalating; it was the year Truman ordered the H-bomb to go into production. 'We had never detested America more violently than we did at that moment.'

For Maurice Merleau-Ponty the Korean War was a turning point. *Les Temps modernes* failed to comment on it for several months: Merleau-Ponty, whose cool intellectualism had previously moderated Sartre's emotional response to politics, decided to remain silent. He would henceforth call Communism 'the opium of the intellectuals'.

*

Nelson had been sending rice, condensed milk, preserved butter and corned beef to Beauvoir's widowed mother, Françoise, who was hard-up and depended on her small allowance from her daughter. Françoise, who lived at 8bis rue Blomet, in the 15th *arrondissement*, often lunched with Beauvoir, and expressed her gratitude. Nelson's letters to Beauvoir grew warmer again. 'I was deeply moved when I read in your letter that you loved, as well as my eyes, my ways in love,' she had written after returning from Wabansia.

> I have always had the same eyes but I never loved anybody in these ways, you have to know, with such pleasure in love and so much love in pleasure, so much fever and peace, in this way which you say you like. I really and wholly felt that I was a woman in a man's arms, and it meant much, so much for me. Nothing better could have been given to me. Good night, honey . . . Just come to me darling, and take me with your strong, soft, greedy hands. I wait for them. I wait for you.

Beauvoir had given up sleeping with Bost when she returned from New York. In April 1948 she'd been to the dentist, to have the tooth replaced which had been knocked out five years earlier: 'I have a brand-new tooth, all gold and white . . . Everybody tells me I am much nicer to see . . . Do you know why I had it done? Yea, you know . . . I want you to have a girl with a whole smile.' And she had asked Stépha to find her a gynaecologist, and been fitted with a diaphragm, all for Nelson.

Now, she brooded over their last parting. If she had had the 'honesty and intelligence' to tell Nelson that she was leaving early at the beginning of their trip up the Mississippi, his disappointment would have been less bitter. She had lied to him, pretending that she had to return to France in mid-July because Sartre needed her to work on a movie script with him. 'But then, suddenly . . . the producers changed their minds.' It is unlikely that Nelson believed her, and her ruthlessness in cutting short the holiday left him aware of all he missed: 'A woman of my own and perhaps a child of my own.' She had 'Sartre and a settled way of life . . . I live a sterile existence,' he wrote. Nelson became involved in another short-lived relationship: 'Because no arms are warm when they're on the other side of the ocean; I know that life is too short and too cold for me to reject all warmth for so many months.'

The affair fizzled out, and Nelson returned 'to my typewriter and my loneliness'. The long-distance relationship with Simone fired up again. Her letters were still loving: 'I still feel your chest so warm against my breasts.' There is no doubt that the little frog wife who wanted to live in her crocodile's stomach was a changed woman. Nelson had penetrated the armour she had built around her emotions, symbolized by her helmet-like turban; aroused, fulfilled, she had become confident in her own sexuality. '[There is] a question every thinking woman in the Western world must have posed herself one time or another,' Angela Carter once wrote. 'Why is a nice girl like Simone wasting her time sucking up to a boring old fart like J.-P.? Her memoirs will be mostly about him; he will scarcely speak about her.'

But Beauvoir could not give up her 'necessary love' for Sartre. It was the central project of her life, the one which gave her life meaning. More rock-solid than marriage, in her eyes, she was less inclined to give it up in July 1948, when she was on the verge of vanquishing Vanetti, than ever before. She tried to explain to Nelson the protective, maternal feelings she had for Sartre. Were she to give him up,

> I should be a dirty creature, a treacherous and selfish woman . . . What you have to know . . . is in which way Sartre needs me. In fact, he is very lonely, very tormented inside himself, very restless, and I am his only true friend, the only one who really understands him, helps him, works with him, gives him some peace and poise. For nearly twenty years he did everything for me; he helped me to live, to find myself . . . Now, since four, five years, it is the time when I can give what he did for me . . . I could not desert him.

It was a touching speech; its only fault was that it omitted any mention of Vanetti, a key player in this game of tug-of-love; of her existence, Nelson was still kept in ignorance. He, like Dolorès, was treated like a mistress.

What Beauvoir really wanted was to integrate Nelson into her life in Paris, and by 1949 she had her own Parisian 'nest' to offer him. In October 1948 she moved into a furnished *atélier*, or studio, in the rue de la Bûcherie, a narrow, pretty street leading down to the banks of the Seine, opposite the Île de la Cité. Pursued by journalists at the Louisiane, she sought privacy, and a home of her own to share with her 'husband'.

From one window in the studio she could look down to the Seine: 'I could see the river, ivy, trees, Notre-Dame.' Opposite was a café, Le Café des Amis, which soon became a favourite. '*Vous ne vous ennuierez jamais*, you'll never be bored,' said her friend Lola, wife of Mouloudji, who had tipped her off about the studio. 'You only have to look out of the window.' Lola was right: in the morning rag-pickers wheeled prams piled high with junk along the road; winos sat on the pavements drinking; cats wandered over the roofs. The vet's, 'under the patronage of the Duke of Windsor', was full of barking dogs. *'Je me plaisais dans mon nouveau logis*, I was very pleased with my new home,' discovered Beauvoir. She put red curtains at the windows and red blankets on the bed, bought some green bronze lamps designed by Giacometti, and hung souvenirs from her travels on the walls and ceiling beam.

One warm day in early June, Simone went to meet Nelson from the boat train at Saint-Lazare station. They had parted badly, and she was apprehensive. Devouring the passengers with her eyes, she waited – and waited. He wasn't there. Slowly she walked back to the studio, sat on the divan and lit a cigarette. *Soudain une voix américaine monta dans la rue.* Algren was in the street outside, weighed down with the mountain of luggage that had prevented him from getting off the train with the other passengers. He had brought her chocolates, whisky and a flowered housecoat. Would he show her the sullen face he had worn in their last days in New York? *Non: il avait l'air rayonnant.* He was radiant.

The four months Simone and Nelson spent together that summer were probably their happiest time. The first hurdle, an introduction to Sartre, was soon overcome, with Michèle Vian ('Zazou') translating. Beauvoir introduced Nelson to her 'leftist' friends, Juliette Gréco, Scipion and Raymond Queneau; he drank cocktails with Gaston Gallimard, went boxing with Jean Cau, drank champagne at the Lido and listened to Yves Montand. In a new *cave*, the Club Saint-Germain started by Boubal from Le Flore, he and Simone danced the bebop. There was all the Old World to see: in Rome Nelson played *boules* with Carlo Levi and lunched in the Piazza Navona; in Naples he snapped the street urchins. 'Ischia remains our paradise,' recalled Simone. The lovers lounged on the beach, walked the ruins of Pompeii, travelled on to Tunis and the island of Djerba. Algiers, Fez, Marrakesh. 'Algren's eyes opened wider and wider.' In the South of France they stayed with Olga and Bost at Cabris, and played roulette in Monte Carlo. Gréco sang, '*Si tu t'imagines*', and Nelson danced with a chair.

September was spent in Paris. An Indian summer. 'Never had we got on better.' Beauvoir's heart closed up as she put Algren on the plane at Orly.

Had it been only a fantasy? The next summer Simone returned to America, glad to escape the torrent of abuse that descended on her when *The Second Sex* was published. Algren, who had won the National Book Award for *The Man with the Golden Gun*, was at his house at Miller, on Lake Michigan.

When she arrived, he told her that he no longer loved her. 'Algren's need to destroy love has to be accepted, finally, as a tragic but undeniable part of his personality,' writes his biographer. His track record with women was abysmal, and his addiction to gambling and alcohol contributed to the breakdown of the relationship, for which Beauvoir cannot wholly be blamed.

One afternoon she walked down the sandy beach beside the lake. 'In the water I took great care not to lose my footing because I could barely swim.' Within minutes she was out of her depth, her head disappearing under the water. Nelson did not hear her shouts of 'Help!' and continued to smile at her. Finally he pulled her out. Back at the house, warming up over a whisky, passion flared up again 'from the scar tissue of our lost love'. But solitary days followed, when Beauvoir watched *Brief Encounter* and soaked the cushions with her tears. On the day that she flew home, Nelson lost all his money at the races. It was the end of the affair.

*

Sartre was, indeed, short of friends, although he had a court of sycophants. Increasingly he turned to the homosexual Jean Genet, whose autobiographical *Journal of a Thief*, dedicated to both Sartre and Beauvoir, showed him a way out of his ethical impasse. Genet's criminal counter-culture had its own morality: 'What I call violence is passive courage infatuated by danger.' Glorifying the life of crime that leads to prison, the only place in which he feels secure, Genet boasts that his courage consists in making up new reasons for living. Reversing the negativity of the slave, who to his master is an object, he discovers his own subjectivity in what his master calls evil. Abject, alienated, controlled by the Other, only in the act of revolt does he realize himself.

In 1950 Sartre alienated the Communists even further by writing a sympathetic preface to a book on Tito: *'Il faut repenser le marxisme, il faut repenser l'homme.* We must rethink Marxism, we must rethink man.' After the failure of the RDR, it became his new project. On holiday with Dolorès in the South of France, he had spent twelve hours a day, to her irritation, struggling to complete his promised work on ethics. Finally, abandoning the unwieldy 360,000-word manuscript, as well as the unfinished fourth novel of *Les Chemins de la liberté*, 'La Dernière Chance, The Last Chance', he began writing a preface to Genet's collected works. 'All I know,' he wrote in a letter, 'is that I'd like to create a morality in which evil is an integral part.' 'What can man do . . . if we admit that evil exists in the world?' Juxtaposing the tragic, brutal history of Europe against that of the young, optimistic America, he argued in 1949 that the problem of evil was integral to European thought:

> If I compare French rationalism to American rationalism, I'd say that American rationalism is white, in the sense of white magic, and that French rationalism is a black rationalism . . . it is always a pessimism.

Now Sartre, who had condemned Baudelaire for his passivity, confessed his profound admiration for Genet's moral extremism: Genet, the gay thief, was 'a hero of our time'. The preface grew, out of control. It became an extended essay on Good and Evil, but also a form of possession, a literary rape of Genet, who was never able to write again after the publication of Sartre's monstrous *Saint Genet, Comédien et Martyr*.

Sartre's stepping-stones to Communism were joining up. The contradiction tearing him apart had become intolerable. His notebooks trace his anguish: 'For my liberty implied the liberty of other men. And all men were not free . . . And I could not be free alone.' He took a final step towards the abnegation of individual freedom in *The Devil and the Good Lord*, a play about the Peasants' War in the sixteenth century. Of all his plays it was the one of which he was most proud. There are many resemblances between Genet and Sartre's protagonist, Goetz, another bastard 'who seeks the Absolute in Evil', but in Goetz's journey from theoretical *engagement* to liberation struggle, the audience may have guessed they were witnessing Sartre's own. 'There is this war to fight, and I will fight it,' says Goetz, as he stabs an officer to death. In this gratuitous act of violence, Sartre signs his submission to the Party.

In Koestler's novel *Darkness at Noon*, the prisoner Rubashov disputes morality with Ivanov, his interrogator. ' "*Apage Satanas!* Get thee behind me, Satan!" repeated Ivanov . . . "I would like to write a Passion Play in which God and the Devil dispute for the soul of Saint Rubashov." ' Now Sartre had written that play, and sided with Stalin, a slaughterer of lambs. *The Devil and the Good Lord*, wrote Beauvoir, was 'the mirror of Sartre's entire ideological evolution'. 'I was a victim and an accomplice in the class struggle,' he wrote.

> A victim because I was hated by an entire class. An accomplice because I felt both responsible and powerless . . . After ten years of

rumination, I had reached breaking point: one light tap was all that was required. In the language of the Church, this was my conversion.

Sartre's political *rapprochement* with the French Communist Party followed soon after. He was approached over the case of Henri Martin, a Communist sailor in the French navy sentenced to five years imprisonment in May 1950 for protesting the conduct of the war in Indochina. Martin's outraged letters to his family over the deaths of the Vietnamese people at the hands of the French colonial forces resonated for Sartre, whose own father had died from a fever caught in the service of French imperial ambition. Martin's letters, dated 'On the Mekong ... 1947', reminded him of Jean-Baptiste's. 'We can be proud of today's toll,' wrote the sailor. 'One child dead and one woman wounded, without considering all the other bodies we have left in the ricefields ... This is how we pacify them. Peace everywhere.' Sartre took the case right to the top, to President Auriol. His theme, *'Il faut rétablir la justice'*, we must restore justice, was as powerful as Voltaire's in the case of Calas, and there is little doubt that Sartre felt he was taking up the baton of Voltaire and Gide in his fight for the 'little people'.

The 'breaking point' came with the arrest of Jacques Duclos, Thorez's deputy in the PCF, put in handcuffs by over-zealous police on 28 May 1952 when the pigeons in his car, which he was bringing home to his wife for dinner, were suspected of being carrier pigeons en route for Moscow, and thus evidence of a Communist plot against the state. Sartre was in Italy with Michèle Vian, writing 'La Reine Albemarle' in his black moleskin notebook, when he read of Duclos's arrest, on the eve of a 20,000-strong Communist demonstration against the arrival in Paris of American General Matthew Ridgeway, apologist for the use of chemical weapons against the Koreans. The PCF had moved into a new militant phase, their sense of national persecution fuelled by McCarthyism in America. Sartre exploded with rage. *'Il fut submergé de colère,'* recalled Beauvoir, when the writer read of the triumph of the Right as the Communist strike of 4 June was brutally crushed.

An anti-Communist is a dog ... In the name of Liberty, Equality and Fraternity, I swore a hatred to the bourgeoisie that would die only with my own death. When I returned abruptly to Paris I had to write or choke.

For five *nuits blanches* he went without sleep. *J'écrivis, le jour et la nuit, la première partie des Communistes et la Paix*. Night and day, I wrote the first part of 'The Communists and the Peace'. In July Sartre's article appeared in *Les Temps modernes*: 'My aim is to declare my agreement with the Communist Party.'

Like an old pony, Sartre went between the shafts. Broken, blinkered, it would only take a tap of the whip for him to trot in whichever direction his Soviet masters pleased.

31

Body Trouble

Woman, like man, *is* her body; but her body is other than herself.'
Simone de Beauvoir, The Second Sex, 1949

'WE DO IT ON THE PREMISES, OURSELVES', read the poster on the door of the offices of *Les Temps modernes*, put up by the secretary, tired of people banging on the door demanding the name and address of an abortionist. In the rue de la Bûcherie, Beauvoir was woken by a young man in the middle of the night: 'My wife is pregnant. Give me an address!' 'But I don't know any,' she protested. 'It wasn't very pleasant to discover that I was apparently thought of as a professional abortionist.' It was June 1949, and Gallimard had sold 22,000 copies of volume one of *The Second Sex* in one week, while monthly editions of *Les Temps modernes*, in which Beauvoir's call to female liberation was serialized, were going like hot cakes.

Attacking the male myths which made of woman the Other, the object of the male gaze, she wrote: 'Man put himself forward as the Subject and considered the woman as the object . . . She is the incidental, the inessential as opposed to the essential . . . he is the Absolute . . . Woman has always been man's dependent, if not his slave.' With startling originality and intellectual courage, Beauvoir took the existentialist idea of the human being as a free consciousness in a world riven by conflict, and applied it to women. Her fundamental argument, that the sexes are equal but different, and that that difference is largely culturally determined, broke the mould of patriarchal thinking as she demonstrated how, the world over, women were oppressed.

Beauvoir's idea of the Self and the Other, developed while writing *She Came to Stay*, when she and Sartre debated Hegel's master/slave theories, was further tuned by the experience of war and the realization of the importance of situation. The belief that 'existence precedes essence', that people create meaning throughout their lives through the power of choice, remained axiomatic to her. And if identity and meaning are continually constructed through existential choices which only end with death, the opportunity to become the author of one's own life is, argued Beauvoir, as much a woman's prerogative as a man's. As beings-for-death, we must live urgently, with passion and conviction. But in 1940s France she saw women's lives cramped and circumscribed in the 'prison-house of home': *On ne nait pas femme: on le devient'*, one is not born a woman, one becomes one.

'The destiny of a woman and her sole glory are to make beat the hearts of men,' wrote Balzac. 'She is a chattel and properly speaking only a subsidiary to man.' It was an opinion shared by Pétain, who made abortion a crime against the state in 1941. But Beauvoir was furious at the double standard of morality she saw ruin the lives of young women. In February 1949 she had told Nelson about the girls she helped: 'There are a lot of abortion affairs just now in France, and I feel quite indignant.' There were one million abortions a year, as many as live births, 'but it is absolutely forbidden. They just arrested one doctor I knew very well and to whom I had sent a lot of worried girls. Another surgeon jumped by [sic] the window last week, because he had been taken in this kind of bad affair.' When a child is born you can send it to war to be killed, 'but when he is in the mother's belly, then it is murder to go anything against him'.

It was only six years since the guillotining of Marie-Jeanne Latour for performing abortions, an act which so outraged Sartre that he created Estelle the baby-killer in *No Exit* in response to it. Simone, who had watched Olga's torment when she aborted in her grandmother's flat during the war, would in 1971 call for abortion to be legalized. But contraception was illegal in France until 1967, abortion outlawed until 1974.

Under the Code Napoléon of 1804 French women had few legal rights. 'Women should stick to knitting,' observed Napoleon to the son of Madame de Staël, and he rolled back the freedoms that women had previously enjoyed under the *ancien régime* and legislated for their total subordination to men. 'The husband must possess the absolute power and right to say to his wife, "Madam, you shall not go to the theatre, you shall not receive such and such a person," ' said Napoleon, ' "for the children you will bear shall be mine." ' Frenchwomen had no parental rights over their own children, unlike in Britain, where the fierce campaign waged by Caroline Norton for custody of her children resulted in the Marriage and Divorce Act of 1857. Nor did they have the equivalent of the British Married Women's Property Act of 1882, which, despite the objection of Lord Fraser that a married woman was already sufficiently protected – 'and why she should be allowed to have money in her pocket to deal with as she thinks fit I cannot understand' – allowed married women in Britain to own property. In Britain a man's right to beat his wife provided that the stick was no thicker than his thumb and to imprison her to force the restitution of his conjugal rights was finally abolished in the case of *Jackson v. Jackson* in 1891. In France a woman remained the sole property of her husband. There was much for Beauvoir to complain about.

Yet in America, where the women of Wyoming won the vote as early as 1869, women still appeared to her as the Other, in a similar relation of *altérité* to men as black slaves to their white masters. In 1947 Algren sent Simone Gunnar Myrdal's *An American Dilemma*, on the race problem. 'I would like to write a book about women as important as [Myrdal's] is about blacks,' she replied. Her friendship with Richard and Ellen Wright, her travels through the Deep South, and Sartre's own shocked encounter with racism, which led him to write *La Putain respectueuse*, were significant factors in formulating her analysis. 'Of all my books [*The Second Sex*] was truly the easiest to write, especially in the beginning,' she discovered. Begun in October 1946 and finished in June 1949, with a six-month gap in between in which she wrote *America Day by Day*, it was also the book of which she remained most proud: 'When all is said and done, it is possibly the book that has brought me the greatest satisfaction of all those I have written.'

Yet there is a sense in which, paradoxically, Beauvoir's message underpins the patriarchy. In 1949, and today in the twenty-first century, her views on motherhood attract criticism. When volume two of *The Second Sex*, on *L'Expérience Vécue*, women's lived experience, burst off the press it created an even greater scandal. Catholic writer Claude Mauriac wrote to one of the contributors to *Les Temps modernes*: 'Your employer's vagina has no secrets from me.' Dubbed indecent, frigid, priapic, nymphomaniac, lesbian, a hundred times aborted, an unmarried mother, Beauvoir was stunned by the reaction to her chapters on 'the Lesbian' and 'Maternity'. She should not have been. Men declared that she had no right to discuss motherhood as she had not herself given birth: 'and they?' was her retort. Feminists criticized her for her negative view of the female body and her rejection of the birth experience.

'Desire,' writes Sartre, 'is defined as *trouble*. If the desiring conscious-ness is *troubled* it is because it is analogous to troubled water.' Desire muddies the clear waters of consciousness, of the translucent cogito. Reason collapses into the chaos of the body and, in the Sartrean philosophy, this is always a failure, a descent into facticity.

For Beauvoir too, the body is lesser. The body is trouble, particularly for a woman. As well as accepting the Cartesian mind/body split, she is complicit with Sartre in privileging the male body, although she goes further than him in worshipping the phallus 'as simple and neat as a finger' and denigrating the female body with its mysterious womb. 'What is a woman?' demands Beauvoir. '*Tota mulier in utero*, woman is a womb.' The uterus, which the ancients thought wandered around the female body causing hysteria, is an object of disgust: 'Concealed, mucous and humid, as it is, it bleeds each month, it is often sullied with bodily fluids, it has a secret and perilous life of its own.' Every female rite of passage is a crisis to be endured, from puberty, which makes of wo-man an 'alienated thing', to the onset of desire:

> Feminine sex desire is the soft throbbing of a mollusc . . . Man dives upon his prey like the eagle and the hawk; woman lies in wait like the carnivorous plant, the bog in which insects and children are swallowed up. She is absorption, leech-like suction, inhalation, she is pitch and glue, a passive demand, insinuating and viscous.

Signifying woman as a flesh-eating plant, a bottomless swamp, a leech, Beauvoir employs many of the same metaphors as Sartre in his own horrified account of *le visqueux*, the slime at the heart of existence, in *Being and Nothingness*. His fear of the viscous represents his fear of the female:

> What it teaches me about the world [is] that it is like a leech sucking me . . . The slimy is *docile*. Only at the very moment when I believe that I possess it, behold, by a curious reversal, *it* possesses me. Here appears its essential character: its softness is leech-like

. . . The For-itself is suddenly *compromised*. I open my hands, I want to let go of the slimy and it sticks to me, it draws me, it sucks at me . . . It is a soft, yielding action, a moist and feminine sucking, it lives obscurely under my fingers, and I sense it like a dizziness; it draws me to it as the bottom of a precipice might draw me . . . I am no longer the master.

Sartre's phobias blossom bizarrely in the next few pages, as he expands on the 'snare of the slimy', which symbolises the 'sugary death of the For-itself'.

The obscenity of the feminine sex is that of everything which 'gapes open' . . . In herself woman appeals to a strange flesh which is to transform her into a fullness of being by penetration and dissolution. Conversely woman senses her condition as an appeal precisely because she is 'in the form of a hole' . . . Beyond any doubt her sex is a mouth and a voracious mouth which devours the penis – a fact which can easily lead to the fear of castration. The amorous act is the castration of the male . . .

Sartre's revulsion from the engulfment he dreaded led him to see the act of love as something to be got over as soon as possible. For him, the penis is 'an instrument which one manages, which one makes penetrate, which one withdraws, which one utilizes'. Emotions are not engaged, as Jean-Paul hurriedly snatches his body back from the death-dealing praying mantis which is woman.

Beauvoir, by contrast, idealizes the male. Man soars like an eagle, woman mustn't even move. Flat on her back in the missionary position, she represents immanence, he transcendence. In a sense, Beauvoir's description of sexual intercourse can be read as a hymn to Algren's penis, the 'pleasure machine' she craves in *The Mandarins*:

I held myself tight against him . . . It was his warmth, his smell, and I no longer had either pride or caution. I found his mouth again, and as my hand crept over his warm belly my body burned with desire. Something was beginning again that night. I was sure of it.

But that night, at Miller, sex happens between 'Anne' and 'Lewis' so fast that she is 'dumbfounded'. Their bodies have become strangers, and she weeps hysterically:

He gave me his heart. With his hands, his lips, his whole body. That was yesterday. All those nights the memories of which were still burning inside me – under the Mexican blanket, in our berth rocked by the Mississippi, in the shadow of mosquito netting, in front of a fire which smelled of resin – all those nights.

'Is that your programme for the summer?' asks Lewis, irritated. 'Spending a pleasant day and then crying all night?'

'Don't sound so superior,' says Anne hotly. 'Sleeping together cold like that, it's . . . horrible! You shouldn't have . . .'

'You wanted it so much. I didn't want to refuse.'

*

If the man is 'infinitely favoured' in love-making, he is even more privileged in not bearing children. Beauvoir's choice to remain childless had logical roots: like the majority of first-wave feminists, she chose career over children in part because there was no other option. Her bohemian lifestyle, spent up to the age of forty-one living in hotels, eating in cafés, bonded to Sartre but taking chance lovers, did not admit children; it was an easy choice, because at no time in her life did she experience maternal longing.

When Bianca Lamblin returned to Paris after the war and met Beauvoir and Sartre in the Jardins du Ranelagh in 1946, she never forgot their twin expressions of horror at the sight of her 'big belly'. Bianca had asked the couple to meet her in order to extract a 'solemn oath' that they would not use her as material for a novel: a promise not worth the paper it was written on, given their routine cannibalization of the family in fiction:

> It was as if I were a slug or some other disgusting animal. They gazed nervously straight ahead. I always knew they had this attitude. They found motherhood, which brings into play organic forces and bodily fluids, deeply revolting.

Pregnant, the female body is passive and alienated, tenanted by the foetus, writes Beauvoir. Her disgust is linked to the identification of the mother with death, the womb as an oceanic source of annihilation. Man is cursed to fall from his 'bright and ordered heaven into the chaotic shadows of his mother's womb'. The fire of the spirit:

is imprisoned by woman in the mud of the earth . . . She also dooms him to death. This quivering jelly which is elaborated in the womb (the womb, secret and sealed like the tomb) evokes too clearly the soft viscosity of carrion. Wherever life is in the making . . . it arouses disgust . . . The slimy embryo begins the cycle that is completed in the putrefaction of death.

Undoubtedly Beauvoir retained from her Catholic childhood the message of the early Christian fathers that woman is, in the words of Tertullian, 'the devil's doorway'. Despite berating St Paul for demanding that women submit to their husbands ('For the husband is the head of the wife, even as Christ is head of the church'), or St Ambrose for arguing that since 'Adam was led to sin by Eve . . . it is just and right that she accept as lord and master him whom she led to sin', Beauvoir had herself internalized the idea that woman's flesh is accursed. Pregnancy is the ultimate annihilation:

The foetus is a part of her body, and it is a parasite that feeds on it; she possesses it and is possessed by it . . . This very opulence annihilates her . . . Ensnared by nature, the pregnant woman is plant and animal . . . an incubator, an egg, she scares children proud of their young straight bodies and makes young people titter contemptuously because she is a human being, a conscious and free individual, who has become life's passive instrument.

Carrying a baby makes woman 'the prey of the species' for Beauvoir. Her shuddering, visceral contempt for mothers and babies, which would prove highly influential in the denigration of marriage and motherhood in 1970s feminism, may have originated in her own difficult relationship with her bullying mother, Françoise. It can also be linked to Beauvoir's bisexuality. Becoming 'prey' in heterosexual intercourse was something with which she would continue to have difficulty. In her lesbian relationships she relished taking the masculine role of 'seducer', as well as that of 'prey'. It was a reason for finding 'the homosexual embrace most satisfying'.

It is only when her fingers trace the body of a woman whose fingers in turn trace her body that the miracle of the mirror is accomplished. Between women . . . separateness is abolished, there is no struggle, no victory, no defeat; in exact reciprocity each is at once subject and object, sovereign and slave.

Knowing the secrets of the female body, the woman makes an expert lover. Approvingly Beauvoir quotes Colette: 'The close resemblance gives certitude of pleasure.' She suggests also that 'mirroring' may have a maternal as well as a sexual aspect, and that in cradling 'a soft carnal object in her arms', the lesbian expresses a love for the child that she has not borne: 'In you I love my child, my darling, and my sister.'

It would, however, be a mistake to label Beauvoir a lesbian. Her place on the sexual continuum would shift at different stages in her life. Her orientation towards same-sex love which would resurface in the future, but in 1947–9 it was her passionate relationship with Nelson that provided the energy and stimulus which brought *The Second Sex* into being, in a country which had no existing feminist movement, despite the foundation of the French Union for Women Suffrage in 1909 by Mme Brunschwig, and female enfranchisement in 1945. Beauvoir's bold call to women to demand reciprocity and respect aroused howls of horror. Fame, for which she had once longed, had become infamy. Sartre was sent pictures of himself covered with excrement. Existentialism had become known as 'excrementalism'. No wonder that when Nelson invited Simone to stay again in September 1951, she was tempted to accept.

*

Sartre had broken up with Dolorès in 1950, after she insisted on dragging him through Mexico and the Yucatán following exactly the same itinerary as Simone and Nelson. Sartre, who was used to Simone making all the arrangements, proved a disappointment to Dolorès when he refused to book tickets or take decisions; her complaints and tears exhausted him. When they returned he ran for cover to his mother's in rue Bonaparte; Dolorès returned to her husband in New York.

When the affair ended, Beauvoir could finally relax. She had feared that Sartre would give in to Vanetti's persistent demands for marriage, or at least to live with her in Paris. Now she and Sartre could continue with the routine which suited them both, spending evenings together in the rue de la Bûcherie listening to music on her new record-player bought with her earnings from *The Second Sex*, eating scrappy meals of ham and bread, and drinking whisky. He sat in her single shabby armchair, she on the single divan. They could forget about the hate mail he received, sometimes twenty letters a day, and the death threats:

I think it was when Dolorès went back to New York that I knew for the first time that, no matter what, Sartre and I would always be together. I still had Algren, and I had no doubt that for Sartre there would always be other women. But we had become necessary to each other in a way that I don't think people ever really understood. They [critics] all said that we had become like a little old married couple, and they snickered at us . . . It's true, we knew each other so well, no one ever understood us as we understood each other . . . All our shared experience made us supremely at ease and comfortable with each other.

In her memoirs Beauvoir said that if Sartre gave her an appointment to meet him at a certain hour of a certain day and year in a strange place many miles away, 'I would go there in complete faith to find him waiting, because I knew I could always depend on him. Well, after so many years, this was still true. In spite of everything – no, perhaps *because* of everything we had been through together – we always depended on each other. He would never disappoint me; I would never let him down.'

Yet there was unfinished business with Algren. Her last contact with him had been at the end of her disastrous summer visit, when she had pinned the purple orchid he had given her on to her breast as she flew from Chicago for New York. From the Hotel Lincoln she had written on 30 September 1950 to 'Nelson, my dearest sweetest one', that 'I am better at dry sadness than at cold anger, for I remained dry-eyed until now . . . but my heart is a kind of dirty soft custard inside.'

Algren told her that he intended to remarry his ex-wife, Amanda, whom he had seen in Hollywood. But the following year he invited her to stay again. In March 1951 Beauvoir wrote to her 'own beastish beast' from 'a lovely port called Saint-Tropez' (where Michèle Vian had a house) that, since he asked her so politely, it would be impolite not to accept. 'I'll be a very decent guest this year, I promise. I shall not cry more than twice a day, nor scream more than twice a week, nor bite more than once a month.'

By July she was close to tears, despite having vowed to 'weep no more'. 'Your piggish pig of countryish country does not seem to want me to go to the States,' she wrote miserably to Algren. Beauvoir had signed a petition organized by the French Women's League, which had links with the Communists, and the American embassy was refusing her a visa. What if they examined *America Day by Day*, now translated into English, or read articles in *Les Temps modernes* against MacArthur and American policy? Beauvoir was 'deeply scared' that she would never see Algren again. If only he would come to Paris: it was easy for him. Americans were 'kings of the world', from whom no visa was demanded.

Much as it went against the grain of her imperious personality, Beauvoir meekly confessed, explained, apologized: 'It was *really humiliating*.' She had wanted to 'kick' the whole American embassy. 'Had it been only a pleasure trip, I should have enjoyed kicking them and saying farewell to the States for ever. But I want *so much* to see you.'

In August 'the swinish swines' at the embassy were still holding out. Cau continued supplicating the officials on Beauvoir's behalf while she and Sartre visited Iceland, Scotland – the people are 'ugly, thrifty out of date', the scenery 'rainy, misty, gloomy' – and London. Sartre and Beauvoir put up at the Park Lane Hotel, and saw Laurence Olivier and Vivien Leigh in *Anthony and Cleopatra*. She approved of the British, who 'don't worship America as much as the French do' and, even in 1951, were still suffering the after-effects of the war: 'They still don't have butter, chocolate, food and clothes free; they are quite poor, but they live in a much more dignified way.'

Finally, on 19 September, Simone arrived at Forrest Avenue. She had not slept with a man in Paris for two years, for Bost had found a new lover, the novelist Marguerite Duras. What did Beauvoir hope for? Perhaps that passion would flare again between them. She had assured her 'dearest monster' that she had given up drinking whisky, a bone of contention with Nelson, who didn't like Beauvoir when she was drunk. She had had to 'gulp' a lot of brandy on Bastille Day in order to keep warm, she explained, but 'I was not drunk. Now no Scotch, no wine, nothing: it is not allowed.' She hoped, she added wistfully, that she would be allowed to kiss Nelson that summer. In the event, she spent most of the month in the house by Lake Michigan writing an essay on the Marquis de Sade ('Just fancy: from eighteen to thirty-six years old, he savagely beated [sic] and fucked women, and maybe men and beasts too . . .'). It was a decoy. She did not let Algren see the manuscript of *The Mandarins*, in which he featured so heavily, although she had shown it to Sartre, who told her that it would be her best book yet, though it still needed a lot of work. Later she would write:

Of all my characters, Lewis is the one who approaches closest to a living model . . . It so happened – a rare coincidence – that Algren, in his reality, was very representative of what I wanted to represent . . . I used [him] to invent a character who would exist without reference to the world of real people.

Towards the end of her stay, as she walked along the beach during the last days of October, Simone lamented that she would never see Algren again, nor the house, nor the lake, nor the sand dotted with little white waders. But she congratulated herself on at least keeping his friendship. 'It's not friendship,' responded Algren brutally. 'I could never give you less than love.' Beauvoir was thrown into turmoil, a fever; she felt physically sick at the prospect of 'the gift of his love' being returned to her. Her love for him was as strong as ever. 'The great new sexual longing and happiness you aroused in me' flooded over her. But the next day Algren clarified his position: 'To have a woman who does not belong to you, who puts other things and other people before you, without there ever being any question of your taking first place, is something that just isn't acceptable . . . Now I want a different kind of life, with a woman and a house of my own.'

'I always felt guilty towards you, from the very first day, because I could give you so little, loving you so much,' replied Beauvoir painfully from the Hotel Lincoln in New York. 'You would never have accepted to come and live in France for keeps, and . . . I *could* not desert Sartre and writing and France.' Her tears brimmed over. 'I felt guilty, always, and it is the bitterest feeling I ever knew when it is toward the very man you love. And as much as I hurt you, deserted you, it hurted me.'

She was about to hurt him much more. Soon Simone would lose even the dying embers of love. *The Mandarins*, in the process of being typed, would appear to Algren as the ultimate betrayal.

32

My Last Good Friend

Camus was probably the last who was a good friend.
Jean-Paul Sartre, 1972

SARTRE SHIFTED UNEASILY in his chair. He and Camus were having a drink in the Pont-Royal. It was April 1952, and Camus was joking about the hostile reviews of his new book, *The Rebel* (*L'Homme révolté*), which had been published the previous October. 'He just took it for granted that we liked it,' recalled Beauvoir. But the book was posing a problem at *Les Temps modernes*, where Sartre had called for a volunteer to review it: 'He wouldn't let anyone say anything bad about it because of their friendship; unfortunately none of us could think of anything good. We wondered how we were going to get out of the dilemma.' Finally twenty-nine-year-old Francis Jeanson, the paper's nominal manager after Merleau-Ponty's departure, put up his hand. 'The review may be *reservé*, severe even,' muttered Sartre, unable to meet Camus's eyes. He knew Jeanson despised Camus's 'pseudo-philosophy and pseudo-history', but Sartre had no idea that he was sailing into the eye of the storm.

He did, however, know what *The Rebel* had cost Camus. Although the friendship between the two men was under increasing strain as their political paths parted, and their last meeting, at the opening of *The Devil and the Good Lord* on 7 June 1951, had been 'a pretty dismal meal' at which, said Beauvoir, 'the old warmth between Camus and ourselves seemed beyond recall', Sartre knew enough about the difficulties of literary creation not to feel sympathetic towards the younger, sicker man. Camus had suffered a serious relapse of his TB, which had brought him to the brink of suicide in 1950. He had spent the winter in Cabris, a favourite village of André Gide's, high in the hills of the Alpes-Maritimes above Grasse, and had taken a year's *congé de maladie* from Gallimard. Streptomycin and a special holistic cure from a Dr Ménétrier, who prescribed minerals such as zinc, iron and magnesium, allowed him to slowly recover his energy; for months he pondered in front of the wood-burning stove at the Chèvre d'Or hotel. He had been working on his essay on revolt since 1943, and was afraid that he would die before it was finished. Only thirty-six, he gloomily compared himself to his heroes, Tolstoy, who had written *War and Peace* between the age of thirty-five and forty-one, Herman Melville, thirty-two when he wrote *Moby Dick*, and another tubercular artist, Keats, who died young.

For three years between 1949 and 1951 Camus returned to Cabris to work on *The Rebel*. He could not be hurried: 'I'm not a philosopher, and for me thought is an interior adventure that matures, that hurts or transports one,' he wrote to his wife Francine. 'It's a meditation that takes days and years to formulate, to move forward, and to find expression.' Far away from the bustle of the Gallimard office at rue Sébastien-Bottin, and the feuds of Parisian literary cabals, he worked for ten hours a day. Francine sent him, as requested, Lenin's analysis of Hegel, and Bertrand Russell's *History of Western Philosophy*, but he preferred Plato to the Germans. 'Only work keeps the soul standing tall,' he told Francine. On 27 February 1951 he complained to his friend René Char that 'the childbirth is long and difficult, and it seems to me that the baby is quite ugly and this effort is exhausting'. But by 8 March he was able to announce to both Francine and Maria that it had been born.

The Rebel was dedicated to Jean Grenier, the teacher who had been a major influence on Camus in encouraging him to join the Communist Party before the war. The first hint of trouble came when Grenier, after reading the manuscript, told Camus that it reminded him of 'the reactionary line of Maurras', the fascist leader of the Action Française movement in the 1930s, which Sartre had satirized in his famous short story 'The Childhood of a Leader'. 'Too bad,' replied Camus. 'The book will make you a lot of enemies,' cautioned Grenier. Camus shrugged: 'Yes, no doubt my friendships are not very solid.'

By the summer of 1952 the Cold War was forcing writers to take sides. 'The post-war period was over,' wrote Beauvoir. 'No more postponements, no more conciliations were possible. We had been forced into making clear-cut choices.' Stalin's terror was about to reach its acme with the alleged 'doctors' plot' of January 1953, when nine doctors, seven of them Jews, were accused of the murder of Andrei Zhdanov in 1948, and a vicious anti-Semitic purge followed. There were 2.6 million in the gulags; it was a strange time for Sartre to choose to become France's most famous fellow traveller or *compagnon de route*, and, in Camus's eyes, showed his 'taste for servitude', as he wrote in his *Carnets* in February 1952. 'Sartre, *l'homme et l'esprit*, *déloyal* [Sartre, man and mind, *disloyal*]', he scribbled angrily, outraged that the existentialist leader, who predicated his philosophy on freedom, was now the leading apologist for Stalin.

In the last chapter of his book Camus threw down the gauntlet, attacking the existentialists and their 'cult of history', without naming Sartre. Not to name him, given his world reputation, was in itself an insult. To avoid a quarrel, Sartre had published an earlier chapter from *The Rebel*, on Nietzsche, in *Les Temps modernes* in August 1951; but when Jeanson's scorching, twenty-page review appeared in May 1952, the split between Sartre and Camus, which in retrospect appears inevitable, burst open like rotten fruit.

Taunting Camus with his glowing right-wing notices in *Le Figaro* and *Aspects de la France*, organ of Action Française, which saw the book as a return to nationalism and to God, Jeanson ironically entitles his own review 'Albert Camus ou l'âme révoltée, Albert Camus or the Soul in Revolt'. This is a punning reference to Hegel's *belle âme*, beautiful soul, doomed, in his *Phenomenology of Spirit*, in its effort to remain pure, but robustly defended by Camus against the German philosopher. To the young journalist Jeanson, a fanatical disciple of Sartre's, Camus's 'revolted soul', which recoils from the gulag, is moralizing and ineffective, preaching quietism and defeatism in the face of the USSR's 'triumphant rebellion'.

Camus intended to separate the idea of individual revolt from that of the revolutionary who seeks victory at any price. He praises the 'man who says no' to life's absurdity, who refuses, and in so doing 'is also saying yes', creating positive values, dignity, solidarity: 'I revolt, therefore I am.' Ahead of his time in setting limits to violence, he argues instead for a revolt 'limited in scope'. Further he will not go: it was a brave and prescient step to question the French and Russian revolutions, to link Robespierre to Stalin, and to claim that historical revolt can lead to nihilism, the end of God, the 'divinization' of man,

24. Beauvoir and Sartre broadcast together, 1946

25. 'She gave me America': Dolorès Vanetti

26. Simone de Beauvoir and Sartre
at Madame Morel's, 1948

27. Beauvoir in the bathroom, Chicago 1948

28. Nelson Algren washes his hair in the sink at Wabansia Avenue

29. Beauvoir and Nelson Algren at the house on Lake Michigan, summer 1950

30. Beauvoir and Nelson Algren at the house on Lake Michigan, summer 1950

31. Claude Lanzmann and Simone de Beauvoir, Summer 1952. 'A mon "first-rate mind," he dedicated this photograph, but by night she was "ma reine d'Afrique," my African queen'

32. Sartre, Boris and Michelle Vian and Simone de Beauvoir at the Café Procope, 1951

33. Sartre and André Gide at Cabris, during the filming of the Marc Allegret documentary, 1950

34. Sartre and Beauvoir with Fidel Castro

35. Beauvoir and Sartre with
Che Guevara in Cuba, 1960

36. Simone de
Beauvoir and
Lena Zonina,
Russia, 1962
or 63

37. Arlette Elkaïm and Sartre,
January 1965

38. Sartre and
Beauvoir with
Nikita Kruschev,
1963

39. Beauvoir and Sartre selling *La Cause du Peuple*, Paris 1970

40. Sylvie Le Bon and Simone de Beauvoir on the terrace of the Hotel Nazionale, Rome, 1971

41. A remorseful Sartre? This handwritten note, acknowledging that he has made mistakes, but 'not on purpose', was found among Sartre's papers after his death

42. Beauvoir and Sartre celebrate a half century of companionship on Sartre's birthday, 21 June 1979

43. Sylvie Le Bon and Beauvoir at a Women's Liberation (MLF) demonstration, June 1974

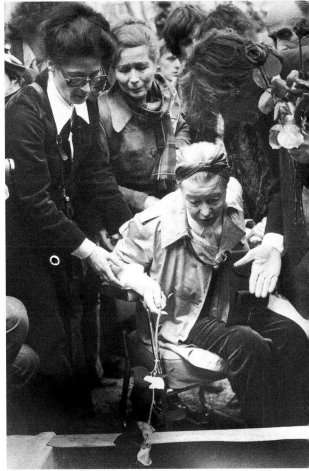

44. Beauvoir casts a rose into Sartre's grave at his funeral, April 1980, supported by Sylvie Le Bon and Hélène de Beauvoir

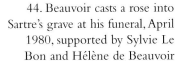

and state murder. In so doing, Camus raised his lone standard of defiance against a virtually unanimous Left Bank intelligentsia, and brought insults raining down on his head. The surrealist André Bréton, also attacked by Camus, was one of the first to view the author as a reactionary hiding behind a 'phantom of revolt . . . Once revolt has been emptied of its passionate substance, what could possibly remain?'

In Jeanson's eyes, Camus's greatest sin is his refusal to live in history, and to understand the socio-economic forces that shape it. Philosophy, claims Camus, transforms 'murderers into judges': but his obsession with Stalinist terror led him to ignore violence in other quarters, French colonial repression in Vietnam, and the smouldering tinderbox which was Algeria. 'A missed opportunity to write a great book,' says Jeanson. The young tyro's withering review was a bitter blow to Camus; but perhaps the greatest insult was that Sartre had chosen a nobody to write it, rather than doing the job himself.

'Monsieur le Directeur', Camus magisterially addresses Sartre in his seventeen-page reply, dated 30 June 1952, and printed in *Les Temps modernes* in August. Disdaining to mention Jeanson by name, he holds Sartre as editor responsible for the article. Furious at the accusation that he is 'detached from reality and history', Camus too gets personal: 'I am beginning to get a little tired of seeing myself – and even more, of seeing former militants who have never refused the struggles of their time – endlessly receive lessons in efficacy from critics who have never done anything more than turn their theatre seat in the direction of history.' It was a sharp reminder of Sartre's ineffectiveness in August 1944, when he had fallen asleep in his seat while 'liberating' the Comédie-Française, only to be woken by Camus with the remark: 'You have turned your theatre seat in the direction of history.' The former editor of *Combat*, who had given Sartre the chance to turn around his murky war record, had not, after all, forgotten his history.

Sartre and Camus were shaping up like two boxers in the ring. Sartre, from his corner, responded with a flurry of blows: in July he published *The Communists and the Peace* and declared himself a revolutionary. In August he delivered the *coup de grâce*: a reply which was cruelty personified:

My dear Camus: Our friendship was not easy, but I will miss it. If you end it today, that doubtless means it had to end. Unfortunately, you have so deliberately put me on trial, and in such an ugly tone of voice, that I can no longer remain silent without losing face . . . Your combination of dreary conceit and vulnerability always discouraged people from telling you unvarnished truths. The result is that you have become the victim of dismal self-importance . . . I would have so much preferred that our present quarrel went straight to the heart of the matter without getting confused with the nasty smell of wounded vanity . . .

The heart of the matter for Camus was the existence of the camps, which he accused Sartre of refusing to discuss and 'even justify' in *Les Temps modernes*. 'Yes, Camus, like you, I find these camps inadmissible,' replies Sartre. 'But equally inadmissible is the use that the "so-called bourgeois press" makes of them every day . . . For, to my way of thinking, the scandal of the camps puts us all on trial – you as well as me, and all the others. The Iron Curtain is only a mirror, in which each half of the world reflects the other. Each turn of the screw *here* corresponds with a twist there, and finally, both here and there, we are both the screwers and the screwed.'

In this thrust, Sartre reminds Camus of French state violence both towards its colonial subjects and towards French workers. In his view, Camus has failed to grow; he is 'stuck' in Liberation France, in 1944. By contrast, argues Sartre, he himself has evolved, and is marching to the drum of history. 'To merit the right to influence men who are struggling, one must first participate in their struggle, and this means accepting many things, if you hope to change a few of them.'

Sartre's letter ends with a lament for the Camus he once had loved:

You had been for us – you could again be tomorrow – the admirable conjunction of a person, an action and a work . . . How we loved you then.

In 1944 the Resistance leader had transcended the contradictions of the times through his 'ardour to live them'. He and Sartre had shared the same 'contact with History . . . If I call it *yours*, it is because you *lived* it more deeply and fully than many of us (myself included).' In this final sentence, Sartre acknowledged who had been the hero then; now it is he who will keep his rendezvous with his century.

Robert Gallimard, who somehow managed to remain friends with both Sartre and Camus, called the break the end of a love story. Camus, said Sartre after his death, was his last good friend. Without him, Sartre would drift rudderless on the sea of politics.

*

Beauvoir had her own break-up to deal with. 'Voilà, c'est fini,' she said to herself. 'I shall never sleep again warmed by another body. Never: what a knell . . . I felt myself sinking into death.' The void seemed again to engulf her, the thin black line to draw closer. But she had one consolation: a car, which became her pride and joy. In 1951, on Genet's advice, she purchased a new model Simca Aronde, and began driving lessons. Soon both she and Bost had their licences, and were able to go for Sunday spins outside Paris. Olga came too: 'I loved the spring in Normandy, the tarns of the Sologne, the villages of Touraine,' wrote Beauvoir. 'I discovered churches, abbeys, châteaux.'

But it was hard to adapt to being on her own. Celebrity had stolen Sartre from her. Although success had not changed him, it had changed his habits: he no longer set foot in the cafés they had 'so loved' before, or took her to the cinema. He was no longer her Baladin, her playboy, sharing flâneries, strolls along the Parisian boulevards: 'I missed his old insouciance and the golden age when we always had so much time.' Not only had he become a public figure, he was engaged on his own political journey, in which Beauvoir claimed to take no interest. 'Read this,' he would say, pointing at the pile of books on his desk. 'C'est passionnant, it's fascinating.' But, writes Beauvoir in her memoirs, she had no desire to play even the smallest political role.

At Les Temps modernes, new, young bloods were 'repoliticizing' the magazine in the direction of Communist fellow-travelling. Beauvoir spotted one of them at the Sunday afternoon meetings at Sartre's flat: Claude Lanzmann, a dark, good-looking journalist seventeen years younger than herself. Claude was a product of the khâgne at Louis-le-Grand, like Cau, who had introduced him to Sartre. Great things were expected of him. 'He was meant to be Proust and Malraux rolled into one,' recalls Olivier Todd. 'He was very dashing and suave.' 'Many women found him attractive,' remembered Beauvoir; 'so did I.' His deadpan humour, the way his mind worked, reminded her of Sartre. At the rue Bonaparte sessions, they drank framboise together and hotly debated politics and literature.

The meetings were red-letter days in one of the darkest periods of Beauvoir's life. Her typist, Lucienne, had just died of breast cancer, and in the spring of 1952 Beauvoir herself became aware of a stabbing pain in her right breast. She fingered the swelling which had appeared, and asked Sartre what to do. 'See a doctor and set your mind at rest.' When Beauvoir woke up from the biopsy, she heard a voice saying that there was nothing wrong with her: 'Angels came and rocked me to sleep.'

Beauvoir told herself that she was too old for Lanzmann. She was forty-four, he only twenty-seven: a toyboy. As a girl she had listened with disgust to her parents' love-making on the other side of the bedroom wall ('still fucking at forty!') and long held the opinion that women over forty were too old for sex: 'Certain aspects of love, well, after forty one has to give them up . . . I promised myself that when I reached that stage, I would dutifully retire to the shelf.' She had been thirty-nine when she began the affair with Algren. Now, at passing forty, she was tempted to break her own rules. In July Bost and Jean Cau invited her to celebrate their imminent departure for Brazil, where they were researching material for a guide, Beauvoir asked if she could bring Lanzmann with her for a dish of aïoli. The merry party ended late, and the next morning Beauvoir's telephone rang:

'I'd like to take you to the cinema,' said Lanzmann.

'To the cinema? What film do you want to see?'

'Any one.'

Beauvoir hesitated. She was on the point of driving down to Milan to meet Sartre, now 'intimately connected' to Michèle Vian, who had left her husband, Boris. But she knew that she couldn't refuse. She agreed to meet Claude, hung up – and burst into tears.

Five days later Beauvoir left for Italy. Lanzmann waved as she crunched the gears and headed for the suburbs. 'Something had happened . . . I had rediscovered my body.'

According to Olivier Todd, who was seventeen when he met Lanzmann, matters were not so simple. After Algren broke it off with Simone de Beauvoir, Sartre confided his worries to Cau: '"Let's toss for her,"' said the secretary, at a *Temps modernes* meeting. Lanzmann won the toss. Shortly afterwards he began living with Beauvoir.'

Like Algren, Lanzmann was Jewish; unlike Algren, he defined himself as a Jew. Determined to prove that his people were not destined for martyrdom, he fought in the Maquis from 1944, and considered Marxism a self-evident truth. When Beauvoir returned from Italy, Lanzmann from Israel, the couple were reunited: 'Our bodies met each other again with joy.' Rather than alarming Beauvoir, the age gap between them provided a welcome distance, as Lanzmann presented no sort of rival to Sartre. Nor did he expect as much of her as Algren had: 'His youth doomed me to being only a moment in his life,' wrote Beauvoir, but it also excused her from giving him the whole of hers. Sartre agreed that Lanzmann could share their joint summer holidays. After a winter holiday with Beauvoir in Holland, he moved into her flat in the rue de la Bûcherie. 'I had loved my solitude,' wrote Beauvoir, 'but I did not regret it.'

Lanzmann, for his part, never forgot the strange rituals which marked his first holiday with Beauvoir and Sartre at Saint-Tropez, the following spring.

> We were living together, and she continued her relationship with Sartre, but it was one which was no longer at all sexual . . . One evening she would see me, and Sartre would remain alone, the following evening she'd see Sartre, and I'd be alone, and we'd meet up, Simone de Beauvoir and I, as soon as dinner was over. But the funny thing was that at that time, at Saint-Tropez that spring, there were only two restaurants open at the port, beside each other. Simone de Beauvoir has always had a loud voice, so when she dined with Sartre in restaurant X, and I was in restaurant Y next door, they were the only customers in restaurant X and I was the only customer in restaurant Y. And I heard Beauvoir tell Sartre – because they told each other everything, that was the rule – I heard Beauvoir tell Sartre everything she'd done with me during the day . . .

After dinner, Beauvoir in turn repeated to the patient Lanzmann Sartre's replies, which he'd already heard . . . and on the third night, when all three dined together, the conversation was repeated again. The 'rule of transparency' was observed ad infinitum.

Lanzmann gave Beauvoir back her youth. Overnight, her anxiety attacks disappeared: 'I leapt back enthralled into happiness.' The roof leaked, the floor was covered in books, but, snuggled up together in the single divan, Simone at last found the intimacy she yearned for. Their temperaments were similar: when upset, Claude burst into tears or had vomiting fits; Simone, equally frenzied, was given to paroxysms of weeping. But with Claude, unlike the puritanical Sartre, there was no longer any need to restrain herself.

*

Rejuvenated by her new lover, Beauvoir had less time for Sartre, who had confessed in 1950 to Koestler that his friendships were melting away under the heat of his politics. Koestler and Mamaine had felt sorry for him. But new friends were waiting in the wings: at the Vienna Peace Congress of December 1952, to which he was invited after publishing the second part of The Communist and the Peace in November, Sartre drank vodka with Ilya Ehrenbourg and Alexander Fadayev, who had called Sartre 'a hyena with a fountain pen' at the Peace Congress just four years earlier, and accepted their invitation to visit the USSR. Only days before, Slansky and ten other Czech Communist leaders, all of them Jews, had been hanged for alleged treason. The star of the show, Sartre was asked to give the inaugural address and his presence attracted autograph hunters by the thousand. Under Communist pressure, he practised self-censorship, banning Vienna performances of *Dirty Hands*, which Ehrenbourg had trashed in the Communist press as pro-American propaganda. At the height of the Cold War, Sartre had turned to putty in Russian hands. It was, opined one American Communist journalist, 'the greatest turnabout that has ever occurred in Western Europe'.

On 23 December Sartre stepped on to the platform at the Val d'Hiv with the French Communist leader, Jacques Duclos. 'We are happy to have amongst us Jean-Paul Sartre,' Duclos announced, to gasps of surprise. The idyll was about to begin.

The Congress for Cultural Freedom, centrepiece of America's covert propaganda operation, which from 1950 to 1967 was run by CIA agent Michael Josselson, was increasingly alarmed at Sartre and Beauvoir's intellectual hegemony. 'Who was the real antagonist?' asked one historian. 'It wasn't the Soviet Union or Moscow. What they were really obsessed with was Sartre and Beauvoir. *That* was the other side.' 'The Left Bank intellectuals were the target,' confirmed Diana Josselson. In a vain attempt to break the Sartrean stranglehold, the Americans launched their own house journal, *Preuves* ('proof' or 'evidence') under the editorship of a Swiss writer, François Bondy, in October 1951; it faced *une hostilité presque totale*.

In Venice with Michèle in June 1953, Sartre picked up his newspaper and read that Julius and Ethel Rosenberg, who had been convicted in March 1951 of betraying American atomic secrets to the Soviets, had been sent to the electric chair by President Dwight D. Eisenhower. Choking with rage, he dictated an article for *Libération* down the telephone:

> This is a legal lynching that covers a whole nation in blood . . . When two innocents are sentenced to death, it is the whole world's business . . . Decidedly, there is something rotten in America . . . *Attention, l'Amérique a la rage*. Watch out, America has rabies! We must cut all ties with her, or we'll also get sick.

The death of Stalin on 5 March 1953 smoothed the way for Sartre to

visit the USSR. His successor, Nikita Krushchev, would admit to being
'up to his elbows' in the blood of his victims in the Ukraine, where he,
too, had displayed a brutal anti-Semitism towards the 'Abramoviches'
who were preying on his fiefdom 'like crows'. But the Jewish 'murderers
in white coats' were released by Malenkov. 'Strangely relieved', Sartre's
hatred of the bourgeoisie continued to blind him to Soviet repression.
In his notes he wrote: 'I held but one thread in my hand, but Theseus
had no more, and it was enough for me too: the inexhaustible and
difficult experience of class struggle . . . There were still closed doors in
my head. I broke them down, not without an exhausting effort.'

Arriving in Moscow on 24 May 1954, Sartre found himself no match
for the Soviet minotaur. He was already suffering from hypertension,
but had refused his doctor's orders to rest. From a window in the Hotel
National on Red Square he watched a million-strong parade of the Red
Army, visited the university, toured factories. The writer Konstantin
Simonov invited Sartre to a four-hour banquet at his dacha. There
were twenty toasts in vodka; Sartre's glass was refilled with Armenian
vin rosé and red wine from Georgia. 'I managed to keep the use of my
senses, but I did partially lose the use of my legs,' he confessed to
Beauvoir.

Shoehorned on to a train to Leningrad, he saw palaces, watched the
ballet, flew on to Uzbekistan, then to Stockholm to meet Ilya
Ehrenbourg for a Peace Movement meeting. There he collapsed.
Alerted by Bost, who was informed by Ehrenbourg that Sartre had been
admitted to a hospital in Moscow, Beauvoir was as frightened as on the
day in 1940 when she had received a letter informing her that Sartre
was in the *Kranken-revier*. She marched round to the Soviet embassy,
who told her that she had only to pick up the phone to call Sartre in
hospital. Was it so easy to penetrate the Iron Curtain? Nervously she
made the call from the rue de la Bûcherie. After three minutes she
heard his voice:

'*Comment allez-vous?*

'*Mais très bien.*'

But Sartre was not 'very well'. In Tashkent an engineer 'as strong as
three cart horses' had challenged him to a vodka duel. Although it was
the engineer who collapsed first, sinking into a heap on the airport
tarmac, Sartre arrived back in Moscow so ill that he begged his
interpreter for a day's rest. But Simonov was waiting. Over yet another
banquet he presented Sartre with a huge drinking horn brimming with
wine: 'Empty or full, you shall take it with you.' Sartre drained the horn
dry but, that afternoon, walking along the bank of the Moskova, he felt

his heart battering against his ribs. The next morning, his blood pressure dangerously high, he was admitted to hospital.

Had Sartre suffered a mini-stroke? He seemed changed to Beauvoir when he returned to Paris, finding it an immense effort to talk, sleeping a great deal, and barely able to 'put two ideas together'. Minded by his 'aides', both his interpreter and a member of the Writers' Union, at all times, Sartre had been unaware that he was an 'object of cultivation' to the KGB and was always 'in the company of KGB agents'. The Union of Writers, whose leaders were Fadeev, Simonov, Riourikov, Korneitchouk, Ehrenbourg and the first secretary, Sourkov, was 'ninety per cent penetrated by the KGB', according to Colonel Oleg Gordievsky, a senior KGB double agent from 1974, who escaped to London with the help of the British Secret Intelligence Service (MI6) in 1985. 'The Peace World Council,' he says, 'was regarded by the KGB as their arm.'

And in 1954 the political stakes were high. Ehrenbourg, for twenty years a KGB agent, had been one of the first prominent Jews to sign a letter calling on all Soviet Jews to follow the instructions of 'our wise Communist Party' in the autumn of 1952, when the Jewish population was 'petrified' at the arrest of their creative intelligentsia. In 1954 he gave Sartre a copy of his latest novel, The Thaw, to read, a public relations exercise suggesting that the frozen gulags were releasing their victims. Khruschev and Malenkov wanted allies, and Sartre's prestige made him an important prize. He was handled carefully. When he demanded privacy, his interpreter waved his arms and shooed everyone away: 'And now Jean-Paul Sartre wishes to be alone.' Deluded into thinking that he enjoyed a measure of autonomy in Russia, Sartre had yet to learn the truth of two Russian sayings: 'One is "alcohol doesn't affect me"; and the other is: "I understand the Russians."'

*

Seduced by his first voyage offert, free trip, Sartre fell into the trap set for him. On his return he gave interviews to Libération, published in July 1954 as 'Jean-Paul Sartre's Impressions of his Trip to the USSR', in which he said: 'La liberté de critique est totale en URSS, there is total freedom of criticism in the USSR.' Blind or duplicitous, he had become both agent and victim of Soviet propaganda.

Seduced first by the Germans, Sartre had slipped into bed with the Russians without a murmur. He had fallen in love with the Soviet paradise just eighteen months before the historic Twentieth Congress, at which Stalin's crimes would be unveiled to the world. By contrast, Nizan had visited the USSR in 1934 and returned deeply troubled. In 1938 Gide's famous *Retour de l'URRS* had denounced Stalin's show trials and purges. Their eyes were opened. Did Sartre's really remain tight shut?

Later Sartre admitted: *'J'ai menti*, I lied.' His lies were many and various. He told Claude Roy, stupefied by Sartre's statement that there was complete freedom of expression in the USSR: 'Obviously, it's not true yet. But if you want it to become so, you have to help them.' In other words, the end justifies the means. In 1975 he admitted to Michel Contat in his *Self Portrait at Seventy* that he had said 'nice things' about the Soviets that he didn't believe. This damning statement is amplified by the letter he wrote to Apletine, head of the foreign commission of the Writers' Union, in July 1954, in which he betrays his obsession with André Gide:

> I believe you accompanied André Gide to the airport twenty years ago. And last month you kindly accompanied me. But the resemblance stops there [. . .] You will see that I am not André Gide.

Explains Contat: 'When you've just accepted someone's invitation, you don't dump shit on them the moment you're home.' The allusion was clear: Gide hadn't hesitated to *verser de la merde*, pour shit on his hosts. Sartre had better manners. Bourgeois good behaviour is more important than telling the truth.

Just before Gide's death, the two writers had met for the last time in Cabris. The awkward body language of the photograph indicates that it was not an easy meeting, but at Gide's death in 1951 Sartre wrote a moving eulogy. Barely four years later he turned on his rival, eager to prove that he, Sartre, was the greater writer, the greater traveller.

So had Sartre lied? Perhaps not. With hindsight, he may have preferred to confess to mendacity rather than to naïveté and credulity. Ehrenbourg was walking a tightrope in 1954. In the autumn of 1952, says Gordievsky, he had been 'active in denouncing Jews while the KGB saw him as just another "filthy Jew", and asked Stalin to let them arrest him'. But despite his own precarious situation, he tried to drop hints to Sartre about the propaganda and lies he would encounter. It was in vain, Ehrenbourg told the director of *Libération*: Sartre swallowed everything he was told hook, line and sinker. 'I honestly thought that Sartre had been warned enough *pour comprendre ma* comédie, that he wouldn't believe me. *Le con!* The bloody fool! Not only did he believe me, but, on his return to France, he repeated everything word for word.'

Still so ill at the end of August that he could barely write, Sartre travelled to Salzburg with Beauvoir. Slumped in a chair in the bedroom of their hotel, he sat for a long time, his hands resting on his knees, his eyes blank: *'La littérature, m'a-t-il déclarée, c'est de la merde.* Literature is crap.'

*

Beauvoir, meanwhile, was settling her own scores with Camus. In October 1954 *The Mandarins* was published, the title chosen by Lanzmann to represent their circle of leftist intellectuals. Forty thousand copies were sold in the first month.

'They're putting you up for the Goncourt,' said Jean Cau. Beauvoir was shocked. She was 'too old'. The evening before the judgement was announced, she went into hiding with Lanzmann. After her victory, she refused to speak to the media: 'At thirty-five I should have enjoyed exhibiting myself; now I found it repugnant.' Journalists camped out on the steps outside her flat, photographers waited at the door of the Café des Amis – Beauvoir gave them the slip by making her exit through the vet's surgery – but she was determined not to become their 'prey'. She who once had longed for fame had become *prisonnier de la gloire*.

On the other hand, the shoals of readers' letters which dropped through her letter-box thrilled her. The dream which Beauvoir had had at twenty, to make herself loved through her books, had finally come true.

The only fly in the ointment was the fact that everybody believed the novel to be autobiographical. 'Re the Mandarins,' reported Camus sourly on 12 December 1954, unhappy at his enforced return to the Parisian *ronde*. 'It seems that I am its hero.' Incensed at being identified as the character Henri Perron, editor of a Resistance paper, whose unhappy wife, Paule, was likewise considered a portrait of Francine, and his girlfriend Josette, Maria Casarès, Camus recorded that all the 'dubious acts of Sartre's life have been generously heaped onto my back' by the author: in the novel 'Henri' has a play produced by a Nazi collaborator, but in fact, Camus confided to a friend, 'I didn't give a play to Simone Berriau during the occupation, Sartre did.'

Beauvoir denies in her memoirs that she had written a 'denunciation' of Camus: 'For Henri, whatever people have said, is not

Camus; not at all.' She claims that the rupture between Perron and his close friend Robert Dubreuilh chronicled in *The Mandarins* is merely 'prophetic'. But the novel is not as fictional as she claims: the paper, *L'Espoir*, which 'Henri' edits, is the name of the series Camus was editing at Gallimard. In the letters 'Henri' and 'Robert' exchange, Beauvoir borrows actual words used by the two combatants. It was an act of piracy on her part, as well as an act of revenge.

'She couldn't stand the friendship between Sartre and me,' said Camus. 'One day she came into my office to tell me that she had a woman friend who wanted to sleep with me, but I replied that in these matters, I was accustomed to choosing for myself. That was a humiliation that such a woman never forgets.' His friends, Brice Parain, Michel and Robert Gallimard, concerned at the denigration of Camus in the book, urged him to reply, but Camus didn't bother, 'Because you don't discuss things with a sewer.'

Influenced by Lanzmann as well as by Sartre, Beauvoir had 'liquidated' her old beliefs and followed Sartre on his journey towards Marxism. Was she the passive partner? Or, as Todd argues, was she not merely complicit but the twin who 'goaded him on . . . the evil cardinal behind him'?

33

~~~

Freedom Fighters

In the first days of the revolt you must kill: to shoot
down a European is to kill two birds with one stone, to
destroy an oppressor and the man he oppresses . . .
                                    Jean-Paul Sartre, 1961

BEAUVOIR WAS RIPE for grooming. When Ehrenbourg met her, fresh
from her triumph with *The Mandarins*, at the Helsinki Peace Congress
in June 1955, she was his principal target. She never forgot the
impression the spy made on her as he sidled up, dressed like 'old
Montparnasse', in a pale green tweed suit, orange shirt and woollen tie,
and told her that every Muscovite intellectual who could speak French
was reading her novel. Before the war he had been hirsute and well
built; now he had lost weight and his hair was white. Ilya – or Elias as
his father, Gersh, had named him in 1891 in Kiev, when it was
forbidden to give Jewish children Russian first names – was still suave
at sixty-four and knew how to flatter the forty-seven-year-old Simone.
Were it not for Russian prudery, the book would be translated, he
assured her. He, who had coined the word *dégel* or thaw, was eager to
make contacts with the West. He hoped that he could count on her.

He succeeded beyond his wildest dreams. The Helsinki Congress
affected Beauvoir as powerfully as Vienna had affected Sartre. 'For us,
the Iron Curtain had dissolved,' wrote Communism's newest recruit.
'No further embargo, no more exile: the realms of socialism were now

part of our world.' She drank Georgian wine with Sourkov under the midnight sun, and talked of her heart's desire, to see China.

Sartre, who in December 1954 had been elected President of the Franco-Soviet Friendship Association, fixed the invitation. When Merleau-Ponty attacked him for alleged 'ultra Bolshevism', Beauvoir leapt to the Kobra's defence. The virulence of her reply in *Les Temps modernes* astonished members of the non-Communist Left, and signalled the strength of her own conversion. After years of fighting against the current, 'I once more felt borne upon the stream of History,' she wrote, 'and I wanted to plunge deeper into it.' She had a new, seemingly innocuous, aim: *servir de quelque chose*, to be useful.

There is no doubt that Beauvoir was a sincere, if naïve, convert to the cause. Undeterred by the 'exotic veil' which seemed to hide China from its Western visitors, and left her feeling that she was faced with a world to which she could not find the key, she wrote *The Long March*, extolling the Chinese Revolution. It was her way of 'giving the lie' to American propaganda, although in so doing she, too, became a Soviet weapon in the *kulturkampf*. Her intoxication with her new creed grew when she and Sartre stopped off in Moscow for a week on the way back from two austere months in China. Dazzled by luxury, cabarets at the Sovietskaia, plates of caviar – 'the sort of food and drink one can get high on!' – enchanted at the old-fashioned ruffled curtains, beaded lampshades and plush wallpaper of the décor, fêted by Simonov and his actress wife at the theatre, lectured by the sister of Elsa Triolet, the *éspionne* wife of Aragon, on the need for the bourgeoisie to accept Communist 'hygiene', Beauvoir fell prey to the two traps against which Gide had warned recipients of *voyages offerts* or freebies: seduction by your hosts, and the smiling faces which everywhere greet you. Both she and Sartre were particularly vulnerable: they were avid travellers, who, with the onset of middle age, had grown tired of roughing it. *Voyageurs sans billet*, increasingly in flight from *la nausée* of their life in Paris, they sought a new validation to their existence through allegiance to the Party. As the comrades handed out the tickets, they dreamt of changing the world.

Beauvoir was more chary than Sartre of accepting the Russian writers' 'imperious' offers of hospitality. Once again Simonov invited Sartre to lunch. 'Excellent! But I won't drink,' said Sartre. All the same, there were four bottles of different kinds of vodka on the restaurant table, and ten bottles of wine. 'Just sample the vodkas,' said Simonov, as he filled their glasses four times. At the 'barbaric' banquet of spit-roasted lamb, running with blood, the Muscovites and

Georgians noisily challenged each other to drinking duels. Beauvoir's head was on fire; she had caught a cold. On her last day she went to bed with a book.

*

For four years after the Sartre–Camus rupture, both writers felt 'dried up'. Sartre wrote little but his turgid, three-part *Communists and the Peace*, in which he attempted to push contingency, choice and freedom into a Marxist pot, and conspicuously failed. The moral and existential crisis he faced took its toll on his health. His multiple addictions deepened. Whisky, tobacco, 'speed' and sex became his crutches as he struggled with the impossible task of reconciling existentialism and determinism in the monumental *Critique of Dialetical Reason*.

Hard as he tried to ignore the ugly face of Soviet Communism, Kruschchev's 'secret speech' of March 1956 at the Twentieth Party Congress spelt out Stalin's crimes: the 'doctors'' plot, the East European show trials, the death camps. Sartre claimed at the time of the Henri Martin affair that 'the intellectual's duty is to denounce injustice wherever it occurs,' but instead he practised double standards, turning his blind eye to Soviet injustice even as he hysterically denounced America and the Free World. Justifying his hypocrisy in the name of realism, it nevertheless tugged at his conscience. 'There is a morality in politics – a difficult subject, and never clearly treated – and when politics must betray its morality, to choose morality is to betray politics,' he wrote at the death of Merleau-Ponty. 'I began to give way to the political realism of . . . Communism,' he admitted in 1973.

> All right, you do it because it works, and you . . . evaluate it according to its efficacy rather than some vague notions having to do with morality, which would only slow things down. But as you can well imagine . . . it upset me no end, despite the fact that – ignoring my own better judgement – I carried it through and finally arrived at a pure realism . . . And when I reached that point, what it meant was that I had blocked out all ideas of morality.

In 1960 Sartre, who had put his 'conversion' to Communism in religious terms, viewed his past sins in the language of the Old Testament: he had worshipped 'at the golden calf of realism'.

Sloughing off his writer's skin in favour of political activism was a slow, anguished business. Like Beauvoir, who was writing *Memoirs of a Dutiful Daughter*, Sartre turned to autobiography, beginning 'Jean-sans-terre,' the first version of *Words*, in 1953, as a way of 'saying goodbye to a certain kind of literature . . . The literature I'd pursued in my youth and then in my novels and short stories. I wanted to show that it was over and done with, and I wanted to emphasize the fact by writing a very literary book about my childhood.'

Yes, agreed Beauvoir, he'd been disgusted with literature. 'You used to say, "Literature is crap."' Did he mean that you should write 'just anyhow'? That there's no point in writing well?

'It's a queer thing, style,' replied Sartre. 'Many left-wing writers think that style, taking too much care of words and all that, is a terrible bore, and that one ought to go straight to the point, not worrying about the rest.'

Protested Beauvoir: 'But very often the result can be disastrous.'

She was, no doubt, thinking of the *Critique de la Raison Dialectique*, or the monstrous size to which his biography of Flaubert would grow. Swollen, grotesque, often unfinished, his 'literature of *praxis*' was a form of suicide. 'I write faster because I'm used to it now,' said Sartre. But he no longer wrote as he did formerly, pausing to think and make corrections:

> For hours at a stretch he raced across sheet after sheet without rereading them, as though absorbed by ideas that his pen . . . couldn't keep up with; to maintain this pace I could hear him crunching corydrane capsules, of which he managed to get through a tube a day.

Chewing the harmless-looking tablets, the drug of choice for intellectuals in the 1950s, with his coffee, Sartre's drug habit grew. Each tube of twenty tablets contained 50 mg of aspirin and 144 mg of amphetamines: lucidity in a pill, which not until 1971 was declared toxic and taken off the market. Sartre needed his uppers after his downers, four or five sleeping pills at night. Black coffee, two or three pipes of rich tobacco, two packs of cigarettes, a heavy lunch with a litre of red wine, meant that he lived on a chemical roller-coaster. The results were disastrous. By the end of an afternoon's work on the *Critique* in 1957 he would be exhausted. Dizzy, stumbling, his gestures became vague, his words 'all mixed up'. In the evenings, in her new apartment at 11bis rue Schoelcher, beside the Montparnasse cemetery, which Beauvoir had bought with her prize money from the Goncourt, she tried to restrain Sartre; but as soon as he drank a glass of whisky it went straight to his head.

'"That's enough," I'd say to him; but for him it was not enough.' Against her will, Beauvoir handed him a second glass. He would ask for a third. Sartre quickly lost control of his movements and his speech. 'That's enough,' repeated Beauvoir. Two or three times she flew into violent tempers, smashing a glass on the tiled floor of the kitchen. Generally she found it too exhausting to quarrel before the fourth glass.

Only Beauvoir, who daily witnessed the harsh process of Sartre's adieu to the novel, his forcing of himself, against his nature, to throw himself into politics, knew the price he paid. 'To think against oneself is all very well,' she wrote in her diary. 'It has fertile results – but in the long run it tears one to pieces; by forcibly smashing a way through to new ideas, he has done damage to his nerves.' She became doubly protective of her 'little man', who in his turn sometimes found her mothering smothering.

Camus, meanwhile, had recovered his voice. In a few weeks in 1956 he wrote *La Chute* (*The Fall*), his reply to *The Mandarins*. In the book, which won him the Nobel Prize for Literature the following year, he portrays the protagonist, Clamence, in the outer circle of hell, the circle reserved for betrayers. Many people thought he was referring to Sartre.

There is no doubt that Sartre defined himself against Camus, as well as against himself. He had described Camus as a *vedette*, meaning either a 'media star' or a 'patrol boat', and himself as a battleship. But the patrol boat slid effortlessly past the battleship with the acquisition of the Nobel Prize, to Sartre's irritation. After Camus's death, in January 1960, Sartre wrote a generous eulogy: '*Une brouille, ce n'est rien...tout juste une autre manière de vivre ensemble*, a quarrel is nothing, just another way of living together and not losing sight of each other in the narrow little world which is given to us.' But it was much more than that. The hostility Sartre and Beauvoir shared towards Camus both united and radicalized them, profoundly affecting their attitude towards violence between 1952 and 1960.

*

When Russian tanks rolled into Budapest in 1956 to crush the Hungarian uprising, living in bad faith finally proved too much for

Sartre. In *The Ghost of Stalin* he unreservedly condemned Soviet aggression, reserving particular venom for the leaders of the French Communist Party and their 'thirty years of lying and sclerosis'.

He, too, had found his voice again. The catalyst was not only events in Eastern Europe, but also those in North Africa, where the Algerian war had been coming to a head ever since the fall of Dien Bien Phu to the liberation army of the Viet Minh in May 1954, Sartre had seen that the writing was on the wall for colonialism. But although Pierre Mendès-France agreed peace with the division of Vietnam, and Morocco and Tunisia gained their independence, to the French, Algeria was different. Not only was it important, after the humiliation of the war, to regain national grandeur, but a deep-seated belief in the European civilizing mission underpinned opposition to decolonization. 'It is not just the status of colonialism which is at issue but the destiny of the white race, and with that of Western civilization, of which it is the guarantee, the only guarantee,' argued the conservative writer André Siegfried in *Le Figaro* in January 1950, unable to recognize that the equation of civilization with Caucasian culture, in itself unacceptable, was no justification for colonial conquest. It soon become obvious that both Mendès-France and Mitterand had given up Indo-China in order to consolidate a more restricted imperial power in Africa, and still believed in a France which ran 'from the Channel to the Sahara'. And, within the context of the Cold War, a defeat for colonialism was viewed by many as a defeat for the West.

After 124 years of occupation, the one million European *colons*, probably known as *pied noirs* because the original soldiers and settlers wore black boots, felt they belonged in Algeria. It was this sense of sharing an inclusive Mediterranean culture common to both *pieds noirs* and Moslems that would cloud Camus's judgement. But for Sartre, on the other hand, the issue of Algerian independence was one which awakened his most passionate feelings. Through the lens of existentialism he saw the oppression inherent in colonialism, the subjugation of the slave to the master as Europeans made black races the Other: 'The impossible dehumanization of the oppressed returns and becomes the alienation of the oppressor.'

Ironically, it was Sartre who brought to the liberation struggles of the second half of the twentieth century the revolt, freedom and passion so powerfully articulated by Camus. Sisyphean stoicism and suffering would be his lot, too, as he stood in solidarity with *Les damnés de la terre*, the wretched of the earth, the eponymous title of the book by the

Martinican psychiatrist Frantz Fanon, in the preface to which Sartre made his notorious statement that, to shoot a European is to 'kill two birds with one stone'.

On 1 November 1954 the Algerian National Liberation Front (FLN) launched an insurrection: the following August dozens of Europeans were massacred at Philippeville. In January 1956 Camus flew to Algeria, just as the new Prime Minister, Guy Mollet, was forming his government, to demand a truce. It was too little too late, and Sartre taunted Camus for being a neo-con. At the Salle Wagram in Paris he made a passionate appeal to the French people not to prop up colonialism, but 'to help it die', and 'to fight side by side with the Algerian people'. From that date his faith in the proletariat would be transferred to colonized peoples.

*

In 1958 Beauvoir began a new diary. It was, as usual, a form of therapy for her in a year in which her political and personal distress converged. 'Mad with rage' at the torture inflicted on Muslims by the French army, Sartre and Beauvoir now felt exiles in their own country. In Paris, she recoiled from the people in the street:

> all murderers, all guilty. Myself as well. 'I'm French.' The words scalded my throat like an admission of hideous deformity. For millions of men and women, old men and children, I was just one of the people who were torturing them, burning them, machine-gunning them, slashing their throats, starving them: I deserved their hatred.

In Stockholm, where he received his Nobel Prize, Camus, on the other hand, refused to speak out on behalf of the Arabs. To him, the FLN *fellaghas* were terrorists. Instead, he declared: 'I love Justice; but I will fight for my mother before Justice' – an admission, wrote the disgusted Beauvoir, that 'he was on the side of the *pieds noirs*'.

Unwilling accomplices to the war, the couple's fury escalated as the country called for the return of de Gaulle. On 26 May, as the French licked their wounds after the battle of Algiers and de Gaulle left Colombey-les Deux-Églises for Paris, Beauvoir poured her despair into her notebook. On Monday, 29 September, news came that de Gaulle had won 80 per cent in the Referendum: 'I began to cry. I'd never have believed it could affect me so much . . . Nightmares the whole night . . .

I can feel death in my heart.' For the French, it is 'a repudiation of themselves, an enormous collective suicide'.

A fortnight later, she had a new shock. Lunching with his producer, Simone Berriau, to show her the first draft of his new play, Sartre carefully put his glass down an inch from the table. As it shattered on the floor, Berriau immediately picked up the phone and made an appointment with the doctor. 'Days of horror,' wrote Beauvoir on 14 October. 'He stumbles over words, has difficulty walking, his handwriting and spelling are appalling, and I am appalled . . . Our death is inside us, but not like the pit in the fruit, like the meaning of life; inside us, but a stranger to us, an enemy, a thing of fear.' Too upset to continue writing, she stuffed the pages of her journal into a folder, which she labelled: 'Diary of a Defeat'. At fifty-three, Sartre had just missed having a heart attack. 'He is a very emotional man,' said the specialist. 'He has overworked himself intellectually, but even more so emotionally. He must have moral calm. Let him work a bit if he insists, but he mustn't try racing against the clock. If he does, I don't give him six months.' Sartre was ordered to stay off alcohol and cigarettes. When Beauvoir asked if he was tired, he answered confusedly: 'You know perfectly well: the thickets of the heart.'

At the end of the year another thread snapped. Lanzmann, who had met a rich widow of thirty-five, decided to separate from Beauvoir. She was fifty, and had never felt older.

*

Rome offered a refuge from French politics. In the summer of 1958 the city became their new *querencia*. 'Marvellous Italy! One slips into the atmosphere immediately,' wrote Beauvoir, when she and Sartre arrived in Milan on 16 June. On their twelfth trip to Venice they fell into their usual rhythm of work: up at 9.30, long breakfast with the papers in the Piazza San Marco. Work till 2.30. A snack and sight-seeing. Work from five till nine. Dinner. A Scotch at Harry's Bar. A last Scotch at midnight on the Piazza where, finally free of the musicians, the tourists and the pigeons, the square regained the beauty captured by Tintoretto, Sartre's favourite artist, in his *Abduction of St Mark*.

In Ravenna Beauvoir's spirits fell: six years ago she had arrived there with Lanzmann, at the beginning of their affair. Claude may have moved in with her initially through self-interest, or even simply as a bet, but his and Simone's relationship had become a full one. Claude's brother, Jacques, recalled that when he travelled with the couple in

Spain in 1954, he heard loud love-making in their bedroom. 'I thought Beauvoir a beautiful woman, beautiful and icy. In bed, I think she was the opposite.' The mystery that was Beauvoir, austere by day, passionate by night, proved attractive to Lanzmann: 'I found you very beautiful, with your smooth face,' he said; 'and I wanted to see what lay behind that impassive exterior.' On the back of his favourite photograph of the two of them, he wrote a dedication: 'Daytime: to my "first rate mind", the greatest female genius in humanity. Night time: to my African queen.'

Now, in Rome, the rain suited her grey mood. Sartre was struggling to write *The Condemned of Altona*, Beauvoir the second volume of her memoirs. In the Hotel Senato in the Piazza Rotonda they listened to the rumble of thunder, saw the rain drumming on the dome of the Pantheon. The storm cleared the air and, strolling through the Piazza Navona under a dark blue sky, they felt the calm of the Roman night. But it was a bitter moment for Beauvoir when she left Sartre at Pisa with Michèle, with whom he spent three weeks every summer (as well as two weeks with Wanda), and returned alone to Paris. In her *atelier d'artiste*, surrounded by mementos of trips she had taken with Lanzmann, she rued her first summer without him.

The rupture was all the harder to bear because Sartre was enjoying a fiery relationship with Lanzmann's younger sister, Evelyne. When Claude first introduced her to Beauvoir, she was a plump, red-haired actress from the provinces, whom she viewed as no threat. A year in Paris wrought its magic: Evelyne reinvented herself as a slim, platinum blonde. She divorced her husband, Serge Rezvani, and had a nose job, sacrificing her Semitic nose for a fashionable *retroussé*, which she hoped would help her get work. Her sexualized appearance belied her real personality: 'Evelyne was . . . so pretty,' wrote Beauvoir disingenuously, 'that people were amazed by her intelligence.'

Acting under the stage name Evelyne Rey, in the spring of 1953 the twenty-three-year-old actress won rave reviews as Estelle in *No Exit*. Intrigued, Sartre asked Claude to arrange a meeting. After a post-performance dinner with Beauvoir, Claude and Evelyne, the smitten playwright enthusiastically embarked upon a new affair. Did Claude act as procurer for his sister, as her former husband later claimed? According to Jacques Lanzmann, 'Claude regularly served as a "Madame" for Evelyne.' As a member of the Sartrean family, he had absorbed its mores.

How ironic for Beauvoir, and how painful, to see Sartre set Evelyne up as his mistress in a flat at 26 rue Jacob, just round the corner from his mother's flat in rue Bonaparte. Sartre was in love again. 'Evelyne was one of the women Sartre was most attached to,' Beauvoir later told John Gerassi. 'He was extremely jealous.'

Once again, Sartre had chosen a 'dark, drowning woman', like Olga and Kos. Abandoned by her mother, Paulette, at the age of six, Evelyne had been brought up by her Jewish father and Catholic stepmother, and had converted to Catholicism. Although she later rediscovered her mother, who lived in Paris with her second husband, the Jewish Yugoslav poet Monny de Boully, she was also 'a little crazy', like her brother Claude, who told Beauvoir, 'I want to kill, all the time.' Insecure and melancholic, a blue-eyed Jewish girl who had remade herself as an Aryan, she brought her own demons to her relationship with Sartre. To begin with, her relationship with him overlapped with her brother's with Beauvoir, and followed the incestuous pattern first established with Olga, for Beauvoir confessed to Nelson that 'the young guy I live with now (so much younger than me) is for me rather a kind of incestuous son than a lover . . . he asks for a motherly tenderness rather than something else'. The 'magic' she had had with Nelson had gone. 'It has been, and never will be again.' But, 'the fact is [Claude] has won my heart by his own stubborn love and faithfulness, and the way he gave himself entirely to me – as a child could do'.

After Lanzmann broke up with Beauvoir, Sartre had Evelyne all to himself. Sensually she pleased him very much, although he worried that being so much taller, she made him a figure of fun. But in her height may have lain her appeal, reminding him of his beloved, but ageing, Anne-Marie, who towered over her Poulou. Twenty-five years younger than Sartre, Evelyne, too, brought the 'fire and ice' of a prohibited relationship to her lover, representing the 'younger sister' he said in *The Words* he unconsciously sought.

But Evelyne was never acknowledged in public, like Castor, Wanda and Michèle Vian, now divorced. Michèle was kept in the dark so successfully that she never discovered that Sartre, who continued his sexual relationship with her, was also making energetic love to Evelyne. Jean Cau, listening to the tissue of lies tumbling from Sartre's lips as he phoned his girlfriends, watched as he replaced the receiver.

'It's difficult sometimes.'

'*Hé oui*', I say. *Hé oui*. I wonder how you manage. A tricky situation.

'*Mon cher Cau*, you've hit the nail on the head. There are some situations that I call *rotten*. You try to resolve them, but it's impossible to escape undamaged externally. *Vous voyez?*'

'Oh, absolutely . . . But what about internally? How do you manage that?'

'It's necessary, in some cases, to adopt a provisional morality.'

Michèle's morals, however, could be as 'provisional' as Sartre's. But in the fatal summer of '58 she let the cat out of the bag when her other lover, a musician named André Reweliotty, with whom she had been two-timing Sartre for the last nine years, knocked on the door of the room she was sharing with Sartre in Rome. Despite his own infidelity, Sartre was devastated. On 14 September he took the train back to Paris, to be met by the faithful Beauvoir, and worked for twenty-eight hours at a stretch, without sleep and almost without a break, on an article he had promised *L'Express* on de Gaulle. When he collapsed, Beauvoir rescued the scattered pages of smudged and spidery writing, and edited them in time for his deadline.

Sartre's feminine satellites increased in number yet further in 1956, perhaps in competition with Camus, who had at least four women, Francine, Maria, Catherine Sellers, and the latest addition, Mi. The newest planet around the Sartrean sun was Arlette Elkaïm, a nineteen-year-old student from Algeria, who also had a troubled past. Distressed at her mother's suicide, which took place when Arlette was fourteen, confused as to her identity – her father was a Sephardic Jew, her mother Arab – Arlette, too, rapidly became emotionally and financially dependent on Sartre. Fragile as a doe, she, too, was seduced.

*

By 1958 the actresses were at war. Evelyne Rey wanted to usurp Wanda as the star of Sartre's plays. In Venice with Arlette in the summer of '59, the writer's money was running out, but he had promised Evelyne a play: *The Condemned*. He and Arlette moved into a seedy hotel by the station, reminiscent of his old haunts in Le Havre. In the heat, dripping with sweat, Sartre finished the final monologue. Stripping off his shirt, he walked up and down, declaiming it 'in a very lyrical and melo-dramatic way, imbued with the same kind of cheap romanticism that made him play an extremely tearful Chopin on the piano', recalled Arlette. 'It was so odd that it rather scared me.' The completed play had a part for Wanda, whom he had also mollified by having Gallimard print two special copies of *La Critique* dedicated 'to Wanda', while dedicating the rest 'to the Beaver'. But after four years' silence, and the failure of *Nekrassov*, few critics expected him to recapture the success of *Kean*, his adaptation of Alexandre Dumas's play about the English actor Edmund Kean.

But this time Sartre had something to say. The question of torture in Algeria had become a pressing one. From Francis Jeanson, author of *Outlaw Algeria*, and founder of a French clandestine network, modelled on the Resistance, of *porteurs de valises*, suitcase carriers, who smuggled money raised for the FLN back to Algeria, he learnt of atrocities committed by the French army and publicized them in *Les Temps modernes* in a sarcastic article, 'Vous êtes formidables' ('You're Terrific'), in May 1957. André Malraux, former Resistant and Minister of Culture, stepped into the fray, publicly accusing Sartre of never having resisted the Germans, and even of having collaborated by allowing his plays to be put on during the Occupation. When in May 1958 Malraux announced: 'The use of torture has ceased,' Sartre was incandescent. Ever since the war, the theme of torture had obsessed him, in *No Exit*, in *Morts sans sépulture* in 1946, in *The Witches of Salem* screenplay (adapted in 1956 from Arthur Miller's *The Crucible*), and now in 1959 in *The Condemned*. Underlining the comparison between the Nazis and the French army by making his hero, Frantz von Gerlach, an SS officer, Sartre's powerful message is that humankind is responsible for its actions. 'Here is my century, solitary and deformed,' says Frantz. 'I, Frantz von Gerlach, here in this room, have taken the century upon my shoulders, and have said: "I will answer for it. This day and forever."' The final monologue was the best bit.

Beauvoir, hiding behind a pillar on the first night, was so apprehensive that the play would fail that she nearly fainted. But at the final curtain, the applause was so loud that 'I knew we had won.' Sartre's play affected her powerfully because of her own involvement in *La Question*, the issue of torture. In May 1960 the radical lawyer Gisèle Halimi had asked Beauvoir if she would publicize the case of a young Algerian girl, Djamila Boupacha, who was on trial as a militant and claimed to have been tortured. It was the time of the Alleg case, when the former editor of *Alger républicain*, whose book about his imprisonment and torture had been seized by the police, was causing a sensation. Beauvoir wrote an article for *Le Monde*. The editor telephoned her reproachfully. Djamila was, he said, under the gravest suspicion. 'I don't see that's any justification for sticking a Coke bottle into her,' retorted Beauvoir. The editor sighed. Could she at least change 'vagina' to 'womb' in the piece?

Joining Halimi's delegation to see the Minister of Justice on

Djamila's behalf, Beauvoir had her first taste of campaigning. Later she wrote the preface to Halimi's book on the Boupacha case. By then public hostility to her position, and that of Sartre's, had grown so great that she was virtually a prisoner in her studio.

*

In the 1960s Beauvoir made a last attempt to recapture the 'magic' she had once known with Nelson Algren, whose own life had become even more rootless and unhappy since his second divorce from Amanda. Walking out of his beloved cottage on the lake, quarrelling with Otto Preminger, Hollywood producer of the film of his book *The Man with the Golden Gun*, and losing all his money, Algren's outrage exploded in 1956 when he read *The Mandarins* in English and recognized himself as Lewis. He booked a trunk call from Chicago to complain, and Beauvoir waited nervously for the call, for the sound of his voice after five years. It never came.

The silence was broken when Beauvoir learnt that Algren had fallen through a hole in the ice and nearly drowned: 'It's so much like you, honey, to fall in a hole! But take care not to die. I had a pang in my heart when I heard it.' In September 1959 she urged him to 'Come to Paris in the spring to fill the magic-bag!' Living on his poker winnings in a furnished room in Chicago, Algren's thoughts returned fondly to his 'frog', who was offering her studio, her car and her cooking ('that, I know, scares you'). She even had a bathroom.

When Algren arrived, in February 1960, Beauvoir was in Cuba with Sartre: '*C'est la lune de miel de la Révolution*, it's the honeymoon of the revolution,' he said. Invited by the editor of the largest newspaper in Cuba, *Revolucíon*, the couple were fêted by Fidel Castro and Che Guavara, then Finance Minister. 'In Cuba and Brazil,' says Sylvie Le Bon de Beauvoir, 'Beauvoir and Sartre were in total accord.' Politically, yes: the energy and vigour of the young Castro, with whom they toured the streets of Havana in an open car, enchanted them. 'No old people in power!' remarked Sartre. 'I have met only people who could be my children.' Photographs show his and Beauvoir's rapt, adoring expressions as they listen to Castro's speeches, or perch on a sofa in front of Che. 'Is it my fault that reality is Marxist?' demanded the young revolutionary. This rhetorical question impressed Sartre so much that he often repeated it, as he and Beauvoir embarked on the love affair with a string of Third World leaders which would mark their future globe-trotting.

On 20 March Beauvoir rang her front door bell at rue Schoelcher. Nelson opened the door. 'It's you?' he asked in surprise, having expected her to arrive the next day. Beauvoir, in her turn, barely recognized Nelson without his glasses, which he had abandoned for contact lenses. Both had aged; but to Beauvoir all that mattered was 'that it was Algren'.

When the American held his 'poor little Gauloise' in his arms again, his anger over *The Mandarins* evaporated. He was wearing the same corduroy trousers, the same worn jacket, the same cap as in 1947. Soon they were sitting side by side on her divan reading the *New York Herald Tribune* and listening to Bessie Smith and Charlie Parker. Algren claimed to feel as much of an exile in America as Beauvoir did in France; but when he put his electric typewriter and reams of yellow paper on her desk, and piled up cans of American food, books, newspapers and records on the floor, 'Chicago came alive again in my studio.'

On occasions Algren behaved like a tourist, embarrassing Beauvoir by flashing the red bulb in the middle of his bow tie when he was introduced to visitors, or filming the prostitutes on the rue Saint-Denis until they spat at him. But otherwise the crocodile and the frog felt as close as in 'the best days of 1949'. The reconciliation was all the sweeter for the time they had wasted. Simone hung on Nelson's arm as they strolled through Paris, dined with him at the Akvavit, watched the flamenco at Les Catalans, drank onion soup at Les Halles and admired the striptease at the Crazy Horse. Together they travelled to Istanbul and Greece. From Beauvoir's account it seems that they resumed sexual relations. When they returned from a last, idyllic week in Crete she wrote wistfully: 'Not a single shadow of disagreement has troubled our five months together.'

It was the last time she would see him. '*J'ai quelque remords vers Algren*,' Beauvoir would tell Le Bon. The remorse she felt over Algren, her most important male lover, lingered because, in the elegiac serenity of their farewells, 'was a reminder of my true condition. *J'étais vieille*. I was an old woman.'

*

Beauvoir's political accord with Sartre hid her private pain. Wrenched from her intimacy with Algren to go on an exhausting, political tour of Brazil with Sartre, at the invitation of the novelist Jorge Amado, she wrote bitterly to her 'Dearest wonderful thing', her 'beautiful flower', her 'subversive beast of my heart, my faraway love,' of Sartre's neglect.

> You'll be proud of Sartre. He decided it wasn't enough to have one dark Algerian girl, one fair-haired Russian, and two fake blondes. What was he lacking? A red-headed one! He found her and began an affair with her. She is twenty-five and a virgin . . .

When Sartre followed the girl to Recife, Beauvoir fell seriously ill. As her fever climbed and the doctor diagnosed typhoid, Sartre 'went mad'. Abandoning Beauvoir, he spent his time with the girl, who, when he tried to seduce her, decided he was the Devil, broke glasses with her naked hands and threatened to bleed to death. Beauvoir dosed her up with sleeping pills and slept in bed with her, holding her wrist all night to prevent her jumping out of the window.

But Sartre's womanizing was secondary to his politics. He had arrived in Brazil in the wake of Malraux, Minister of Culture since July 1958, who had spent the summer of 1959 on propaganda trips through Latin America. 'In Brazil, I want to be the anti-Malraux,' he said, determined to counter Malraux's Gaullist propaganda with his own call for Algerian self-determination. Huge audiences flocked to hear him. 'Viva Cuba! Viva Sartre!' shouted the students. 'Cuba sí, Yankee no,' read the posters. Urging the youth of Latin America to follow the example of the Cuban revolution and unite against 'US imperialism', preaching anarchy as well as Marxism, Sartre became intoxicated by the power of his own rhetoric. But he also became the tool of his official hosts, as Beauvoir uneasily recognized. Warned by Jeanson not to return by plane to Paris, where members of the Organization Armée Secrète (OAS), the right-wing terrorist organization fighting for l'Algérie Française, would be waiting for them at the airport, the couple were 'kidnapped' by the Cuban consul, flown to Cuba, and 'detained' for a week in Caracas. 'We have to visit a big plant, lunch with the workers, then we see Fidel,' complained Beauvoir to Nelson.

Pawns of the Cubans, perhaps, Sartre and Beauvoir had also become powerful, global symbols of revolution and the counter-culture. Their return to France in November was a media event which met Sartre's hunger for danger, his deep-seated need to smash the 'glass prison' of his youth, to cancel out his cowardice and to prove himself a hero. On 5 September 1960, the trial of the 'Jeanson network' had opened in the same court in which Dreyfus had been tried, at a time when many Frenchmen were refusing to take up arms against the Algerians. Before leaving for Brazil, Sartre and Beauvoir had signed the 'Manifesto of the

121', the declaration by writers and artists of the 'right to insubordination in the Algerian War'. 'Use me as you want,' Sartre told his lieutenants, Lanzmann, Jean Pouillon, Péju and Bost. They forged his signature on an inflammatory letter he dictated from Brazil, defending Jeanson, and Sartre's immense prestige swung opinion behind the struggle for Algerian independence.

'Shoot Sartre!' shouted 5,000 veterans marching down the Champs Élysées. 'Al-gér-ie Fran-çaise' honked the horns outside the courtroom. But 'The great shadow of Sartre stood before [us] like a shield, tremendous,' said the defence counsel, Roland Dumas. 'His name alone tipped the scales, pulling in the leftist intelligentsia and initiating a reversal of public opinion.'

At the Spanish frontier, the Commissioner advised Paris that the writer had returned. In Paris, he and Beauvoir were determined to get themselves charged, but de Gaulle announced: 'You do not imprison Voltaire.' The following June a bomb exploded in the hall of 42 rue Bonaparte: Sartre moved Mme Mancy into a hotel and went into hiding with Beauvoir.

In Rome in July 1961, Frantz Fanon, who was dying of leukaemia, came to meet Sartre. It was an important encounter. Fanon, author of *Peaux Noirs, Masques Blancs* (*Black Skins, White Masks*) convinced Sartre that 'it is only in violence that the oppressed can attain their human status'. The Catholic journal *Témoignage chrétien* had already argued that the French themselves were responsible for the violence of their colonial subjects through their own misrule and brutality, and throughout the fifties this theme of the 'mirror image' of violence had been applied to Tunisia and Morocco. Written at the height of the Algerian war, at a time when Algerians were being herded into the Vel d'Hiv just as once the Jews had been, Fanon's book is a searing indictment of colonialism. Febrile and agitated, the dying man talked till two in the morning. Afterwards, Sartre wrote in his preface: 'This irrepressible violence . . . is man re-creating himself.' To his critics, it was an invitation to terrorism.

*

But OAS terror spread to metropolitan France after de Gaulle affirmed Algeria's right to self-determination. As Sartre continued to speak widely, he was pelted with rotten eggs and received death threats. In January 1962, at two in the morning, Beauvoir was wakened by a dull thud: a bomb had gone off in the rue Saint-Guillaume. 'Well, they've nosed us out,' she said to Sartre, who was standing on the balcony. In fact the bomb had been aimed at a *pied noir*. Three days later, on 7 January, Sartre's new secretary, Claude Faux, telephoned to say that 42 rue Bonaparte had been blown up. '*Cette fois ils voulaient votre peau.* This time they were after your blood.'

'I've got keys,' Faux had told the policeman standing guard outside the flat.

'Oh, you won't need keys.'

The bomb had been left on the flat above Sartre's, and had destroyed the two fifth-floor apartments, and torn off the door to his flat. Above the third storey, the staircase had collapsed. *Les plastiquers*, the bombers, had made the attempt on Sartre and Beauvoir's lives as a reprisal for his last press conference in Rome.

The couple immediately left their borrowed flat on boulevard Saint-Germain and moved to a new refuge on the Quai Louis-Blériot, overlooking the Seine, where they were given police protection. The day after the publication of Halimi's book on Djamila Boupacha, to which Beauvoir had lent her name as co-author, her concierge at the rue Schoelcher received a phone call: '*Attention! Simone de Beauvoir saute cette nuit!* Simone de Beauvoir will be blown up tonight.' As students moved into her flat to guard it, both Sartre and Beauvoir continued to speak and to demonstrate, despite the risks they ran as chief targets of the OAS.

On 1 July, Algerian independence was declared. Too many had died in seven years of war for either writer to rejoice. Estranged from their homeland, they had rediscovered their old 'paradise', Soviet Russia, and were busy walking its Elysian fields.

34

⁓

Madame Z(artre)

> You are my wife.
> Jean-Paul Sartre to Lena Zonina, July 1962

AT A DINNER party at the Soviet embassy in Paris, in 1958, Elsa
Triolet, grey-haired and blue-eyed, sat opposite Beauvoir and com-
miserated with her on the problems of ageing; as the two fifty-year-olds
laughingly agreed that they would like every looking-glass smashed,
Triolet, a KGB agent and wife of Louis Aragon, Communist leader of
the Comité National des Écrivains, congratulated herself on a job well
done. The Soviet aim was to bring Sartre and Beauvoir back into the
Communist orbit after the Russian intervention in Hungary. Following
the couple's visit to Cuba and an introduction to Krushchev at yet
another embassy reception, they were invited to return to Moscow by
the Union of Writers of the USSR. 'We would like very much to go,'
replied a delighted Sartre.

Despite his fierce denunciation of Soviet policy since World War II
as 'twelve years of terror and stupidity' in *L'Express* on 9 November
1956, and his statement that, 'It is not, and never will be possible to
resume relations with the men who are currently running the French
Communist Party', Sartre was performing a startling volte-face. The
Algerian war and the Bay of Pigs fiasco had drawn him closer to the
Communists, as the world seemed to tremble on the verge of a third
world war. 'It seems your dirty Kennedy is going to make serious trouble

for Castro,' wrote Beauvoir to Algren on 14 April 1961. 'I hate this grinning boy and his grinning wife.' As the Berlin Wall went up, Sartre's commitment to Marxism and revolutionary 'counter-violence' grew even firmer. Repeating to himself Che Guevara's remark: 'It's not my fault that reality is Marxist', he blamed himself in his preface to Paul Nizan's *Aden-Arabie* for not having rebelled earlier like his old friend, and decided that if Nizan were alive in 1961 he would have rejoined the Party.

Arriving in Moscow on 1 June 1962, Sartre and Beauvoir were greeted at the airport by thirty-nine-year-old Lena Zonina, 'Consultant' to the Foreign Commission of the Writers' Union. Their new interpreter spoke flawless French and was a literary critic who had already written articles on their work. Slim, *petite* and curvaceous, with lustrous dark eyes and hair, she was also tough and highly intelligent.

But Sartre was on his guard. Angry that in 1954 he had been 'led by the nose' and told the expedient lie that 'freedom of criticism is complete in the USSR', he was determined not to be fooled again. Instead of being shown a construction site in Nove-Peschanaya Street, or being forced to sit through a conference on collective farming, as on his last visit to Moscow from 25 October to 1 November 1955, he wanted to visit *kolkhozes*, meet peasants. On that occasion, as the unsigned Soviet report on his visit records, Sartre had protested that 'My questions were not answered . . . I needed a sincere discussion.' He complained that the puppet play, *Divorce Case* he was taken to see was 'too long . . . We didn't find anything funny in this play,' and that in Simonov's play, *One Love Story*, which they saw at the Mossovet Theatre, the characters were 'hackneyed' and stereotypical. When shown the Komsomolskaya underground station, he remarked that it 'lacked taste . . . due to the desire to show off the wealth of the USSR'. At the Tretyakov Gallery, he criticized Soviet painting; after being shown round GUM, he observed, 'shop windows in Moscow are a lot more vulgar' than those in Paris. From the point of view of his Soviet hosts, he was a difficult customer.

But Sartre had been even more on the defensive with the Western media in Moscow. When the correspondent from *France-Soir* asked if he liked being in the USSR, Sartre replied, yes, he felt among friends. 'You are a person of a bourgeois way of life and a decadent,' retorted the journalist. 'Do you really think that they can feel at home with you?' 'What fools they are,' said Sartre to his Soviet minders in 1955 of the 'reactionary journalists' who pursued him from the *New York Herald Tribune* and other papers. 'They live in the USSR and . . . they don't understand all the changes that have taken place.' By the end of the trip, he had assured his Soviet hosts that his 'main impression' from the visit was that 'the Soviet people' had become 'more simple and free', and he expressed a wish to visit again with Beauvoir in the summer of 1956.

Hungary had intervened. Truly shocked by the brutal Soviet actions in crushing the green shoots of democracy, Sartre was wary and suspicious when he stepped on to Russian soil in June 1962. Of this, his Soviet hosts were well aware. 'He had made declarations in the press about his break-up with Soviet writers following the events in Hungary in 1956,' notes Zonina in her first report, 'and continued to regard the Soviet Union with suspicion in the years that followed'; his relations with the French Communist Party were 'complex and strained', so it was difficult to organize his programme: 'His past literary connections had to be restored with great caution.' She warned superiors against Sartre's 'absolute intolerance towards anything that he could define as "propaganda"'.

But what a rare prize Sartre was. What a coup for the Soviets, at the height of the cultural Cold War, if they could bring him on side again. 'The importance of his visit cannot be overestimated,' continues Zonina. 'He now enjoys immense authority among the progressive intelligentsia abroad.' Known as a writer and philosopher in the post-war period, in the last ten years he had become 'even more famous as a social and political figure' commanding 'immense influence over wide circles of the intelligentsia who fear the revival of Fascism'. His magazine *Les Temps modernes* formed opinion, his opposition to the Algerian war had made him a towering symbol of the 'anti-fascist, anti-war and anti-colonial struggle', popular not only with the French and Algerian intelligentsia, but with the Arab, African and Latin-American avant-garde.

And Sartre is ready to jump. As a mark of their opposition to de Gaulle, he and Beauvoir have broken their cultural exchange agreement with the French government and refused to allow the Ministry of the Interior to pay for their tickets to Moscow. As well as paying for themselves, they refused to meet anyone from the French embassy in Moscow. Knowing how much was riding on the visit, the Soviets choose their interpreter with the utmost care. By providing Zonina as Sartre's guide, they would manage their target even more effectively than in 1954.

Was Lena a spy? 'My mother was no Mata Hari,' says her daughter, Macha, in response to allegations that Lena was a sting. Zonina was 'a *grande dame* of Russian letters and not a "direct or indirect agent of the KGB",' writes Gilbert Dagron, at the time cultural attaché at the French embassy in Moscow, and a close friend of Zonina's. 'A woman of slightly austere and haughty beauty, not a seductive spy under orders to fool a naïve philosopher.' Others who met her in France had a different opinion: '*Elle était effectivement agent du gouvernement,*' says Sartre's publisher, Robert Gallimard.

'The story that Lena was just a translator who fell in love with Sartre is a fairytale,' states Oleg Gordievksy, the highest ranking KGB officer ever to work for Britain. For eleven years, 1974 to 1985, Gordievsky, as a double agent, reported to MI5 while continuing to work for the KGB, first in Copenhagen and then in London; in 1963 he was already a KGB officer familiar with the circumstances surrounding her recruitment. 'Lena was Jewish, and her story cannot be understood without knowing what it meant to be a Jew in the USSR,' he says. Stalin's anti-Semitic campaign, unleashed in 1948, had begun slowly but soon became brutal:

> Jews who had taken Russian names were ordered to reveal their 'real' names. The outstanding Jewish theatre director, Solomon Mikhoels, head of the Jewish anti-Fascist committee, was killed by the KGB in Minsk, Belarus, in a fake car-crash.

In 1949, Lena Zonina's father, Alex Zonin, a writer, was arrested as an 'enemy of the people' and sent to the gulag in Kazakhstan. For Lena, a diminutive of 'Lenina', the name given to her by her Bolshevik mother, to be the daughter of a traitor was a 'great disgrace'. Barred from finishing her university studies, 'she would have been scared of what could happen to her, especially in 1952. By then a rumour was going round that the entire Jewish population was going to be sent to Siberia.' At that point Ilya Ehrenbourg allegedly rescued Lena from social death by employing her as his secretary, and after her father's release in 1955 she completed her postgraduate degree in French.

But Russian Jews had long been a source of officers, including 'very senior generals, colonels and majors', for the KGB, and its predecessor, the NKVD, as well as a large numbers of agents, says Gordievsky: 'Just members of the public, who were never dropped, but on the contrary, recruited more Jews, because Jews felt ever more helpless. Practically all Jews of any position of influence were recruited to the KGB. They would sign a form stating: "I commit myself to clandestinely co-operate with the Soviet government, and I am prepared to keep my relationship secret." They signed papers in their hundreds,' he recalls. In the war Zonina served in the navy, possibly as an intelligence officer rather than just 'scrubbing decks' as she claimed.

> She would have been recruited either in the navy or at university, but certainly before she joined Ehrenbourg, and was possibly suggested by the KGB to him. As his secretary, she was sure to be vetted by the KGB. Ehrenbourg was a national figure, a long-serving KGB agent, and a man of influence. His secretary was an important person who would be carefully chosen.

By 1962 the Writers' Union was 90 per cent penetrated by the KGB. 'All translators and interpreters were in the KGB without exception, including everyone who had contact with overseas,' says Gordievsky. 'Between 1962 and '66 the KGB was total master of everything international. At this time the Fifth Directorate was established in the KGB with an ideological function: it was responsible for spying on intellectuals. Lena Zonina would have been under its control. If she did well, if her superior officers approved of her, she would get money presents on her birthday, and at Christmas.'

From the 200,000 KGB agents in Moscow at the time, Lena would have been carefully selected to work with 'such an important target'. But she was not the KGB's first choice. Another interpreter, V. Gak, from the Institute of International Relations, was picked. Gak, reports Zonina, in language which to a Russian reader indicates 'without the slightest doubt' that she is a KGB agent, 'is a Party member [and] among his acquaintances are many of *our comrades* [my italics] who had studied at the same time as him at the Military Institute for Foreign Languages'. But Gak enraged Sartre and Beauvoir with tactless questions about their relationship with the French Communist Party.

> 'What sort of propaganda are you carrying on here?' demanded Sartre. 'Who do you take me for?' Even Simone de Beauvoir who, as I later learned, usually checks Sartre when he loses control of his temper, flew into a rage and started repeating:
> 'This isn't propaganda, it's a provocation. Why are you provoking us? What's the purpose of this?'

Back at their hotel, on that first evening, she and Sartre decided to cut their visit short. Zonina, about to leave for a literary colloquium, was ordered to cancel her trip and take over. 'It cost me a lot of effort afterwards to convince Sartre that Gak's statements in no way expressed the attitude of . . . the Soviet Union,' she reported. 'This incident increased Sartre's suspicion towards all things Soviet'.

She was the KGB's last hope if their project was not to be derailed. But in asking Lena to handle the prickly couple, they had made the ideal choice. Attractive, flirtatious, feminine and perceptive, but scared as to her own future, and with a daughter to care for, Zonina was highly motivated. 'She would have asked what ideas she had to put into Sartre's head when she met him,' explains Gordievsky. Zonina's cold, businesslike prose confirms this: 'What Sartre was shown . . . was extremely important.' His 'reaction to what he sees would attract interest . . . all over the world'. Therefore, his programme, was

> set up in such a way as to give him a complete illusion that he meets with anyone he wants to meet, that he chooses the subjects for conversation, and that he works out his own programme rather than follows one imposed on him.

Sartre's hotel room, and Beauvoir's, were bugged. Microphones were installed in the walls and an army of 'listeners', like Gordievsky's wife, Yelena, transcribed the tapes. Time lapses or passages of silence in the tapes were given their own abbreviations, such as 'PA', which stood for *polovoi akt,* sexual intercourse. The listeners would not have long to wait before 'PA' featured in their transcripts. Within days Sartre was falling in love with the beautiful Russian.

*

Beauvoir also fell prey to Soviet spin. 'No more banquets . . . no more propaganda,' she recorded approvingly in the third volume of her memoirs, *Force of Circumstance.* She defended the camps, 'really rehabilitation centres', and argued that the internees they met approved 'in principle' of the system that required their incarceration. Russia, she claimed in 1962, had emerged from the Dark Ages into the dawn of a Renaissance in which Kafka, Saint-Exupéry, and even the bourgeois Dostoevsky were once again read, and students everywhere cried: 'Translate Camus, Sartre, Sagan, everything!'

Sartre's initial aim had been to see the Virgin Soils (in Russian, *tselina*), a pet project of Brezhnev's since the Central Party resolution of 2 March 1954 had made the decision to plough up virgin land, for example the steppe of Kazakhstan, and resettle it. But Sartre never got to see the virgin soils around Kiev and Leningrad; instead he and Beauvoir were persuaded to go to Rostov, a large village 120 miles outside Moscow to meet Party *apparatchiks*. Unaware that their 'friend' Alexis Sourkov, First Secretary of the Union of Writers was, according to Gordievsky, 'a KGB agent 150%', or that Fadeev, head of the Union, had denounced many dissidents and sent them to the gulag (he would commit suicide when internees were released and he was obliged to face up to his past), the unsuspecting couple believed that when they dined with Simonov in his country *dacha*, their wishes to meet 'real peasants' were being met. They were introduced to the art historian Dorosh who, gushes Beauvoir, 'loves the peasants' so much that he has rented a simple room in an *isba* to get to know them better. He talks Sartre into abandoning the idea of 'virgin soils'. Far better to go to Rostov, where he can introduce them to 'interesting people . . . Comrade Karabanov, a Party organizer' and 'I.A. Fedoseev, People's Deputy and retired chairman of a collective farm'.

Closely shadowed by Lena and three officials, Sartre and Beauvoir finally reach the village; they are told that all the peasants have gone home. One woman remains in a barn. 'Can we visit her *isba?*' 'No, she has just washed all her laundry.' The couple peer at a lamp burning in front of an icon. 'Are there a lot of peasants who are practising Christians?' 'They can all decide for themselves,' answers the Head of Propaganda briskly. At this point Sartre begins shouting, 'I am interested in people and their psychology and not in the beans you've planted this year.' Once again, Lena tries to save the day:

> I made an attempt to speak to the comrades, having chosen a convenient moment when neither Sartre nor Beauvoir was around. Comrades replied that they could not entrust Dorosh with the role of leader as his view of the processes . . . in the oblast differed from their view.

As the Communists argue, Sartre repeats over dinner: 'Tomorrow we want to see some peasants.' The next morning he refuses to visit a collective farm; Lena announces that she is taking them to a shoe factory. 'We refused,' said Beauvoir. As they returned to Moscow a day early, Zonina reported on her 'target':

> This episode has shown that . . . standard, 'protocol' forms of communication irritate him and bring undesirable results.

The spy redoubled her efforts to create an 'element of "spontaneity"' in Sartre's meetings. From that moment, Sartre and Beauvoir were both, once again, led by the nose. The 'illusion' that Sartre was not a 'famous foreigner' but a 'human being, a writer with whom it is interesting to discuss pressing issues', was cultivated by Lena; peasants were forgotten and informal 'encounters' substituted. It was time to play her trump card: sex.

Enchanted by 'white nights' in St Petersburg, Beauvoir drank a vodka toast at the spot where Pushkin fought his last duel, inspected the courtyard where the old woman moneylender killed by Raskolnikov lived, and peered into the dark depths of the canal where he disposed of the axe. But as she ticked the boxes on their three-week sightseeing tour of Russia, Sartre's hand was in Lena's, and her thighs were warming his. At night in the Peking hotel in Moscow, the hidden cameras rolled as Sartre made love to Lena. '*Je t'aime*,' he whispered, to the crash of an imaginary Wagnerian orchestra. He loved her body and soul: she was his wife. In the ten-page letter he wrote on his return, he remembered how, in Russia, she had been his wife 'officially'. Down there, they married us. '*Tu me manques terriblement*, I miss you terribly.'

Sartre believed that Lena was in love with him. Sexually she aroused him in a way he, at fifty-seven, could barely believe. '*Tout était pour moi sexuel*,' he wrote wonderingly, as he remembered how she had rejuvenated him. Wild nights, not white nights, filled his memory: her flesh with its *odeurs sauvages*, animal smells, her bare breasts, her soft skin. Her smile as she closed her eyes last thing at night, and lay in his arms. You love me as much as I love you, he wrote: you are as hungry for me as I am for you, you fill me up, you satisfy me, you overwhelm me. '*Ton amour existe*,' he wrote. She had convinced him that she loved him. He was ill-favoured, older, but she gave him the gift of herself.

A better-looking man might have been less gullible. 'Sartre was a little barrel of a man, and as ugly as a human being can be,' wrote the film director John Huston in 1958, when Sartre wrote a screenplay on Freud for him. 'His face was both bloated and pitted, his teeth were yellowed and he was wall-eyed. He wore a grey suit, black shoes, white shirt, tie and vest.' Sartre's other women remembered how grateful he was for sexual favours. In his biography of Flaubert, *L'Idiot de la Famille*, which reads as a 'disguised autobiography', Sartre attacks the novelist's mother, Caroline, for turning her son into the daughter she wanted: 'Putting her imprint on him, she has condemned him for ever to have only an *imaginary* sexual life. An unreal woman in men's hands he will be an unreal man in his relations with women.' Sartre still blamed his own mother, who had hoped for a daughter named 'Annie', for bringing him up as a girl, passive and feminized. But with Lena, fiery and sexually experienced, the 'unreal man' felt the blood sing in his veins. So powerful was his own passion that it did not occur to him that Lena's might be counterfeit.

But Lena was under intense pressure. Twice married and divorced, she lived with her mother, and two-year-old Macha, in a fifth-floor apartment in Moscow. Ill with diabetes, she was often on the verge of collapse. Sartre talks of her heavy body sprawled in the armchair after sex, unaware of what 'giving herself totally' had cost her. Insulin-dependent, Lena injected herself three times a day, and carried bread with her in case of a hypoglycaemic attack. Even so, on one occasion she fainted in front of Sartre and Beauvoir. The animal insulin available in the USSR did not suit her, and she nursed the hope that her new lover could bring her human insulin from France.

The pressure ratcheted up on Ehrenbourg too, whose own survival hung in the balance. As the flight of intellectuals from the French Communist Party intensified, Sartre's own global prestige was soaring: the prize had to be courted assiduously and relentlessly. My approach has brought 'positive results', reports Zonina triumphantly to her KGB superiors. The target has made 'certain positive political conclusions regarding changes in the atmosphere of our country following the 20th and 22nd Party Congresses', and now considers it in a 'period of bloom'. He has given an interview to the Polish press, published on 23 June 1962 in *Politika*, in which he declares that today 'Russian writers and left-wing Western European writers once can speak . . . with freedom . . . without fearing to stumble against a taboo'; he has also agreed to publish Soviet authors regularly in *Les Temps modernes*. Before Sartre and Beauvoir left the USSR, Ehrenbourg and Zonina extracted another promise from him: to speak at the forthcoming World Congress for Peace and Disarmament.

Sartre's infatuation with Lena meant he danced to the Soviet tune. He would return eight times within four years. Within a fortnight of leaving, Sartre had dumped Beauvoir and returned alone to Moscow to speak on 'The Demilitarization of Culture' at the Congress from 11 to 16 July. From the moment that the project of a congress of intellectuals against disarmament was proposed, wrote Sartre gleefully to Lena, he had 'a valid reason to go to the USSR without recanting'. His presence lent weight to Soviet 'peace' propaganda at a time when the Russians were developing and stockpiling arms. Irresponsible and gullible, Sartre's motivation was chiefly sexual: to be alone with Lena, who was again his interpreter and staying in the same hotel. There, behind drawn curtains, drinking vodka together, Sartre congratulated himself on his Macchiavellian skill in escaping the other delegates as well as Beauvoir's tiresome chaperonage.

'On ne fait qu'un, we are one,' had been Beauvoir and Sartre's mantra. Now Sartre recalled how, after sex with Lena, he lay spent on her stomach as she slept, and underlined the words: 'Tout à fait un, pas tout à fait deux.' They were completely one: again he underlined the fact that he was saying it for the *first time*. He had shed his skin in Moscow, wrote the old Kobra, in a final death, in words that recall the French expression for orgasm, le petit mort. Now the 'ancien serpent' had new skin on his old bones, and had become her 'bébé serpent'. In words which echo his 1929 proposal to Simone, he proposed a 'pacte' with Lena in which he promised to be 'faithful unto death – or senility'.

Caught up in a whirlwind of passion, Sartre barely spared a thought for his 'old wife', Castor, who was dismayed by the new threat posed by her young and sensual Russian rival. It was hard to bear. In the poignant epilogue to Force of Circumstance, which she finished in March 1963, Simone de Beauvoir bravely asserts: 'There has been one undoubted success in my life: my relationship with Sartre. In more than thirty years, we have only once gone to sleep disunited.' But even as she affirmed their perfect harmony, her memoir charted their increasing distance from each other.

Afraid that Lena would become 'another Dolorès', Beauvoir followed her usual practice of making friends with her rival. 'We liked her very much,' she wrote dolefully in her memoir. Few of her readers knew what it cost her to write those lines. A photograph of herself beside a glowing, triumphant 'Madame Z' tells a different story of pain and displacement.

Celibate and alone, her partnership with Sartre increasingly diverging from the legend of the model couple, fifty-four-year-old Beauvoir loathed her appearance: 'I often stop, flabbergasted, at the sight of this incredible thing that serves me as a face . . . The eyebrows slipping down toward the eyes, the bags underneath, the excessive fullness of the cheeks, and that air of sadness around the mouth that wrinkles always bring.' While the middle-aged Sartre made love to Lena, she faced a different fate: the 'pox of time', as she called it, for which there was no cure, had stolen her beauty. 'Jamais plus un homme, never again a man,' she lamented.

Her depression was due not only to ageing, but to the public hostility she still encountered. 'You've won. You've made all the right enemies,'

Nelson Algren had said to Beauvoir in 1960, after the success of *Prime of Life*. But insults were often hard to take. 'In France, if you are a writer, to be a woman is simply to provide a stick to be beaten with,' she wrote. 'The fact is that I am a writer – a woman writer, which doesn't mean a housewife who writes but someone whose whole existence is governed by her writing.' But because of her message that women were 'not just a tribe of moral cripples from birth', she had the rat pack at the heels. Whispers, looks, sneering laughter, dogged her movements. She hid in her studio and refused to give interviews to the press. In March 1963, on the last page of her memoir, she wrote bitterly: 'The promises have all been kept. And yet, turning an incredulous gaze towards that young and credulous girl, I realize with stupor just how much I've been swindled.'

'*Je mésure avec stupeur à quel point j'ai été flouée.*' 'In 1929 everything was possible for Simone de Beauvoir,' recalls Le Bon. 'Now the dreams of youth had faded. She felt she'd been swindled, because of the malice towards her, the hostility.' But it was not the only reason Castor felt cheated; she was terrified of losing Sartre's love.

*

Sartre would do anything for his Lentchka, his new 'wife'. When at the Peace Congress in July 1962, Zonina and Ehrenbourg sternly criticised his Round Table speech appealing to Marxists to assimilate the 'best things in Western culture', and told him that it implied a rejection of the 'ideological struggle', he at once agreed to change it. His next address to Congress emphasised 'the importance of ideological struggle'. Lena was pleased to find him so obedient. Sartre 'is intolerant when ideas are imposed on him,' she reported, 'but respects sensible arguments if they are presented with tact'.

In the 900 pages of outpouring of his love, Sartre shows no signs of suspicion that Zonina might be *une espionne*, a spy. Despite his intellectual gifts and his harem of women, he was woefully unprepared for entrapment by a fragile but skilful woman who knew that her life might depend on the successful seduction of an ageing writer.

*

From Rome, where he and Beauvoir stayed in August, Sartre wrote that he felt like Orpheus, forbidden to gaze upon his Eurydice. Physically, he was frustrated, in 'hell'. It was too dangerous to entrust their letters to the post, and so he depended on Ehrenbourg, Sourkov and others as couriers. But this time it was the Italian writer Carlo Levi, just back from Moscow, who handed Sartre a letter from Zonina.

His memories of her flooded back: his Lentchka, unhappy, ill, tired, but blossoming like a flower of the night. His Lentchka, holding Macha in her arms. But Sartre's reply, which included his journal about his 'women' and his outings with Beauvoir, Olga and Bost, who were staying in a nearby studio, seemed to arouse Lena's jealousy.

Don't be jealous, he remonstrated with his '*petite bête sauvage et blessée*', his wild, wounded little animal. He loved her, diabetes and all. There are only two people in my life: 'You and le Castor.' His other mistresses didn't exist, they were merely his 'patients'. That Lena's own illness and vulnerability might have been part of her attraction for 'Dr' Sartre seems not to have occurred to him, as he related '*la tournée du médécin*', his 'medical round' in Paris, which consisted of going from one tearful woman to another. His patients told him their troubles with men, the tricks they got up to, their little lies, quite shamelessly, as if he were a woman, or their mother. He, in his turn, was in the habit of lying to them. It took only three seconds for a 'patient' to start crying when he entered her room, he related. Like a pet dog, he put up with his mistresses' whims: '*Bref, je m'ennuie à mourir*, I'm bored to death.'

Cynical, yet at heart sympathetic to feminine frailty, Sartre stressed to Zonina that he merely played a 'maternal role' with his women. His love he reserved for her. But it is no coincidence that in 1963, while writing *Les Mots*, Sartre asked his old friend, J.B. Pontalis, to psycho-analyse him. Sartre had made an intensive study of Freud, whose biography by Ernest Jones had been translated for him by Michèle Vian, and although he dissociated himself from the film Huston ultimately made with Montgomery Clift, he retained his interest in Freud. Pontalis wisely refused to become Sartre's therapist, although he commented that the treacherous narrative of 'Jean-sans-terre' should have been entitled 'Jean-sans-père'. Sartre began analysing his own dreams. Henceforth he would see himself in the therapeutic role with his 'patients', complaining, like his doctor grandfather, of the tediousness of his daily rounds, which had, he told Lena, cast a heavy shadow over his recent years in Paris.

Olga was one of his principal 'patients'. Unhappy in her marriage to Bost, who was having an affair with an American woman in Paris, Barbara Aptekman, she quarrelled with him constantly. On more than one occasion Bost had left home. On 8 September Sartre explained to Lena how fond he remained of Olga, despite her 'ravaged face', which was like a death's head, or a dead butterfly's, marked by the effects of tuberculosis and anorexia and, to cap it all, failed plastic surgery. She had gambled on 'le hasard du couteau, the luck of the knife' six years ago, when the septum of her nose had collapsed, probably due to cocaine addiction or the rags soaked in ether she was accustomed to stuff up her nose. Castor and he, said Sartre, although not in principle in favour of cosmetic surgery, had offered her a 'new nose'. But Olga had felt uncomfortable among the rich women in their furs in the waiting-room, and had refused her follow-up appointments with her surgeon. As a result, her 'nez de nouveau' had cartilage in the wrong place, and she was distressed at her appearance, her pale eyes, bad skin and lifeless hair. Castor, sighed Sartre, visited Olga once a week, but she was a burden.

As for her forty-four-year-old sister, Wanda, she was 'drunk with unhappiness and hate'. She'd acted in his plays under the stage name Marie Olivier, without the slightest success. He had written *Huis Clos* for Wanda, explained Sartre, but the problem was that the more she acted, the more the critics tore her to pieces. Nobody employed her but him, and the result was 'total failure . . . She's *really* mad.' Michèle was nervous, but Wanda was psychotic, paranoid. They'd been intimate from 1941 to '44, until she had made their break-up inevitable by sleeping with Camus. But despite her pathological rages, he couldn't abandon her. He saw her three times a week, for two hours a time.

On 1 October, after his return to Paris, Sartre stayed with Beauvoir in rue Schoelcher, and his description of their life together hints at the impregnability of their routine. He slept on the divan, Beauvoir in the little bedroom at the top of the spiral staircase. There was a big bay window overlooking the Montparnasse cemetery. Castor was accustomed to leaving out the leftover ham from the evening meal on the windowsill for the birds, until the Italian woman in the flat above accused her of feeding the dead. The graves in the cemetery were so old, wrote Sartre, that the tragedy of death was effaced. He and Castor liked the peaceful atmosphere, and the view over the cemetery of trees and flowers. The following year, when he moved to a tenth-floor flat at 222 boulevard Raspail, Sartre drew Lena a careful map showing his village, Montparnasse, and 'my view' over the green pastures of the cemetery.

His next letter was turning into a 128-page 'document', which he didn't dare trust to anyone. All he wanted was to spend Christmas in her arms.

*

But when Sartre and Beauvoir returned to Moscow in December, Zonina was strangely unavailable. Sartre's fervour reached even dizzier heights. Outside it was freezing, inside he lay on the bed masturbating. 'It's not my fault, nor is it yours.' Other people had separated them, and he was bursting with frustration, like a Siamese twin severed from his other half. 'C'est que je *te désire*', wrote Lena's unhappy suitor: 'I want to enter you.' But they were never left alone, and he could only survive on memories of her rounded stomach, the rosy cheeks of her *derrière* and her bush, black as a Russian night.

'I have lived in Hell for two hours,' wrote Sartre on 15 December. He had promised to return to Paris on the 10th, and he was still waiting on the 15th. There was surely some misunderstanding. It was minus twenty; he *had* to see her. Manipulated by the KGB, Sartre was a puppet on a string. He and Beauvoir were allowed to meet dissident writers such as Solzhenitsyn, whose novel about his experience of the camps, *A Day in the Life of Ivan Denisovich*, had been published by *Novy Mir*: 'There is great hope that [they] will win in this stupid battle the old academic people and Kroutchtchev began against them,' wrote Beauvoir to Algren in April 1963. But the thaw was going into sharp reverse. Krushchev had attacked modern art after visiting an exhibition of painting and sculpture. His propaganda chief Ilyichev made an anti-Semitic speech denouncing 'ideological coexistence'. Sartre, crazy with desire, remained blinkered. Drawn into a web spun by Lena, who must have marvelled at his naiveté, he failed, unlike Gide, to take the unique opportunity to look under the surface of Soviet totalitarianism or to report from the front line.

From the Soviet point of view, Sartre and Beauvoir were, states Gordievsky: 'Useful idiots . . . There is not the slightest doubt that Lena Zonina was a secret agent of the KGB.' Her reports to the Soviet Writers Union, parts of which Sartre may have been allowed to see, only tell half the story. Her KGB 'information files' on Sartre and Beauvoir, which reveal her true opinion of her targets, are buried in the KGB archives which are closed to Western researchers.

*

Finally the KGB allowed Sartre his heart's desire. Nights in the 'big bedroom' with his seductress. Touched by her courage, afraid of her '*fragilité*' and her illness, he swore that nothing but atomic warfare would stop him returning to see her. '*Je t'aime, ma chérie . . . tu es ma femme, mon amour.*'

He kept his promise in August 1963, when he and Beauvoir returned to the Soviet Union for the COMES Congress (Community of European Writers) meeting in Leningrad. COMES had been set up in Italy with the intention of bridging the gap between writers of the East and West, but when the french couple arrived Soviet writers expressed their contempt for Western literature, particularly Proust and Joyce. Dostoevsky's thesis that, with the death of God, anything is allowed, was realized to the full in the 'rotten, corrupted' West, said Leonov.

Flying down to Georgia to meet Krushchev at his country house, Beauvoir was surprised to find herself and Sartre subjected to an aggressive speech by the leader, as if they were 'so many henchmen of capitalism'. 'You were very rough on them,' said Sourkov afterwards to Krushchev. 'They must understand,' he replied sharply. Afterwards Sartre heard that Thorez had called on Krushchev that morning and warned him to be on his guard against the anti-Communists he was going to meet, who were all the more dangerous because they pretended to belong to the Left. Ehrenbourg was also accused by Krushchev of inciting Sartre to leave the Communist Party. Ehrenbourg observed that Sartre had never belonged to it; but it was no use.

Sartre and Beauvoir travelled on for six weeks, through the Crimea to Armenia, escorted by Lena. This time, Sartre was in the Soviet Union long enough to appreciate the unstable political situation. 'Ma Lentchka, ma femme,' he wrote from Rome, he loved her more than ever: 'beaucoup plus'. Concerned at the risks she ran, he had suggested marriage to her. Apart from his 'angel', he was going entirely without sex, he told her; if she came to Paris they could be together, and he could provide her with far better healthcare.

But Sartre was also growing jealous of Lena's coquetterie. She was 'très coquette', casting spells on men. It was a theme that would become recurrent, as he reproached her for being 'tellement coquette, such a flirt', while repeating that he trusted her. 'I can't see any reason why she should be in love with Sartre,' says Gordievsky.

Soviet reality made people very cynical and double-faced. It was easy for Zonina to play the part of a woman in love. It is likely that the KGB would have given her another man to target as well. She probably exaggerated her illness, because Sartre himself was not strong, and because he had a great interest in sick women.

Lena procrastinated when Sartre urged her to come to Paris. Had there been a strong 'operational need', she would have been allowed to visit, as she did in 1960. But 'it was too dangerous to allow her to *settle* in Paris and marry Sartre. She knew too much about the KGB, and about the gulag, at a time when the Soviets wanted Westerners to forget about it.'

As Sartre waited for Lena's reply at the Hotel Minerva, his favourite hotel in Rome, he stared out gloomily at Bernini's carved elephant, emblem of luck, on its obelisk in the square opposite; he worried ceaselessly over his lover's health, and her fidelity. He could not write: the pen fell from his hands. '*Je suis plongé dans la stupeur.*' With trembling hands, he tore open her letter.

It was the death knell to his hopes. Lena had read Beauvoir's memoir, *Force of Circumstance*, which provided her with a convenient excuse. 'It does not just depend on us,' she wrote to Sartre. 'The more I read the Beaver's memoirs, the more I understand that I could never decide to change things. And this kills something in me. You know that I feel friendship for the Beaver. I respect her. I admire the relationship you have . . . But you and the Beaver have together created a remarkable and dazzling thing which is so dangerous for those people who get close to you.' 'She never wanted to marry him,' recalls Lena's daughter, Macha. 'It was very difficult to choose, because of me, because of leaving her mother, and because she could not return. My mother was very independent, she could never accept dependence.'

Sartre's torment grew. 'You *are* the meeting of East and West, or rather the West meets the East (without any ideological struggle) in our bed,' he wrote. '*O mon bel Orient*, my rising sun.' How he loved her, how happy and young she made him. What would he do without her? For the first time he tried to telephone Lena from the Beaver's apartment. She wasn't in. He was told that she wouldn't be returning until midnight. What was she doing, out till midnight? Who was she with? At whom was she making eyes? 'I trust you,' he repeated hopelessly.

Sartre's love for Lena expressed itself in his dedication of *The Words*, 'To Madame Z'. In Lena's own copy he wrote a personal dedication: 'To Madame Z(artre), My beautiful sun. *Words* will never suffice to express the strength of my love for you.' When Arlette, Evelyne, Wanda and Michèle questioned him, he merely replied that Zonina was his and Beauvoir's 'Russian friend'.

*

Morosely Sartre sank back into his daily medical rounds: 1.30 to 4 p.m., Arlette, 4 to 6 p.m., Evelyne, 6.30 to 9 p.m., Michèle, 9 to midnight

Wanda. His patients were more troublesome than ever. '*On m'a fait la gueule*, I'm fed up with it,' he complained to Lena. Arlette was intelligent but ill; Sartre had got Arlette a job at Gallimard, but he had his doubts as to whether it would work out.

As for Evelyne (whom he saw for an hour and a half, three times a week), she'd been sobbing on his sofa, troubled by her 'double failure (theatre, passion)'. After failing in *Les Séquestrés d'Altona*, her big chance, she'd taken refuge in a violent love affair with her doctor, Norbit Ben, an Algerian Jew, who was unfortunately married. 'I listened and I gave her some money,' said Sartre. 'It's always the most effective remedy.'

Michèle had arrived at 6.30 pm, also tearful. Her boyfriend, jazz musician André Reweliotty, had been killed in a car crash in 1962, and Michèle had been in a clinic, but was still depressed. Sitting alone in her flat all day, playing jazz records, drinking and crying, she was couldn't sleep, couldn't work. Sartre took her out to the Pont Royal bar, where they talked about Michèle's daughter, Carole, for whom he'd found an excellent private school as she was failing at the *lycée*. He and Boris Vian had helped Michèle buy a three-room apartment. Only forty-three, Michèle, 'sad and mad', clutching her Pekingese, was already an old woman.

And there was a new drain on Sartre's purse, as well as his time: Olga. Bost had finally confessed that he'd been cheating on her with Barbara for the last six years. Barbara herself was having an affair with the film director, Nico Papatakis, and the distraught Bost was sleeping at Castor's. Now the problem was that Olga was too proud to ask Bost for money, which he and Sartre gave, fifty-fifty, to her father each month. 'I gave her 40,000 francs,' sighed Sartre. His compulsive generosity towards his decayed mistresses, in terms of both time and cash, contributed to their dependence. But, as Sartre wrote of Flaubert, he carried a wound from his childhood. Sartre, the wounded healer, needed his 'patients'.

*

And in October it was the turn of Beauvoir's mother to fall ill. Alerted by a telephone call from Bost that Françoise had fallen and broken her hip, Simone hurried back from Rome to be by her side. Her seventy-seven-year-old mother had lived alone in her flat on the rue Blomet since 1942, growing increasingly arthritic. When she slipped in the bathroom, it took her two hours to crawl to the telephone. In hospital she was told to rest, but she also suffered abdominal pain, at first diagnosed as diverticulitis.

'Do not go gentle into that good night, old age should burn and rage at close of day; Rage, rage against the dying of the light,' were the lines from Dylan Thomas which Beauvoir chose as the epigraph to *A Very Easy Death*, her account of her mother's last days. She dedicated it to her sister, Poupette, with whom she shared the nursing of their mother. 'How these old women cling to life,' she wrote to Algren. 'She was nearest my heart during this month than she had been since my early childhood.'

Poupette and Simone colluded in a merciful deception, telling their mother that she was getting better after an operation revealed that she had cancer of the colon. '*Un cancer! C'était dans l'air*,' wrote Simone. You could see it in Maman's eyes, in the bags under her eyes, her skinniness. Simone remembered her mother's courage after her father's death. He had left her without a *sou* at fifty-four; but she had 'turned a page', studying for a certificate as an assistant librarian, remounting her old bicycle and wobbling her way to work with the Red Cross. As a young woman she had longed to be an explorer, and, as a widow, she had accepted every invitation to travel. She had made new friends, rebuilt *sa petite vie*, her little life, as the doctor patronizingly called it.

'Dying is hard work, when you love life so much,' wrote Beauvoir. Their mother could hang on for two or three months; but Françoise developed bed sores, and the sisters could not bear to witness her pain. Her ears were full of the sound of our lies, wrote Beauvoir, as their mother clung to the hope of recovery: 'We *ordered* the doctors to give her a lot of morphine and in fact to kill her slowly.' Remembering their uncle, who had demanded his revolver to kill himself in the final agony of stomach cancer, the two women insisted that Françoise should not suffer. And in her final weeks, Beauvoir rediscovered a compassion she had lost for the old woman she had sharply ordered to 'Hurry up!' only weeks previously at a visit to the family grave in Père Lachaise cemetery. 'Where will you and your sister go?' asked Françoise, as she put flowers on the grave. 'There is only room for me . . . Of course, I should like to go to heaven, but not all alone, not without my daughters.'

For four nights Beauvoir slept on a cot bed beside her dying mother. Her mind returned to the time when she was twenty, and her mother had turned timidly towards her and said: 'I know you don't think I'm intelligent.' Intimidated by her fierce, brilliant daughter, Françoise added: '*Toi, tu me fais peur*, you frighten me.'

'You frighten me.' It was a remark Françoise often repeated, staring intensely at the woman her daughter had become. But as time passed, the silence between them had softened; materially, Françoise depended on Simone: 'I was the family's support, in a way her son.' The little girl with a man's mind had become the head of the family, to whom Françoise deferred, accepting her 'free union' with Sartre, which she regarded as less shameful than a registry office wedding.

At the end of the 'long, sad month' of November, and her mother's burial, Simone was devoured by her own cancer: remorse. Sartre was sympathetic. He and Castor didn't love their mothers very much, he confided to Lena. They'd counted up to the ages of ten or eleven and then, after that, not at all. As for him, he'd broken seriously with his when she remarried: 'This first rupture dried up my heart.' When Françoise first fell ill, he urged Beauvoir to write about her mother's death. Beauvoir was shocked. 'Not straight away,' she replied. But Sartre knew that Castor had embarked on a 'tragic and passionate adventure, to be part of another's agony'.

As Sartre flew to Prague to meet Lena, who in his dreams was now his wife, Beauvoir turned to a new friend: Sylvie Le Bon, thirty-three years her junior.

35

~

Betrayal

I don't understand why everything is so black in your
letter and in your heart.
Jean-Paul Sartre to Lena Zonina, 1966

SYLVIE LE BON was seventeen when she first met Simone de Beauvoir.
The schoolgirl from Rennes, Brittany, had come up to Paris to prepare
for her entrance examination to L'École Normale, which now admitted
women. Like her heroine, Beauvoir, Sylvie was hoping to study
philosophy, and wrote her a fan letter in the spring of 1960. In
November Beauvoir invited her to rue Schoelcher.

It was the first time Sylvie had entered an *atelier*, and she was
impressed by the yellow sofa, the original *objets d'art* and, most of all, by
her hostess, who was wearing a black and mauve Greek skirt and
earrings, but no turban: 'Never in Paris,' recalls Sylvie. 'She only wore
it for trips abroad.' Beauvoir asked Le Bon if she was interested in
politics. 'I said, "No." She was scandalized. She went straight out to the
kiosk and returned with her arms full of newspapers, which she dropped
in my lap. *Elle avait une vitalité très grande.* Beauvoir was a force of
nature. She was a living flame.'

'I was wrong in 1962 when I thought nothing significant would
happen to me any more, apart from calamities,' recalled Beauvoir. 'Now
once again a piece of great good fortune was offered to me.' That
evening she took Sylvie out to dinner, and the schoolgirl shyly

confessed that she had won first prize at her *lycée*. Over the next two years they met occasionally. Beauvoir was surprised, however, to receive a letter from Mme Le Bon, who had read her daughter's diary and found an entry showing that Beauvoir thought she beat Sylvie. Beauvoir wrote a civil reply saying that Sylvie never spoke of her family, but to Sylvie the correspondence between her parent and Beauvoir was a betrayal. When she was fourteen, Sylvie had formed a close friendship with a girl the same age at school, named Danièle, which her parents tried to break up on the ground that it was 'unnatural'. '*Notre histoire à quatorze ans, c'était un grand amour*' recalls Sylvie. 'It was very hard for me.' Beauvoir, recalling her own relationship with Zaza, was sympathetic to Sylvie's position, to the rebellion of daughters against mothers. Their reconciliation after their 'almost-quarrel' brought the two closer together. But it was in 1963, at the time of her mother's death, when Beauvoir's black dog of depression, the 'giant beast which settles on my breast', crushed her so that she could no longer breathe, that Sylvie's succour became indispensable.

'You are my reincarnation,' Beauvoir told her young acolyte, as Sylvie's professional path followed in her own footsteps. After studying at Sèvres, the women's teacher training college, Le Bon requested a post at Rouen, where she, like Beauvoir, taught at the Lycée Jeanne d'Arc. The notorious Hôtel du Petit Mouton had closed down, but Sylvie found somewhere equally filthy: the Hôtel Le Rochefoucauld. 'The dirtier it was, the more it amused me,' she recalls. 'I was short of money.' But she was able to return to Paris two or three nights a week, to a flat in the boulevard Jourdan and, four years later, her provincial exile over, took up a post at the Lycée Clemenceau in Paris.

'Beauvoir made me think about death.' Beauvoir's fear of the terrible emptiness on the other side of the 'black line' amused Sylvie at first, but as the older woman insisted on talking about the tragic truth at the heart of life, the anguish of knowing that there is no God to pardon, no remission of sins, and that man is only what he makes of himself, they became more intimate. '*L'homme doit souffrir*, man must suffer,' Sartre told Sylvie. On the other hand, wrote Beauvoir, when you seize life, 'either in joy, action or revolt, death draws back'. Sylvie, like herself, 'was an intellectual and passionately in love with life. And she was like me in many other ways . . . She had one very rare gift: she knew how to listen . . . I loved her enthusiasms and her anger, her gravity, her gaiety, her horror of the commonplace, her uncalculating generosity.' Slowly the oxygen of youth worked its magic again. Beauvoir's spirits lifted. '[Sylvie] is as thoroughly interwoven in my life as I am in hers,' she wrote warmly in *All Said and Done*, the last volume of her memoirs dedicated to Sylvie: 'We read the same books, we see shows together, and we go for long drives in the car. There is such an interchange between us that I lose the sense of my age.'

In August 1965 Beauvoir took Le Bon away on holiday for the first time, to Corsica. Recalls Sylvie: 'It was our honeymoon.'

*

In 1963 Sartre, too, was contemplating 'the happiness and gaiety of *ma vie en rose*' with Lena. He was also still viewing the Soviet Union through rose-tinted spectacles. That November he praised 'Communist optimism', and underlined his message: '*Notre époque a de la chance*, our era is a lucky one.' When *Les Mots* was published in January 1964, and widely hailed as his return to literature, Sartre responded: 'In comparison with the death of one child, *La Nausée* isn't up to scratch.' His belief in revolutionary violence remained unchanged. In May 1964, despite the publication of a virulently anti-Semitic pamphlet by a professor at Kiev University named Kichko, he and Beauvoir agreed to attend the celebrations taking place at Kiev to mark the 150th anniversary of the birth of the Ukrainian poet Shevchenko.

All Moscow was talking about the Brodsky affair, the trial of a young Jewish poet and translator who was sentenced to five years' forced labour. Ehrenbourg translated the trial notes for Sartre, but the little man only had eyes for Lena, as, with Beauvoir as chaperone, they travelled together for six weeks through Estonia before returning to Leningrad. His passion for his Lentchka, fuelled by jealousy that in his absence she was in the arms of another man, reached new heights. When they lay skin to skin, he forgot his 'interior confusion'. 'When I was inside you, parasite to your pleasure, looking at your beauty,' he wrote, 'I no longer existed except as a joyful witness.' Her smile, looking up at him, was that of a young girl.

Money was plentiful. Lena had translated *Les Mots* into Russian, and Sartre's royalties in the USSR were piling up. Regretfully, he returned to Rome where he waited desperately for a letter from the spy, daydreaming about her black hair, her proud gait, her little hands, the red nails which caressed him. Finally, on 30 August, her reply arrived. He read it with tears in his eyes, reassured that 'Sainte Lena' loved him as he did her.

Sartre's correspondence reveals in pitiful clarity how access to Zonina was used as a bargaining chip by the Soviets. When he begs to see her in May, he is told by Sourkov that he cannot visit the USSR until October. At times he is shown an envelope containing a letter from her, but it is not handed over. He is finally allowed to come on 1 June. Hurt to discover that the Soviet press has misrepresented his proposals for an international 'Congress of Culture Workers' which, reports Zonina, the writer Korneichuck 'has asked Sartre to make', as a plan to set up an 'international government of the intelligentsia', Sartre protests bitterly that Korneichuck has done nothing to defend him or refute this 'absurd idea'.

'I have come to the Soviet Union as a friend,' complains Sartre, as they sit in Korneichuck's dacha in Kiev.

> I have the right to expect to be treated as a friend . . . If they are going to fling mud at me for the things that I do at the request of my friends . . . I will have to give up my collaboration with my Soviet friends . . . I cannot allow lies to be told about me without any refutation by the people who share my cause, fighting for the peaceful co-existence of states, the protection of culture from the threat of a new war, and against re-emergence of the Cold War.

In Sartre's defence, it must be said that his intention to work for peace and cultural coexistence was sincere and heartfelt. During the long summer in Novgorod, Tallin and Tartu, he discussed with the Estonians his hopes for his coming meeting with Ben Bella in October to celebrate Algerian Independence Day and to foster contacts between European and African writers. But the Russians knew that he was caught fast in their honey trap, and they laughed in his face: his threats were empty. Feebly Sartre agreed to write again for *Les Lettres françaises* after an eight-year gap, and in order to 'facilitate our relationship with the USSR', Beauvoir yielded to the French Communist Courtade's demand for an article on Yalta.

Jean Cau was partly right when he wrote that Sartre loved to boast about how he outranked Simonov, but he never took himself seriously as a political figure: 'Sartre *moquait son* personnage *politique* . . . Sartre the *man* regarded Sartre the *personality* with irony.' Politics bored him. 'It was a chore. *L'ennui noir. La nausée.*' Sartre, who never read a newspaper, was no political animal like Aron. His virtuosity allowed him to knock out a speech on Marxism, and then return to his 'true and secret loves . . . Genet or Flaubert'.

In October 1964 the Soviets achieved their greatest propaganda coup: Sartre's refusal of the Nobel Prize for Literature. Early that autumn Sartre was astonished to be asked by an Italian friend, the philosopher Enzo Paci, for the text of his speech of acceptance. He hesitated over his decision, but not for long. Tempting as the 250,000 kroner was, politically he was determined to show his solidarity with the Eastern bloc – and his beloved Lena. Had he taken the prize, it would have sent a message to the world that he was committed to the West.

Sartre knew the fate of the dissident Russian Boris Pasternak, who had won the Nobel Prize in 1958 for *Dr Zhivago*, a novel critical of post-revolutionary Russia. Drummed out of the Writers' Union, he had been attacked by the head of the KGB as 'a pig who soils his own stable', denounced as a 'traitor' and threatened with exile. No non-dissident Soviet writer had been given the prize. Camus, yes, but no Western Communist.

In mid-October *Le Figaro littéraire* tipped Sartre as that year's winner, despite his 'controversial political past'. That means they've pardoned me, Sartre sarcastically told Lena. Lanzmann rang at once saying he needed an article on Sartre, who retorted that he didn't want the prize, nor any publicity. The next day, 14 October, Sartre wrote a polite letter to the Secretary of the Swedish Academy declining the prize 'for strictly personal and other, more objective reasons, which it would not be appropriate to explain here'. It did not reach its destination in time, and on 22 October the Swedes announced that the Nobel Prize had had been awarded to Sartre 'for his work, which, in the spirit of freedom and in the name of truth, has had a great impact on our era'.

'People are going to think that you're refusing it because Camus got it first,' said Castor. André Maurois claimed in *Paris-Jour* that Sartre was afraid of making Simone jealous. But on 19 October Sartre lunched with the journalist Olivier Todd – 'a guy I really like' – and his first wife, Nizan's daughter, irritated, he confessed, at the scandal about to burst over his head. 'Sartre was a genius,' says Todd:

> He wasn't driven by petty feelings, by pique that Camus got the prize first. When Camus won, Sartre laughed and said: '*Il le mérite bien*, he deserves it.' Nor was it to do with publicity: he knew that he would get far more publicity by refusing it. He was not perturbed but convinced that he had to refuse. He believed that if he took it he would be a pawn in the East–West relationship.

It was the first ever refusal of the Nobel, and Sartre's hiding place with Castor in rue Schoelcher was quickly rumbled by journalists. He fled from the paparazzi to the office of Simone Gallimard, where he gave his only interview to a Swedish journalist, Carl-Gustav Bjurström, who drafted a statement in French, to which Sartre added the note 'translated from the Swedish', in the desire not to offend the Swedish people. He had, he said, always declined official distinctions, such as the Legion of Honour after the war. But he made his political position clear: 'Today, the Nobel Prize appears to be a distinction reserved to leaders of the Western bloc and rebels of the Eastern bloc . . . I do not mean to say that the Nobel Prize is a "bourgeois" prize . . . [but] I am particularly sensitive to the conflict between these two cultures . . . Of course, I hope that "the best wins", that is to say, socialism . . . It is regrettable that the prize was given to Pasternak before Sholokhov, and that the only Soviet work to be honoured should be a work published abroad and banned at home.'

Sartre's women were furious at the loss of a fortune. He was pursued by a vengeful Wanda: 'You're spitting on 26 million [old francs]!' Old contacts, like Mauriac and René Maheu, praised his rejection of the prize. Others saw it as an example of Sartre's increasing isolation, expressed both in his texts and his acts.

*

At Christmas Sartre sat, as so often, in the bar of the Pont Royal. This time he was waiting for Lena, who was coming to spend three weeks with him. Beauvoir lent him her studio and moved into his spartan apartment but, despite sweet nights with his 'beautiful witch', and lazy days in the place de la Contrescarpe and the place des Vosges, a cloud hung over Lena's visit. Both she and Ehrenbourg, with whom he 'disputed amicably', did not approve of his refusal of the Nobel Prize which, they told him, sent out the signal that he supported the growingly repressive, neo-Stalinist successors to Krushchev, Brezhnev and Kosygin. Nor was the Cossack novelist Mikhail Sholokhov worthy of the Nobel: he'd been a favourite of Stalin's, a government creature. In 1937 Sholokhov had had an affair with literary groupie Yevgenia Yezhova, wife of NKVD chief Nikolai 'Blackberry' Yezhov, who bugged Sholokhov's room and listened in fury to the blow-by-blow account of their love-making. When Sholokhov complained to Stalin and Beria, Stalin ordered Yezhov to the Politburo to apologize to Sholokhov. Now in 1964 the KGB were listening to blow-by-blow accounts of Sartre's love-making, and copying, studying and placing in the KGB archives (where there are several entries under the name of Sartre) his forty-page letters, before passing them on to Lena. This Lena knew well: but she dared not tell him.

In her reports, Zonina put into Sartre's mouth occasional critical comments about 'arranged' meetings, for example with Illitchev, head of the 'Ideological Department' of the Central Committee, or complaints about the harmful influence in France of Elsa Triolet, and praise for 'threatened' writers such as Tvardovsky, Doroch, and Voznensky, who wrote for the 'liberal' review *Iunost*. To Gilbert Dagron, sending such 'hostile messages' to the Party and its *apparatchiks* required 'a certain courage', but in fact to criticize Tvardovsky, the editor of the literary journal *Novy Mir*, or the popular young poet Vosnensky was 'no sin', says Gordievsky; indeed, it was quite the fashion to criticize Illitchev.

As her obituary by Lev Kopelev, who features in Solzhenitskyn's *First Circle*, and Raïssa Orlova stated in 1985, Zonina was one of the first Russians to pierce the cultural Iron Curtain with her article on *The Mandarins* in 1955, but 'she was never part of any opposition group or dissidents and never opposed the authorities. Not only because of her feeling of responsibility towards her family, but also because she considered overt resistance to be hopeless.' Instead: '*Toute sa vie, Lena Zonina joua le jeu d'une soumision au système*, she played the game of submission to the system.'

But the game was a dangerous one. As KGB collaborators in a climate of vicious anti-Semitism, Zonina and Ehrenbourg's position was perilous. Many times Zonina hinted at the risks she ran; but Sartre was as deaf as he was blind. He wrote in March 1965 that he never lost sight of the 'difficulty of our relations', but to him that difficulty centred on her illness, his suspicions that she had another lover, and the burgeoning crisis of his adoption of his latest mistress, Arlette Elkaïm.

*

Sartre applied to adopt twenty-eight-year-old Arlette in January 1965, and on 18 March the adoption became legal. To all his women it seemed a betrayal; to Beauvoir it must have appeared the ultimate act of disloyalty. It had been falsely rumoured in 1958 that Arlette was pregnant by Sartre, and that he was ready to marry her. It was said that in the face of Simone's distress, he had relented on that occasion. Now Arlette's jealousy of Evelyne had grown, and in order to placate her, states Le Bon, he proposed to make the doe-eyed Arlette his daughter: This time he refused to be swayed. His other ageing, discarded mistresses were outraged when they heard the news. 'At four o'clock, to Evelyne's,' reported Sartre to Lena. 'You've no right to do this to me,' raged the distraught actress. 'I was as cold as an ice cube,' recorded Sartre. Evelyne's motives, which he believed to be economic, revolted him. Wanda was even more hysterical. '*Tuez-moi, achevez-moi!*' *she* screamed. 'Kill me, finish me off!' She began smashing her furniture. But Sartre was adamant. He knew Wanda wanted him to buy her a flat.

But if the storms of tears from the other women were based on the belief that they were missing out financially, Beauvoir had real grounds for complaint. To adopt Arlette was to make her Sartre's literary heir, unless he made a will to the contrary. Beauvoir had devoted the last thirty-six years to Sartre as his 'morganatic wife', his 'little judge', who had edited, drafted and even written 'his' work; she had put loyalty to their pact above her love for Algren; she was the old wife now displaced by the new in a final act of Sartrean spite against the bourgeoisie, for in making his mistress his daughter the Kobra created the ultimate fulfilment of his fantasy of incest.

By adopting Arlette, at a time when Algerians in France were being threatened with deportation, Sartre was assuring her future. Gerassi recalls Sartre's own version of events: 'One day [he] was walking with Arlette and invited her to go into a florist's they were passing to select a bunch of flowers. The patron asked "Monsieur" what he would like to buy for his "beautiful daughter".' Sartre looked at Arlette and said something like, 'Well, I'm not so good in bed any more and this guy makes a lot of sense. If you are my daughter, you become a French citizen and then nobody can deport you, because you won't be an Algerian Jew any more.'

Sartre told Gerassi that he needed someone younger than Castor to keep distributing his royalties to the five women he kept (including Elkaïm) after his death. 'But,' he adds, 'Sartre certainly expected Castor to decide which of his published works to publish posthumously, not Elkaïm.'

Beauvoir was devastated. She had always assumed that she would be Sartre's literary executor. 'She had so many of Sartre's things,' recalls Le Bon. 'He left all his papers with her. *Elle gardait tout.*' Archives, packet of letters. 'Arlette never said anything, so Simone had no idea that there would be any problems after his death.'

Putting on a brave face, Beauvoir acted as sponsor to the adoption. And she comforted Sartre's newest 'child', another fragile Jewish girl named Liliane Siegel, known as *la clandestine* because her existence was meant to be secret. Liliane had felt close to Arlette, who had herself met Sartre only a short while before, also through writing a letter. She was shocked when Sartre announced:

> 'By the way, child, I mean to adopt Arlette, but I'll never do so without your consent.'
> I felt myself grow pale. My heart beat faster.
> 'You're joking. Are you serious? Why would you do such a thing to me? Adopt anyone you like, but not Arlette!'
> '. . . I tell you, I'll never do it without your consent . . .'

What did Castor think? demanded Liliane.

> 'She disapproves. She says I'm going to damage you and Evelyne.'
> 'Oh yes, that's true, there's Evelyne, poor Evelyne! Have you told her?
> 'No, not yet. I tell you, I'm thinking of doing it, but it won't be right away.'

But a few months later *France-Soir* announced that Sartre had adopted a daughter. It was headline news. Sobbing, Liliane rang Castor: 'He had promised! Without my consent . . .' Sartre eventually placated Liliane with a special 'contract' between 'Poulou' and the 'Bastard', assuring her that he loved his bastard daughter as much as his legal one.

Sartre's lies were catching up with him. Arlette had taken the discovery of Lena's existence in Paris as badly as Lena had taken the news that her lover was adopting another woman. The adoption compensated Arlette for her displacement by Lena, but it also fulfilled Sartre's need for a docile, acquiescent, musical presence in his life – a role previously filled by his mother. Arlette was learning the piano and flute; she and Sartre sang together in the afternoons after his daily lunch at La Coupole. A favourite aria was the song of the King of Thule from Gounod's *Faust*, which he sang with great brio.

Nineteen sixty-five signalled a parting of ways, the establishment of rival courts. Instead of Sartre and Beauvoir, the king and queen of existentialism, there were now two kings, as Beauvoir grew closer to Sylvie, with whom she spent weekends driving into the country around Paris or holidaying. Sartre spent more time with Arlette, for whom he bought a house in the Junas, in the South of France. The women continued to exist as satellites around the Sartrean sun, Arlette in a flat close to La Coupole, Michèle Vian on the boulevard du Montparnasse, Wanda on the rue du Dragon and, of course, Mme Mancy on the boulevard Raspail. Sartre lunched with her every Sunday. The menu was always the same: roast pork and mashed potatoes.

Sylvie, who had rejected Beauvoir's offer to maintain her if she gave up her teaching career in favour of retaining her independence, did not approve of the way in which Sartre supported his women: 'All these parasites,' as she described them, 'oppressed him. His generosity was maladroit, misplaced; he wanted to help them, but then they became dependent . . . like whores, always asking for money. Once Sartre had slept with a woman, he felt responsible. It wasn't like the *machismo* of Camus, who bedded a woman and washed his hands of her . . . Sartre was *paternaliste*. I said to him:

'You don't treat them as equals if you pay them.'

'*Oui, mais je ne peux pas changer.*'

As Castor predicted, Evelyne was deeply hurt by Sartre's action. On 18 October 1967, she killed herself. Evelyne took good care that no one found her before the barbiturates she had swallowed took effect; she left behind six letters to the Sartre family, exonerating them from blame. Sartre was stupefied, because Evelyne had seemed on the verge of turning her life around; she had made her first film for television and reconnected with an old lover named Lourçars, a TV producer. But she was, Beauvoir believed, 'scarred enormously' by her liaison with Sartre, which he never officially acknowledged. She wanted babies, which he would not give her.

'For sure, there is guilt,' Sartre wrote to Lena. 'It's not your fault,' Castor and Sylvie told him. But Sartre was overcome with desolation as he contemplated Evelyne's poor failure of a life. He felt 'withered and funereal', staring at the Parisian rain and writing his Flaubert.

Perhaps Sartre meant to assuage his guilt towards the Jews by adopting Arlette; if so, his guilt was now all the greater at the suicide of Evelyne, another Jewish girl caught in the Sartrean web. Yevgenia Yezhova has been described as a 'silly sensual woman [who] unwittingly was to play the terrible role of the black widow spider: most of her lovers were to die'. Sartre was almost as merciless.

*

Lena's visit to Paris, which she repeated the following year, revealed the immutability of Sartre and Beauvoir's relationship to her. To Zonina, like Bienenfeld, Sartre and Beauvoir were as implacable as the two-faced Janus stone. Castor patronized and excluded her. In his letters, Sartre reproached Lena for her 'hatred' of Castor, her jealousy.

'*Ma fausse Madame Z,* my false Madame Z,' he called her in October 1965, complaining of his lost innocence. He was sure that she had another lover in Milan.

The West aroused ambiguous feelings in Zonina. She disliked its materialism, but wanted a better life for herself and Macha. Sartre's offer for her to live in Paris with him was tempting. He professed to want them to be 'a real couple', he adored their 'double life and unique love', but she had too many anchors in the USSR. 'It was a tactic of the KGB to keep hostages. She would have been afraid for her mother,' writes Gordievsky. 'Zonina could not marry Sartre because the KGB did not want their agent to live abroad; they were concerned that their secrets would be compromised.'

Ehrenbourg urged Sartre to write to Mikoyan to ask for a pardon for Brodsky, who had been sent to a state farm near Archangel. He did so, in a remarkably servile letter. Shortly afterwards Brodsky was pardoned. But by October 1965, when Sartre met Ehrenbourg, Sourkov, Tvardovsky and other Russian 'friends' at a COMES conference in Rome, there was an ominous new development. Two Russian dissident writers, Andrev Sinyavsky and Yuli Daniel, had been arrested and charged with publishing anti-Soviet books abroad, although they had expressed only a 'timid criticism' of the regime. Their work was being circulated clandestinely, dog-eared typewritten pages passed from hand to hand and known as *samizdat.* Lena Zonina signed a petition, initiated by Ehrenbourg, calling for the release of Sinyavsky and Daniel; it was an apparently daring move. She was one of only sixty-two members of the Writers Union to do so out of a membership of 6,000, although she did not take the more extreme step of resigning from the Union. 'The act of signing the petition for Sinyavsky and Daniel in 1967 was not exactly a dissident move,' says Gordievsky. 'It was regarded as a moral gesture . . . Many obvious KGB agents signed it in spite of some annoyance to their KGB handlers.' Doroch was another to do so. At this point some KGB collaborators took advantage of the brief opportunity to emigrate to Israel.

Beauvoir misunderstood the situation when she wrote that: 'Putting one's name to this petition meant taking the risk of never being sent abroad again, of losing one's job and of remaining unpublished for ever.' As a KGB agent, Lena went where she was sent. But, as time went by, Lena and Ehrenbourg, both vulnerable Jews playing a dangerous game but whose true sympathies often lay with the dissidents, privately despised Sartre, for whom being 'a friend of the USSR' meant toeing the Party line rather than using his immense influence in the cause of freedom. At the Rome COMES congress he ferociously attacked 'phoney *avant-garde*' writers such as Solzhenitsyn, James Joyce, Céline and Breton. His opposition to International PEN, the worldwide association of writers which defends freedom of expression, was virulent. 'Sartre was utterly against the PEN Club,' reported Zonina, and was 'astonished' that Soviet writers agreed to sit at the same table as anti-Soviet figures. On one of his last visits to Moscow, in July 1965, Sartre watched the latest Soviet films, *The Great Patriotic War* and *The First Teacher*, and enthusiastically praised their 'revolutionary essence', before going on with Beauvoir to celebrate the twenty-fifth anniversary of the establishment of the Soviet regime in Lithuania.

'When I learnt about Sartre and Beauvoir, I lost all respect for Western civilization,' recalls Gordievsky, who had once put his faith in the development of 'socialism with a human face'. 'They should have been on the side of justice and democracy but turned out to be on the side of brutality.'

The trial of Sinyavsky and Daniel in February 1966 was followed by the Twenty-Third Congress, at which Sholokhov, who the previous year had been awarded the Nobel Prize as Sartre suggested, denounced the 'bourgeois defenders' of the young writers. He ranted that seven years in the gulag was far too lenient a sentence: 'In Stalin's time, they would have been shot!'

The trial disturbed Western Communists. In France, Aragon and the PCF condemned it in *L'Humanité*, and the paper was banned in Moscow; the Italian Communist Party did likewise. When Sartre and Beauvoir arrived in Moscow on 2 May, their very presence proclaiming their support for Brezhnev and Mikoyan's hard line against Sinyavsky and Daniel, of whose brutal treatment there were new, alarming reports, Ehrenbourg turned on them in a rage. 'What are you doing here in the midst of all this?' he demanded. 'The situation for intellectuals is a tragedy.' Even *samizdat* could only be used with extreme caution.

Sartre remained wilfully blind. He and Beauvoir asked Lena to arrange a meeting with Solzhenitsyn, whose short story 'Matriona's House' they had published in *Les Temps modernes*. The great novelist telephoned: he wanted to see Zonina. She returned with a glum face: 'He does not want to see you,' she said to Sartre, who was hurt by this rejection. Beauvoir comforted him. What Solzhenitsyn was saying, in effect, was this: 'Sartre, do you see, is a writer whose work has all been published. Every time he writes a book he knows it will be read. So I really do not feel that I can talk to him: I should suffer too much.'

But the Russian was saying something very different: it was not his *amour-propre* that was wounded, but his conscience. 'He didn't want to see people for whom he had profound contempt,' says Gordievsky. 'He refused to see them because of deep ideological conviction.'

*

Sartre's virulent anti-Americanism prolonged the time he spent as a tool of the Soviet Union. In February 1965 the Americans bombed North Vietnam. Sartre was on the point of flying to the States to speak at Cornell University, but immediately cancelled his trip and went to the Helsinki Peace Congress in July, in order 'to be helpful to the Soviet cause', still unaware that the Peace Movement was 'an arm of the KGB'. Ehrenbourg met him in Moscow beforehand to ensure that the speech he was to make followed the Party line. This interview, reported Zonina, clarified that Sartre was:

> ready for co-operation with the Soviet delegation, that his views were openly anti-American, and that he was convinced that immediate . . . aid was to be given to the Vietnamese people . . . Following a request from the leadership of the Soviet delegation, Sartre attended the two final days of the Congress (14 and 15 July) where he gave a speech that denounced American imperialism.

As Sartre demanded that there should be no yielding to 'American blackmail' but whole-hearted support for the Vietnamese, the seventy-four-year-old Ehrenbourg reproached him for taking sides with the Chinese. The puppet had deviated from his brief. The old fox was so angry that he nearly had a stroke.

Beauvoir, too, was feeling the strain. On their regular visits to Italy, Sartre generally flew while she sped down the *autostrada*, impatient for a new stretch of motorway to open. Beauvoir was a fast driver: 'I was enchanted the first time I did the Milan–Bologna run in two and a half hours.' But in the summer of 1965, driving on the wrong side of the road from Milan to Paris as she raced to meet Sartre, she saw a red tanker coming down the hill towards her. It swerved. A head-on collision was avoided, but the whole of her Peugeot 404 was smashed in. Miraculously, she stepped out of the car with only four broken ribs.

Shocked and in pain, she spent three weeks in bed. 'Castor has a big black eye,' Sartre informed Lena in November. It was the only sign, apart from a bit of breathlessness, of her accident. But a short story she wrote the following year, 'Misunderstanding in Moscow', Beauvoir revealed the mental pain Sartre caused her.

In this story it is June 1966, and André and Nicole, a French couple in their sixties, have arrived in Moscow to see his daughter Macha (the real name of Zonina's daughter). Nicole, a retired schoolteacher, at once feels the contrast between her own middle-aged appearance and that of the 'beautiful young woman' who acts as their guide. André is delighted to be back in Moscow; Nicole, by contrast, finds the city hideous. But it is not the architecture, but the loving relationship between André, a famous writer, and Macha, which irks her. André and Macha sit close together, look into each other's eyes, call each other 'tu'. They dutifully address Nicole as '*vous*'. She counts the days until their departure, unaware that André has extended their stay:

'You've decided that without even telling me!' Nicole said.

Suddenly there was red smoke in her head, a red fog in front of her eyes, something red was screaming in her throat. He doesn't give a damn about me! He didn't say a word . . . All his smiles, all his tenderness went towards Macha.

The fictional ending is a happy one, the reconciliation of André and Nicole; but in real life the knots were not so easily retied. Beauvoir was probably expressing in 'Malentendu à Moscou' not only her jealousy of Lena, but her miserable sense of usurpation by Arlette, the daughter at whose flat Sartre now wrote as well as making music. It was a double exile. And in September 1966, when she and Sartre flew into Tokyo to be greeted by more than 100 photographers at the airport, and a pretty, petite Japanese guide bowed smilingly to Sartre, her heart once again sank into her boots. Tomiko Asabuki became his lover. As in America, in Brazil and in Russia, it was a woman who gave Sartre a new country. Sartre and Beauvoir travelled on to Egypt, where the crowds shouted, 'Long live Nasser! Long live Sartre! Long live Simone!' and to Israel. 'Disillusioned with Russia', writes the novelist Shusha Guppy, Sartre and other fellow travellers 'kept finding promised lands, in China, Cuba . . .' As one god toppled, Stalin or Krushchev, Sartre substituted a new, young, virile figure, Castro, Nasser, before whom to abase himself. As Camus had realized long ago, something in Sartre aspired to servitude.

'*Nous étions complices*,' Sartre had written to Lena at the beginning of their affair, in words redolent of those once used to Castor. But collusion was collapsing under the burden of betrayal, both personal and political. The majority of European intellectuals had left the Party or been expelled after the 1957 Hungarian uprising, but Sartre kept the faith: later, when asked why he concealed the existence of the concentration camps, about which he had known for a long time, he answered: 'One should not drive Billancourt [i.e. the Renault car workers] to despair' – a quote that has become famous as an example of '*la trahison des clercs*', the treason of the intellectuals.

In June 1966, after the trip to the Soviet Union about which Beauvoir wrote so unhappily, he was still brimming with confidence: '*Mon amour, comme tu es belle*,' he wrote to Lena. He carried a vision of her before him, bold and colourful, that moved him profoundly; the last kisses she had given him in front of Sourkov and Georg were still warm on his lips, he felt her skin against his cheeks: he was cut in two. Despite the grave and depressing atmosphere in Moscow, she had given him '*un bonheur si parfait*', so perfect a happiness that it could withstand any absence, a phrase reminiscent of those 'perfect moments' Roquentin wistfully recalled with Annie in *La Nausée*. 'I still have a moment of confidence in our future,' wrote Sartre, 'in spite of everything.'

But Lena's reply triggered another outburst from her lover. Why did she say that she *had* to touch the Italian, he demanded: 'I can very easily get jealous of you.' At the same time liked the fact that she pleased men. Sartre promised to return to the USSR in September, after Japan. It was agreed that Zonina would translate *La Nausée* and Beauvoir's latest novel, *Les Belles Images*, but the proposed trip was cut short after he and Beauvoir accepted an invitation to join Bertrand Russell's Tribunal to investigate American war crimes in Vietnam in July. Sartre's diary became 'too full' to find a window for Lena. Her letters in return were pregnant with meaning.

'I haven't been able to understand your life, you tell me,' he wrote, as she accused him of only seeing the details. The coded message mystified Sartre. He knew all her difficulties, he responded, he'd seen her faint, he'd seen her on the verge of swooning, he'd seen her with *mal au foie*, a bad liver. '*In spite of all that* I don't understand why everything is black in your letter and in your heart.' Why, once had she said to him: 'I *can't* go on living'?

On 31 August 1967, Ilya Ehrenbourg died. Sartre felt it like 'a personal bereavement'. Bereft of her protector, the darkness closed over Lena. She sent Sartre a last, despairing message: '*Ne me laisse pas tomber!* Don't let me fall.'

On 21 August 1968, Soviet tanks rolled into Czechoslovakia to crush the 'Prague Spring'. Sartre, on holiday with Beauvoir in Rome, condemned the Soviets as 'war criminals' and, finally, broke off relations with the USSR. 'I believe I shall never see Moscow again,' wrote Beauvoir, not without a sigh of relief.

Part Five

The Farewell Ceremony

1969–86

36

Feminist Mother

Simone de Beauvoir was a living flame.

Sylvie Le Bon, April 2005

IN 1969 *The Second Sex* sold 750,000 copies in the USA, as the Women's Liberation Movement leapt into life and took Beauvoir as its bible. Betty Friedan, who had described the housewife's 'sickness' in *The Feminine Mystique*, founded NOW in 1966, a feminist organization soon outstripped by radical groups like SCUM, the Society for Cutting Up Men. A flood of new books raised the consciousness of women: Kate Millett's *Sexual Politics*, Germaine Greer's *The Female Eunuch* and Shulamith Firestone's *Dialectic of Sex*. In France, the embryonic Mouvement de Libération des Femmes (MLF) turned to Simone de Beauvoir, whose confidence in socialism was fast evaporating. In 1949 she had written: '*En gros, nous avons gagné la partie*, by and large, we have won the game.' Now she was not so sure.

Her path to militancy lay via the May 1968 student uprising in Paris, a watershed in Sartre and Beauvoir's revolutionary trajectory which smashed the celebrity bubble and returned them to French street politics. By 1968 Sartre was a towering figure on the world stage. He and Beauvoir were superstars, a globe-trotting couple as controversial and newsworthy as Burton and Taylor, who lived in a parallel universe of private jets, security and luxury hotels. 'No private plane, no magnificent banquets,' complained Beauvoir in Israel in March 1967, although despite refusing to visit the Israeli army, 'a small military plane was put at our disposal for our return to Tel Aviv', so that she let the chauffeur go. Annoyed that the helicopter intended to whisk them south from the King David Hotel in Jerusalem was grounded by bad weather, so that they were forced to travel by car, she was disappointed at the size of her retinue ('Only Monique and Ely travelled with us; not a single journalist . . .') and the 'indifferent' food of Tel Aviv.

What a contrast to Egypt, where Nasser had rolled out the red carpet for them. In February, after the customary press conference at the airport, the government provided 'a light plane' for the literary power couple, who were planning a special issue of Les Temps modernes on the Arab–Israeli conflict. Lanzmann and a 'swarm' of photographers and journalists accompanied them. At Abu Simbel, the Ministry of Culture offered the engineers' plane. Tours of inspection of a chemical factory, an iron and steel complex, the blossoming desert followed, before Sartre and Beauvoir paraded in a jeep with an army general, greeted by lines of cheering soldiers waving French and Egyptian flags. Medals were presented at a banquet, before another 'spontaneous' acclamation by peasants took place. The villagers took such 'a genuine interest in us', wrote Beauvoir ingenuously, that her bodyguards struggled to clear a way for her. At a final feast before whirling dervishes and belly-dancers, she and Sartre were presented with two priceless funerary masks.

When Sartre asked Nasser to free eighteen prisoners, he did so. 'Handsome conduct', concluded Beauvoir, seemingly unaware of the propaganda coup she and Sartre represented to the Marxist camp. In Israel, Sartre addressed General Dayan; in Nazareth he received Arab delegations and met Prime Minister Levi Eshkol, although, to the horror of their Egyptian friends, Lufti el-Kholi, editor of a left-wing review, Al Talia, and his wife Liliane, Sartre signed a statement upholding the sovereignty of Israel, with whom he and Beauvoir sided in the Six Day War of June 1967.

As president of the Russell Tribunal, Sartre took the President of the Republic of France to task for refusing a visa to Vladimir Dedijier, the Yugoslav writer and militant who acted as chairman, for the planned meeting of the Tribunal in Paris. 'I want to believe, dear Sir,' wrote Sartre magisterially to de Gaulle, on 13 April 1967, on squared school paper of the sort used by his lycée pupils, 'that my fears are not justified and that our government will grant a visa to both Mr Dedijier and all the other members of the tribunal . . .' 'Mon cher Maître,' replied de Gaulle, using a form of address which implied that he recognized Sartre as a writer but not as president of the Tribunal: 'you will not be the one to teach me that all justice, in principle as well as practice, belongs to the state.' There was no question of offending his American allies: de Gaulle forbade any talk of American atrocities on French soil.

The outraged writer gave an interview to *Le Nouvel observateur*. 'Only café waiters who know that I write have the right to call me "Maître",' fumed Sartre. The difficulties de Gaulle and others were putting in his way proved the legitimacy of the Tribunal. 'People are afraid of us. Not of course of Bertrand Russell, who is ninety-four years old, or of myself, who am pushing seventy . . . So, why do they fear us? Because we are bringing up an issue that that no Western government wants to confront: that of war crimes, which everyone wants to retain the right to commit.'

The human rights of colonized peoples never failed to fire Sartre's blood, whether in Indo-China or Algeria, and he had been quick to accept when Ralph Schoenman, Russell's American secretary, approached Beauvoir in July 1966 and asked her and Sartre to join the Tribunal. In view of Russell's great age, Schoenman invited Sartre to take on the presidency. Urged to accept by Tito Gerassi, who was already campaigning on behalf of the Vietnamese, Beauvoir, 'utterly disgusted by the Americans' . . . contempt for the Vietnamese people's right to self-determination', agreed.

In January 1967 Sartre met Schoenman in London. After de Gaulle's veto of the Paris meeting, Sartre and Beauvoir flew to Stockholm in May, where the self-important Schoenman was already holding three press conferences a day and talking wildly to journalists as if he were his master himself: 'Lord Russell would not allow . . . Lord Russell insists . . .'

'Don't carry on like de Gaulle, who says *France* when he means *I*,' protested Sartre. Schoenman's vainglory as the mouthpiece of an ageing philosopher amused Sartre, although he was often angered by his overbearing manner, unaware of the appeal that another ambitious young man would soon hold for him.

In the meantime Beauvoir had become deeply involved in the meetings of the Tribunal, where Sartre took the lead in accusing the Americans of genocide. Her conscientious attendance was not unconnected to the presence of Dedijer, a tall, broad-shouldered hero of the Yugoslav resistance. Shards of the shell which had struck him were still lodged in his head, which often ached from his old wound and triggered violent rages. 'His intransigent character, his life and his warmth quite won us over,' wrote Beauvoir coyly, as she began a relationship with the

Yugoslav. In November she shared convivial evenings with him in Copenhagen, and in 1968 they met up again in Yugoslavia. But Dedijer, a married man, also had an affair with Arlette, whom he escorted on her annual holidays with Sartre for three years. Sylvie did not approve either of Dedijer's politics or his personal relationships, and under her influence Beauvoir broke off the relationship. 'Sylvie didn't like him, so I saw no sense in continuing,' Beauvoir told her biographer. 'It wasn't anything serious and it didn't last very long,' added Le Bon. 'She ended it when I told her what I thought of him.'

*

By 1968 de Gaulle had been in power for ten years, and his government was moribund. 'France is bored,' declared *Le Monde* in March. 'Our young people are bored.' The lid flew off the pressure cooker as students surged on to the streets in Nanterre, a western suburb of Paris housing marginalized immigrants from the Maghreb. On 22 March, the Nanterre students, led by a German named Daniel Cohn-Bendit, who had already invaded the women's quarters, roaring, 'Down with sexual ghettos,' began a sit-in at the university. They invaded the Sorbonne. On 6 May riot police clashed with students in the Latin Quarter, and soon the smell of tear gas was drifting down the boulevard Saint-Michel. Six hundred thousand demonstrators chanted: 'Ten years is enough!' as they erected barricades, tore up *pavés*, the street cobbles, and hurled them at the police as they sang the 'Internationale'.

On 9 May Sartre, Beauvoir, Jacques Lacan and Lefebvre published a manifesto expressing their solidarity with the students or *contestaires* who were challenging the establishment. When the Sorbonne reopened and the students occupied it, Beauvoir hurried down to join them: 'Neither in my studious youth nor even at the beginning of this year of 1968 could I ever possibly have imagined such a party.' There were jazz bands and orchestras, sandwiches and sleeping-bags. As the red flag flew over the chapel, Sartre, joyfully voicing his youthful anarchy, spoke on Radio Luxembourg: 'These young people don't want the future of our fathers – our future – a future which has proved we were cowardly, worn out, weary . . . Violence is the only thing that remains, whatever the regime, for students who have not yet entered into their fathers' system . . . The only relationship they can have to this university is to smash it.'

Unable to resist the opportunity to take a swipe at his old rival, the academic Raymond Aron, Sartre added in *Le Nouvel observateur*:

'When an ageing Aron endlessly repeats the main tenets of a thesis he wrote in 1939 . . . We must abolish the current system . . . Each teacher must agree to be judged and questioned by his pupils . . . It is time that students be allowed to see . . . a naked Aron.' Excited by Cohn-Bendit's energy, expressing his deep-rooted revulsion at the 'idiocies' of traditional pedagogy, Sartre interviewed the young leader for *Le Nouvel observateur*, an act which conferred respectability upon him. On 20 May, in the gilded amphitheatre of the Sorbonne, he debated with thousands of students who casually addressed him as Jean-Paul, the name that even his intimates had never used to him.

The contagion was spreading. The red flag of the Sorbonne was carried to the Renault car factory at Billancourt, and soon nine million workers were on strike. Alan Geismar, the student union leader, led his followers to the Stock Exchange and set it on fire. But, as 'beatniks, whores and tramps' moved into the Sorbonne, and drug-dealers sold marijuana in its corridors, the tide began to ebb. In June de Gaulle won the election. 'The revolution,' wrote Beauvoir, 'was stillborn.'

Laying its failure squarely at the feet of the French Communist Party, Sartre and Beauvoir stayed in close touch with the *gauchistes*. In Rome in 1969 they met the two Cohn-Bendit brothers and other disheartened young extremists, Marc Kravetz and François Georges, who were harshly critical of *Les Temps modernes*, accusing it of having become an institution. By 1970 the Maoist Proletarian Left was in crisis, weak and isolated; its paper, *La Cause du peuple* (*The People's Cause*), was outlawed and confiscated, its editors arrested. Sartre, who had been irritated when de Gaulle said, 'You don't arrest Voltaire,' now saw the value of his privileged position and offered to become the nominal editor. The crudely printed red and black broadsheet, with his name and Beauvoir's on the back page, proclaimed itself to be 'communist, revolutionary and proletarian', and represented his own dramatic move leftwards, which split the editorial board of *Les Temps modernes* and led even the loyal Pontalis to resign. 'What this is about,' declared Sartre in *Le Monde*, 'is making it possible through prolonged effort . . . for ninety-seven per cent of the French people one day to make a revolution.' Henceforth the old Kobra would be *un nouvel intellectuel*, a new intellectual at one with the masses. The events of 10 May 1968 had led him to shed another skin: never again would he wear a suit or tie, but turned out in his black pullover and moth-eaten fur-lined jacket to protest at the trial of Le Dantec and Le Bris, the paper's editors, who were sentenced to a year and eight months respectively.

Beauvoir was equally revitalized by the struggle for 'justice and freedom'. She held a press conference in her flat and formed an association with Michel Leiris, of 'Friends of *La Cause du peuple*'. A week later the main leftist groups formed *Secours Rouge*, an organization to aid imprisoned militants. Thirty volunteer sellers of the paper had been thrown into prison on a charge of reviving La Gauche Prolétarienne, so on 20 June 1970 she and Sartre decided to sell the paper themselves, accompanied by the inevitable crowd of paparazzi. 'Read *La Cause du peuple! Pour la liberté de la presse!*' On the avenue du Géneral-Leclerc, as they pushed through the crowd distributing the paper, a *flic* grasped Sartre by the arm and began steering him towards the police station.

Flash bulbs popped. '*Vous arrêtez un prix Nobel!* You're arresting a Nobel Prize [*sic*],' shouted an onlooker. The cop let go. Six days later Sartre and Beauvoir, the latter still looking like a respectable bourgeoise in her neat white polo-neck, dark costume and turban, repeated the exercise, but although she and her friends were bundled into a Black Maria, no one touched Sartre. 'His thirst for martyrdom,' wrote François Mauriac sourly in *Le Figaro littéraire*, was 'no reason for putting this incurably insufferable person in prison'.

Yet despite his speeches and TV appearances, Sartre's influence was waning. When he hoisted himself up to the lectern at the Mutualité to speak to the students in February 1969, he saw some words scribbled on a sheet of paper: 'Sartre, be clear, be brief.' It was Michel Foucault, Lévi-Strauss and Jacques Lacan who filled the lecture halls, as structuralism made existentialism old hat and the New Novel and Françoise Sagan superseded the literature of *engagement*.

And as Sartre stood on a barrel at Billancourt to speak to the bewildered workers, he appeared a curiously diminished figure. To many of the media, he had become a laughing stock, a man they despised. 'At any demonstration, he and Beauvoir would be there in the front, like a pantomime,' remembers Jean-Claude Sauer, photo-journalist for *Paris-Match*. 'It became a joke to everyone. Sartre's biggest mistake was to allow himself to be used by others. He was completely wrong to give young people hope that everything will change. Nothing will change . . . They were naïve. Dishonest. They played a role . . . And even though he was a kind of dwarf, he attacked those little girls.'

*

It is August 1968. In the Piazza Santa Maria di Trastavere, Rome, as Sartre steps out of Beauvoir's car, his legs crumple beneath him. He clutches at Beauvoir and Sylvie's arms, and the two women support him until the giddy spell passes. 'I did not think it of much consequence,' writes Beauvoir, 'but I was surprised, since he had drunk nothing.'

Unaware that smoking two packs of Boyards a day, the big, fat brown cigarettes of which Sartre is so fond, is narrowing his arteries, she puts him on the train from Rome to Paris in September 1970, confident that his condition has stabilized. On her return, he resumes his usual precise routine, sleeping two nights a week at Arlette's, but spending the others with Beauvoir in rue Schoelcher in the comfortable intimacy enjoyed by many old married couples. In the evening they picnic on hard-boiled eggs or a slice of ham, washed down with 'un peu de scotch', and listen to 'home concerts' on her gramophone: Monteverdi, Gesualdo, Verdi, Mozart – above all Così fan tutte – varied by modern composers like Stockhausen and Xenakis. Then Beauvoir climbs the spiral staircase to the bedroom, while Sartre sleeps on the divan in the studio. In the morning they share a cup of tea, before Liliane Siegel, a yoga teacher, comes to collect him for breakfast. This is always two double expressos and four pieces of bread and butter. Sartre can be observed giving Liliane 500-franc notes over the meal; afterwards he shuffles back to his studio flat in boulevard Raspail to work, in reduced circumstances which Liliane claims distressed her.

Instead of the room she had first seen at rue Bonaparte, where Sartre had sat at a 'splendid desk', flanked by 'imposing bookshelves – the whole atmosphere was what I thought appropriate to a writer', he has a light, modern room with a tiny, toy-like desk cluttered with books, papers, cigarettes, ashtrays, pens and a lamp. Against the wall is a white Formica table. A standard lamp from the flea-market is almost the only other object in the room apart from the quantities of books on the floor, and a wooden chair, shiny with age, conspicuously out of keeping with the undistinguished quality of the rest of the furniture.

Sartre notices Liliane's gaze resting on the chair.

'Do you like it? It belonged to my great-grandfather. This chair is the only thing I care about – except my books of course.'

'It's very beautiful, but it looks uncomfortable.'

'I like to be uncomfortable. I don't like seats that corrupt.'

Puritan to the end, Sartre has virtually no possessions apart from pen and paper. Instead he finds reassurance in the regularity of his habits, invariably meeting Beauvoir for lunch. Afterwards they go back to his flat, where she works at the Formica table. On Saturday evenings Sylvie joins them for dinner, and on Sunday all three lunch together at La

Coupole; but one evening towards the end of September, after dinner with Sylvie at Dominique's, where Sartre has drunk a great deal of vodka, he falls asleep, dropping his cigarette on the floor. The next morning, when Beauvoir and Sylvie collect him from his flat for lunch, he bumps against the furniture. At La Coupole he staggers into the tables, and when the two women take him round to Wanda's in the rue du Dragon, he falls as he climbs out of the taxi.

The next morning his physician, Dr Zaidmann, refers him for further tests, and refuses to allow him to go with the Maoists on a tour of industrial centres. Sartre is to begin a course of injections to stimulate his failing circulation. He is to rest. Instead he struggles to finish the third, 2,000-page tome of his Flaubert, *The Family Idiot*, on which he has been labouring from the ages of fifty to sixty-seven. As he speculates on Flaubert's childhood, finding parallels with his own and slipping into disguised autobiography, Sartre again has recourse to stimulants: his old favourites, corydrane, tobacco and alcohol. 'Doping the animal,' his old secretary, Jean Cau, called it, fascinated by the tic Sartre had developed, as, sitting at his desk, he raised his right shoulder and opened and shut his folded arm. Cau believed it dated from Sartre's boxing days, describing his master as an 'intellectual boxer', for whom every conversation was a match. But now the boxing tic has morphed into something more ornithological. 'Monsieur Poulou', as Eugénie, the maid from Alsace, used to call Sartre, is flapping his arms like a pair of wings. The little chicken is living up to his nickname.

'These new disturbances,' writes Beauvoir, 'compelled me to become dramatically aware of a fragility that in fact I had been conscious of all the time.' She feels a sense of premonition: of 'life set between parentheses': delight and dread.

*

Beauvoir's own fragility, which she had revealed to her readers at the end of *Force of Circumstance* when she wrote, 'I have been gypped,' and for which she had been widely reviled by women who condemned her defiant defence of her free union with Sartre and blamed her fear of old age on her unwise rejection of marriage, had been temporarily overcome. Her method had been the usual one: writing, to which she had always turned, 'like a prayer', at times of vulnerability, dissecting her own sorrow with a surgeon's skill.

From the 'deep wounds' of Sartre's adoption of Arlette in 1965 sprang a new novel, *Les Belles Images*, which Beauvoir dashed off between October and January 1966 while recovering from her motor accident. 'Writing about myself would have meant pouring salt all over.' Instead Beauvoir set this slight but prescient novel in an advertising office, where her heroine, Laurence, is a copywriter who sells 'beautiful images'. A promiscuous, materialistic working mother who pops pills and worries about tummy tucks while sending her daughter to a psychiatrist, Laurence believes that she has 'lost the game' and invests her hopes in her child. The novel leapt up the best-seller list, despite poor reviews accusing the author of apeing Sagan.

But it was Beauvoir's next book, *La Femme Rompue* (*The Woman Destroyed*) that brought a storm crashing about her head. The most recurrent criticism of her work was that her stories were auto-biographical; once again she was said to be the subject of these three tales of abandoned, neurotic womanhood, which touched a nerve with her readers. According to Le Bon, however, Beauvoir was writing about *'la femme mariée qui n'avait pas gagné la vie,'* married women who didn't earn their own living, and Olga was her model for the eponymous 'destroyed woman', Monique, whose dependence on men brings only unhappiness. Monique's husband Maurice is on the verge of leaving her for the mistress she loathes, Noëllie. 'Women who do nothing can't stand those who work,' says Maurice, uttering his mistress's thoughts. Monique, gulping down spirits, tranquillizers and sleeping pills, con-templates suicide. Olga, her face ravaged by botched plastic surgery as she sits beside Beauvoir at a feminist meeting in 1972, Olga who talks of killing herself and Bost and 'raves, rages and sometimes bites', represents woman as victim in this modern morality tale.

Murielle, another lonely forty-something whose story is a prequel to Bridget Jones, drowns in self-pity alone in her flat on New Year's Eve:

> I keep my end up but a woman alone is spat on . . . Die alone live alone no I can't bear it. I need to have a man I want Tristan to come back lousy dunghill of a world . . . they are laughing and here I am withering on the shelf: forty-three it's too soon . . . Nobody takes me out any more I just stay here stewing in my own shit. I'm sick of it sick sick sick . . . What a dirty trick to have pushed me into that marriage me so vital alive a burning flame and him stuffy middle-class cold-hearted prick like limp macaroni . . .

In this monologue Beauvoir hammers home her message that women are the losers in marriage unless they forge an independent life, but there is an unmentioned subtext to these poignant portraits of angry, disappointed females. Economic self-sufficiency was no guarantee against the pangs of love. *The Woman Destroyed* was published in 1967, on the eve of Beauvoir's sixtieth birthday. She had continued writing to Nelson Algren, inviting herself to spend a week with him in Chicago in May 1965 when Sartre planned to lecture at Cornell. 'I should like to see you again before *you* die,' she told her 'dearest own rat' on Bastille Day, 14 July 1964.

Her timing was abysmal. Despite his apparent forgiveness of Beauvoir in 1960, when he had visited her in Paris, Algren had been wounded by his portrait in *The Mandarins*. When she returned from Brazil to rue Schoelcher, where he had stayed on in her absence before returning to America , she found no letter from him, only a few photographs of Istanbul; to her chagrin, he continued writing long, newsy letters to Olga. The writer Gillian Tindall recalls meeting Algren at a party given by Peggy Guggenheim in 1961, when he was 'spewing bile' about Beauvoir to anyone who would listen. Guggenheim, meanwhile, wrote an unpublished novel about her affair with Algren, in which his fictional character makes vituperative comments about his affair with his French lover. She sent the manuscript to Beauvoir with a sarcastic letter, which Beauvoir translated and forwarded to Algren. 'Dearest beast, are you still breathing? Or dead, or what?' demanded Beauvoir in December 1961. 'Did you marry Mary G, not daring to tell me?'

Subsequently Beauvoir sent a French-Canadian journalist, Madeleine Gobeil, whom she had befriended, to interview Algren. He at once began a copycat affair with her, taking her to the same cottage at Miller in which he and Beauvoir had stayed. Gobeil's blow-by-blow accounts of the relationship were sent to Beauvoir at Algren's instigation, so she believed. The war continued through third parties.

Algren vented some of his spleen in *Who Lost an American?* dedicated to Simone de Beauvoir and published in 1963. It was a book which had 'no right to be written', Beauvoir protested to him in October, hoping – perhaps tongue-in-cheek – that her own new book, *Force of Circumstance*, would not be so hated, and that he would not be 'unpleased' by it; it was, she explained, written 'with all my heart'.

Her fears were well founded. The anger Algren felt over *The Mandarins* was minor compared to the volcanic fury which now erupted when he read *Force of Circumstance*, which first appeared in the United States in the December 1964 issue of *Harper's* magazine under the provocative heading: 'The Question of Fidelity'. Opening up the magazine, the scales finally dropped from his eyes. For the first time he understood that Beauvoir had sought an American lover as tit-for-tat

for Sartre's seduction of Dolorès. But while she was disguised as 'M', he
was named and shamed as Beauvoir's beau. To add insult to injury, he
(like many of Beauvoir and Sartre's lovers) began to feel like a lab rat
in a psychiatric experiment when he read about their pact:

> To maintain throughout all deviations from the main path a
> 'certain fidelity'.
> 'I have been faithful to thee, Cynara! in my fashion.' Such an
> undertaking has its risks . . .
> If the two allies allow themselves only passing sexual liaisons,
> then there is no difficulty, but it also means that the freedom they
> allow themselves is not worthy of the name. Sartre and I have
> been more ambitious. It has been our wish to experience
> 'contingent loves': but there is one question we have deliberately
> avoided: How would the third person feel about the arrangement?

Reviewing the book in *Harper's*, Algren vented his outrage:

> Anybody who can experience love contingently has a mind that
> has recently snapped. How can love be *contingent*? Contingent
> upon *what*? . . . Procurers are more honest than philosophers.

In place of his 'good, affectionate' letters and audiotape to Beauvoir
in December 1963, there would only be silence. He never forgave his
'frog wife', although, according to Madeline Gobeil, he continued to
admire her achievements. For her part Beauvoir, despite her rage at
Algren's 'contemptuous' remarks about Sartre and her in *Who Lost an
American?*, retained a wistful affection for him. In her last letter to
Algren, in November 1964, she said she would find him wherever he
was hiding when she came over to the States in May 1965. But the
Vietnam war intervened. After becoming president of the Russell
Tribunal denouncing American war crimes, Sartre cancelled his visit
to Cornell.

Algren remained bitter at his lack of recognition, in contrast to
Beauvoir's global fame. One of the most poignant pieces of evidence is
a mutilated photograph in the Ohio University archives, showing the
former lovers beside Lake Michigan in the summer of 1952; in other
copies of this photograph Beauvoir's hair lies loose around her
shoulders as she smiles for the camera, but in this picture her image has
been ripped out. The culprit seems to have been Nelson.

By May 1981 Algren was slightly mollified to find himself elected to the élite American Academy of Arts and Letters. He was seventy-two, had recently moved to Sag Harbour, New York, and was finally feeling at home in the literary community of eastern Long Island; he decided to ask his friends to a party.

But when W.J. Weatherby, *The Times* correspondent, arrived to interview Algren, he found that the years had not, after all, softened his rage. Snapping at the journalist like the crocodile to which Beauvoir had once compared him, he declared: 'I've been in whorehouses all over the world and the woman there always closes the door . . . but this woman flung the door open and called in the public and the press . . . I don't have any malice against her but I think it was an appalling thing to do.'

When the first guest arrived for Algren's party on 9 May, he found his body, surrounded by unopened bottles of alcohol. He had died of a heart attack.

'Aren't you sorry?' enquired Beauvoir's sister, Poupette, when the news reached France. 'Don't you feel anything for him?'

'Why should I?' replied Beauvoir, who never appreciated how used and thrown away like a worn glove she and Sartre made their victims feel.

'What did he feel for me, that he could have written those horrible things?'

But she continued to keep his letters in the upstairs bedroom in her studio, and to wear his ring until her death.

Hatred was coming to Beauvoir from another source. Wanda, high on cocaine, had made a voodoo doll of Beauvoir and was sticking pins in it. Her grudge was that Beauvoir had left her out of her memoirs, which, like Algren, she considered not autobiography but 'autofiction'. In 1965 Sylvie became concerned at Wanda's behaviour when the actress bought a pistol and threatened to murder Beauvoir. Posing as a journalist from *Elle*, Sylvie and two of her student friends tricked Wanda into opening the door of her flat, where they held her down and searched her room. Sylvie returned in triumph to Beauvoir, brandishing Wanda's revolver. '[Wanda] was a miserable drug addict,' recalls Sylvie. She had proved her devotion to Beauvoir.

Few knew better than strong-minded Sylvie, who physically so closely resembled her companion, the price Beauvoir had paid for her independence. 'The Independent Woman' in *The Second Sex* reads as her personal confession of the sacrifices involved in 'a life of freedom':

Liaison or marriage . . . can be reconciled with a career much less easily for [a woman] than a man. Sometimes her lover . . . asks her to renounce it: she hesitates, like Colette's *Vagabonde*, who ardently desires the presence of a man at her side but dreads the fetters of marriage. If she yields, she is once more a vassal; if she refuses, she condemns herself to withering solitude.

How much easier to be a Baladin or Playboy than a female *Vagabonde*. Wistfully Beauvoir imagines a 'man that acts as devoted servant,' like George Eliot's husband, Lewes, who created the domestic harmony that 'the wife usually creates around the husband-overlord'. Independent woman, on the other hand, is 'torn between her professional interests and the problems of her sexual life; it is difficult for her to strike a balance between the two; if she does, it is at the price of concessions, sacrifices, acrobatics, which require her to be in a constant state of tension'. 'Nervousness and frailty' are the price of singledom.

The pact – so glibly described in *Force of Circumstance* – had proved an almost impossible juggling act. Keeping all the balls in the air, Sartre and her other lovers, had cost Beauvoir dearly. Sensing this, her readers identified with Beauvoir the woman. It was the secret of her popularity. On journeys with Sartre she was mobbed, like the Pope, she said. It was time to creep out from under the shadow of the man who had taken her 'under his wing' in 1929, and answer the question women everywhere were asking: was she a feminist?

Beauvoir had expected socialism to deliver sexual equality. It had not done so, and in 1970 she crossed her personal Rubicon. She had already noticed in the May '68 demonstrations that even *gauchiste* men did not treat women as equals.

> Men made the speeches, but women typed them. Men were on the soapboxes and on the podiums, but women were in the kitchens making coffee. So they got fed up with this because they were intelligent women. They realized that they would have to take their fate into their own hands . . . I agreed with them because I understood that women could not expect their emancipation to come from general revolution but would have to create their own. Men were always telling them that the needs of the revolution came first and their turn as women came later . . .

When at the end of 1970 Gisèle Halimi and other members of the *Mouvement de Libération des Femmes* asked Beauvoir to join their campaign, she agreed, signing the 'Manifesto of the 343', which proclaimed: '*Je me suis fait avorter*, I have had an abortion.' The

Manifesto, signed not only by 'names' such as Colette Audry, Dominique Desanti and Simone Signoret, but also by members of the Sartre family, Olga, Arlette, Michèle, Hélène de Beauvoir and Liliane Siegel, secretaries, office workers and housewives, was published in *Le Nouvel observateur* on 5 April 1971. Above arrest, like Sartre, Beauvoir believed that she was not as courageous as ordinary women who risked losing their jobs; as for the negative publicity, she was used to it. In November she and 4,000 women marched through Paris to demand a woman's right to choose: militants handed out parsley, the symbol of clandestine abortion, and at the Nation a few brave spirits climbed a statue and burnt dishcloths, symbol of female servitude.

Beauvoir herself had never had an abortion, states Le Bon, she had continued to feel fervently for women forced to turn to back-street abortionists. 'She gave money very freely, allowing abortions to be carried out in her flat,' recalls Michèle Vian, who also clubbed together with her friends to obtain instruments and towels so that terminations could take place in her own flat. 'It was very difficult, very hard, we were working at the same time . . . There were *flics* around, it was illegal. But these pregnant girls were so ashamed, these girls raped by their *patron*. Their families showed them the door. They had nowhere to go.'

Three months later, in July 1971, Halimi formed Choisir la Cause des Femmes, with the aim of repealing the 1920 law against abortion. Beauvoir was its first president; the other founders included Jacques Monod, Nobel Prize winner for medicine. Having distinguished medical men on board, some of them Catholic, proved vital in the association's first battle against the state: the famous Bobigny trial, in which Choisir took on the defence of Marie-Claire, a sixteen-year-old girl accused of having had an abortion with the agreement of her mother.

'Halimi was brilliant,' recalls Laurence Nguyen, a member of the National Secretariat of Choisir. 'First she was beautiful. She represented women so well.' Women were judged on their appearance; at the trial they ran the gauntlet of a hostile, jeering crowd who shouted insults at them: 'Lesbian!' '*Grosse et moche et mal baisée! Fat and ugly and badly fucked.' 'Si nous sommes mal baisées, à qui la faute?*' the women retorted. 'If we aren't properly fucked, whose fault is it?'

Encouraged by their first victory, *la loi Veil*, reform of the abortion law overseen by the Minister, Simone Veil, women decided to stand for the national assembly. In the elections of March 1978, 100 women candidates came forward, their slogans, '*Cent femmes pour les femmes*', 'Vote for Choisir', 'Choose change', showing that change was truly in the air. Men could barely believe it. 'When we asked them to help, they didn't take it seriously,' recalls Nguyen, then the thirty-six-year-old candidate for Fontainebleau. 'They said they'd put up our posters, but they forgot the water for the glue. They came back laughing: we made *pipi* in the glue for you.'

Shocked that the status of women had barely changed in the last ten years, by 1972 Beauvoir had undergone a Damascene conversion: '*Je me déclare féministe*, I declare myself a feminist,' she wrote at the end of *All Said and Done*. 'No, we have not won the game; in fact we have won almost nothing since 1950.' In 1949 she had based *The Second Sex* on philosophical grounds. If she were to write it again, she said, she would base the oppression of women on economics, but she would not modify her basic tenet, 'that all male ideologies are directed at justifying the oppression of women, and that women are so conditioned by society that they consent to this oppression'. Convinced that nurture, not nature, shapes women, she stood by her original idea: 'You are not born a woman; you become one . . . No feminist questions the statement that women are manufactured by civilization, not biologically determined.' Angry that 'difference' restricted women to 'the act of wiping – of wiping babies, the sick, the old', she, like Firestone, advocated the abolition of the family and deplored the 'slavery' of childrearing.

For a writer to metamorphose into an icon, he or she must personify the spirit of the age. Beauvoir personified seventies feminism: strong, single, feisty. Her lifestyle was as inspirational as her ideas in mobilizing women, although some young French feminists had reservations about her reputation for free love. 'It is difficult for us,' said some; 'We admire what she wrote, but we don't like the life she leads.' Others had breathed the zeitgeist she had bred. 'It wasn't only the *parapluies*, the figureheads, who did it,' says Michèle. 'We women made the revolution.' *The Second Sex* had outgrown its reputation in Catholic France as '*un truc scandaleux*': it had started an unstoppable process.

At the time of the Liberation, Beauvoir had written that it was her turn, Sartre's and hers, to carry the torch. After the existentialist boom, Beauvoir had taken that torch and carried it in an entirely different direction. She had taken the existentialist message of freedom and self-realization and applied it to her own sex. She had made it relevant to millions of women across the globe; she had become an inspiration, a model and a beloved mother. No wonder women reached out as she passed and touched the hem of her skirt: she carried the aura of royalty, the sanctity and mystique of Mother Teresa.

Fighting for a cause separate from Sartre's, Beauvoir had finally triumphed in the fame game. She was, at last, a woman in her own right. But behind the public persona lay the private. She had lit the fire of women's liberation but once, long ago, she had betrayed her pupils' trust: Olga, Bianca, Nathalie, women all now damaged or dead. She had violated adolescent girls and pimped for Sartre. In 1972 she made a point of retracting another important statement in *The Second Sex*: 'the first penetration is always a rape'. Beauvoir had not forgotten her past. Her change of heart had its roots in her own murky history of bad faith. There could be no more glaring contradiction than that between the principles enshrined in *The Second Sex* and her past practice of what was, by any contemporary standard, child abuse. At sixty-four, was it too late to save her 'children'?

37

The Abduction of an Old Man

Comment expliquer ce 'détournement de vieillard'?
How can one explain this 'abduction of an old man'?
Simone de Beauvoir, *La cérémonie des adieux*

AT ST PAUL-DE-VENCE that spring, the orange trees were in blossom.
At the end of the garden at the Hôtel Colombe d'Or, Simone and
Sylvie shared a small cottage while Sartre and Arlette stayed in the
hotel itself. The days passed pleasantly, lunching together and visiting
Fondation Maeght to admire the pictures. In the evenings, Sartre
joined Beauvoir in the cool, white sitting-room, hung with Calder's
paintings, where they talked, drank whisky and ate *saucisson* and
chocolate together.

On their return to Paris in May 1971, Sartre lovingly opened the
heavy box he had received from Gallimard; it was full of copies of *The
Family Idiot*. He told Beauvoir that the 2,000-page book gave him as
much pleasure as the publication of *Nausea*. She was more concerned,
however, at the perilous pastures into which the Maoists were leading
him. On 13 February Sartre had accompanied Liliane to the Sacré
Coeur, which La Gauche Prolétarienne had decided to occupy after a
young militant, Richard Deshayes, had been disfigured by a tear-gas
grenade during a demonstration. The Maoists assured Sartre that they
had the agreement of the priest, Monseigneur Charles. But when Sartre
and Liliane entered there were only a few elderly parishioners praying.

'I've been taken for a ride again,' Sartre told Liliane. 'It's a stupid gimmick.'

Gradually the church filled up with young men. The doors were shut. Minutes later the riot police stormed the building. Sartre, propped against a wall, escaped injury, but in the violent clash which followed a man had his thigh pierced by a spiked railing. Angry at having been trapped, alarmed at the power of the Maoists within Secours Rouge, Sartre withdrew from its management.

He continued to visit Michèle Vian at St Bernard's Chapel at Montparnasse station, where she was on hunger strike in solidarity with Geismar, locked up in Santé prison; she and Sartre had rekindled their old intimacy against a public backdrop of hostility to the *gauchistes*, who were increasingly viewed as terrorists. 'I went on all the demonstrations,' recalls Michèle. Increasingly, as Choisir claimed Beauvoir's time, she left Michèle and Liliane to accompany Sartre on his outings with the Maoists, whose demos he still attended. 'Castor always made Sartre's women her friends,' says Michèle. In practical matters, such as their annual holidays, arranged according to their old *heures de professeur*, 'She was the leader, she made the rules.' Although their political paths were diverging, with Beauvoir in charge the rigid Sartrean routine still functioned smoothly.

Castor kept a firm eye on Sartre, who often stayed with her because the lift was broken in his block of flats and it tired him to walk up ten flights of stairs. But on Tuesday, 18 May, when he arrived at her flat from Arlette's and Beauvoir asked casually: '*Comment ça va?*' he replied: 'Well, not so good.' His mouth was twisted, his words indistinct, and he could barely walk. He had had a third stroke. That evening, after Sartre had seen his doctor, Sylvie drove him to Beauvoir's. As Sartre sipped his fruit juice, and Sylvie replaced the cigarette between his paralysed lips, Beauvoir put on Verdi's *Requiem*. 'Most appropriate,' murmured Sartre.

Within a week, Sartre had recovered his powers of speech and his good humour, although when Bost came to dinner Beauvoir told him that she could see trouble ahead as she tried to persuade Sartre to cut down his consumption of alcohol, caffeine and stimulants. Quietly Sartre climbed the stairs to the balcony which overhung her studio. His tenor voice as light and pure as in his youth, he sang: 'I don't want to cause my Castor even the slightest pain.'

That June his own suffering increased as a painful tongue made eating difficult.

'What a horrible year,' remarked Beauvoir. '*Tout le temps vous avez eu des ennuis.*'

'Oh! *Ça ne fait rien,*' replied Sartre. 'When you're old it no longer has any importance.'

'You mean because one's going to die?'

'Yes. It's natural to come to pieces little by little.'

From that time Beauvoir noticed a new detachment in Sartre. He was, if not sad, remote and indifferent to his fate. And when, that summer, she had a last lunch with him at La Coupole before they parted, he to Junas with Arlette, she to Italy with Sylvie, he smiled and said: '*Alors, c'est la cérémonie des adieux!* So this is the farewell ceremony!'

'I won't live beyond seventy,' Sartre confided to Beauvoir in December. 'You told me yourself that people find it hard to recover from a third stroke.' 'But your strokes were very slight,' protested Beauvoir. Sartre continued: 'I'm afraid I shan't finish the Flaubert.' 'Does that grieve you?' 'Yes, it does.' He began to make plans for his funeral, insisting, above all else, that he was not to be buried in the family vault at Père Lachaise cemetery between his mother, who had died in January 1969, and his stepfather, Joseph Mancy.

At the funeral of Overney, a sacked Renault worker killed by a security guard, Sartre struggled to follow the coffin with Beauvoir and Michèle. His legs would not carry him. Although his enthusiasm for the Maoists' 'violence, spontaneity and morality' led him into another daring escapade, in which he was smuggled into the Renault works in the back of a van in February 1972, his relationship with alcohol was taking its toll. Beauvoir noticed that after a single glass of whisky he began talking nonsense and staggering on his way to bed. And when his secretary, Puig, arrived at Arlette's flat where Sartre had been watching television while she was out, he found him lying on the floor, drunk. It took Puig half an hour to rouse Sartre, and when he walked the ailing writer home, Sartre fell and bloodied his nose.

It began to be obvious that Sartre needed careful watching. When in August Beauvoir went to the station in Rome to meet him, he had given her the slip. She found him back at the hotel, his speech slurred. 'I'll be all right in a minute,' he told her. He had taken advantage of being alone to drink two half-bottles of wine in the restaurant car. 'Why do you drink too much whenever you get the chance?' asked Beauvoir. '*C'est agréable,*' came the defiant reply. But liking alcohol was not answer enough for Beauvoir, who suspected that Sartre had lost interest even in 'his garden, Flaubert'. After delivering the third volume to Gallimard, he toyed with the idea of basing the fourth on *Madame Bovary* on structuralism, which she knew he disliked. Instead of writing, the couple took to playing draughts, of which they soon became passionately fond.

One afternoon, as they were walking back towards the Panthéon, Sartre stopped and said: 'Cats have just pissed on me.' Sylvie laughed and believed him; Beauvoir said nothing. She had already noticed that he often left a damp patch on the chair in her studio, and had taken the bull by the horns: 'You are incontinent. You ought to tell the doctor.' To her surprise, Sartre confessed that he had already told him. 'It has been going on a long while now. It's those cells I've lost.' 'Don't you find it embarrassing?' protested Beauvoir. He answered with a smile. 'When you're old you can't expect too much, your claims have to be modest.'

*

Perhaps it is to escape these interrogations over his bodily functions that Sartre submits himself to a new interrogation. In November he agrees to be interviewed by two *gauchistes*, a young stateless Egyptian Jew named Benny Lévy, who at the time uses the pseudonym Pierre Victor, and journalist Philippe Gavi. Victor, a philosophy graduate from the École Normale and leader of La Gauche Prolétarienne with Geismar, has known Sartre since 1970. Sartre liked him immediately, detecting in this thin, wild-looking man with the 'profile of an eagle' 'feminine qualities' which appealed to him. To the surprise of the 'family', Victor, in his grey-green parka, false beard and sunglasses, a seventies hoodie, charmless but forceful, seems to Sartre, the prototype 'worker-intellectual', *un mec*, a guy with whom he can have the sort of conversations that he 'very much likes to have with women'.

'Sartre didn't want to discuss ideas with Beauvoir at this time in his life,' recalls Michèle. 'He admired youth and its philosophy. He preferred the young, the men for their ideas, the women for their charm.' Irreverent, familiar, Philippe and Pierre address Sartre as *tu*. The two *jeunes camarades* who, in these interviews published as *On a raison de se révolter* (*We are Right to Revolt*), treat Sartre without deference but as an equal, resurrect for him the gaiety of his youth with Nizan, with whom he was a 'couple' before Beauvoir.

Sartre believes himself to be free of illusions. 'Of course I exist for you only in so far as I am useful to you,' he tells Victor. Age, he says, has turned him into 'a mere image', only able to join a demo with the young if he is brought there in a car with a folding chair. There are tensions with the Maos: he disagrees with the kidnapping of Nogrette, the Renault official responsible for the dismissal of the workers, by an underground group, La Nouvelle Résistance Populaire. 'I am not a Maoist,' he often asserts, but he takes on the editorship of two more Maoist papers, *Tout* and *J'accuse*, which merges with *La Cause du peuple*, in order to serve as a shield against the authorities. Radicalized by these editorships, urged by Victor to abandon Flaubert, in February 1973 Sartre, with Victor, Serge July and Gavi, takes a bold and provocative step in launching a new daily paper, *Libération*, and announcing: 'I believe in illegality.'

Independent, sacrilegious, the revolutionary paper features scatological cartoons and taboo sexual subjects. It also gives voice to Sartre's anti-colonialism, felt even more viscerally after the May Lai massacre, and his opposition to the PCF, at a time when the publication of Alexander Solzhenitsyn's *The Gulag Archipelago* in translation is revealing to young intellectuals everywhere the murderous truth of totalitarianism. As, during that Roman summer, Beauvoir reads aloud to Sartre the greatest work of the exiled novelist who once refused to shake hands with them, the full realization of the USSR as 'paradise lost' perhaps hits home; but it is doubtful whether, even with eyes wide open, they are courageous enough to admit to each other the part they played in prolonging the agony of the Russian and Chinese peoples by propping up a bankrupt system.

'You don't regret anything about your relationship with Communism and the Communists?' asks Olivier Todd.

'Non,' replies Sartre. *Je ne regrette rien.* 'I couldn't have acted differently.' 'No one will ever get him to admit that he made a mistake in becoming the most famous fellow traveller ever,' comments Todd. Nor does Sartre publicly acknowledge that his old friend, the right-wing liberal Raymond Aron, who had attacked Marxism as 'the opium of the intellectuals' years ago, has been right all along. But in his study, alone with his conscience, Sartre finds cold comfort as he pens the words: 'I became a traitor and remained one.'

Other chickens are coming home to roost. In 1971–2 Marcel Ophuls's television documentary *Le Chagrin et la pitié*, which probes French collaboration with the Germans during the Occupation and demonstrates that France was never *la nation résistante* of Gaullist myth, plays to full houses in the cinema, despite its TV ban. Many believe it has opened a can of worms. Nevertheless, that year President Pompidou pardons the notorious leader of the Lyon Milice, Paul

Touvier, who emerges from hiding twenty years after his death sentence for hounding resistants. The state, like many individuals, prefers to draw a convenient veil over the past: Sartre is one of those who campaigns to save Touvier from the guillotine.

*

So far Sartre had remained entirely rational, although, aware perhaps of his deteriorating health, he admits: 'May '68 may have come too late for me.' On 5 March 1973 a crisis occurred. Sartre had been forced to meet a tight deadline the day before, writing an article on the parliamentary elections for the first issue of *Libé*; he was proud of dashing it off so fast and efficiently in the din of the editorial office in rue de Bretagne. The next day, after lunch with Michèle at La Coupole – 'who always made him drink too much,' wrote Beauvoir crossly – he had another stroke. His arm was paralysed. The next morning she was panic-stricken. Sartre was talking gibberish.

It was two days before Sartre was able to see a neurologist at the Salpêtrière hospital. He told Beauvoir that the patient had had an attack of anoxia, lack of oxygen to the brain, caused partly by tobacco but also by the state of his arteries, and ordered Sartre to stop smoking and to cut down his drinking. He took no notice. Alarmed at his confused state of mind, Arlette took him to the South of France for a holiday, where he sat in the sun reading *romans policiers*. 'Just why am I here?' he demanded. 'Is it because we are expecting Hercule Poirot?'

Tearfully Beauvoir toured Languedoc with Sartre and Sylvie, but as she steered the car past *garrigues* and vineyards, fruit trees in blossom and distant blue hills, he continued to talk nonsense, jumbling his words and imagining there was a young man in the back of the car. Back in Paris, the neurologist took his blood pressure: 200/120. 'I'm not stupid. But I'm empty,' Sartre told the specialist. His fits of dizziness increased, and in June he had a triple haemorrhage at the back of his 'good' eye.

Sartre's growing blindness was becoming an embarrassment, although not to him. In Menton, he tipped a bowl of fish soup over his feet; in Venice, he spilt spaghetti and the ice cream his diabetic appetite craved, and refused to let Beauvoir cut up his meat. Her anxiety grew: torn between compassion for Sartre and worry that Sylvie was growing bored, she was trying to please two people with incompatible needs. Wanda, who had also come to Venice to mind Sartre, gave him his medication with meticulous care, but she was concerned when, unable any longer to see the clock, he began getting dressed in the middle of the night.

It was clear that Sartre could no longer live alone. Once again Beauvoir turned to his women for help. In 1973 Arlette and Liliane found him a larger, two-bedroom flat, also on the tenth floor, but with two lifts, on boulevard Edgar-Quinet, near the new Tour Montparnasse. It still overlooked the waving fronds of the trees in the cemetery, but this was no longer of comfort to Sartre, who that autumn entered the valley of darkness. 'My occupation as a writer is completely destroyed,' he told Michel Contat, who was disturbed to find this 'marvellous guy', a great writer who lived the simplest of lives, 'not despairing but cruelly lucid' when he interviewed him on the eve of his seventieth birthday in June 1975 for the *Nouvel observateur*. Sartre wanted his self-portrait to be as unsparing as that which Rembrandt painted of himself as an old man. He took no interest in the move to the new flat, which he disliked. 'This apartment is the place where I don't work any more,' he told Beauvoir flatly.

Beauvoir and Arlette shared Sartre's care at nights, Beauvoir sleeping over for five nights a week and Arlette two. Most mornings Beauvoir read aloud to Sartre, book reviews from *Le Monde*, chapters from *Madame Bovary*. On Saturday, 15 December she arrived to find him sitting at his worktable. In a heartbroken voice he said: 'I have no ideas.' His task was to draw up an appeal for *Libération*, which was doing badly and into which he had already put 30,000 francs of his own money, the entire payment he had received for *On a raison de se révolter*. Beauvoir sat down beside him. He gave her, she wrote in her memoir, *La cérémonie des adieux*, 'the essential lines', and when Gavi came for the piece he was pleased. Not for the first time, Beauvoir had written it. Afterwards, as she gave him his medicine, Sartre said: 'You're a good wife.'

But 'wifely' care was wearing her out. The desiccated prose of her final memoir, its language as 'dry as dust', betrays Beauvoir's deepening depression as Sartre referred to himself as '*un mort vivant*, a living corpse', or told Lanzmann, when he kissed him goodbye, that he was kissing 'a piece of tomb'. His piteous query: 'Shall I ever get my eyes back?' rang in her ears. 'Not completely,' she replied. The white lie was necessary, for Sartre had confessed to Contat: 'Obviously it's bearable only if you think it's temporary.' Liliane noted Beauvoir's own 'worried eyes' when, after giving the customary three little rings of the bell which was their special code, she hurried into the flat for her night shift, asking: 'Have you had a good day?' Sartre's blindness and apathy meant that Beauvoir was also carrying the burden of *Les Temps modernes* on her shoulders. At the editorial meetings in rue Schoelcher, he often slept through the discussion, and it was Lanzmann and Bost on whom she depended. When, therefore, she learnt from Sartre in September 1973 that he had decided to hire Pierre Victor as his secretary in addition to Puig, her first reaction was one of relief.

Sartre, for his part, valued his friendship with Pierre too highly to see it ended now that he could no longer function as a journalist. He asked Liliane to act as go-between. But when she suggested to Pierre that he come to Sartre's flat on Mondays, Wednesdays and Fridays from eleven to one to read to him and to help him work, Pierre lowered his head and remained silent for a long time, before saying curtly: 'I've got things to do. I'll think about it.'

Liliane was flabbergasted.

'How dare you tell me you've got things to do? You've squeezed him like a lemon for three years, you can certainly give him a few hours a week!'

'I've got things to do.'

Finally Liliane was forced to reveal that Sartre himself was behind the proposal. Geismar had told him that since the collapse of La Gauche Proletarienne that year, Victor, whose family had fled Egypt after the 1956 Suez crisis, was in danger of being deported: Georges Pompidou had refused to allow his naturalization. After much coaxing, the young militant agreed to his new role. The *sous* Sartre would give him would get him out of his financial difficulties. Arlette, on the other hand, made furious phone calls to both Liliane and Castor: she was afraid that Victor would become Sartre's Schoenmann.

*

In 1972 Beauvoir went public about her relationship with Sylvie. Whispers arose as to the nature of their friendship, as they were seen side by side at MLF demos such as that at the Bois de Vincennes on 22 June 1974. Sylvie, her glossy dark hair swept up on her head in a younger, more stylish version of Beauvoir's, her flashing eyes hidden behind dark glasses, her eager smile as she turns towards her companion, the resolute set of whose mouth as she gazes into the distance suggestive of her visionary role, appears the devoted disciple of the woman who had shown her, when she first read *Memoirs of a Dutiful Daughter*, that one could 'invent a free life, proud and joyful, outside the old paths'. But the photo suggests a deeper intimacy also.

'Do not think this is boastful,' said Sylvie, 'but Beauvoir often told me, "My relationship with you is almost as important as that with Sartre. I could not have such a relationship with another man, because I have Sartre. But with a woman I have always desired it, and since Zaza I have only found it with you." So it is important to say that with me she had something she had always wanted, always missed, and tried to have in her life with other women, but with them it never worked. In front of me one day, she said to Sartre, "I have always desired, let us say, a feminine friendship." Well, he said he always knew it, and then he encouraged her to have it. 'Fine, fine,' he would say, 'bring your little friend, bring her to Rome with us.'

Speculation grew that Beauvoir was lesbian. The German feminist Alice Schwartzer asked her whether she had ever had 'a sexual relationship with a woman'. 'No,' answered Beauvoir. 'I have had some very important relationships with women, of course, some very close relationships, sometimes close in a physical sense. But they never aroused erotic passion on my part.' 'Why not?' asked the journalist. Because her upbringing directed her towards heterosexuality, replied Beauvoir.

> 'Do you mean that you accept homosexuality on a theoretical level, for yourself as well?
>
> Yes, completely and utterly. Women should not let themselves be conditioned exclusively to male desire any more . . . And in any case, I think that these days every woman is a bit . . . a bit homosexual. Quite simply, because women are more desirable than men.
>
> How so?
>
> Because they are more attractive, softer, their skin is nicer. And generally they have more charm. It is quite often the case with the usual married couple that the woman is nicer, more lively, more attractive, more amusing, even on an intellectual level.

These teasing remarks to Schwartzer must have amused Beauvoir, whose letters to Sartre prove beyond doubt that young women aroused an 'erotic passion' in her which invariably ended in their seduction. But Le Bon denies that this was so in her own case: 'Simone de Beauvoir was profoundly heterosexual . . . She had very little sex with Olga. Bienenfeld desired it, it was very important to her. Simone de Beauvoir and I shared *un amour très fort,* we shared tenderness and affection, *je l'admirais tellement,* I admired her so much. *Pour moi, c'était l'amour.* But even in Corsica, which Castor called our *lune de miel*, there was no question of sex.'

Beauvoir was not bisexual, in the sense that she felt equally attracted to both sexes, asserts Le Bon: 'She admired the beauty of women, she enjoyed intimacy, tenderness, sensuality; she was not interested in the sexual side . . . Her love for Zaza was not carnal love.' But it had been an ardent, all-encompassing love, as Beauvoir's memoirs and her obsessive attempts to fictionalize the most formative experience of her youth testify. Zaza's death had branded itself into Beauvoir's consciousness. In discovering 'Zaza reborn' in the person of Sylvie, her instinct was to leap with delight into a relationship which, finally, healed the scar of loss.

'She encouraged me to do everything, to experience everything,' recalls Sylvie. Following the heterosexual path already trodden by Beauvoir, Sylvie had an affair with Bost: 'Sartre was so *séduisant*, charming, captivating, to men as well as women. It was his whole manner of being, so intelligent, attentive and generous . . . but not handsome. Bost was *beau et séduisant*.' In Rome, recalls Le Bon, 'Sartre told a thousand stories: he was funny, light-hearted, not sad at all.' In 1977, after a Sunday lunch of stuffed duck and excellent wine with Sartre's former Japanese interpreter, Tomiko, at her house in Versailles, Sylvie, 'who was a little tipsy, made ardent declarations to Sartre, who was delighted', records Beauvoir. Did Sylvie have an affair with Sartre also? She declined to answer, repeating only that Beauvoir wanted her to experience '*everything* you want'.

What Beauvoir did not want was to be defined as a radical lesbian within the Women's Movement, although she defended the right to be homosexual. In the seventies, after publishing her monumental study *La Vieillesse* (*Old Age*), Beauvoir planned to write a sequel to *The Second Sex*. But the MLF splintered into warring factions: there was no room at the top for competing feminist divas, and Beauvoir and Halimi became quarrelsome rivals. In the hot seat as editor of the journal *Nouvelles féministes*, where, as Sartre had done for *Libération*, Beauvoir agreed to act as a shield against government persecution, she found herself the punchbag between leftists and separatists on the editorial board. Beauvoir sided with Christine Delphy, Emmanuèle de Lesseps and Claude Hennequin against those who 'proudly proclaimed their separatism and defined their struggle as strictly lesbian'. In 1976, while praising the fact that it was now possible for women to come out as lesbian, she objected to other women who 'become lesbian because of their political engagement . . . who think it's a political act to be lesbian' and therefore 'dogmatically' excluded men from their struggle.

When the American feminist Margaret A. Simons asked Beauvoir whether the biological difference between men and women is an *essential* difference, one which should be 'the centre of a woman's existence', she replied:

> I am against this opposition . . . Here there are a certain number of women who exalt menstruation, maternity etc . . . I am absolutely against all this since it means falling once more into the masculine trap of wishing to enclose ourselves in our difference . . . One should not make the body the centre of the universe . . . It [is] playing man's game to say that woman is essentially different from the man. There exists a biological difference, but this difference is not the foundation for sociological difference.

In 1982 she spoke out even more plainly about the friction which led to the dissolution of the magazine in 1980. 'What these women are not telling you is that they are not only "separatist" but "*lesbian* separatist". Although I support every woman's right to choose how she expresses her sexuality, I cannot support any ideology which exalts one and excludes all the other.' Unlike Sartre, Beauvoir never deviated from that existentialist given: freedom of choice.

Her feminist 'children' continued to criticize her, often violently, and particularly in her own country: the majority of her obituaries would be hostile. The reverence paid to Simone Veil, Marguerite Duras or Nathalie Sarraute was not accorded to Beauvoir. French post-structuralist feminists like the Psych et Po group considered her 'a phallic woman, complicit with the dominant forms of masculine power'. It was said that her answer to the 'woman question' was the adoption by women of male habits and values, and that in counselling women against marriage and motherhood and rejecting home-making and housework, she had been brainwashed by the patriarchy. Her message was confusing: did the call to rise up against female subordination simply mean becoming a surrogate man? But Beauvoir was a pioneering woman of her time, for whom entry into male professions was the key to emancipation. With hindsight it is easy to see that becoming a doctor or a lawyer may mean assuming a double or triple burden for those who try to have it all. Beauvoir fulfilled her own passionately intellectual nature; she never believed that one size fits all, only that men should not make woman the 'Other' in a relationship or in society.

*

'I often felt like quitting,' said Benny Lévy, Sartre's new secretary, who was still calling himself Pierre Victor. Sartre, small, blind and corpulent, was also somnolent. He dozed in his chair as Lévy read to him: 'It was a constant struggle against death . . . At first I was involved in a sort of resuscitation.' Very soon the young man abandoned Flaubert to return to philosophy. He had studied Sartre's work in depth, and the writer was delighted to find that his disciple remembered his ideas better than he did himself. Levy's eyes and energy allowed Sartre to escape the prison of his decaying body. Captain Pardaillon's adventures in the backs of lorries were over; there remained the adventure of the mind. Sartre, who had all his life long thought 'against himself', alone at his desk, who had once said, 'to think is to think alone', now declared that *nous formons les pensées ensemble*.

It was a delusion. Lévy was in search of his own identity. After arriving in Europe post-Suez, 'My problem,' he wrote, 'shared by most Jews in a similar situation, was that of "figuring out" where I was, and what France was to me . . . Sartre helped me solve it, when I was fourteen or fifteen: through him, I felt part of the French language.' Now Sartre helped the twenty-eight-year-old whom he thought of as the 'living prolongation of himself' become a citizen of France by writing to President Giscard d'Estaing, who replied in his own hand that he was glad to do this favour for Sartre.

But Lévy's quest was leading him 'from Mao to Moses'. At first suspicious of the militant leader, Arlette rapidly became Lévy's friend and accomplice and, after Aron and Lanzmann, he became 'the fourth Jewish figure' (apart from Bianca Bienenfeld) in the life of Jean-Paul Sartre. Together Benny Lévy and Arlette learnt Hebrew and studied the Kabbalah. 'What next? Maybe he'll decide to become a rabbi!' joked Sartre. But in November 1976, at the Israeli embassy in Paris, Sartre received an honorary degree from the University of Jersualem and delivered a carefully memorized speech in which he said: 'I have been Israel's friend for a long while,' remarking shortly afterwards that he would write *Anti-Semite and Jew* differently, were he to write it at the present time. Challenged by Lévy, he owned up to the Jewish blood running in his own veins as a Schweitzer. And, after the failure of Sartre's planned TV series on 'The Meaning of Revolt in the Twentieth Century', in September 1975, he relied more and more heavily on the young man's invitations to eat with him in the suburbs at Groslay, where his 'commune' of wife and friends practised Orthodox

Judaism and absorbed him into a new, rival 'family', sharing jokes and meals far from the rituals of old Montparnasse.

There were tensions with the newly militant Beauvoir, her consciousness raised by the women's struggle. In a confrontational 1975 interview with Sartre on the 'woman question', she accuses him of speaking out on behalf of all oppressed groups, workers, blacks and Jews, except women. Mildly Sartre replies that, having grown up as a child surrounded by women, '*J'ai toujours pensé qu'il y avait en moi une sorte de femme*', he'd always thought that inside himself there *was* a kind of woman.

'But you're an adult now!' Beauvoir upbraids him. 'Why have you ignored that oppression which makes of women victims?' Because obedience is a characteristic trait of women, replies Sartre with more spirit. They rather like male 'imperialism'. Beauvoir changes tack: on rereading his books, she has detected 'traces of machismo, even of male chauvinism'.

'You exaggerate a bit,' murmurs Sartre. 'But I suppose it's true.'

'But don't you yourself feel like a chauvinist?'

In a touching reply, Sartre protests that, as far as she is concerned, he has never considered himself superior to her, or more intelligent, or more active: 'We are equals.' Mollified, Beauvoir concedes that he had never 'oppressed' her. Assuring her that he approves absolutely of *la lutte féministe*, the feminist struggle, Sartre nevertheless prophesies that it will shake society to its roots and may end by overturning it completely. But, shaken by her accusations of being an MCP (male chauvinist pig), he begins to spend even more time with Arlette and Lévy.

The show-down came in 1978. At *Les Temps modernes*, where Bost's deafness kept him away from board meetings and Lanzmann was busy making his film of the holocaust, *Shoah*, Beauvoir had made the mistake of co-opting Lévy on to the committee in the hope that his presence would encourage Sartre to attend: the secretary's vanity soon became apparent. In February, in the wake of Egyptian President Sadat's visit to Israel, Sartre was taken by Lévy and Arlette to Jerusalem. A wheelchair was provided; the sky was blue. He enjoyed the five-day holiday, and his meetings with Eli Ben Gal and other Jewish and Palestinian intellectuals. But on his return, when Lévy dashed off an article on the visit for *Le Nouvel observateur*, suggesting that he could continue Sadat's mission, Sartre had his reservations. 'You Maos, you always go too fast for me,' he muttered. Nevertheless, he let Victor send off the piece under both their names. Bost rang:

'*C'est horriblement mauvais.* Here at the paper, we're all horrified. Do persuade Sartre to withdraw it.' Having read the article herself and found it 'very weak', Beauvoir informed Sartre that she was horrified at 'the idea of Benny Lévy as the new Messiah – the one for whom we all wait to bring peace in the land'. Sartre was 'furious' remembers Jean Pouillon, at her veto. Lévy flew into a rage, and walked out of a meeting in her flat with Pouillon, Horst and the *Temps modernes* board, shouting '*Vous etes tous des morts,* you're all corpses!'

Never again would he allow himself to be bested by Beauvoir. Henceforth Lévy's conversations with Sartre would be secret.

*

'I've never been so popular with women before!' boasted Sartre to Beauvoir, with 'naïve self-satisfaction'. His harem was growing larger and younger. The latest addition was a young Greek woman named Hélène Lassithiotakis, whom he had been seeing since 1972, when she had knocked on his door in Paris and reminded him that they had met in Athens. Professing himself in love again, Sartre set her up in a flat in Paris, where she had a psychotic episode in the street. Stabilized, plump and silent on her medication, she returned to the University of Athens, where she invited Sartre to lecture in February 1977. After speaking for an hour on 'What is philosophy?' before an audience of 1,500 people, he sat down to thunderous applause, but, on returning to Paris a few days later, he collapsed in the street. His blood pressure was 220. Beauvoir and Liliane took him to the Brossuet Hospital, where, after tests, his specialist sternly warned him that if he did not give up smoking, he risked having his legs amputated. Sartre was diabetic, and suffering from peripheral arterial damage: 'the diabetes way of death'. 'Your toes will have to be cut off, and then your feet, and then your legs.' 'Sartre was impressed,' recorded Beauvoir. Two days later he handed her his Boyards and his lighter. It was his final renunciation: of tobacco, and also of Hélène.

When Beauvoir and Liliane steamed open the neurologist's report, they learnt that Sartre had only 30 per cent circulation in his legs. 'With care,' wrote Professor Housset, 'he may live a few years more.' A *few* years! 'I fell to pieces.' Beauvoir opened the tube of valium she had taken from Sartre's flat and gulped the pills down with swigs of whisky. That July, on holiday with Sylvie in Austria, she drank so heavily in the evenings that she nearly fell into a lake.

By 1978 Sartre was haemorrhaging money. In debt to Gallimard, paying monthly salaries to both Puig and Victor, he was also paying allowances to a growing number of women. Realizing that Sartre had not long to live, Liliane took the decision to introduce him to a bevy of her friends, with whom he lunched and talked about sex. 'Do you realize, child, that not counting Castor and Sylvie,' he remarked to her, 'there are nine women in my life at the moment!' Frail and blind, leaning on the arm of a young woman, Sartre would take slow, prudent steps towards La Coupole, where his companion would cut up his food for him, chatter to him as he drank a bottle of Bordeaux blanc, and wipe his lips as he rounded off the meal with a creamy Irish coffee. When Beauvoir told him he needed a new pair of shoes, he replied: 'I can't afford it.' But he was always ready to pay for a meal for a pretty young woman who made him feel alive.

Nevertheless, the doctor's warnings persuaded Sartre to go on a diet. He would eat only once a day, steak *au poivre* and green beans, until he had lost the six kilos he had put on during his last holiday in Rome. For five weeks he ate nothing else until he had achieved his goal, only to return to the cuisine of Alsace he had known as a child, and for which he never lost the taste: saveloy and sauerkraut with an enormous glass of beer.

So far Beauvoir had tolerated the presence of Sartre's women. But one Sunday, after Michèle had spent the previous night sleeping at Sartre's flat, he appeared in a stupor over lunch at La Palette the next day. That evening he felt so ill that Beauvoir rang the emergency services: Sartre's blood pressure had risen to 250. 'Has he been drinking?' asked the doctor. It transpired that Michèle had given Sartre half a bottle of whisky. Beauvoir rang her in a temper, forbidding her from spending another Saturday night with Sartre. Michèle was upset; she and Beauvoir had been good friends for many years. 'Bravo!' Beauvoir used to say, when Michèle returned Sartre to her at the end of their holiday. '*Il est bien bronzé*. You're a good nurse.' Now Michèle was defiant: 'Yes, I gave him alcohol. He was blind; he couldn't make love, he couldn't write, he couldn't smoke; there was only alcohol left. *Je n'aime pas boire seule*, I don't like drinking alone. And he was unhappy.' Beauvoir took to hiding the bottle of whisky, after she had given him a small tot. Often Sylvie would water down the bottle with water. But Sartre was alcohol-dependent, and short rations made him angry. He began to view Beauvoir as his gaoler, and resent her control. She, on the other hand, often treated him like a naughty little boy.

Battle was joined between two camps. Beauvoir and Victor no longer spoke to each other: 'It was an unpleasant situation. Up until then

Sartre's real friends had always been mine too.' She watched from a distance as Victor organized an Israeli–Palestinian meeting in Paris in March 1979, which the old *Temps modernes* team boycotted. She worried more than ever when, shortly afterwards, a Belgian psychiatric patient battered at Sartre's door demanding money and stabbed him in the hand. But Sartre never ceased to amaze her with his ability to emerge from the abyss and appear once more, despite the fact that he could scarcely walk, *vraiment lui-même*, truly himself. On his last birthday, 21 June 1979, Françoise Sagan sent him a 'Love Letter to Jean-Paul Sartre', and he began a new friendship. Unlike Beauvoir, whom she criticized for her clinical chronicle of Sartre's decline, Sagan laughed and ignored the mess, and the stares of onlookers, as the great intellectual dropped food all over his trousers.

Yet their final Roman holiday together was a peaceful one. Sartre and Beauvoir took their familiar air-conditioned rooms in the Albergo Nazionale, overlooking the 'ghostly white' dome of St Peter's. The old couple returned to their gentle routine of reading aloud, dozing, eating ice cream and people-watching. Friends who expected to find Sartre a broken man, wrote Beauvoir defiantly, were struck by his 'indomitable vitality'. She, who once had written the poignant phrase, 'I knew that no harm would ever come to me through him, so long as he did not die before me,' continued to spit in the face of death. But Raymond Aron was shocked when, on 26 June, at Sartre's last but one public appearance to plead the plight of the Vietnamese boat people, he had to whisper '*mon petit camarade*' into his ear in order to be recognized by his old friend and rival as he supported him down the steps of the Elysée Palace. Sartre was, thought Aron, 'a dead man walking'.

One Sunday morning at the beginning of March 1980, Arlette almost tripped over Sartre's supine form on the floor of his bedroom when she arrived at his flat. He was dead drunk. His young women had been bringing in bottles of whisky and vodka and hiding them behind books. Beauvoir at once emptied the hiding places, rang the women to ask them not to bring in any more alcohol, and gave Sartre a good scolding. Angrily he protested: 'You're fond of a drink too.' It was true. Beauvoir was no better than the rest, complained Arlette. 'Arlette thinks Castor is going to be the death of me, by encouraging me to drink, because she drinks too,' Sartre confided to Liliane, who had also faced his wrath when she tried to limit his consumption of vodka.

'Give me something to drink, these glasses are minute.'
'The last, I warn you!'

'You warn me of what! You get on my bloody nerves the lot of you, trying to run my life!'

He had raised his voice.

'Alcohol isn't your life, it's your death.'

'What are you up to these days?' asked Olivier Todd, on his last visit to Sartre in February 1980. 'I'm writing a *bouquin de philo* with Victor,' came the reply. But 'writing' was a misnomer. Sartre still thought, but slowly; Victor talked non-stop. Drowned in a torrent of words, unable to reread what Victor wrote, Sartre confessed to Contat that authorial self-criticism, always present 'when you read a text with your own eyes, is never very clear when someone else is reading in a loud voice'. To Liliane he was more stark: 'Pierre would quite like to absorb me. Some days he baits me, we have a row, sometimes that amuses me and I stand up to him, but at other times it bores me so I give in.' Befuddled by alcohol, bullied and bewildered, Sartre, who had once disagreed when Victor insisted that 'the whole origin of morals is in the Torah', became the mouthpiece for messianic Judaism.

Or so it seemed to the Sartreans, when they read the first extract from *Power and Liberty* in *Le Nouvel observateur* in March 1980. When Beauvoir read the manuscript of Sartre's conversations with Lévy, she burst into tears and threw it on to the floor of his flat. It was only weeks before the piece was due to appear, because up to that moment Sartre had fobbed her off by saying that the 800-page transcript was 'not ready'. Beauvoir begged Sartre not to publish. '*Elle était folle de fureur*, she was mad with rage,' recalls Michèle. Affronted by the tone of the conversations, the *tutoiement* of Sartre by the unknown, unpublished Lévy, his assumption of 'arrogant superiority', Beauvoir was even more horrified to find that Sartre had reneged on his own thought to submit to the opinions of an ersatz philosopher. Under the barrage of Levy's questioning, the author of *Nausea* stutters that he has 'never felt despair', that he only studied Kierkegaard because it was the fashion, even: 'My works are a failure.' In a final apostasy, the ventriloquist's doll is manipulated into reciting Lévy's own muddled thoughts: 'Well, this idea of ethics as the ultimate end of revolution – it's by a sort of messianism that you can truly conceive it.'

Yet Sartre had started with high hopes. He had unfinished philosophical business: the famous 'Morale' promised at the end of *Being and Nothingness*. Beaten by Hegel in *The Critique*, he returned to his first premise: the 'death of God'. There are indications that Sartre was wavering in his non-belief. 'Atheism is a long, cruel business,' he had written in *Les Mots*. 'I have been a man who no longer has any idea what to do with his life. I have become once again the traveller without a ticket that I was at seven.' The 'silence of the transcendental is as permanent as man's yearning for God,' he confessed earlier. 'Everything in me cries out for God, I don't know how to forget him.' Marvelling at Gide's courage in confronting his doubts, he told Jeanson in 1951: 'The most precious thing Gide offers us is his decision to live right to the end the agony and the death of God.' Questioned by Beauvoir in 1974, he finally admitted:

> I don't see myself as so much dust that has appeared in the world, but as a being that was expected, prefigured, called forth. In short, as a being that could, it seems, come only from a creator; and this idea of a creating hand that created me refers me back to God.

Looking for a rope to haul him out of the howling existential void, Sartre clung to Lévy and the God of Israel.

It was his last betrayal; but one to which he went willingly.

*

In order to avoid the 'tantrums' of '78, Lévy took the text in person to Jean Daniel, editor of *Le Nouvel observateur*. All night Daniel's phone rang with Sartreans begging him not to publish. Lanzmann rang on behalf of Beauvoir; Bost, Jean Pouillon added their voices to her plea. The editor hesitated. 'They are all defending the Temple,' said André Horst, who was himself in favour of publication. The next day Sartre himself rang. His voice was loud, clear and authoritative:

> I, Sartre, ask you to publish this manuscript, and to publish it in its entirety . . . I know my friends have got in touch with you, but their reasons for doing so are entirely wrong: the itinerary of my thought eludes them all, including Simone de Beauvoir.

Thereafter, according to Arlette, Beauvoir and Sylvie behaved coolly towards Sartre. Allegedly he described them as those 'two austere muses', complaining to her that at lunch they did not speak to him once; nor was the argument 'fully made up' during the last two months of life which remained to him. Beauvoir and Le Bon, on the other hand, claim that they were more 'affectionate and solicitous' than ever after the interviews appeared, as they wanted to reassure him that, whatever he published, nothing would interfere with their personal relationship. 'There was an argument, yes,' said Beauvoir, 'but there was never, never a break.'

All the same, his conversations with Lévy haunted Sartre. 'At the *Temps modernes* this morning, did anyone talk about the conversation?' asked the worried writer, after the first interview came out on 10 March in *Le Nouvel observateur*. 'I said no, which was true,' recorded Beauvoir; others who attended the meeting remembered that they spoke of little else. Nervously Beauvoir denied the facts because she was afraid of widening the gulf between Sartre and herself and the old guard. She was touched by his response: 'As if I were a little child, who had to be told gently something she did not want to hear,' he said: 'You know, Castor, I am still alive and thinking. You must allow me to continue to do so.'

But within days Sartre learnt of the strength of the reaction of his old associates: the 'sinister' interviews, published under the remarkably un-Sartrean title 'L'Espoir maintenant' ('Hope Now'), on 10, 17 and 24 March, were 'embarrassing, appalling, Victor's words not Sartre's', writes Todd. Sartre was deeply hurt; literary Paris was savaging his piece, perhaps even laughing at him. 'Sartre realized, afterwards, that the whole thing was very bad, and didn't reflect his thought at all,' said Claude Lanzmann. 'Even worse, it was poorly received.' Lanzmann even went so far as to suggest that the furore 'gave Sartre the *coup de grâce*'.

Certainly the dates support this possibility; two days after the publication of the second conversation on 17 March, Bost spent the evening with Beauvoir and Sartre. Pointedly, no reference was made to his 'abduction' by Lévy. The next morning, 20 March, when Beauvoir went in to wake Sartre at nine o'clock, she found him sitting on the edge of the bed, gasping for breath. She tried to call an ambulance, but the phone was cut off: Puig had failed to pay the bill. Throwing on her clothes, Beauvoir ran to the concierge, who summoned the emergency services. Sartre was taken to Broussais hospital. Unfazed, Beauvoir kept a lunch appointment with the Pouillons.

When she arrived at the hospital, Sartre was in intensive care. He had a pulmonary oedema, fluid on the lung, a high fever, and was delirious. But his fever abated and Beauvoir was hopeful that he would recover; they talked of going to Belle-Île in Brittany for Easter. Hours with Sartre were strictly divided, Arlette taking the morning and Beauvoir the afternoons. Victor flew back from Cairo; Jean Pouillon visited. At Sartre's bedside, he handed him a glass of water. 'Next time, whisky at my place,' said the dying philosopher.

'When will he come out?' Beauvoir asked Professor Houssuet.

'I can't say,' replied the doctor hesitantly. '*Il est fragile, très fragile.*'

Sartre was moved back into intensive care. As Beauvoir kept vigil beside him, he became agitated: 'I don't care for this place.' She squeezed his hand. 'Fortunately we'll be leaving soon,' he murmured. 'I love the idea of going to a little island.'

Sartre worried constantly about how he would pay for his funeral, but Beauvoir calmed him by saying that his hospital costs and everything else would be taken care of by social services. When he developed bedsores she knew the end was near, and threw herself into Professor Houssuet's arms in a storm of tears, begging him not to let Sartre suffer. 'I promise you that, Madame,' said the doctor. Calling her into the corridor, he assured her that he would keep his word.

Sartre slept as the April days passed, but one afternoon, with closed eyes, he caught Beauvoir by the wrist and said, 'I love you very much, my dear Castor.' On 14 April he was asleep when she came in; he woke and said a few words without opening his eyes, and then held his lips up to Beauvoir. 'I kissed his mouth, his cheek.' The next day he fell into a coma; Beauvoir sat all day with him until it was six o'clock, when Arlette arrived. At 9 p.m. Arlette rang: 'It's over.'

Sylvie telephoned Bost, Pouillon and Horst, who came at once. They stayed all night with Beauvoir, drinking whisky and talking about Sartre. Outside there was a scuffle: two journalists dressed as male nurses had tried to get in, but were prevented by the staff. At one point Beauvoir asked to be left alone with Sartre, and tried to lie down beside him under the sheet. A nurse stopped her. '*Non. Attention . . . la gangrène.*' Only then did Beauvoir understand the nature of Sartre's bedsores. She lay on top of the sheet and slept fitfully until five, when the body was taken away.

'You are in your little box; you will not come out of it and I shall not join you there,' wrote Beauvoir in *Adieux*. 'Even if I am buried next to you there will be no communication between your ashes and mine.'

38

Adieux

His death separates us. My death will not reunite us . . .
It is splendid that we were able to live our lives in
harmony for so long.

Simone de Beauvoir

THE CROWD BEGAN to form early in the morning outside the Broussais hospital in the rue Didot. Students with copies of *Libé* stuffed in their pockets, housewives with shopping baskets, French, English, Jews and Arabs, stood silently in the street, waiting. It was Saturday, 19 April 1980, four days after Sartre's death. He lay in his coffin, dressed in the maroon velvet suit and tie which Sylvie had bought for his last outing to the opera with her and Beauvoir; beside his face an unknown admirer had placed a red rose. Beauvoir bent to kiss him, and the undertakers closed the lid.

Among those who had previously come to the hospital to pay their respects was Giscard d'Estaing, who told the Sartreans that he knew Sartre would not have wished for a state ceremony, but that he was ready to pay the funeral expenses. Beauvoir, holed up at Sylvie's to escape the media, declined. The Sartreans clubbed together to pay for Sartre's burial at Montparnasse cemetery, on whose doorstep he had lived so long. His grave would be only steps away from that of Baudelaire, doomed to the fate which Sartre had been determined to avoid, of being placed in the same tomb as his stepfather, General Aplink.

On the morning of the funeral, Beauvoir was prostrate with grief. Barely able to walk, she had numbed her feelings with whisky and valium, only allowing herself to be comforted by her sister, Hélène, and brother-in-law Lionel de Roulet, who had arrived from Alsace. Lanzmann, Bost, Pouillon and Sylvie had seen to the funeral arrangements; of Arlette, there had been little sign.

Supported by Sylvie and Poupette, Beauvoir climbed into a limousine. As the hospital gates opened and the hearse moved forward, the crowd, which soon amounted to 50,000, surged forward, pressing against the vehicle. TV crews and photographers held their cameras up to the windows, and the flash-guns popped as Beauvoir opened her handbag and fumbled for her pills, stuffing them into her mouth as tears streamed down her cheeks. Sylvie wiped them away with a tissue. Outside, the 'obscene' paparazzi pursued Yves Montand and Simone Signoret, as the cortège wound its way down avenue Général Leclerc. Students climbed on to the bronze Lion of Belfort, just as they had in '68, and the crowd took up the Resistance cry: 'Nous sommes tous des Juifs allemands, we are all German Jews.' It was Sartre's last demo.

A symbolic detour was made by way of boulevard Raspail as far as the Vavin crossroads, passing in front of number 222, where Sartre had lived. Slowly the cortege wended its way past La Coupole, where Sartre's corner seat remained empty, and the waiters stood with bowed heads; up the boulevard Montparnasse to the cemetery, where a folding chair was found for Simone beside the open grave. In a final, pathetic gesture of love, she cast a white rose on to the coffin. After the ceremony was over, Lanzmann and Sartre's friend Georges Michel tried to help her to her feet, but the press of the crowd nearly pushed her into the grave; one onlooker fell in, as Beauvoir was half dragged, half pushed back to the car and taken to Lanzmann's apartment in rue Boulard.

The old guard dined together that night at the nearby Café Zeyer on the rue d'Alésia. Beauvoir was beyond help. 'That's enough, Castor . . . be careful . . . it's too much, you will take an overdose,' warned Sylvie, as her charge, oblivious to those around her, swallowed another valium and drank whisky, her tears still flowing unchecked. At midnight she asked to be taken home, and Michel and Sylvie put her into Michel's car. 'For the second time that day I had to put my arms round her neck and carry her the few metres into her apartment,' recalls Michel. 'I put her on the sofa. Sylvie took over: "I'll undress her and put her to bed." I embraced them both and left.'

On 23 April Sartre's body was disinterred and taken to Père Lachaise cemetery for cremation, after which his ashes were returned to the Montparnasse tomb. Beauvoir was too ill to attend. When Sylvie and Lanzmann returned from the cremation to Sylvie's flat, where they had left her, she had fallen out of bed and was feverish and delirious, talking to an imaginary Sartre. In the Hôpital Cochin, she was diagnosed with pneumonia and depression. Few thought she would survive.

Beauvoir spent a month in hospital, detoxing and resting. Holding herself together during the seven years of Sartre's subservience to Lévy had brought her to breaking point, and during his long-drawn-out disintegration she too had crumbled physically. 'I took too many tranquillizers and drank too much alcohol, while he was ill, to try to hold on, not to break down. I was in a very bad shape when he died. My lungs were congested, I could no longer walk,' she told her biographers, Francis and Gontier, in 1985. 'But they cured me at the hospital. They gave me fortifying medication and brought me back to life. When I returned home I was tired and weak, but I was walking, and since then I'm better.'

The immediate crisis had passed; Sylvie's fear that Beauvoir would, as she had often sworn, commit suicide after Sartre's death, was assuaged when in August she asked to be taken to Norway. But before she could cruise the fjords with Le Bon, another crisis faced her.

*

'Vipère, sale bonne femme,' hisses Michèle Vian at the mention of the name of Liliane Siegel, whose description of the last act of the 'abduction' has coloured the public memory of the immediate period after Sartre's death, when Arlette and Lévy stripped Sartre's flat of its possessions. Arlette, who had taken Lévy's side during the infamous quarrel over the Nouvel observateur articles, and was no longer on speaking terms with Beauvoir, voiced her displeasure with her rival to Liliane: 'Castor wants him for herself, now he's dead.' No Medusa, with her head of snakes, could feel greater fury than Elkaïm-Sartre, as she now called herself, and Beauvoir, two women, one old, one young, each believing herself to be high priestess and true guardian of the Sartrean flame, who launched themselves into a war of Amazonian dimensions. In the snakepit, the women fought dirty.

As Beauvoir lay in her hospital bed, Arlette and Lévy tussled with Liliane over Sartre's few chattels. The quarrel centred on Sartre's chair, inherited from his great-grandfather. Liliane was already enraged, because Lévy had taken her mother's lamp, which she had lent Sartre, as well as 'vacating' the flat of all Sartre's books and furniture. She demanded to meet Arlette at the Dôme.

'I've come to ask you for the chair. Castor is particularly attached to it.'

'So am I particularly attached to it.'

'How can you compare yourself to Castor? Do you think Sartre would have wanted that?

'You've come to lecture me . . .'

'I've come to ask you for the chair, you've no right . . .'

'I'm just as attached to the chair as she is.'

Twelve days later the chair was delivered to Castor's flat. It was a Pyrrhic victory. Lévy's suburban study was soon furnished with Sartre's desk, books and lamps, in imitation of his master. Not 'the smallest souvenir, the oldest pipe', was given to Beauvoir, recalled Bianca Lamblin. 'It made me tremble to realize how much she was hated.' Grudgingly, after further arguments between Sylvie and Arlette, Sartre's *Pléiade* collection of plays from the repertory of the Comédie-Française, which Beauvoir had inherited from her parents and given him, were returned to her; Arlette kept the Picasso drawing which the artist had given Sartre and Beauvoir.

Beauvoir had hardly been able to believe her ears when she heard the rumour that Arlette was emptying Sartre's apartment, since French law requires the residence of a citizen who dies intestate to be sealed until the contents are evaluated for tax purposes. Arlette incurred a hefty fine for disobeying the law, but to her it was a price worth paying. Much more was at stake than a few sticks of furniture: Sartre's manuscripts and papers.

Michèle Vian defends Arlette's actions: 'After Sartre's death, he left debts of forty thousand francs (€70,000). It was terrible for her. She had to sell the apartment very quickly . . . All the money went in debts.' Sartre's dependent women, Michèle among them, now turned to Arlette for their allowances: 'She gave me my money, because I had none.'

Beauvoir, on the other hand, was certain that Arlette's main motive was to retain control of the manuscripts. They were the heart of the matter. Much as it went against the grain to beg favours from Sartre's adopted daughter and literary executor, Beauvoir was hardly out of hospital before she took a taxi to Arlette's and 'humbled' herself to ask for the manuscript she wanted above all else: that of *Cahiers pour une morale*, Sartre's 600 unpublished pages on ethics promised in the conclusion to *Being and Nothingness*. Sartre had given her the manuscript of his greatest philosophical work, and dedicated it to Castor; now she wanted the manuscript which completed it. But Arlette was obdurate: her answer was *non*.

This harsh revelation of the legitimate heir's power confirmed Beauvoir in the decision she had made while still in hospital, to adopt Le Bon in turn as her daughter. Arlette had been so doelike that 'Beauvoir never imagined that there would be any problems after his death', said Sylvie. 'She never guessed.' But now 'the doe transformed herself into a vulture', as Georges Michel put it. And there was, in Beauvoir's eyes, another vulture at the feast, her sister, Hélène, her nearest relative and heir. *'J'ai tous les droits*, I have all the rights,' said Hélène. 'I am the family.' 'I saw the sister arrive at the hospital and chase me away,' recalls Sylvie, visualizing a similar feud erupting between herself and Hélène to that which now existed between Castor and Arlette. And Beauvoir had said 'terrible things' against Poupette in her letters, just as Sartre had said 'terrible things' against Arlette in his letters to Lena Zonina. Were any of these letters to fall into the wrong hands, they were in danger of being destroyed. Beauvoir knew that in Sylvie she would have a devoted, scholarly literary executor, younger and more energetic than her sister.

During the summer of 1980, Beauvoir urged Sylvie to accept, but her first reaction was one of dismay. 'We were a couple, we had *une amitié d'amour*, a loving friendship. I hated the idea of being the same as Arlette, an adopted daughter. But on holiday in Norway, Beauvoir said: "I am ill, you must accept." She repeated it over and over again . . . She had a lot of Sartre's things; he used to leave his papers with her. There were several packets, envelopes, and she often went through the archives. *Elle gardait tout.* There were her letters to Sartre and his to her. There were allusions, to her liaison with Bost, which Beauvoir didn't want to become public because she wanted to protect Olga.' In the end, Sylvie agreed.

Hélène ultimately accepted her elder sister's decision. Beauvoir was seventy-two, but Poupette was only two years younger, and understood the reasons for choosing Le Bon. Beauvoir's fear, that if she were to become too frail to care for herself, her sister might take her to live with her in her farmhouse 400 miles from Paris in the village of Goxwiller in Alsace, receded.

In an interview with Alice Schwarzer, Beauvoir hinted at her sexual secrets:

> I have always spoken my mind as far as I have been able. I have
> always followed my desires and my impulses . . . If I had my

memoirs to write over, I would give a frank and balanced account of my own sexuality. A truly sincere one, from a feminist point of view; I would like to tell women about my life in terms of my own sexuality because it is not just a personal matter but a political one too.

I did not write about it at the time because I did not appreciate the importance of this question, or the need for personal honesty.

Beauvoir's reticence in her memoirs had not been matched in her letters, which she knew were a ticking time-bomb as far as her reputation was concerned. She left them in their envelopes, trusting to Sylvie's judgement, as Sartre had trusted to hers. The story of the girls she had manipulated in order to bind Sartre closer as her own sexual power faded, the 'dangerous liaisons' in which she and Sartre had colluded like the wicked Viscount de Valmont and the Marquise de Merteuil, could wait. In the meantime, it was Sylvie's affection which kept her alive. 'I knew for certain that without Sylvie, Castor wouldn't go on living,' said Liliane, recalling the day in April 1982 when she had taken Sylvie, who had broken her ankle in London, to a clinic. Sylvie required an operation. When Liliane told Beauvoir the news:

'She sobbed and moaned, "No, not Sylvie, not my Sylvie, not today."
I knelt down, and she threw herself into my arms.
'What if she doesn't wake up, not today . . .'

Liliane agreed to take Beauvoir to the clinic, where they waited for Sylvie to return from the operating theatre. When she came round, Sylvie saw that Beauvoir had been crying. 'Castor, you must go home and give poor little Liliane something to eat,' she said, squeezing Liliane's hand hard to make her understand that she mustn't leave Castor alone. Reassured, Beauvoir agreed to go home. Sylvie had stocked the freezer: the meal was waiting. As Liliane laid the table, Beauvoir chose a good bottle of red Bordeaux.

In Bianca's opinion, Beauvoir took advantage of Le Bon's devotion. 'Sylvie did all the housework, the driving,' recalls Bianca. 'I said to Castor, "Cette Sylvie, elle fait le ménage de votre studio. Don't you feel ashamed?" I was shocked. She was professeur at the lycée.' Beauvoir flushed: 'I do feel a bit guilty. But Sylvie likes doing it . . . and it's not much work.'

Le Bon's task was not always easy. In the Breton thalassothérapie clinic which Beauvoir attended after leaving hospital, massage and sea-water could not undo the damage already done to her liver by alcohol and substance abuse: she had cirrhosis, and was warned by the doctors to stop drinking. She refused to give up whisky and vodka. 'Sylvie wasn't always kind to her,' said Michèle. '*Elle faisait la gueule très souvent à Beauvoir*, she often sulked.' But if Sylvie was grumpy at times, it was because she was anxious about the extent of Beauvoir's addiction.

Interviewed at five o'clock on a May day in 1985, a frail Beauvoir's first 'ritual' question to her biographers is: 'Should we have something to drink?' Walking slowly to the refrigerator, she takes out three chilled glasses and a cold bottle of whisky. She measures the whisky carefully in a pewter jigger. She settles herself comfortably in her favourite place on the sofa, under the Giacometti lamp, her pills, telephone and appointment book beside her. Beauvoir, in her cherry-red robe, with matching turban, Algren's silver ring glinting on her index finger, sips her whisky as the tape recorder whirrs. Soon, she pours another jigger.

*

Anger drove Beauvoir's recovery in the summer of 1980. She was determined to show the world what she had been to Sartre. Within a year she published her account of his last ten years, *La Cérémonie des Adieux* (*Adieux: A Farewell to Sartre*), sometimes described as her fifth volume of memoirs, together with the conversations she had recorded with him in Rome in 1974. The dispassionate voice, relating, in merciless detail, Sartre's physical deterioration, attracted criticism, but it did not surprise readers already familiar with *Une morte si douce*, Beauvoir's poignant account of her mother's death. Writing against death had always been her way of exorcizing her fear of annihilation, but in *Adieux* her voice lacks the energy and tenderness of her writing about Françoise: it is flat and exhausted, straining to hide her devastation at Sartre's final betrayal, his choice to privilege youth, Lévy and Arlette, over the pact. This is Beauvoir at the end of her tether, loving, loyal – and terrified.

Her opening salvo provoked a response from Arlette, who published an 'open' letter in *Libération* in December 1981:

> Sartre is well and truly dead then, in your eyes, it seems, since you take advantage of it so harshly and resolutely trample on the faces of people whom he loved, with the aim of discrediting the interviews he did, the year he died, with Benny Lévy . . .
>
> Before his death, Sartre was quite alive . . . he heard and understood, and you treated him as a dead man who

inconveniently enough, appeared in public – this last comparison is not mine but his.

Beauvoir did not reply. One vulture pecking at the corpse was enough. Grimly she prepared her next broadside, the publication of Sartre's letters to her, which she had begun planning even before his death. Although she was in physical possession of the letters, the copyright rested with Arlette as his literary executor. The Sartreans urged her not to antagonize Sartre's daughter, for fear that she might withhold permission. Beauvoir took no notice. 'After all,' she said, 'he wrote these letters to me and they were in my possession. Why should I not publish them?'

Olga was 'very angry' when Beauvoir told her that she intended also to include Sartre's love letters to her, and refused permission. 'Je le ferai tout de même,' said the wilful writer. 'I'll do it anyway.' Bianca was equally shocked to be told by Beauvoir that, 'completely by chance', she had found nineteen letters that Sartre had written to Bianca. Convinced at first that she had thrown all Sartre's letters into a friend's furnace in a fury in 1942, she then remembered lending some of them to Beauvoir to read in 1939: 'She "forgot" to give them back, and I forgot to ask for them. In other words, she had carefully put them aside and kept them for forty years, in order to bring them out again when she deemed appropriate.'

Upset at Beauvoir's 'hypocrisy', but sympathetic to her pain during Sartre's illness, Bianca reluctantly gave permission, on condition that she was given a pseudonym. Arlette, meanwhile, was racing ahead of Beauvoir in the literary war, publishing Sartre's Cahiers pour une morale and War Diaries in 1983. Finally, triumphantly, Beauvoir published Lettres à Castor: 'Anyone who reads his letters to me will know what I meant to him.'

But Bianca and Olga did not want people to know what they had meant to Sartre. 'I was a victim, I was deceived,' says Bianca, 'but I was not the only one. Sartre wanted to brutalize his ugliness. It was because of his ugliness that he had such a great need for women, to prove himself . . . Afterwards I wanted to destroy the letters in their totality.' Outraged to find herself disguised by a French name, 'Louise Védrine', the name of Beauvoir's childhood nanny, she asked Beauvoir why she had obliterated her Jewish identity. There was no answer; nor, when she asked Beauvoir for the letters back, were they ever forthcoming.

Month after month, for nearly three years, that is to say until her death . . . She would arrive empty-handed at the restaurants where we met.

'Did you bring me Sartre's letters?'

No, she had forgotten them again.

At their last lunch together, in a restaurant on the avenue de Neuilly near Bianca's flat, Beauvoir arrived and exclaimed: 'Oh! I prepared the envelope for you, but I left it on my desk.' After Beauvoir's death, Bianca met Sylvie and asked why Beauvoir had never returned the letters, as she had promised. 'It's obvious,' said Sylvie. 'She was afraid you would burn them.' Sylvie herself handed the letters back to Bianca. As for Olga, she died without ever speaking to Beauvoir again.

Sartre's letters to Castor caused a sensation, allowing readers to glimpse the private lives behind the public image, and leaving them hungry for more. The' model couple' of the free-loving counter-culture were morphing into something more destructive and amoral. Beauvoir and Sartre's symbiotic need for each other, set out in the pact over fifty years ago, overrode all other relationships. 'I had never known anything like the dimension of their love for each other; their tranquil certainty that only death could separate them . . . the authenticity of their relationship,' wrote Liliane. 'I loved them as a single entity.' At the centre of each other's lives, two faces of a single Janus stone, Sartre and Beauvoir had fulfilled their promise to exist, to think, to write as one.

But where were the Beaver's letters to Sartre? demanded critics. An 'infuriated' Beauvoir insisted to journalists and biographers that she had lost them. She had gone as far as she was prepared to in exploiting the insatiable demand of celebrity, that it should strip itself naked, and reveal its 'true' inner core for its public. Sartre's lovers had been hung out to dry. She had shown the flaws at the heart of the artist, and titillated her audience. Still she held tight to her own mask. But once the striptease had started, the public wanted to see the show to the end. Like the audience at the Moulin Rouge, they wanted the whole spectacle. Beauvoir, however, was more tease than strip; only Sylvie knew the whereabouts of the incriminating letters. Only posthumously would Beauvoir strip to the buff.

She continued to gather laurels. Awarded the Jerusalem prize for promoting individual freedom in 1975, Beauvoir made an auto-biographical film with Josée Dayan and Malka Ribowska, which paralleled the film *Sartre by Himself* by Alexandre Astruc and Michel Contat. In 1983 the Danish government awarded her the Sonning

Prize for her work, and she used the $23,000 prize money to fly with Sylvie in Concorde to the United States, where she met Kate Millett. Beauvoir's influence led directly to the establishment of the first Ministry of Women's Rights in France, under Yvette Roudy, and the Beauvoir Commission on Women and Culture. She signed appeals, made a TV adaptation of *The Second Sex*. The rebel had become an icon.

In April 1986 Beauvoir was rushed to hospital with appendicitis. After an operation, she developed a pulmonary oedema, just as Sartre had done. Sylvie phoned Liliane on 14 April, to tell her that Castor had died. The two women returned together to the hospital, where Beauvoir's body was wheeled in, dressed in her red dressing-gown. Algren's ring was still on her finger. Sylvie asked Liliane to raise Castor's head, and, as she took the cold head in her hands, 'patiently and tenderly, as she had so often done before, Sylvie tied the red scarf round Castor's face for the last time'.

On 19 April, the same day as Sartre's own burial, 5,000 people followed Beauvoir's coffin. As she was laid in the same tomb as Sartre in Montparnasse cemetery, Claude Lanzmann read her adieu to Sartre: 'His death separates us. My death will not reunite us.'

Selected Bibliography

This bibliography includes only those books, articles and interviews mentioned in the text.

Works by Simone de Beauvoir

L'Invitée (Paris: Gallimard 1943); *She Came to Stay*, translated by Yvonne Moyse and Roger Senhouse (London: Flamingo, 1984).

Pyrrhus et Cinéas (Paris: Gallimard, 1944).

Le Sang des Autres (Paris: Gallimard 1945); *The Blood of Others*, translated by Yvonne Moyse and Roger Senhouse (London: Penguin, 1964).

Tous les Hommes sont Mortels (Paris: Gallimard, 1946), *All Men Are Mortal*, translated by Euan Cameron (London: Virago, 1995).

The Ethics of Ambiguity, translated by Bernard Frechtman (New York: Citadel Press, 1948).

L'Amérique au jour le jour (Paris: Gallimard, 1948); *America Day by Day*, translated by Carol Cosman (Phoenix, 1991).

Le Deuxième Sexe, vols. 1 and 2 (Paris: Gallimard, 1949); *The Second Sex*, translated by H. M. Parshley (London: Everyman's Library, 1993).

Les Mandarins (Gallimard, 1954): *The Mandarins*, translated by Leonard M. Friedman (London: Flamingo, 1984).

La Longue Marche (Paris: Gallimard, 1957).

Mémoires d'une jeune fille rangée (Paris: Gallimard, 1958); *Memoirs of a Dutiful Daughter*, translated by James Kirkup (London: Penguin, 1963).

La Force de l'Âge (Paris: Gallimard, 1960); The Prime of Life, translated by Peter Green (London, Penguin, 1965).

Djamila Boupacha, with Gisèle Halimi (Paris: Gallimard, 1962), translated by Peter Green (New York: Macmillan, 1962).

La Force des choses, 1 and 2 (Paris: Gallimard, 1963); Force of Circumstance I, translated by Richard Howard (New York: Putnam); Hard Times, Force of Circumstance II, 1952–1962, translated by Richard Howard with a new introduction by Toril Moi (New York: Paragon House, 1992).

Une Mort Très Douce (Paris: Gallimard, 1964).

Les Belles Images (Paris: Gallimard, 1966).

La Femme Rompue (Paris: Gallimard, 1968); Woman Destroyed, translated by Patrick O'Brian (New York: Putnam, 1974).

La Vieillesse (Paris: Gallimard, 1970); The Coming of Age (New York: Putnam, 1974).

Tout Compte Fait (Paris: Gallimard, 1972); All Said and Done, translated by Patrick O'Brian (London: André Deutsch and Weidenfeld & Nicolson, 1974).

Les Ecrits de Simone de Beauvoir, ed. Claude Francis and Fernande Gontier (Paris: Gallimard, 1979).

Quand prime le Spirituel (Paris: Gallimard 1979); When Things of the Spirit Come First, translated by Patrick O'Brian (London: Flamingo, 1983).

La Cérémonie des Adieux (Paris: Gallimard, 1981); Adieux, A Farewell to Sartre, translated by Patrick O'Brian (London: André Deutsch and Weidenfeld & Nicolson, 1984).

Posthumous publications

Correspondance Croisée 1937–1940, Simone de Beauvoir, Jacques-Laurent Bost, ed. Sylvie Le Bon de Beauvoir (Paris: Gallimard, 2004).

Lettres à Sartre, ed. Sylvie Le Bon de Beauvoir (Paris: Gallimard, 1990); Letters to Sartre, translated and edited by Quintin Hoare (London: Vintage, 1992).

Journal de Guerre, Septembre 1939–Janvier 1941, ed. Sylvie Le Bon de Beauvoir (Paris: Gallimard, 1990).

Beloved Chicago Man: Letters to Nelson Algren 1947–1964, ed. Sylvie Le Bon de Beauvoir (Phoenix, 1999), first published in French translation by Gallimard, 1997.

Works by Jean-Paul Sartre

La Nausée (Paris: Gallimard, 1938); *Nausea*, translated by Robert Baldick, with an introduction by James Wood (London: Penguin, 2000).

Le Mur (Paris: Gallimard, 1939); *The Wall and Other Stories*, translated by Lloyd Alexander (New York: New Directions, 1948).

L'Être et le Néant (Paris: Gallimard, 1943); *Being and Nothingness*, translated by Hazel E. Barnes, with an introduction by Mary Warnock (Routledge: 1989).

Les Chemins de la Liberté (The Roads to Freedom):

Vol. I, *L'Âge de Raison*, (Paris: Gallimard, 1945); *The Age of Reason*, translated by Eric Sutton (London: Penguin, 1961).

Vol. II, *Le Sursis* (Paris: Gallimard: 1945); *The Reprieve*, translated by Eric Sutton (London: Penguin, 2001).

Vol. III, *La Mort dans l'âme* (Paris: Gallimard, 1949); *Iron in the Soul*, translated by Gerald Hopkins (London: Penguin, 1963).

Baudelaire (Paris: Gallimard, 1947).

L'Existentialisme est un humanisme (Paris: Nagel, 1946); *Existentialism and Humanism*, translated by Philip Mairet (London: Methuen, 1973).

Réflexions sur la question juive (Paris: Gallimard, 1948); *Anti-Semite and Jew*, translated by George J. Becker (New York: Schocken, 1948).

Qu'est-ce que la Littérature? (Paris: Gallimard, 1948); *What is Literature?* translated by Bernard Frechtman (London: Routledge, 2001).

Existentialism and Human Emotions (New York: Philosophical Library, 1957), translated by Bernard Frechtman and Hazel E. Barnes.

Huis Clos (Paris: Gallimard, 1944), translated by Stuart Gilbert, in *No Exit and Three Other Plays*, *The Flies*, *Dirty Hands*, *The Respectful Prostitute* (London: Vintage, 1989).

Morts sans sépulture (Paris: Gallimard, 1946); *Men Without Shadows* (London: Penguin, 1962).

Situations I, Critiques littéraires (Paris: Gallimard, 1947).

Situations I and III (Paris: Gallimard, 1955); *Literary and Philosophical Essays*, translated by Annette Michelson (Rider, 1955).

Situations X (Paris: Gallimard, 1975), translated by Paul Auster and Lydia Davis as *Life/Situations: Essays Written and Spoken by Jean-Paul Sartre* (New York: Random House, 1977).

Le Diable et le Bon Dieu (Paris: Gallimard, 1951); *The Devil and the Good Lord and Two Other Plays* (New York: Knopf, 1960).

Saint Genet, comédien et martyr (Paris: Gallimard, 1952); *Saint Genet,*

Actor and Martyr, translated by Bernard Frechtman (New York: Pantheon, 1983).

Les Séquestrés d'Altona (Paris: Gallimard, 1959); *The Condemned of Altona*, translated by Sylvia and George Leeson (New York: Knopf, 1961).

Critique de la raison dialectique (Paris: Gallimard, 1960); *The Critique of Dialectical Reason*, translated by Alan Sheridan-Smith (London: Verso, 1976).

Les Mots (Paris: Gallimard, 1964); *Words*, translated by Irene Clephane (London: Penguin, 1967).

Les Ecrits de Sartre, ed. Michel Contat and Michel Rybalka (Paris: Gallimard, 1970).

The Family Idiot, Gustave Flaubert, 1821–1857, vols. 1 and 2 (Paris: Gallimard, 1971), translated by Carol Cosman (University of Chicago Press, 1981 and 1987).

On a raison de se révolter, with Philippe Gavi and Pierre Victor (Paris: Gallimard, 1974).

Un théâtre de situations, ed. Michel Contat and Michel Rybalka (Paris: Gallimard, 1972); *Sartre on Theater*, translated by Frank Jellinek (New York: Pantheon Books, 1976).

Posthumous publications

Oeuvres Romanesques, ed. Michel Contat and Michel Rybalka (Paris: Pléiade, Gallimard, 1981).

Les Carnets de la Drôle de Guerre: Novembre 1939–Mars 1940 (Paris: Gallimard, 1983); *War Diaries: Notebooks from a Phoney War*, translated by Quintin Hoare (Verso, 1984).

Lettres au Castor et à quelques autres, vols. 1 and 2 (Paris: Gallimard, 1983).

Critique de la raison dialectique (Paris: Gallimard, 1985).

La Reine Albermarle ou le dernier touriste (Paris: Gallimard, 1991).

Witness to My Life: The Letters of Jean-Paul Sartre to Simone de Beauvoir, 1926–1939, ed. Simone de Beauvoir, translated by Lee Fahnstock and Norman MacAfee (Hamish Hamilton, 1992).

Quiet Moments in a War: The Letters of Jean-Paul Sartre to Simone de Beauvoir, 1940–1963, ed. Simone de Beauvoir, translated by Lee Fahnstock and Norman MacAfee (New York: Charles Scribner's Sons, 1993).

Beauvoir and Sartre: Documents, articles, interviews, audiovisual material

Beauvoir, unpublished journals, 1926–30, Bibliothèque Nationale de France (BNF).

Beauvoir, Sylvie Le Bon de, unpublished letters to Simone de Beauvoir.

Galster, Ingrid, 'Le couple modèle?' *L'Histoire, Numéro Spécial, Sartre: portrait sans tabou*, février 2005.

Gobeil, Madeleine, 'Interview with Simone de Beauvoir', *American Vogue*, 1965.

Maugarlone, François, 'Une drôle de famille', *L'Histoire*, février 2005.

Ophuls, Marcel, *Le Chagrin et la Pitié* (*The Sorrow and the Pity*), film, 1969.

'Sartre et les femmes', interview with Catherine Chaîne, *Le Nouvel observateur*, 31 January 1977.

'Sartre, autoportrait à 70ans', Entretiens avec Michel Contat, 6CD (Gallimard/France Culture, 2001), complete transcripts of tapes made in 1975 as basis for 'Self-Portrait at Seventy', interview with Michel Contat, *Le Nouvel observateur*, June and July 1975, reprinted in *Life/Situations*.

Sartre, unpublished letters to Lena Zonina, private archive of Macha Zonina.

Scruton, Roger, 'The Power of Negative Thinking', *Spectator*, 25 June 2005.

Weatherby, W.J., 'The Life and Hard Times of Nelson Algren', *The Times*, 10 May 1981.

Winock, Michel, 'Que reste-t-il de Sartre?', interview with Michel Winock, in *Chroniques de la Bibliothèque nationale de France*, No. 30, avril–juin 2005.

Zonina, Lena, 'Reports on Working with Jean-Paul Sartre and Simone de Beauvoir', 1962–1965, Archives on the Writers' Union of the USSR, Moscow State Archives of Art and Literature.

Secondary sources

Algren, Nelson, *Who Lost an American?* (London: Macmillan, 1963).

Algren, Nelson, *Conversations with Nelson Algren* (Hill & Wang, 1964).

Appignanesi, Lisa, *Simone de Beauvoir* (London: Penguin, 1988).

Aronson, Ronald, *Camus and Sartre: The Story of a Friendship and the Quarrel that Ended It* (University of Chicago Press, 2004).

Bair, Deirdre, *Simone de Beauvoir: A Biography* (London: Vintage, 2001).

Beach, Sylvia, *Shakespeare and Company* (University of Nebraska Press, 1991).

Beever, Anthony, and Cooper, Artemis, *Paris After the Liberation* (London: Hamish Hamilton, 1994).

Bérard, Ewa, *La Vie tumultueuse d'Ilya Ehrenbourg, Juif, Russe et Soviétique* (Paris: Ramsay, 1991).

Berne, Mauricette (ed.), *Sartre*, catalogue of the Exposition Sartre, Paris, 2005, (Bibliothèque Nationale de France/Gallimard, 2005).

Bonal, Gérard, and Ribowska, Malka, *Simone de Beauvoir* (Paris: Seuil/Jazz Editions, 2001).

Brassaï, *The Secret Paris of the Thirties*, translated by Richard Miller (London: Thames & Hudson, 1976).

Brinnin, John Malcolm, *Truman Capote, A Memoir* (London: Sidgwick & Jackson, 1987).

Camus, Albert, *L'Etranger* (Paris: Gallimard, 1939), *The Outsider* (London: Penguin, 1961).

Camus, Albert, *Le Mythe de Sisyphe* (Paris: Gallimard, 1942), *The Myth of Sisyphus* (London: Penguin, 1975).

Camus, Albert, *La Peste* (Paris: Gallimard, 1947), *The Plague* (London: Penguin, 1960).

Camus, Albert, *L'Homme revolté* (Paris: Gallimard, 1952), *The Rebel* (London: Penguin, 1971).

Camus, Albert, *Essais* (Paris: Gallimard, 1965).

Camus, Albert, *Carnets III, mars 1951–décembre 1959* (Paris: Gallimard, 1989).

Caracalla, *Montparnasse: L'Âge d'or* (Paris: Denoël, 1997).

Card, Claudia (ed.), *The Cambridge Companion to Simone de Beauvoir* (Cambridge University Press, 2003).

Cocteau, Jean, *Journal: Le Passé Défini* (Paris: Gallimard, 1985).

Cohen-Solal, Annie, *Sartre: a life* (London: Heinemann, 1987).

Contat, Michel, *Sartre, L'invention de la Liberté* (Paris: Editions Textuel, 2005).

Crosland, Margaret, *Simone de Beauvoir: The Woman and her Work* (London: Heinemann, 1992).

Curtis, Michael, *Verdict on Vichy: Power and Prejudice in the Vichy France Regime*, (London: Weidenfeld & Nicolson, 2002).

Dayan, Josée, and Ribowska, Malka, *Simone de Beauvoir*, texte intégral de la bande sonore du film, *Simone de Beauvoir* (Paris: Gallimard, 1979).

Drew, Bettina, *Nelson Algren: A Life on the Wild Side* (London: Bloomsbury, 1990).

Evans, Mary, *Simone de Beauvoir: A Feminist Mandarin* (London: Tavistock, 1985).

Fanon, Frantz, *The Wretched of the Earth* (London: Penguin, 1967).

Francis, Claude, and Gontier, Fernande, *Simone de Beauvoir*, translated by Lisa Nesselson (London: Sidgwick & Jackson, 1987).

Friedan, Betty, *The Feminine Mystique* (London: Penguin, 1963).

Fryer, Jonathan, *Oscar and André* (London: Constable, 1997).

Fullbrook, Kate, and Fullbrook, Edward, *Simone de Beauvoir and Jean-Paul Sartre: The Remaking of a Twentieth-Century Legend* (Harvester Wheatsheaf, 1993).

Galster, Ingrid, *Sartre, Vichy et les intellectuels* (Paris: L'Harmattan, 2001).

Gerassi, John, *Jean-Paul Sartre, Hated Conscience of His Century* (University of Chicago Press, 1989).

Gide, André, *Journal* (Paris: Gallimard, 1946); *The Journals of André Gide*, translated by Justin O'Brien (London: Secker & Warburg, 1947).

Gide, André, *Les Nourritures Terrestres* (*Fruits of the Earth*), 1897.

Gildea, Robert, *Marianne in Chains: In Search of the German Occupation of France 1940–45* (London: Pan, 2003).

Guéhenno, Jean, *Journal des Années Noires* (Paris: Gallimard, 1947).

Guppy, Shusha, *A Girl in Paris* (London: Minerva, 1992).

Hawthorne, Melanie C. (ed.), *Contingent Loves: Simone de Beauvoir and Sexuality* (University Press of Virginia, 2000).

Hayman, Ronald, *Writing Against: A Biography of Sartre* (London: Weidenfeld & Nicolson, 1986).

Heller, Gerhard, *Un Allemand à Paris: 1940–1944*, avec le concours de Jean Grand (Paris: Seuil, 1981).

Hewitt, Leah D., *Autobiographical Tightropes: Simone de Beauvoir et al* (University of Nebraska Press, 1990).

Jeanson, Francis, *Sartre par lui-même* (Paris: Seuil, 1955); *Sartre dans sa vie* (Paris: Seuil, 1966).

Joseph, Gilbert, *Une Si Douce Occupation: Simone de Beauvoir et Jean-Paul Sartre, 1940–1944* (Paris: Albin Michel, 1991).

Kedward, Rod, *La Vie en bleu: France and the French since 1900* (London: Penguin, 2006).

Klarsfeld, Serge, *Le Mémorial de la déportation des Juifs de France* (Paris: 1978).

Koestler, Arthur, *Darkness at Noon* (1940), translated by Daphne Hardy (London: Vintage, 2005).

Lamblin, Bianca, *Mémoires d'une jeune fille dérangée* (Paris: Balland, 1993); *A Disgraceful Affair: Simone de Beauvoir, Jean-Paul Sartre and Bianca Lamblin*, translated by Julie Plovnick (Boston: North Eastern University Press, 1996).

Lanzmann, Claude et al., *Témoins de Sartre* (Paris: Gallimard, 2005).

Lanzmann, Claude, *Shoah, the complete text of the Holocaust film*, with a preface by Simone de Beauvoir (New York: Da Capo Press, 1995).

Lehmann, John, *Christopher Isherwood: A Personal Memoir* (New York: Henry Holt, 1987).

Lévy, Bernard-Henri, *Le Siècle de Sartre: enquête philosophique* (Paris: Grasset, 2000).

Lévy, Claude, and Tillard, Paul, *La Grande Rafle du Vel d'Hiv* (Paris: Laffont, 1967).

Lottmann, Herbert R., *Albert Camus: A Biography* (Corte Madera, CA, 1997).

Madsen, Axel, *Hearts and Minds: The Common Journey of Simone de Beauvoir and Jean-Paul Sartre* (New York: William Morrow and Company, 1977).

Merleau-Ponty, Maurice, *Phénoménologie de la perception* (Paris: Gallimard, 1945).

Michel, Georges, *Mes Années Sartre: Histoire d'une amitié* (Paris: Hachette, 1981).

Miles, Rosalind, *The Women's History of the World* (London: Paladin, 1989).

Moi, Toril, *Feminist Theory and Simone de Beauvoir* (London: Blackwell, 1990).

Moi, Toril, *Simone de Beauvoir: The Making of an Intellectual Woman* (London: Blackwell, 1994).

Moreau, Jean-Luc, *Sartre, voyageur sans billet* (Paris: Fayard, 2005).

Murdoch, Iris, *Sartre: Romantic Rationalist* (London: Fontana, 1969).

Nizan, Paul, *Aden-Arabie* (Paris: Maspero, 1960).

Nizan, Paul, *Le Cheval de Troie* (Paris: Grasset, 1935).

Papatakis, Nico, *Tous les désespoirs sont permis* (Paris: Fayard, 2003).

Paxton, Robert O., *Vichy France: Old Guard and New Order, 1940–1944* (London: Barrie & Jenkins, 1972).

Perrin, Marius, *Avec Sartre au Stalag XIID* (Paris: Delarge, 1980).

Pryce-Jones, David, *Paris in the Third Reich: A History of the German Occupation 1940–1944* (London: Collins, 1981).

Rees, William (ed. and trans.), *The Penguin Book of French Poetry 1920–1850* (London: Penguin, 1990).

Rousso, Henry, *The Vichy Syndrome: History and Memory in France since*

1944, translated by Arthur Goldhammer (Cambridge, Mass.: Harvard University Press, 1991).

Rowley, Hazel, *Tête-à-Tête: Simone de Beauvoir and Jean-Paul Sartre* (London: HarperCollins, 2005).

Russell, Bertrand, *History of Western Philosophy* (London: George Allen and Unwin, 1961).

'Simone de Beauvoir aujourd'hui: Six entretiens' (Paris: Mercure de France, 1984).

Schwarzer, Alice, *After 'The Second Sex': Conversations with Simone de Beauvoir 1972–1982*, translated by Marianne Howarth (London: Chatto & Windus, 1984).

Sebag Montefiore, Simon, *Stalin: The Court of the Red Tsar* (London: Phoenix, 2004).

Showalter, Elaine, *Inventing Herself: Claiming a Feminist Intellectual Heritage* (London: Picador, 2001).

Siegel, Liliane, *In the Shadow of Sartre*, translated by Barbara Wright (London: Collins, 1990).

Signoret, Simone, *Nostalgia Isn't What It Used to Be* (London: Weidenfeld & Nicolson, 1978).

Stonor Saunders, Frances, *Who Paid the Piper? The CIA and the Cultural Cold War* (London: Granta Books, 2000).

Strachey, Ray, *The Cause: A Short History of the Women's Movement in Great Britain* (London: Virago, 1978).

Thibault, Richard, *Les Normands sous l'Occupation: vie quotidienne et années noires* (Paris: Charles Corlet, 1998).

Thompson, Kenneth A. (ed.), *Sartre, Life and Works* (New York: Facts on File, 1984).

Todd, Olivier, *Albert Camus: A Life*, translated by Benjamin Ivry (New York: Alfred A. Knopf, 1997).

Todd, Olivier, *Un fils rebelle* (Paris: Grasset & Fasquelle, 1981).

Warnock, Mary, *Existentialism* (Oxford University Press, 1970).

Notes

Full details of works cited in these notes can be found in the Bibliography on page 495. Where another translator is not cited, I have translated from the French.

Preface

page xi 'Je peux me tromper . . .' Jean-paul Sartre, handwritten noted dated '29.6.71', Michel Contat, *Sartre, l'invention de la liberté* (Paris: Les Éditions Textuels, 2005) p. 147.

page xii '*The* biographical question . . .' Bernard-Henri Lévy, *Le Siècle de Sartre* (Paris: Éditions Grasset, 2000) p. 407.

page xiv '*Mais les vôtres, Castor?*' Sylvie Le Bon de Beauvoir, ed., introduction to Simone de Beauvoir, *Lettres à Sartre, 1930–39* (Paris: Éditions Gallimard, 1990) p. 9.

page xiv 'to tell all . . . (*de tout dire pour dire vrai*)' ibid., p. 10.

page xiv 'making even the best of them . . .' Quintin Hoare, translator, Introduction to Simone de Beauvoir, *Letters to Sartre* (Vintage: 1992) p. viii.

page xvii '*L'athéisme est une enterprise cruelle* . . .' *Les Mots*, p. 210.

Chapter 1: Becoming

page 3 '*Elle a dit "non"* . . .': interview with Sylvie Le Bon de Beauvoir, 29 November 2005.

page 3 'What we have is an *essential* love . . .': Simone de Beauvoir, *The Prime of Life*, translated by Peter Green (Penguin, 1965), p. 22, first published as *La Force de l'Âge* (Gallimard, 1960).

page 4 'I think she's beautiful . . .': Sartre, quoted by Madeleine Gobeil, interview with Jean-Paul Sartre, *American Vogue*, 1965.

page 4 '[He] corresponded exactly to the dream-companion . . .': Simone de Beauvoir, *Memoirs of a Dutiful Daughter*, translated by James Kirkup (Penguin, 1963), p. 345, first published as *Mémoires d'une jeune fille rangée* (Gallimard, 1958).

page 5 'She didn't look very nice . . .': interview with Stépha Gerassi, née Estépha Awdykovicz, in Deirdre Bair, *Simone de Beauvoir* (Vintage, 1991), p. 116.

page 5 'Take off that hideous frock . . .': Simone de Beauvoir, 'Marguerite', in *When Things of the Spirit Come First*, translated by Patrick O'Brian (Flamingo, 1983), first published as *Quand prime le spirituel* (Gallimard, 1979), p. 187; in her preface to the English edition, Beauvoir writes (p. 8): 'I give Marguerite my own childhood at the Cours Désir, and my own adolescent religious crisis . . . In the end her eyes are opened; she tosses mysteries, mirages and myths overboard, and looks the world in the face . . . I wrote it . . . with a fellow-feeling for the heroine.'

page 5 'You have a lovely body . . .': ibid., p. 187.

page 5 'From the very first . . .': Bair, *Simone de Beauvoir*, p. 116.

page 6 'From the owner . . .': Brassaï, 'Sodom and Gomorrah', in *The Secret Paris of the 30s* (Gallimard, 1976), translated from the French by Richard Miller (Thames & Hudson, 1978), describes Le Monocle [no page numbers].

page 6 'I love Stépha . . .': Simone de Beauvoir, 31 December 1928, unpublished journal, Bibliothèque Nationale de France.

page 6 'Physical love . . .': Beauvoir, *Memoirs of a Dutiful Daughter*, p. 307.

page 6 'There is within me . . .': ibid.

page 7 'The upholstery was of red moquette . . .': ibid., p. 5.

page 8 Seigneurs de Beauvoir: *Histoire Genealogique et Chronologique de la Maison Royale de France, des Pairs, Grand Officiers de la Couronne et de la Maison du Roy*, Tome second (La Compagnie des Libraries), M.DDC.XXVI, pp. 14, 16, 236; Tome huitième, p. 654.

page 8 'In the ranks of high society . . .': Beauvoir, *Memoirs of a Dutiful Daughter*, p. 33.

page 8 'He was contemptuous . . .': ibid.

page 9 'She believed herself to be dishonoured . . .': Simone de Beauvoir, *Une Mort très douce* (Gallimard), 1964, p. 49 (my translation).

page 9 'I was very happy . . .': Claude Francis and Fernande Gontier, *Simone de Beauvoir*, translated from the French by Lisa Nesselson (Sidgwick & Jackson), 1987, p. 370.

page 10 'I am given a red plum . . .': Beauvoir, *Memoirs of a Dutiful Daughter*, p. 11.

page 10 '*Pauvre petite!*': Beauvoir, *Mémoires d'une jeune fille rangée*, p. 18; 'Poor little thing': Beauvoir, *Memoirs of a Dutiful Daughter*, p. 11.

page 10 'If you raise . . .': ibid., p. 13.

page 10 'She was provincial . . .': Beauvoir, *Une Mort très douce*, p. 48.

page 11 'There's Monsieur and Madame fighting again': Beauvoir, *Memoirs of a Dutiful Daughter*, p. 16.

page 11 'I don't blame my father . . .': Beauvoir, *Une Mort très douce*, p. 51.

page 11 '*Chez l'homme, l'habitude tue le désir*': ibid., p. 51.

page 11 'was enough to convince me . . .': ibid., p. 51.

page 12 '*Je me sacrifie*': ibid., p. 50.

page 12 'I've never been an egoist . . .': ibid., p. 54.

page 12 'It's my right' ('*J'ai bien le droit*'): ibid., p. 56.

page 13 '[Mama] was washing the plates . . .': Beauvoir, *Memoirs of a Dutiful Daughter*, p.104.

page 13 'We lived on the fifth floor . . .': Beauvoir, *When Things of the Spirit Come First*, pp. 187–8.

page 14 'one must make use of everything . . .': Beauvoir, *Memoirs of a Dutiful Daughter*, p. 66.

page 14 'My father was totally ruined': ibid., p. 72.

page 14 'Papa used to say with pride . . .': ibid., p.121.
page 15 'How I longed . . .': ibid.
page 15 'Simone looks like a monkey . . .': ibid., pp. 61–2.
page 16 *'Ne gratte pas tes boutons'*: Beauvoir, *Mémoires d'une jeune fille rangée*, p. 141.

Chapter 2: The Frog Prince

page 17 'I loathe my childhood . . .': Jean-Paul Sartre, *Words* (Penguin, 1967), translated by Irene Clephane, first published as *Les Mots* (Gallimard, 1964), p. 104.
page 17 'I am pink and fair . . .': ibid., p. 20.
page 18 'I'd have preferred a trip to Japan . . .': Jean-Baptiste Sartre, quoted in Annie Cohen-Solal, *Sartre* (Heinemann, 1987), p. 15.
page 18 'My little Paul . . .': ibid., p. 24.
page 18 'Families naturally prefer widows . . .': Sartre, *Words*, p. 14.
page 19 'I was shown a young giantess . . .': ibid., p. 16.
page 19 'bore so close a resemblance . . .': ibid.
page 20 'My young pupil . . .': Cohen-Solal, *Sartre*, p. 32; Charles Schweitzer was reading Victor Hugo's *L'Art d'être grandpère*.
page 20 *'Aime'* was spelt *'ême'*: Sartre, *Words*, p. 50.
page 20 'Until the age of ten . . .': ibid., p. 53.
page 20 'Oui, ma petite maman,' Beauvoir V L Bost, 31 May 1939, S de Beauvoir–Jacques Laurent Bost, *Correspondence Croisée* (Gallimard, 2004), p. 380.
page 20 'the booming voice of his grandfather . . .': see François George Maugarlone, 'Une drôle de famille', *L'Histoire*, 2005 février, p. 46.
page 21 'a shrimp that interested no one': Sartre, *Words*, p. 84.
page 21 'I was in danger of . . .': ibid., p. 85.
page 21 'You're making a girl of him . . .': ibid., p. 65.
page 21 'My name is Lucien . . .' Jean-Paul Sartre, 'The Childhood of a Leader', in *The Wall* (New York: New Directions Paperback, 1948), translated by Lloyd Alexander, p. 84.
page 22 'He had gone out with his wonder child . . .': Sartre, *Words*, p. 66.
page 22 'He still went to the salon . . .': Sartre, *The Wall*, p. 90.
page 22 *'Il s'en va, froid . . .'*: Tristan Corbière, 'Le Crapaud', *The Penguin Book of French Poetry 1820–1850*, selected and translated by William Rees (Penguin, 1990); Corbière, self-conscious and abrasive, caricatured himself as 'the toad', and, according to his translator, hid his insecurities and failures in love behind a mask of irony and black humour, but the mask did not conceal his pain any more than Sartre's irony does in *Words*.
page 24 'I was born from writing . . .': Sartre, *Words*, p. 97.
page 24 'My little fellow will write': ibid., p. 96.
page 24 'You're spoilt, boy . . .': ibid., p. 137.
page 25 'Name, profession . . .': ibid., p. 142.

Chapter Three: Jacques

page 26 'I comforted myself . . .': Beauvoir, *Memoirs of a Dutiful Daughter*, p. 89.

page 26 'eyes of a lover . . .': ibid., p. 73.

page 27 'We'll have plenty of time . . .': ibid., p. 75.

page 27 'Do as your mother says': ibid., p. 107.

page 27 'I no longer believe . . .': ibid., p. 137.

page 28 'A girl has two friends . . .':quoted in Gérard Bonal and Malka Ribowska, *Simone de Beauvoir* (Paris: Seuil/Jazz Éditions, 2001), p. 13.

page 28 'Now thank Madame de Beauvoir . . .' Beauvoir, *Memoirs of a Dutiful Daughter*, p. 120.

page 28 Beauvoir refuses to be separated from Zaza, whose Catholic Lacoin family ('Mabille' in the memoirs) would never have allowed her to go to a lay institution: Beauvoir, *All Said and Done*, translated by Patrick O'Brian (André Deutsch and Weidenfeld & Nicolson, 1974), p. 10, first published as *Tout Compte Fait* (Gallimard, 1972); in the memoirs (*Memoirs of a Dutiful Daughter*, p. 150, *Memoires d'une jeune fille rangee*, p. 209), Beauvoir relates, however, how M. Lacoin, an engineer, demanded that his daughter should sit the more difficult 'masculine' *baccalauréat*, in order that she should get a good grounding in science, as well as the easier new *bac*, introduced in 1902, known as 'Latin and languages,' which most girls took, leaving philosophy and mathematics to the boys. An extra teacher was brought in to teach Zaza algebra, trigonometry and physics at the Cours Désir, and Simone was allowed to join her lessons. Both girls took both *bacs*; without this opportunity, it would not have been possible for Simone to study philosophy at university level.

page 28 'What do you want to do . . .': Beauvoir, *Memoirs of a Dutiful Daughter*, p. 141.

page 28 'Bringing nine children . . .': ibid., p. 140.

page 29 'I allowed myself . . .': ibid., p. 95.

page 29 '*Est-ce que j'aime* . . .': Beauvoir, unpublished journal, 12 August 1926 (my translation).

page 29 'calling for a man's body . . .': Beauvoir, *Memoirs of a Dutiful Daughter*, p. 100.

page 30 'With his rosy cheeks . . .': ibid., p. 60.

page 30 'I should be in love . . .': ibid., p. 90.

page 30 'finish Verlaine . . .': Beauvoir, unpublished journal, 12 August 1926.

page 30 'I can no longer change . . .': ibid.

page 30 '*Un jour je me marierai*, one day I'll get married': ibid., 17 August 1926.

page 31 'If I am to set up home . . .': Beauvoir, *Memoirs of a Dutiful Daughter*, p. 200.

page 31 'What a catch . . .': ibid., p. 201.

page 31 'The name of Champigneulles . . .': ibid., p. 198.

page 31 'It's like a railway accident . . .': ibid., p. 202.

page 31 'beautiful apartment . . .': ibid., p. 209.

page 31 'You girls will never marry . . .': ibid., p. 104.

page 32 Law Camille Sée: see Toril Moi, *Simone de Beauvoir: The Making of an Intellectual Woman* (Oxford: Blackwell, 1994), pp. 42–7.

page 32 'How I should love . . .': Beauvoir, *Memoirs of a Dutiful Daughter*, p. 160.

page 32 'it requires such strength . . .' quoted in Elaine Showalter, *Inventing Herself: Claiming a Feminist Intellectual Heritage* (Picador, 2001), p. 205. Léontine Zanta, in her 1921 novel, *La Science et l'Amour*, claims that the teacher of philosophy must have 'an elevated soul, galvanized by struggle and constant self-mastery', and compares teaching to the priesthood; Moi, *Simone de Beauvoir*, p. 58.

page 33 'I wanted to be one of those pioneers': Beauvoir, *Memoirs of a Dutiful Daughter*, p.160; the École Normale Supérieure (ENS) was not opened to women until 1927.

page 33 'By and large we have won . . .' 'En gros, nous avons gagné la partie,': Beauvoir, *The Second Sex*, and Toute Compte Fait, p. 623.

page 33 'My feminine status . . .': Beauvoir, *The Prime of Life*, p. 292.

page 33 'Am I proud?': Beauvoir, journal, 16 September 1926.

page 34 'solitude and anguish': ibid., 6 September 1926.

page 34 'it pleased her to love': ibid., 7 October 1926.

page 34 'Mama thinks she's making me very happy [*Maman croit de me faire un immense plaisir en m'envoyant chez Jacques*]': ibid., 20 October 1926.

page 34 'Is it any business . . .': Beauvoir, *Memoirs of a Dutiful Daughter*, p. 212.

page 34 'Action is the last refuge . . .': quotation from Oscar Wilde in Beauvoir, journal, 29 October 1926.

page 34 'I only torture myself': ibid., 20 October 1926.

page 34 'It is only necessary . . .': ibid., 29 October 1926.

page 34 'Eight days without seeing you': ibid., 6 November 1926.

page 34 '*Pardon! A toi, Jacques* . . .': ibid., 7 November 1926.

page 34 'Simone is very pretty . . .' Beauvoir, *Memoirs of a Dutiful Daughter*, p. 215.

page 35 'The idea of marrying him revolted me . . .': ibid., p. 209.

page 35 'everything in my life . . .': ibid., p. 217.

Chapter 4: La Rochelle

page 36 'The mirror was a great help . . .': Sartre, *Words*, p. 69.

page 37 'One thing is certain . . .': Sartre, interview with Gerassi, quoted in Sartre, *Oeuvres romanesques* (Paris: Pléiade, Gallimard, 1981) and Cohen-Solal, *Sartre*, p. 42.

page 37 'Philippe awoke with a start . . .': Jean-Paul Sartre, *The Reprieve (Le Sursis)*, first published 1945, translated by Eric Sutton (Penguin, 2001), p. 161.

page 37 'I certainly did have a fairly sexual feeling . . .': Simone de Beauvoir, *Adieux: A Farewell to Sartre*, translated by Patrick O'Brian (André Deutsch and Weidenfeld & Nicolson, London, 1984), p. 292.

page 38 'I found my mother's letting go very disagreeable': ibid., pp. 312–16.

page 38 'What attracted me . . .': Sartre, *Words*, p. 36, note; 'I had an older sister, my mother, and I wanted a younger,' Sartre writes. 'Even today – 1963 – it is the only family relationship which appeals to me. I made the serious mistake of often looking among women for this sister who never turned up.'

page 38 'We rolled on the ground . . .': Beauvoir, *Adieux*, p. 147.

page 39 'Who's this bum . . . [*Vieux con avec un oeil qui dit merde à l'autre*]': John Gerassi, *Jean-Paul Sartre: Hated Conscience of his Country* (University of Chicago Press, 1989), p. 61.

page 39 'one thing that was always . . .': Beauvoir, *Adieux*, p. 309.

page 40 'I had no true self . . .': Sartre, *Words*, p. 69.

page 40 'At first I played . . .': Beauvoir, *Adieux*, p. 220.

page 40 'Very pretty . . .': ibid., p. 144.

page 40 'Writing against': ibid.

page 40 'a poor devil . . .': ibid., p. 431.

page 41 'a pitiful character': ibid., p. 134.

page 41 'big hooked nose . . .': 'Jésus la Chouette', *Les Écrits de Sartre*, ed. Michel Contat and Michel Rybalka (Gallimard, 1970), p. 511; the French master in this story has also promised Anne-Marie to 'make a man' of Poulou ('*Je lui ai juré de faire de vous un homme*').

page 41 'He never did survive the ridicule . . .': 'Jésus', Gerassi, *Jean-Paul Sartre*, p. 59. In fact Michel Contat and Michel Rybalka established that the teacher in question never did kill himself, although Sartre continued to believe that he did.

page 41 'tumbled down into the blue sky . . .': Sartre, *Words*, p. 155.

page 41 'I grew up . . .': ibid.

page 42 'What's all this money?': Beauvoir, *Adieux*, pp. 146–7.

page 42 'Like a voodoo drum . . .': Sartre, *Words*, p. 79.

page 43 'Careful! . . .': ibid., p. 56.

page 43 'How could I continue? . . .': Gerassi, *Jean-Paul Sartre*, p. 60.

page 45 'I *had* my tomb . . .': Sartre, *Words*, p. 130.

page 45 '*J'en ai été saisi*': 'Une Vie pour la Philosophie', entretien avec Jean-Paul Sartre, 1975, choisi par Michel Rybalka à partir du texte original français, *Le Magazine littéraire*, no. 7, March–May 2005, p. 56, extracts from *The Philosophy of Jean-Paul Sartre*, ed. Paul A. Schilpp (Open Court, 1981). Sartre read Henri Bergson, *L'Essai sur les données immédiates de la conscience*.

page 45 'What I at that time . . .': quoted in Cohen-Solal, *Sartre*, p. 57.

page 45 'spent all my time despairing . . .': Sartre, *War Diaries: Notebooks from a Phoney War, November 1939–March 1940*, translated by Quintin Hoare (Verso, 1984), p. 268.

page 45 'It was more tempestuous . . .': unpublished text, part published in *Le Magazine littéraire*, issue on Sartre, 1970, quoted Cohen-Solal, *Sartre*, p. 56.

page 46 'I desired her . . .': Sartre, *War Diaries*, pp. 267–8.

page 46 Simone Jollivet: Camille in Beauvoir's memoirs. Born Simone-Camille Sans, she took Simone Jollivet as her stage name.

page 46 'When I think of glory . . .': Jean-Paul Sartre to Simone Jollivet (1926), *Witness to My Life, The Letters of Jean-Paul Sartre to Simone de Beauvoir 1926–1939*, ed. Simone de Beauvoir, translated by Lee Fahnestock and Norman MacAfee (Hamish Hamilton, 1992), first published as *Lettres au Castor et à quelques autres* (Gallimard, 1983), p. 3.

page 46 'Mirabeau effect': Beauvoir, *Adieux*, p. 310.

page 47 'So how come . . .': Gerassi, *Jean-Paul Sartre*, p. 61.

Chapter 5: Zaza

page 48 'Who could believe . . .': Beauvoir, journal, 29 September 1928.

page 49 'borrowed, in a spirit of irony, from Maritain': Claude Francis and Fernande Gontier, *Les Écrits de Simone de Beauvoir* (Gallimard, 1979), p. 39; Beauvoir intended her collection of short stories to be called *Primauté du spirituel* (the title of Jacques Maritain's book), when she began writing them in 1935, but for copyright reasons changed it to *Quand prime le spirituel* (*When Things of the Spirit Come First*).

page 49 'the harm done by religiosity . . .': Simone de Beauvoir, preface to the English translation, *When Things of the Spirit Come First*, p. 9.

page 49 'I knew perfectly well . . .': Beauvoir, 'Marguerite', ibid., p. 169.

page 50 'It is not by methodically . . .': ibid., pp. 167–8.

page 51 'Miracles exploded . . .': Beauvoir, *Memoirs of a Dutiful Daughter*, p. 269; the idea of the *acte gratuit* as a miracle is explored both in Beauvoir's memoirs and in her fiction.

page 51 'I have too much real regard . . .': ibid., p. 270.

page 51 'My mother used to count . . .': Francis and Gontier, *Les Ecrits de Simone de Beauvoir*, p. 376.

page 52 'as solid as a rock': Beauvoir, *Memoirs of a Dutiful Daughter*, p. 247.

page 52 'ruined girl': Beauvoir, 'Anne', *When Things of the Spirit Come First*, p. 119.

page 52 'I think of Zaza . . .': Beauvoir, journal, 24 September 1928.

page 52 'She had no idea . . . [*Elle ne savait*]': ibid., 29 September 1928.

page 53 'I find a letter . . . [*Je trouve un lettre de Zaza*]': ibid., 2 October 1928.

page 53 Maurice de Gandillac: 'Clairaut' in the memoirs; *talas* may also be a contraction of *ils vont à la messe*, they go to mass, i.e. practising Catholics.

page 53 'passionately desired . . .': Beauvoir, journal, 31 December 1928.

page 53 '*Jacques, pour toi, le bonheur* . . .': ibid., 31 December 1928.

page 53 'It's easy to see . . .': ibid., p. 239.

page 54 'If I *have* got genius . . .': ibid.; Beauvoir quotes her journal, p. 265.

page 54 'I hated the family . . .': André Gide, *Les Nourritures terrestres* (*Fruits of the Earth*), 1897.

page 54 'When you have read me . . .': André Gide, quoted in Justin O'Brien, translation and introduction to *The Journals of André Gide*, vol. 1, 1889–1913 (Secker & Warburg, 1947), p. ix.

page 55 'The egotistic note . . .' quoted in Jonathan Fryer, *Oscar and André* (Constable, 1997), p. 202.

page 55 'Live dangerously . . .': Beauvoir, *Memoirs of a Dutiful Daughter*, p. 273.

page 55 'serious as the rain': Sartre to Simone Jollivet, 'Summer 1928', *Witness to My Life*, p. 29.

page 56 'so that you will not be Madame Bovary . . .': Sartre to Simone Jollivet, '1926', ibid., p. 13.

page 56 'Until last year I was very melancholy . . .': ibid., p. 21.

page 56 'You look like Dorothée Reviers . . .': Sartre to Simone Jollivet, '1928', ibid., p. 15.

page 56 'I don't like to hear . . .': Sartre to Simone Jollivet, '1927', ibid., p. 24.

page 57 'He loved the big body . . .': 'Une Défaite', pp. 81–2, in Cohen-Solal, *Sartre*, p. 72.

page 57 'Tell me whether . . .': *Witness to My Life*, p. 8.

page 57 '*La laideur* . . .': quoted by Bernard-Henri Lévy, *Le Siècle de Sartre* (Paris: Grasset, 2000), p. 393.

page 57 'Jésus had killed himself': Gerassi, *Jean-Paul Sartre*, p. 59.

Chapter 6: Rivals: The Kobra and the Llama

Journal quotations in this chapter are from Simone de Beauvoir's unpublished 'Cahier de 1929', Bibliothèque Nationale de France (BNF), Paris.

page 59 'I love him profoundly . . .': Beauvoir, journal, 10 September 1929.

page 60 'The jutting jaw . . .': Beauvoir, *Memoirs of a Dutiful Daughter*, p. 313.

page 61 'The Eugene tries . . .': ibid., p. 322.

page 61 'How fast you walk . . .': ibid., p. 323.

page 61 'Any news of Jacques?': ibid., p. 315.

page 61 '*Ce type-là, il a foutu le camp* . . .': Beauvoir, *Memoires d'une jeune fille rangée*, p. 441.

page 62 'A very pretty girl . . .': Gerassi, *Jean-Paul Sartre*, p. 91.

page 62 'I think she's beautiful . . .': Sartre, interview with Madeleine Gobeil, *American Vogue*, 1965, cited in Ronald Hayman, *Writing Against: A Biography of Sartre* (Weidenfeld & Nicolson, 1986), p. 70.

page 62 'Maheu was . . . very jealous': Gerassi, *Jean-Paul Sartre*, p. 91.

page 63 'a gorgeous practical joke': Sartre to Simone Jollivet, 25 May 1927, *Witness to My Life*, p. 25.

page 63 'I took a bottle . . .': interview with Sartre, 'Sartre et les femmes', Catherine Chaîne, *Le Nouvel observateur*, February 1977.

page 63 'BEAUVOIR = BEAVER . . .': Beauvoir, *Mémoires d'une jeune fille rangée*, p. 452 ['*Les Castors vont en bande et ils ont l'esprit constructeur*']; *Memoirs of a Dutiful Daughter*, p. 323.

page 64 'We understood each other . . .': *Memoirs of a Dutiful Daughter*, p. 323.

page 64 'I should hope so . . .': ibid., p. 321.

page 64 'Women should be as free . . .': ibid., pp. 324–5.

page 64 'I find it impossible to respect any woman . . .': ibid., p. 325.

page 65 'Do you think I haven't . . .': ibid., p. 324.

page 65 a 'little, well-brought-up young lady': Bair, *Simone de Beauvoir*, p. 129.

page 65 'I never even kissed . . .': ibid.

page 65 '*J'apprends la douceur* . . .' Beauvoir, journal, 11 September 1929.

page 66 'Maheu was in love with her . . .': interview with Sartre, 26 March 1971, Gerassi, *Jean-Paul Sartre*, p. 90.

page 66 'Sartre was incredibly generous . . .': Maheu, telephone conversation with John Gerassi, 5 October 1989, in Bair, *Simone de Beauvoir*, p. 628n.

page 66 'The people . . . are dreaming': Bair, *Simone de Beauvoir*, p. 628.

page 66 'Gerassi is a liar . . .': interview with Sylvie Le Bon, 29 November 2005.

page 66 '*Bonne chance, Castor*': Beauvoir, *Mémoires d'une jeune fille rangée*, p. 460.

page 67 'That is pure invention': Beauvoir, *Memoirs of a Dutiful Daughter*, p. 332.

page 67 'I don't think I slept . . .': ibid., p. 334.

Chapter 7: The Summer of Love

Journal quotations in this chapter are from Simone de Beauvoir's unpublished 'Cahier 1929–30', Bibliothèque Nationale de France (BNF), Paris.

page 68 'I need Sartre . . .': Beauvoir, journal, 8 August 1928.

page 69 'No, this evening . . .': Beauvoir, *Memoirs of a Dutiful Daughter*, p. 337.

page 70 'She's a sly puss!': ibid., p. 335.

page 70 '*l'homme seul* . . .': see Jean-Luc Moreau, *Sartre, voyageur sans billet* (Paris:

Fayard, 2005), pp. 57–88, for an analysis of the topic of man alone, and the relationship between Sartre and Nizan.

page 71 'Concerning God . . .': Beauvoir, *Memoirs of a Dutiful Daughter*, p. 335.

page 71 'If God does not exist . . .': Sartre, 'Camus's *The Outsider*', in *Literary and Philosophical Essays*, translated by Annette Michelson (Rider & Co., 1955), p. 27.

page 71 'Brutal adventure . . .': Beauvoir, *Memoirs of a Dutiful Daughter*, p. 336.

page 71 'From now on, *je vous prends* . . .': Beauvoir, *Mémoires d'une jeune fille rangée*, p. 473; *Memoirs of a Dutiful Daughter*, p. 339.

page 72 'Whatever happens . . .': Beauvoir, *Memoirs of a Dutiful Daughter*, p. 340.

page 72 'theory of contingency': ibid., p. 343.

page 72 'Contingency: there are two kinds of events . . .': this lost letter to Simone Jollivet is summarized in Gerassi, *Jean-Paul Sartre*, p. 87.

page 72 'to be in dread of nothing': Søren Kierkegaard, *The Concept of Dread* (London, 1944), in Sartre, *War Diaries*, pp. 131,132.

page 73 'We are as free as you like . . .': Beauvoir, *Memoirs of Dutiful Daughter*, p. 343.

page 73 'to tick Castor off': see Sartre to Simone Jollivet, *Lettres au Castor*, p. 15.

page 73 '*Il la mit en pièces* . . .': Beauvoir, *Mémoires d'une jeune fille rangée*, p. 480.

page 73 'I was simply not in his class . . .': Beauvoir, *Memoirs of a Dutiful Daughter*, p. 344.

page 74 'I no longer asked myself . . .': ibid., p. 345; '*Je ne me demandai plus: que faire?*': Beauvoir, *Mémoires d'une jeune fille rangée*, p. 481.

page 74 'Their culture . . .': Beauvoir, *Memoirs of a Dutiful Daughter*, p. 344.

page 74 'I wasn't the One and Only [*Je n'étais pas l'unique, ni la première*]': Beauvoir, *Mémoires d'une jeune fille rangée*, p. 480.

page 74 'rigorous, demanding, precise . . .': Maurice de Gandillac, cited in Bair, *Simone de Beauvoir*, pp. 145–6; see also Gerassi, *Jean-Paul Sartre*, p. 91; Kate Fullbrook and Edward Fullbrook, *Simone de Beauvoir and Jean-Paul Sartre: The Remaking of a Twentieth-Century Legend* (Harvester Wheatsheaf, 1993), p. 61.

page 75 second to Sartre: see Moi, *Simone de Beauvoir*, p. 15.

Chapter 8: A Month in the Country

Journal quotations in this chapter are from Simone de Beauvoir's unpublished 'Cahier 1928–1929' and 'Cahier 1929–30', Bibliothèque Nationale de France (BNF), Paris.

page 76 'I'm only a desire for beauty . . .' Sartre, *War Diaries*, p. 282.

page 77 'Very soon I realized': Simone de Beauvoir, *The Prime of Life*, translated by Peter Green (Penguin, 1965), first published as *La Force de l'Âge* (Gallimard, 1960), p. 13.

page 77 'suspicious, ugly . . .': Sartre, *War Diaries*, p. 44.

page 77 'trapped between two nations . . .': Sartre, *Words*, p. 99.

page 78 'a thousand Socrates': Sartre, *War Diaries*, p. 73.

page 78 'small, honest figure . . .': unpublished letter, Jean-Paul Sartre to Simone de Beauvoir, 'mai 1948', personal archive Sylvie Le Bon de Beauvoir.

page 79 'Women's company': Sartre, *War Diaries*, p. 282.

page 79 'She peeled the bark . . .': Beauvoir, two unpublished chapters of *L'Invitée*, Francis and Gontier, *Les Écrits de Simone de Beauvoir*, p. 279 (my translation).

page 80 'The pleasures of love-making . . .': Beauvoir, *Prime of Life*, p. 63.
page 80 'the light of battle . . .': ibid., p. 14.
page 81 'Don't be silly!': Bair, *Simone de Beauvoir*, pp. 150, 155, 156. In 1984 Beauvoir said, 'Oh, he felt he had to propose to me after my father accosted us at La Grillère.' See also Fullbrook and Fullbrook, *Simone de Beauvoir and Jean-Paul Sartre*, p. 62.
page 81 'Sartre corresponded . . .': Beauvoir, *Memoirs of a Dutiful Daughter*, p. 345.
page 81 'certain facts': Beauvoir, preface to *Prime of Life*, pp. 8–9.
page 82 'morally I don't esteem him . . .': Beauvoir journal, 10 September 1929.

Chapter 9: A 'Morganatic' Marriage

Journal quotations in this chapter, and chapter ten, are from Simone de Beauvoir's unpublished 'Cahier 1929–1930', Bibliothèque Nationale de France (BNF), Paris.

page 83 'I was hoist . . .': Sartre, 1 December 1939, *War Diaries*, p. 75.
page 84 'There was a desk . . .': Beauvoir, *Prime of Life*, p. 11.
page 84 'Paris seemed the centre of the world . . .': ibid., p. 28.
page 85 The 'wasteland' of his future . . . : Sartre to Beauvoir, 1930, *Witness to My Life*, p.32.
page 86 'It will all depend . . .': Beauvoir, *Memories of a Dutiful Daughter*, p. 346.
page 86 'Marriage was impossible . . .': Bair, *Simone de Beauvoir*, p. 156. Jacques' business failed and he died an alcoholic at forty-six.
page 87 'was not inclined to be monogamous . . .': Beauvoir, *Prime of Life*, p. 22.
page 87 'I was hoist . . .': Sartre, 1 December 1939, *War Diaries*, p. 75.
page 87 'She didn't want marriage . . .': interview with Sylvie Le Bon de Beauvoir, 29 November 2005.
page 87 'essential love . . .': Beauvoir, *Prime of Life*, p. 22.
page 88 'There was a balustrade . . .': ibid., p. 23.
page 88 '*Toi et moi* . . .': Beauvoir, *L'Invitée* (Gallimard,1943), p. 29, translated by Yvonne Moyse and Roger Senhouse as *She Came to Stay* (Flamingo, 1984).
page 89 'There's no need to talk of faithfulness . . .': Beauvoir, *She Came to Stay*, p. 17.
page 89 'We intended to give ourselves . . .': Beauvoir, *Prime of Life*, p. 23.
page 89 'I have never met anyone . . .': ibid., p. 28.
page 89 'It's a morganatic marriage . . .': ibid., p.19.
page 90 'By the time I met . . .': ibid., p. 14.
page 91 'Do you hate me . . .': Beauvoir, *Memoirs of a Dutiful Daughter*, p. 359.
page 91 'N'ayez-pas de chagrin . . .': Beauvoir, *Mémoires d'une jeune fille rangée*, p. 502.
page 91 'I should have turned . . .': Beauvoir, *All Said and Done*, p. 10.

Chapter 10: On Her Paris Honeymoon

page 93 'To love is to relinquish . . .': Beauvoir, The *Second Sex*, translated by H. M. Parshley (Jonathan Cape, 1953; Everyman's Library, 1993), p. 674, first published as *Le Deuxième Sexe* (Gallimard, 1949).
page 93 'I belong to you . . .': Beauvoir, journal, 'Sunday night', 3 November 1929.

page 93 'to embrace all experience . . .': Beauvoir, *Prime of Life*, p. 25.

page 93 'Playboy soul . . .': Beauvoir, journal, 20 September 1929; see, too, '*Il avait emprunté à Synge le mythe du "Baladin", éternel errant qui déguise sous de belles histoires mensongères la médiocrité de la vie*', Beauvoir, *La Force de l'Âge*, p. 25.

page 93 'I have never wished to be serious . . .': Sartre, *War Diaries*, p. 326.

page 94 'recreate Man': Beauvoir, *Prime of Life*, p. 15.

page 94 'Then *he* arrives . . .': Beauvoir, journal, 9 November 1929.

page 94 'I knew no harm . . .': Beauvoir, *Prime of Life*, p. 23.

page 94 'She's on her Paris honeymoon,' ibid., p. 53.

page 94 'I wanted to relax . . .': Alice Schwarzer, *After the Second Sex: Conversations with Simone de Beauvoir* (New York: Pantheon Books, 1984), p. 110.

page 94 'he supplied me . . .': Beauvoir, *Prime of Life*, p. 27.

page 95 'With Sartre, who is not sensual . . .': Beauvoir, journal, 10 September 1929.

page 95 branches ['*Je cherchais les branches . . . Maheu? Une branche – Sartre? Lui surtout*']: Beauvoir, journal, 12 December 1929.

page 95 'I take the liberty . . .': letter from Maheu to Beauvoir, copied by Beauvoir for Sartre, 6 January 1930, *Letters to Sartre*, translated and edited by Quintin Hoare, (Vintage, 1992), p. 4.

page 95 'I shall assure him . . .': Beauvoir to Sartre, 6 January 1930, *Letters*, p. 5.

page 96 'What is this sadness . . . [*tristesse de corps, tristesse de chair*]': Beauvoir, journal, 8 January 1930.

page 96 'Their violence overrode . . .': Beauvoir, *Prime of Life*, p. 63.

page 96 'hidden disease . . .': ibid.

page 96 'I am feeble [*Je suis faible, je suis lâche – j'ai du chagrin*]': Beauvoir, journal, 8 January 1930.

page 97 'a woman of ardent . . .': Beauvoir, *The Second Sex*, pp. 411, 417, 674, 724.

page 97 'I should perhaps . . .': Sartre, *War Diaries*, p. 293.

page 97 'So as I was reasonably well equipped . . .': Beauvoir, *Adieux*, p. 314.

page 97 'Uncomfortable with his body . . .': see Asa Moberg, 'Sensuality and Brutality: Contradictions in Simone de Beauvoir's Writings about Sexuality', in Melanie C. Hawthorne (ed.), *Contingent Loves: Simone de Beauvoir and Sexuality* (University Press of Virginia, 298), pp. 98–9.

page 98 '[Sartre] is a warm . . .': Beauvoir, *Beloved Chicago Man: Letters to Nelson Algren 1947–64* (Phoenix, 1999), p. 212.

page 98 'the first penetration . . .': Beauvoir, *Second Sex*, p. 403.

page 98 a patient on an operating table: 'It was as though he were a doctor preparing for an operation, and I had only to let myself be taken,' recalls Bianca Bienenfeld Lamblin, *A Disgraceful Affair*, p. 44; Anne Dubreuilh, in bed with Victor Scriassine in Beauvoir's *The Mandarins*, says: 'I sensed a presence without feeling it, as you sense a dentist's steel tool against a swollen gum'; in *The Second Sex* the comparison between love-making and the chilly atmosphere of the doctor's or dentist's is often made, as translator Asa Moberg points out; Sartre himself, describing how hard he found it to endure 'the pressure of another presence constantly upon me', stated that from the age of seventeen, 'a pitiless clarity ruled over my mind: it was an operating-room, hygienic, without nooks or crannies, without microbes, beneath a cold light', *War Diaries*, p. 271.

page 98 'I've got a new theory': Beauvoir, *Prime of Life*, p. 41.

page 98 'Except when he's asleep . . .': Beauvoir, *Memoirs of a Dutiful Daughter*, p. 337.

page 98 Sartre was under the influence of Spinoza: see Mauricette Berne (ed.), *Sartre*, catalogue de l'exposition 'Sartre' présentée à la Bibliothèque Nationale de France (8 mars–31 août 2005) (Gallimard, 2005), p. 41.

page 98 'To be moral . . .': Sartre, *War Diaries*, pp. 82–4.

page 98 'really good': ibid.; see 'Spinoza and the Good', Bertrand Russell, *History of Western Philosophy* (Allen & Unwin, 1961), p. 553.

page 99 'Do you have . . .': Beauvoir, *Prime of Life*, p. 52.

page 99 'I must try [*Il faut que j'éssaie d'écrire*]': Beauvoir, journal, 9 June 1930.

page 99 '*Ma petite épouse* . . .': Sartre to Beauvoir, '1930', Berne, *Sartre*, p. 38; Beauvoir, *Witness to My Life*, p. 32.

page 100 'went to bed . . .': Francis and Gontier, *Simone de Beauvoir*, p. 379.

page 100 'in arid, obscure prose . . .': Sartre to Beauvoir, '1930', *Witness to My Life*, p. 34.

page 100 'I can't let Pierre down': Beauvoir, *Prime of Life*, p. 56; Guille is 'Pagniez' in the memoirs, Maheu 'Herbaud'.

page 100 'slept with Guille': Bair, *Simone de Beauvoir*, p. 172.

page 101 'She profited . . .': interview with Sylvie Le Bon de Beauvoir, 21 April 2005.

page 101 'It's not in some retreat . . .': Sartre, *Situations I*, quoted in Moreau, *Sartre*, p. 9.

page 101 'public affairs . . .': Beauvoir, *Prime of Life*, p. 15.

page 101 'dabble in politics . . .': *Witness to My Life*, pp. 160, 376.

page 102 'If we got married . . .': Beauvoir, *Prime of Life*, pp. 65–6.

page 102 'I didn't feel . . .': *Sartre, by himself*, film by Michel Contat.

page 102 'A child . . .': Beauvoir, *Prime of Life*, p. 78.

page 102 'She made her free . . .': interview with Sylvie Le Bon de Beauvoir, 21 April 2005.

Chapter 11: Marooned in Mudtown

page 103 'I *was* Roquentin . . .': Sartre, *Words*, p. 157.

page 103 'Nothing new will ever happen . . .': Beauvoir, *Prime of Life*, p. 207.

page 104 'How unpleasant it was!': Sartre, *Nausea* (first published as *La Nausée*, Gallimard, 1938), translated by Robert Baldick (Penguin, 2104), p. 22.

page 104 'I understood . . . what a tree is': *Witness to My Life*, p. 37.

page 105 'He invariably took my advice': Beauvoir, *Prime of Life*, p. 106.

page 105 'I live alone . . .': quoted in Sartre, *Oeuvres Romanesques*, p. xliv (my translation).

page 105 'Why is it . . .': Sartre, *War Diaries*, 14 March 1940, p. 338.

page 106 'We would watch . . .': Cohen-Solal, *Sartre*, p. 82.

page 106 'Everyone called him . . .': Gerassi, *Jean-Paul Sartre*, p. 107.

page 106 'Sartre was very elitist . . .': ibid., p. 108.

page 107 '*Traîne tes coquilles* . . .': Sartre, *La Mort dans l'âme* (Gallimard 1949); *Iron in the Soul*, translated by Gerard Hopkins (Penguin, 1963); Cohen-Solal, *Sartre*, p. 83.

page 107 'The motion picture . . .': Cohen-Solal, *Sartre*, pp. 78–9.

page 108 '*Dans la tristesse* . . .': ibid., p. 81.

page 108 'I couldn't do it': Sartre, *Nausea*, p. 22.

page 109 'If you look at yourself . . .': ibid., p. 31; Iris Murdoch, *Sartre: Romantic Rationalist* (1953; Fontana, 1969), p. 11.

page 109 'it grabs you . . .': Sartre's summary of *Nausea*, Gerassi, *Jean-Paul Sartre*, p. 118.
page 109 'special sense . . .': Murdoch, *Sartre*, p. 12.
page 110 Roquentin: Michel Contat and Michel Rybalka, in *Oeuvres Romanesques*; Moreau, *Sartre*, p. 34.
page 110 'a comedy!': Sartre, *Nausea*, p. 111.
page 110 'A spy from the world . . .': James Wood, introduction to *Nausea*, p. viii.
page 110 'the magic of adventures . . .': Sartre, *Nausea*, p. 57.
page 111 'see *everything*': Beauvoir, *Prime of Life*, p. 91.
page 112 'fighting off . . .': Bair, *Simone de Beauvoir*, p. 177.
page 112 'I had subdued . . .': Beauvoir, *Prime of Life*, p. 100.
page 113 'She seized me . . .': ibid., p. 98.

Chapter 12: The Little Russian

page 114 'She felt Xavière's . . .': Beauvoir, *She Came to Stay*, p. 246.
page 115 '*Vous verrez*, You'll see . . .': Beauvoir, *L'Invitée*, p. 45 (translation modified), *She Came to Stay*, pp. 29–30.
page 116 'excessively well brought up . . .': Bonal and Ribowska, *Simone de Beauvoir*, p. 48.
page 116 'We had a profession . . .': Beauvoir, *Prime of Life*, p. 288; see Serge Julienne-Caffié, 'Variations on Triangular Relationships', *Contingent Loves*, p. 41.
page 117 '*vous autres*': Sartre to Beauvoir, 3–4 September 1934, *Witness to My Life*, p. 45, n.5, translators' note on the couple's private language; Lee Fahnestock and Norman MacAfee give the example of the neologism '*vous autre*' invented by Sartre.
page 117 'this allowed a shameful . . .': Beauvoir, *L'Invitée*, p. 30, *She Came to Stay*, p. 17.
page 117 '[Beauvoir's] influence . . .': interview with Colette Audry, in Bair, *Simone de Beauvoir*, p. 183.
page 118 'They seemed to think . . .': Olivier Todd, quoted in Julienne-Caffié, 'Variations on Triangular Relationships', in *Contingent Loves*, p. 44.
page 118 Ricardo Ainslie, *The Psychology of Twinship*: quoted ibid., p. 45.
page 118 'We are truly one person . . .': Beauvoir to Sartre, 7 November 1939, *Letters*, p. 100.
page 119 '*Il y a un élan passionnée que lui manqué* . . . There's no surge of passion in him': Beauvoir to J.-L. Bost, Sylvie Le Bon de Beauvoir (ed.), *Simone de Beauvoir, Jacques-Laurent Bost, Correspondance croisée 1937–1940* (Gallimard, 2004), p. 212 (my translation).
page 119 'Marcelle . . .': Beauvoir, *When Things of the Spirit Come First*, pp. 32–3.
page 120 'lights the flame': Hawthorne, 'Leçon de Philo', in *Contingent Loves*, p. 67; Sylvie Le Bon de Beauvoir refers to Beauvoir's force and vitality as 'a living flame', interview with Sylvie Le Bon de Beauvoir, 21 April 2005.
page 120 'At first it was Olga . . .': Beauvoir, *Prime of Life*, p. 227.
page 120 'You are much too close . . .': Beauvoir to Olga Kosackiewicz, July 1934 (undated), Sylvie Le Bon de Beauvoir archives, quoted in Hazel Rowley, *Tête-à-Tête: Simone de Beauvoir and Jean-Paul Sartre* (HarperCollins, 2005), p. 54.
page 121 'I want you to know . . .': ibid.

page 121 'felt himself united body and soul . . .': Sartre, *Baudelaire* (Gallimard, 1947), p. 18 (my translation).

page 121 'When you have a son . . .': ibid. p.19.

page 122 '*Je suis un autre* . . .': ibid., p. 22.

page 122 'which was in itself reason . . .': Paul Nizan, quoted by Olivier Todd, *Un fils rebelle* (Grasset 1981), pp. 65–6; Todd found Nizan's portrait of Sartre as Lange 'biased but revelatory'.

page 123 'It was [Lange's] fate . . .': quotations from Paul Nizan, *Le Cheval de Troie* (1935), in Moreau, *Sartre, voyageur sans billet*, pp. 60–62 (my translation).

page 124 '*Un événement m'est arrivé*, something happened to me . . .': Sartre, *Nausea*, p. 183.

page 124 'I *was* the root . . .': ibid., p. 188.

page 124 'When the town dies': ibid., p. 221–2.

Chapter 13: Berlin

page 126 '*Les Juifs* . . .': Beauvoir, *La Force de l'âge*, p. 191, *Prime of Life*, p. 165.

page 126 'like altars . . .': John Lehmann, *Christopher Isherwood: A Personal Memoir* (New York: Henry Holt and Co., 1987), p. 13.

page 127 'You see, *mon petit camarade*': Beauvoir, *La Force de l'âge*, p. 157, *Prime of Life*, p. 135.

page 127 'I counted on my power of speech . . .': Sartre, *War Diaries*, pp. 284–5.

page 128 'Most of the time we have no choice . . .': Gerassi, *Jean-Paul Sartre*, p. 120.

page 128 'A strong sensual passion . . .': Sartre, *War Diaries*, p. 284.

page 128 'There's one half of humanity . . .': ibid., p. 281.

page 129 'What does it *really* mean . . .': Beauvoir, *Prime of Life*, p. 165.

page 129 'did not look as if it were crushed . . .': ibid., p. 180.

page 129 'Otherwise we would have had . . .': ibid.

page 129 'If there's another war . . .': Beauvoir, *Prime of Life*, p. 192.

page 130 'Despite all the efforts by my grandfather . . .': Gerassi, *Jean-Paul Sartre*, p. 120.

page 131 'The true condition . . .': Beauvoir, *Prime of Life*, p. 193.

page 131 'I met her . . .': ibid., p. 184.

page 131 'I was always free . . .': Gerassi, *Jean-Paul Sartre*, p. 105.

page 132 'This affair neither took me by surprise . . .': Beauvoir, *Prime of Life*, p. 184.

page 132 'I've had three . . .': Sartre, *War Diaries*, p. 328.

page 132 'I saw everything . . .': ibid., p. 184.

page 132 'tabula rasa . . .': Sartre, *Oeuvres romanesques*, p. 1728.

page 132 'All consciousness . . .': Sartre, *War Diaries*, p. 232.

page 133 'disciple . . .': ibid., p. 184.

page 133 'The Ego . . .': 'La Transcendance de l'ego; esquisse d'une description phénoménologique', in *Recherches philosophiques*, Vol. 6, 1936–7, republished Paris: Librairie Vin, 1965; *The Transcendence of the Ego*, pp. 85–123, translated by Forrest Williams and Robert Kirkpatrick (New York: Farrar, Straus, & Giroux, n.d.), p. 93.

page 133 'Every consciousness . . .': Sartre, *War Diaries*, p. 232.

page 133 The rejection of rationalism: Axel Madsen, *Hearts and Minds: The Common Journey of Simone de Beauvoir and Jean-Paul Sartre* (New York: William Morrow and Co.,1977), p. 64.

page 134 'Didn't you meet . . .': Beauvoir, *Prime of Life*, p. 184.
page 135 'If I needed . . . .': ibid., p. 158.
page 135 '*rouges, dorés* . . .': Beauvoir, *La Force de l'âge*, p. 228.
page 135 'Is it absolutely . . .': Beauvoir, *She Came to Stay*, p. 27.
page 135 'I only remember . . .': ibid., p 13.
page 136 '[Xavière] had not let go . . .': ibid., p. 246.
page 136 'tea, honey and flesh . . .': ibid., p. 148.
page 136 'She could think . . .': ibid., p. 246.
page 136 'The smiles . . .': Beauvoir, *Prime of Life*, p. 230.
page 136 '*très peu*': interview with Sylvie Le Bon de Beauvoir, 29 November 2005.

Chapter 14: Bewitched

page 137 'We fell, the Beaver and I . . .': Sartre, *War Diaries*, p. 78.
page 137 'What are you doing . . .': Beauvoir, *Prime of Life*, p. 149.
page 138 'Hemingway's lovers . . .': ibid., p. 138.
page 138 'with thick black . . .': Sartre, *Nausea*, pp. 249–51.
page 139 'beautiful and hard . . .': ibid., p. 252.
page 139 'To free oneself . . .': Justin O'Brien, introduction to *The Journals of André Gide, vol 1: 1889–1913* (Secker & Warburg, 1947), p. ix.
page 139 'the Communist ideal . . .': ibid, p. xii.
page 139 'Thus, paradoxically . . .': Beauvoir, *Prime of Life*, p. 141.
page 140 '*On ne fait qu'un*': Beauvoir, *La Force de l'âge,* pp. 166–8, *Prime of Life*, pp. 143–5.
page 141 'a lie to oneself . . .': Sartre, *Being and Nothingness*, first published as *L'Etre et le Néant* (Gallimard, 1943) translated by Hazel Barnes (Methuen, 1958), pp. 48–9, 55–6.
page 141 'There is myself . . .': ibid.
page 141 'We rejoiced . . .': Beauvoir, *Prime of Life*, p. 128.
page 141 'I put life first . . .': Beauvoir, *La Force de l'âge,* p. 168 (my translation).
page 142 'I did not regard . . .': Beauvoir, *Prime of Life*, p. 221.
page 142 'How can anyone . . .': Beauvoir, *She Came to Stay*, p. 49.
page 143 'An effort . . .': ibid., p. 45.
page 143 'I'm not an intellectual . . .': ibid., p. 54.
page 143 'In the red-light . . .': ibid., p.10.
page 143 'What were we really . . .': Beauvoir, *Prime of Life*, p. 157.
page 144 'I was recaptured . . .': Sartre, *War Diaries*, p. 77.
page 145 'A monster . . .': Sartre, *Nausea*, p. 116.
page 145 'I know what the matter with me is . . .': Beauvoir, *Prime of Life*, p. 210.
page 146 'Psychology was not . . .': ibid., p. 213.
page 146 'about our respective . . .': Colette Audry, *La Statue* (Paris: Gallimard, 1983), p. 212.
page 146 'I loathe being touched': Sartre, *The Age of Reason*, translated by Eric Sutton (Penguin, 1961), p. 56, first published as *L'Âge de Raison* (Gallimard, 1945).
page 147 'I was at the nadir . . .': Sartre, *War Diaries*, p. 78.
page 148 'I do not understand . . .': Marthe Kosakiewicz to Beauvoir, 11 August 1935; Sylvie Le Bon de Beauvoir archives, in Hazel Rowley, *Tête-à-Tête*, p. 57.

page 148 'By her *maladresse* . . .' Beauvoir, *Prime of Life*, p. 243, *La Force de l'âge*, p. 278 (translation modified).

page 150 'A violent and undefined . . .': Sartre, *Age of Reason*, p. 58.

page 150 'vast, empty beach . . .': Beauvoir, *Prime of Life*, p. 240.

page 150 'She became . . .': ibid., p. 242.

Chapter 15 : The Trio

page 151 'Each conscience . . .': Hegel. This quotation was chosen by Beauvoir as the epigraph to *L'Invitée*.

page 151 'The anguish . . .': Beauvoir, *She Came to Stay*, p. 126.

page 152 'with water . . .': ibid., p. 81.

page 152 'They were ageing . . .': ibid., p. 139.

page 152 'I frequently told myself . . .': Beauvoir, *Prime of Life*, p. 242.

page 153 'short stories . . .': Sartre, *War Diaries*, p. 145. Sartre lost 'Le Soleil de minuit'.

page 153 'Dépaysement': short story in Sartre, *Oeuvres Romanesques*, ed. Michel Contat and Michel Rybalka (Gallimard: Bibliothèque de la Pléiade, 1981), appendix 1, p. 1549.

page 154 'I therefore determined . . .': Beauvoir, *Prime of Life*, p. 241, *La Force de l'âge*, p. 276.

page 154 '*les rapports humains* . . .': Beauvoir, *La Force de l'âge*, p. 278.

page 154 'Henceforth, Xavière . . .': Beauvoir, *She Came to Stay*, p. 112.

page 154 'an old corpse': ibid., p. 160.

page 154 'When I created . . .': Beauvoir, *Prime of Life*, p. 242.

page 155 'the positions of Pompeii': in Sartre, 'Dépaysement', *Oeuvres Romanesques*, Appendix I, pp. 1549–55 (my translation).

page 156 'He was nineteen . . .': Beauvoir, Prime of Life, p. 246.

page 157 'Sartre painted . . .': Beauvoir, *La Force de l'âge*, p. 282, n. 1

page 157 'handsome, hesitant . . .': Sartre, *War Diaries*, pp. 273–4.

page 157 'He did not possess . . .': Beauvoir, *Prime of Life*, p. 246.

page 157 Sylvie Le Bon confirms that Olga's marriage certificate (in the *mairie* of the sixth *arrondissement*) is incorrect. As her birth certificate was in the USSR, she was able to fabricate her date of birth as 6 November 1917, to make herself look younger than Bost. Rowley, *Tête-à-Tête*, p. 359, n. 30.

page 157 'nymph-like': Sartre, *War Diaries*, p. 276.

page 158 'J'étais terrifiée': Beauvoir, *La Force de l'âge*, p. 292.

page 158 'It seems queer . . .': Beauvoir, *She Came to Stay*, p. 97.

page 159 'You can rely on us . . .': ibid., p. 105, *L'Invitée*, p. 135 (translation modified).

page 159 'You both have . . .': ibid., p. 57.

page 159 'It was an awful . . .': quoted in Bair, *Simone de Beauvoir*, p. 194.

page 159 '[Olga's] role . . .': Beauvoir, *Prime of Life*, p. 257, *La Force de l'âge*, p. 294 (translation modified).

page 160 'The crowd was moving . . .': Moreau, *Sartre*, p. 23 (my translation).

page 160 'I was well aware . . .': Sartre, interview no. 11, Gerassi, *Jean-Paul Sartre*, p. 124.

page 161 'Naples: just big . . .': Sartre to Olga Kosackiewicz, Summer 1936, *Witness to My Life*, p. 51.

page 161 'The Beaver was . . .': ibid, p. 57.

page 161 '*un gâteau* . . .': Sartre, 'Dépaysement', *Oeuvres Romanesques*, p. 1544.

page 163 'Friends, comrades . . .': Gerassi, Jean-Paul Sartre, p. 123.

page 165 'wobbly and alone': Carolyn Smith, *Cutting it Out: A Journey through Psychotherapy and Self-Harm* (published by Jessica Kingsley, 2006); 'Unkindest Cut of All', *The Times*, 4 February 2006.

page 165 The scene Beauvoir paints: see Beauvoir, *Prime of Life*, p. 258.

page 165 'Françoise could not help . . .': Beauvoir, *She Came to Stay*, pp. 284–5, *L'Invitée*, p. 354 (translation modified).

page 166 'Mathieu looked . . . .': Sartre, *Age of Reason*, pp. 194–5, *L'Âge de Raison*, p. 240.

page 167 The deeper the cut: conversation with psychiatrist Dr Jonathan Pimm, University College London, 16 June 2006; Dr Pimm conducted a 'psychological autopsy' on Olga in which he emphasized the significant division between superficial and deep self-harmers, and that 'deep cutting is a sign that patients have sustained profound psychological damage in early life'. In Britain, 15–20 per cent of self-harmers go on to kill themselves, and after one episode of self-harm the likelihood of suicide is multiplied one-hundred-fold.

page 167 'positively maniacal': Beauvoir, *Prime of Life*, p. 258.

page 167 '*ce rictus maniaque*': Beauvoir, *L'Invitée*, p. 354.

page 167 '*visage maniaque*': Sartre, *L'âge de raison*, p. 239.

page 167 'Be careful . . .': Beauvoir, *She Came to Stay*, p. 343.

page 167 'Sartre was already . . .': Beauvoir, interview in Gerassi, *Jean-Paul Sartre*, p. 99.

Chapter 16: Notoriety

page 169 'Why do you write . . .': Mme Mancy to Sartre, quoted in *Correspondance croisée*, p. 239.

page 169 'Now you seem . . .': Sartre to Beauvoir, April 1937, *Witness to My Life*, p. 76.

page 169 'Someone had taken charge . . .': Beauvoir, *Prime of Life*, p. 293.

page 170 'two consciousnesses . . .': Sartre to Beauvoir, 15 September 1937, *Witness to My Life*, p. 122.

page 171 'I didn't much care . . .': Beauvoir, *Adieux*, pp. 304–6.

page 173 'Being powerless . . .': Beauvoir, Prime of Life, p. 294.

page 172 The sudden death of Maxim Gorky: see Simon Sebag Montefiore, *Stalin: The Court of the Red Tsar* (Phoenix, 2004), pp. 191–2; Gorky's medical records in the NKVD archives suggest that he in fact died naturally of TB and pneumonia.

page 172 'I believe . . .': André Gide, quoted in Justin O'Brien, introduction to *The Journals of André Gide, vol. 1* (Secker & Warburg, 1947), p. xiii.

page 172 'deeply disconcerted': Beauvoir, *Prime of Life*, p. 288.

page 172 'We in the West . . .': Moreau, *Sartre*, p. 302 (my translation).

page 172 '*Mon cher amour* . . .': Sartre to Beauvoir, Laon, April 1937; Berne, *Sartre*, p. 46.

page 172 'Dear Toulouse . . .': Sartre to Simone Jollivet, March 1937, *Witness to My Life*, p. 75.

page 173 'Enquire of Pierre Bost . . .': Beauvoir, *Prime of Life*, p. 299.

page 173 'I made my magnificent . . .': Beauvoir, *La Force de l'âge*, pp. 339–42, *Prime of Life*, pp. 296–9; *Witness to My Life*, p. 92.

page 174 'At the precise moment . . .': Sartre, *War Diaries*, p. 78.

page 175 'There are times . . .': Sartre–Beauvoir, 3 May 1937, *Witness to My Life*, p. 100.

page 175 'and very appealing . . .': Sartre to Beauvoir, 26 April 1937, ibid., p. 91.

page 175 'I just wish . . .': Beauvoir to Sartre, probably early 1937, *Letters to Sartre*, p. 8.

page 175 'And I love you . . .': Sartre to Beauvoir, 3 May 1937, *Witness to My Life*, p. 99.

page 176 'You terrorize me . . .': Sartre to Beauvoir, 'Wednesday', ibid., p. 105.

page 176 'Who is this new Jean-Paul?': André Gide to Jean Paulhan, 27 July 1937, Jean Paulhan Archives, quoted in Cohen-Solal, *Sartre*, p. 120.

page 176 'One of the most striking . . .': Sartre, *Oeuvres Romanesques*, pp. 1701–11.

page 176 'I'll grow . . .': Sartre, 'L'Enfance d'un Chef [The Childhood of a Leader]', *The Wall*, translated by Lloyd Alexander (New York: New Directions Paperback, 1975), p. 144.

page 177 'But why do you . . .': Mme Mancy to Sartre, quoted by Simone de Beauvoir, 7 February 1937, *Simone de Beauvoir–Jacques-Laurent Bost, Correspondance croisée*, p. 239.

page 177 'A family . . .': Sartre to Beauvoir, 3–4 September 1934, *Witness to My Life*, p. 44.

page 177 'It's not always . . .': Sartre to Beauvoir, September 1937, ibid., pp. 142–4.

page 177 'Lola lies to herself': Sartre to Serge Roullet, 10 January 1967, Contat and Rybalka, *Les Écrits de Sartre*, pp. 70–71 (my translation).

page 178 'I'd like to talk . . .': 'Lettres à Wanda', in 'Témoins de Sartre', *Les Temps modernes*, nos. 531–3, 1990, quoted in Moreau, *Sartre*, p. 115 (my translation).

page 179 'I'm delighted . . .': ibid., p. 134.

page 179 'obscure . . . artificial . . .': Sartre to Beauvoir, 26 April 1937, *Witness to My Life*, p. 90.

page 179 'I showed you . . .': Bonal and Ribowska, *Simone de Beauvoir*, p. 51 (my translation).

page 179 'little voice . . .': Sartre to Beauvoir, 15 September 1937, *Witness to My Life*, p. 128.

page 180 'Harmony . . .': Beauvoir, *Prime of Life*, p. 260.

page 180 'We were all like snakes . . .': Bair, *Simone de Beauvoir*, p. 194.

page 180 'the pleasure . . .': Sartre to Beauvoir, 5 May 1937, *Witness to My Life*, p. 106.

Chapter 17: Breaking the Rules

page 181 'Bienenfeld arrived . . .': Beauvoir to J.-L. Bost, 28 November 1938, *Correspondance croisée*, pp. 135–6, 5 February 1939, p. 233.

page 181 'Maman didn't want . . .': interview with Bianca Bienenfeld Lamblin, 8 November 2004.

page 181 'We were all thrilled . . .': Bianca Lamblin, *A Disgraceful Affair: Simone de Beauvoir, Jean-Paul Sartre, Bianca Lamblin*, translated by Julie Plovnick (Northeastern University Press: Boston, 1996), p. 15; Lamblin, *Mémoires d'une jeune fille dérangée* (Paris: Éditions Balland, 1993), p. 23.

page 182 'She came in . . .': interview with Sarah Hirschmann, 11 October 2002.

page 183 'I expected to wait . . .': interview with Bianca Bienenfeld Lamblin, 8 November 2004.

page 183 'She was like . . .': Lamblin, *A Disgraceful Affair*, p. 19.

page 184 'The one who was . . .': ibid., p. 23.

page 184 '*Elle était frustrée* . . .': interview with Bianca Bienenfeld Lamblin, 8 November 2004.

page 184 'She was a little . . .': ibid.

page 184 'I found Bost . . .': Beauvoir to Sartre, 15 July 1938, *Letters to Sartre*, p. 16.

page 185 'I kissed that fiery girl . . .': Sartre to Beauvoir, 14 July 1938, *Witness to My Life*, p. 151.

page 186 'She wanted to give me . . .': Sartre to Beauvoir, [July] 1938, ibid., p. 156.

page 186 'You're very sweet . . .': Beauvoir to Sartre, 22 July 1938, *Letters to Sartre*, pp. 19–20.

page 186 'I slept with Little Bost . . .': Beauvoir to Sartre, 27 July 1938, ibid., p. 21.

page 186 'Why on earth . . .': Sartre to Beauvoir, *Witness to My Life*, pp. 157–8.

Chapter 18: In the Shadow of War

page 188 'I didn't want to admit . . .': Beauvoir, *Prime of Life*, p. 319.

page 188 'I was drunk with joy . . .': Beauvoir to J.-L. Bost, 30 July 1938, *Correspondance croisée*, pp. 32–3 (my translation).

page 189 'Sartre! It's the great Sartre': Beauvoir to J.-L. Bost, 31 July 1938, ibid., p. 35.

page 189 '*Je t'aime avec violence*': Beauvoir to J.-L. Bost, 3 August 1938, ibid., p. 49.

page 190 'What would Bost say . . .': Beauvoir to J.-L. Bost, 30 August 1938, ibid., p. 66.

page 190 '*Des remords, pas de regrets*': Sylvie Le Bon de Beauvoir, *Avant-propos*, ibid., p 12.

page 190 'no intention . . .': Beauvoir, preface to *The Prime of Life*, p. 8.

page 190 'Without doubt [*sans doute le silence sur sa liaison*] . . .': Le Bon, *Avant-propos*, *Correspondance croisée*, p. 12 (my translation); in editing and publishing this important correspondence, Le Bon has remedied this omission, but the letters still await an English translator.

page 191 '*Une vieille dame* . . .': Beauvoir to J.-L. Bost, 30 August 1938, Le Bon, *Correspondance croisée*, p. 69.

page 191 'But now I've put matters in order . . .': Beauvoir to J.-L. Bost, 25 August 1938, ibid., p. 60.

page 192 'southern hell': Beauvoir, *Prime of Life*, p. 334.

page 192 'I refused to admit . . .': ibid., p. 318.

page 192 'Perhaps this is the place . . .': Sartre to Beauvoir [September], *Witness to My Life*, pp. 175–6.

page 192 'O my beloved . . .': Beauvoir to J.-L. Bost, 21 September 1938, *Correspondance croisée*, p. 85.

page 192 'Bost was convinced . . .': Beauvoir, *Prime of Life*, p. 321.

page 193 'I retain only . . .': ibid.

page 193 'I saw him . . .': interview with Bianca Bienenfeld Lamblin, 28 April 2005.

page 193 'voluble, flirtatious . . .': Lamblin, *A Disgraceful Affair*, p. 34.

page 193 '*un peu de phénoménologie*': Beauvoir to J.-L. Bost, 7 November 1938, *Correspondance croisée*, p. 93.

page 193 'mental faculties . . .': Sartre to Beauvoir, [end of July] 1938, *Witness to My Life*, p. 172.

page 194 'I played the whore . . .': Sartre to Beauvoir, Sunday morning, [July] 1938, ibid., p. 167.

page 194 'I froze her out . . .': Sartre to Beauvoir, [end of July] 1938, ibid., p. 172.

page 194 'the scent of a masterpiece': Sartre to Beauvoir, [September] 1938, ibid., p. 179.

page 194 *Nausea* defined existence: Sartre to Jean Paulhan, Monday [autumn] 1938, ibid., p. 180.

page 194 'He's read my second chapter . . .': Beauvoir to J.-L. Bost, [9 November] 1938, *Correspondance croisée*, p. 104.

page 194 'Only later, when he had won': Beauvoir, *Prime of Life*, p. 338.

page 195 'throat was as tight . . .': ibid., p. 340.

page 195 'Spend the greatest . . .': Beauvoir to J.-L. Bost, [11 November] 1938, *Correspondance croisée*, p. 106.

page 196 'I went into the lavatory . . .': Beauvoir to J.-L. Bost, [24 November] 1938, ibid., p. 122.

page 196 'You make me afraid': J.-L. Bost to Beauvoir, 29 November 1938, ibid., p. 138.

page 196 'a sort of faded . . .': Lamblin, *A Disgraceful Affair*, p. 36.

page 197 'I was not so strongly . . .': interview with Bianca Bienenfeld Lamblin, 8 November 2004.

page 197 'It was as if he wanted to brutalize . . .': Lamblin, *A Disgraceful Affair*, p. 43.

page 197 'He wanted to brutalize . . .': interview with Bianca Bienenfeld Lamblin, 28 April 2005.

page 198 'Simone was the princess . . .': ibid., 8 November 2004.

page 198 'complete communism . . .': Beauvoir to J.-L. Bost [18 January] 1939, *Correspondance croisée*, p. 207.

page 198 'Our future . . .': Sartre to Louise Védrine (the name Beauvoir gave Bianca in Sartre's letters, which deeply offended Bianca, as it was the name of Beauvoir's former maid), July 1939, *Witness to My Life*, p. 190.

page 198 'I want to stress . . .': Sartre to Louise Védrine, [July] 1939, ibid., p. 191.

page 199 'very nice': Sartre to Beauvoir, [July] 1939, ibid., pp. 200–202.

page 199 'the nothingness of the flesh': Sartre to Beauvoir, [June] 1939, ibid., p. 185.

page 199 'the obscenity of Shakespeare': Albert Camus, review of *Le Mur*, *Algér republicain*, 12 March 1939, Michel Contat, *Sartre: L'Invention de la Liberté* (Paris: Les Éditions Textuel), p. 54.

page 199 'God is not an artist . . .': Sartre, 'M. François Mauriac et la Liberté', *Situations I* (Gallimard, 1947), p. 52.

page 199 'We lead completely separate . . .': Beauvoir to J.-L. Bost, 17 February 1939, *Correspondance croisée*, p. 257.

page 199 'fragile little iron-willed . . .': Sartre to Beauvoir, [June] 1939,*Witness to My Life*, p. 183.

page 199 'The plot moves . . .': Beauvoir to J.-L. Bost, 22 February 1939, *Correspondance croisée*, p. 262.

page 200 'In the end I think . . .': Beauvoir to J.-L. Bost, [4 June] 1939, ibid., p. 386.

page 200 'I find that frighteningly obscene': J.-L. Bost to Beauvoir, [7 June] 1939, ibid., p. 391.

page 201 'I have only *one* sensual life . . .': Beauvoir to J.-L. Bost, [8 June] 1939, *Correspondance croisée*, p. 397.

page 201 *'Je ne regrette rien'*: J.-L. Bost to Beauvoir, [19 August] 1939, ibid., p. 414.

page 201 *'J'ai une espèce de remords*, I have a kind of remorse . . .': Beauvoir to J.-L. Bost, 6 June 1939, ibid., p. 390.

page 201 'I saw the little blue flowers . . .': Beauvoir to J.-L. Bost, [12 April] 1939, ibid., p. 325.

page 201 'Don't lose heart . . .': Sartre to Louise Védrine, 31 August 1939, *Witness to My Life*, p. 225.

page 202 'Everything is ready, *Tout est prêt* . . .': J.-L. Bost to Beauvoir, [25 August] 1939, *Correspondance croisée*, p. 419.

page 202 'In 1939, History . . .': Beauvoir, *Prime of Life*, p. 359.

Chapter 19: Women in Love

page 205 'I feel abandoned . . . [*On se sent abandonné de Dieu et des homes*]': Beauvoir to J.-L. Bost, 9 October 1939, *Correspondance croisée*, p. 546.

page 206 'That Jew, Pieter . . .': Sartre to Beauvoir, Tuesday, 5 September 1939, *Witness to My Life*, p. 233. Sartre referred to his letters as 'a witness to my life', as Beauvoir notes in her preface, but he also described Beauvoir as his 'witness'. The phrase recalls Adèle Hugo's memoir of her husband: *Victor Hugo, by a Witness to His Life*. Hugo's funeral was the largest of any literary figure of the nineteenth century, Sartre's the largest in the twentieth century. It was a comparison that Sartre, who liked to keep company with the immortals, would have relished.

page 206 'I've never had . . .': Sartre to Beauvoir, 7 September 1939, *Witness to My Life*, p. 237.

page 206 'hemmed in . . .': Sartre to Beauvoir, 3 September 1939, ibid., p. 230.

page 206 'Eat up . . .': Sartre to Beauvoir, 9 September 1939, ibid., p. 240.

page 207 'We are respected . . .': Sartre to Beauvoir, 23 September 1939, ibid., p. 262.

page 207 'Would you send me . . .': Sartre to Beauvoir, 12 September 1939, ibid., p. 243.

page 207 'being-for-the-war': Sartre to Beauvoir, 28 September 1939, ibid., p. 267.

page 207 'Whoever reads . . .': Sartre to Beauvoir, 16 September 1939, ibid., p. 249.

page 207 'abandoned in the world . . .': Sartre, 24 November 1939, *War Diaries*, p. 38.

page 207 '*Video meliora* . . .': Ovid, *Metamorphoses*, VII, 20.

page 207 Franz Kafka's *Das Schloss* (1926), translated as *The Castle* (1937), has been interpreted as an exercise in Kierkegaardian existentialist theology; it portrays society as pointless and irrational.

page 207 'Was it quiet . . .': Sartre to Beauvoir, 14 September 1939, *Witness to My Life*, p. 250.

page 208 'I felt a profound peace . . .': Sartre to Beauvoir, 12 September 1939, ibid., p. 241.

page 208 'If the war . . .': Sartre to Beauvoir, 13 September 1939, ibid., p. 247.

page 208 'We two are one . . .': Sartre to Beauvoir, 2 October 1939, ibid., p. 275.

page 208 'My dearest love . . .': Sartre to Beauvoir, 6 October 1939, ibid., p. 280.

page 209 '*have the two* . . .' : Sartre to Beauvoir, 26 September 1939, ibid., p. 264.

page 209 'On the occasion . . .': Sartre, *War Diaries*, p. 139.

page 209 Gerassi and Beauvoir slept together: interview with Sylvie Le Bon de Beauvoir, 29 November 2005.

page 209 'I have the impression . . .': Beauvoir to J.-L. Bost, 3 September 1939, *Correspondance croisée*, p. 439.

page 210 'I'm scared . . .': Beauvoir to Sartre, 7 September 1939, *Letters to Sartre*, p. 43.

page 210 'God knows, he repels me': Beauvoir to Sartre, 8 September 1939, *Letters to Sartre*, p. 47.

page 210 'Kos is a magnificent . . .': Beauvoir to Sartre, 10 September 1939, *Letters to Sartre*, p. 52.

page 211 'I don't know . . .': J.-L. Bost to Beauvoir, 17 September 1939, *Correspondance croisée*, p. 469.

page 211 '*Je voudrais que vous* . . .': J.-L. Bost to Beauvoir, 16 September 1939, ibid., p. 467.

page 211 'I'm almost convinced . . .': Beauvoir to Sartre, 17 September 1939, *Letters to Sartre*, p. 63.

page 211 Privileging happiness: Beauvoir to Sartre, 20 September 1939, ibid., p. 72.

page 212 'femininity is neither . . .': Beauvoir, *Prime of Life*, p. 367.

page 212 'completely mutilated . . .': Beauvoir to J.-L. Bost, 25 September 1939, *Correspondance croisée*, p. 500.

page 212 'She's lying': Beauvoir to J.-L. Bost, 20 September 1939, ibid., p. 483.

page 212 '*Sale bonne femme* . . .': Beauvoir to J.-L. Bost, 21 September 1939, ibid., p. 486.

page 212 'B. arrived . . .': Beauvoir to J.-L. Bost, 22 September 1939, ibid., p. 491.

page 213 'we petted . . .': Beauvoir to Sartre, 22 September 1939, *Letters to Sartre*, p. 77.

page 213 'You will let me . . .': Beauvoir to Sartre, 21 September 1939, ibid., p. 74.

page 213 'We had so much happiness . . .': Beauvoir to Sartre, 5 October 1939, ibid., p. 95.

page 214 'I already have turbans . . .': Beauvoir to J.-L. Bost, 29 September 1939, *Correspondance croisée*, p. 512.

page 214 'I have the most wonderful . . .': Beauvoir to Sartre, 23 September 1939, *Letters to Sartre*, p. 78.

page 214 'Better wait until . . .': Beauvoir to J.-L. Bost, 5 October 1939, *Correspondance croisée*, p. 531.

page 214 '*dédoublement* . . . kingdom of the shades': Beauvoir to J.-L. Bost, 10 October 1939, ibid., p. 551.

page 214 'as precious as the devil . . .': J.-L. Bost to Beauvoir, 8 October 1939, ibid., p. 545.

page 215 '*C'est gênant* . . .': Beauvoir to J.-L. Bost, 9 October 1939, ibid., p. 546.

page 215 '*Je vous aime tellement* . . .': Beauvoir to J.-L. Bost, 11 October 1939, ibid., p. 557.

page 215 'pulled me on to the bed . . .': Beauvoir to Sartre, 11 October 1939, *Lettres à Sartre*, p. 178, *Letters*, p. 111.

page 216 'It's so unfair . . .': Beauvoir to J.-L. Bost, 12 October 1939, *Correspondance croisée*, p. 561.

page 216 '*le plus grand menteur du monde*': J.-L. Bost to Beauvoir, 1939.

page 216 'a little tamed animal [*une petite bête apprivoisée*]': Beauvoir to Sartre, 15 October 1939, *Lettres à Sartre*, p. 191.

page 216 'When I am sixty . . .': Beauvoir to J.-L. Bost, 22 October 1939, *Correspondance croisée*, p. 594.

page 216 'You look like a lesbian, a coke-addict . . .': J.-L. Bost to Beauvoir, 25 October 1939, ibid., p. 608.

page 216 'The strength of . . . .': Beauvoir to Sartre, 10 November 1939, *Letters*, p. 155.

page 217 'I am physiologically . . .': Beauvoir to J.-L. Bost, 20 December 1939, *Correspondance croisée*, p. 831.

page 217 *'You're not allowed . . .'*: Sartre to Beauvoir, 2 October 1939, *Witness to My Life*, p. 275.

page 217 *'Merde!'*: Sartre, *L'âge de raison*, p. 21, *The Age of Reason*, p. 15.

page 218 'for the blister . . .': Sartre, *The Age of Reason*, p. 44, *L'âge de raison*, p. 62.

page 218 'I can hardly endure . . .': Sartre, *War Journal*, pp. 122, 138.

page 218 'We were so intent on love . . .': Sartre to Beauvoir, 7 November 1939, *Witness to My Life*, p. 329.

page 218 'your presence . . .': Sartre to Beauvoir, 6 November 1939, ibid., p. 327.

page 219 'frothing with rage': Sartre to Beauvoir, 8 November 1939, ibid., p. 330.

page 219 'I shall soon . . .': Beauvoir, *Prime of Life*, p. 418.

page 219 'I'm on holiday . . .': ibid.

page 219 'I've absolutely decided . . .': Beauvoir to J.-L. Bost, 31 October 1939, *Correspondance croisée*, p. 632.

page 219 'I don't want you . . .': J.-L. Bost to Beauvoir, 4 November 1939, ibid., p. 654.

page 220 *'un peu trop sur la bouche . . .'*: J.-L. Bost to Beauvoir, 6 November 1939, ibid., p. 661.

page 220 'Everyone was on heat . . .': Beauvoir to J.-L. Bost, 14 October 1939, ibid., p. 565.

page 220 'Sartre says . . .': Beauvoir to J.-L. Bost, 15 December 1939, ibid., p. 814.

page 220 'bare-legged . . .': Beauvoir–Sartre, 7 November 1939, ibid., p. 150.

page 220 'Normally it's only . . .': Beauvoir to Sartre, 10 December 1939, *Letters to Sartre*, p. 202.

Chapter 20: The Turn of the Screw

page 221 'Drunk as donkeys': Journal de Bost, 24 December 1939, *Correspondance croisée*, p. 843.

page 221 'The leaves fall . . .': Sartre, *War Diaries*, p. 29.

page 221 'Never have I . . .': Beauvoir, 18 December 1939, *Journal de Guerre*, ed., Sylvie Le Bon de Beauvoir (Gallimard, 1990), p. 203.

page 222 'Well, Sartre . . .': Beauvoir to J.-L. Bost, 27 December 1939, *Correspondance croisée*, p. 854.

page 222 'Threesomes . . .': Beauvoir to Sartre, 11 November 1939, *Letters to Sartre*, p. 157.

page 223 'those ten years . . .': Beauvoir to Sartre, 12 November 1939, ibid., p. 160.

page 223 'stop the affair . . .': Beauvoir to Sartre, 17 December 1939, ibid., p. 217.

page 223 'wailing on the wall . . .': Beauvoir to J.-L. Bost, 10 November 1939, *Correspondance croisée*, p. 673.

page 223 'nights of passion . . .': Beauvoir to J.-L. Bost, 13 November 1939, ibid., p. 690.

page 223 'I think that . . .': J.-L. Bost to Beauvoir, 15 November 1939, ibid., p. 696.

page 224 a caricature of herself: Beauvoir to J.-L. Bost, 11 November 1939, ibid., p. 678.

page 224 'sickened by passion': Beauvoir to Sartre, 12 November 1939, *Letters*, p. 161.

page 224 'the first time . . .': Beauvoir to Sartre, 22 December 1939, ibid., p. 226.

page 224 'I asked her . . .': Beauvoir to Sartre, 5 January 1940, ibid., p. 242.

page 225 'Her body had . . .': Beauvoir to Sartre, 12 January 1940, ibid., p. 252.

page 225 'sentences so terrible': interview with Bianca Bienenfeld Lamblin, 8 November 2004.

page 225 'rid France . . .': Bair, *Simone de Beauvoir*, p. 242.

page 225 'She weeps . . .': Beauvoir, 10 December 1939, *Journal de Guerre*, translated by Lamblin, A *Disgraceful Affair*, pp. 70–71.

page 225 'so perfect and charming . . .': Beauvoir to Sartre, 14 January 1940, *Letters*, p. 255.

page 225 'grew languid . . .': Beauvoir to Sartre, 24 January 1940, ibid., p. 268.

page 225 '*Elle me plaît physiquement* . . .':Beauvoir, 25 January 1940, *Journal de Guerre*, p. 258.

page 225 'Never have I felt . . .': Sartre to Beauvoir, 15 November 1939, *Witness to My Life*, p. 345.

page 226 'this war . . .': Sartre to Beauvoir, 20 December 1939, ibid., p. 419.

page 226 'Everyone finds me . . .': Beauvoir, 1 February 1940, *Journal de Guerre*, p. 162.

page 226 'How united . . .': Beauvoir, February 1940, *Journal de Guerre*, p. 165.

page 226 '*une profiteuse de guerre*': Beauvoir to J.-L. Bost, 16 November 1939, *Correspondance croisée*, p. 703.

page 227 'Heidegger rightly . . .': Sartre, 24 November 1939, *War Diaries*, p. 40.

page 227 'A being thrown . . .': ibid., p. 38.

page 227 '*Existenz*': Lévy, *Le Siècle de Sartre*, p. 182.

page 227 'but I must . . .': Beauvoir to J.-L. Bost, 5 February 1939, *Correspondance croisée*, pp. 232–3.

page 227 'revelation . . .': Beauvoir to J.-L. Bost, ibid., 10 February 1939, p. 244.

page 227 'scrumptious': Sartre to Beauvoir, 16 November 1939, *Witness to My Life*, p. 340.

page 227 'dared, in the postwar . . .': *Bifur*, 8, ed. du Carrefour, quoted in Lévy, *Le Siecle de Sartre*, pp. 179–80 (my translation).

page 228 'Kierkegaard's image': see Murdoch, *Sartre*, p. 8.

page 228 'I can see clearly . . .': Sartre, 27 November 1939, *War Diaries*, pp. 53–4.

page 228 'I have reread . . .': Sartre, 9 January 1940, *Lettres au Castor*, vol. 2, p. 27, translation taken from Cohen-Solal, *Sartre*, p. 142.

page 228 'It takes me . . .': Sartre, *Sartre by Himself*, film directed by Alexandre Astruc and Michel Contat, translated by Richard Seaver (New York: Urizen, 1978), pp. 29–30.

page 229 'It lay there . . .': Beauvoir, *She Came to Stay*, p. 54.

page 229 When I perceive . . . : see Fullbrook and Fullbrook, *Simone de Beauvoir and Jean-Paul Sartre*, p. 111.

page 229 *The Ethics of Ambiguity*: see Margaret A. Simons, 'Beauvoir and Sartre: The philosophical relationship', *Yale French Studies*, no. 172, 1986, pp. 165–79.

page 229 looking through a keyhole: Sartre, 'The Look', *Being and Nothingness*, p. 259.

page 229 'We start with . . .': ibid., p. 364.

page 230 'mother lode': Fullbrook and Fullbrook, *Simone de Beauvoir and Jean-Paul Sartre*, p. 116.

page 230 'The Beaver has taught me something new': Sartre, 17 February 1940, *War Diaries*, p. 197.

page 230 'I feel strangely bashful . . .': Sartre, 18 February 1940, ibid., p. 208.

page 230 'Time is the opaque . . .': quoted in Fullbrook and Fullbrook, *Simone de Beauvoir and Jean-Paul Sartre*, p. 119.

page 230 'It struck me . . .': Beauvoir to Sartre, 16 February 1940, *Letters to Sartre*, p. 273.

page 231 'I am more . . .': Sartre, *War Diaries*, p. 29; 'It's true; I'm not authentic', p. 61.

page 231 'My love . . .': Beauvoir to Sartre, 27 February 1940, *Letters to Sartre*, p. 279.

page 231 '*La guerre* . . .': interview with Bianca Bienenfeld Lamblin, 28 April 2005.

page 232 'I can't believe . . .': Beauvoir, 16 February 1940, *Journal de Guerre*, p. 284.

page 232 'his precious, miraculous, fragile presence . . .': Beauvoir, 17 February 1940, ibid., p. 286.

page 232 'There's one thing . . .': Beauvoir to Sartre, 18 February 1940, *Letters to Sartre*, p. 277.

page 232 'There's something ignoble . . .' Sartre to Beauvoir, 28 February 1940, *Quiet Moments in a War: The Letters of Jean-Paul Sartre to Simone de Beauvoir 1940–1963* (Paris: 1983), translated by Lee Fahnstock and Norman MacAfee, p. 233.

page 233 '*une* histoire . . .' Beauvoir, 18 February 1940, *Journal de Guerre*, p. 287.

page 233 'I feel neither jealousy . . .' Beauvoir, 21 February 1940, *Journal de Guerre*, p. 291.

page 233 'ten days . . .' Beauvoir – Sartre, 19 March 1940, *Letters to Sartre*, p. 299.

Chapter 21: Occupation

page 235 'The reign of evil . . .': Sartre, *Iron in the Soul*, p. 95.

page 236 'I should worry . . . .': ibid., p. 79.

page 236 '50,000 and 70,000 children': Robert Gildea, *Marianne in Chains: In Search of the German Occupation of France 1940–45* (Pan Books, 2003), p. 88.

page 236 'One evening . . .': Beauvoir, *Adieux*, p. 388.

page 237 'You've come . . .': quoted in Gilbert Joseph, *Une Si Douce Occupation: Simone de Beauvoir et Jean-Paul Sartre 1940–1944* (Paris: Albin Michel, 1991), p. 29.

page 237 'Crushed by . . .': quoted in Gildea, *Marianne in Chains*, p. 43.

page 238 'I shall save . . .': Sartre, *Iron in the Soul*, p. 179.

page 238 'Mathieu turned . . .': ibid., pp. 217, 218.

page 238 'Mathieu went on . . .': ibid., p. 225.

page 238 '*la connerie* . . .': J.-L. Bost to Beauvoir, 3 February 1940, *Correspondance croisée*, p. 967.

page 238 'the man with . . .': Cohen-Solal, *Sartre*, p. 139.

page 239 'The prisoners . . .': Sartre, *Iron in the Soul*, p. 329.

page 239 'I thought . . .': Beauvoir, *Adieux*, p. 389.

page 239 'Bloody hell': ibid., p. 345.

page 239 'Perhaps Hitler . . .': Beauvoir, *Prime of Life*, p. 436.

page 239 'Not to be . . .': ibid., p. 437.

page 239 'A like-mindedness . . .': Lamblin, *A Disgraceful Affair*, p. 25.

page 240 'As far as I . . .': Beauvoir, *Prime of Life*, p. 438.

page 240 'I asked . . . .': Lamblin, *A Disgraceful Affair*, p. 77.

page 240 'a precious cloth . . .': Beauvoir, *Journal de Guerre*, p. 304.

page 240 'Would you take . . . ?': Sartre, *The Reprieve*, quoted in Lamblin, *A Disgraceful Affair*, p. 72.

page 241 'an invention . . .': Benny Lévy, interview with Jean-Paul Sartre, *Le Nouvel observateur*, March 1980, quoted in Lamblin, *A Disgraceful Affair*, p. 179.

page 241 'Why don't they . . .': ibid., p. 78.

page 241 'A guttural voice . . .': Beauvoir, *Prime of Life*, p. 444.

page 241 'the shedding of French blood . . .': ibid.

page 242 'I haven't had . . .': ibid., p. 454.

page 242 'I misconstrued . . .': ibid., p. 445.

page 243 'It is with honour . . .': quoted by Michael Curtis, *Verdict on Vichy: Power and Prejudice in the Vichy France Regime* (Weidenfeld & Nicolson, 2002), p. 12.

page 243 'opportunities for profit and pleasure': see Gildea, *Marianne in Chains*, p. 14.

page 243 'I have high hopes . . .': Sartre to Beauvoir, 8 July 1940, *Quiet Moments*, p. 233.

page 243 'I breathe . . .': Beauvoir, *Prime of Life*, p. 457.

page 243 'purely physical . . .': Sartre to Wanda, 26 May 1940, Sylvie Le Bon de Beauvoir archives, quoted in Rowley, *Tête-à-Tête*, p. 363 n. 45.

page 243 'I don't imagine . . .': Sartre to Beauvoir, 12 May 1940, *Quiet Moments*, p. 180.

page 243 Papatakis was not told: Niko Papatakis, *Tous les désespoirs sont permis* (Paris: Fayard, 2003), pp. 260–61.

page 244 'dirty Jew': Sartre, *The Age of Reason*, p. 62.

page 244 'Mathieu was barring . . .': ibid., p. 44.

page 244 the mother, and what is happening to her body: Sara Heinaman, 'The Body as an Instrument of Expression', in Claudia Card (ed.), *The Cambridge Companion to Simone de Beauvoir* (CUP, 2003), p. 66.

page 244 '*un sale type*, a dirty beast . . .': Beauvoir, *Le Sang des autres* (Gallimard, 1945), p. 125, *The Blood of Others*, translated by Yvonne Moyse and Roger Senhouse, (Penguin, 1964), p. 97.

page 244 'Oh, she said . . .': Beauvoir, *The Blood of Others*, p. 99.

page 245 'I looked at her . . . *Une avorteuse* . . .': Beauvoir, *The Blood of Others*, p. 100, *Le Sang des autres*, p. 129.

page 245 'I don't like babies': 'At the Bay', in *The Short Stories of Katherine Mansfield*, pp. 279–80, quoted in Beauvoir, *The Second Sex*, p. 537.

page 245 'I'm not a little dog . . .': Beauvoir, *Le Sang des autres*, p. 131, *The Blood of Others*, p. 102.

Chapter 22: Stalag

page 247 'I shall bend my knee . . .': Sartre, *Bariona, ou le Fils de tonnerre*, in *Écrits de Sartre*, pp. 565–633.

page 247 'I can picture you . . .': Beauvoir to Sartre, 11 July 1940, *Letters to Sartre*, p. 313.

page 247 'To be a prisoner . . .': quoted in Cohen-Solal, *Sartre*, p. 150.

page 248 'In a strange way . . .': Beauvoir, *Adieux*, p. 390.

page 248 'In the Stalag . . .': Sartre, interview with John Gerassi, 1973, quoted in *Oeuvres Romanesques*, p. lxi.

page 248 'an ugly . . .': *Les Temps modernes*, September 1982, p. 472.

page 248 'Which I found . . .': Beauvoir, *Adieux*, p. 410.

page 248 '[The Germans] can . . .': *Les Temps modernes*, September 1982, p. 457.

page 249 'Stop, gentlemen': Joseph, *Une Si Douce Occupation*, p. 73.

page 249 'I'd been repulsively . . .': Sartre to Beauvoir, 29 July 1940, *Quiet Moments*, p. 240.

page 249 'I ruled against . . .': Sartre to Beauvoir, December 1940, *Quiet Moments*, p. 244.

page 249 'It is quite advantageous . . .': Marius Perrin, *Avec Sartre au Stalag XII D* (Paris: Delarge, 1980), pp. 128–9, translation quoted in Cohen-Solal, p. 154.

page 250 'Is this the Sartre . . .': Joseph, *Une Si Douce Occupation*, p. 59.

page 250 'I want you to know . . .': Sartre to Beauvoir, December 1940, *Quiet Moments*, pp. 244–5.

page 250 the subject had been chosen . . . : Sartre, 31 October 1962, *Les Écrits de Sartre*, p. 565.

page 250 'The Germans didn't . . .': Beauvoir, *Adieux*, p. 183.

page 250 'I must be free . . .': Sartre, Scene VII, *Bariona, ou le Fils de tonnerre*, *Écrits de Sartre*, p. 627 (my translation).

page 251 'I realized . . .': *Sartre on Theatre*, ed. Michael Contat and Michael Rybalka, translated by Frank Jellinek (New York: Pantheon Books, 1976), p. 39.

page 251 'There are moments . . .': Sartre to Beauvoir, 27 May 1943, *Lettres au Castor*, p. 251, *Quiet Moments*, p. 203 (translation modified).

page 251 'Till the war . . .': Perrin, *Avec Sartre*, p. 463.

page 251 'I shall follow no one . . .': Sartre, unposted letter, quoted in Hayman, *Writing Against*, p. 158.

page 251 'Sartre does not like . . .': Perrin, *Avec Sartre*, pp. 127–8, Cohen-Solal, *Sartre*, p. 157.

page 252 'Poulou': Sartre to Beauvoir, n.d. 1940, *Quiet Moments*, p. 246.

page 252 'sad . . . dear little letters': Sartre to Beauvoir, n.d. 1940, *Quiet Moments*, p. 247.

page 252 'It was a childish falsification . . .': Joseph, *Une Si Douce Occupation*, p. 101.

Chapter 23: The New Order

page 253 'Never were we more free . . .': Sartre, 'La république du silence', in *Situations III*, pp. 11–13.

page 253 '*Ils nous prennent tout*': David Pryce-Jones, *Paris in the Third Reich: A History of the German Occupation, 1940–1944* (Collins, 1981), p. 94.

page 254 'car crash': Léon Blum compared France to an 'accident victim', Robert Paxton, *Vichy France: Old Guard and New Order, 1940–1944* (Barrie & Jenkins, 1972), p. 237.

page 254 Glouglou: nickname of the janitor, Pierre Théodore, in Serge Lifar, *Ma Vie*, quoted in Pryce-Jones, *Paris in the Third Reich*, p. 12.

page 254 'I knew none . . .': Beauvoir, *Prime of Life*, p. 471.

page 254 'desire to get along . . .': witness testimony, *Le Chagrin et la Pitié*, a film by Marcel Ophuls (1969).

page 255 'repugnant . . .': Beauvoir, *Prime of Life*, p. 464.

page 255 '*Il n'y avait...*': *La Force de l'âge*, p. 549, *Prime of Life*, p. 464.

page 255 'terrifying': *Prime of Life*, p. 459.

page 255 'I had foreseen . . .': ibid., p. 460.

page 255 'I spotted Bienenfeld . . .': Beauvoir to Sartre, 31 December 1940, *Letters to Sartre*, p. 360.

page 255 'The misfortunes of others [*le malheur d'autrui*] . . .': Beauvoir, *Journal de Guerre*, p. 335.

page 255 'Bianca's father': Lamblin, *A Disgraceful Affair*, p. 91.

page 256 'The yellow star . . .': quoted in Pryce-Jones, *Paris in the Third Reich*, p. 138.

page 256 'The abundance of Jews . . .': ibid.

page 256 'You really shouldn't . . .': Lamblin, *A Disgraceful Affair*, p. 100, *Mémoires d'une jeune fille dérangée*, p. 118.

page 256 'Optimism remained so obstinately rooted . . .': Beauvoir, *Prime of Life*, p. 512.

page 256 'forgotten': Simone Signoret, *Nostalgia Isn't What It Used To Be* (Weidenfeld & Nicolson, 1978), p. 49.

page 257 'double execution . . . *J'ai porté* . . .': Lamblin, *A Disgraceful Affair*, p. 90, *Mémoires d'une jeune fille dérangée*, p. 107.

page 257 'I break things . . .': Beauvoir to Sartre, 11 July 1940, *Letters to Sartre*, p. 319.

page 257 'When I tried . . .': Beauvoir to Sartre, 14 July 1940, ibid., p. 329.

page 258 'It's still all roses . . .': Beauvoir to Sartre, 29 November 1940, ibid., p. 349.

page 258 'I couldn't get on better . . .': Beauvoir to Sartre, 1 January 1941, ibid., p. 361.

page 258 'My heart's breaking . . .': Beauvoir to Sartre, 7 January 1941, ibid., p. 365.

page 258 'a beloved cat . . .': Sartre to Beauvoir, n.d. 1941, *Quiet Moments*, p. 251.

page 258 'Sartre completely baffled me . . .': Beauvoir, *Prime of Life*, p. 478.

page 259 'What *did* disorientate . . . *La raideur de son moralisme*': ibid., p. 479, *La Force de l'âge*, p. 549.

page 259 fundamentally anti-fascist: for a discussion of Sartre's anti-fascism, and its continuity in his political life, see Lévy, *Le Siècle de Sartre*, pp. 360–406.

page 259 'some sort of compromise': Beauvoir, *Prime of Life*, p. 480.

page 259 Valkyrie: Beauvoir to Sartre, 24 July 1940, *Letters to Sartre*, p. 38.

page 259 'completely disgusted': Sartre to Beauvoir, 29 July 1940, *Quiet Moments*, p. 240.

page 259 'Take the point of view . . .': Sartre, *Que' est-ce qu'un collaborateur?* Situations *III* (Gallimard, 1976), pp. 51–6.

page 259 '*Le Mal*': Lévy, *Le Siècle de Sartre*, pp. 400–406.

page 260 'camaraderie joyeuse': talk by Dominique Descanti, 11 January 2008, Colloque Simone de Beauvoir 2008, Paris.

page 260 'smash in': conversation with George Chazelas, quoted in Cohen-Solal, *Sartre*, p. 167.

page 260 'If we accept . . .': quoted ibid., p. 165.

page 260 George Chazelas: ibid., p. 164.

page 261 navigate the treacherous reefs: see Gildea, 'Trimmers', in *Marianne in Chains*, p. 175.

page 261 Georges Davy: in Ingrid Galster, *Sartre, Vichy et les intellectuels* (Paris:

L'Harmattan, 2001), pp. 108–9: '*Il valait mieux donner le poste à Sartre qu'à un pétainiste.*' Beauvoir, *Prime of Life*, p. 481.

page 261 'I should sign' . . . 'a secret resistant': Gerassi, interview October 1971, *Jean-Paul Sartre*, p. 175. It is probable that Sartre signed the oath and lied to Gerassi.

page 262 'In one sense [*en un sens c'est la guerre qui rend si précieux tous les instants que je vis*]':Beauvoir, quoted in Bonal and Ribowska, *Simone de Beauvoir*, p. 53.

page 262 'Well,' remarked Gide . . . : Beauvoir, *Prime of Life*, p. 495.

page 262 'So this is death': ibid., p. 496.

page 262 'returned to nothingness': ibid., p. 490.

page 263 '*The* biographical question [La *question biographique*]': Lévy, *Le Siècle de Sartre*, p. 407.

page 263 'q young and brilliant . . .': Jean Daniel, editorial of 16 October 1997, *Le Nouvel observateur*, quoted by Galster, *Sartre, Vichy et les intellectuels*, p. 87; Dreyfus was given notice according to the Statute of the Israelites in a letter from the Ministry of November 1941, and provisionally nominated to a post in Lyon, but in fact he remained as *professeur de philosophie* at Condorcet until 21 January 1941, Galster, ibid., p. 100.

page 263 'I've been sacked . . .': quoted ibid., p. 102, Galster interview with Dreyfus's son and daughter-in-law, Dr Michel Dreyfus-Le-Foyer and his wife, June 2000.

page 263 'the supreme mark . . .': Sartre, *Réflexions sur la question juive* (Gallimard, 1954), quoted in Galster, *Sartre, Vichy et les intellectuels*, p. 89. Sartre's emphasis on the role of look is expressed in his remark: '*Le Juif est un homme que les autres hommes tiennent pour Juif.*'

page 264 'I hold Flaubert . . .': Sartre, *Les Temps modernes*, no. 1, October 1945, p. 5.

Chapter 24: Supping with the Devil

page 265 'You know what it means . . .': Sartre, *Huis Clos.*

page 265 Sartre slept with Sorokine, who also seduced Bost: Joseph, *Une Si Douce Occupation*, p. 220; see also Rowley, *Tête-à-Tête*, p. 130; Sorokine's mother alleged this in her report to the Ministry of Education, and Sylvie Le Bon de Beauvoir confirmed that Sorokine slept with both men.

page 266 'the senior wife . . .': John Weightman, 'The End of the Affair', *Times Literary Supplement,* 25 December 1981, p. 1482, quoted in Galster, *Sartre, Vichy et les intellectuels*, p. 157.

page 266 'I've never known . . .': Sartre to Beauvoir, 24 February 1940, ibid., pp. 75–6.

page 266 'using Sartre as a sex-toy ['*Sartre est, de telle sorte, le "porte-sex"*']', Galster, *Sartre, Vichy et les intellectuels*, p. 161.

page 266 'the power of . . .': Sartre to Beauvoir, 24 February 1940, *Quiet Moments*, p. 75.

page 266 'I have decided . . .': Sartre to Beauvoir, n.d. 1941, *Quiet Moments*, p. 251.

page 266 'Find an author [*trouvez un auteur*]': Sartre to Jean-Louis Barrault, 9 July 1942, unpublished letter, quoted in Galster, *Sartre, Vichy et les intellectuels*, p.41; Beauvoir, *Prime of Life*, p. 485.

page 266 'After what I've done . . .': quoted in Joseph, *Une Si Douce Occupation*, p. 243.

page 267 'represented the one form . . .': Beauvoir, *Prime of Life*, p. 500.

page 267 'We have come . . .': quoted in Joseph, *Une Si Douce Occupation*, p. 172.

page 267 'Nevertheless, I decided . . .': Sartre to Judge Zoussman, in ibid., p. 174.

page 267 'Hommage à Jean Giraudoux': *Comoedia*, 5 February 1944, *Les Écrits de Sartre*, p. 95.

page 268 'To present . . .': Gerhard Heller, *Un Allemand à Paris 1940–1944, avec le concours de Jean Grand* (Éditions du Seuil,1981), p. 28.

page 268 'on collaborating': Olivier Todd, *Albert Camus: A Life, translated by Benjamin Ivry* (New York: Alfred A. Knopf, 1997), p. 176.

page 268 'preserving the tone . . .': Heller, *Un Allemand à Paris*, p. 100.

page 268 'Haven't you seen . . .': ibid., p. 144.

page 269 '*avec ma gratitude*': ibid., p. 146.

page 269 close to Sartre and Beauvoir: Heller's memoir contradicts Beauvoir's statement in *Prime of Life*, p. 475, that she went to the Flore 'where no member of the occupation forces ever set foot'.

page 269 'I judged the approach . . .': Heller, *Un Allemand à Paris*, p. 159.

page 269 'Olga has never . . .': Sartre to Jean-Louis Barrault, 9 July 1942, unpublished letter quoted in Galster, *Sartre, Vichy et les intellectuels*, p. 43.

page 270 'raising his glass': Marc Bénard in Joseph, *Une Si Douce Occupation*, p. 266.

page 271 'The man who wanted to become a playwright . . . [*l'homme qui voulait devenir dramaturge et faire jouer des amis a eu moins le souci des Juifs que de sa carrière et de ses proches*]': Michel Contat, *Le Monde*, 25 July 1985, quoted in Galster, *Sartre, Vichy et les intellectuels*, p. 14.

page 271 Michel Leiris: letter to Ingrid Galster, 1 July 1981, Galster, *Sartre, Vichy et les intellectuels*, p. 21. In the film *Sartre par lui-même*, Sartre claimed that *Les Mouches* had compromised him.

page 271 Goebbels: in *Das Reich*, German weekly which was the official organ of Goebbels; see Galster, *Sartre, Vichy et les intellectuels*, p. 23.

page 271 'a writer who resisted . . .': unpublished interview with John Gerassi, quoted in Cohen-Solal, *Sartre*, p. 190.

page 271 'Our hotel rooms . . .': Gerassi, *Jean-Paul Sartre*, p. 176.

page 273 'I tried to arrive . . .': Beauvoir, *Prime of Life*, p. 529.

page 273 'When they die . . .': ibid., p. 533.

page 273 'Never were we more . . .': Sartre , 'La République du silence', *Les Lettres françaises*, 7 September 1944.

page 273 'people were cheerful . . .': Boris Vian, quoted in Pryce-Jones, *Paris in the Third Reich*, p. 168.

page 274 'corrupting a minor': Beauvoir, *Prime of Life*, p. 540; Joseph, *Une Si Douce Occupation*, p. 220.

page 275 'at a time when France . . . [*à l'heure où la France aspire à la restauration de ses valeurs morales et familiales*]': Joseph, *Une Si Douce Occupation*, p. 221.

page 275 June 1943: on 30 July 1945 Beauvoir was reinstated as a teacher at the Lycée Fénelon, but she turned down the post and never taught again.

page 275 'I can't remember . . .': Beauvoir, *Prime of Life*, p. 540.

page 275 'No one was to write . . .': ibid., p. 514.

page 275 'Delange . . .': Sartre to Beauvoir, 'Thursday, 8' [Summer] 1943, *Quiet Moments*, p. 255.

page 275 deportation quota: Paxton, *Vichy France*, pp.181–3. Leval negotiated to send French Jews only if foreign Jews fell short of Himmler's quota. Some 60–65,000 foreign

Jews were deported from France, and 6,000 French Jews. Only 2,800 deportees returned.

page 275 'I had become, overnight . . .': Beauvoir, *Prime of Life*, p. 558.

page 276 'I'm reading Beauvoir's book . . . [*Je lis le livre de Beauvoir*, L'Invitée, *dont tout le monde parle*]': Jean Cocteau, *Journal 1942–1945* (Gallimard, 1989), quoted in Joseph, *Une Si Douce Occupation*, p. 302.

page 276 '*Vive la paix honteuse*': in Pryce-Jones, *Paris in the Third Reich*, p. 165.

page 276 'All the grocers . . .': Raymond Queneau, cited by Patrick Lorriot in *Le Nouvel observateur*, 21–27 April 1980, Gerassi, *Jean-Paul Sartre*, p. 180.

page 276 'Anyone who is an existentialist . . .': Mary Warnock, introduction, *Being and Nothingness: An Essay on Phenomenological Ontology*, translated by Hazel Barnes (Routledge, 1989), p. xiii.

page 276 'lies at the heart': ibid., p. x.

page 277 'the *Ens causa sui* [cause of his own being], which religions call God . . .': ibid., p. 615.

page 277 'There will be a few . . .': *Lettres au Castor*, vol. 1.

page 278 'We were like two dogs . . .': Bair, *Simone de Beauvoir*, pp. 290–92.

page 278 'Why are you going to . . .': Todd, *Albert Camus*, p. 174.

page 278 '*Merde* . . .': Sartre to Beauvoir, Summer 1943, *Lettres au Castor*, vol. 2, p. 312.

page 278 'each of us will act . . .': *No Exit (Huis Clos)* (Vintage, 1989), p. 17.

page 278 'guillotined an abortionist': Galster, *Sartre, Vichy et les intellectuels*, p. 31; Beauvoir, *Prime of Life*, p. 362.

page 279 'I wanted the dough . . .': Sartre to Beauvoir, Summer 1943, *Quiet Moments*, p. 254.

page 279 'With nobody in the whole world . . .': Sartre to Beauvoir, July 1945, ibid., p. 266.

page 280 'I would offer . . .': Beauvoir, *Prime of Life*, p. 562.

page 281 'very few intellectuals . . .': interview with Olivier Todd, 20 April 2005.

page 282 'I've sold my soul . . .': Beauvoir, *Prime of Life*, p. 570.

Chapter 25: Liberation

page 283 'The Allied air forces . . .': Beauvoir, *Prime of Life*, p. 566.

page 284 plot to kill Hitler: the plot to plant a bomb due to explode during Hitler's daily military conference was instigated by Colonel Claus Schenk von Stauffenberg, who had sent a leading conspirator, Count Fritz von der Schulenberg, to raise support from the military staffs in France at the end of 1943; Heinrich von Stülpnagel was contacted by der Schulenberg, according to the journal of Ernst Jünger, 31 May 1944, Pryce-Jones, *Paris in the Third Reich*, p. 193.

page 284 'the objective . . .': ibid., p. 141.

page 284 French-born children: the strict French definition of a Jew, which included those who did not practise any religion, was used in preference to the German definition of one who had two Jewish grandparents *and* belonged to the Jewish faith; see Robert Gildea, *Marianne in Chains*, p. 273.

page 284 'The representatives of the French . . .': Dannecker's telegram, 'President Laval has proposed . . .', 6 July 1942, Pryce-Jones, *Paris in the Third Reich*, p. 142. When Oberg arrived, Reinhard Heydrich, head of the *Sicherheitsdienst* (SD), who answered to

Himmler, briefed the SD and Gestapo on the decision, taken in February 1942 at the Wannsee Conference by the leaders of the SD and Gestapo, to kill all Jews. He subsequently held a conference in the Ritz on 5 May, with Oberg, Bousquet and Darquier de Pellepoix, where, in order to deport Jews for the 'Final Solution', he demanded that the French police forces should be subordinated directly to Oberg.

page 284 'as in a supermarket . . .': Robert Paxton, *Vichy France*, p. 184.

page 284 'moat of blood': ibid., p. 298.

page 285 'I saw a train pass . . .': Edith Thomas in *Les Lettres françaises*, no. 2, quoted in Claude Lévy and Paul Tillard, *La Grande Rafle du Vel d'Hiv* (Paris, 1967), p. 176. There were eighty-five transports from Drancy, and the names of the deportees have been traced by Serge Klarsfeld in his *Le Mémorial de la déportation des Juifs de France* (1978).

page 285 'Well, this time . . .': Max Jacob's letter, quoted in Francis Steegmuller, *Cocteau*, and Pryce-Jones, *Paris in the Third Reich*, p. 146.

page 286 'They were both killed . . .': Beauvoir, *Prime of Life*, p. 578.

page 286 'convoy seventy-one': see Klarsfeld, *Le Mémorial de la déportation des Juifs de France*. Bourla's full name was Bourla-Benjamin.

page 286 'I'm more intelligent . . .': Todd, *Albert Camus*, p. 174.

page 286 'greatness and truth [*la grandeur et la vérité*]': Albert Camus, 'On Jean-Paul Sartre's *The Wall and Other Stories*', in *Lyrical and Critical Essays*, p. 206, quoted in Ronald Aronson, *Camus and Sartre: the story of a friendship and the quarrel that ended it* (University of Chicago Press, 2004), p. 13.

page 286 'Getting up . . .': Jean-Paul Sartre, 'Camus's *The Outsider*', in *Literary and Philosophical Essays*, quoted in Aronson, *Camus and Sartre*, p. 13.

page 287 'only one leader . . .': Todd, *Albert Camus*, p. 179.

page 287 'I never touched a gun . . .': ibid., p. 170.

page 287 'this doesn't concern me': Aronson, *Camus and Sartre*, p. 52.

page 288 'If you are brave . . .': Todd, *Albert Camus*, p. 180.

page 288 'You gave yourself . . .': Sartre, 'Reply to Albert Camus', in *Situations I*, p. 71, cited in Aronson, *Camus and Sartre*, p. 37.

page 288 'I became a member': Beauvoir, *Adieux*, p. 267; in saying, '*Je suis entré dans son groupe de résistance, peu avant la Libération,*' Sartre suggests a degree of involvement he never had.

page 288 'Sartre's resistance . . .': interview with Olivier Todd, 19 April 2005.

page 289 'In the Catalan . . .': Hervé le Boterf, *La Vie parisienne sous l'occupation*, in Pryce-Jones, *Paris in the Third Reich*, p. 30.

page 289 'We became . . .': Beauvoir, *Prime of Life*, pp. 573–5.

page 290 'Monsieur Sartre . . .': unpublished letter, J.-L. Bost to Beauvoir, April 1944, quoted in Rowley, *Tête-à-Tête*, p. 144.

page 290 'absolute opposite . . .': Cohen-Solal, *Sartre*, p. 233.

page 290 'Beauvoir wanted . . .': interview with Olivier Todd, 19 April 2005; see also Todd, *Albert Camus*, p. 231.

page 290 'I asked myself . . .': Michel Contat and Michel Rybalka (eds), *Un théâtre de situations* (Paris: Gallimard, 1972), *Sartre on Theater*, translated by Frank Jellinek (New York: Pantheon Books, 1976), p. 199.

page 290 'the lion of his generation': Alfred Fabre-Luce, cited in Joseph, *Un Si Douce Occupation*, p. 340.

page 291 'night people [who] . . .': Brassaï, *The Secret Paris of the 30s*, p. 5.

page **291** 'How we loved you . . .': Jean Daniel, *Le Temps qui reste: Essai d'une autobiographie professionelle* (Paris, 1984), p. 72.

page **291** 'his last good friend': *Sartre, autoportrait à 70 ans, entretiens avec Michel Contat* (Gallimard, 2005), Jean-Paul Sartre, *Self-Portrait at Seventy*, in *Life/Situations* (New York, 1976), p. 107.

page **292** 'We hastily packed up . . .': Beauvoir, *Prime of Life*, p. 590.

page **293** 'with two flaxen-haired . . .': ibid., p. 594.

page **293** 'Walking around Paris . . .': *Un Promeneur dans Paris insurgé*, series of seven articles on the Liberation of Paris, *Combat*, 28 August 1944, written, according to Michel Contat and Michel Rybalka, with 'the collaboration of Simone de Beauvoir'; *Les Écrits de Sartre*, p. 103.

page **293** 'we wrote reports . . .': Quoted in Aronson, *Camus and Sartre*, p. 24.

page **293** 'too busy': Bair, *Simone de Beauvoir*, p. 293.

page **294** 'the Republic': see Lamblin, *A Disgraceful Affair*, p. 118.

page **294** 'You have turned . . .': Todd, *Albert Camus*, p. 188, translation modified, Aronson, *Camus and Sartre*, p. 25. The original reads: '*Tu as mis ton fauteuil dans le sens de l'histoire*', Todd, French edition, p. 355.

page **294** 'The Resistance was . . .': Sartre, 'Paris under the Occupation,' *Sartre Studies International* 4, no. 2 (1998), 8, cited in Aronson, *Camus and Sartre*, p. 40.

page **294** '*Chacun son boche*': cited in Pryce-Jones, *Paris in the Third Reich*, p. 204.

page **295** '900 FFI . . .': Rod Kedward, *La Vie en bleu: France and the French since 1900* (Penguin, 2006), p. 303.

page **295** '30,000 Poles died': Pryce-Jones, *Paris in the Third Reich*, p. 204.

page **295** 'a Gaullist myth': see Henry Rousso, *The Vichy Syndrome*, p. 16. Only at the end of his speech did de Gaulle mention 'our beloved and admirable allies'.

Chapter 26: Retribution and Remorse

page **299** '*C'est fini* . . .': Beauvoir, *La Force des choses* (Gallimard, 1963), p. 13.

page **299** 'freedom incarnate . . .': Beauvoir, *Force of Circumstance*, first published as *La Force des Choses*, translated by Richard Howard (New York: G. Putnam's Sons), p. 4.

page **299** 'The arrival . . .': Beauvoir, *Adieux*, p. 362.

page **300** '*On nous déportait* . . .': Sartre, 'La République du silence', in *Les Lettres françaises*, 9 September 1944 (first legal edition), text reproduced in Mauricette Berne (ed.), *Sartre*, catalogue, p. 93 (my translation).

page **300** only 28,000: After the war the Minister of Anciens Combattants recognized that during the Occupation in Paris there were 28,817 resisters, an annual percentage of 0.5 per cent of the population, Henri Michel, *Paris résistant* (Albin Michel, 1982), cited in Joseph, *Un Si Douce Occupation*, p. 358.

page **300** 'fearless and active . . .': Aronson, *Camus and Sartre*, p. 38, cites the introduction to an American compilation, *The Republic of Silence* (1947), which gives the text of Sartre's article.

page **301** 20,000 women: Kedward, *La Vie en bleu*, p. 308.

page **302** 'but,' said Sartre . . . : Gerassi, *Jean-Paul Sartre*, p. 179; Beauvoir, *Force of Circumstance*, p. 6.

page **302** 'We could count . . .': Beauvoir, *Force of Circumstance*, p. 4.

page **302** 'The less they . . .': Todd, *Albert Camus*, p. 198.

page 303 'another Communist tract': ibid., p. 182.

page 303 'Until our last moment . . .': ibid., p. 199.

page 303 'You have given me . . .': ibid., pp. 200–201.

page 304 'I did not want to hear . . .': Beauvoir, *Force of Circumstance*, pp. 20–22.

page 304 'The Vichy regime . . .': Paxton, *Vichy France*, p. 381.

page 304 'Any blame . . .': Sartre, Gallimard Archives, cited Joseph, *Un Si Douce Occupation*, pp. 361–2.

page 304 'I'm just a poor paper dealer': Cohen-Solal, *Sartre*, p. 218.

page 304 '*Il avait mal mené* . . .': Jean Cocteau journal, cited Joseph, *Un Si Douce Occupation*, p. 361.

page 304 'taken an active part . . .': ibid., p. 366.

page 305 'I'm upset . . .': Beauvoir to Sartre, 13 December 1945, *Letters to Sartre*, pp. 389–90.

page 305 'Above the gas chamber . . .': Jacques-Laurent Bost, *Combat*, in Cohen-Solal, *Sartre*, p. 247.

page 306 'I was pinned . . .': Lamblin, *A Disgraceful Affair*, p. 132.

page 306 'After the war . . .': interview with Sylvie Le Bon de Beauvoir, 29 November 2005.

page 306 'This then is . . .': Beauvoir, *Pyrrhus and Cinéas*, translated by Christopher Freemantle, *Partisan Review*, vol. 3, pt 3, 1946, p. 333.

page 306 'an order of precedence': Fullbrook and Fullbrook, *Simone de Beauvoir and Jean-Paul Sartre*, p. 142.

page 307 'Simone said . . .': interview with Bianca Bienenfeld Lamblin, 28 April 2005.

page 307 'forced into silence': Kedward, *La Vie en bleu*, p. 314.

page 307 *The Sorrow and the Pity*: Le Chagrin et la Pitié was made in 1971 but not shown on French television until 1981. It was condemned by Sartre, 'whose "complex" on the subject of commitment to the Resistance is well known': Henry Rousso, 'The Broken Mirror', in *The Vichy Syndrome*, pp. 98–130.

page 307 'usurped by someone . . .': Bianca Lamblin to Ingrid Galster, October 1996, letter quoted by Galster in *Sartre, Vichy et les intellectuels*, p. 82.

page 307 'quite visible . . .': Beauvoir, *Force of Circumstance*, p. 11.

page 307 'I have so often advised women . . .': ibid., p. 13.

page 308 'Would you and Sartre like to meet . . .': ibid., p. 15.

page 308 'You're a general! . . .': ibid., p. 16.

page 308 'I've never seen Sartre . . .': ibid., p. 17.

Chapter 27: Dolorès

page 309 'Do you realize . . .': Todd, *Albert Camus*, p. 218.

page 309 'each, in his own way . . .': Sartre, 'On *The Sound and the Fury*: Time in the Work of Faulkner', in *Literary and Philosophical Essays*, p. 84, and 'John Dos Passos and "1919"', ibid., pp. 88, 89.

page 309 'I didn't know . . .': Sartre, 'New York, the Colonial City', ibid., p. 118.

page 310 'The American street . . .': Sartre, 'American Cities', ibid., p. 115.

page 310 'It all shone . . .': Beauvoir, *Adieux*, p. 236.

page 311 'At the very end': testimony of Dolorès Vanetti, 4 May 1983, Cohen-Solal, *Sartre*, p. 237.

page 311 'That's what they say . . .': Todd, *Albert Camus*, p. 218.

page 311 'devoted himself to underground . . .': cited in Cohen-Solal, *Sartre*, p. 228.

page 312 'I have never . . .': *New York Times*, 1 February 1945, Cohen-Solal, *Sartre*, p. 231.

page 312 '*L'effort de guerre* . . .': Beauvoir, *Cérémonie*, p.336.

page 312 'As he shakes . . .': *Le Figaro*, 11–12 March 1945, *Les Ecrits de Sartre*, p. 119.

page 313 'The Resistance taught . . .': *Vogue*, July 1945, *Les Écrits*, p. 124.

page 313 'In publishing . . .': quoted by Aronson, *Camus and Sartre*, p. 54; Cohen-Solal, *Sartre*, p. 233; see Aronson's discussion of Sartre's debt to Camus, pp. 52–5.

page 313 'I draw from the absurd . . .': Albert Camus, *The Myth of Sisyphus* (Penguin, 1975), p. 62.

page 313 'the Self . . .': Roger Scruton, 'The Power of Negative Thinking', *Spectator*, 25 June 2005, p. 30.

page 314 'Since the writer . . .': introduction to *Les Temps modernes*, quoted in Aronson, *Camus and Sartre*, pp. 56–7.

page 314 'two black army officers': anecdote related by Pizella, *Les Nuits*, quoted in Cohen-Solal, *Sartre*, p. 242.

page 314 'In this land . . .': *Situations III*, pp. 99–100.

page 315 'I have five . . .': Sartre, *The Respectful Prostitute* (New York: Vintage Books, 1989) p. 254.

page 315 'They caught . . .': ibid., p. 273.

page 315 'Like everybody else . . .': Sartre, 'Individualism and Conformism in the United States', *Essays*, p. 98.

page 315 'I believe . . .': ibid., p. 101.

page 315 '*Ça ne vous gênait pas* . . .': *Cérémonie*, p. 342, *Adieux*, p. 239.

page 316 'Whenever you asked . . .': Beauvoir, *Force of Circumstance*, p. 16.

page 316 'a furious solidarity . . .': ibid., p. 23.

page 316 'What are those clogs . . .': ibid., p.'25.

page 317 'to sleep with Beauvoir': interview with Sylvie Le Bon de Beauvoir, 29 November 2005.

page 317 'To my very dear Llama . . .': Rowley, *Tête-à-Tête*, p. 152.

page 317 'double bed . . .': LS, 26 July 1945, pp. 387, 388.

page 318 'This is my third marriage': Beauvoir, *All Said and Done*, p. 91.

page 319 '*très belle* . . .': Jean Cau, 'Croquis de mémoire', *Témoins de Sartre* (Gallimard, 2005), pp. 47, 48.

page 319 'At present . . .': Beauvoir, *Force of Circumstance*, pp. 68–9.

page 319 'I didn't want people . . .' Bair, p 302

page 320 'My philosophy . . .': ibid., p. 58; according to Beauvoir's testimony to Deirdre Bair, this lunch with Salacrou took place in May 1945, not 1946 as appears from *Force of Circumstance*.

page 320 'What about you, madame?': *La Force de l'âge*, p. 625, *Prime of Life*, p. 547.

page 320 'We are alone without excuses . . .': Sartre, *Existentialism and Human Emotions*, translations by Bernard Frechtman and Hazel E. Barnes (New York: Citadel Press, 1987), p. 23.

page 321 'Every woman in love . . .': Beauvoir, *Second Sex*, p. 686; see Moi, *Simone de Beauvoir*, p. 218, for a discussion of the role of the *amoureuse*, 'the speechless mermaid', in Beauvoir's fiction.

Chapter 28: The Abyss

page 322 'Death suddenly appeared . . . [*Brusquement la mort m'est apparue. Je me suis tordue les mains, j'ai pleuré, je me suis cogné la tête aux murs*]': Beauvoir, *La Force de l'âge*, p. 688, *Prime of Life*, p. 603.

page 322 'false prophet': Roger Garaudy, a Communist intellectual, attacked Sartre in *Les Lettres françaises*, 28 December 1945; Camus was also under attack by Pierre Hervé in *Action*, who described both Sartre and Camus as the 'popes of existentialism'.

page 322 *Vies, Vits*: Beauvoir, *Force of Circumstance*, p. 91; the oral pun is on the French words for *life* and *penis*.

page 322 troglodytes: 'Voici comment vivent les troglodytes de Saint-Germain-des-Prés', 3 May 1947, *Samedi-Soir*.

page 322 'Hell is all . . .': Beauvoir, *Force of Circumstance*, p. 111.

page 323 'I spent a marvellous . . .': Beauvoir to Sartre, 13 December 1945, *Letters to Sartre*, p. 392.

page 323 'You have to choose . . .': Beauvoir, *Force of Circumstance*, p. 53.

page 323 'He doesn't have . . .': Beauvoir to Sartre, 13 December 1945, *Letters to Sartre*, p. 391.

page 323 'Six years ago . . .' Beauvoir to Sartre, 27 December 1945, ibid., p. 395.

page 323 '*Tué*, killed . . .': Sartre to Beauvoir [January] 1946, *Quiet Moments in a War*, p. 275.

page 324 'Dolorès's love for me . . .': Sartre to Beauvoir, [January] 1946, ibid., p. 274.

page 324 'a poor and charming creature . . .': Sartre to Beauvoir, [February] 1946, ibid., p. 275.

page 324 '*particularly* to the Beaver': Todd, *Un fils rebelle*, p. 116.

page 324 'He told me . . .': testimony of Vanetti, May 1983, Cohen-Solal, *Sartre*, p. 278.

page 324 'literature had become . . .': Beauvoir, *Prime of Life*, p. 606; Moi, *Simone de Beauvoir*, pp. 244–51.

page 324 'At those times . . .': Beauvoir, *All Said and Done*, p. 135.

page 325 'There are sometimes . . .': Beauvoir, *Force of Circumstance*, p. 75.

page 325 'To exorcize death . . .': Beauvoir, *Prime of Life*, p. 603.

page 325 'the banal image . . .': ibid., p. 604.

page 325 'peril of loneliness . . .': ibid., p. 607.

page 326 'Already it evokes . . .': Beauvoir, *Force of Circumstance*, p. 82.

page 326 'I always . . .': Beauvoir, *Prime of Life*, p. 606.

page 326 'reinventing himself': Jacqueline Rose, introduction to *All Men Are Mortal*, translated by Euan Cameron (Gallimard, 1946, Virago, 1995), p. viii.

page 326 'a fleck of foam . . .': Beauvoir, *All Men Are Mortal*, p. 403.

page 326 'to make himself God': Beauvoir, *The Ethics of Ambiguity* (*Pour une morale de l'amibiguité*), translated by Bernard Frechtman (New York: Citadel Press, 1948), p. 10; Beauvoir argues that 'the synthesis of the for-itself [consciousness] and the in-itself [objects, which have essences]' by which man tries to make himself a god, is impossible.

page 326 'Man makes himself man . . .': Sartre, 'Ethical Implications', *Being and Nothingness*, p. 626.

page 327 'No man really is God': *Second Sex*, p. 686.

page 327 'engaged freedom . . .': Beauvoir, *Ethics of Ambiguity*, p. 11.

page 327 'irritated': Beauvoir, *Force of Circumstance*, p. 67.

page 327 'The earth turned . . .': Beauvoir, *Prime of Life*, p. 599.

page 328 'schizophrenic delirium . . .': Beauvoir, *La Force de l'âge*, p. 685, *Prime of Life*, p. 600, translation modified; see Moi, *Simone de Beauvoir*, p. 228, on Beauvoir's 'schizophrenia'.

page 328 'What about this Dolorès . . .': Cohen-Solal, *Sartre*, p. 279.

page 329 'Lucie' in *Morts sans Sépulture* may have been inspired by the story of Lucie Aubrac, a famous woman Resistant who freed her husband from the Gestapo in Lyon; Galster, *Sartre, Vichy et les intellectuels*, p. 50, n. 26. Sartre situated the play in the Vercors, possibly under the influence of Bianca Lamblin's account of the Resistance in the Vercors in which she had participated.

page 329 The play dominated . . . : *Écrits de Sartre*, pp. 132–4.

page 329 'I am not an existentialist': *Les Nouvelles littéraires*, November 1945, in Cohen-Solal, *Sartre*, p. 263.

page 329 'Camus is not an existentialist': interview in *Paru*, December 1945, ibid.

page 329 Sartre–Salacrou duel: Galster, *Sartre, Vichy et les intellectuels*, pp. 59–60.

page 329 '*une sorte de compensation maladive*': Vladimir Jankélévitch, *Libération*, 10 juin 1985, p. 35, quoted in Galster, *Sartre, Vichy et les intellectuels*, pp. 93–4; Jankélévitch was a professor of philosophy at the University of Lille before being dismissed under the Vichy racial laws.

page 330 'Stunningly attractive': Beauvoir to Sartre, 18 January 1946, *Letters to Sartre*, p. 395.

page 330 'Saw the charming . . .': Todd, *Albert Camus*, p. 232.

page 331 'You don't want to! . . .': Beauvoir, *Les Mandarins* (Gallimard, 1954), *The Mandarins*, translated by Leonard M. Friedman (Flamingo, 1984), pp. 98–9.

page 332 'I hate challenge . . .': Beauvoir to Nelson Algren, 28 September 1947, *Beloved Chicago Man: Letters to Nelson Algren 1947–1964* (Gallimard, 1997, Orion 1999), p. 72.

page 332 '[Koestler] was a hell of a raper': quoted in Asa Moberg, 'Sensuality and Brutality', in *Contingent Loves*, p. 105.

page 332 'composite character . . .': testimony of Beauvoir to Deirdre Bair, in Bair, *Simone de Beauvoir*, p. 644, n. 14, in which Beauvoir says that Koestler was not 'the only model . . . for Scriassine'.

page 332 'a doctor': *Mandarins*, p. 97.

page 332 'Michèle Vian to his harem . . .': testimony of Beauvoir to Deirdre Bair: 'Everyone knows that Michèle succumbed to Sartre shortly after they met, even while he was still involved with Dolorès', Bair, *Simone de Beauvoir*, p. 644, n. 13.

page 332 'Of course I want to . . .': Beauvoir, *Force of Circumstance*, p. 85.

page 332 'You don't dress . . .': ibid., pp. 120.

page 332 'I was a person . . .': ibid., p. 119.

page 333 '*Que vous avez* . . .': Beauvoir, *La Force des choses* 1, p. 135, *Force of Circumstance*, p. 94; Shusha Guppy, 'Feminist Witness to the Century', *The Times Higher Educational Supplement*, 25 February 2000.

Chapter 29: Nelson, My Sweet Crocodile

page 334 'I am your wife . . .': Beauvoir to Nelson Algren, 4 June 1947.

page 334 'the leading French . . .': Mary McCarthy, quoted in Elaine Showalter,

Inventing Herself: Claiming a Feminist Intellectual Heritage (Picador, 2002), p. 197.

page 334 'I was prepared . . .': Beauvoir, *America Day by Day*, translated by Carol Cosman (*L'Amérique au jour le jour*, Gallimard, 1954, Phoenix, 1999), p. 123.

page 334 'free peoples': President Truman, quoted in Frances Stonor Saunders, *Who Paid the Piper? The CIA and the Cultural Cold War* (Granta Books, 2335,) p. 25.

page 335 ideological chasm: Dean Acheson, ibid., p. 25.

page 335 'It seems my statements . . .': Beauvoir, *America*, p. 51; Maurice Merleau-Ponty, 'The Yogi and the Proletarian', *Les Temps modernes*, no. 3 (December 1945) was a critique of Koestler's *The Yogi and the Commissar*.

page 336 'the beautiful, cold novelist . . .': ibid., p. 322.

page 336 'felt the command . . .': Showalter, *Inventing Herself*, p. 198.

page 336 'How pretty . . .': Beauvoir, *America*, pp. 58–9.

page 337 'These women who . . .': ibid., p. 60.

page 337 'the relation between the sexes . . .': ibid., p. 325.

page 337 'obsessed by . . .': ibid., p. 323.

page 337 'It was a strange stirring . . .': Betty Friedan, *The Feminine Mystique* (1963), in Rosalind Miles, *The Women's History of the World* (Paladin, 1989), p. 274.

page 338 'Far from suffering . . .': Beauvoir, *Force of Circumstance*, p. 189; see Mary Evans, *Simone de Beauvoir: A Feminist Mandarin* (Tavistock, 1985), pp. 56–9, for a discussion of Beauvoir's awakening consciousness of women's oppression in 1947.

page 338 'I wanted to have . . .': Beauvoir, *Force of Circumstance*, p. 122.

page 338 'a stunningly beautiful . . .': Bair, *Simone de Beauvoir*, p. 329.

page 339 'She had the prettiest smile . . .': Beauvoir, *Force of Circumstance*, p. 122.

page 339 'It was as if . . .': Bair, *Simone de Beauvoir*, pp. 329–30.

page 339 'Dolorès was as dainty . . .': Beauvoir to Sartre, 31 January 1947, *Letters to Sartre*, p. 417.

page 339 'crazy': Beauvoir to Sartre, 30 January 1947, ibid., p. 425.

page 339 'I like her a lot . . .': ibid.

page 339 'That Simone de Boudoir sounds . . .': Nelson Algren to Mary Guggenheim, 10 February 1947, in Bettina Drew, *Nelson Algren: A Life on the Wild Side* (Bloomsbury, 1990), pp. 177–8.

page 340 'a taste of Chicago . . .': Beauvoir, *America*, pp. 103–4.

page 340 'Somebody hollered into the phone . . .': Nelson Algren, *Conversations with Nelson Algren* (Hill & Wang, 1964), p. 180.

page 340 'Mlle de Beauvoir . . .': Bair, *Simone de Beauvoir*, p. 330.

page 340 'complicity . . .': Beauvoir, ed. Sylvie Le Bon de Beauvoir, *Beloved Chicago Man: Letters to Nelson Algren 1947–64* (Victor Gollancz, 1999), p. 13.

page 341 'I introduced her to stick-up men . . .': Nelson Algren, 'Last Rounds in Small Cafés: Remembrances of Jean-Paul Sartre and Simone de Beauvoir', *Chicago*, 1980, p. 213, in Bair, *Simone de Beauvoir*, p. 335.

page 341 'furious curiosity': Algren, *Conversations*, p. 180.

page 341 'Simone de Beauvoir's eyes . . .': Nelson Algren, *Who Lost an American?* (Macmillan, 1963), p. 96.

page 341 'It is beautiful,': Beauvoir, *America*, p. 105.

page 341 'I'm very comfortable . . .': Beauvoir, *Mandarins*, p. 423.

page 342 'My impetuosity . . .': Bair, *Simone de Beauvoir*, p. 336.

page 342 'Nelson liked one-night stands . . .': interview with Ted Liss, November 1987, Drew, *Nelson Algren*, p. 180.

page 343 'He's more or less . . .': Beauvoir to Sartre, 28 February 1947, *Letters to Sartre*, p. 434.

page 343 'an authentic native . . .':Beauvoir, *America*, p. 109.

page 343 'Before going to sleep . . .': Beauvoir to Nelson Algren, 23 February 1947, *Beloved Chicago Man*, p. 14.

page 343 'Get your douche-bag . . .': Drew, *Nelson Algren*, p. 180.

page 343 'Nelson constantly got angry . . .': interview with Ted Liss, November 1987, Drew, *Nelson Algren*, p. 180.

page 343 'Little Gauloise': *Mandarins*, p. 436.

page 343 'ardour and the vitality . . .': testimony of Ivan Moffatt, Bair, *Simone de Beauvoir*, p. 337.

page 344 'unpleasant comments': Beauvoir, *America*, p. 47.

page 344 'Everywhere we go . . .': ibid., p. 231.

page 344 'I love you . . .': Beauvoir to Sartre, 9 March 1947, *Letters to Sartre*, p. 441.

page 344 'I depend . . .': Beauvoir to Sartre, 13 March 1947, ibid., p. 442.

page 345 'I mean seeing . . .': Beauvoir to Sartre, 14 April 1947, ibid., p. 449.

page 345 'I had a dreadful . . .': Beauvoir to Sartre, 8 May 1947, ibid., p. 454.

page 345 'I wanted to walk about . . .': Beauvoir, *Force of Circumstance*, p. 126.

page 345 'We shall never . . .': Beauvoir to Nelson Algren, 17 May 1947, *Beloved Chicago Man*, p. 17.

page 345 'complete orgasm': Bair, *Simone de Beauvoir*, p. 333.

page 345 'the intoxication . . .': Beauvoir, *Force of Circumstance*, p. 126.

page 345 'virility incarnate': testimony of Mary Guggenheim, Bair, *Simone de Beauvoir*, p. 334.

page 345 'profound self-abandonment': Beauvoir, *Second Sex*, p. 681.

page 346 'beloved husband': Beauvoir to Nelson Algren, 17 May 1947, *Beloved Chicago Man*, p. 17.

page 346 'garrulous little frog': Beauvoir to Nelson Algren, 3 October 1947, ibid., p. 74.

page 346 'He possessed . . .': Beauvoir, *Force of Circumstance*, p. 126.

page 346 'I send this book . . .': Beauvoir, *Beloved Chicago Man*, p. 17.

Chapter 30: Breaking Point

page 349 'An anti-Communist is a dog . . .': Beauvoir, *Force of Circumstance*, p. 261.

page 349 'mocking oracle . . .': Arthur Koestler, *Darkness at Noon* (Vintage, 1994), p. 18.

page 349 'The worst artists . . .': Sartre, *What is Literature?* (Librairie Gallimard, 1948), translated by Bernand Frechtman (Routledge, 2001), p. xxii.

page 349 from a Marxist point of view: John Malcolm Brinnin, *Truman Capote: A Memoir* (Sidgwick & Jackson, 1987), p. 8; Capote discussed this with Brinnin at the artists' colony Yaddo in 1946.

page 349 'empire of signs': Sartre, *What is Literature?*, p. 5.

page 350 'loaded pistols': ibid., p. 15; Sartre was quoting a remark made by Bruce Parain.

page 350 'The politics . . .': ibid., p. 197.

page 350 'Former communists . . .': ibid., p. 220.

page 350 'setback': ibid., p. 222.

page 350 'art for art's sake': ibid., introduction by David Caute, p. xii.

page 351 'corrosive lucidity': ibid., p. xiii.

page 351 'Terror is legitimized . . .': Camus, *Neither Victims nor Executioners, Combat,* 19 and 30 November, 1946 (New York, 1960), translated by Dwight Macdonald, Aronson, *Camus and Sartre*, p. 97.

page 351 'You're a Marxist now?': Camus, *Carnets II, 1942–51* (Gallimard, 1964), pp. 147–8, in Aronson, *Camus and Sartre*, pp. 88–9.

page 352 'I am coming . . .': Beauvoir, *Force of Circumstance*, p. 126.

page 352 'dull, dark . . .': Beauvoir to Nelson Algren, 18 May 1947, *Beloved Chicago Man*, p. 18.

page 352 'I deeply regret . . .': Beauvoir to Nelson Algren, 21 May 1947, ibid., p. 19.

page 352 'The version . . .': Beauvoir to Nelson Algren, 2 July 1947, ibid., p. 42.

page 352 'I feel unhappy . . .': Beauvoir to Nelson Algren, 4 June 1947, ibid., p. 46.

page 352 *Chavirée*: Beauvoir, *La Force des choses*, p. 179; '[I experienced] an anxiety . . .': *Force of Circumstance*, p. 128.

page 353 'She was the only woman . . .' Beauvoir, *Adieux*, p. 305.

page 353 'To maintain through all . . .': Beauvoir, *Force of Circumstance*, p. 124.

page 353 'incredible cruelty': Cohen-Solal, *Sartre*, p. 323.

page 353 'I wondered in terror . . .': Beauvoir, *Force of Circumstance*, p. 133.

page 354 'take me in your arms . . .': Beauvoir to Nelson Algren, 19 July 1947, *Beloved Chicago Man*, p. 53.

page 354 'cooking his pot roast . . .': testimony of Beauvoir, 1983, Bair, *Simone de Beauvoir*, p. 356.

page 354 'Nelson, I love you . . .': Beauvoir to Nelson Algren, 23 July 1947, *Beloved Chicago Man*, p. 54.

page 354 'You see, it has never . . .': Beauvoir to Nelson Algren, 3 July 1947, ibid., p. 43.

page 354 'When I think . . .': Beauvoir to Nelson Algren, 10 August 1947, ibid., p. 61.

page 355 'to keep his figure in shape . . .': Art Shay, quoted in Bonal and Robowska, *Simone de Beauvoir*, p. 88.

page 355 'For some reason . . .': ibid., p. 86.

page 355 'The reason I do not stay . . .': Beauvoir to Nelson Algren, 26 September 1947, *Beloved Chicago Man*, p. 69.

page 355 'O my love . . .': Beauvoir to Nelson Algren, 28 September 1947, ibid., p. 71.

page 355 'Please, please don't take . . .': Beauvoir to Nelson Algren, 21 October 1947, ibid., p. 88.

page 356 'M. Jean-Paul Sartre . . .': *Combat*, 11 March 1948.

page 356 'revolutionary romanticism': Cohen-Solal, *Sartre*, p. 304.

page 356 'a jackal with a fountain pen': Beauvoir, *Force of Circumstance*, p. 169.

page 356 Ehrenbourg, who had spied for the Soviets: interview with Oleg Gordievsky,12 May 2006; Ewa Bérard, *La vie tumulteuse d'Ilya Ehrenbourg, Juif, Russe et Soviétique* (Éditions Ramsay: Paris, 1991), p. 199, relates that Hemingway had too many doubts about Ehrenbourg to allow him to join the International Brigade, although they worked together on the film *Terre d'Espagne*.

page 356 Koestler had probably also spied: Stonor Saunders, *Who Paid the Piper?*, p. 61.

page 356 'broadly on the side of . . .': Maurice Merleau-Ponty and Sartre both signed the article in the January 1950 issue of *Les Temps modernes*, quoted in Hayman, p. 262.

page 357 'Splitting up . . .': Beauvoir, *Force of Circumstance*, p. 176.

page 357 The CIA was created by the National Security Act of 26 July 1947.

page 357 'Discussed need . . .': Stonor Saunders, *Who Paid the Piper?*, p. 61.

page 357 'He was my friend . . .': Beauvoir, *Force of Circumstance*, p. 140.

page 358 '*Mon Dieu*, how wonderful . . .': Sartre to Beauvoir, unpublished, 'Mai 1948', archive Sylvie Le Bon de Beauvoir (my translation).

page 358 'she kills me . . .': Sartre to Beauvoir, 18 May 1948, *Quiet Moments*, p. 282.

page 358 '*bon camarade*': Sartre to Beauvoir, 'Mai 1948', archive Sylvie Le Bon de Beauvoir (my translation).

page 358 '*Plaque Simone . . .*': ibid.

page 359 'She'd lost her lighter . . .': ibid.

page 359 'frog commandments': Drew, *Nelson Algren*, p. 190.

page 359 'The frog would give everything . . .': Beauvoir to Nelson Algren, 19 April 1948, *Beloved Chicago Man*.

page 360 'I have to be back . . .': Beauvoir, *Force of Circumstance*, pp. 158–60.

page 360 'Nelson *very bad*': Nelson Algren and Simone de Beauvoir's joint diary, courtesy of Ohio State University Libraries.

page 360 'I learnt it from poverty': Camus, 'Première Response', *Essais*, in Aronson, *Camus and Sartre*, p. 107.

page 361 'personal episode': Beauvoir, *Adieux*, p. 268.

page 361 'Have you thought . . . ?': Beauvoir, *Force of Circumstance*, pp. 231–2.

page 362 'I was deeply moved . . .': Beauvoir to Nelson Algren, 30 October 1947, *Beloved Chicago Man*, p. 94.

page 362 'I have a brand-new . . .': Beauvoir to Nelson Algren, 2 April 1948, ibid., p. 191.

page 362 'honesty and intelligence . . .': Beauvoir, *Force of Circumstance*, p. 160.

page 362 'But then, suddenly . . .': Beauvoir to Nelson Algren, 19 July 1948, *Beloved Chicago Man*, p. 206.

page 362 'A woman of my own . . .': Beauvoir, *Force of Circumstance*, pp. 166–7.

page 363 'I still feel your chest . . .': Beauvoir to Nelson Algren, 17 July 1948, *Beloved Chicago Man*, p. 203.

page 363 '[There is] a question . . .': Angela Carter, 'Colette', *London Review of Books Anthology One*, ed. Michael Mason (London: Junction Books, 1981), p. 135: Moi, *Simone de Beauvoir*, p. 253.

page 363 'I should be . . .': Beauvoir–Nelson Algren, 19 July 1948, *Beloved Chicago Man*, p. 205.

page 363 '*Vous ne vous ennuierez jamais . . .*': Beauvoir, *La Force des choses*, p. 231.

page 363 '*Je me plaisais . . .*': ibid., p. 232.

page 364 'Ischia remains . . .': Beauvoir, *Force of Circumstance*, p. 182.

page 365 'Algren's need . . .': Drew, *Nelson Algren*, p. 324.

page 365 'In the water . . .': Beauvoir, *Force of Circumstance*, p. 226.

page 365 '*Il faut repenser le marxisme . . .*': Sartre, preface to Louis Dalmas, *Le Communisme yougoslave depuis la rupture avec avec Mouscou*, July 1950, *Écrits de Sartre*, p. 223.

page 366 'What can man do . . . [*que peut faire . . . un homme, si'il est admis que le mal est dans le monde?*]': *Défence de la culture française par la culture européenne*, lecture by Sartre, 24 April 1949, *Écrits*, p. 214.

page 366 'a hero of our time': Sartre's italics, *Saint Genet, Comédien et Martyr* (Gallimard, 1952), p. 549, *Écrits*, p. 244.

page 366 'For my liberty . . .': Beauvoir, *Force of Circumstance*, p. 243.

page 366 '*Apage Satanas* . . .': Koestler, *Darkness at Noon*, p. 122.

page 367 'I was a victim . . .': Beauvoir, *Force of Circumstance*, p. 261.

page 367 'We can be proud . . .': Henri Martin, letter from Saigon, in Cohen-Solal, *Sartre*, p. 326.

page 367 '*Il faut rétablir* . . .': *Action*, 24 janvier 1952, *Écrits*, p. 246.

page 367 '*Il fut submergé* . . .': Beauvoir, *La Force des choses*, p. 281.

Chapter 31: Body Trouble

page 369 'Woman, like man . . .': Beauvoir, *Second Sex*, p. 61.

page 369 'We do it on the premises, ourselves . . .': Beauvoir, *La Force des choses*, p. 266, *Force of Circumstance*, p. 191.

page 369 'Man put himself forward . . .': Beauvoir, *La Force des choses*, p. 258, *Force of Circumstance*, p. 185.

page 369 'She is the incidental . . .': Beauvoir, *Second Sex*, pp. xl, xliv.

page 370 'The destiny of a woman . . .': Balzac, *Physiologie du marriage*; *Second Sex*, p. 117.

page 370 'There are a lot . . .': Beauvoir to Nelson Algren, 9 February 1949, *Beloved Chicago Man*, p. 267.

page 370 'Women should stick to knitting': Rosalind Miles, *The Women's History of the World*, p. 229.

page 371 'and why she should be allowed . . .': Ray Strachey, *The Cause: A Short History of the Women's Movement in Great Britain* (1928, Virago, 1978), p. 275.

page 371 'When all is said and done . . .': Beauvoir, *Force of Circumstance*, p. 191.

page 372 'Desire is defined . . .': Sartre, *Being and Nothingness*, p. 387.

page 372 The body is trouble: for a discussion of this subject see Moi, *Simone de Beauvoir*, pp. 164–71; on Beauvoir's ambivalence towards the female body see also Evans, *Simone de Beauvoir*, pp. 66–7.

page 372 'What is a woman?': Beauvoir, *Second Sex*, p. xxxvi.

page 372 'Feminine sex desire . . .': ibid., p. 406.

page 372 'What it teaches me . . .': Sartre, *Being and Nothingness*, p. 606.

page 372 'The snare of the slimy . . .': ibid., p. 609.

page 372 'The obscenity . . .': ibid., pp. 613–14.

page 373 'pleasure machine . . .': Beauvoir, *Mandarins*, p. 683.

page 374 'It was as if I were a slug . . .': Lamblin, *A Disgraceful Affair*, p. 136.

page 374 'bright and ordered heaven . . .': Beauvoir, *Second Sex*, p. 154.

page 375 'the devil's doorway': ibid., p. 104.

page 375 'For the husband . . .': ibid., p. 103.

page 375 'The foetus is part . . .': ibid., p. 520.

page 375 'It is only when her fingers . . .': ibid., p. 438.

page 376 'a soft carnal object . . .': ibid., p. 439.

page 376 'In you I love . . .': Renée Vivien, *Sortilèges*; *Second Sex*, p. 438.

page 377 'I think it was when . . .': Bair, *Simone de Beauvoir*, pp. 414–15.

page 377 'I am better at dry sadness . . .': Beauvoir to Nelson Algren, 30 September 1950, *Beloved Chicago Man*, p. 376.

page 377 'own beastish beast': Beauvoir to Nelson Algren, 5 March 1951, ibid., p. 420.

page 377 'I'll be a very decent . . .': Beauvoir to Nelson Algren, 27 March 1951, ibid., p. 422.

page 378 'It was *really* . . .': Beauvoir to Nelson Algren, 13 July 1951, ibid., p. 437.

page 378 'ugly, thrifty . . .': Beauvoir to Nelson Algren, 24 August 1951, ibid., p. 441.

page 378 'I was not drunk . . .': Beauvoir to Nelson Algren, 23 July 1951, ibid., p. 438.

page 378 'Of all my characters . . .': Beauvoir, *Force of Circumstance*, p. 267.

page 379 'It's not friendship . . .': ibid., pp. 250–51.

page 379 'I always felt guilty . . .': Beauvoir to Nelson Algren, 30 October 1951, *Beloved Chicago Man*, p. 442.

Chapter 32: My Last Good Friend

page 380 'Camus was probably . . .' Camus to John Gerassi in Todd, *Albert Camus*, p. 426.

page 380 'He just took it for granted . . .': Beauvoir, *Force of Circumstance*, p. 259.

page 380 'pseudo-philosophy . . .': Francis Jeanson, 'Albert Camus ou l'âme révoltée [Albert Camus or the soul in revolt]', *Les Temps modernes*, no. 79, mai 1952, *Écrits*, p. 250.

page 381 'a year's *congé de maladie* . . .': Herbert R. Lottman, *Albert Camus* (Weidenfeld & Nicolson, 1979), p. 476.

page 381 'I'm not a philosopher . . .': Todd, *Albert Camus*, p. 280; in 1945 Camus had published a fifteen-page article, 'Remarks on Revolt', in the magazine *L'Existence*. The remarks he made then on revolt were repeated almost word for word in the first chapter of *L'Homme révolté*.

page 381 'Only work . . .': ibid., p. 295.

page 381 'the childbirth . . .': ibid., p. 295.

page 381 'the reactionary line . . .': ibid., p. 300.

page 382 'The post-war period . . .': Beauvoir, *Force of Circumstance*, p. 262.

page 382 2.6 million in the gulags: Sebag Montefiore, *Stalin*, p. 625.

page 382 'taste for servitude': Albert Camus, *Carnets III, mars 1951–décembre 1959* (Gallimard, 1989), p. 90; Camus applied to Sartre and the progressives a quote originally from de Tocqueville's *De la démocratie en Amérique*, in saying that '*Ces esprits "qui semblent faire du goût de la servitude une sorte d'ingrédient de la vertu. S'applique à Sartre et aux progressistes."*'

page 382 '*Sartre, l'homme et l'esprit, déloyal* [Sartre, man and mind, disloyal]': Camus, *Carnets*, p. 62.

page 382 Jeanson's . . . review: Jeanson, 'Albert Camus *ou l'âme révoltée*', *Écrits*, p. 250.

page 382 'triumphant rebellion': Jeanson, in Aronson, *Camus and Sartre*, p. 141 (translation by Adrian van den Hoven).

page 382 'man who says no': Camus, 'Remarque sur la Révolte' (in *Essais*, 1945), quoted Todd, *Albert Camus*, p. 300.

page 382 'limited in scope': Aronson, *Camus and Sartre*, p. 116.

page 383 'phantom of revolt . . .': André Breton in *Arts*, October 1951, quoted ibid., p. 133.

page 383 'Philosophy . . . transforms': Albert Camus, *The Rebel*, p. 226.

page 383 'A missed opportunity . . .': Jeanson, in Todd, *Albert Camus*, p. 307.

page 383 'Monsieur le Directeur': Cohen-Solal, *Sartre*, p. 332.

page 383 'I am beginning . . .': Aronson, *Camus and Sartre*, p. 145.

page 383 'My dear Camus': 'Réponse à Albert Camus', *Les Temps modernes*, no. 82, August 1952, in *Situations* (New York) p. 71, and Cohen-Solal, *Sartre*, pp. 332–3.

page 384 'Yes, Camus, like you . . .': *Situations*, p. 71, Aronson, *Camus and Sartre*, p. 150 (translation modified by Adrian van den Hoven).

page 384 'To merit the right . . .': Aronson, *Camus and Sartre*, p. 151.

page 384 'You had been for us . . .': ibid., p. 152.

page 385 '*Voilà, c'est fini, plus jamais je ne dormirai pas* . . .': Beauvoir, *Force des choses*, p. 347.

page 385 'I shall never sleep . . .': Beauvoir, *Force of Circumstance*, p. 254.

page 385 'I missed his old insouciance . . .': ibid., p. 255.

page 385 'Read this . . .': Beauvoir, *Force des choses*, p. 349, *Force of Circumstance*, p. 255.

page 385 'He was meant to be Proust . . .': interview with Olivier Todd, 27 April 2005.

page 385 'Many women . . .': Beauvoir, *Force of Circumstance*, p. 252.

page 386 'still fucking at forty': Bair, *Simone de Beauvoir*, p. 70.

page 386 'I'd like to take you . . .': Beauvoir, *Force des choses II*, p. 10, *Force of Circumstance*, p. 279 (translation modified).

page 386 'Something had happened . . .': Beauvoir, *Force des choses II*, p. 10, *Force of Circumstance*, p. 280.

page 386 'Let's toss for her . . .': interview with Olivier Todd, 27 April 2005.

page 386 'Our bodies met . . .': Beauvoir, *Force of Circumstance*, p. 282.

page 387 'We were living together . . .': Claude Lanzmann, *Témoins de Sartre* (Gallimard, 2005), pp. 34–5 (my translation).

page 387 'I leapt back . . .': Beauvoir, *Force of Circumstance*, p. 285.

page 387 Sartre confessed to Koestler . . . : this conversation took place on 23 June, 1950; Stonor Saunders, *Who Paid the Piper?*, pp. 73–4.

page 388 'the greatest turnabout . . .': Jo Starobin, quoted in Cohen-Solal, Sartre, p. 337.

page 388 'We are happy . . .': Beauvoir, *Force of Circumstance*, p. 288.

page 388 'It wasn't the Soviet Union . . .': Carol Brightman in Stonor Saunders, *Who Paid the Piper?*, p. 101.

page 388 'The Left Bank intellectuals . . .': Diana Josselson in ibid.

page 388 'This is a legal lynching . . .': *Écrits*, pp. 704–8.

page 389 'up to his elbows': Sebag Montefiore, *Stalin*, p. 669.

page 389 'Abramoviches': ibid., p. 559.

page 389 'Strangely relieved': Beauvoir, *Force of Circumstance*, p. 290.

page 389 'I held but one thread . . .': ibid., p. 288.

page 389 'I managed to keep . . .': ibid., p. 304.

page 389 '*Comment allez-vous?*': Beauvoir, *La Force des choses*, p. 45.

page 389 'Empty or full . . .': Beauvoir, *Force of Circumstance*, p. 307.

page 390 'in the company of KGB . . .': email from Oleg Gordievsky, 27 April 2006.

page 390 'Fadeev, Simonov . . .': Ewa Bérard, *La Vie tumultueuse d'Ilya Ehrenbourg, Juif, Russe et Soviétique* (Éditions Ramsay, 1991), pp. 304–5.

page 390 Ehrenbourg, for twenty years a KGB agent: interview with Oleg Gordievsky, 12 May 2006.

page 390 'And now Jean-Paul Sartre . . .': Beauvoir, *Force of Circumstance*, p. 307.

page 390 'One is "alcohol doesn't affect me" . . .': Stonor Saunders, *Who Paid the Piper?*, p. 36.

page 390 '*La liberté de critique* . . .': *Libération*, 15 July 1954, *Écrits de Sartre*, p. 279.

page 390 'both agent and victim': see Moreau, *Sartre*, p. 309.

page 391 '*J'ai menti* . . .': Sartre, *Entretiens avec moi-même*, interviews with Michel Contat, 1975, *Situations* X, p. 220.

page 391 'I believe you accompanied André Gide . . .': letter quoted by Ewa Bérard-Zarzika, in Moreau, *Sartre*, p. 315 (my translation).

page 391 'When you've just accepted . . .': Michel Contat, quoted ibid., p. 316 (my translation).

page 391 'I honestly thought . . .': Ilya Ehrenbourg to Emmanuel Astier de la Vigerie, director of *Libération*, in ibid., pp. 331–2 (my translation).

page 392 '*La littérature* . . .': *La Force des choses II* (Gallimard, 1963), p. 51.

page 392 'Re the Mandarins . . .': Camus, 12 December 1954, *Carnets III*, p. 209.

page 392 'dubious acts . . .': ibid.

page 392 'I didn't give a play to Simone Berriau . . .': Todd, *Albert Camus*, p. 322.

page 393 'denunciation': Beauvoir, *Force of Circumstance*, p. 315.

page 393 'For Henri . . .': Aronson, *Camus and Sartre*, p. 180.

page 393 'She couldn't stand . . .': Todd, *Albert Camus*, p. 322.

page 393 'Because you don't discuss . . .': ibid., p. 325.

page 393 'goaded him on . . .': interview with Olivier Todd, 27 April 2005.

Chapter 33: Freedom Fighters

page 394 'In the first days . . .': Sartre, preface to Franz Fanon, *The Wretched of the Earth*, translated by Constance Farrington (Penguin, 1967, first published 1961), p. 19.

page 394 'For us the Iron Curtain . . .': Beauvoir, *Force of Circumstance*, p. 324.

page 395 Beauvoir leapt to the Kobra's defence: Beauvoir, 'Merleau-Ponty et le pseudo-sartrisme', *Les Temps modernes*, June 1955, *Écrits*, p. 62.

page 395 'I once more felt borne . . .': Beauvoir, *Force of Circumstance*, p. 326.

page 395 'Giving the lie': ibid., p. 344.

page 395 'the sort of food . . .': ibid., p. 352.

page 395 'Excellent! . . .': ibid., p. 334.

page 396 'the intellectual's duty . . .': Aronson, *Camus and Sartre*, p. 170.

page 396 'There is a morality in politics . . .': eulogy at the death of Merleau-Ponty, ibid., p. 172.

page 396 'the golden calf of realism': Sartre, 'Albert Camus', 7 January 1960, eulogy on the death of Camus, in Aronson, *Camus and Sartre*, p. 217.

page 397 'saying goodbye . . .': Beauvoir, *Adieux*, pp. 214–15.

page 397 'I write faster . . .': ibid., p. 215.

page 397 'For hours at a stretch . . .': Beauvoir, *Force of Circumstance*, p. 385.

page 398 'To think against oneself . . .': ibid., p. 453.

page 398 'the outer circle of hell . . .': Camus refers in *The Fall* to a 'bourgeois hell' where, as one goes through the circles, the crimes become 'denser and darker. Here we are in the last circle. The circle of the . . . Ah, you know that?' quoted in Aronson, *Camus and Sartre*, p. 199.

page 398 *vedette*: according to Jean Cau, in Todd, *Albert Camus*, p. 310.

page 398 '*Une brouille, ce n'est rien . . .*': Sartre, 'Albert Camus', *France-Observateur*, 7 janvier 1960, *Écrits*, p. 352

page 399 'thirty years of lying . . .': 'Après Budapest, Sartre parle', *L'Exprèss*, 9 November 1956, *Écrits*, p. 306.

page 399 'It is not just the status . . .': André Siegfried, in Kedward, *La Vie en bleu*, p. 325.

page 399 'from the Channel . . .': ibid., p. 329.

page 399 'the impossible dehumanisation . . . [*L'impossible déshumanisation*]': Sartre, 'Portrait du colonisé', *Les Temps modernes*, July–August 1957, *Écrits*, p. 313 (my translation).

page 400 'to help it die': Sartre, *Le colonialisme est un système*, *Les Temps modernes*, March–April 1956, *Écrits*, p. 297.

page 400 'Mad with rage': Beauvoir, *Force of Circumstance*, p. 340.

page 400 'all murderers . . .': ibid., p. 384.

page 400 'I love Justice . . .': ibid., p. 383.

page 400 'I began to cry . . .': Beauvoir's 'Diary of a Defeat', ibid., pp. 448–9.

page 401 'Days of horror . . .': ibid., p. 451.

page 401 'Marvellous Italy!': ibid., p. 414.

page 402 'I thought Beauvoir . . .' Jacques Lanzmann, in Rowley, p. 372 n.25.

page 402 'I found you very beautiful [*Je te trouvais très belle*]': Claude Lanzmann to Beauvoir, Bonal and Ribowska, *Simone de Beauvoir*, p. 126 (my translation).

page 402 'Claude regularly served . . .': Jacques Lanzmann, in Rowley, *Tête-à-Tête*, p. 223.

page 403 'the young guy I live . . .': Beauvoir to Nelson Algren, 15 February 1954.

page 403 'It's difficult sometimes . . .': Jean Cau, 'Croquis de Mémoire', *Témoins de Sartre*, pp. 55–6 (my translation).

page 404 an article he had promised *L'Express*: this was 'Les Grenouilles qui demandent un roi [The Frogs who want a King]', *L'Espress*, 25 September 1958, *Écrits*, p. 320, and *Situations V*.

page 404 'in a very lyrical . . .': in Cohen-Solal, *Sartre*, p. 383.

page 405 '*Vous êtes formidables*': Sartre, *Les Temps modernes*, May 1957, *Écrits*, p. 309, and *Situations V*. Sartre had been asked by *Le Monde* to comment on the testimonies of young soldiers who had witnessed incidents of torture, but his article was judged 'too violent'. Subsequently he published it in *Les Temps modernes*.

page 405 'The use of torture . . .': Beauvoir, *Force of Circumstance*, p. 469.

page 405 'Here is my century . . .': Sartre, *The Condemned of Altona* (*Les Sequestrés d'Altona*), translated by Sylvia and George Leeson (New York: Knopf, 1961), p. 177.

page 405 'I knew we had won': Beauvoir, *Force of Circumstance*, p. 473.

page 405 *La Question*, by Henri Alleg (Éditions de Minuit), 1958, was seized on 27 March 1958 on the grounds that it demoralized the army and was harmful to national defence.

page 405 'I don't see that's any justification . . .': Beauvoir, *Force of Circumstance*, p. 501.

page 406 'It's so much like you, honey . . .': Beauvoir to Nelson Algren, January 1958.

page 406 'Come to Paris . . .': Beauvoir to Nelson Algren, September 1959.

page 406 '*C'est la lune de miel . . .*': *La Force des choses II*, p. 286, *Force of Circumstance*, p. 491.

page 406 'In Cuba and Brazil . . .': interview with Sylvie Le Bon de Beauvoir, 21 April 2005.

page 406 'No old people . . .': Sartre, 'Ouragan sur le sucre [Hurricane over the Sugarcane]', *France-Soir*, 10 and 11 July.

page 406 'Is it my fault that reality is Marxist?': Che Guevara, in Bonal and Ribowska, *Simone de Beauvoir*, p. 139.

page 407 *'J'ai quelque remords . . .'*: interview with Sylvie Le Bon de Beauvoir, April 2005.

page 407 'was a reminder . . . *J'étais vieille*': *La Force des choses II*, p. 310, *Force of Circumstance*, p. 509.

page 407 'Dearest wonderful thing': Beauvoir to Nelson Algren, Rio, 26 August 1960, p. 545.

page 408 'Subversive beast of my heart . . .' Beauvoir to Nelson Algren, 23 September 1960, pp. 347–8.

page 408 'went mad': Beauvoir to Nelson Algren, Havana, 28 October 1960, p. 549.

page 408 'In Brazil, I want to be the anti-Malraux': Sartre in Cohen-Solal, *Sartre*, p. 400.

page 408 'Viva Cuba! . . .': Beauvoir, *Force of Circumstance*, p. 543.

page 408 'US imperialism': Cohen-Solal, *Sartre*, p. 402.

page 408 'kidnapped': Beauvoir to Nelson Algren, 28 October 1960, p. 550.

page 408 hunger for danger: Gerassi, *Jean-Paul Sartre*, p. 187, quotes Vladimir Jankelevitch: 'Sartre's postwar commitment was a sort of sickly compensation, remorse, hunger for the danger he did not want to risk during the war. He invested everything into the after-war.'

page 409 'Use me as you want': conversation with Dionys Mascolo, Cohen-Solal, *Sartre*, p. 417.

page 409 'Shoot Sartre!': Beauvoir, *Force of Circumstance*, p. 567.

page 409 'The great shadow of Sartre . . .': Roland Dumas, in Cohen-Solal, *Sartre*, p. 420.

page 409 'it is only in violence . . .': Beauvoir, *Force of Circumstance*, p. 591.

page 409 'mirror image': Kedward, *La Vie en bleu*, p. 328.

page 409 'This irrepressible violence . . .' Sartre, preface to Fanon, *The Wretched of the Earth*, p. 18.

page 410 'I've got keys': Beauvoir, *Force of Circumstance*, p. 611.

Chapter 34: Madame Z(artre)

page 411 'You are my wife': Sartre to Lena Zonina, n.d. [July 1962], unpublished letter, Macha Zonina private archives; these letters, which include long extracts from Sartre's journals, are generally not dated. All quotations from Sartre's letters to Lena Zonina are taken from his unpublished letters, Macha Zonina private archives.

page 411 'We would like . . .': Beauvoir, *Force of Circumstance*, p. 576.

page 411 'twelve years of terror . . .': Sartre, 9 November 1956, *L'Express*.

page 411 'It seems your dirty Kennedy . . .': Beauvoir to Nelson Algren, 14 April 1961, p. 559.

page 412 'It's not my fault that reality is Marxist': Ronald Hayman, *Writing Against: A Biography of Sartre*, p. 342. [check text]

page 412 'Consultant': 'Consultant to the Foreign Commission of the Union of

Writers of the USSR' is the title with which Lena Zonina signs her first unpublished 'Report on Working with Simone de Beauvoir and Jean-Paul Sartre (1–24 June 1962)', RGALI Fond 631/Op.26/Delo 2950 (Archives of the Writers Union of the USSR in the the Moscow State Archives of Art and Literature), translated by Dr Lyuba Vinagradova. Six reports exist, the first a summary of Sartre and Beauvoir's previous visit in 1955. Five reports by Zonina chronicle their visits between June 1962 and August 1965: Report 1, 1–24 June 1962, with postcript on Sartre's visit alone to the Peace Congress in Moscow; Report 2, 28 December 1962–13 January 1963, Report 3, 4 August–14 September 1963, Report 4, 1 June–10 July 1964, Report 5, 1 July–5 August 1965. Some brief quotations from the Zonina reports have previously appeared in Ewa Bérard-Zarzycka , 'Sartre et Beauvoir en U.R.S.S.', in *Commentaire* 14, no. 53 (Spring, 1991), pp. 161–8.

page 412 'My questions were not answered . . .': 'Unsigned Report to the Union of Writers of the USSR, Jean-Paul Sartre and Simone de Beauvoir' (1955), RGALI, Fond 631/ Opus 26/ D 2672.

page 412 'too long . . .': ibid.

page 412 'lacked taste . . .': ibid.

page 412 'shop windows . . .': ibid.

page 412 'You are a person . . .': ibid.

page 412 'What fools they are . . .': ibid.

page 413 'more simple and free': ibid.

page 413 'He had made declarations . . .' Lena Zonina, Report 1, 1–24 June 1962.

page 413 'His past literary connections . . .': ibid.

page 413 'absolute intolerance . . .': ibid.

page 413 'The importance of his visit': ibid.

page 413 'immense influence . . .': ibid.

page 413 'My mother was . . .': interview with Macha Zonina, 2 May 2006.

page 414 'a *grande dame* . . .': Gilbert Dagron, 'Pour l'honneur de Mme Z . . .', unpublished article, n.d., private archive of Macha Zonina.

page 414 '*Elle était effectivement* . . .': conversation with Robert Gallimard, who has read Sartre's letters to Zonina, 26 April 2005.

page 414 'The story that Lena Zonina . . .': interview with Oleg Gordievsky, 12 May 2006.

page 415 'is a Party member . . .': Lena Zonina, Report 1, Visit of Sartre and Beauvoir, 1–24 June 1962.

page 415 'many of *our comrades* . . . ': Dr Lyuba Vinagradova, Russian translator of these reports, states that 'to every Russian this would sound the same as "many of our comrades from the KGB". There isn't the slightest doubt about this.' Email from Vinagrodova, 14 August 2007.

page 415 'What sort of propaganda . . .': Zonina, Report 1, June 1962.

page 416 'It cost me . . .': ibid.

page 416 'She would have asked . . .': interview with Oleg Gordievsky, 12 May 2006.

page 416 'What Sartre was shown . . .': Zonina, Report 1, June 1962.

page 416 'set up . . .': ibid.

page 416 '*polovoi akt*': Oleg Gordievsky, see *Next Stop Execution: The Autobiography of Oleg Gordievsky* (Macmillan, 1995), p. 181; in July 1985 Gordievsky escaped to the West. He has been credited with doing more than any other individual in the West to accelerate the collapse of Communism.

page 416 'No more banquets . . .': Beauvoir, *Force of Circumstance*, p. 633.

page 417 Alexei Sourkov: Sourkov was 'a KGB agent 150%', email from Oleg Gordievsky, 27 April 2006.

page 417 'Can we visit . . .': Beauvoir, *Force of Circumstance*, p. 634.

page 418 '*Je t'aime*': Sartre to Lena Zonina, n.d., Macha Zonina private archive.

page 418 'Sartre was a little barrel . . .': John Huston, *An Open Book* (New York: Knopf, 1980), p. 295.

page 418 'Putting her imprint on him . . .': Sartre, *L'Idiot de la Famille*, p. 657.

page 419 'a valid reason . . .': Sartre to Lena Zonina, 25–26 May 1962, Macha Zonina private archive.

page 420 '*Tout à fait un* . . .': Sartre to Lena Zonina, n.d., Macha Zonina private archive.

page 420 'There has been one . . .': Beauvoir, *Force of Circumstance*, p. 642; see Toril Moi, introduction to *Hard Times*, *Force of Circumstance II, 1952–1962*, translated by Peter Green (New York: Paragon, 1992), p. ix, for a discussion of how difficult Beauvoir found it to acknowledge her depressive feelings, which she displaced on to ideas of age and death.

page 420 'I often stop, flabbergasted . . .': Beauvoir, *Force of Circumstance*, p. 656.

page 420 '*Jamais plus un homme*': Beauvoir, *La Force des choses II*, p. 506.

page 420 'You've won . . .': Beauvoir, *Force of Circumstance*, p. 646.

page 421 'In France, if you are . . .': ibid., p. 645.

page 421 'The promises have all been kept . . .': ibid., p. 658, *La Force des choses II*, p. 508 (translation modified).

page 421 'In 1929 everything was possible . . .': interview with Sylvie Le Bon de Beauvoir, 29 November 2005.

page 421 'the best things in Western culture': Zonina, handwritten postcript to Report 1 on the Congress for Peace and Disarmament, 10–16 July 1962; Sartre had planned to return to Europe on 14 July, but stayed until the 16th at the request of A.A. Sourkov. His first speech on the 'Demilitarization of Culture' did not please the KGB.

page 422 '*petite bête sauvage* . . .': Sartre to Lena Zonina, 31 August 1962, Rome, Macha Zonina private archives.

page 422 '*la tournée du médecin*', ibid.

page 422 'Jean-sans-père': Pontalis is quoted by Hayman, *Writing Against*, p. 364.

page 422 '*le hasard du couteau* . . .': Sartre to Lena Zonina, n.d., Macha Zonina private archives.

page 423 Map of Montparnasse: sketched by Sartre, showing the position of his flat and Beauvoir's on each side of the cemetery, Sartre to Lena Zonina, 27 October 1963, Macha Zonina private archive.

page 424 'It's not my fault . . .': Sartre to Lena Zonina, n.d., 'Moscow', Macha Zonina private archive. Zonina's 'Report on Working with Simone de Beauvoir and Jean-Paul Sartre, 28 December 1962–13 January 1963' makes clear that the Soviet purpose was to follow up the meetings between Sourkov and Sartre which had taken place in November 1962 in Paris with the aim of setting up an 'International Meeting of Writers' following Sartre's proposal at the July 1962 Congress. Her report on the negotiations between Sourkov and Sartre, followed by Sartre's promise to form a committee in Paris and to publish E. Dorosh and other Soviet writers in *Les Temps modernes* in a special edition dedicated to Soviet literature, show how different her agenda was from Sartre's.

page **424** 'There is great hope . . .': Beauvoir to Nelson Algren, April 1963, *Beloved Chicago Man*, p. 567.

page **424** 'Useful idiots': interview with Oleg Gordievsky, 12 May 2006.

page **424** 'There is not the slightest doubt . . .': email from Oleg Gordievsky, 21 April 2006.

page **425** 'You were very rough . . .': Beauvoir, *Tout Compte Fait*, p. 398, *All Said and Done*, p. 290.

page **425** '*Ma Lentchka, ma femme* . . .': Sartre to Lena Zonina, n.d. [after return from USSR] 1963, private archives of Macha Zonina.

page **425** 'I can't see any reason': interview with Oleg Gordievsky, 12 May 2006, email 21 April 2006.

page **426** 'It does not just depend . . .': Lena Zonina to Sartre, n.d., courtesy of Macha Zonina, quoted by Gonzague de Saint-Bris and Vladimir Fedorovksi in *Les Egéries russes* (Paris: Jean-Claude Lattès, 1994), p. 282, and Rowley, *Tête-à-Tête*, p. 278.

page **426** 'She never wanted to marry him . . .': interview with Macha Zonina, 29 November 2005.

page **426** 'You *are* the meeting . . .': Sartre to Lena Zonina, n.d. [1963], private archive of Macha Zonina.

page **426** 'To Madame Z(artre)': Sartre wrote this dedication in the copy of *Les Mots* he presented to Lena; private archives of Macha Zonina.

page **427** Nico Papatakis made *Les Abysses* in 1963.

page **428** 'Do not go gentle . . .': Dylan Thomas, epigraph to Beauvoir, *Une Mort très douce*.

page **428** 'How these old women . . .': Beauvoir to Nelson Algren, n.d. [December 1963], *Beloved Chicago Man*, p. 571.

page **428** '*Un cancer* . . .': Beauvoir, *Une Mort très douce*, p. 36.

page **428** 'We *ordered* the doctors . . .': Beauvoir to Nelson Algren, *Beloved Chicago Man*, p. 571.

page **429** 'I know you don't think I'm intelligent [*Je sais que tu ne me trouves pas intelligente*]': Beauvoir, *Une Mort très douce'*, p. 98 (my translation).

page **429** '*Toi, tu me fais peur* . . .': ibid., pp. 94, 98.

page **429** 'I was the family's . . .': p. 96.

page **429** her own cancer: remorse [*Et moi aussi un cancer me dévorait: le remords*]': p. 80.

page **429** 'This first rupture . . .': Sartre to Lena Zonina, n.d. [October 1963], Macha Zonina private archives.

Chapter 35: Betrayal

page **430** 'I don't understand why . . .': Sartre to Lena Zonina, 1966.

page **430** 'Never in Paris . . .': interview with Sylvie Le Bon de Beauvoir, 21 April 2005.

page **430** 'I was wrong in 1962': Beauvoir, *All Said and Done*, p. 58.

page **431** '*Notre histoire* . . .': interview with Sylvie Le Bon de Beauvoir, April 2005.

page **431** '*L'homme doit souffrir* . . .': interview with Sylvie Le Bon de Beauvoir, 29 November 2005.

page **431** 'either in joy, action or revolt . . .': Beauvoir, *All Said and Done*, p. 159.

page **431** 'was an intellectual': ibid., p. 63.

page **431** '[Sylvie] is as thoroughly . . .': ibid., p. 64.

page 432 'Communist optimism': Sartre to Lena Zonina, November 1963, Macha Zonina private archive.

page 432 'In comparison with the death . . .': *Le Monde*, 18 April 1964.

page 432 'The Brodsky affair': Beauvoir, *All Said and Done*, p. 304.

page 432 'interior confusion': Sartre to Lena Zonina, 11 July 1964, Macha Zonina private archive.

page 433 Korneichuck 'has asked Sartre to make . . .': Lena Zonina, Report 3, 'On Working with Jean-Paul Sartre and Simone de Beauvoir (1 June –10 July 1964), RGALI Fond 631/Op 26/D 2995.

page 433 'I have come to the Soviet Union as a friend': ibid.; Sartre was concerned that the European Association of Writers should promote cultural enrichment.

page 433 'facilitate our relationship': Sartre to Lena Zonina, n.d. [November 1963], Macha Zonina private archive; Sartre allowed *Les Lettres françaises* to publish his *Hommage à Nazim Hikmet*, 10–16 December 1964, *Écrits*, p. 407.

page 433 '*Sartre moquait son* personnage . . .': Jean Cau, 'Croquis de mémoire', *Témoins de Sartre*, p. 61.

page 434 'a pig who soils . . .': Bérard, *Ehrenbourg*, p. 328.

page 434 'for strictly personal and other . . .': Sartre to Lena Zonina, copy of 14 October 1964 letter to Swedish Academy.

page 434 'People are going to think . . .': Sartre to Lena Zonina, 19 October 1964, Macha Zonina private archive.

page 434 'Sartre was a genius . . .': conversation with Olivier Todd, 6 May 2006.

page 435 'Today, the Nobel Prize . . .': Cohen-Solal, *Sartre*, p. 448.

page 435 'You're spitting on . . .': Sartre to Lena Zonina, n.d. [January 1965], Macha Zonina private archive.

page 435 Mikhail Sholokhov and Yevgenia Yezhova, see Sebag Montefiore, *Stalin*, p. 26.

page 436 'arranged' meetings: Gilbert Dagron, 'Pour l'honneur de Mme Z . . .', unpublished article, n.d., private archive of Macha Zonina.

page 436 'no sin': interview with Oleg Gordievsky, 12 May 2006.

page 436 'she was never part of . . .': article (in Russian) by Lev Kopelev and Raïssa Orlova, *Russkaja mysl'* (Russian Thought), Paris, 12 February 1985, Macha Zonina archive (my translation).

page 436 '*Toute sa vie* Lena Zonina . . .': Dominique Dhombres, *Le Monde*, 8 February 1985.

page 436 'rumoured that Arlette was pregnant . . .': Axel Madsen, *Hearts and Minds*, pp. 194, 206; Kenneth A Thompson: *Sartre: Life and Works*, p. 111; Le Bon denies this. Letter to the author, 5 December 2007.

page 437 '*Tuez-moi* . . .': Sartre to Lena Zonina, n.d., Macha Zonina archive.

page 437 'One day [he] was walking . . .': Bair, *Simone de Beauvoir*, p. 496, quotes John Gerassi interview, 7 December 1971.

page 437 'But Sartre certainly expected . . .': Gerassi, *Sartre*, p. 158.

page 437 'She had so many . . .': interview with Sylvie Le Bon de Beauvoir, 21 April 2005; Hayman describes Sartre's adoption of Arlette as 'an act of aggression . . . an act of vengeance', p. 374.

page 438 'By the way, child . . .': Liliane Siegel, *In the Shadow of Sartre* (William Collins, 1990) originally published as *La Clandestine* (Éditions Maren Sell, 1988), translated by Barbara Wright, p. 56.

page 438 'She disapproves . . .': ibid., p. 58.

page 439 'All these parasites . . .': interview with Sylvie Le Bon de Beauvoir, 29 November 2005. It was not the adoption which annoyed Beauvoir, states Le Bon, but the fact that Sartre did not urge Arlette to work, and instead supported her; letter of 5 December 2007.

page 439 'scarred enormously': Bair, *Simone de Beauvoir*, p. 462.

page 439 'For sure, there is guilt': Sartre to Lena Zonina, November 1967, Macha Zonina private archive.

page 439 'It's not your fault': interview with Sylvie Le Bon de Beauvoir, 29 November 2005.

page 439 'silly sensual woman': Sebag Montefiore, *Stalin*, p. 287.

page 440 '*Ma fausse Madame Z*': Sartre to Lena Zonina, October 1965, Macha Zonina private archive.

page 440 'a real couple [*un vrai couple*]': Sartre to Lena Zonina, n.d. [1965].

page 440 'It was a tactic of the KGB . . .': interview with Oleg Gordievsky, 12 May 2006.

page 440 'did not take the more extreme step of resigning . . .': interview with Macha Zonina, 30 November 2005; Lena Zonina did not resign from the Union 'in disgust', as Rowley claims in *Tête-à-Tête*, p. 291.

page 440 'The act of signing . . .': email from Oleg Gordievsky, 24 April 2006.

page 440 'Putting one's name . . .': Beauvoir, *All Said and Done*, p. 320.

page 441 'Sartre was utterly against the PEN Club': Lena Zonina, 'Report on Working with Jean-Paul Sartre and Simone de Beauvoir (1 July–5 August 1965)', RGALI Fond/Op 26/D 3017. Zonina reports that Sartre discussed with Sourkov his opposition to Soviet writers participating in PEN meetings, and agreed to accept the Vice-Chairmanship of the European Writers' Association, if elected, at the Congress of October 1965, in order to strengthen it against International PEN.

page 441 'When I learnt about . . .': interview with Oleg Gordievsky, 12 May 2006.

page 441 'In Stalin's time . . .': ibid.

page 441 'What are you doing here . . .': Beauvoir, *All Said and Done*, p. 321.

page 441 'He does not want to see you': ibid.

page 442 'He didn't want to see . . .': interview with Gordievsky, 12 May 2006.

page 442 'ready for co-operation . . .': Lena Zonina 'Report on Working with Jean-Paul Sartre and Simone de Beauvoir (1 July–5 August 1965)', RGALI Fond 631/Op 26/D 3017.

page 442 'American blackmail': Beauvoir, *All Said and Done*, p. 318.

page 442 'Castor has a big black eye': Sartre to Lena Zonina, 9 November 1965.

page 443 'You've decided that without . . .': Beauvoir, 'Malentendu à Moscou', *Roman d'étude du XX siècle* 13 (juin 1992), quoted in Rowley, *Tête-à-Tête*, p. 293.

page 443 'Disillusioned with Russia': Shusha Guppy, *A Girl in Paris* (Minerva, 1992), p. 248.

page 443 '*Nous étions complices*': Sartre to Lena Zonina, 1st letter, Macha Zonina archive.

page 444 'One should not drive Billancourt . . .': Guppy, *A Girl in Paris*, p. 248.

page 444 '*Mon amour* . . .': Sartre to Lena Zonina, n.d. [1966], Macha Zonina archive.

page 444 'a personal bereavement': Sartre and Beauvoir, personal statement on the death of Ilya Ehrenbourg, *L'Unità*, 3 September 1967, *Écrits*, p. 451.

page 444 '*Ne me laisse pas* . . .': Sartre to Lena Zonina, n.d., 1966, Macha Zonina archive.

page 445 'I believe I shall never see . . .': Beauvoir, *All Said and Done*, p. 337; in her memoirs, Beauvoir wrote that 'not without regret' she believed she would never see Moscow again; as so often, the official version did not reflect her true feelings.

Chapter 36: Feminist Mother

page 449 'Simone de Beauvoir was a living flame': interview with Sylvie Le Bon de Beauvoir, 21 April 2005.

page 449 'sickness': Beauvoir, *All Said and Done*, p. 453.

page 449 'En gros, nous avons gagné . . .: Beauvoir, *Tout Compte Fait*, p. 623.

page 450 'No private plane . . .': ibid., p. 398.

page 450 'a genuine interest': ibid., p. 376.

page 450 Lufti el-Kholi: ibid., p. 402.

page 450 'I want to believe . . .': Sartre, *Lettre au Président de la République*, *Le Monde*, 25 April 1967, *Écrits*, p. 446; Cohen-Solal, *Sartre*, p. 456.

page 451 'you will not be the one . . .': Hayman, *Writing Against*, p. 389.

page 451 'Only café waiters . . . [Je ne suis "maître" que pour les garçons de café . . .]', Sartre, interview, *Le Nouvel observateur*, 26 April–3 May 1967, *Écrits*, p. 447; Cohen-Solal, *Sartre*, p. 456.

page 451 'utterly disgusted . . .': Beauvoir, *All Said and Done*, p. 338.

page 451 'Lord Russell would not . . .': ibid., p. 345.

page 451 'His intransigent character . . .': ibid., p. 342.

page 452 an affair with Arlette: Rowley, *Tête-à-Tête*, p. 318.

page 452 'Sylvie didn't like him . . .': Bair, *Simone de Beauvoir*, p. 520, p. 672 n. 14.

page 452 'It wasn't anything serious . . .': ibid.

page 452 'France is bored . . .': Pierre Viansson-Ponté, 15 March 1968, quoted in Cohen-Solal, *Sartre*, p. 457.

page 452 'These young people . . .': Hayman, *Writing Against*, p. 393; in his broadcast of 12 May Sartre repeated sentiments already expressed in the preface to *Aden-Arabie*.

page 453 'When an ageing Aron . . .': *Le Nouvel observateur*, 19 and 26 June, 1968, Cohen-Solal, *Sartre*, p. 461.

page 453 'beatniks, whores . . .': Beauvoir, *All Said and Done*, p. 429.

page 453 'The revolution . . .': ibid., p. 430.

page 453 'What this is about . . .': *Le Monde*, 17–18 May 1970, quoted Hayman, *Writing Against*, p. 407.

page 453 'un nouvel intellectuel': Beauvoir, *Cérémonie*, p. 13; against the 'classic intellectual', Sartre set the 'new intellectual' who endeavours to become integrated with the masses.

page 454 'Read *La Cause du peuple*!': Beauvoir, *Tout compte fait*, p. 593, *All Said and Done*, p. 434.

page 454 'Vous arrêtez un prix Nobel!': *Tout compte fait*, p. 594.

page 454 'His thirst for martyrdom . . .': Hayman, *Writing Against*, p. 408.

page 454 'Sartre, be clear . . .': Cohen-Solal, *Sartre*, p. 463.

page 454 'At any demonstration . . .': interview with Jean-Claude Sauer, 19 April 2005; Sauer believes that Jean Cau was particularly badly treated by Sartre, who refused to be a 'yes man'. When Cau won the Prix Goncourt, Sartre never sent him a word of congratulation.

page 455 'giving Liliane 500-franc notes': conversation with Olivier Todd, 14 June 2007.

page 455 'splendid desk': Siegel, *In the Shadow of Sartre*, p. 23.

page 455 'Do you like it? . . .': ibid. p. 24.

page 456 'disguised autobiography': Hayman remarks that 'the more a biographer speculates, the more he is liable to slip into disguised autobiography', *Writing Against*, p. 384.

page 456 'Doping the animal': Jean Cau, 'Croquis de mémoire', *Témoins de Sartre*, p. 51.

page 456 fascinated by the tic ('*il y un tic qui toujours me fascine*'): ibid., p. 42.

page 456 'These new disturbances . . .': *Adieux*, p. 20.

page 456 'Dissecting her own sorrow': see Moi, *Simone de Beauvoir*, p. 251.

page 456 *Les Belles Images* (Gallimard, 1966) was dedicated to Claude Lanzmann; anxious not to fall into the fault of didacticism which she felt had marked her previous novels, Beauvoir said: 'I'm not giving any lesson,' in an interview with Jacqueline Piatier, *Le Monde*, 23 December 1966, but said her motivation was to convey her sense of apprehension at the modern 'world of lies'. *Écrits*, p. 224.

page 457 'Writing about myself . . .': Bair, *Simone de Beauvoir*, p. 524.

page 457 '*la femme mariée . . .*': interview with Sylvie Le Bon de Beauvoir, 29 November 2005.

page 457 Olga was her model: ibid.

page 457 'Women who do nothing . . .': Beauvoir, *The Woman Destroyed*, first published as *La Femme Rompue* (Gallimard, 1967), translated by Patrick O'Brian (Collins, 1969), p. 154.

page 457 Olga who talks of killing herself: Beauvoir to Nelson Algren, April 1964, *Beloved Chicago Man*, p. 573.

page 457 'raves, rages and sometimes bites': Beauvoir to Nelson Algren, November 1964, ibid., p. 575.

page 457 'I keep my end up . . .': Beauvoir, 'The Monologue', *The Woman Destroyed*, pp. 91–3; Beauvoir took as her epigraph Flaubert's saying: 'The monologue is her form of revenge.'

page 458 'I should like to see . . .': Beauvoir to Nelson Algren, 14 July 1964, *Beloved Chicago Man*, p. 574.

page 458 'spewing bile': conversation with Gillian Tindall, 4 June 2007.

page 458 'Dearest beast . . .': Beauvoir to Nelson Algren, December 1961, *Beloved Chicago Man*, p. 561.

page 458 'Madeleine Gobeil': Bair, *Simone de Beauvoir*, p. 501.

page 458 'unpleased': Beauvoir to Nelson Algren, October 1963, *Beloved Chicago Man*, p. 570.

page 459 'Anybody who can experience . . .': quoted in Rowley, *Tête-à-Tête*, p. 303.

page 459 'According to Madleine Gobeil, he continued to admire . . .': conversation with Madleine Gobeil-Noël, 11 January 2008. Colloque Simone de Beauvoir, Paris.

page 460 I've been in whorehouses . . .': W. J. Weatherby, 'The Life and Hard Times of Nelson Algren', *The Times*, 10 May 1981.

page 460 'Aren't you sorry?': Bair, *Simone de Beauvoir*, pp. 502–3.

page 460 high on cocaine: interview with Sylvie Le Bon de Beauvoir, 29 November 2005.

page 460 'autofiction': Bair, *Simone de Beauvoir*, p. 500.

page 460 '[Wanda] was a miserable . . .': interview with Sylvie Le Bon de Beauvoir, 29 November 2005.

page 460 'a life of freedom . . .': Beauvoir, 'The Independent Woman', *Second Sex*, p. 728.

page 461 'torn between her professional interests . . .': ibid, p. 731.

page 461 'Men made the speeches . . .': Deirdre Bair, interview with Beauvoir, 'Women's Rights in Today's World', 1984 *Britannica Book of the Year*, p. 25.

page 462 'Beauvoir herself never had an abortion': Letter from Sylvie Le Bon de Beauvoir, 5 December 2007.

page 462 'She gave money . . .': interview with Michèle Vian, 25 June 2007.

page 462 'Choisir la cause des femmes': leaflet, March 2005.

page 462 'Halimi was brilliant . . .': interview with Laurence Nguyen, 24 June 2007.

page 462 'Choose change': Choisir election leaflet, 'Avec Gisèle Halimi et Laurence Nguygen', March 1978; by then Halimi was president of Choisir.

page 463 '*Je me déclare féministe*, I declare myself a feminist . . .': Beauvoir, Tout Compte Fait, p. 623. *All Said and Done*, p. 455.

page 463 'that all male ideologies . . .': ibid., p. 448.

page 463 'the act of wiping . . .': ibid., p. 453.

page 463 'slavery': ibid., p. 457.

page 463 'It is difficult for us . . .': interview with Laurence Nguyen, 24 June 2007.

page 463 'It wasn't the *parapluies* . . .': interview with Michèle Vian, 25 June 2007.

page 464 'the first penetration is always rape': retraction in Beauvoir, All Said and Done, p. 458.

Chapter 37: The Abduction of an Old Man

page 465 '*Comment expliquer* . . .': *Cérémonie*, p. 166, *Adieux*, p. 119; Beauvoir quotes the expression '*détournement de vieillard*' (a variant of the usual '*détournement de mineur*' the abduction of a young person, usually for immoral purposes), which was used by Olivier Todd to describe Benny Lévy's influence over Sartre in *Un fils rebelle*; Cohen-Solal refers to the 'corruption of an old man', *Sartre*, p. 498.

page 466 'I've been taken for a ride . . .': Siegel, *In the Shadow of Sartre*, p. 117.

page 466 'I went on all . . .': interview with Michèle Vian, 26 June 2007.

page 466 '*Comment ça va?*': *Cérémonie*, p. 31, *Adieux*, p. 17.

page 466 'I don't want to cause . . .': *Adieux*, p. 19 (translation modified).

page 467 'What a horrible year': *Cérémonie*, p. 35, *Adieux*, p. 19.

page 467 '*Alors, c'est la cérémonie des adieux*': *Cérémonie*, p. 35, *Adieux*, p. 20.

page 467 'I won't live . . .': *Adieux*, p. 22.

page 467 'I'll be all right': ibid., p. 33.

page 468 'Cats have just pissed': *Adieux*, p. 34.

page 468 'profile of an eagle': Lévy, *Sartre*, p. 724.

page 468 'feminine qualities': *Pouvoir et Liberté*: actualité de Sartre: interview with Benny Lévy, *Liberation*, 6 January 1977, in Lévy, *Sartre*, p. 726; in this interview Benny Lévy emphasized that despite any feminine traits detected by Sartre, he was not homosexual.

page 468 'Sartre didn't want to discuss . . .': interview with Michèle Vian, 26 June 2007.

page 468 address Sartre as '*tu*': Lévy, *Sartre*, pp. 736–7; Lévy defends Benny Lévy against the charge of manipulating or bullying Sartre, at least at the beginning of their relationship.

page 468 'Of course I exist . . .': Beauvoir, *Adieux*, p. 37.

page 469 'I am not a Maoist': Sartre, *Life/Situations*, p. 162.

page 469 'I believe in illegality': Beauvoir, *Adieux*, p. 39.

page 469 'Independent, sacrilegious': Kedward, *La Vie en bleu*, pp. 461–3.

page 469 'You don't regret anything . . . [*Vous ne regrettez rien*]': Todd, *Un fils rebelle*, p. 14.

page 469 'I became a traitor . . .': Sartre, *Words*, p. 148.

page 469 'Marcel Ophuls': Kedward, *La Vie en bleu*, p. 459; Paul Touvier was condemned to death in 1945 and 1947, and then twice to five years' imprisonment and ten years' local banishment for theft in 1949. Despite angry demonstrations by Resistance organizations, in September 1972 Pompidou defended his pardon of Touvier. Sartre objected on legal grounds to the headline in *La Cause du peuple*: 'The Guillotine, but for Touvier.' Beauvoir, *Adieux*, p. 38.

page 470 'who always made him drink': ibid., p. 40.

page 470 'Just why am I here?': ibid., p. 42.

page 471 'My occupation as a writer . . .': *Sartre, autoportrait à 70 ans, entretiens avec Michel Contat*; Contat recorded his conversations with Sartre in March 1975 at Arlette's house in Junas, and they were published in June in *Le Nouvel observateur*, and republished on CD in 2005, his centenary.

page 471 'This apartment is the place where . . .': Beauvoir, *Adieux*, p. 64.

page 471 'You're a good *wife*': ibid.

page 472 'I've got things to do . . .' Siegel, *In the Shadow of Sartre*, p. 125.

page 472 Sartre's Schoenmann: Beauvoir, *Adieux*, p. 65.

page 472 'invent a free life . . .': Beauvoir said of Herbaud (Maheu) in *Mémoires d'une jeune fille rangée*, '*Il m'avait montré qu'on pouvait, en dehors des sentiers battus, inventer une vie libre, orgueilleuse et joyeuse.*' Quoted with photograph of Beauvoir and Sylvie Le Bon de Beauvoir at the MLF (Mouvement pour la Libération des Femmes) demonstration at the Cartoucherie du Bois de Vincennes, 22 June 1974, in Bonal and Ribowska, *Simone de Beauvoir*, pp. 152–5.

page 473 'Do not think this is boastful . . .': Bair, *Simone de Beauvoir*, p. 510.

page 473 'I have had some very important . . .': Schwarzer, *After the Second Sex*, pp. 108–9.

page 473 'Simone de Beauvoir was profoundly . . .': interview with Sylvie Le Bon de Beauvoir, 29 November 2005.

page 474 'She encouraged me . . .': ibid.

page 474 'who was a little tipsy . . .': Beauvoir, *Adieux*, p. 102.

page 474 'proudly proclaimed . . .': '*Le Deuxieme Sexe vingt-cinq ans après*', interview de John Gerassi, *Society*, Janvier–Fevrier, 1976, in *Écrits de Simone de Beauvoir*, p. 555.

page 475 'I am against this opposition . . .': Margaret A. Simons and Jessica Benjamin, 'Simone de Beauvoir: an interview', Bair, *Simone de Beauvoir*, p. 551.

page 475 'What these women are not telling you . . .': ibid., p. 552.

page 475 'a phallic woman . . .': Moi, *Simone de Beauvoir*, p. 77; Elaine Marks, in her anthology *Critical Essays on Simone de Beauvoir*, notes that over half of the essays included in her book are 'discreetly or obtrusively sarcastic'. Beauvoir is presented as 'a slightly ridiculous figure, naïve in her passions, sloppy in her scholarship, inaccurate in her documentation, generally out of her depth and inferior as a writer. Indeed, the tone of superiority that many critics, of both sexes, adopt when writing about Simone de Beauvoir deserves special attention' (p. 2).

page 475 the 'woman question': Evans, *Simone de Beauvoir*, p. xi.

page 476 'I often felt like quitting': interview with Benny Lévy in Cohen-Solal, *Sartre*, p. 496.

page 476 '*Nous formons des pensées ensemble*': Beauvoir, *Adieux*, p. 120

page 476 'My problem . . .': *Le Monde*, 16 January 1982, ibid., p. 556.

page 476 'living prolongation . . .': Beauvoir, *Adieux*, p. 12.

page 476 'from Mao to Moses': Lévy, *Le Siècle de Sartre*, p. 725.

page 476 'What next? Maybe . . .': Cohen-Solal, Sartre, p. 510.

page 477 '*J'ai toujours pensé . . .*' 'Simone de Beauvoir interroge Jean-Paul Sartre', *L'Arc*, no 61, 1975, p. 3–12, *Ecrits*, p. 533–46 (my translation).

page 477 'You Maos . . .': Beauvoir, *Adieux*, p. 110.

page 478 '*C'est horriblement mauvais*': Beauvoir, *Cérémonie*, p. 154, *Adieux*, p. 110.

page 478 'the idea of Benny . . .': Bair, *Simone de Beauvoir*, p. 576.

page 478 'furious': Cohen-Solal, *Sartre*, p. 511.

page 478 'the diabetes way of death': Dr Thomas Stuttaford, *The Times*, 5 July 2007.

page 478 'A *few* years: Beauvoir, *Adieux*, p. 105.

page 479 'Do you realize, child . . .': Siegel, *In the Shadow of Sartre*, p. 157.

page 479 'steak *au poivre* and green beans': ibid., p. 135.

page 479 'Has he been drinking?': Beauvoir, *Adieux*, p. 100.

page 479 'Yes, I gave him alcohol . . .': interview with Michèle Vian, 26 June 2007.

page 479 'It was an unpleasant . . .': Beauvoir, *Adieux*, p. 110.

page 480 'You're fond of a drink too': ibid., p. 118.

page 480 'Give me something to drink . . .': Siegel, *In the Shadow of Sartre*, p. 145.

page 481 'What are you up to?': Todd, *Un fils rebelle*, p. 12.

page 481 'when you read . . .': Beauvoir, *Adieux*, p. 120.

page 481 'Pierre would quite like . . .': Siegel, op cit, p. 137.

page 481 'she burst into tears': interview with Arlette Elkaïm-Sartre in Cohen-Solal, *Sartre*, p. 514.

page 481 '*Elle était folle de fureur . . .*': interview with Michèle Vian, 26 June 2007.

page 481 'never felt despair': *Pouvoir et Liberté*, in Lévy, *Le Siècle de Sartre*, p. 729.

page 481 'My works are a failure (*Mes oeuvres sont un échec*)': ibid.

page 481 'Well, this idea of ethics . . .': Hayman's translation, *Writing Against*, p. 472.

page 481 'Atheism is a long . . .': Sartre, *Words*, p. 157.

page 482 'The silence of the transcendental . . .': 'Un nouveau mystique', *Situations 1*, pp. 142–3.

page 482 'The most precious thing Gide offers . . .': Francis Jeanson, 'Gide vivant' (1951), in *Sartre dans sa vie* (Paris: Seuil, 1974), p. 271 (my translation).

page 482 'I don't see myself . . .': Beauvoir, *Adieux*, p. 438.

page 482 'I, Sartre, ask you . . .': conversation with Jean Daniel in Cohen-Solal, *Sartre*, p. 514.

page 482 'two austere muses': ibid., p. 515.

page 483 'There was an argument . . .': Bair, *Simone de Beauvoir*, p. 582.

page 483 'At the *Temps modernes* . . .': Beauvoir, *Adieux*, p. 120.

page 483 'embarrassing, appalling . . .': Todd, *Un fils rebelle*, p. 12.

page 484 'I love you very much . . .': Beauvoir, *Adieux*, p. 120.

page 484 'Non. Attention . . .': Beauvoir, *Cérémonie*, p. 174.

page 484 'You are in your little box': Beauvoir, *Adieux*, p. 3.

Chapter 38: Adieux

page 485 'His death separates us . . .': Beauvoir, *Adieux*, preface.

page 486 'obscene', Todd, *Un fils rebelle*, p. 300.

page 486 'Nous sommes tous . . .': ibid.

page 486 'That's enough, Castor': Bair, *Simone de Beauvoir*, p. 587.

page 486 'For the second time . . .': Georges Michel, *Mes Années Sartre* (Paris: Hachette, 1981), p. 41.

page 487 'I took too many tranquillizers . . .': Francis and Gontier, *Simone de Beauvoir*, p. 356.

page 487 'Vipère': interview with Michèle Vian, 26 June 2007.

page 487 'Castor wants him for herself . . .': Siegel, *In the Shadow of Sartre*, p. 170.

page 488 'I've come to ask you . . .': ibid., p. 177.

page 488 'the smallest souvenir . . .': Lamblin, *A Disgraceful Affair*, p. 160.

page 488 'humbled': Bair, *Simone de Beauvoir*, p. 589.

page 489 'Beauvoir never imagined . . .': interview with Sylvie Le Bon de Beauvoir, 21 April 2005.

page 489 'the doe transformed herself . . .': Michel, *Mes Années Sartre*, p. 201.

page 489 'J'ai tous les droits . . .': interview with Sylvie Le Bon de Beauvoir, 21 April 2005.

page 489 'I have always spoken my mind,' Schwarzer, *After the Second Sex*, pp. 84–5.

page 490 'She sobbed and moaned . . .': Siegel, *In the Shadow of Sartre*, pp. 178–9.

page 490 'Sylvie did all the housework . . .': interview with Bianca Bienenfeld Lamblin, 28 April 2005.

page 491 'Sylvie wasn't always kind . . .': interview with Michèle Vian, 26 June 2007.

page 491 'Should we have something to drink?': Francis and Gontier, *Simone de Beauvoir*, p. 357.

page 491 'Sartre is well and truly dead . . .': Arlette Elkaïm-Sartre, *Libération*, 3 December 1981, p. 26.

page 492 'very angry': interview with Bianca Bienenfeld Lamblin, 28 April 2005.

page 492 'Je le ferai . . .': ibid.

page 492 'She "forgot" to give them back . . .': Lamblin, *A Disgraceful Affair*, p. 163.

page 492 'Anyone who reads . . .': Bair, *Simone de Beauvoir*, p. 599.

page 492 'I was a victim . . .': interview with Bianca Bienenfeld Lamblin, 28 April 2005.

page 492 'Month after month . . .': Lamblin, *A Disgraceful Affair*, pp. 167–8.

page 493 'Sylvie herself handed the letters . . .': interview with Bianca Bienenfeld Lamblin, 28 April 2005.

page 493 'I had never known . . .': Siegel, *In the Shadow of Sartre*, p.174

page 493 'infuriated': Bair, *Simone de Beauvoir*, p. 601; Beauvoir lied to Deirdre Bair about the existence of the letters for three years, from 1983 to her death.

page 494 'His death separates us . . .': Beauvoir, *Adieux*, preface.

Index